WRITING COMPILERS AND INTERPRETERS

An Applied Approach

Ronald Mak

WILEY

John Wiley & Sons, Inc.

New York • Chichester • Brisbane • Toronto • Singapore

To my parents, teachers, students, coworkers, and friends.
I have learned from you all.

In recognition of the importance of preserving what has been written, it is a policy of John Wiley & Sons, Inc. to have books of enduring value published in the United States printed on acid-free paper, and we exert our best efforts to that end.

Copyright © 1991 by Ronald Mak
Published by John Wiley & Sons, Inc.

Library of Congress Cataloging-in-Publication Data

Mak, Ronald, 1953-
    Writing compilers and interpreters : an applied approach / Ronald Mak.
      p. cm.
    Includes index.
    ISBN 0-471-50968-X (paper) 0-471-54712-3 (cloth) 0-471-55580-0 (book/disk)
    1. Compilers (Computer programs) 2. Interpreters (Computer
programs) 3. IBM Personal Computer—Programming. 4. Pascal
(Computer program language) I. Title.
QA76.76.C65M35 1991
005.4'53—dc20   90-48155

Printed in the United States of America
91 92 10 9 8 7 6 5 4 3 2 1

Preface

This book teaches you how to write compilers and interpreters by *doing*. In this book, we will write a working Pascal interpreter, an interactive symbolic debugger, and a compiler that generates code for a real computer, the 8086 processor of the IBM PC. Along the way, we will also write a set of useful utility programs.

I wrote this book for the practicing programmer who needs to learn how to write a compiler or interpreter but who does not want to study a more traditional theoretical textbook. Whether you are a professional programmer who needs to write a compiler at work, or a personal programmer who wants to write an interpreter for an experimental language you've developed, this book will quickly show you what you need to know.

If you are taking a computer science course on compiler writing, you will also find that this book is a good laboratory text. The programs are all examples of how to apply the theory, and you can make numerous exercises and projects out of improving them.

A skills approach

Writing a compiler or an interpreter is not a simple task. I believe the best way to learn how to do it is to learn the necessary skills first. You can best learn these skills by using them in working programs. This theme runs throughout all the chapters. Each chapter teaches a set of skills, and in the first eight chapters, you see how these skills can be applied in practical utility programs. These programs include a program lister, a source file compactor, a cross-reference generator, an interactive calculator, a syntax checker, and a pretty-printer.

Each chapter's programs also build upon the ones in the previous chapters. When we finally complete our interpreter in Chapter 10, we will have utilized parts from all the programs that came before it. The interactive debugger in Chapter 11 is built on top of the interpreter. The compiler that we complete in Chapter 14 is the culmination of all the previous chapters' skills and programs. The program chart in Figure P-1 shows how the programs are related. This approach enables you to see an interpreter and a compiler evolve in stages. If you study the utility programs in each chapter, you can be certain of your understanding of the skills at each stage before you move on to the next stage.

By design, this book teaches you essentially one way to write a compiler or an interpreter. The techniques that you will see will not always be the best or most efficient ones, just ones that do the job and are easy to learn and understand. I hope that you will be inspired to study more advanced texts and replace some of the routines with better ones. We'll write the code in a modular fashion to make it easier to do just that.

Why learn how to write compilers and interpreters?

As a competent programmer, you can no longer afford not to know something about writing compilers and interpreters. Today's computing environment places strong emphasis on "user-friendly" software. The languages we use to communicate with the computer play a major role in determining just how friendly software is.

After a period of relative inactivity, a revolution is beginning in software science. Recently, we have seen the development of new third generation programming languages such as C++, Modula 2, and Ada. The new object-oriented programming paradigm promises to be as important today for improving programmer productivity as was structured programming yesterday.

Even "non-programmer" developers of applications software have seen advances. So-called fourth generation, or specification, languages enable developers to specify *what* to do, and the software is responsible for deciding *how* to do it. People who have never considered themselves programmers in the traditional sense are now developing sophisticated applications using HyperCard software on the Apple Macintosh, which includes a language called HyperTalk for writing scripts.

As users become more sophisticated, they demand systems with greater flexibility. They are less willing to accept preset, unmodifiable parameters or behavior. One way to satisfy these users is to offer systems that are extensible. This can be achieved with a programming language. A prime example is the use of the PostScript language to program laser printers and control graphical displays.

If you wish to keep abreast of these software advances, you must understand the workings of the language compilers and interpreters. If you wish to make new advances yourself, you must also be able to write your own compilers and interpreters. I hope this book helps.

Organization

This book is organized into three parts. The first part teaches you the basic skills of reading a source program and producing a listing, decomposing the program into tokens (scanning), and analyzing the program based on its syntax (parsing).

FIGURE P-1 The Program Chart.

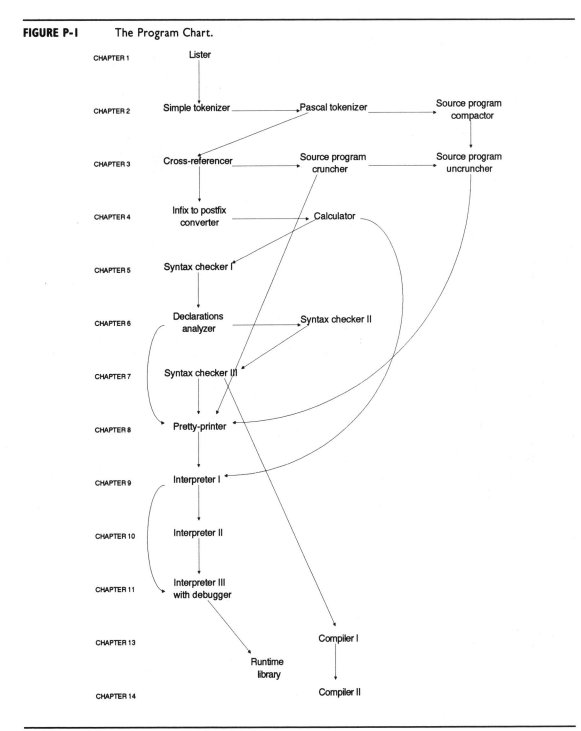

By the second part of the book, you will have built up a sufficient repertoire of skills to write a Pascal interpreter. But we won't stop with merely executing a program. We'll add a symbolic debugger with an interactive command language that allows you to set breakpoints and watchpoints, single-step and trace the flow of the program, and print and modify the values of variables.

In the third part of the book, we'll write a compiler that will translate a Pascal source program into an equivalent 8086 assembly language object program. You will then be able to assemble the compiler's output and run it on an IBM PC-compatible computer. In the very last chapter, we will take a brief look at some advanced concepts that are beyond the scope of this book.

Prerequisites

I assume that you can already program well in C, and that you understand concepts like recursion and data structures, especially stacks, pointers, linked lists, and binary trees. A reading knowledge of Pascal is helpful. You should also have some experience writing and managing large programs consisting of several modules.

We will write all our programs in C, a language that is becoming the standard for writing such systems software. The language that we will interpret and compile is Pascal, a popular language with a relatively simple syntax but which nevertheless contains many important features.

System requirements

All of the C programs in this book were developed with Microsoft's Quick C and Borland's Turbo C development environments. The assembly language programs generated by the compiler can be assembled by Microsoft's Quick Assembler or by Borland's Turbo Assembler. Both the C and assembly language programs can be run on an IBM PC-compatible machine. The C programs should also run with few if any changes on most UNIX systems.

The Pascal source language is acceptable by Microsoft's Quick Pascal compiler and by Borland's Turbo Pascal compiler.

Acknowledgments

Bill Gladstone first got me going on this book, and then my editors at Wiley, including Ellen Greenberg, Katherine Schowalter, and Laura Lewin, kept me on track. The technical reviewer my editors provided did an excellent job. The improvements from the first to the second draft are mostly due to his suggestions. Joyce Jackson supervised the final layout.

Several people knew that I was writing a book. My neighbors always asked about it whenever we saw each other. My coworkers often knew it was better not to ask when I wandered the halls in a daze. I hope my friends forgive me for being always too busy.

Special thanks to my good friend who is an excellent cook, house painter, plumber, electrician, and computer repairman. He helped me find more time for writing by pulling me through two house remodelings.

Final thanks go to Freundin, who made sure her master went for a walk every evening, and who was nice to him even though he didn't pay quite enough attention to her.

A final word on bugs

I always got upset whenever I bought a computer book and found bugs in the programs. How can the author do such shoddy work, I would ask myself.

Well, now that I have written a book myself under a tight schedule, I know how that happens. The compiler and the interpreter in this book are complex programs. The ones that I have worked on professionally went through extensive quality assurance testing. Unfortunately, the programs in this book were not tested nearly so thoroughly.

So, the question is not whether there are any bugs left, or even how many. I only hope that they aren't too embarrassing. I apologize in advance for them.

If you find a bug, or if you have a suggestion for an improvement, please write to me.

Contents

PART II   Interpreting   171

PART III   Compiling   281

PART I

Scanning and Parsing

CHAPTER I

Introduction

1.1 What are compilers and interpreters?

MISSING SEMICOLON. SYNTAX ERROR.

Well, so much for respect for your latest programming masterpiece! We programmers swear and curse at compilers more than just about any other systems software. Yet, they enable us to concentrate more on our algorithms than on the intricacies of machine language. And, as we are often reminded, compilers meticulously check our programs for syntactic correctness.

The main purpose of a compiler and of its close cousin, the interpreter, is to translate a program written in a high-level programming language like Pascal into a form that a computer can understand in order to execute the program. In the context of this translation, the high-level language is the *source language*.

A compiler translates a program written in a high-level language into a low-level language, which can be the assembly language or even the machine language of a particular computer. In the context of this translation, the low-level language is the *object language*. The program that you write in the high-level language is called the *source program*. Its translated version is the *object program*.

Once created, an object program is a separate program in its own right. If it is in machine language, it must be loaded into the computer's memory and then executed. If it is in assembly language, it must first be translated by an assembler to machine language, and then loaded and executed.

On the other hand, an interpreter does not produce an object program. It may translate the source program into an internal intermediate form that it can execute, or it may simply execute the source language statements directly. The net result is that an interpreter translates a program into the actions that the program describes.

1.1.1 Differences between compilers and interpreters

What an interpreter does with a source program is very similar to what you would do if you had to figure it out without a computer. Suppose that you are handed a Pascal program. You first look it over to check for syntax errors. Then, you locate the start of the main program, and you start to execute the statements one at a time by hand. You have a pencil and a scratch pad by your side to keep track of the values of the variables. For example, if you encounter the statement

$$i := j + k$$

you look up the current values of j and k on your scratch pad, add the values, and write down the sum as the new value for i.

An interpreter essentially does what you just did. It is a program that runs on the computer. A Pascal interpreter reads in a Pascal source program, checks it for syntax errors, and executes the source statements one at a time. Using some of its own variables as a scratch pad, the interpreter keeps track of the values of the source program's variables.

A compiler is also a program that runs on the computer. A Pascal compiler reads in a Pascal source program and checks it for syntax errors. But then, instead of executing the source program, it translates the source program into the object program. For example, if a compiler generates an assembly language object program, it translates the same statement into the following assembly statements:

```
mov ax,WORD PTR j
add ax,WORD PTR k
mov WORD PTR i,ax
```

(Of course, if it generates a machine language object program, the output is even more cryptic!)

1.1.2 Advantages and disadvantages of compilers and interpreters

Which is easier to use, a compiler or an interpreter? To execute a source program with an interpreter, you simply feed the source program into the interpreter, and the interpreter takes over to check and execute the program. A compiler, however, checks the source program and then produces an object program. After running the compiler, you need to load the object program into memory in order to execute it. If the compiler generates an assembly language object program, you also must first run an assembler. So, an interpreter definitely has advantages over a compiler when it comes to the effort required to execute a source program.

An interpreter is also more versatile than a compiler. Remember that they are themselves programs, and like any other programs, they can run on different computers. A Pascal interpreter can run on both an IBM PC and an Apple Macintosh and it will execute Pascal source programs on either computer. A compiler, however, generates object programs for a particular computer. Therefore, if you make a Pascal compiler for the PC to run on the Macintosh, it still generates object programs in the assembly language or the machine language of the PC.

What happens if the source program contains a logic error that does not show up until run time, such as an attempt to divide by a variable whose value is zero? Since an interpreter is in control when it is executing a source program, it can stop and indicate the line number of the offending statement and the name of the variable. It can even prompt you for some corrective action (like changing the value of the variable) before resuming execution. The object program generated by a compiler, on the other hand, usually runs by itself. Information from the source program, such as line numbers and names of variables, might not be in the object program. When a runtime error occurs, the program may simply abort, and perhaps print a message containing the address of the offending instruction. It is then up to you to figure out what source statement that address corresponds to, and what variable has the wrong value.

When it comes to debugging, an interpreter is generally the way to go. However, some modern program-development environments now give compilers debugging capabilities almost as good as those of interpreters. You can compile a program and then run it under the control of the environment. If a runtime error occurs, you are given the information and control you need to correct the error. Then, you can either resume the execution of the program, or compile and run it again. Such compilers, though, usually generate extra information or instructions in the object program to keep the environment informed of the current state of the program's execution. This may cause the compiler to generate less efficient code than it otherwise would.

The most important concern may be how *fast* a source program executes. As we saw, an interpreter executes the statements of the source program pretty much the way you would by hand. Each time it executes a statement, it looks it over to figure out what operations the statement says to do. With a compiler, the computer executes a machine language program, either generated directly by the compiler or indirectly via an assembler. Since a computer directly executes a machine language program at top speed, such a program can run ten to 100 times faster than the interpreted source program. A compiler is definitely the winner when it comes to speed. This is certainly true with an optimizing compiler that knows how to generate especially efficient code.

So, we see that compilers and interpreters have advantages and disadvantages. It depends on what aspects of program development and execution we consider. A compromise may be to have both a compiler and an interpreter for the same source language. Then we have the best of both worlds, easy development and fast execution.

That is the ultimate goal of this book. By the time you finish, you will have written a Pascal interpreter with interactive debugging facilities, and a Pascal compiler that generates assembly language object programs.

1.2 Writing compilers and interpreters

Until recently, only the most advanced systems programmers were privy to the arcane art of writing compilers and interpreters. That was part of the mystique of being considered the Grand Guru of the programming department.

That no longer needs to be so! Even though writing a compiler or an interpreter is a complex task, we can tackle it if we start by learning the individual concepts. The best way to learn a concept is to apply it in a program, and once we understand it well, that concept becomes a skill we can use in other programs. That will be our approach: we'll acquire the necessary skills to write compilers and interpreters by writing programs.

Compiler and interpreter concepts deal with operations on source programs. Many of these operations are actually quite useful in their own right. We will write programs that perform these useful operations, so not only will we acquire skills, but we'll also end up with a good set of source program utilities.

1.2.1 The parts of a compiler and an interpreter

To see what we're getting ourselves into, we will first take a high-level overview of what compilers and interpreters are made of. In later chapters, we'll examine these parts in much greater detail. Figure 1-1 shows the parts of a compiler, and Figure 1-2 shows the parts of an interpreter.

The brain of a compiler is its *parser*. The parser knows the *syntax* of the source language, or the "grammar rules" that determine how the source statements are written. Armed with such knowledge, the parser controls the compilation process.

Whenever the parser needs more of the source program to work on, it calls upon the *scanner*. The scanner reads in the source program and breaks it apart into a sequence of *tokens*—numbers, identifiers, operators, etc. It hands them one at a time to the parser whenever the parser calls for the next one.

The parser also knows the *semantics* of the source language. The semantics of a language determine the meaning of its expressions and statements. For example, Pascal's syntax tells us that i + j is a correct way to write an expression. Its semantics tell us that the values of i and j should be added together to obtain a new value.

The parser's knowledge of the source language's syntax allows it to know whenever it has obtained enough tokens from the scanner to form a syntactic entity, such as an expression. Its knowledge of the language's semantics enables it to then call the *code generator* to produce object code that performs the op-

FIGURE I-I   The parts of a compiler.

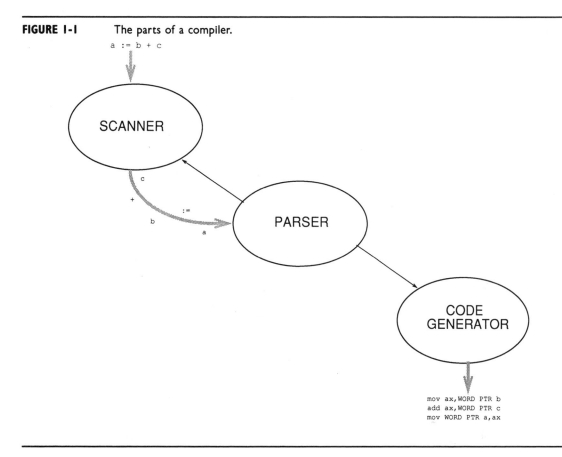

```
a := b + c
```

```
mov ax,WORD PTR b
add ax,WORD PTR c
mov WORD PTR a,ax
```

erations specified by the expression. This continues until the entire source program has been read in. The result is an equivalent object program.

An interpreter also has a parser that controls it. Its scanner does the same job as the one in a compiler. However, an interpreter has an *executor* instead of a code generator. For every syntactic entity, the parser calls upon the executor to perform the operations specified by the semantics of the entity. Whenever the source program loops, the parser goes back in the program and reprocesses the statements in the loop. If the program calls a procedure, the parser goes off to process the statements in that procedure until it returns. This continues until the entire program is finished.

In this book, we will write an interpreter and then a compiler. We will develop these programs incrementally—the utility programs in each chapter build upon the ones in previous chapters. In the first part of the book, we will concentrate on the parser and the scanner, which are common to both compilers and interpreters. The first task is one of the scanner: generating a program listing.

FIGURE 1-2   The parts of an interpreter.

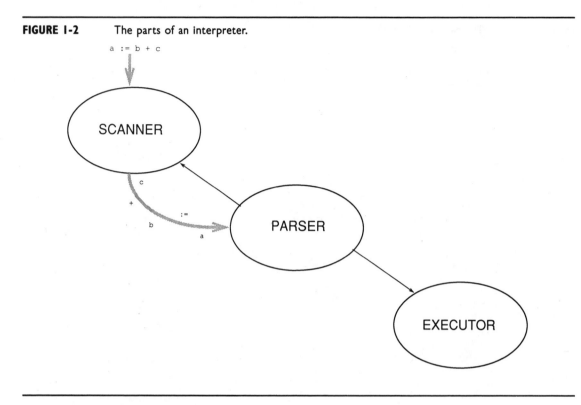

1.3 The program listing

In the rest of this chapter, we will write our first utility program. In doing so, we will develop the following skills:

- open a source file named in the command line
- read the file one line at a time into a source buffer
- print lines with line numbers and page headers

The scanner's main role is to hand tokens over to the parser. Since it reads in the source program, it can also print it out. The printed version is called a *program listing*.

A program listing contains each line of the source program printed on a separate line. Each printed line usually begins with a line number. Each page can have a page header that contains the page number, the name of the source file, and the current date and time.

1.4 Program 1-1: A Source Program Lister

Our first utility program does the scanner's job of listing the source file. Shown in Figure 1-3, this program is also the framework upon which we will build the rest of the scanner in the next chapter.

FIGURE 1-3   A source program lister.

```
/************************************************************/
/*                                                          */
/*       Program 1-1:  Source File Lister                   */
/*                                                          */
/*       Print the contents of a source file                */
/*       with line numbers and page headings.               */
/*                                                          */
/*       FILE:       list.c                                 */
/*                                                          */
/*       USAGE:      list sourcefile                        */
/*                                                          */
/*           sourcefile     name of source file to list     */
/*                                                          */
/************************************************************/

#include <stdio.h>
#include <sys/types.h>
#include <sys/timeb.h>

#define FORM_FEED_CHAR          '\f'

#define MAX_FILE_NAME_LENGTH     32
#define MAX_SOURCE_LINE_LENGTH   256
#define MAX_PRINT_LINE_LENGTH    80
#define MAX_LINES_PER_PAGE       50
#define DATE_STRING_LENGTH       26

typedef enum {
    FALSE, TRUE,
} BOOLEAN;

/*----------------------------------------------------------*/
/* Globals                                                  */
/*----------------------------------------------------------*/

int line_number = 0;                /* current line number */
int page_number = 0;                /* current page number */
int level       = 0;                /* current nesting level */
int line_count  = MAX_LINES_PER_PAGE;  /* no. lines on current pg */

char source_buffer[MAX_SOURCE_LINE_LENGTH]; /* source file buffer */

char source_name[MAX_FILE_NAME_LENGTH]; /* name of source file */
char date[DATE_STRING_LENGTH];          /* current date and time */

FILE *source_file;

/*----------------------------------------------------------*/
/* main              Contains the main loop that drives     */
/*                   the lister.                            */
/*----------------------------------------------------------*/

main(argc, argv)
```

```
int  argc;
char *argv[];

{
    BOOLEAN get_source_line();

    init_lister(argv[1]);

    /*
    -- Repeatedly call get_source_line to read and print
    -- the next source line until the end of file.
    */
    while (get_source_line());
}

/*----------------------------------------------------------*/
/* init_lister       Initialize the lister globals.         */
/*----------------------------------------------------------*/

init_lister(name)

    char *name;                /* name of source file */

{
    time_t timer;

    /*
    -- Copy the source file name and open the source file.
    */
    strcpy(source_name, name);
    source_file = fopen(source_name, "r");

    /*
    -- Set the current date and time in the date string.
    */
    time(&timer);
    strcpy(date, asctime(localtime(&timer)));
}

/*----------------------------------------------------------*/
/* get_source_line   Read the next line from the source     */
/*                   file.  If there was one, print it out  */
/*                   and return TRUE.  Else at end of file,  */
/*                   so return FALSE.                        */
/*----------------------------------------------------------*/

    BOOLEAN
get_source_line()

{
    char print_buffer[MAX_SOURCE_LINE_LENGTH + 9];

    if ((fgets(source_buffer, MAX_SOURCE_LINE_LENGTH,
```

```
                              source_file)) != NULL) {                  line_count = 1;
    ++line_number;                                                  };

    sprintf(print_buffer, "%4d %d: %s",                    if (strlen(line) > MAX_PRINT_LINE_LENGTH)
                    line_number, level, source_buffer);        save_chp = &line[MAX_PRINT_LINE_LENGTH];
    print_line(print_buffer);
                                                           if (save_chp) {
    return(TRUE);                                              save_ch  = *save_chp;
    }                                                          *save_chp = '\0';
    else return(FALSE);                                    }
}
                                                           printf("%s", line);
/*-------------------------------------------------*/
/* print_line        Print out a line.  Start a new page if */    if (save_chp) *save_chp = save_ch;
/*                   the current page is full.      */   }
/*-------------------------------------------------*/
                                                      /*-------------------------------------------------*/
print_line(line)                                      /* print_page_header   Print the page header at the top of  */
                                                      /*                    the next page.            */
    char line[];        /* line to be printed */      /*-------------------------------------------------*/

{                                                     print_page_header()
    char save_ch;
    char *save_chp = NULL;                            {
                                                          putchar(FORM_FEED_CHAR);
    if (++line_count > MAX_LINES_PER_PAGE) {              printf("Page %d   %s   %s\n\n", ++page_number, source_name, date);
        print_page_header();                         }
```

The basic idea is to read each line from the source file into the buffer named source_buffer and then to print each line to the standard output file. We want each source line to be numbered and each page to have a header. Figure 1-4 shows a sample listing with these features.

FIGURE I-4   A sample source program listing.

```
Page 1   newton.pas   Mon Jul 09 01:51:57 1990      18 0:        ELSE IF number < 0 THEN BEGIN
                                                    19 0:            writeln('*** ERROR:  number < 0');
  1 0: PROGRAM newton (input, output);              20 0:        END
  2 0:                                              21 0:        ELSE BEGIN
  3 0: CONST                                        22 0:            sqroot := sqrt(number);
  4 0:     epsilon = 1e-6;                          23 0:            writeln(number:12:6, sqroot:12:6);
  5 0:                                              24 0:            writeln;
  6 0: VAR                                          25 0:
  7 0:     number, root, sqroot : real;            26 0:            root := 1;
  8 0:                                              27 0:            REPEAT
  9 0: BEGIN                                        28 0:                root := (number/root + root)/2;
 10 0:     REPEAT                                   29 0:                writeln(root:24:6,
 11 0:         writeln;                             30 0:                    100*abs(root - sqroot)/sqroot:12:2,
 12 0:         write('Enter new number (0 to quit): ');  31 0:                    '%')
 13 0:         read(number);                        32 0:            UNTIL abs(number/sqr(root) - 1) < epsilon;
 14 0:                                              33 0:        END
 15 0:         IF number = 0 THEN BEGIN            34 0:     UNTIL number = 0
 16 0:             writeln(number:12:6, 0.0:12:6);  35 0: END.
 17 0:         END
```

The lister utility requires that the name of the source file be in the command line when it is run. In the main routine, we fetch this name as argv[1] and pass it to function init_lister. There, we copy the name into variable source_name, open the source file source_file, and set the date and time string.

In the main routine's while loop, we call boolean function get_source_line repeatedly to read and print source lines. That function returns TRUE if it successfully read and printed a line. If it reached the end of the source file instead, it returns FALSE.

In function get_source_line, we call fgets to fill source_buffer with the contents of the next source line. Variable line_number keeps track of the line number. Variable level is zero for now and the next few chapters. In later chapters, its value will be the current nesting level. We call sprintf to print the source line, along with its line number and level, into print_buffer. We then ship print_buffer off to function print_line to print it.

In function print_line, variable line_count keeps track of how many lines have been printed on the current page. If the number of lines exceeds MAX_LINES_PER_PAGE, we call function print_page_header to skip to the top of the next page and print a page header. In any case, we make sure that the current line will fit on one printed line. If the line is too long, we truncate it before printing it, and then restore it to its original length.

Note the difference between variables line_number and line_count. We initialize line_number to zero and increment it by one for each source line. Its final value is the total number of source lines. line_count counts the number of lines on the current page. We reset it to one for each new page. Initializing it to MAX_LINES_PER_PAGE is a clever trick to force the very first source line to trigger a new page and page header.

Questions and exercises

1. A compiler translates a source program into an equivalent object program. How can we determine that two programs written in two different languages are equivalent for all possible input? Does this uncertainty about compilers make interpreters more desirable?

2. A *cross compiler* runs on one computer but generates object programs written in the machine or assembly language of another computer. How can this be useful?

3. Explain the statement: A computer is an interpreter for its machine language.

4. Modify the lister utility to wrap a long line to the next line instead of truncating it.

CHAPTER 2

Scanning

Now that we've taken care of the scanner's task of producing a source program listing, we can tackle its main business: scanning. In this chapter, we will write a complete scanner to serve us, with only a few changes, throughout the rest of this book.

In order to better understand what a scanner does and how it works, we will write a utility program that uses the scanner. It reads in a Pascal program and then lists the words, numbers, strings, and special symbols that are in the program. Then, to further show how a scanner can be used, we will write another utility program that compacts a source program. In this chapter, we will develop the following skills:

- scan words, numbers, strings, and special characters
- determine the value of a number
- recognize reserved words

We will also begin to organize our code into separate modules. This will make writing the compiler and the interpreter, which are large and complex programs, much more manageable.

2.1 How to scan for tokens

Scanning is going through and breaking up the text of a program into its language components, such as words, numbers, and special symbols. These components are called *tokens*. For example, you can scan the following sentence:

They cried, "54-40 or fight!"

to obtain the following tokens:

word:	They
word:	cried
comma:	,
quotation mark:	"
number:	54
hyphen:	-
number:	40
word:	or
word:	fight
exclamation mark:	!
quotation mark:	"

Now how do you manage to do that? You visually scan the characters of the sentence from left to right. As soon as you have seen enough characters to make up a token, you mentally extract it from the sentence. You begin to recognize the type of token by its first character: If it's a letter, you have a word, and if it's a digit, you have a number. If it is any other character, you have a special symbol. Each time you have extracted a token, you resume scanning the sentence from where you last left off.

The scanner that we'll write will work just like that. To see what is happening in greater detail, we begin with three simple tokens: word, number, and period. A word is made of letters, and a number is made of digits. Suppose you read the following line into the character array source_buffer:

Add 12 and 34.

You want to extract each token in turn from source_buffer and place its characters into the empty character array token_string. This is shown in Figure 2-1.

At the start of a word token, you fetch its first letter and each subsequent letter from source_buffer. You append each letter to the contents of token_string. As soon as you fetch a character that is not a letter, you stop. All the letters in token_string make up the word token.

Similarly, at the start of a number token, you fetch its first digit and each subsequent digit from source_buffer. You append each digit to the contents of token_string. As soon as you fetch a character that is not a digit, you stop. All the digits in token_string make up the number token.

If you have a period, you fetch that character and place it into token_string. You must then fetch the next character.

Once you are done extracting a token, you have the first character after the token. (That is why you fetched the character after a period.) This character tells you that you have finished extracting the token. If the character is a blank, you

FIGURE 2-1   Extracting tokens from source_buffer and placing them into token_string.

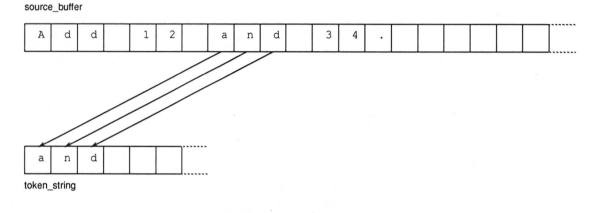

skip it and any subsequent blanks until you are looking again at a nonblank character. This character is the start of the next token.

You extract this next token the same way you extracted the previous one. This process continues until all the tokens have been extracted from the source buffer. Between extracting tokens, you must reset token_string to the empty string to prepare it for the next token.

Let's work this out with the sample input line. Variable bufferp points to a character in source_buffer. Variable ch is the character pointed to by bufferp, that is, ch has the value of *bufferp. You begin with the first nonblank character in the buffer. Since it is the letter A, you extract a word token:

```
    source_buffer:   Add 12 and 34.
        bufferp:     ^
            ch:      A
    token_string:    A

    source_buffer:   Add 12 and 34.
        bufferp:       ^
            ch:      d
    token_string:    Ad

    source_buffer:   Add 12 and 34.
        bufferp:        ^
            ch:      d
    token_string:    Add

    source_buffer:   Add 12 and 34.
        bufferp:         ^
            ch:
```

When `bufferp` points to a character that is not a letter, you are done extracting the word token Add. You can now print it out or otherwise process it. Afterwards, you can clear `token_string` and skip `bufferp` up to the next nonblank character. Since that character is the digit 1, you extract a number token:

```
     source_buffer:   Add 12 and 34.
           bufferp:              ^
                ch:   1
      token_string:   1


     source_buffer:   Add 12 and 34.
           bufferp:               ^
                ch:   2
      token_string:   12


     source_buffer:   Add 12 and 34.
           bufferp:                 ^
                ch:
```

When `bufferp` points to a character that is not a digit, you are done extracting the number token 12. You can clear `token_string` and skip `bufferp` up to the next nonblank character.

You continue to extract the word token and and the number token 34. Now, `bufferp` points to the period:

```
     source_buffer:   Add 12 and 34.
           bufferp:                 ^
                ch:   .
```

Since ch is not a blank, no skipping is necessary. Extracting the period token leaves us with the following:

```
      token_string:   .


     source_buffer:   Add 12 and 34.❖
           bufferp:                  ^
                ch:   ❖
```

Here, `bufferp` points to the character after the period which for now, we will represent with ❖.

Following are the basic steps to scanning:

1. Skip any blanks up to the next nonblank character. This character is the first character of the token to extract, and it indicates the token type.

2. Fetch characters of the token up to a character that does not belong. You are done extracting that token.

3. Now you have the first character after the token. Process the token you have just extracted. Then repeat these steps to extract the next token.

2.2 Program 2-1: A Simple Tokenizer

A scanner for Pascal source programs must, of course, recognize Pascal tokens. The Pascal language contains several types of tokens: identifiers, reserved words, numbers, strings, and special symbols. Our first utility program is a simple tokenizer that reads a source file and lists the tokens that it finds. The first version recognizes only words, numbers, and the period, but it provides the foundation upon which we will build the full Pascal scanner in the second version of the tokenizer.

A Pascal word token is made up of a letter followed by any number of letters and digits (including zero). For now, we restrict a number token to a Pascal unsigned integer, which is one or more consecutive digits. (We'll handle signs, decimal points, fractions, and exponents later.) And, we use the rule that an input file must have a period as its last token.

The tokenizer prints its output in the source listing. For example, the following input lines:

```
The sum of 123
and 456 is 579.
```

produce the following listing:

```
1 0: The sum of 123
   >> <WORD>          The
   >> <WORD>          sum
   >> <WORD>          of
   >> <NUMBER>        123
2 0: and 456 is 579.
   >> <WORD>          and
   >> <NUMBER>        456
   >> <WORD>          is
   >> <NUMBER>        579
   >> <PERIOD>        .
```

What is not immediately obvious from the example is that we are not just printing the digits that make up each number, but the number's value. Thus, the simple tokenizer needs to know how to calculate integer values.

As shown in Figure 2-2, the simple tokenizer borrows code from the source program lister in Chapter 1 to initialize itself and to read and print the source file. The other functions make up the rudimentary scanner.

FIGURE 2-2   A simple tokenizer.

```
/****************************************************************/
/*                                                            */
/*      Program 2-1:  Simple Tokenizer                        */
/*                                                            */
/*      Recognize words, small integers, and the period.      */
/*                                                            */
/*      FILE:      token1.c                                   */
/*                                                            */
/*      USAGE:      token1 sourcefile                         */
/*                                                            */
/*          sourcefile    name of source file to tokenize     */
/*                                                            */
/****************************************************************/

#include <stdio.h>
#include <math.h>
#include <sys/types.h>
#include <sys/timeb.h>

#define FORM_FEED_CHAR          '\f'
#define EOF_CHAR                '\x7f'

#define MAX_FILE_NAME_LENGTH    32
#define MAX_SOURCE_LINE_LENGTH  256
#define MAX_PRINT_LINE_LENGTH   80
#define MAX_LINES_PER_PAGE      50
#define DATE_STRING_LENGTH      26
#define MAX_TOKEN_STRING_LENGTH MAX_SOURCE_LINE_LENGTH
#define MAX_CODE_BUFFER_SIZE    4096

#define MAX_INTEGER             32767
#define MAX_DIGIT_COUNT         20

typedef enum {
    FALSE, TRUE,
} BOOLEAN;

/*------------------------------------------------------------*/
/*  Character codes                                           */
/*------------------------------------------------------------*/

typedef enum {
    LETTER, DIGIT, SPECIAL, EOF_CODE,
} CHAR_CODE;

/*------------------------------------------------------------*/
/*  Token codes                                               */
/*------------------------------------------------------------*/

typedef enum {
    NO_TOKEN, WORD, NUMBER, PERIOD,
    END_OF_FILE, ERROR,
} TOKEN_CODE;

/*------------------------------------------------------------*/
/*  Token name strings                                        */
/*------------------------------------------------------------*/
```

```
char *symbol_strings[] = {
    "<no token>", "<WORD>", "<NUMBER>", "<PERIOD>",
    "<END OF FILE>", "<ERROR>",
};

/*------------------------------------------------------------*/
/*  Literal structure                                         */
/*------------------------------------------------------------*/

typedef enum {
    INTEGER_LIT, STRING_LIT,
} LITERAL_TYPE;

typedef struct {
    LITERAL_TYPE type;
    union {
        int  integer;
        char string[MAX_SOURCE_LINE_LENGTH];
    } value;
} LITERAL;

/*------------------------------------------------------------*/
/*  Globals                                                   */
/*------------------------------------------------------------*/

char       ch;              /* current input character */
TOKEN_CODE token;           /* code of current token */
LITERAL    literal;         /* value of literal */
int        buffer_offset;   /* char offset into source buffer */
int        level = 0;       /* current nesting level */
int        line_number = 0; /* current line number */

char source_buffer[MAX_SOURCE_LINE_LENGTH]; /* source file buffer */
char token_string[MAX_TOKEN_STRING_LENGTH]; /* token string */
char *bufferp = source_buffer;              /* source buffer ptr */
char *tokenp = token_string;                /* token string ptr */

int     digit_count;        /* total no. of digits in number */
BOOLEAN count_error;        /* too many digits in number? */

int page_number = 0;
int line_count  = MAX_LINES_PER_PAGE;    /* no. lines on current pg */

char source_name[MAX_FILE_NAME_LENGTH]; /* name of source file */
char date[DATE_STRING_LENGTH];          /* current date and time */

FILE *source_file;

CHAR_CODE char_table[256];

/*------------------------------------------------------------*/
/*  char_code          Return the character code of ch.       */
/*------------------------------------------------------------*/

#define char_code(ch)   char_table[ch]
```

```
/*------------------------------------------------*/
/* main              Loop to tokenize source file.      */
/*------------------------------------------------*/

main(argc, argv)

    int  argc;
    char *argv[];

{
    /*
    -- Initialize the scanner.
    */
    init_scanner(argv[1]);

    /*
    -- Repeatedly fetch tokens until a period
    -- or the end of file.
    */
    do {
        get_token();
        if (token == END_OF_FILE) {
            print_line("*** ERROR: Unexpected end of file.\n");
            break;
        }

        print_token();
    } while (token != PERIOD);

    quit_scanner();
}

/*------------------------------------------------*/
/* print_token       Print a line describing the current    */
/*                   token.                               */
/*------------------------------------------------*/

print_token()

{
    char line[MAX_PRINT_LINE_LENGTH];
    char *symbol_string = symbol_strings[token];

    switch (token) {

        case NUMBER:
            sprintf(line, "    >> %-16s %d\n",
                        symbol_string, literal.value.integer);
            break;

        default:
            sprintf(line, "    >> %-16s %-s\n",
                        symbol_string, token_string);
            break;
    }
    print_line(line);
}

        /********************************/
        /*                              */
        /*        Initialization        */
        /*                              */
        /********************************/

/*------------------------------------------------*/
/* init_scanner      Initialize the scanner globals     */
/*                   and open the source file.          */
```

```
/*------------------------------------------------*/

init_scanner(name)

    char *name;        /* name of source file */

{
    int ch;

    /*
    -- Initialize character table.
    */
    for (ch = 0;   ch < 256;  ++ch) char_table[ch] = SPECIAL;
    for (ch = '0'; ch <= '9'; ++ch) char_table[ch] = DIGIT;
    for (ch = 'A'; ch <= 'Z'; ++ch) char_table[ch] = LETTER;
    for (ch = 'a'; ch <= 'z'; ++ch) char_table[ch] = LETTER;
    char_table[EOF_CHAR] = EOF_CODE;

    init_page_header(name);
    open_source_file(name);
}

/*------------------------------------------------*/
/* quit_scanner      Terminate the scanner.             */
/*------------------------------------------------*/

quit_scanner()

{
    close_source_file();
}

        /********************************/
        /*                              */
        /*        Character routines    */
        /*                              */
        /********************************/

/*------------------------------------------------*/
/* get_char          Set ch to the next character from the   */
/*                   source buffer.                     */
/*------------------------------------------------*/

get_char()

{
    BOOLEAN get_source_line();

    /*
    -- If at end of current source line, read another line.
    -- If at end of file, set ch to the EOF character and return.
    */
    if (*bufferp == '\0') {
        if (! get_source_line()) {
            ch = EOF_CHAR;
            return;
        }
        bufferp = source_buffer;
        buffer_offset = 0;
    }

    ch = *bufferp++;    /* next character in the buffer */

    if ((ch == '\n') || (ch == '\t')) ch = ' ';
}

/*------------------------------------------------*/
/* skip_blanks       Skip past any blanks at the current    */
```

```
/*                      location in the source buffer.  Set      */
/*                      ch to the next nonblank character.        */
/*-----------------------------------------------------------*/

skip_blanks()

{
    while (ch == ' ') get_char();
}

                /********************************/
                /*                              */
                /*      Token routines          */
                /*                              */
                /********************************/

        /* Note that after a token has been extracted, */
        /* ch is the first character after the token.   */

/*-----------------------------------------------------------*/
/* get_token           Extract the next token from the source  */
/*                     buffer.                                  */
/*-----------------------------------------------------------*/

get_token()

{
    skip_blanks();
    tokenp = token_string;

    switch (char_code(ch)) {
        case LETTER:    get_word();             break;
        case DIGIT:     get_number();           break;
        case EOF_CODE:  token = END_OF_FILE;    break;
        default:        get_special();          break;
    }
}

/*-----------------------------------------------------------*/
/* get_word            Extract a word token and set token to   */
/*                     IDENTIFIER.                              */
/*-----------------------------------------------------------*/

get_word()

{
    BOOLEAN is_reserved_word();

    /*
    -- Extract the word.
    */
    while ((char_code(ch) == LETTER) || (char_code(ch) == DIGIT)) {
        *tokenp++ = ch;
        get_char();
    }

    *tokenp = '\0';
    token   = WORD;
}

/*-----------------------------------------------------------*/
/* get_number          Extract a number token and set literal  */
/*                     to its value.  Set token to NUMBER.      */
/*-----------------------------------------------------------*/

get_number()

{
```

```
    int     nvalue      = 0;      /* value of number */
    int     digit_count = 0;      /* total no. of digits in number */
    BOOLEAN count_error = FALSE;  /* too many digits in number? */

    do {
        *tokenp++ = ch;

        if (++digit_count <= MAX_DIGIT_COUNT)
            nvalue = 10*nvalue + (ch - '0');
        else count_error = TRUE;

        get_char();
    } while (char_code(ch) == DIGIT);

    if (count_error) {
        token = ERROR;
        return;
    }

    literal.type          = INTEGER_LIT;
    literal.value.integer = nvalue;
    *tokenp = '\0';
    token   = NUMBER;
}

/*-----------------------------------------------------------*/
/* get_special          Extract a special token.  The only     */
/*                      special token we recognize so far is   */
/*                      PERIOD.  All others are ERRORs.        */
/*-----------------------------------------------------------*/

get_special()

{
    *tokenp++ = ch;
    token = (ch == '.') ? PERIOD : ERROR;
    get_char();
    *tokenp = '\0';
}

                /********************************/
                /*                              */
                /*      Source file routines    */
                /*                              */
                /********************************/

/*-----------------------------------------------------------*/
/* open_source_file    Open the source file and fetch its      */
/*                     first character.                        */
/*-----------------------------------------------------------*/

open_source_file(name)

    char *name;         /* name of source file */

{
    if ((name == NULL) ||
        ((source_file = fopen(name, "r")) == NULL)) {
        printf("*** Error:  Failed to open source file.\n");
        exit(-1);
    }

    /*
    -- Fetch the first character.
    */
    bufferp = ""        ;
    get_char();
```

```
}
/*-----------------------------------------------------*/
/* close_source_file   Close the source file.          */
/*-----------------------------------------------------*/

close_source_file()

{
    fclose(source_file);
}


/*-----------------------------------------------------*/
/* get_source_line     Read the next line from the source */
/*                     file.  If there is one, print it out */
/*                     and return TRUE.  Else return FALSE  */
/*                     for the end of file.             */
/*-----------------------------------------------------*/

    BOOLEAN
get_source_line()

{
    char print_buffer[MAX_SOURCE_LINE_LENGTH + 9];

    if ((fgets(source_buffer, MAX_SOURCE_LINE_LENGTH,
                              source_file)) != NULL) {
        ++line_number;

        sprintf(print_buffer, "%4d %d: %s",
                        line_number, level, source_buffer);
        print_line(print_buffer);

        return(TRUE);
    }
    else return(FALSE);
}

            /******************************/
            /*                            */
            /*       Printout routines    */
            /*                            */
            /******************************/

/*-----------------------------------------------------*/
/* print_line          Print out a line.  Start a new page if */
/*                     the current page is full.        */
/*-----------------------------------------------------*/

print_line(line)

    char line[];        /* line to be printed */

{
```

```
    char save_ch;
    char *save_chp = NULL;

    if (++line_count > MAX_LINES_PER_PAGE) {
        print_page_header();
        line_count = 1;
    };

    if (strlen(line) > MAX_PRINT_LINE_LENGTH)
        save_chp = &line[MAX_PRINT_LINE_LENGTH];

    if (save_chp) {
        save_ch   = *save_chp;
        *save_chp = '\0';
    }

    printf("%s", line);

    if (save_chp) *save_chp = save_ch;
}

/*-----------------------------------------------------*/
/* init_page_header    Initialize the fields of the page */
/*                     header.                          */
/*-----------------------------------------------------*/

init_page_header(name)

    char *name;         /* name of source file */

{
    time_t timer;

    strncpy(source_name, name, MAX_FILE_NAME_LENGTH - 1);

    /*
    -- Set the current date and time in the date string.
    */
    time(&timer);
    strcpy(date, asctime(localtime(&timer)));
}

/*-----------------------------------------------------*/
/* print_page_header   Print the page header at the top of */
/*                     the next page.                   */
/*-----------------------------------------------------*/

print_page_header()

{
    putchar(FORM_FEED_CHAR);
    printf("Page %d   %s   %s\n\n", ++page_number, source_name, date);
}
```

The scanner has two important enumeration types. CHAR_CODE defines constants that represent the different types of characters that the scanner can fetch. For now, these are LETTER (the characters A through Z and a through z), DIGIT (the characters 0 through 9), SPECIAL (only the character . for now), and EOF_ CODE (to represent the end of file). TOKEN_CODE defines constants that represent the different types of tokens that the scanner recognizes. For now, these are WORD,

NUMBER, PERIOD, END_OF_FILE, and (when all else fails) ERROR. When indexed by a token code, string array symbol_strings returns the name string of the corresponding token type.

Global variables for the tokenizer include ch (the current character from source_buffer), token (the token code of the current token), and bufferp (which points to characters in source_buffer). Variable token_string contains each token as it is extracted, and variable literal contains the value of literals. Enumeration type LITERAL_TYPE defines the possible literal types. (We only care about integer for now.)

Array char_table maps characters to character codes. Macro char_code indexes into the array with a character to obtain and return the character's code. For example, the value of char_table['a'] is LETTER. char_table is initialized in routine init_scanner.

The main routine's loop is simple. We call function get_token to extract the next token from the source file and function print_token to print it. This happens repeatedly until get_token extracts a period. Since the period token must be the last in the file, it is an error to extract the END_OF_FILE token.

Function print_token obtains the name string of the token from symbol_strings. Then, if the token is a number, we print the value of literal.value. integer. In all other cases, we just print the value of token_string.

As we said before, function init_scanner initializes char_table. We also call function init_page_header to initialize the information in the page header, and function open_source_file to open the source file. Function quit_scanner closes the source file.

Function get_char fetches the next character from source_buffer. We set ch to *bufferp and advance bufferp to the next character. If the last character of the source line has already been fetched from source_buffer (bufferp points to the null character \0), we call function get_source_line to refill the buffer.

In get_char, we take a few liberties with each character we fetch. We set ch to EOF_CHAR if we have reached the end of the file. Since Pascal dictates that we treat the end-of-line and tab characters as blanks, we set ch to a blank if \n or \t is fetched.

The real workhorse of the scanner is routine get_token. We first call function skip_blanks to skip up to the next nonblank character. Then ch is the first character of the next token. Based on this character's code, we call function get_word, get_number, or get_special to extract a word, number, or period token. If we are at the end of the file, we set token to the END_OF_FILE code.

Function get_word works much the same. We repeatedly call get_char to fetch characters and append them to the contents of token_string. We don't stop until we fetch a character that does not belong to the token, one that is not a letter or a digit. When the function returns, ch is the first character after the token.

Routine get_special so far only knows the period. Everything else is an error. After fetching the period, we call get_char so that ch is the first character after the token.

Function get_number not only extracts a number token (an unsigned integer literal for now), but it also calculates the number's value. It is calculated in local variable nvalue, and at the end of the function, we set literal.value.integer to the value.

Each time we call get_number, nvalue is initially zero. To accumulate the value as each digit of the number is fetched from left to right, we multiply nvalue by ten, and then add the numeric value of the digit. For example:

```
              nvalue:   0

       source_buffer:   386
             bufferp:   ^
                  ch:   3
              nvalue:   10*0 + 3 = 3

       source_buffer:   386
             bufferp:    ^
                  ch:   8
              nvalue:   10*3 + 8 = 38

       source_buffer:   386
             bufferp:     ^
                  ch:   6
              nvalue:   10*38 + 6 = 386
```

When the value of ch is a digit, the value of the expression

$$ch - \text{'0'}$$

is the numeric value of the digit. This works because the ASCII codes of the characters '0' through '9' are 48 through 57. If, for example, ch has the value '5', then '5'-'0' is simply 53–48, or five.

We must also guard against an overflow caused by a number with too many digits. Since the maximum integer value is 32767, we define MAX_DIGIT_COUNT to be four. (Of course, in the full scanner, we allow a much greater range of values!) If a number has too many digits, we set local boolean variable count_error to TRUE and stop accumulating the value. Then, after all the digits have been fetched, we set token to ERROR.

Function open_source_file opens the source file. Then, to force get_char to fill the source buffer before attempting to fetch the file's first character, we initialize bufferp to point to the null character in the empty string "". Function close_source_file closes the source file.

Functions get_source_line, print_line, and print_header are taken directly from the lister utility program. Function init_page_header also uses code from that program.

2.3 Modularizing the code

Before beginning the second version of the tokenizer utility, we should prepare to modularize our code by breaking it apart into separate files. We will now create two modules, the scanner module and the error module.

Scanner Module

scanner.h	*n*	Scanner header file
scanner.c	*n*	Scanner routines

Error Module

error.h	*n*	Error header file
error.c	*n*	Error routines

Miscellaneous

common.h	*n*	Common header file

Where: *n*   new file

Each chapter builds upon the organization we will establish here. We may create new modules, add new files to existing modules, or modify existing files.

Figure 2-3 shows file common.h. It defines various constants and the boolean type that we saw in the simple tokenizer. These definitions will be useful throughout the various modules. We also define three memory allocation macros that we will frequently use.

FIGURE 2-3   File common.h.

```
/****************************************************************/
/*                                                            */
/*      C O M M O N   R O U T I N E S   (Header)              */
/*                                                            */
/*      FILE:     common.h                                    */
/*                                                            */
/*      MODULE:   common                                      */
/*                                                            */
/****************************************************************/

#ifndef common_h
#define common_h

#define FORM_FEED_CHAR         '\f'

#define MAX_FILE_NAME_LENGTH   32
```

```
#define MAX_SOURCE_LINE_LENGTH   256
#define MAX_PRINT_LINE_LENGTH    80
#define MAX_LINES_PER_PAGE       50
#define DATE_STRING_LENGTH       26
#define MAX_TOKEN_STRING_LENGTH MAX_SOURCE_LINE_LENGTH
#define MAX_CODE_BUFFER_SIZE     4096
#define MAX_NESTING_LEVEL        16

typedef enum {
    FALSE, TRUE,
} BOOLEAN;

        /****************************************/
        /*                                    */
        /*      Macros for memory allocation   */
        /*                                    */
        /****************************************/
```

```
#define alloc_struct(type)        (type *) malloc(sizeof(type))      #define alloc_bytes(length)        (char *) malloc(length)
#define alloc_array(type, count)  (type *) malloc(count*sizeof(type))
                                                                     #endif
```

At the beginning of each header file, we test for and define a special pre-processor flag. For example, in common.h, we begin with the following:

```
#ifndef common_h
#define common_h
```

At the end of the file, we have:

```
#endif
```

These flags ensure that whenever all the modules are compiled together, each header file is included only once, since the flag is defined the first time the file is included.

2.4 Program 2-2: A Pascal Tokenizer

Now that you understand how a simple scanner works, we can write the second version of the tokenizer utility. This version uses a scanner that recognizes all Pascal tokens: words (identifiers and reserved words), numbers (integer and real), strings, and all the special symbols.

Figure 2-4 shows the main file of the utility, token2.c. Most of the globals are gone. They've been moved to file scanner.h, and only three are used in the main file: token, token_string, and literal. String array symbol_strings now has entries for all the Pascal tokens. Function print_token now distinguishes between integer and real numbers and it can print string tokens.

FIGURE 2-4   Main file of the Pascal tokenizer.

```
/*****************************************************************/    #include <stdio.h>
/*                                                             */     #include "common.h"
/*      Program 2-2:  Pascal Source Tokenizer                  */     #include "error.h"
/*                                                             */     #include "scanner.h"
/*      Recognize Pascal tokens.                               */
/*                                                             */     /*------------------------------------------------------------*/
/*      FILE:     token2.c                                     */     /* Token name strings                                         */
/*                                                             */     /*------------------------------------------------------------*/
/*      REQUIRES:  Modules error, scanner                      */
/*                                                             */     char *symbol_strings[] = {
/*      USAGE:     token2 sourcefile                           */         "<no token>", "<IDENTIFIER>", "<NUMBER>", "<STRING>",
/*                                                             */         " ", "*", "(", ")", "-", "+", "=", "[", "]", ".", ";",
/*        sourcefile     name of source file to tokenize       */         "<", ">", ",", ":", "/", ":=", "<=", ">=", "<>", "..",
/*                                                             */         "<END OF FILE>", "<ERROR>",
/*****************************************************************/         "AND", "ARRAY", "BEGIN", "CASE", "CONST", "DIV", "DO", "DOWNTO",
```

```
    "ELSE", "END", "FILE", "FOR", "FUNCTION", "GOTO", "IF", "IN",
    "LABEL", "MOD", "NIL", "NOT", "OF", "OR", "PACKED", "PROCEDURE",
    "PROGRAM", "RECORD", "REPEAT", "SET", "THEN", "TO", "TYPE",
    "UNTIL", "VAR", "WHILE", "WITH",
};

/*-------------------------------------------------------------*/
/* Externals                                                   */
/*-------------------------------------------------------------*/

extern TOKEN_CODE token;
extern char       token_string[];
extern LITERAL    literal;

/*-------------------------------------------------------------*/
/* main                 Loop to tokenize source file.          */
/*-------------------------------------------------------------*/

main(argc, argv)

    int  argc;
    char *argv[];

{
    /*
    -- Initialize the scanner.
    */
    init_scanner(argv[1]);

    /*
    -- Repeatedly fetch tokens until a period
    -- or the end of file.
    */
    do {
        get_token();
        if (token == END_OF_FILE) {
            error(UNEXPECTED_END_OF_FILE);
            break;
        }
```

```
        print_token();
    } while (token != PERIOD);

    quit_scanner();

}

/*-------------------------------------------------------------*/
/* print_token          Print a line describing the current    */
/*                      token.                                 */
/*-------------------------------------------------------------*/

print_token()

{
    char line[MAX_SOURCE_LINE_LENGTH + 32];
    char *symbol_string = symbol_strings[token];

    switch (token) {

        case NUMBER:
            if (literal.type == INTEGER_LIT)
                sprintf(line, "      >> %-16s %d (integer)\n",
                                symbol_string, literal.value.integer);
            else
                sprintf(line, "      >> %-16s %g (real)\n",
                                symbol_string, literal.value.real);
            break;

        case STRING:
            sprintf(line, "      >> %-16s '%-s'\n",
                                symbol_string, literal.value.string);
            break;

        default:
            sprintf(line, "      >> %-16s %-s\n",
                                symbol_string, token_string);
            break;
    }
    print_line(line);
}
```

The Pascal tokenizer works similarly to the simple tokenizer, only smarter. For example, if we give it the Pascal program shown in Figure 2-5, we can expect the output shown in Figure 2-6.

FIGURE 2-5   Sample input file for the Pascal tokenizer.

```
PROGRAM hello (output);                            BEGIN {hello}
                                                       FOR i := 1 TO 10 DO BEGIN
{Write 'Hello, world.' ten times.}                        writeln('Hello, world.');
                                                       END;
VAR                                                END {hello}.
    i : integer;
```

FIGURE 2-6 Sample output from the Pascal tokenizer.

```
Page 1   hello.pas  Mon Jul 09 23:18:52 1990

  1 0: PROGRAM hello (output);
  >> PROGRAM          PROGRAM
  >> <IDENTIFIER>     hello
  >> (                (
  >> <IDENTIFIER>     output
  >> )                )
  >> ;                ;
  2 0:
  3 0: {Write 'Hello, world.' ten times.}
  4 0:
  5 0: VAR
  >> VAR              VAR
  6 0:    i : integer;
  >> <IDENTIFIER>     i
  >> :                :
  >> <IDENTIFIER>     integer
  >> ;                ;
  7 0:
  8 0: BEGIN {hello}
```

```
  >> BEGIN            BEGIN
  9 0:    FOR i := 1 TO 10 DO BEGIN
  >> FOR              FOR
  >> <IDENTIFIER>     i
  >> :=               :=
  >> <NUMBER>         1 (integer)
  >> TO               TO
  >> <NUMBER>         10 (integer)
  >> DO               DO
  >> BEGIN            BEGIN
 10 0:       writeln('Hello, world.');
  >> <IDENTIFIER>     writeln
  >> (                (
  >> <STRING>         'Hello, world.'
  >> )                )
  >> ;                ;
 11 0:    END;
  >> END              END
  >> ;                ;
 12 0: END {hello}.
  >> END              END
  >> .                .
```

Figure 2-7 shows file scanner.h. It contains three of the types that were originally defined by the simple tokenizer. We move them to this header file because other modules will use these types. Note that token_code now defines constants for all Pascal tokens. In particular, it defines a separate constant for each reserved word.

FIGURE 2-7 File scanner.h.

```
/***************************************************************/
/*                                                             */
/*     S C A N N E R   (Header)                                */
/*                                                             */
/*     FILE:    scanner.h                                      */
/*                                                             */
/*     MODULE:  scanner                                        */
/*                                                             */
/***************************************************************/

#ifndef scanner_h
#define scanner_h

#include "common.h"

/*------------------------------------------------------------*/
/* Token codes                                                */
/*------------------------------------------------------------*/

typedef enum {
    NO_TOKEN, IDENTIFIER, NUMBER, STRING,
    UPARROW, STAR, LPAREN, RPAREN, MINUS, PLUS, EQUAL,
    LBRACKET, RBRACKET, COLON, SEMICOLON, LT, GT, COMMA, PERIOD,
    SLASH, COLONEQUAL, LE, GE, NE, DOTDOT, END_OF_FILE, ERROR,
    AND, ARRAY, BEGIN, CASE, CONST, DIV, DO, DOWNTO, ELSE, END,
    FFILE, FOR, FUNCTION, GOTO, IF, IN, LABEL, MOD, NIL, NOT,
    OF, OR, PACKED, PROCEDURE, PROGRAM, RECORD, REPEAT, SET,
    THEN, TO, TYPE, UNTIL, VAR, WHILE, WITH,
} TOKEN_CODE;

/*------------------------------------------------------------*/
/* Literal structure                                          */
/*------------------------------------------------------------*/

typedef enum {
    INTEGER_LIT, REAL_LIT, STRING_LIT,
} LITERAL_TYPE;

typedef struct {
    LITERAL_TYPE type;
    union {
        int   integer;
```

```
        float real;                                    } LITERAL;
        char  string[MAX_SOURCE_LINE_LENGTH];
    } value;                                           #endif
```

Figure 2-8 shows file scanner.c. Although it retains the structure of the scanner in the simple tokenizer, this version is greatly expanded. The CHAR_CODE enumeration type now defines QUOTE. We now have reserved word tables and several new global variables, buffer_offset, print_flag, and word_string. Note that digit_count and count_error, formerly local variables, are now global.

FIGURE 2-8   File scanner.c.

```
/***************************************************************/      RW_STRUCT rw_2[] = {
/*                                                  */              {"do", DO}, {"if", IF}, {"in", IN}, {"of", OF}, {"or", OR},
/*        S C A N N E R                             */              {"to", TO}, {NULL, 0 },
/*                                                  */          };
/*        Scanner for Pascal tokens.                */
/*                                                  */          RW_STRUCT rw_3[] = {
/*        FILE:      scanner.c                       */              {"and", AND}, {"div", DIV}, {"end", END}, {"for", FOR},
/*                                                  */              {"mod", MOD}, {"nil", NIL}, {"not", NOT}, {"set", SET},
/*        MODULE:    scanner                         */              {"var", VAR}, {NULL, 0 },
/*                                                  */          };
/***************************************************************/
                                                                  RW_STRUCT rw_4[] = {
#include <stdio.h>                                                    {"case", CASE}, {"else", ELSE}, {"file", FFILE},
#include <math.h>                                                     {"goto", GOTO}, {"then", THEN}, {"type", TYPE},
#include <sys/types.h>                                                {"with", WITH}, {NULL , 0 },
#include <sys/timeb.h>                                             };
#include "common.h"
#include "error.h"                                                RW_STRUCT rw_5[] = {
#include "scanner.h"                                                  {"array", ARRAY}, {"begin", BEGIN}, {"const", CONST},
                                                                     {"label", LABEL}, {"until", UNTIL}, {"while", WHILE},
#define EOF_CHAR          '\x7f'                                      {NULL , 0 },
#define TAB_SIZE          8                                       };

#define MAX_INTEGER       32767                                   RW_STRUCT rw_6[] = {
#define MAX_DIGIT_COUNT   20                                          {"downto", DOWNTO}, {"packed", PACKED}, {"record", RECORD},
#define MAX_EXPONENT      37                                          {"repeat", REPEAT}, {NULL , 0 },
                                                                  };
#define MIN_RESERVED_WORD_LENGTH    2
#define MAX_RESERVED_WORD_LENGTH    9                             RW_STRUCT rw_7[] = {
                                                                     {"program", PROGRAM}, {NULL, 0},
/*------------------------------------------------*/              };
/* Character codes                                */
/*------------------------------------------------*/              RW_STRUCT rw_8[] = {
                                                                     {"function", FUNCTION}, {NULL, 0},
typedef enum {                                                    };
    LETTER, DIGIT, QUOTE, SPECIAL, EOF_CODE,
} CHAR_CODE;                                                       RW_STRUCT rw_9[] = {
                                                                     {"procedure", PROCEDURE}, {NULL, 0},
/*------------------------------------------------*/              };
/* Reserved word tables                           */
/*------------------------------------------------*/              RW_STRUCT *rw_table[] = {
                                                                     NULL, NULL, rw_2, rw_3, rw_4, rw_5, rw_6, rw_7, rw_8, rw_9,
typedef struct {                                                  };
    char      *string;
    TOKEN_CODE token_code;                                        /*------------------------------------------------*/
} RW_STRUCT;                                                      /* Globals                                        */
                                                                  /*------------------------------------------------*/
```

```
char        ch;              /* current input character */
TOKEN_CODE  token;           /* code of current token */
LITERAL     literal;         /* value of literal */
int         buffer_offset;   /* char offset into source buffer */
int         level = 0;       /* current nesting level */
int         line_number = 0; /* current line number */
BOOLEAN     print_flag = TRUE; /* TRUE to print source lines */

char source_buffer[MAX_SOURCE_LINE_LENGTH]; /* source file buffer */
char token_string[MAX_TOKEN_STRING_LENGTH]; /* token string */
char word_string[MAX_TOKEN_STRING_LENGTH];  /* downshifted */
char *bufferp = source_buffer;              /* source buffer ptr */
char *tokenp  = token_string;               /* token string ptr */

int     digit_count;         /* total no. of digits in number */
BOOLEAN count_error;         /* too many digits in number? */

int page_number = 0;
int line_count  = MAX_LINES_PER_PAGE;     /* no. lines on current pg */

char source_name[MAX_FILE_NAME_LENGTH]; /* name of source file */
char date[DATE_STRING_LENGTH];          /* current date and time */

FILE *source_file;

CHAR_CODE char_table[256];

/*-------------------------------------------------------*/
/* char_code          Return the character code of ch.   */
/*-------------------------------------------------------*/

#define char_code(ch)   char_table[ch]

                 /********************************/
                 /*                              */
                 /*        Initialization        */
                 /*                              */
                 /********************************/

/*-------------------------------------------------------*/
/* init_scanner      Initialize the scanner globals      */
/*                   and open the source file.           */
/*-------------------------------------------------------*/

init_scanner(name)

    char *name;      /* name of source file */

{
    int ch;

    /*
    -- Initialize character table.
    */
    for (ch = 0;   ch < 256; ++ch) char_table[ch] = SPECIAL;
    for (ch = '0'; ch <= '9'; ++ch) char_table[ch] = DIGIT;
    for (ch = 'A'; ch <= 'Z'; ++ch) char_table[ch] = LETTER;
    for (ch = 'a'; ch <= 'z'; ++ch) char_table[ch] = LETTER;
    char_table['\''] = QUOTE;
    char_table[EOF_CHAR] = EOF_CODE;

    init_page_header(name);
    open_source_file(name);
}

/*-------------------------------------------------------*/
/* quit_scanner      Terminate the scanner.              */
```

```
/*-------------------------------------------------------*/

quit_scanner()

{
    close_source_file();
}

                 /********************************/
                 /*                              */
                 /*        Character routines     */
                 /*                              */
                 /********************************/

/*-------------------------------------------------------*/
/* get_char          Set ch to the next character from the */
/*                   source buffer.                      */
/*-------------------------------------------------------*/

get_char()

{
    BOOLEAN get_source_line();

    /*
    -- If at end of current source line, read another line.
    -- If at end of file, set ch to the EOF character and return.
    */
    if (*bufferp == '\0') {
        if (! get_source_line()) {
            ch = EOF_CHAR;
            return;
        }
        bufferp = source_buffer;
        buffer_offset = 0;
    }

    ch = *bufferp++;     /* next character in the buffer */

    /*
    -- Special character processing:
    --
    --      tab        Increment buffer_offset up to the next
    --                 multiple of TAB_SIZE, and replace ch with
    --                 a blank.
    --
    --      new-line   Replace ch with a blank.
    --
    --      {          Start of comment:  Skip over comment and
    --                 replace it with a blank.
    */
    switch (ch) {

        case '\t': buffer_offset += TAB_SIZE -
                                buffer_offset%TAB_SIZE;
                   ch = ' ';
                   break;

        case '\n': ++buffer_offset;
                   ch = ' ';
                   break;

        case '{': ++buffer_offset;
                  skip_comment();
                  ch = ' ';
                  break;

        default:   ++buffer_offset;
```

```
        }
    }
    /*------------------------------------------------------*/
    /*  skip_comment      Skip over a comment.  Set ch to ']'.  */
    /*------------------------------------------------------*/

    skip_comment()

    {
        do {
            get_char();
        } while ((ch != ']') && (ch != EOF_CHAR));
    }

    /*------------------------------------------------------*/
    /*  skip_blanks       Skip past any blanks at the current  */
    /*                    location in the source buffer.  Set  */
    /*                    ch to the next nonblank character.   */
    /*------------------------------------------------------*/

    skip_blanks()

    {
        while (ch == ' ') get_char();
    }

            /*******************************/
            /*                             */
            /*        Token routines       */
            /*                             */
            /*******************************/

        /* Note that after a token has been extracted, */
        /* ch is the first character after the token.  */

    /*------------------------------------------------------*/
    /*  get_token         Extract the next token from the source  */
    /*                    buffer.                               */
    /*------------------------------------------------------*/

    get_token()

    {
        skip_blanks();
        tokenp = token_string;

        switch (char_code(ch)) {
            case LETTER:   get_word();     break;
            case DIGIT:    get_number();   break;
            case QUOTE:    get_string();   break;
            case EOF_CODE: token = END_OF_FILE;  break;
            default:       get_special();  break;
        }
    }

    /*------------------------------------------------------*/
    /*  get_word          Extract a word token and downshift its  */
    /*                    characters.  Check if it's a reserved  */
    /*                    word.  Set token to IDENTIFIER if it's  */
    /*                    not.                                  */
    /*------------------------------------------------------*/

    get_word()

    {
        BOOLEAN is_reserved_word();
```

```
    /*
    -- Extract the word.
    */
    while ((char_code(ch) == LETTER) || (char_code(ch) == DIGIT)) {
        *tokenp++ = ch;
        get_char();
    }
    *tokenp = '\0';
    downshift_word();

    if (! is_reserved_word()) token = IDENTIFIER;
}

/*------------------------------------------------------*/
/*  get_number         Extract a number token and set literal  */
/*                     to its value.  Set token to NUMBER.  */
/*------------------------------------------------------*/

get_number()

{
    int    whole_count    = 0;      /* no. digits in whole part */
    int    decimal_offset = 0;      /* no. digits to move decimal */
    char   exponent_sign  = '+';
    int    exponent       = 0;      /* value of exponent */
    float  nvalue         = 0.0;    /* value of number */
    float  evalue         = 0.0;    /* value of exponent */
    BOOLEAN saw_dotdot    = FALSE;  /* TRUE if encounter .. */

    digit_count = 0;
    count_error = FALSE;
    token       = NO_TOKEN;

    literal.type = INTEGER_LIT;     /* assume it's an integer */

    /*
    -- Extract the whole part of the number by accumulating
    -- the values of its digits into nvalue.  whole_count keeps
    -- track of the number of digits in this part.
    */
    accumulate_value(&nvalue, INVALID_NUMBER);
    if (token == ERROR) return;
    whole_count = digit_count;

    /*
    -- If the current character is a dot, then either we have a
    -- fraction part or we are seeing the first character of a ..
    -- token.  To find out, we must fetch the next character.
    */
    if (ch == '.') {
        get_char();

        if (ch == '.') {
            /*
            -- We have a .. token.  Back up bufferp so that the
            -- token can be extracted next.
            */
            saw_dotdot = TRUE;
            --bufferp;
        }
        else {
            literal.type = REAL_LIT;
            *tokenp++ = '.';

            /*
            -- We have a fraction part.  Accumulate it into nvalue.
            -- decimal_offset keeps track of how many digits to move
```

```
            --  the decimal point back.
            */
            accumulate_value(&nvalue, INVALID_FRACTION);
            if (token == ERROR) return;
            decimal_offset = whole_count - digit_count;
        }
    }

    /*
    -- Extract the exponent part, if any. There cannot be an
    -- exponent part if the .. token has been seen.
    */
    if (!saw_dotdot && ((ch == 'E') || (ch == 'e'))) {
        literal.type = REAL_LIT;
        *tokenp++ = ch;
        get_char();

        /*
        -- Fetch the exponent's sign, if any.
        */
        if ((ch == '+') || (ch == '-')) {
            *tokenp++ = exponent_sign = ch;
            get_char();
        }

        /*
        -- Extract the exponent.  Accumulate it into evalue.
        */
        accumulate_value(&evalue, INVALID_EXPONENT);
        if (token == ERROR) return;
        if (exponent_sign == '-') evalue = -evalue;
    }

    /*
    -- Were there too many digits?
    */
    if (count_error) {
        error(TOO_MANY_DIGITS);
        token = ERROR;
        return;
    }

    /*
    -- Adjust the number's value using
    -- decimal_offset and the exponent.
    */
    exponent = evalue + decimal_offset;
    if ((exponent + whole_count < -MAX_EXPONENT) ||
        (exponent + whole_count >  MAX_EXPONENT)) {
        error(REAL_OUT_OF_RANGE);
        token = ERROR;
        return;
    }
    if (exponent != 0) nvalue *= pow(10, exponent);

    /*
    -- Set the literal's value.
    */
    if (literal.type == INTEGER_LIT) {
        if ((nvalue < -MAX_INTEGER) || (nvalue > MAX_INTEGER)) {
            error(INTEGER_OUT_OF_RANGE);
            token = ERROR;
            return;
        }
        literal.value.integer = nvalue;
    }
    else literal.value.real = nvalue;
```

```
    *tokenp = '\0';
    token   = NUMBER;
}

/*------------------------------------------------------------*/
/*  get_string        Extract a string token.  Set token to   */
/*                    STRING.  Note that the quotes are        */
/*                    stored as part of token_string but not   */
/*                    literal.value.string.                    */
/*------------------------------------------------------------*/

get_string()

{
    char *sp = literal.value.string;

    *tokenp++ = '\'';
    get_char();

    /*
    --  Extract the string.
    */
    while (ch != EOF_CHAR) {
        /*
        -- Two consecutive single quotes represent
        -- a single quote in the string.
        */
        if (ch == '\'') {
            *tokenp++ = ch;
            get_char();
            if (ch != '\'') break;
        }
        *tokenp++ = ch;
        *sp++     = ch;
        get_char();
    }

    *tokenp      = '\0';
    *sp          = '\0';
    token        = STRING;
    literal.type = STRING_LIT;
}

/*------------------------------------------------------------*/
/*  get_special       Extract a special token.  Most are       */
/*                    single-character.  Some are double-       */
/*                    character.  Set token appropriately.      */
/*------------------------------------------------------------*/

get_special()

{
    *tokenp++ = ch;
    switch (ch) {
        case '^':  token = UPARROW;    get_char(); break;
        case '*':  token = STAR;       get_char(); break;
        case '(':  token = LPAREN;     get_char(); break;
        case ')':  token = RPAREN;     get_char(); break;
        case '-':  token = MINUS;      get_char(); break;
        case '+':  token = PLUS;       get_char(); break;
        case '=':  token = EQUAL;      get_char(); break;
        case '[':  token = LBRACKET;   get_char(); break;
        case ']':  token = RBRACKET;   get_char(); break;
        case ';':  token = SEMICOLON;  get_char(); break;
        case ',':  token = COMMA;      get_char(); break;
        case '/':  token = SLASH;      get_char(); break;
```

```
case ':':   get_char();         /* : or := */
            if (ch == '=') {
                *tokenp++ = '=';
                token    = COLONEQUAL;
                get_char();
            }
            else token = COLON;
            break;

case '<':   get_char();         /* < or <= or <> */
            if (ch == '=') {
                *tokenp++ = '=';
                token    = LE;
                get_char();
            }
            else if (ch == '>') {
                *tokenp++ = '>';
                token    = NE;
                get_char();
            }
            else token = LT;
            break;

case '>':   get_char();         /* > or >= */
            if (ch == '=') {
                *tokenp++ = '=';
                token    = GE;
                get_char();
            }
            else token = GT;
            break;

case '.':   get_char();         /* . or .. */
            if (ch == '.') {
                *tokenp++ = '.';
                token    = DOTDOT;
                get_char();
            }
            else token = PERIOD;
            break;

default:    token = ERROR;
            get_char();
            break;
    }
    *tokenp = '\0';
}
```

```
/*----------------------------------------------------------*/
/*  downshift_word        Copy a word token into word_string */
/*                        with all letters downshifted.     */
/*----------------------------------------------------------*/

downshift_word()

{
    int  offset = 'a' - 'A';    /* offset to downshift a letter */
    char *wp    = word_string;
    char *tp    = token_string;

    /*
    -- Copy word into word_string.
    */
    do {
        *wp++ = (*tp >= 'A') && (*tp <= 'Z')    /* if a letter, */
                ? *tp + offset                  /* then downshift */
                : *tp;                          /* else just copy */
```

```
        ++tp;
    } while (*tp != '\0');

    *wp = '\0';
}
```

```
/*----------------------------------------------------------*/
/*  accumulate_value    Extract a number part and accumulate */
/*                      its value.  Flag the error if the first */
/*                      character is not a digit.           */
/*----------------------------------------------------------*/

accumulate_value(valuep, error_code)

    float     *valuep;
    ERROR_CODE error_code;

{
    float value = *valuep;

    /*
    -- Error if the first character is not a digit.
    */
    if (char_code(ch) != DIGIT) {
        error(error_code);
        token = ERROR;
        return;
    }

    /*
    -- Accumulate the value as long as the total allowable
    -- number of digits has not been exceeded.
    */
    do {
        *tokenp++ = ch;

        if (++digit_count <= MAX_DIGIT_COUNT)
            value = 10*value + (ch - '0');
        else count_error = TRUE;

        get_char();
    } while (char_code(ch) == DIGIT);

    *valuep = value;

}
```

```
/*----------------------------------------------------------*/
/*  is_reserved_word    Check to see if a word token is a   */
/*                      reserved word.  If so, set token    */
/*                      appropriately and return TRUE.  Else, */
/*                      return FALSE.                       */
/*----------------------------------------------------------*/

    BOOLEAN
is_reserved_word()

{
    int       word_length = strlen(word_string);
    RW_STRUCT *rwp;

    /*
    -- Is it the right length?
    */
    if ((word_length >= MIN_RESERVED_WORD_LENGTH) &&
        (word_length <= MAX_RESERVED_WORD_LENGTH)) {
        /*
```

```
    --  Yes.  Pick the appropriate reserved word list
    --  and check to see if the word is in there.
    */
    for (rwp = rw_table[word_length];
         rwp->string != NULL;
         ++rwp) {
        if (strcmp(word_string, rwp->string) == 0) {
            token = rwp->token_code;
            return(TRUE);              /* yes, a reserved word */
        }
    }
}

    return(FALSE);                     /* no, it's not */
}


            /*******************************/
            /*                             */
            /*     Source file routines    */
            /*                             */
            /*******************************/

/*------------------------------------------------------*/
/*  open_source_file    Open the source file and fetch its  */
/*                      first character.                    */
/*------------------------------------------------------*/

open_source_file(name)

    char *name;        /* name of source file */

{
    if ((name == NULL) ||
        ((source_file = fopen(name, "r")) == NULL)) {
        error(FAILED_SOURCE_FILE_OPEN);
        exit(-FAILED_SOURCE_FILE_OPEN);
    }

    /*
    -- Fetch the first character.
    */
    bufferp = ""       ;
    get_char();
}

/*------------------------------------------------------*/
/*  close_source_file  Close the source file.          */
/*------------------------------------------------------*/

close_source_file()

{
    fclose(source_file);
}

/*------------------------------------------------------*/
/*  get_source_line    Read the next line from the source  */
/*                     file.  If there is one, print it out */
/*                     and return TRUE.  Else return FALSE  */
/*                     for the end of file.             */
/*------------------------------------------------------*/

    BOOLEAN
get_source_line()

{
    char print_buffer[MAX_SOURCE_LINE_LENGTH + 9];
```

```
    if ((fgets(source_buffer, MAX_SOURCE_LINE_LENGTH,
                            source_file)) != NULL) {
        ++line_number;

        if (print_flag) {
            sprintf(print_buffer, "%4d %d: %s",
                    line_number, level, source_buffer);
            print_line(print_buffer);
        }

        return(TRUE);
    }
    else return(FALSE);
}

            /*******************************/
            /*                             */
            /*     Printout routines       */
            /*                             */
            /*******************************/

/*------------------------------------------------------*/
/*  print_line        Print out a line.  Start a new page if  */
/*                    the current page is full.         */
/*------------------------------------------------------*/

print_line(line)

    char line[];        /* line to be printed */

{
    char save_ch;
    char *save_chp = NULL;

    if (++line_count > MAX_LINES_PER_PAGE) {
        print_page_header();
        line_count = 1;
    };

    if (strlen(line) > MAX_PRINT_LINE_LENGTH) {
        save_chp  = &line[MAX_PRINT_LINE_LENGTH];
        save_ch   = *save_chp;
        *save_chp = '\0';
    }

    printf(line);

    if (save_chp) *save_chp = save_ch;
}

/*------------------------------------------------------*/
/*  init_page_header   Initialize the fields of the page  */
/*                     header.                          */
/*------------------------------------------------------*/

init_page_header(name)

    char *name;        /* name of source file */

{
    time_t timer;

    strncpy(source_name, name, MAX_FILE_NAME_LENGTH - 1);

    /*
    -- Set the current date and time in the date string.
    */
```

```
    time(&timer);
    strcpy(date, asctime(localtime(&timer)));
}
/*---------------------------------------------------*/
/* print_page_header  Print the page header at the top of  */
/*                    the next page.                       */
/*---------------------------------------------------*/
```

```
print_page_header()

{
    putchar(FORM_FEED_CHAR);
    printf("Page %d   %s   %s\n\n", ++page_number, source_name, date);
}
```

Functions init_scanner and get_token have small changes. The former now initializes the QUOTE element of char_table, and the latter now calls the new function get_string whenever char_code(ch) is QUOTE. Function get_source_line now does not print the line if print_flag is FALSE.

The rest of the changes to the scanner enable it to scan Pascal programs more intelligently. We will begin with the ability to scan comments.

2.4.1 Comments

In Pascal, a comment is enclosed in curly braces: {This is a comment.} A comment can appear anywhere a blank can appear; in fact, a comment is treated as a single blank. We add this feature to the scanner by making function get_char a bit smarter. Whenever we fetch the character {, we call function skip_comment to skip over a comment, and then we set ch to a blank.

With the comment-smart get_char, the following input lines:

```
{This is a comment
 that spans two lines.}


Two{comments in}{a row}here.
```

produce the following output:

```
1 0: {This is a comment
2 0:  that spans two lines.}
3 0:
4 0: Two{comments in}{a row}here.
   >> <IDENTIFIER>    Two
   >> <IDENTIFIER>    here
   >> .                     .
```

We now also update global variable buffer_offset. When the contents of source_buffer is printed, the value of buffer_offset is the character offset from the beginning of source_buffer to the current character. Thus, we set it to zero each time we read a new source line, and for each non-tab character, we increment it by one. For each tab character, we bump it up to the next multiple of TAB_ SIZE. Later, we will see how buffer_offset helps us print error messages that point to the current character when an error occurs.

2.4.2 Identifiers and reserved words

A Pascal word token is either an identifier or a reserved word. Function get_ word now makes this distinction. Your first thought might be to simply list all the reserved words in a string array:

```
char *reserved_words[] = {"and", "array", "begin", ... };
```

Then, whenever you extract a word token, you can compare the token against the elements of the string array. If a match is found, the token is a reserved word; otherwise, it's an identifier.

This would work fine, except Pascal ignores case in its word tokens. Thus, the scanner must recognize all of the following to be the same identifier:

lastname   LASTNAME   LastName

and all of the following to be the same reserved word:

begin   BEGIN   Begin   BeGiN

The solution to this problem is quite simple. You downshift all the letters of word tokens to lowercase, and store the downshifted word token in the new global variable word_string. You can then reliably compare them against a list of down-shifted reserved words.

Instead of putting all the reserved words in one string array, you can speed up the comparisons by grouping the reserved words based on their lengths into several short arrays. These are the reserved word arrays at the beginning of file scanner.c. Array rw_table is actually an array of pointers to these lists. For example, rw_table[5] is a pointer to the list of five-letter reserved words.

In get_word, we extract a word token and store it in token_string, just as before. But now we call function downshift_word to copy the token into word_ string with all of its letters downshifted. Then, we call the boolean function is_ reserved_word to determine whether or not we have a reserved word. If not, we set token to IDENTIFIER.

In function is_reserved_word, we use the length of the word token to pick the current reserved word list from rw_table. If the word is found in the list, we set token appropriately and return TRUE. Otherwise, we return FALSE.

We saw how the scanner recognizes identifiers and reserved words in Figures 2-5 and 2-6.

2.4.3 Strings

A Pascal scanner must recognize Pascal strings and special symbols. Whenever it fetches a single-quote character, function `get_token` calls function `get_string` to extract a string token. In function `get_string`, we repeatedly fetch characters and append them to `token_string` and to `literal.value.string` until we encounter the other single quote. We include the leading and trailing quote characters in `token_string` but not in `literal.value.string`. (We'll see in a later chapter why it is useful to keep the quote characters.)

In Pascal, two consecutive single quotes represent one single quote in a string: the string `'don''t'` contains the characters `don't`. Otherwise, one single quote terminates the string. Given the following input:

```
'This is a string.'
'Don''t skip this'.
```

the tokenizer outputs:

```
1 0: 'This is a string.'
  >> <STRING>            'This is a string.'
2 0: 'Don''t skip this'.
  >> <STRING>            'Don't skip this'
  >> .                    .
```

2.4.4 Special symbols

Most of Pascal's special symbol tokens are single character, like + and =. Some are double character, like .. and :=. The double-character special symbols have an extra bit of complexity: the first character looks just like a single-character special symbol token. If the scanner fetches a character that can either be a single-character special symbol or the first character of a double-character special symbol, it must fetch the following character. From this second character, the scanner can tell whether it has a single-character or a double-character special symbol token.

Function `get_special` now knows how to extract all the special symbol tokens. Like the other token extraction functions, it always leaves `ch` at the first character after the token. Given the following input:

```
+ - : = := < <= <> .
```

the tokenizer outputs:

```
1 0: + - : = := < <= <> .
  >> +                   +
  >> -                   -
```

```
>> :                    :
>> =                    =
>> :=                   :=
>> <                    <
>> <=                   <=
>> <>                   <>
>> .                    .
```

2.4.5 Numbers

Now we are ready to tackle scanning both integer and real numbers. The definition of a Pascal number begins with an *unsigned integer*. An unsigned integer consists of one or more consecutive digits. The simplest form of a number token is an unsigned integer:

$$3 \quad 75 \quad 13456$$

A number token can also be an unsigned integer (the whole part) followed by a fraction part. A fraction part consists of a decimal point followed by an unsigned integer, such as:

$$123.45 \quad 0.967$$

These numbers have whole parts 123 and 0, and fraction parts .45 and .967, respectively.

A number token can also be a whole part followed by an exponent part. An exponent part consists of the letter E or e followed by an unsigned integer. An optional exponent sign + or - can appear between the letter and the first exponent digit. Examples are:

$$152e3 \quad 2E53 \quad 345e-12 \quad 7825E+5$$

Finally, a number token can be a whole part followed by a fraction part *and* an exponent part, in that order:

$$163.98E7 \quad 0.000123e-45$$

The scanner now limits the number of digits in the number to 20 (see constant MAX_DIGIT_COUNT). Also, the exponent value must be in the range of -37 through $+37$ (see constant MAX_EXPONENT). The specific values we use here depend on how real numbers are represented on a particular computer.

Function get_number is the longest function in the scanner, but it is easy to follow in light of the definition of what a number is and what we have already seen in the simple tokenizer. Note that local variable nvalue is now real and we can accumulate values greater than 9999.

In function get_number, we extract up to three unsigned integers. We always extract the whole part, and we can extract neither, one, or both of the fraction and the exponent parts. For each part, we call function accumulate_value. In this function, we first check that the current character is a digit, and then we accumulate the number's value just as we did before. If the current character is not a digit, we call function error with the error code that was passed in. (Function error will be explained when we discuss how to flag syntax errors.)

After we have accumulated the value of the whole part in nvalue, we set whole_count to the number of digits in that part. We then look for a decimal point. If we find one, we call accumulate_value again to further accumulate the value into nvalue. After this call, we set local variable decimal_offset to the number of places we need to move the decimal point back from the right end of nvalue. decimal_offset is always either zero or a negative value.

For example, suppose get_number is called to extract the number token 386.07. After the first call to accumulate_value to obtain the value of the whole part, the situation is as follows:

```
          nvalue:   386
   decimal_offset:   0

   source_buffer:   386.07
         bufferp:        ^
              ch:   .
```

We call accumulate_value a second time for the fraction part, and then we have the following:

```
          nvalue:   38607
   decimal_offset:   -2

   source_buffer:   386.07❖
         bufferp:            ^
              ch:   ❖
```

We now look for an exponent part. There is one if the current character is an E or an e. The next character after that can be a + or -. If so, we save that character in exponent_sign. We call accumulate_value for the exponent, but this time we use a fresh local variable evalue. If exponent_sign is -, then we negate evalue and we have the following:

```
          nvalue:   38607
   decimal_offset:   -2
          evalue:   -3
```

```
source_buffer:   386.07e-3❖
     bufferp:              ^
         ch:    ❖
```

At this point, we check to see if there were too many digits in the number token. If so, we call function error with the TOO_MANY_DIGITS error code.

Now, to compute the final value of nvalue, we first set local variable exponent to the sum of evalue and decimal_offset. We check to see if we are still within the valid range for exponents, and if so, exponent is the power of ten by which to multiply nvalue. If the number is an integer, we check to see if it is within the valid range of integers. Finally, we set either literal.value.integer or literal.value.real to the value of nvalue.

We have one more thing to consider. Pascal uses the token .. as a subrange specifier, as in the following:

```
TYPE
    teenyears = 11..19;
```

When get_number has fetched the first period, we must fetch another character to see if we have a decimal point or the .. token. If we find a second period, we don't have a fraction part, nor can we have an exponent part. We just back bufferp up to put the second period back, and we are done fetching the digits of the number token. The next time get_token is called, it will extract the .. token. Given the following input:

```
123 -456 12..34 +123.45 -0.00012 .... 0012.3e001
123.4e27 0 000 00000.100000 -123.4567E-27.
```

the tokenizer outputs the following:

```
1 0: 123 -456 12..34 +123.45 -0.00012 .... 0012.3e001
    >> <NUMBER>        123 (integer)
    >> -               -
    >> <NUMBER>        456 (integer)
    >> <NUMBER>        12 (integer)
    >> ..              ..
    >> <NUMBER>        34 (integer)
    >> +               +
    >> <NUMBER>        123.45 (real)
    >> -               -
    >> <NUMBER>        0.00012 (real)
    >> ..              ..
    >> ..              ..
    >> <NUMBER>        123 (real)
```

```
2 0: 123.4e27 0 000 00000.100000 -123.4567E-27.
   >> <NUMBER>        1.234e+029 (real)
   >> <NUMBER>        0 (integer)
   >> <NUMBER>        0 (integer)
   >> <NUMBER>        0.1 (real)
   >> -               -
   >> <NUMBER>        1.23457e-025 (real)
   >> .               .
```

2.4.6 Flagging errors

What should the scanner do when it encounters an error? It should print out an error message. A nice touch is to point to the error itself. For example, the following input:

```
123e99 123456 1234567890.123457890e12
1234.56e.
```

should produce the following output:

```
 1 0: 123e99 123456 1234567890.123457890e12
        ^

*** ERROR: Real literal out of range.
   >> <ERROR>         123e99
                         ^

*** ERROR: Integer literal out of range.
   >> <ERROR>         123456
                                          ^

*** ERROR: Too many digits.
   >> <ERROR>         1234567890.123457890e12
 2 0: 1234.56e.
         ^

*** ERROR: Invalid exponent.
   >> <ERROR>         1234.56e
   >> .               .
```

Figures 2-9 and 2-10 show files error.h and error.c of the error module. File error.h defines the maximum number of syntax errors that we will tolerate. It also defines all the syntax error codes that we will use in the rest of the modules.

FIGURE 2-9   File error.h.

```
/****************************************************************/
/*                                                            */
/*      E R R O R   R O U T I N E S   (Header)                */
/*                                                            */
/*      FILE:      error.h                                    */
/*                                                            */
/*      MODULE:    error                                      */
/*                                                            */
/****************************************************************/

#ifndef error_h
#define error_h

#define MAX_SYNTAX_ERRORS 25

/*----------------------------------------------------------*/
/* Error codes                                              */
/*----------------------------------------------------------*/

typedef enum {
    NO_ERROR,
    SYNTAX_ERROR,
    TOO_MANY_SYNTAX_ERRORS,
    FAILED_SOURCE_FILE_OPEN,
    UNEXPECTED_END_OF_FILE,
    INVALID_NUMBER,
    INVALID_FRACTION,
    INVALID_EXPONENT,
    TOO_MANY_DIGITS,
    REAL_OUT_OF_RANGE,
    INTEGER_OUT_OF_RANGE,
    MISSING_RPAREN,
    INVALID_EXPRESSION,
    INVALID_ASSIGNMENT,
    MISSING_IDENTIFIER,
    MISSING_COLONEQUAL,
    UNDEFINED_IDENTIFIER,
    STACK_OVERFLOW,
    INVALID_STATEMENT,
    UNEXPECTED_TOKEN,
    MISSING_SEMICOLON,
    MISSING_DO,
    MISSING_UNTIL,
    MISSING_THEN,
    INVALID_FOR_CONTROL,
    MISSING_OF,
    INVALID_CONSTANT,
    MISSING_CONSTANT,
    MISSING_COLON,
    MISSING_END,
    MISSING_TO_OR_DOWNTO,
    REDEFINED_IDENTIFIER,
    MISSING_EQUAL,
    INVALID_TYPE,
    NOT_A_TYPE_IDENTIFIER,
    INVALID_SUBRANGE_TYPE,
    NOT_A_CONSTANT_IDENTIFIER,
    MISSING_DOTDOT,
    INCOMPATIBLE_TYPES,
    INVALID_TARGET,
    INVALID_IDENTIFIER_USAGE,
    INCOMPATIBLE_ASSIGNMENT,
    MIN_GT_MAX,
    MISSING_LBRACKET,
    MISSING_RBRACKET,
    INVALID_INDEX_TYPE,
    MISSING_BEGIN,
    MISSING_PERIOD,
    TOO_MANY_SUBSCRIPTS,
    INVALID_FIELD,
    NESTING_TOO_DEEP,
    MISSING_PROGRAM,
    ALREADY_FORWARDED,
    WRONG_NUMBER_OF_PARMS,
    INVALID_VAR_PARM,
    NOT_A_RECORD_VARIABLE,
    MISSING_VARIABLE,
    CODE_SEGMENT_OVERFLOW,
    UNIMPLEMENTED_FEATURE,
} ERROR_CODE;

#endif
```

FIGURE 2-10   File error.c.

```
/****************************************************************/
/*                                                            */
/*      E R R O R   R O U T I N E S                           */
/*                                                            */
/*      Error messages and routines to print them.            */
/*                                                            */
/*      FILE:      error.c                                    */
/*                                                            */
/*      MODULE:    error                                      */
/*                                                            */
/****************************************************************/

#include <stdio.h>
#include "common.h"
#include "error.h"

/*----------------------------------------------------------*/
/* Externals                                                */
/*----------------------------------------------------------*/

extern char    *tokenp;
extern BOOLEAN print_flag;
extern char    source_buffer[];
extern char    *bufferp;

/*----------------------------------------------------------*/
/* Error messages    Keyed to enumeration type ERROR_CODE   */
/*                   in file error.h.                       */
/*----------------------------------------------------------*/

char *error_messages[] = {
```

```
"No error",                                    "Unimplemented feature",
"Syntax error",                            };
"Too many syntax errors",
"Failed to open source file",              /*------------------------------------------------------------*/
"Unexpected end of file",                  /* Globals                                                  */
"Invalid number",                          /*------------------------------------------------------------*/
"Invalid fraction",
"Invalid exponent",                        int error_count = 0;    /* number of syntax errors */
"Too many digits",
"Real literal out of range",                        /******************************/
"Integer literal out of range",                     /*                            */
"Missing right parenthesis",                        /*      Error routines        */
"Invalid expression",                               /*                            */
"Invalid assignment statement",                     /******************************/
"Missing identifier",
"Missing := ",                             /*------------------------------------------------------------*/
"Undefined identifier",                    /* error          Print an arrow under the error and then */
"Stack overflow",                          /*                print the error message.                */
"Invalid statement",                       /*------------------------------------------------------------*/
"Unexpected token",
"Missing ; ",                              error(code)
"Missing DO",
"Missing UNTIL",                               ERROR_CODE code;    /* error code */
"Missing THEN",
"Invalid FOR control variable",            {
"Missing OF",
"Invalid constant",                            extern int buffer_offset;
"Missing constant",                            char message_buffer[MAX_PRINT_LINE_LENGTH];
"Missing : ",                                  char *message = error_messages[code];
"Missing END",                                 int  offset   = buffer_offset - 2;
"Missing TO or DOWNTO",
"Redefined identifier",                        /*
"Missing = ",                                  -- Print the arrow pointing to the token just scanned.
"Invalid type",                                */
"Not a type identifier",                       if (print_flag) offset += 8;
"Invalid subrangetype",                        sprintf(message_buffer, "%*s^\n", offset, " ");
"Not a constant identifier",                   if (print_flag) print_line(message_buffer);
"Missing .. ",                                 else            printf(message_buffer);
"Incompatible types",
"Invalid assignment target",                   /*
"Invalid identifier usage",                    -- Print the error message.
"Incompatible assignment",                     */
"Min limit greater than max limit",            sprintf(message_buffer, " *** ERROR: %s.\n", message);
"Missing [ ",                                  if (print_flag) print_line(message_buffer);
"Missing ] ",                                  else            printf(message_buffer);
"Invalid index type",
"Missing BEGIN",                               *tokenp = '\0';
"Missing period",                              ++error_count;
"Too many subscripts",
"Invalid field",                               if (error_count > MAX_SYNTAX_ERRORS) {
"Nesting too deep",                                sprintf(message_buffer,
"Missing PROGRAM",                                         "Too many syntax errors.  Aborted.\n");
"Already specified in FORWARD",                    if (print_flag) print_line(message_buffer);
"Wrong number of actual parameters",               else            printf(message_buffer);
"Invalid VAR parameter",
"Not a record variable",                           exit(-TOO_MANY_SYNTAX_ERRORS);
"Missing variable",                            }
"Code segment overflow",                   }
```

In file `error.c`, string array `error_message` contains the messages that correspond to the error codes. In function `error`, we index into this array with an error code. We use global variable `buffer_offset` to print an arrow under the end of the last token we scanned, which is the token that caused the error. We then print the error message.

If we have too many errors, we simply abort. Of course, this is just the sort of action that drives programmers crazy about compilers. We put this in as a last resort and hope that it does not occur often.

2.5 Program 2-3: A Source Program Compactor

The tokenizer utility calls the scanner to provide it with tokens, just like a compiler or an interpreter. To demonstrate that you have indeed written a good general-purpose Pascal scanner, here is another utility to use it.

Pascal programs are written to be read by people, with line breaks, blanks, indentation, and comments to improve readability. But suppose you want to save disk space, even at the expense of readability. You can then store a compacted version of the Pascal source file with all comments and unnecessary blanks removed. Line breaks only serve to keep line lengths at, say, 80 characters or less. For example, the following Pascal program:

```
PROGRAM hello (output);

{Write 'Hello, world.' ten times.}

VAR
    i : integer;

BEGIN {hello}
    FOR i := 1 TO 10 DO BEGIN
        writeln ('Hello, world.');
    END;
END {hello}.
```

can be compacted to:

```
PROGRAM hello(output);VAR i:integer;BEGIN FOR i:=1 TO 10 DO BEGIN
writeln('Hello, world.');END;END.
```

The output is a compacted Pascal program that can still be correctly compiled by a Pascal compiler. As far as the Pascal compiler is concerned, the two versions are equivalent. In fact, the Pascal scanner would process the compacted version faster!

Note how all the comments and unnecessary blanks are removed. Wherever a blank is still required, only one is used. One blank is required between two words, between two numbers, or between a word and a number. No blank is required between a word and a special symbol, or between a number and a special symbol. Any blanks in a string are not removed.

The source compactor utility uses the Pascal scanner to read in a Pascal source program and outputs a compacted version. We depend on the scanner to read the source file, and we call get_token each time we want the next token. We set the scanner's print_flag to FALSE so that the compactor does not produce a listing.

The compactor needs to classify each token it obtains from the scanner as a *delimiter* or a *nondelimiter*. A delimiter is a token that establishes a boundary for itself and any adjacent token. Thus, a special symbol is a delimiter. In the expression alpha*pi, it is clear that there are three tokens. Words and numbers are not delimiters. The identifier alpha and the number 3 cannot be written together; alpha3 is scanned as a single identifier token. In Pascal, blanks, tabs, and line breaks also serve as delimiters. The compactor defines an enumeration type as follows:

```
typedef enum {
    DELIMITER, NONDELIMITER,
} TOKEN_CLASS;
```

We call function token_class to return the class of the current token. All special symbols and strings are in class DELIMITER. All other tokens (identifiers, reserved words, and numbers) are in class NONDELIMITER. Global variable token_class records the class of the current token.

Figure 2-11 shows the main file of the compactor utility, compact.c. The scanner has done most of the work. We call the scanner to extract tokens which we then output. We keep track of the class of current token and that of the previous token. If the previous token and the current token are both nondelimiters, we output a blank between them. In all other cases, we can output the current token adjacent to the previous one. See routines append_blank and append_token.

FIGURE 2-11   A source program compactor.

```
/****************************************************************/
/*                                                              */
/*      Program 2-3:  Pascal Source Compactor                   */
/*                                                              */
/*      Compact a Pascal source file by removing                */
/*      all comments and unnecessary blanks.                    */
/*                                                              */
/*      FILE:      compact.c                                    */
/*                                                              */
/*      REQUIRES:  Modules error, scanner                       */
/*                                                              */
/*      USAGE:     compact sourcefile                           */
/*                                                              */
/*          sourcefile     name of source file to compact       */
/*                                                              */
/****************************************************************/

#include <stdio.h>
```

```
#include "common.h"
#include "scanner.h"

#define MAX_OUTPUT_RECORD_LENGTH        80

/*------------------------------------------------------------*/
/* Token classes                                            */
/*------------------------------------------------------------*/

typedef enum {
    DELIMITER, NONDELIMITER,
} TOKEN_CLASS;

/*------------------------------------------------------------*/
/* Externals                                                */
/*------------------------------------------------------------*/
```

```
extern TOKEN_CODE token;
extern char       token_string[];
extern BOOLEAN    print_flag;

/*------------------------------------------------------*/
/*  Globals                                             */
/*------------------------------------------------------*/

int  record_length;          /* length of output record */
char *recp;                  /* pointer into output record */

char output_record[MAX_OUTPUT_RECORD_LENGTH];

/*------------------------------------------------------*/
/*  main             Loop to process tokens.            */
/*------------------------------------------------------*/

main(argc, argv)

    int  argc;
    char *argv[];

{
    TOKEN_CLASS class;           /* current token class */
    TOKEN_CLASS prev_class;      /* previous token class */
    TOKEN_CLASS token_class();

    /*
    -- Initialize the scanner.
    */
    print_flag = FALSE;
    init_scanner(argv[1]);

    /*
    -- Initialize the compactor.
    */
    prev_class = DELIMITER;
    recp  = output_record;
    *recp = '\0';
    record_length = 0;

    /*
    -- Repeatedly process tokens until a period
    -- or the end of file.
    */
    do {
        get_token();
        if (token == END_OF_FILE) break;
        class = token_class();

        /*
        -- Append a blank only if two adjacent nondelimiters.
        -- Then append the token string.
        */
        if ((prev_class == NONDELIMITER) && (class == NONDELIMITER))
            append_blank();
        append_token();

        prev_class = class;
    } while (token != PERIOD);

    /*
    -- Flush the last output record if it is partially filled.
    */
    if (record_length > 0) flush_output_record();

    quit_scanner();
```

```
}

/*------------------------------------------------------*/
/*  token_class        Return the class of the current token. */
/*------------------------------------------------------*/

    TOKEN_CLASS
token_class()

{
    /*
    -- Nondelimiters:  identifiers, numbers, and reserved words
    -- Delimiters:     strings and special symbols
    */
    switch (token) {

    case IDENTIFIER:
    case NUMBER:
        return(NONDELIMITER);

    default:
        return(token < AND ? DELIMITER : NONDELIMITER);
    }
}

/*------------------------------------------------------*/
/*  append_blank       Append a blank to the output record,  */
/*                     or flush the record if it is full.    */
/*------------------------------------------------------*/

append_blank()

{
    if (++record_length == MAX_OUTPUT_RECORD_LENGTH - 1)
        flush_output_record();
    else strcat(output_record, " ");
}

/*------------------------------------------------------*/
/*  append_token       Append the token string to the output */
/*                     record if it fits.  If not, flush the */
/*                     current record and append the string  */
/*                     to append to the new record.          */
/*------------------------------------------------------*/

append_token()

{
    int token_length;            /* length of token string */

    token_length = strlen(token_string);
    if (record_length + token_length
                        >= MAX_OUTPUT_RECORD_LENGTH - 1)
        flush_output_record();

    strcat(output_record, token_string);
    record_length += token_length;
}

/*------------------------------------------------------*/
/*  flush_output_record          Flush the current output    */
/*                               record.                     */
/*------------------------------------------------------*/

flush_output_record()
```

```
{                                                      *recp = '\0';
    printf("%s\n", output_record);                     record_length = 0;
    recp = output_record;                          }
```

This compactor has a maximum output record length of 80 characters. To fill each output record as much as possible, we start a new output record only when the current token cannot fit in the current output record. In function flush_output_record, we write out the current record and start a new one. It is also called at the very end of the program to write out the last record.

Questions and exercises

1. Suppose the syntax rules of Pascal stated that a comment is to be completely ignored. Then, if the source contains:

   al{comment}pha 123{another}45

   the scanner would extract the word token alpha and the number token 12345. What changes would need to be made to function get_char to implement this rule?

2. Number tokens in Pascal are all represented as unsigned values. How does our scanner process input like -3?

3. The final calculation in routine get_number may be time consuming.

   nvalue *= pow(10, exponent)

   Rewrite the routine to avoid such a calculation.

CHAPTER 3

The Symbol Table

Compilers and interpreters build and maintain a data structure used throughout the translation process. This structure is commonly called the *symbol table*, and it is where all the information about a source program's identifiers are kept.

Maintaining a well-organized symbol table is an important skill for all compiler writers. As a compiler or an interpreter parses a source program, it relies on the symbol table to provide information about each identifier. It must be able to access and update existing information and enter new information quickly and efficiently. Otherwise, the translation process is slowed, or worse, it produces incorrect results.

In this chapter, we will write three utility programs to develop our symbol table skills. These skills enable us to:

- create a symbol table organized as a binary tree
- search for and update information in the symbol table

The first program generates a cross-reference listing by keeping line number information in the symbol table. The second program uses the symbol table to keep track of identifiers as it crunches a source program into a compressed form. The third program restores a crunched program.

3.1 Symbol table entries and operations

What information about an identifier is kept in the symbol table? Any information that is useful! Information about an identifier is stored as an *entry* in the table.

Such information typically includes the identifier's name string, its type, and how it is defined.

No matter what information a symbol table keeps about each identifier or how it is organized, certain operations are fundamental. You *enter* information about an identifier into the table by creating an entry. You *search* the table to look up an identifier's entry and make available the information stored there. You can then *update* the entry to modify the stored information.

There can be only one entry per identifier in a symbol table. Therefore, for each identifier, you first search the table to see if it already has an entry, and if so, you just access or update that entry. Otherwise, you must create a new entry.

In order to maintain the modularity of our code, we will keep the symbol table routines in their own files. In this chapter, we will introduce the new symbol table module.

Scanner Module

scanner.h	*u*	Scanner header file
scanner.c	*u*	Scanner routines

Symbol Table Module

symtab.h	*n*	Symbol table header file
symtab.c	*n*	Symbol table routines

Error Module

error.h	*u*	Error header file
error.c	*u*	Error routines

Miscellaneous

common.h	*u*	Common header file

Where: *u*   file unchanged from the previous chapter
        n   new file

3.2 Binary tree organization

How should you organize the symbol table? You can choose from many different data structures, such as arrays, linked lists, trees, and hash tables. The most common operations that are performed on a symbol table are creating new entries and searching for existing entries. You also want the entries to be sorted alphabetically to aid searching. These operations can be done very efficiently if you organize a symbol table as a binary tree, and then the functions to do the operations are not hard to write. Figure 3-1 shows a small symbol table organized as a binary tree.

FIGURE 3-1   A symbol table organized as a binary tree. To keep the node diagrams simple, we show the name string inside the name field. Actually, the name field points to the name string.

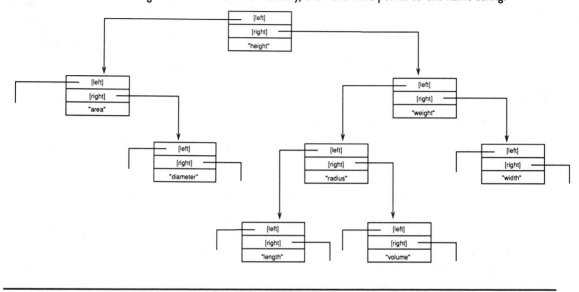

Each entry of the symbol table is stored as a node of the binary tree. Each node contains a pointer to the identifier's name string and pointers to its left and right subtrees. At any given node, that node's left subtree is either empty or contains nodes whose name strings are alphabetically less than the given node's name string. The given node's right subtree is either empty or contains nodes whose name strings are alphabetically greater than the given node's name string.

Figure 3-2 shows the header file symtab.h. The definition of a symbol table entry, SYMTAB_NODE, reflects this structure. Besides the left and right subtree and name string pointers, the structure contains other fields that will be useful in later chapters. Field level will be the nesting level of the identifier, and field label_ index will be used by the compiler to emit an assembly-language reference to the identifier. Field info is "wild," as we will see later, we can use this field whenever necessary to point to any information specific to a particular utility program.

FIGURE 3-2   File symtab.h.

```
/************************************************************/
/*                                                          */
/*      S Y M B O L   T A B L E   (Header)                  */
/*                                                          */
/*      FILE:    symtab.h                                   */
/*                                                          */
/*      MODULE:  symbol table                               */
/*                                                          */
/************************************************************/

#ifndef symtab_h
#define symtab_h

#include "common.h"

/*----------------------------------------------------------*/
/* Value structure                                          */
/*----------------------------------------------------------*/

typedef union {
    int    integer;
```

```
      float   real;                                        struct symtab_node *parms;
      char    character;                                   struct symtab_node *locals;
      char    *stringp;                                    struct symtab_node *local_symtab;
} VALUE;                                                    char             *code_segment;
                                                       } routine;

/*----------------------------------------------*/          struct {
/* Definition structure                        */              int             offset;
/*----------------------------------------------*/              struct symtab_node *record_idp;
                                                           } data;
typedef enum {                                           } info;
    UNDEFINED,                                       } DEFN_STRUCT;
    CONST_DEFN, TYPE_DEFN, VAR_DEFN, FIELD_DEFN,
    VALPARM_DEFN, VARPARM_DEFN,                      /*----------------------------------------------------*/
    PROG_DEFN, PROC_DEFN, FUNC_DEFN,                 /* Symbol table node                                 */
} DEFN_KEY;                                          /*----------------------------------------------------*/

typedef enum {                                       typedef struct symtab_node {
    DECLARED, FORWARD,                                   struct symtab_node *left, *right;  /* ptrs to subtrees */
    READ, READLN, WRITE, WRITELN,                        struct symtab_node *next;          /* for chaining nodes */
    ABS, ARCTAN, CHR, COS, EOFF, EOLN, EXP, LN, ODD, ORD,   char            *name;            /* name string */
    PRED, ROUND, SIN, SQR, SQRT, SUCC, TRUNC,            char               *info;            /* ptr to generic info */
} ROUTINE_KEY;                                           DEFN_STRUCT        defn;            /* definition struct */
                                                         int                level;           /* nesting level */
typedef struct {                                         int                label_index;     /* index for code label */
    DEFN_KEY key;                                    } SYMTAB_NODE, *SYMTAB_NODE_PTR;
    union {
        struct {                                     /*----------------------------------------------------*/
            VALUE value;                             /* Functions                                         */
        } constant;                                  /*----------------------------------------------------*/

        struct {                                     SYMTAB_NODE_PTR search_symtab();
            ROUTINE_KEY     key;                     SYMTAB_NODE_PTR enter_symtab();
            int             parm_count;
            int             total_parm_size;         #endif
            int             total_local_size;
```

Field defn is a structure of type DEFN_STRUCT. This substructure contains more information when an identifier is defined to be the name of a constant, procedure, function, variable, or parameter. We will see how this information is entered in Chapters 6 and 7.

The DEFN_KEY enumeration type defines constants that specify how an identifier is defined. An identifier is either undefined, or it is the name of a constant, type, variable, record field, value parameter, VAR (reference) parameter, program, procedure, or function. We will set the defn.key field of a symbol table node to the identifier's definition key.

The ROUTINE_KEY enumeration type defines constants that represent the programmer-defined or standard Pascal procedures and functions. Starting in Chapter 7, we will set the defn.info.routine.key field of a symbol table node when the identifier is the name of a procedure or function.

Once we see how to parse Pascal constant definitions, we will enter the value of a constant identifier into the defn.info.constant.value field of the identifier's symbol table node. The field type is defined by the VALUE union type, which is similar to the LITERAL type of the scanner.

An identifier's type is a major piece of information that is missing. We will modify symtab.h to include type information when we see how to parse declarations in Chapter 6.

Figure 3-3 shows file `symtab.c`, which contains the symbol table functions. There are only two functions, one to search the symbol table, and another one to enter information into it.

FIGURE 3-3   File `symtab.c`.

```
/****************************************************************/
/*                                                              */
/*      S Y M B O L   T A B L E                                 */
/*                                                              */
/*      Symbol table routines.                                  */
/*                                                              */
/*      FILE:       symtab.c                                     */
/*                                                              */
/*      MODULE:     symbol table                                */
/*                                                              */
/****************************************************************/

#include <stdio.h>
#include "common.h"
#include "error.h"
#include "symtab.h"

/*--------------------------------------------------------------*/
/*  Globals                                                     */
/*--------------------------------------------------------------*/

SYMTAB_NODE_PTR symtab_root = NULL;      /* symbol table root */

/*--------------------------------------------------------------*/
/*  search_symtab       Search for a name in the symbol table.  */
/*                      Return a pointer of the entry if found, */
/*                      or NULL if not.                         */
/*--------------------------------------------------------------*/

    SYMTAB_NODE_PTR
search_symtab(name, np)

    char            *name;      /* name to search for */
    SYMTAB_NODE_PTR np;         /* ptr to symtab root */

{
    int cmp;

    /*
    -- Loop to check each node.  Return if the node matches,
    -- else continue search down the left or right subtree.
    */
    while (np != NULL) {
        cmp = strcmp(name, np->name);
```

```
        if (cmp == 0) return(np);           /* found */
        np = cmp < 0 ? np->left : np->right;  /* continue search */
    }

    return(NULL);                           /* not found */
}

/*--------------------------------------------------------------*/
/*  enter_symtab        Enter a name into the symbol table,     */
/*                      and return a pointer to the new entry.  */
/*--------------------------------------------------------------*/

    SYMTAB_NODE_PTR
enter_symtab(name, npp)

    char            *name;      /* name to enter */
    SYMTAB_NODE_PTR *npp;       /* ptr to ptr to symtab root */

{
    int             cmp;        /* result of strcmp */
    SYMTAB_NODE_PTR new_nodep;  /* ptr to new entry */
    SYMTAB_NODE_PTR np;         /* ptr to node to test */

    /*
    -- Create the new node for the name.
    */
    new_nodep = alloc_struct(SYMTAB_NODE);
    new_nodep->name = alloc_bytes(strlen(name) + 1);
    strcpy(new_nodep->name, name);
    new_nodep->left = new_nodep->right = new_nodep->next = NULL;
    new_nodep->info = NULL;
    new_nodep->defn.key = UNDEFINED;
    new_nodep->level = new_nodep->label_index = 0;

    /*
    -- Loop to search for the insertion point.
    */
    while ((np = *npp) != NULL) {
        cmp = strcmp(name, np->name);
        npp = cmp < 0 ? &(np->left) : &(np->right);
    }

    *npp = new_nodep;                       /* replace */
    return(new_nodep);
}
```

A complete compiler or interpreter has more than just one symbol table. During the translation process, there is a symbol table for the source program's global identifiers and a separate symbol table for the local identifiers of each procedure and function. Until Chapter 7, we will have a single symbol table. Global variable `symtab_root` points to the root of the symbol table tree. We initialize it to NULL, since the table starts out empty.

Whenever we need to search for an identifier's symbol table node, we pass function search_symtab a pointer to the identifier's name string and a pointer to the root node of the symbol table to search. Until Chapter 7, the value of the second parameter will be the value of symtab_root.

In the while loop of search_symtab, we first check the node pointed to by np. If the names match, we have found the node, so we return the pointer to that node. However, if the name we are searching for is less than the node's name, we set np to point to the node's left subtree. Or, if our name is greater, we set np to point to the node's right subtree. At the top of the loop, we check again. If np becomes NULL, that is, the search went off the bottom of the tree, the name was not in the symbol table and we return NULL.

Whenever we need to create a new symbol table node for an identifier, we pass function enter_symtab a pointer to the identifier's name string and a *pointer to a pointer* to the root of the symbol table. Until Chapter 7, the value of the second parameter will be &symtab_root. We use a pointer to a pointer because inserting a node causes a pointer itself to be changed.

FIGURE 3-4   Inserting a new node into the symbol table. Variable npp is a pointer to a pointer to a symbol table node. Here, it points to the NULL link that will be replaced by the pointer to the new node. Also shown are the three previous node pointers that npp pointed to during the search for the correct insertion point.

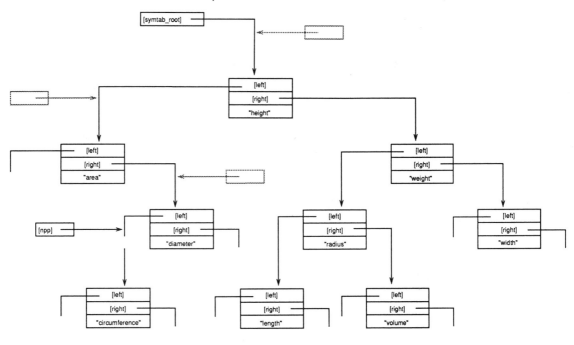

In enter_symtab, we first allocate and initialize a new node. We set the info field to NULL, and since we will not be using them until later chapters, we set the level and label_index fields to zero. We also set the defn.key field to UNDEFINED. Eventually, we will reset this field to another DEFN_KEY value.

Then, as in function search_symtab, we search the binary tree to find where to insert the new node. We find the proper entry point when npp points to a NULL pointer. This is shown in Figure 3-4. We replace the NULL pointer with a pointer to the new node, and we return that pointer.

We have seen how a symbol table can be organized and maintained. Next, we will see how some utility programs can use it. These programs will give us insight into how compilers and interpreters use symbol tables.

3.3 Program 3-1: A Cross-Referencer

A *cross-reference* listing of a source program is an alphabetical listing of all the identifiers that appear in the program. As shown in Figure 3-5, alongside each identifier's name are the source line numbers that contain the identifier. This is useful for tracking where each identifier is used.

FIGURE 3-5   A sample cross-reference listing.

```
Page 1   hello.pas   Mon Jul 09 03:45:59 1990              12 0: END (hello).


 1 0: PROGRAM hello (output);                      Cross-Reference
 2 0:                                              ---------------
 3 0: (Write 'Hello, world.' ten times.)
 4 0:                                              hello          1
 5 0: VAR
 6 0:      i : integer;                            i              6   9
 7 0:
 8 0: BEGIN (hello)                                integer        6
 9 0:      FOR i := 1 TO 10 DO BEGIN
10 0:          writeln('Hello, world.');           output         1
11 0:      END;
                                                   writeln       10
```

Our cross-referencer utility program is built upon the scanner, symbol table, and error modules. The first time the scanner extracts a particular identifier, it is entered into the symbol table along with its line number. Each subsequent time the scanner extracts that same identifier, its node is updated to include the current line number. We use the info field to point to a linked list of line numbers. As soon as the entire program has been scanned, all the identifier names and their line numbers are printed in alphabetical order.

Figure 3-6 shows the main file of the utility xref.c. In the main routine, the scanner loop goes around once for each token until the scanner extracts a period. For each identifier, we call function search_symtab to search the symbol table for the identifier's node. If it is not found, this must be the first time it is used, so we call function `enter_symtab` to create a node for it. Then, whether the node was newly-created or found, we call function `record_line_number` to record the current line number in the entry. When the scanner loop terminates, we call `print_xref` to print the cross-reference listing.

FIGURE 3-6   File xref.c.

```
/**************************************************************/
/*                                                          */
/*      Program 3-1:  Pascal Cross-Referencer               */
/*                                                          */
/*      List all identifiers alphabetically each with the line */
/*      numbers of the lines that reference it.             */
/*                                                          */
/*      FILE:      xref.c                                   */
/*                                                          */
/*      REQUIRES:  Modules symbol table, scanner, error     */
/*                                                          */
/*      USAGE:     xref sourcefile                          */
/*                                                          */
/*         sourcefile      name of source file to cross-ref */
/*                                                          */
/**************************************************************/

#include <stdio.h>
#include "common.h"
#include "scanner.h"
#include "symtab.h"

#define MAX_LINENUMS_PER_LINE   10

/*----------------------------------------------------------*/
/* Line number item and list header                         */
/*----------------------------------------------------------*/

typedef struct linenum_item {
    struct linenum_item *next;       /* ptr to next item */
    int                line_number;
} LINENUM_ITEM, *LINENUM_ITEM_PTR;

typedef struct {
    LINENUM_ITEM_PTR first_linenum, last_linenum;
} LINENUM_HEADER, *LINENUM_HEADER_PTR;

/*----------------------------------------------------------*/
/* Externals                                                */
/*----------------------------------------------------------*/

extern int      line_number;
extern TOKEN_CODE token;
extern char     word_string[];

extern SYMTAB_NODE_PTR symtab_root;

/*----------------------------------------------------------*/
/* main          Loop to process identifiers.  Then         */
/*               print the cross-reference listing.         */
/*----------------------------------------------------------*/

main(argc, argv)
```

```
int  argc;
char *argv[];

{
    SYMTAB_NODE_PTR np;        /* ptr to symtab entry */
    LINENUM_HEADER_PTR hp;     /* ptr to line item list header */

    init_scanner(argv[1]);

    /*
    -- Repeatedly process tokens until a period
    -- or the end of file.
    */
    do {
        get_token();
        if (token == END_OF_FILE) break;

        if (token == IDENTIFIER) {
            /*
            -- Enter each identifier into the symbol table
            -- if it isn't already in there, and record the
            -- current line number in the symbol table entry.
            */
            np = search_symtab(word_string, symtab_root);
            if (np == NULL) {
                np = enter_symtab(word_string, &symtab_root);
                hp = alloc_struct(LINENUM_HEADER);
                hp->first_linenum = hp->last_linenum = NULL;
                np->info = (char *) hp;
            }
            record_line_number(np, line_number);
        }

    } while (token != PERIOD);

    /*
    -- Print out the cross-reference listing.
    */
    printf("\n\nCross-Reference");
    printf(  "\n---------------\n");
    print_xref(symtab_root);

    quit_scanner();
}

/*----------------------------------------------------------*/
/* record_line_number  Record a line number into the symbol */
/*                     table entry.                         */
/*----------------------------------------------------------*/

record_line_number(np, number)

    SYMTAB_NODE_PTR np;        /* ptr to symtab entry */
```

```
int             number;      /* line number */

{
    LINENUM_ITEM_PTR   ip;        /* ptr to line item */
    LINENUM_HEADER_PTR hp;        /* ptr to line item list header */

    /*
    -- Create a new line number item ...
    */
    ip = alloc_struct(LINENUM_ITEM);
    ip->line_number = number;
    ip->next = NULL;

    /*
    -- ... and link it to the end of the list
    -- for this symbol table entry.
    */
    hp = (LINENUM_HEADER_PTR) np->info;
    if (hp->first_linenum == NULL)
        hp->first_linenum = hp->last_linenum = ip;
    else {
        (hp->last_linenum)->next = ip;
        hp->last_linenum = ip;
    }
}
/*------------------------------------------------------*/
/*  print_xref          Print the names and line numbers in   */
/*                       alphabetical order.                   */
/*------------------------------------------------------*/

print_xref(np)

    SYMTAB_NODE_PTR np;        /* ptr to subtree */
```

```
    int n;
    LINENUM_ITEM_PTR ip;           /* ptr to line item */
    LINENUM_HEADER_PTR hp;         /* ptr to line item list header */

    if (np == NULL) return;

    /*
    -- First, print the left subtree.
    */
    print_xref(np->left);

    /*
    -- Then, print the root of the subtree
    -- with at most MAX_LINENUMS_PER_LINE.
    */
    printf("\n%-16s  ", np->name);
    n = strlen(np->name) > 16 ? 0 : MAX_LINENUMS_PER_LINE;
    hp = (LINENUM_HEADER_PTR) np->info;
    for (ip = hp->first_linenum; ip != NULL; ip = ip->next) {
        if (n == 0) {
            printf("\n%-16s  ", " ");
            n = MAX_LINENUMS_PER_LINE;
        }
        printf(" %4d", ip->line_number);
        --n;
    };
    printf("\n");

    /*
    -- Finally, print the right subtree.
    */
    print_xref(np->right);
}
```

Line numbers for an identifier are stored in a linked list of LINENUM_ITEM structures. The LINENUM_HEADER structure points to the head and tail items in the list. We use the info field of each identifier's node to point to this header structure. We pass to function record_line_number a pointer to a symbol table node and a line number. There, we create a line number item for the line number, and then we append the item at the end of the node's linked list of items.

Recursive function print_xref does an *inorder traversal* of the symbol table tree in order to print the names alphabetically. We pass to it a pointer to the root node. First, the function calls itself for the node's left subtree. Then the node's name followed by the list of line numbers is printed. At most MAX_LINENUMS_PER_LINE numbers are printed per line, and multiple lines are printed, if necessary. Finally, print_xref calls itself again for the node's right subtree.

So, with our existing scanner module and a simple symbol table module, we have written a utility program that performs quite adequately.

3.4 Program 3-2: A Source Program Cruncher

In Chapter 2, we wrote a compactor utility program that made Pascal source files smaller by squeezing out comments and all unnecessary blanks. We will now write a source program cruncher that reduces the file size even more by replacing tokens with byte-sized codes. This utility program not only shows another use of a symbol table, but it also prepares us for writing our interpreter. Starting in Chapter 8, we will use this crunched form as the interpreter's intermediate form.

A crunched program is no longer readable by either humans or by Pascal compilers and interpreters. Therefore, we will follow with an uncruncher utility to render a crunched source program back to a form readable by the compilers and interpreters.

Where do you get the byte codes? In file scanner.h of the scanner module, we defined the enumeration type TOKEN_CODE. The values of the enumeration constants will be the byte codes! You can replace, for example, the reserved word token BEGIN with the value of the enumeration constant BEGIN. The TOKEN_CODE constants are small integers.

What about an identifier? You can replace it with the value of the enumeration constant IDENTIFIER, but you also need to indicate which identifier. That is where the symbol table comes into play. Following each IDENTIFIER byte code, you place another code to indicate which symbol table entry represents the identifier. You do the same for the NUMBER and STRING byte codes, which means that you will enter number and string tokens into the symbol table too.

Our cruncher utility makes two passes over the source file—in other words, it reads the source file twice. During the first pass, we build the symbol table and then output the crunched symbol table entries to the crunch file. During the second pass, we crunch the source program and output it to the crunch file after the symbol table.

Figure 3-7 shows the main file of the cruncher utility program, crunch.c. It expects the first argument in the command line, argv[1], to be the name of the input source file, and the second argument, argv[2], to be the name of the output crunch file.

FIGURE 3-7   File crunch.c.

```
/*****************************************************************/
/*                                                             */
/*      Program 3-2:  Pascal Source Cruncher                   */
/*                                                             */
/*      Crunch a Pascal source file.  It can be restored later */
/*      with the uncruncher utility.                           */
/*                                                             */
/*      FILE:     crunch.c                                     */
/*                                                             */
/*      REQUIRES:  Modules symbol table, scanner, error        */
/*                                                             */
/*      USAGE:     crunch sourcefile crunchfile                */
/*                                                             */
/*          sourcefile     [input] source file to crunch       */
/*                                                             */
/*          crunchfile     [output] crunch file                */
/*                                                             */
/*****************************************************************/

#include <stdio.h>
```

```
#include "common.h"
#include "scanner.h"
#include "symtab.h"

/*------------------------------------------------------------*/
/* Externals                                                  */
/*------------------------------------------------------------*/

extern TOKEN_CODE token;
extern char       token_string[];
extern char       word_string[];
extern BOOLEAN    print_flag;

extern SYMTAB_NODE_PTR symtab_root;

/*------------------------------------------------------------*/
/* Globals                                                    */
/*------------------------------------------------------------*/

short index = 0;      /* symtab entry index */
```

```
FILE  *crunch_file;

/*------------------------------------------------------------*/
/*  Main program        Crunch a source file in two passes    */
/*                      over the file.                        */
/*------------------------------------------------------------*/

main(argc, argv)

    int  argc;
    char *argv[];

{
    /*
    -- Initialize the scanner.
    */
    print_flag = FALSE;
    init_scanner(argv[1]);

    /*
    -- Pass 1.
    */
    do_pass_1();
    close_source_file();

    /*
    -- Open the crunch file and output the crunched
    -- symbol table.
    */
    crunch_file = fopen(argv[2], "wb");
    if (crunch_file == NULL) {
        fprintf(stderr, "*** ERROR: Failed to open crunch file.\n");
        exit(-2);
    }
    fwrite(&index, sizeof(short), 1, crunch_file);
    output_crunched_symtab(symtab_root);

    /*
    -- Pass 2.
    */
    open_source_file(argv[1]);
    do_pass_2();

    fclose(crunch_file);
    quit_scanner();
}

/*------------------------------------------------------------*/
/*  do_pass_1          Pass 1: Read the source file to build  */
/*                            the symbol table.               */
/*------------------------------------------------------------*/

do_pass_1()

{
    SYMTAB_NODE_PTR np;          /* ptr to symtab node */

    /*
    -- Repeatedly process tokens until a period
    -- or the end of file.
    */
    do {
        get_token();
        if (token == END_OF_FILE) break;

        /*
        -- Enter each identifier, number, or string into
```

```
        -- the symbol table if it isn't already in there.
        */
        switch (token) {

            case IDENTIFIER:
                if ((np = search_symtab(word_string, symtab_root))
                        == NULL) {
                    np = enter_symtab(word_string, &symtab_root);
                    np->info = (char *) index++;
                }
                break;

            case NUMBER:
            case STRING:
                if ((np = search_symtab(token_string, symtab_root))
                        == NULL) {
                    np = enter_symtab(token_string, &symtab_root);
                    np->info = (char *) index++;
                }
                break;

            default:
                break;
        }

    } while (token != PERIOD);
}

/*------------------------------------------------------------*/
/*  do_pass_2          Pass 2: Reread the source file to      */
/*                            output the crunched program.    */
/*------------------------------------------------------------*/

do_pass_2()

{
    SYMTAB_NODE_PTR np;          /* ptr to symtab node */

    /*
    -- Repeatedly process tokens until a period
    -- or the end of file.
    */
    do {
        get_token();
        if (token == END_OF_FILE) break;

        output_crunched_token();
    } while (token != PERIOD);
}

/*------------------------------------------------------------*/
/*  output_crunched_symtab        Output a crunched symbol table */
/*                                in alphabetical order.      */
/*------------------------------------------------------------*/

output_crunched_symtab(np)

    SYMTAB_NODE_PTR np;          /* ptr to symtab subtree */

{
    char length;                 /* byte-sized string length */

    if (np == NULL) return;

    /*
    -- First, crunch the left subtree.
    */
```

```
    output_crunched_symtab(np->left);

    /*
    -- Then, crunch the root of the subtree.
    */
    length = strlen(np->name) + 1;
    index  = (short) np->info;
    fwrite(&index,  sizeof(short), 1, crunch_file);
    fwrite(&length, 1,             1, crunch_file);
    fwrite(np->name,length,        1, crunch_file);

    /*
    -- Finally, crunch the right subtree.
    */
    output_crunched_symtab(np->right);
}

/*-----------------------------------------------------*/
/*  output_crunched_token       Output a token record.    */
/*-----------------------------------------------------*/

output_crunched_token()

{
    SYMTAB_NODE_PTR np;                /* ptr to symtab node */
    char            token_code = token; /* byte-sized token code */

    /*
```

```
    -- Write the token code.
    */
    fwrite(&token_code, 1, 1, crunch_file);

    /*
    -- If it's an identifier, number, or string,
    -- look up the symbol table entry and write
    -- the entry index.
    */
    switch (token) {

        case IDENTIFIER:
            np = search_symtab(word_string, symtab_root);
            index = (short) np->info;
            fwrite(&index, sizeof(short), 1, crunch_file);
            break;

        case NUMBER:
        case STRING:
            np = search_symtab(token_string, symtab_root);
            index = (short) np->info;
            fwrite(&index, sizeof(short), 1, crunch_file);
            break;

        default:
            break;
    }
}
```

In the main routine, we call functions do_pass_1 and do_pass_2. After the first pass, we open the crunch file and write the number of symbol table entries to the file. Then, we call function output_crunched_symtab to write out the crunched symbol table. In between passes, we close and reopen the source file so that the second pass rereads the source program.

Function do_pass_1 reads the source file the first time to build the symbol table. In this utility, not only do we enter identifier names into the symbol table, but also number and string tokens.

Each time we create a new symbol table node, we set the info field to the value of global variable index. We initialize index to zero, and increment it after each new symbol table node, so that each node has a unique value. We will use this value during the second pass. For example, if the node for identifier gamma has the index value five, then whenever gamma appears in the source program, we will write the value of the enumeration constant IDENTIFIER followed by five to the crunch file. The final first pass value of index is the number of symbol table entries.

Function do_pass_2 reads the source file a second time. We call function output_crunched_token for each token to crunch and output it to the crunch file.

Recursive function output_crunched_symtab does an inorder traversal of the binary tree to output the nodes alphabetically. For each node, we write the index value from the info field, the length of the name string, and the name string itself. Note that we write only as much of the string as necessary.

In function output_crunched_token, we write a byte-sized token code to the crunch file for each token. The value is that of the appropriate TOKEN_CODE enumeration constant. For an identifier, number, or string, we also look up the symbol table node and write the index value from the node's `info` field to the crunch file.

After two passes over the source file, the cruncher utility has written a crunch file consisting of a crunched representation of the source program's symbol table followed by a crunched representation of the source program itself. To uncrunch the source file, we need the uncruncher utility.

3.5 Program 3-3: A Source Program Uncruncher

The uncruncher utility shown in Figure 3-8 uncrunches a crunched Pascal source file to a form acceptable by a compiler or an interpreter. The format of an uncrunched program is similar to the output of the compactor utility we wrote in the previous chapter.

FIGURE 3-8   The uncruncher utility program.

```
/******************************************************************/
/*                                                                */
/*      Program 3-3:  Pascal Source Uncruncher                    */
/*                                                                */
/*      Uncrunch a crunched Pascal source file.                   */
/*                                                                */
/*      FILE:      uncrunch.c                                     */
/*                                                                */
/*      USAGE:     uncrunch crunchfile                            */
/*                                                                */
/*         crunchfile     file to uncrunch, as created by         */
/*                        the cruncher utility                    */
/*                                                                */
/******************************************************************/

#include <stdio.h>
#include "common.h"
#include "scanner.h"

#define MAX_OUTPUT_RECORD_LENGTH     80

/*--------------------------------------------------------------*/
/*  Token classes                                               */
/*--------------------------------------------------------------*/

typedef enum {
    DELIMITER, NONDELIMITER,
} TOKEN_CLASS;

/*--------------------------------------------------------------*/
/*  Globals                                                     */
/*--------------------------------------------------------------*/

FILE *crunch_file;
char token_string[MAX_TOKEN_STRING_LENGTH];
char output_record[MAX_OUTPUT_RECORD_LENGTH];

TOKEN_CODE ctoken;                /* current token from crunch file*/
int     record_length;           /* length of output record */
```

```
char    *recp;                   /* pointer into output record */
char    **symtab_strings;        /* array of symtab strings */

char *symbol_strings[] = {
    "<no token>", "<IDENTIFIER>", "<NUMBER>", "<STRING>",
    "^", "*", "(", ")", "-", "+", "=", "[", "]", ":", ";",
    "<", ">", ",", ".", "/", ":=", "<=", ">=", "<>", "..",
    "<END OF FILE>", "<ERROR>",
    "AND", "ARRAY", "BEGIN", "CASE", "CONST", "DIV", "DO", "DOWNTO",
    "ELSE", "END", "FILE", "FOR", "FUNCTION", "GOTO", "IF", "IN",
    "LABEL", "MOD", "NIL", "NOT", "OF", "OR", "PACKED", "PROCEDURE",
    "PROGRAM", "RECORD", "REPEAT", "SET", "THEN", "TO", "TYPE",
    "UNTIL", "VAR", "WHILE", "WITH",
};

TOKEN_CLASS token_class();

/*--------------------------------------------------------------*/
/*  Main program       Uncrunch a source file.                  */
/*--------------------------------------------------------------*/

main(argc, argv)

    int  argc;
    char *argv[];

{
    TOKEN_CLASS class;           /* current token class */
    TOKEN_CLASS prev_class;      /* previous token class */

    /*
    -- Open the crunch file.
    */
    crunch_file = fopen(argv[1], "rb");
    if (crunch_file == NULL) {
        printf("*** Error: Failed to open crunch file.\n");
        exit(-2);
    }

    /*
```

```
     --  Initialize the uncruncher.
     */
     prev_class = DELIMITER;
     recp = output_record;
     *recp = '\0';
     record_length = 0;

     /*
     --  Read the crunched symbol table.
     */
     read_crunched_symtab();

     /*
     --  Repeatedly process tokens until a period
     --  or the end of file.
     */
     do {
         get_ctoken();
         if (ctoken == END_OF_FILE) break;
         class = token_class();

         /*
         --  Append a blank only if two adjacent nondelimiters.
         --  Then append the token string.
         */
         if ((prev_class == NONDELIMITER) && (class == NONDELIMITER))
             append_blank();
         append_token();

         prev_class = class;
     } while (ctoken != PERIOD);

     /*
     --  Flush the last output record if it is partially filled.
     */
     if (record_length > 0) flush_output_record();
}

/*------------------------------------------------------------*/
/*  read_crunched_symtab      Read the crunched symbol table  */
/*                            and build an array of its name  */
/*                            strings.                        */
/*------------------------------------------------------------*/

read_crunched_symtab()

{
     short count;      /* number of symtab entries */
     short index;      /* symtab entry index */
     char  length;     /* length of name string, incl. '\0' */

     /*
     --  Read the count of symbol table entries and
     --  allocate that many elements for the array.
     */
     fread(&count, sizeof(short), 1, crunch_file);
     symtab_strings = (char **) alloc_bytes(count*sizeof(char *));

     /*
     --  Read each symbol table entry (array index, string length,
     --  and string).  Set the array element.
     */
     do {
         fread(&index, sizeof(short), 1, crunch_file);
         fread(&length, sizeof(char), 1, crunch_file);

         symtab_strings[index] = alloc_bytes(length);
```

```
         fread(symtab_strings[index], length, 1, crunch_file);
     } while (--count > 0);
}

/*------------------------------------------------------------*/
/*  get_ctoken           Read the next token code from the    */
/*                       crunch file.  Uncrunch the token into */
/*                       token _string with a lookup in the   */
/*                       symbol table name strings array or in */
/*                       the symbol strings array.            */
/*------------------------------------------------------------*/

get_ctoken()

{
     /*
     --  Read the crunched token code.
     */
     fread(&ctoken, sizeof(char), 1, crunch_file);

     /*
     --  Identifier, number, and string tokens:  Look up in the
     --  symbol table name strings array.  All other tokens:  Look
     --  up in the symbol strings array.
     */
     switch (ctoken) {

         case IDENTIFIER:
         case NUMBER:
         case STRING:  {
             short index;          /* symtab strings index */

             fread(&index, sizeof(short), 1, crunch_file);
             strcpy(token_string, symtab_strings[index]);
             break;
         }

         default:
             strcpy(token_string, symbol_strings[ctoken]);
             break;
     }
}

/*------------------------------------------------------------*/
/*  token_class        Return the class of the current token. */
/*------------------------------------------------------------*/

     TOKEN_CLASS
token_class()

{
     /*
     --  Nondelimiters:  identifiers, numbers, and reserved words
     --  Delimiters:     strings and special symbols
     */
     switch (ctoken) {

         case IDENTIFIER:
         case NUMBER:
             return(NONDELIMITER);

         default:
             return(ctoken < AND ? DELIMITER : NONDELIMITER);
     }
}

/*------------------------------------------------------------*/
/*  append_blank       Append a blank to the output record,   */
```

```
/*                       or flush the record if it is full.     */
/*-----------------------------------------------------------*/

append_blank()

{
    if (++record_length == MAX_OUTPUT_RECORD_LENGTH - 1)
        flush_output_record();
    else strcat(output_record, " ");
}

/*-----------------------------------------------------------*/
/*  append_token      Append the token string to the output   */
/*                    record if it fits.  If not, flush the   */
/*                    current record and append the string    */
/*                    to append to the new record.            */
/*-----------------------------------------------------------*/

append_token()

{
    int token_length;          /* length of token string */
```

```
    token_length = strlen(token_string);
    if (record_length + token_length
                          >= MAX_OUTPUT_RECORD_LENGTH - 1)
        flush_output_record();

    strcat(output_record, token_string);
    record_length += token_length;
}

/*-----------------------------------------------------------*/
/*  flush_output_record       Flush the current output        */
/*                            record.                         */
/*-----------------------------------------------------------*/

flush_output_record()

{
    printf("%s\n", output_record);
    recp = output_record;
    *recp = '\0';
    record_length = 0;
}
```

The uncruncher borrows the TOKEN_CLASS structure from the compactor. Global variable symtab_strings points to a string array that contains the name strings from the crunched symbol table. This array is allocated and filled in function read_crunched_symtab. String array symbol_strings maps token codes back to their token strings.

The main routine expects the name of the crunch file to be the first command line argument, argv[1]. We open the crunch file, initialize some global variables, and then call function read_crunched_symtab to read the crunched symbol table. The rest of the routine is essentially a copy of the main routine of the compactor: we write token strings with or without a blank in between.

Function read_crunched_symtab reads the crunched symbol table and places the name strings into string array symtab_strings. We first read the number of symbol table entries and then allocate the symbol_strings array large enough to hold that many name strings.

In the cruncher utility, we entered identifier, number, and string tokens into the symbol table. When we crunched each node, we wrote the node's index value followed by the length of the node's name string and then the string itself. Now, when we read it back in, the index value determines which element of symtab_strings to use. For example, if the index value for identifier gamma is five, we set symtab_strings[5] to point to the string "gamma".

Back in the main routine, we call function get_ctoken in a loop to extract tokens from the crunch file. In that function, we read the next value of ctoken from the crunch file. If ctoken is IDENTIFIER, NUMBER, or STRING, we also read the symbol table index and use it to obtain the token string from array symtab_strings, which we copy into token_string. For any other token code, we use the code itself to obtain the token string from array symbol_strings.

Functions token_class, append_blank, append_token, and flush_output_record are all from the compactor utility.

The output of the uncruncher utility is virtually the same as what the compactor utility produced. It can be processed by a Pascal compiler or an interpreter, but not easily read by humans. In Chapter 7, we will write a "pretty-printer" utility that will take any source file, including output from the compactor and uncruncher utilities, and reprint it in a neatly-indented format.

Questions and exercises

1. Functions search_symtab and enter_symtab are *interface routines* of the symbol table module. Reimplement the symbol table as a hash table and rewrite these two functions.

2. If an identifier appears more than once in a source line, the line number appears more than once for that identifier in the cross-reference listing. Fix the cross-referencer so that a line number appears once at most for each identifier.

3. Rewrite the cruncher utility to make only one pass over the source file.

4. One difference between the output of the compactor utility and that of the uncruncher utility is how case is preserved. The compactor preserves the case of identifier name strings and reserved words, while the uncruncher downshifts all name strings and writes all reserved words in uppercase. Rewrite the cruncher and uncruncher utilities to preserve case.

CHAPTER 4

Parsing Expressions

Every programming language has a syntax, the set of "grammar rules" that specify how statements and expressions in that language are correctly written. A language's syntax plays a vital role for a compiler and an interpreter. Pascal compilers and interpreters must know Pascal's syntax in order to translate Pascal programs.

The part of a compiler or an interpreter that knows the source language's syntax is the parser. The parser controls the translation process since it analyzes the source program based on the syntax. It calls the scanner routines to give it tokens, and it calls the symbol table routines to enter and search for identifiers. When a compiler's parser has recognized a syntactic entity, such as an arithmetic expression, it calls the code generator routines to emit the appropriate object code. Similarly, an interpreter's parser calls the executor routines to perform the appropriate operations.

The rest of the chapters in the first part of this book are about parsing. This chapter begins with parsing expressions. We will write two utility programs to develop parsing skills that enable us to:

- write parsing routines based on syntax diagrams
- parse expressions
- interpret expressions

The first program parses simple arithmetic expressions in order to translate them into postfix form. The second program is a calculator for Pascal expressions. It also gives us a preview of interpreting, the topic of the second part of this book.

4.1 Syntax diagrams

Before you can write a parser, you need to be able to describe the source language's syntax. There are several ways to do this, but Pascal's relatively simple syntax lends itself well to *syntax diagrams*. These are graphical representations of the syntax rules.

In Chapter 2, we used a written description of a Pascal number. Figure 4-1 shows the same description using syntax diagrams. For example, the first diagram states that a digit is any of the characters 0 through 9. Figure 4-2 shows the syntax diagram for an identifier. In the diagrams, you follow the lines from left to right, and sometimes, as in the diagram for an unsigned integer, you have a loop. You can also have alternate paths, as in the diagram for a number. Rounded boxes enclose literal text (although case variations are not shown), and square boxes enclose elements that are defined by other diagrams. Not all the details of the syntax rules are shown by the syntax diagrams. For example, the diagram for an unsigned integer does not indicate the maximum number of allowable digits.

We will design our parser so that its structure mirrors the syntax diagrams. Thus, the diagrams not only describe the source language's syntax, but they also help us write the parser. The diagrams representing the lowest-level syntactic

FIGURE 4-1   Syntax diagrams for a number.

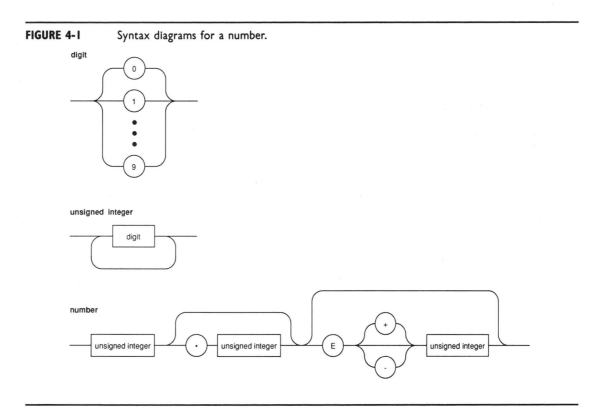

FIGURE 4-2   Syntax diagram for an identifier.

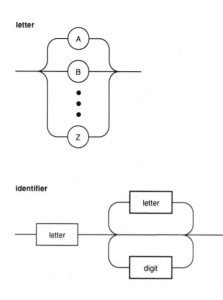

entities, like identifier and number tokens, help us write the scanner. In Chapter 15, we will discuss other ways to describe a language's syntax and other ways to write a parser.

4.2 Simple expressions

We begin our work on an expression parser by considering simple expressions. Figure 4-3 shows the syntax diagrams which we will use to design the parser. The names *simple expression*, *term*, and *factor* are descriptive but are otherwise arbitrary. Such labels are often also used as the names of routines in the parser.

The first diagram states that an expression is a simple expression. (We will deal with the complete Pascal expression syntax later.) The second diagram states that a simple expression is either a single term, or several terms separated by + or - operators. The third diagram states that a term is either a single factor, or several factors separated by * or / operators. The fourth diagram states that a factor is either an identifier, a number, or a parenthesized expression.

Together, these diagrams show how the definitions are nested: expressions are simple expressions, simple expressions are made up of terms, and terms are made up of factors. Expressions are also defined recursively, since a factor can contain an expression. The way the diagrams refer to each other reflects Pascal's operator precedence rules: * and / have higher precedence (bind more tightly) than + and

FIGURE 4-3   Syntax diagram for a simple expression.

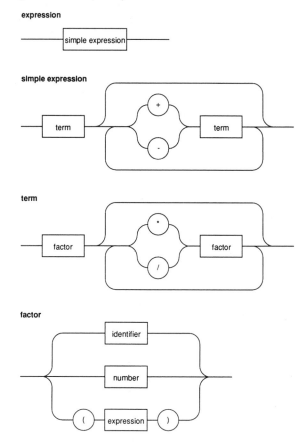

-, and parenthesized subexpressions are evaluated independently. (This will be more obvious when we write the parser.)

Figure 4-4 shows how some sample expressions can be decomposed based on the syntax diagrams. Our first utility program shows how a parser can be written from these diagrams.

4.3 Program 4-1: Infix to Postfix Converter

In both Pascal and normal algebraic notation, expressions are written in *infix* notation, where the operators are in between the operands. For example, a + b.

In *postfix* notation, operators are written after their operands, as in a b +. This notation, also called *Reverse Polish Notation*, or *RPN*, was popularized by

FIGURE 4-4   Decomposing an expression into its parts.

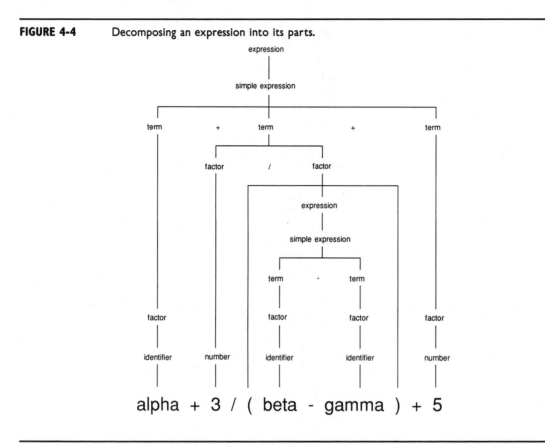

Hewlett-Packard's scientific pocket calculators. It is useful when performing calculations based on a stack. Reading a postfix expression from left to right, each operand pushes its value onto the stack. Each binary operator pops off the top two values, performs the operation on them, and pushes the resulting value back onto the stack. A unary operator pops off the top value, operates on it, and pushes the new value back onto the stack. The following is a more complicated infix expression:

$$((-17 + 49)/4 - 2*3)*(9 - 3 + 2)$$

When converted to postfix, it becomes:

$$17 \text{ neg } 49 + 4 / 2 3 * - 9 3 - 2 + *$$

(We represent the unary - operator as neg to distinguish it from the binary subtraction operator.) We preserve the order of the operands, but we reorder the operators according to the precedence rules. No parentheses are necessary. In the following example, a postfix expression is evaluated on a stack. The stack is shown horizontally: its bottom is at the left, represented by the marker |, and its top is at the right.

Operation	Stack
push 17	| 17
neg	| -17
push 49	| -17 49
+	| 32
push 4	| 32 4
/	| 8
push 2	| 8 2
push 3	| 8 2 3
*	| 8 6
-	| 2
push 9	| 2 9
push 3	| 2 9 3
-	| 2 6
push 2	| 2 6 2
+	| 2 8
*	| 16

Our first utility program, postfix.c, shown in Figure 4-5, converts simple infix expressions to postfix. Its parser follows closely the syntax diagrams of Figure 4-3. Figure 4-6 shows sample output. The program assumes that the expressions are separated by semicolons and that the final expression is terminated by a period.

FIGURE 4-5   File postfix.c.

```
/****************************************************************/
/*                                                              */
/*      Program 4-1:  Infix to Postfix Converter                */
/*                                                              */
/*      Convert simple Pascal expressions from infix to         */
/*      postfix notation.                                       */
/*                                                              */
/*      FILE:       postfix.c                                   */
/*                                                              */
/*      REQUIRES:   Modules scanner, error                      */
/*                                                              */
/*      USAGE:      postfix sourcefile                          */
/*                                                              */
/*          sourcefile      name of source file containing      */
/*                          expressions to convert to postfix   */
/*                                                              */
/****************************************************************/

#include <stdio.h>
```

```
#include "common.h"
#include "error.h"
#include "scanner.h"

/*------------------------------------------------------------*/
/*  Externals                                                 */
/*------------------------------------------------------------*/

extern TOKEN_CODE token;
extern char       token_string[];
extern BOOLEAN    print_flag;

/*------------------------------------------------------------*/
/*  Globals                                                   */
/*------------------------------------------------------------*/

char postfix[MAX_PRINT_LINE_LENGTH];    /* buffer for postfix */
char *pp;                               /* ptr into postfix */
```

```
/*------------------------------------------------------------*/
/*  main                Contains the main loop that drives    */
/*                      the conversion by calling expression  */
/*                      each time through the loop.           */
/*------------------------------------------------------------*/

main(argc, argv)

    int   argc;
    char  *argv[];

{
    /*
    -- Initialize the scanner.
    */
    init_scanner(argv[1]);

    /*
    -- Repeatedly call expression until a period
    -- or the end of file.
    */
    do {
        strcpy(postfix, ">> ");
        pp = postfix + strlen(postfix);

        get_token();
        expression();

        output_postfix("\n");
        print_line(postfix);

        /*
        -- After an expression, there should be a semicolon,
        -- a period, or the end of file.  If not, skip tokens
        -- until there is such a token.
        */
        while ((token != SEMICOLON) && (token != PERIOD) &&
               (token != END_OF_FILE)) {
            error(INVALID_EXPRESSION);
            get_token();
        }
    } while ((token != PERIOD) && (token != END_OF_FILE));
}

/*------------------------------------------------------------*/
/*  expression          Process an expression, which is just a */
/*                      simple expression.                    */
/*------------------------------------------------------------*/

expression()

{
    simple_expression();
}

/*------------------------------------------------------------*/
/*  simple_expression   Process a simple expression consisting */
/*                      of terms separated by + or - operators. */
/*------------------------------------------------------------*/

simple_expression()

{
    TOKEN_CODE op;             /* an operator token */
    char       *op_string;     /* an operator token string */

    term();
```

```
    /*
    -- Loop to process subsequent terms
    -- separated by operators.
    */
    while ((token == PLUS) || (token == MINUS)) {
        op = token;        /* remember operator */

        get_token();
        term();            /* subsequent term */

        switch (op) {
            case PLUS:  op_string = "+";        break;
            case MINUS: op_string = "-";        break;
        }
        output_postfix(op_string);      /* output operator */
    }
}

/*------------------------------------------------------------*/
/*  term                Process a term consisting of factors  */
/*                      separated by * or / operators.        */
/*------------------------------------------------------------*/

term()

{
    TOKEN_CODE op;             /* an operator token */
    char       *op_string;     /* an operator token string */

    factor();

    /*
    -- Loop to process subsequent factors
    -- separated by operators.
    */
    while ((token == STAR) || (token == SLASH)) {
        op = token;        /* remember operator */

        get_token();
        factor();          /* subsequent factor */

        switch (op) {
            case STAR:  op_string = "*";        break;
            case SLASH: op_string = "/";        break;
        }
        output_postfix(op_string);      /* output operator */
    }
}

/*------------------------------------------------------------*/
/*  factor              Process a factor, which is an identi- */
/*                      fier, a number, or a parenthesized    */
/*                      subexpression.                        */
/*------------------------------------------------------------*/

factor()

{
    if ((token == IDENTIFIER) || (token == NUMBER)) {
        output_postfix(token_string);
        get_token();
    }
    else if (token == LPAREN) {
        get_token();
        expression();   /* recursive call for subexpression */

        if (token == RPAREN) get_token();
```

```
        else              error(MISSING_RPAREN);              output_postfix(string)
    }
    else error(INVALID_EXPRESSION);                               char *string;
}

                                                              {
                                                                  *pp++ = ' ';
/*-----------------------------------------------------*/          *pp   = '\0';
/*  output_postfix    Append the string preceded by a blank  */    strcat(pp, string);
/*                    to the postfix buffer.             */        pp += strlen(string);
/*-----------------------------------------------------*/
                                                              }
```

FIGURE 4-6   Sample output from the infix to postfix converter.

```
Page 1   postfix.in   Mon Jul 09 23:34:54 1990          2 0: ((a + b)*c)/(d - e*f) + 3.14159;
                                                     >>  a b + c * d e f * - / 3.14159 +
                                                        3 0: a + b + c.
   1 0: alpha + beta;                               >>  a b + c +
>>  alpha beta +
```

We see our familiar scanner loop in the main routine. Each time through the loop, we call function get_token to extract the first token of an expression, and then we call function expression to process it. At the end of an expression, we look for a semicolon, period, or the end of the file. We flag any other tokens as errors.

In function expression, we call function simple_expression, because an expression is just a simple expression. In function simple_expression, we call function term to process the first term. We then begin a loop where we look for either a + or a - operator, and when found, we call term again. Function term parses a term and outputs it in postfix, so we must call function output_postfix to output either a + or a - after whatever term wrote.

Function term is similar to simple_expression, except it calls function factor and looks for * and / operators. Function factor parses a factor and outputs it in postfix, so we must call function output_postfix to output either a * or a / after whatever factor wrote.

In function factor, if we see an identifier or a number, we output it by calling output_postfix. If we find a left parenthesis, we make a recursive call to function expression to output the subexpression in postfix, and then we expect to see a right parenthesis. If we don't it's an error.

Notice that whenever we call expression, simple_expression, term, or factor, we already have the first token of the expression, simple expression, term, or factor. In each function, we consume tokens until we get one that does not belong to the function. This is analogous to the scanner functions: each time we call function get_word, variable ch already has the first letter of the word, and when get_word returns, ch has the first character after the word.

Now that we have seen how to write a parser for simple expressions, we are ready to tackle nearly complete Pascal expressions.

FIGURE 4-7   Syntax diagrams for (nearly complete) Pascal expressions.

expression

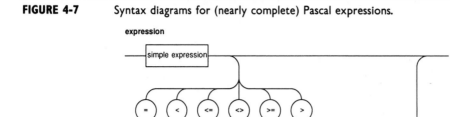

simple expression

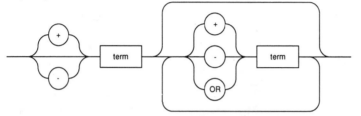

term

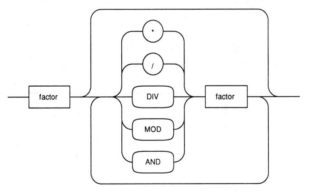

factor

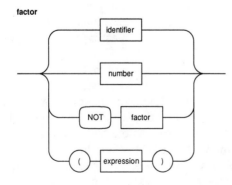

4.4 Pascal expressions

Figure 4-7 shows the syntax diagrams for nearly complete Pascal expressions. We now define an expression to be either a simple expression, or a simple expression followed by a relational operator and then another simple expression. (We won't be doing Pascal's set type in this book, so we leave out the IN operator.)

The complete set of operators now appears in the definitions of simple expression and term. We can have a unary + or - operator before a term, and the definition of factor includes the unary NOT operator. Missing for now are fully-specified variables (with subscripts, pointers, etc.), strings, and function calls. (We'll get to these in later chapters.)

Our latest syntax diagrams implement the full Pascal operator precedence table:

Precedence	Operators
1 (highest)	NOT
2	* / DIV MOD AND
3	+ - OR
4 (lowest)	= < > <> <= >=

4.5 Program 4-2: Calculator

The infix to postfix converter is very much like a compiler since it translates source infix expressions into "object code" for an RPN calculator. Our next utility program is an interpreter that actually performs the stack-based operations specified by infix expressions.

This calculator utility program interprets a language consisting entirely of assignment statements. These statements contain variables that correspond to the calculator's registers. We will keep track of the variables and their values in the symbol table.

Figure 4-8 shows the main file of the calculator, calc.c, which is similar to the infix to postfix converter. The major differences are the addition of the stack, which we implement as an array, and the functions assignment_statement, push, and pop. Function expression now handles relational operators, and function simple_expression now looks for a unary + or - operator before the first term. Function factor now handles a unary NOT and calls itself recursively if it finds one.

FIGURE 4-8   File `calc.c`.

```
/****************************************************************/
/*                                                            */
/*      Program 4-2:  Calculator                              */
/*                                                            */
/*      Interpret Pascal assignment statements with simple    */
/*      variables.  An assignment to "output" prints the value*/
/*      of the expression.                                    */
/*                                                            */
/*      FILE:     calc.c                                      */
/*                                                            */
/*      REQUIRES:  Modules symbol table, scanner, error       */
/*                                                            */
/*      USAGE:     calc sourcefile                            */
/*                                                            */
/*         sourcefile     name of source file containing      */
/*                        assignment statements to interpret  */
/*                                                            */
/****************************************************************/

#include <stdio.h>
#include "common.h"
#include "error.h"
#include "scanner.h"
#include "symtab.h"

#define STACK_SIZE 32

/*------------------------------------------------------------*/
/* Externals                                                  */
/*------------------------------------------------------------*/

extern TOKEN_CODE token;
extern char       token_string[];
extern char       word_string[];
extern LITERAL    literal;
extern BOOLEAN    print_flag;

extern SYMTAB_NODE_PTR symtab_root;

/*------------------------------------------------------------*/
/* Globals                                                    */
/*------------------------------------------------------------*/

float stack[STACK_SIZE];      /* evaluation stack */
float *tos = stack;           /* top of stack pointer */

/*------------------------------------------------------------*/
/* pop              Return the value popped off the stack.    */
/*------------------------------------------------------------*/

#define pop()          *tos--

/*------------------------------------------------------------*/
/* main             Contains the main loop that drives        */
/*                  the interpretation by calling             */
/*                  assignment_statement each time through    */
/*                  the loop.                                 */
/*------------------------------------------------------------*/

main(argc, argv)

    int argc;
    char *argv[];
```

```
{
    /*
    -- Initialize the scanner.
    */
    init_scanner(argv[1]);

    get_token();

    /*
    -- Repeatedly call assignment_statement
    -- until a period or the end of file.
    */
    do {
        if (token == IDENTIFIER) assignment_statement();

        /*
        -- After a statement, there should be a semicolon,
        -- a period, or the end of file.  If not, skip tokens
        -- until there is such a token.
        */
        while ((token != SEMICOLON) && (token != PERIOD) &&
               (token != END_OF_FILE)) {
            error(INVALID_ASSIGNMENT);
            get_token();
        }

        /*
        -- Skip any trailing semicolons.
        */
        while (token == SEMICOLON) get_token();

    } while ((token != PERIOD) && (token != END_OF_FILE));
}

/*------------------------------------------------------------*/
/* assignment_statement      Process an assignment statement  */
/*                           consisting of:                   */
/*                                                            */
/*                              identifier := expression      */
/*------------------------------------------------------------*/

assignment_statement()

{
    SYMTAB_NODE_PTR np;          /* ptr to symtab node */
    float           *vp;         /* ptr to value */
    BOOLEAN         output_flag;  /* TRUE if assign to "output" */

    /*
    -- Look for the identifier.
    */
    if (token != IDENTIFIER) {
        error(MISSING_IDENTIFIER);
        return;
    }

    /*
    -- Enter the identifier into the symbol table
    -- unless it is "output".
    */
    output_flag = strcmp(word_string, "output") == 0;
    if (!output_flag) {
        if ((np = search_symtab(word_string, symtab_root)) == NULL) {
            np = enter_symtab(word_string, &symtab_root);
```

```
            np->defn.key = VAR_DEFN;
        }
    }
    /*
    -- Look for the := .
    */
    get_token();
    if (token != COLONEQUAL) {
        error(MISSING_COLONEQUAL);
        return;
    }
    get_token();

    /*
    -- Process the expression.
    */
    expression();

    /*
    -- Assign the expression value to the identifier.  If
    -- the identifer is "output", print the value instead.
    */
    if (output_flag) printf(">> output: %0.6g\n", pop());
    else {
        vp = alloc_struct(float);
        *vp = pop();
        np->info = (char *) vp;
    }
}

/*-----------------------------------------------------------*/
/* expression          Process an expression consisting of a */
/*                     simple expression optionally followed */
/*                     by a relational operator and a second */
/*                     simple expression.                    */
/*-----------------------------------------------------------*/

expression()

{
    TOKEN_CODE op;                  /* an operator token */
    float      operand_1, operand_2;  /* operand values */

    simple_expression();

    /*
    -- If there is a relational operator, remember it and
    -- process the second simple expression.
    */
    if ((token == EQUAL) || (token == LT) || (token == GT) ||
        (token == NE)   || (token == LE) || (token == GE)) {
        op = token;            /* remember operator */

        get_token();
        simple_expression();   /* second simple expression */
        /*
        -- Pop off the operand values ...
        */
        operand_2 = pop();
        operand_1 = pop();

        /*
        -- ... and perform the operation, leaving the
        -- value on top of the stack.
        */
        switch (op) {
            case EQUAL:
```

```
                push(operand_1 == operand_2 ? 1.0 : 0.0);
                break;

            case LT:
                push(operand_1 <  operand_2 ? 1.0 : 0.0);
                break;

            case GT:
                push(operand_1 >  operand_2 ? 1.0 : 0.0);
                break;

            case NE:
                push(operand_1 != operand_2 ? 1.0 : 0.0);
                break;

            case LE:
                push(operand_1 <= operand_2 ? 1.0 : 0.0);
                break;

            case GE:
                push(operand_1 >= operand_2 ? 1.0 : 0.0);
                break;
        }
    }
}

/*-----------------------------------------------------------*/
/* simple_expression   Process a simple expression consisting */
/*                     of terms separated by +, -, or OR      */
/*                     operators.  There may be a unary + or - */
/*                     before the first term.                 */
/*-----------------------------------------------------------*/

simple_expression()

{
    TOKEN_CODE op;                  /* an operator token */
    TOKEN_CODE unary_op = PLUS;     /* a unary operator token */
    float      operand_1, operand_2;  /* operand values */

    /*
    -- If there is a unary + or -, remember it.
    */
    if ((token == PLUS) || (token == MINUS)) {
        unary_op = token;
        get_token();
    }

    term();

    /*
    -- If there was a unary -, negate the top of stack value.
    */
    if (unary_op == MINUS) *tos = -(*tos);

    /*
    -- Loop to process subsequent terms
    -- separated by operators.
    */
    while ((token == PLUS) || (token == MINUS) || (token == OR)) {
        op = token;     /* remember operator */

        get_token();
        term();         /* subsequent term */

        /*
        -- Pop off the operand values ...
```

```
        */
        operand_2 = pop();
        operand_1 = pop();

        /*
        -- ... and perform the operation, leaving the
        -- value on top of the stack.
        */
        switch (op) {
            case PLUS:  push(operand_1 + operand_2);   break;
            case MINUS: push(operand_1 - operand_2);   break;

            case OR:
                push((operand_1 != 0.0) || (operand_2 != 0.0)
                        ? 1.0 : 0.0);
                break;
        }
    }
}

/*-------------------------------------------------------------*/
/* term              Process a term consisting of factors    */
/*                   separated by *, /, DIV, MOD, or AND       */
/*                   operators.                                */
/*-------------------------------------------------------------*/

term()

{
    TOKEN_CODE op;               /* an operator token */
    float      operand_1, operand_2;   /* operand values */

    factor();

    /*
    -- Loop to process subsequent factors
    -- separated by operators.
    */
    while ((token == STAR) || (token == SLASH) || (token == DIV) ||
           (token == MOD)  || (token == AND)) {
        op = token;     /* remember operator */

        get_token();
        factor();/* subsequent factor */

        /*
        -- Pop off the operand values ...
        */
        operand_2 = pop();
        operand_1 = pop();

        /*
        -- ... and perform the operation, leaving the
        -- value on top of the stack.  Push 0.0 instead of
        -- dividing by zero.
        */
        switch (op) {
            case STAR:
                push(operand_1 * operand_2);
                break;

            case SLASH:
                if (operand_2 != 0.0) push(operand_1/operand_2);
                else {
                    printf("*** Warning:  division by zero.\n");
                    push(0.0);
                }
```

```
                break;

            case DIV:
                if (operand_2 != 0.0)
                    push((float) (  ((int) operand_1)
                                  / ((int) operand_2)));
                else {
                    printf("*** Warning:  division by zero.\n");
                    push(0.0);
                }
                break;

            case MOD:
                if (operand_2 != 0.0)
                    push((float) (  ((int) operand_1)
                                  % ((int) operand_2)));
                else {
                    printf("*** Warning:  division by zero.\n");
                    push(0.0);
                }
                break;

            case AND:
                push((operand_1 != 0.0) && (operand_2 != 0.0)
                        ? 1.0 : 0.0);
                break;
        }
    }
}

/*-------------------------------------------------------------*/
/* factor            Process a factor, which is an identi-   */
/*                   fier, a number, NOT followed by a fac-  */
/*                   tor, or a parenthesized subexpression.  */
/*-------------------------------------------------------------*/

factor()

{
    SYMTAB_NODE_PTR np;          /* ptr to symtab node */

    switch (token) {

        case IDENTIFIER:
            /*
            -- Push the identifier's value, or 0.0 if
            -- the identifier is undefined.
            */
            np = search_symtab(word_string, symtab_root);
            if (np != NULL) push(*((float *) np->info));
            else {
                error(UNDEFINED_IDENTIFIER);
                push(0.0);
            }

            get_token();
            break;

        case NUMBER:
            /*
            -- Push the number's value.  If the number is an
            -- integer, first convert its value to real.
            */
            push(literal.type == INTEGER_LIT
                    ? (float) literal.value.integer
                    : literal.value.real);

            get_token();
```

```
            break;                                                 break;
                                                                }
        case NOT:                                               }
            get_token();                         /*------------------------------------------------------*/
            factor();                            /* push              Push a value onto the stack.       */
            *tos = *tos == 0.0 ? 1.0 : 0.0;   /* NOT tos */   /*------------------------------------------------------*/
            break;
                                                 push(value)
        case LPAREN:
            get_token();                             float value;
            expression();
                                                 {
            if (token == RPAREN) get_token();        if (tos >= &stack[STACK_SIZE]) {
            else                error(MISSING_RPAREN);   error(STACK_OVERFLOW);
                                                         return;
            break;                                   }

        default:                                     *++tos = value;
            error(INVALID_EXPRESSION);
                                                 }
```

Input to the calculator is a sequence of Pascal-like assignment statements. The statements are separated by semicolons, and a period marks the end of the input. An assignment statement is a simple variable (an identifier) followed by := and then by an expression. The appearance of a variable before a := effectively "defines" that variable, and when the statement is executed, the variable is assigned the value of the expression. Using an undefined variable in an expression is an error.

We store a variable's value in the variable identifier's symbol table node. We allocate enough memory to hold a float value, and then we point the node's info field to the value. Whenever a value is assigned to the special variable output, we print that value. Figure 4-9 shows sample output.

FIGURE 4-9   Sample output from the calculator.

```
Page 1   calc.in   Mon Jul 09 23:41:16 1990           >> output: 514.622
                                                        9 0: root := (number/root + root)/2;  output := root;
                                                      >> output: 261.291
   1 0: {Square root of 4096 by Newton's algorithm.}  10 0: root := (number/root + root)/2;  output := root;
   2 0:                                               >> output: 138.483
   3 0: number := 4096;                                11 0: root := (number/root + root)/2;  output := root;
   4 0: root := 1;                                    >> output: 84.0305
   5 0:                                                12 0: root := (number/root + root)/2;  output := root;
   6 0: root := (number/root + root)/2;  output := root;  >> output: 66.3874
>> output: 2048.5                                      13 0: root := (number/root + root)/2;  output := root;
   7 0: root := (number/root + root)/2;  output := root;  >> output: 64.0429
>> output: 1025.25                                     14 0: root := (number/root + root)/2;  output := root;
   8 0: root := (number/root + root)/2;  output := root;  >> output: 64
```

We will not see how to process Pascal type declarations until Chapter 6, so for now, we make do with only the real type. The calculator converts all integer values to real, and uses 0.0 and 1.0 to represent the boolean values false and true, respectively.

Variable tos points to the value at the top of the stack. Function push pushes a value onto the stack by incrementing tos. Function pop returns the value pointed to by tos and then decrements tos.

In the scanner loop of the main routine, we call function assignment_statement to process assignment statements. Each time we call the function, we already have the first token. So in that function, we check if this token is an identifier, and if not, we flag the error and return. Otherwise, unless it is output, we enter the identifier's name into the symbol table if it isn't already in there. We then look for a := and call function expression. At the end of the function, we check if the identifier was output, and if so, we print its value.

In function expression, if there is a relational operator, we pop the two top operand values off of the stack into variables operand_1 and operand_2. We perform the appropriate relational operation and push the result (either 0.0 or 1.0) back onto the stack.

Functions simple_expression and term are similar. For each operator, we pop the top two values off of the stack into operand_1 and operand_2, perform the appropriate operation on those values, and then push the result back onto the stack. In term, to perform the Pascal integer operations DIV and MOD, we first convert the operand values to int, perform the operation, and then convert the result back to float. We also check for an attempt to divide by zero.

If you compare function term of the infix to postfix converter to the corresponding function of the calculator, you can clearly see the difference between a compiler and an interpreter. Function term of the converter (the compiler) outputs code to push two operand values onto the stack, and then it outputs an operator like *. The function in the calculator (the interpreter) actually performs the multiplication on the two values and pushes the product back onto the stack. A compiler *outputs code* to perform an operation, while an interpreter *performs the operation*.

In function factor, we obtain the value of a variable from its symbol table entry, and then we push it onto the stack. We flag an UNDEFINED_IDENTIFIER error if the variable is not in the symbol table, which means the variable was never assigned a value. We push a number's value onto the stack. If the number is an integer, we first convert it to real. For the NOT operator, we call the function recursively, and then we invert the value at the top of stack by replacing a 0.0 value by 1.0, or a nonzero value by 0.0. Finally, we handle a parenthesized expression as before with a recursive call to function expression.

So now we know how to parse assignment statements and expressions. In the next chapter, we will see how to parse the Pascal control statements.

Questions and exercises

1. Trace the function calls of the parser by hand as it converts an expression from infix to postfix.

2. At what point in an expression does the parser detect a missing right parenthesis?

3. The parser does very primitive error checking in the lowest-level function factor. Can better error checking (and recovery from errors) be done in the higher-level functions?

4. Explain how the Pascal operator precedence rules are incorporated in the parser.

5. Pascal has only four operator precedence levels.

   a. Explain why the following expression is incorrect:

      a = b AND c > d

   b. Trace the function calls of the parser as it converts the expression to postfix.

   c. How can Pascal's operator precedence table be modified to have the expressions make sense? How would the expression parser be modified?

6. Is it possible to have an empty expression? What about an empty statement? How does the parser code allow or disallow an empty syntactic construct?

7. Describe the conditions which would cause a stack overflow. Give an example of a statement that causes a stack overflow.

8. Should the parser check for a stack underflow?

9. Extend the calculator program to handle a small set of function calls, such as sqrt and sin.

CHAPTER 5

Parsing Statements

Every Pascal compiler or interpreter checks the source program for syntactic correctness. It flags any errors that it finds with an error message, and only when there are no errors does it output object code or execute the program. Most programmers must sadly admit that their compilers or interpreters do syntax checking more than anything else.

So, a very important task of any parser is syntax checking. In this chapter, we will write a syntax checker to develop the skills to:

- parse Pascal statements
- flag syntax errors in the listing

A syntax checker is a utility program that only does syntax checking. Our first version will only check Pascal statements and expressions. In later chapters, we will write versions that can check other parts of a source program.

5.1 Error reporting and recovery

Programmers are prone to making syntax errors, so it is important to consider how errors are handled. For each syntax error a compiler or an interpreter encounters in the source program, it should:

1. Pinpoint the location of the error.

2. Print a descriptive error message.

3. Recover from the error.

So far, we are taking care of the first two steps by printing an arrow that points to the error and an error message under the erroneous line. The third step is much more difficult. You generally do not generate or execute code if there is even one syntax error. However, you want the parser to continue syntax checking in a meaningful way. So what can a compiler or an interpreter do when it encounters an error?

- It can terminate, crash, or hang; in other words, no recovery is attempted. Thus, at most one syntax error can be uncovered per run.
- It can become hopelessly lost, but still attempt to process the rest of the source program while printing reams of irrelevant error messages. Here, too, there is no error recovery, but the parser does not admit it.
- It can skip tokens until it reaches something that it recognizes. The parser resynchronizes itself at that point and then continues syntax checking as though nothing happened.

The first two options are clearly undesirable. To implement the third option, the parser must look for *synchronization points* after each error. A synchronization point is a location in the source program where syntax checking can be reliably restarted. Ideally, you find such a point as soon after the error as possible.

In this chapter, we begin the parser module. Error reporting and recovery will be a strong theme in the module's routines.

5.2 The parser module

In Chapter 4, we wrote a Pascal expression parser as part of a calculator utility program. Those parsing routines will now be part of the new parser module:

Parser Module

parser.h	*n*	Parser header file
stmt.c	*n*	Parse statements
expr.c	*n*	Parse expressions

Scanner Module

scanner.h	*u*	Scanner header file
scanner.c	*c*	Scanner routines

Symbol Table Module

symtab.h	*u*	Symbol table header file
symtab.c	*u*	Symbol table routines

Error Module

error.h	*u*	Error header file
error.c	*u*	Error routines

Miscellaneous

common.h	*u*	Common header file

Where: *u* file unchanged from the previous chapter
          c file changed from the previous chapter
          n new file

The changes to file scanner.c add new error handling functions. File expr.c contains the expression parsing functions from Chapter 4, and file stmt.c contains new parsing functions for statements. File parser.h is their header file. We will examine each of the new or changed files.

5.3 Parsing Pascal statements with error handling

Figure 5-1 shows the syntax diagrams for the Pascal statements. Note how the first diagram shows that a statement can be empty. Just as we did with expressions, we will design our statement parser from the syntax diagrams.

With the aid of these diagrams, we can understand the changes in file scanner.c. First, we define several global token lists:

```
TOKEN_CODE []                       = {BEGIN, CASE, FOR, IF, REPEAT,
                                       WHILE, IDENTIFIER, 0};

TOKEN_CODE statement_end_list[]     = {SEMICOLON, END, ELSE, UNTIL,
                                       END_OF_FILE, 0};

TOKEN_CODE declaration_start_list[] = {CONST, TYPE, VAR, PROCEDURE,
                                       FUNCTION, 0};
```

The statement_start_list lists the tokens that can start a statement, and the statement_end_list lists the tokens that can end a statement. The declaration_start_list lists the tokens that can start a declaration. We will save this list for Chapter 6, where we parse declarations. A zero terminates each token list. (This explains why we were careful to have a dummy zero value in the TOKEN_CODE enumeration type in file scanner.h.)

Figure 5-2 shows two new functions in scanner.c that use the token lists. Whenever we call boolean function token_in, we pass it a token list. If the current token is in the (nonempty) token list, we return TRUE. Otherwise, we return FALSE.

FIGURE 5-1   Syntax diagrams for Pascal statements.

statement

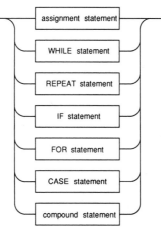

assignment statement

WHILE statement

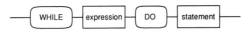

REPEAT statement

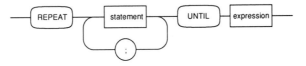

IF statement

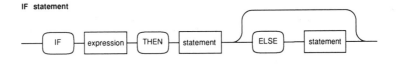

FIGURE 5-1   Continued

FOR statement

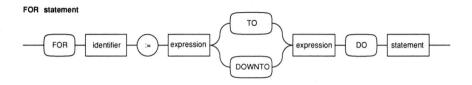

CASE statement

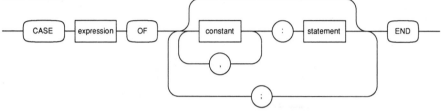

compound statement

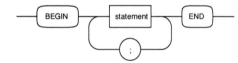

constant

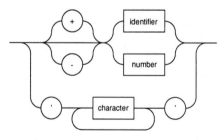

FIGURE 5-2   Functions token_in and synchronize in file scanner.c.

```
/*-------------------------------------------------------------*/
/* token_in          Return TRUE if the current token is in  */
/*                   the token list, else return FALSE.      */
/*-------------------------------------------------------------*/

    BOOLEAN
token_in(token_list)

    TOKEN_CODE token_list[];
```

```
{
    TOKEN_CODE *tokenp;

    if (token_list == NULL) return(FALSE);

    for (tokenp = &token_list[0]; *tokenp; ++tokenp) {
        if (token == *tokenp) return(TRUE);
    }

    return(FALSE);
```

```
}                                                                    (! token_in(token_list3));

/*------------------------------------------------------*/            if (error_flag) {
/*  synchronize      If the current token is not in one of  */            error(token == END_OF_FILE ? UNEXPECTED_END_OF_FILE
/*                   the token lists, flag it as an error.  */                              : UNEXPECTED_TOKEN);
/*                   Then skip tokens until one that is in   */
/*                   one of the token lists.                 */            /*
/*------------------------------------------------------*/                -- Skip tokens to resynchronize.
                                                                          */
synchronize(token_list1, token_list2, token_list3)                        while ((! token_in(token_list1)) &&
                                                                                 (! token_in(token_list2)) &&
    TOKEN_CODE token_list1[], token_list2[], token_list3[];                       (! token_in(token_list3)) &&
                                                                                  (token != END_OF_FILE))
{                                                                             get_token();

    BOOLEAN error_flag = (! token_in(token_list1)) &&              }
                         (! token_in(token_list2)) &&         }
```

We call function synchronize whenever we need to check for a syntax error and then resynchronize the parser. We pass it up to three token lists (any of them can be empty). If the current token is not in any of them, we flag an UNEXPECTED_ TOKEN error. Then, to resynchronize, we repeatedly call get_token to skip tokens until we find a token that is in one of the lists.

We will use function synchronize to do most of our error handling. During parsing, whenever we need to do an error check, we call synchronize to make sure we are looking at a correct token. If not, we flag the error and resynchronize the parser.

Header file parser.h, shown in Figure 5-3, contains two macros, if_token_ get and if_token_get_else_error, that represent two very common code sequences in the parser. We call the second macro whenever we are looking for a specific token. Like function synchronize, it flags an error if the current token is not the one we expect, but the macro does not skip tokens.

FIGURE 5-3   File parser.h.

```
/************************************************************/          /********************************/
/*                                                          */          /*                              */
/*   P A R S I N G   R O U T I N E S   (Header)             */          /*      Macros for parsing      */
/*                                                          */          /*                              */
/*   FILE:     parser.h                                     */          /********************************/
/*                                                          */
/*   MODULE:   parser                                       */          /*-------------------------------------------------------*/
/*                                                          */          /* if_token_get             If token equals token_code, get */
/************************************************************/          /*                          the next token.                  */
                                                                        /*-------------------------------------------------------*/
#ifndef parser_h
#define parser_h                                                        #define if_token_get(token_code)               \
                                                                            if (token == token_code) get_token()
#include "common.h"
#include "symtab.h"                                                     /*-------------------------------------------------------*/
                                                                        /* if_token_get_else_error  If token equals token_code, get */
```

```
/*                           the next token, else error.    */
/*---------------------------------------------------------*/

#define if_token_get_else_error(token_code, error_code) \
```

```
    if (token == token_code) get_token();                \
    else                     error(error_code)

#endif
```

Now look at the parsing routines in file `stmt.c`, shown in Figure 5-4. Like the expression parsing functions, when we call each function we already have the first token of the statement. Function `statement` uses this token to call the appropriate parsing function.

FIGURE 5-4   File `stmt.c`.

```
/*********************************************************/
/*                                                       */
/*      S T A T E M E N T   P A R S E R                  */
/*                                                       */
/*      Parsing routines for statements.                 */
/*                                                       */
/*      FILE:       stmt.c                               */
/*                                                       */
/*      MODULE:     parser                               */
/*                                                       */
/*********************************************************/

#include <stdio.h>
#include "common.h"
#include "error.h"
#include "scanner.h"
#include "symtab.h"
#include "parser.h"

/*---------------------------------------------------------*/
/* Externals                                               */
/*---------------------------------------------------------*/

extern TOKEN_CODE token;
extern LITERAL    literal;
extern TOKEN_CODE statement_start_list[], statement_end_list[];

/*---------------------------------------------------------*/
/* statement            Process a statement by calling the */
/*                      appropriate parsing routine based on*/
/*                      the statement's first token.       */
/*---------------------------------------------------------*/

statement()

{
    /*
    -- Call the appropriate routine based on the first
    -- token of the statement.
    */
    switch (token) {

        case IDENTIFIER:    assignment_statement(); break;
        case REPEAT:        repeat_statement();     break;
        case WHILE:         while_statement();      break;
        case IF:            if_statement();         break;
        case FOR:           for_statement();        break;
        case CASE:          case_statement();       break;
```

```
        case BEGIN:         compound_statement();   break;
    }

    /*
    -- Error synchronization:  Only a semicolon, END, ELSE, or
    --                         UNTIL may follow a statement.
    --                         Check for a missing semicolon.
    */
    synchronize(statement_end_list, statement_start_list, NULL);
    if (token_in(statement_start_list)) error(MISSING_SEMICOLON);
}

/*---------------------------------------------------------*/
/* assignment_statement    Process an assignment statement:*/
/*                                                         */
/*                         <id> := <expr>                  */
/*---------------------------------------------------------*/

assignment_statement()

{
    get_token();
    if_token_get_else_error(COLONEQUAL, MISSING_COLONEQUAL);

    expression();
}

/*---------------------------------------------------------*/
/* repeat_statement    Process a REPEAT statement:         */
/*                                                         */
/*                     REPEAT <stmt-list> UNTIL <expr>     */
/*---------------------------------------------------------*/

repeat_statement()

{
    /*
    -- <stmt-list>
    */
    get_token();
    do {
        statement();
        while (token == SEMICOLON) get_token();
    } while (token_in(statement_start_list));

    if_token_get_else_error(UNTIL, MISSING_UNTIL);
    expression();
```

```
}

/*-----------------------------------------------------*/
/*  while_statement      Process a WHILE statement:    */
/*                                                     */
/*                          WHILE <expr> DO <stmt>     */
/*-----------------------------------------------------*/

while_statement()

{
    get_token();
    expression();

    if_token_get_else_error(DO, MISSING_DO);
    statement();
}

/*-----------------------------------------------------*/
/*  if_statement      Process an IF statement:         */
/*                                                     */
/*                        IF <expr> THEN <stmt>        */
/*                                                     */
/*                  or:                                */
/*                                                     */
/*                        IF <expr> THEN <stmt> ELSE <stmt>  */
/*-----------------------------------------------------*/

if_statement()

{
    get_token();
    expression();

    if_token_get_else_error(THEN, MISSING_THEN);
    statement();

    /*
    -- ELSE branch?
    */
    if (token == ELSE) {
        get_token();
        statement();
    }
}

/*-----------------------------------------------------*/
/*  for_statement      Process a FOR statement:        */
/*                                                     */
/*                        FOR <id> := <expr> TO|DOWNTO <expr> */
/*                        DO <stmt>                    */
/*-----------------------------------------------------*/

for_statement()

{
    get_token();
    if_token_get_else_error(IDENTIFIER, MISSING_IDENTIFIER);

    if_token_get_else_error(COLONEQUAL, MISSING_COLONEQUAL);
    expression();

    if ((token == TO) || (token == DOWNTO)) get_token();
    else error(MISSING_TO_OR_DOWNTO);

    expression();
    if_token_get_else_error(DO, MISSING_DO);
```

```
    statement();
}

/*-----------------------------------------------------*/
/*  case_statement      Process a CASE statement:      */
/*                                                     */
/*                        CASE <expr> OF               */
/*                            <case-branch> ;          */
/*                            ...                      */
/*                        END                          */
/*-----------------------------------------------------*/

TOKEN_CODE follow_expr_list[]      = {OF, SEMICOLON, 0};

TOKEN_CODE case_label_start_list[] = {IDENTIFIER, NUMBER, PLUS,
                                      MINUS, STRING, 0};

case_statement()

{
    BOOLEAN another_branch;

    get_token();
    expression();

    /*
    -- Error synchronization:  Should be OF
    */
    synchronize(follow_expr_list, case_label_start_list, NULL);
    if_token_get_else_error(OF, MISSING_OF);

    /*
    -- Loop to process CASE branches.
    */
    another_branch = token_in(case_label_start_list);
    while (another_branch) {
        if (token_in(case_label_start_list)) case_branch();

        if (token == SEMICOLON) {
            get_token();
            another_branch = TRUE;
        }
        else if (token_in(case_label_start_list)) {
            error(MISSING_SEMICOLON);
            another_branch = TRUE;
        }
        else another_branch = FALSE;
    }

    if_token_get_else_error(END, MISSING_END);
}

/*-----------------------------------------------------*/
/*  case_branch            Process a CASE branch:      */
/*                                                     */
/*                        <case-label-list> : <stmt>   */
/*-----------------------------------------------------*/

TOKEN_CODE follow_case_label_list[] = {COLON, SEMICOLON, 0};

case_branch()

{
    BOOLEAN another_label;

    /*
    -- <case-label-list>
```

```
*/
do {
    case_label();

    get_token();
    if (token == COMMA) {
        get_token();
        if (token_in(case_label_start_list)) another_label = TRUE;
        else {
            error(MISSING_CONSTANT);
            another_label = FALSE;
        }
    }
    else another_label = FALSE;
} while (another_label);

/*
-- Error synchronization:  Should be :
*/
synchronize(follow_case_label_list, statement_start_list, NULL);
if_token_get_else_error(COLON, MISSING_COLON);

statement();
}

/*------------------------------------------------------*/
/* case_label            Process a CASE label and return a  */
/*                       pointer to its type structure.     */
/*------------------------------------------------------*/

case_label()

{
    TOKEN_CODE sign     = PLUS;      /* unary + or - sign */
    BOOLEAN    saw_sign = FALSE;     /* TRUE iff unary sign */

    /*
    -- Unary + or - sign.
    */
    if ((token == PLUS) || (token == MINUS)) {
        sign     = token;
        saw_sign = TRUE;
        get_token();
    }
```

```
/*
-- Number or identifier.
*/
if ((token == NUMBER) || (token == IDENTIFIER)) return;

/*
-- String constant:  Character type only.
*/
else if (token == STRING) {
    if (saw_sign) error(INVALID_CONSTANT);

    if (strlen(literal.value.string) != 1)
        error(INVALID_CONSTANT);
}
}

/*------------------------------------------------------*/
/* compound_statement      Process a compound statement:    */
/*                                                          */
/*                         BEGIN <stmt-list> END            */
/*------------------------------------------------------*/

compound_statement()

{
    /*
    -- <stmt-list>
    */
    get_token();
    do {
        statement();
        while (token == SEMICOLON) get_token();
        if (token == END) break;

        /*
        -- Error synchronization:  Should be at the start of the
        --                         next statement.
        */
        synchronize(statement_start_list, NULL, NULL);
    } while (token_in(statement_start_list));

    if_token_get_else_error(END, MISSING_END);
}
```

When we return from a parsing function to function statement, we have just parsed a statement, and so we are looking at the first token after the statement. We expect that token to be one of the statement ending tokens (a semicolon, END, ELSE, or UNTIL), and to be sure, we call function synchronize, passing both statement_end_list and statement_start_list. We pass the first list because we want to resynchronize at the end of a statement. We pass the second list in case a statement ending token is missing, so then we want to resynchronize at the beginning of the next statement. The token_in(statement_start_list) test checks for and flags a MISSING_SEMICOLON error.

5.3.1 Assignment statement

Function `assignment_statement` is a simplified version of the one in the calculator utility. Since we are only checking syntax, we no longer make calls to the symbol table routines.

5.3.2 WHILE and REPEAT statements

Function `while_statement` is a straightforward transcription of the corresponding syntax diagram. Function `repeat_statement` is similar, but it processes a statement list consisting of one or more statements separated by semicolons. In its outer loop, we parse each statement in the statement list, and we stay in the loop if, after each statement, we see the start of the next statement. We consume the semicolon(s) after the statement in the inner loop.

5.3.3 IF and FOR statements

Pascal syntax supports two forms of the IF statement, one with an ELSE branch and one without. In function `if_statement`, we look for the reserved word token ELSE after processing the statement of the THEN branch. If there is an ELSE, we parse the statement of the ELSE branch.

One potential problem with IF statements is that of the "dangling ELSE." We will explore this further in the questions and exercises at the end of this chapter.

Function `for_statement` is another straightforward transcription of the corresponding syntax diagram.

5.3.4 CASE statement

The CASE statement has the most complex syntax of all the Pascal statements. We need to define two token lists, `follow_expr_list` and `case_label_start_list`, which are the list of the tokens that can follow the CASE expression and the list of the tokens that can start a CASE branch label:

```
TOKEN_CODE follow_expr_list[]      = {OF, SEMICOLON, 0};

TOKEN_CODE case_label_start_list[] = {IDENTIFIER, NUMBER, PLUS,
                                      MINUS, STRING, 0};
```

In function `case_statement`, we first parse the CASE expression. We next call `synchronize` to look for the OF, passing both `follow_expr_list` and `case_label_start_list`. We want to resynchronize at the OF, but if the OF is missing, we will resynchronize at the start of the first CASE label.

Then, as long as we're looking at the start of a CASE label, we call function `case_branch` to parse a CASE branch. After each CASE branch, we look for a semicolon. If we see one, we loop again to parse the next CASE branch. If we find the start of the next CASE label instead, we flag the MISSING_SEMICOLON error and loop again. If there is any other token, we assume that we are done and exit the loop. We finish with a check for the END.

In function case_branch, we parse a CASE branch that consists of a CASE label list followed by a colon and the branch statement. We define the token list follow_ case_label_list to be the list of tokens that can follow the label list:

```
TOKEN_CODE follow_case_label_list[] = {COLON, SEMICOLON, 0};
```

We call function case_label to parse each label. After the last label, we call synchronize, passing both follow_case_label_list and statement_start_list. We want to resynchronize at the colon, but if it is missing, we will settle for the start of the next branch statement.

In function case_label, we parse a CASE label list that consists of one or more constants (numbers, identifiers, or characters) separated by commas. A unary + or - sign can come before a number or an identifier. Note that we do not as yet verify that an identifier is the name of a constant.

5.3.5 Compound statement

In Pascal, a compound statement is a statement list of one or more statements separated by semicolons. The reserved word token BEGIN precedes the statement list, and the reserved word token END follows it. In the outer loop of function compound_statement, we call function statement to parse each statement in the list, and then in the inner loop we consume any semicolons after the statement. If the current token is END, we break out of the outer loop. Otherwise, we call synchronize to make sure we're looking at the start of the next statement instead of one of the other statement ending tokens ELSE or UNTIL. We loop again if we are indeed at the start of the next statement. Outside the loop, we finish by verifying that we have the END.

5.3.6 Expressions

Figure 5-5 shows the other file in the parser module, expr.c. It contains the expression parsing functions from the calculator utility program in Chapter 4. Since we are no longer interpreting the expressions, the stack operations are gone, and function factor no longer makes calls to the symbol table routines. We also take advantage of function token_in and define several new token lists, rel_op_ list, add_op_list, and mult_op_list:

```
TOKEN_CODE rel_op_list[]  = {LT, LE, EQUAL, NE, GE, GT, 0};
TOKEN_CODE add_op_list[]  = {PLUS, MINUS, OR, 0};
TOKEN_CODE mult_op_list[] = {STAR, SLASH, DIV, MOD, AND, 0};
```

FIGURE 5-5   File expr.c.

```
/************************************************************/
/*                                                          */
/*        E X P R E S S I O N   P A R S E R                 */
/*                                                          */
/*        Parsing routines for expressions.                */
/*                                                          */
/*        FILE:       expr.c                                */
/*                                                          */
/*        MODULE:     parser                                */
/*                                                          */
/************************************************************/

#include <stdio.h>
#include "common.h"
#include "error.h"
#include "scanner.h"
#include "parser.h"


/*----------------------------------------------------------*/
/* Externals                                                */
/*----------------------------------------------------------*/

extern TOKEN_CODE token;
extern char       word_string[];

/*----------------------------------------------------------*/
/* expression       Process an expression consisting of a   */
/*                  simple expression optionally followed   */
/*                  by a relational operator and a second   */
/*                  simple expression.                      */
/*----------------------------------------------------------*/

TOKEN_CODE rel_op_list[] = {LT, LE, EQUAL, NE, GE, GT, 0};

expression()

{
    TOKEN_CODE op;              /* an operator token */

    simple_expression();        /* first simple expr */

    /*
    -- If there is a relational operator, remember it and
    -- process the second simple expression.
    */
    if (token_in(rel_op_list)) {
        op = token;             /* remember operator */

        get_token();
        simple_expression();    /* 2nd simple expr */
    }
}

/*----------------------------------------------------------*/
/* simple_expression  Process a simple expression consisting*/
/*                    of terms separated by +, -, or OR     */
/*                    operators.  There may be a unary + or */
/*                    before the first term.                */
/*----------------------------------------------------------*/

TOKEN_CODE add_op_list[] = {PLUS, MINUS, OR, 0};

simple_expression()
```

```
{
    TOKEN_CODE op;                   /* an operator token */
    TOKEN_CODE unary_op = PLUS;      /* a unary operator token */

    /*
    -- If there is a unary + or -, remember it.
    */
    if ((token == PLUS) || (token == MINUS)) {
        unary_op = token;
        get_token();
    }

    term();             /* first term */

    /*
    -- Loop to process subsequent terms separated by operators.
    */
    while (token_in(add_op_list)) {
        op = token;     /* remember operator */

        get_token();
        term();         /* subsequent term */
    }
}

/*----------------------------------------------------------*/
/* term             Process a term consisting of factors    */
/*                  separated by *, /, DIV, MOD, or AND      */
/*                  operators.                               */
/*----------------------------------------------------------*/

TOKEN_CODE mult_op_list[] = {STAR, SLASH, DIV, MOD, AND, 0};

term()

{
    TOKEN_CODE op;      /* an operator token */

    factor();           /* first factor */

    /*
    -- Loop to process subsequent factors
    -- separated by operators.
    */
    while (token_in(mult_op_list)) {
        op = token;     /* remember operator */

        get_token();
        factor();       /* subsequent factor */
    }
}

/*----------------------------------------------------------*/
/* factor           Process a factor, which is a variable,  */
/*                  a number, NOT followed by a factor, or   */
/*                  a parenthesized subexpression.           */
/*----------------------------------------------------------*/

factor()

{
    switch (token) {

        case IDENTIFIER:
```

```
        get_token();                                           break;
        break;
                                                    case LPAREN:
    case NUMBER:                                         get_token();
        get_token();                                        expression();
        break;
                                                            if_token_get_else_error(RPAREN, MISSING_RPAREN);
    case STRING:                                             break;
        get_token();
        break;                                      default:
                                                        error(INVALID_EXPRESSION);
    case NOT:                                               break;
        get_token();                            }
        factor();
                                            }
```

5.4 Program 5-1: Pascal Syntax Checker I

Now that we have all the statement parsing routines, we can put them all together into the first version of our syntax checking utility program. The main file, syntax1.c, is shown in Figure 5-6. We initialize the scanner, extract the first token, and then call function statement to parse a statement, which can be a compound statement. After parsing the statement, we look for the end of file and we print a summary showing the number of source lines read and the number of syntax errors. Figure 5-7 shows sample output.

FIGURE 5-6   File syntax1.c.

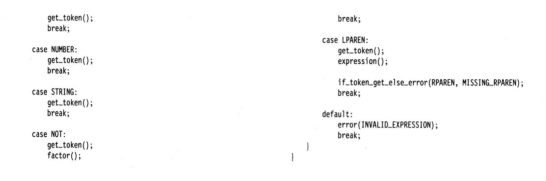

```
/*****************************************************************/      extern int       error_count;
/*                                                             */
/*      Program 5-1:  Syntax Checker I                         */        /*-----------------------------------------------------*/
/*                                                             */        /* Globals                                             */
/*      Check the syntax of Pascal statements.                 */        /*-----------------------------------------------------*/
/*                                                             */
/*      FILE:      syntax1.c                                   */        char buffer[MAX_PRINT_LINE_LENGTH];
/*                                                             */
/*      REQUIRES:  Modules parser, symbol table, scanner,      */        /*-----------------------------------------------------*/
/*                     error                                   */        /* main              Initialize the scanner and call the */
/*                                                             */        /*                   statement routine.                */
/*      USAGE:     syntax1 sourcefile                          */        /*-----------------------------------------------------*/
/*                                                             */
/*        sourcefile    name of source file containing         */        main(argc, argv)
/*                      statements to be checked               */
/*                                                             */            int   argc;
/*****************************************************************/          char *argv[];

#include <stdio.h>                                                       {
#include "common.h"                                                          /*
#include "error.h"                                                           -- Initialize the scanner.
#include "scanner.h"                                                         */
                                                                            init_scanner(argv[1]);
/*-----------------------------------------------*/
/* Externals                                     */                          /*
/*-----------------------------------------------*/                          -- Parse a statement.
                                                                            */
extern TOKEN_CODE token;                                                     get_token();
extern int       line_number;                                               statement();
```

```
/*
-- Look for the end of file.
*/
while (token != END_OF_FILE) {
    error(UNEXPECTED_TOKEN);
    get_token();
}

quit_scanner();

/*
-- Print the parser's summary.
```

```
*/
print_line("\n");
print_line("\n");
sprintf(buffer, "%20d Source lines.\n", line_number);
print_line(buffer);
sprintf(buffer, "%20d Source errors.\n", error_count);
print_line(buffer);

if (error_count == 0) exit(0);
else                  exit(-SYNTAX_ERROR);
}
```

FIGURE 5-7   Sample output from the syntax checker I.

```
Page 1   syntax1.in   Tue Jul 10 00:15:58 1990

  1 0: BEGIN
  2 0:     alpha := beta - gamma;
  3 0:
  4 0:     IF alpha <> theta THEN BEGIN
  5 0:         area := length*width
  6 0:         volume := area*height + ;
                                       ^
*** ERROR: Missing ; .
                         ^
*** ERROR: Invalid expression.
  7 0:     END
  8 0:     ELSE x := ((a - b/c) MOD f;

*** ERROR: Missing right parenthesis.
  9 0:
 10 0:     CASE switch OF
```

```
 11 0:         one, 2, three: z := -123.45;
 12 0:
 13 0:         four, -'5':  BEGIN
                        ^
*** ERROR: Invalid constant.
 14 0:             n := n + 1;
 15 0:             k := k - 1;
 16 0:         END
 17 0:     END
 18 0:
            ^
*** ERROR: Unexpected end of file.
          ^
*** ERROR: Missing END.


                  18 Source lines.
                   6 Source errors.
```

5.5 Type checking

A statement that follows the syntax rules as described by the syntax diagrams is not necessarily correct. For example, the diagrams do not indicate type. Type checking must wait until we can parse declarations, which we will do in the next chapter. Nevertheless, the syntax checker is useful for flagging some of the most common errors.

Questions and exercises

1. In Pascal, a compound statement can appear anywhere a simple statement appears. Explain how the statement parsing routines support this rule.

2. *Dangling* ELSE. In the following, the THEN branch of one IF statement contains

another IF statement. The question is, to which IF statement does the ELSE branch belong?

$$\text{IF a = b THEN IF c = d THEN a := c ELSE a := d}$$

In Pascal, the ELSE always belongs to the IF immediately preceding it, so in the above example, it belongs to the second IF. Explain how function if_ statement supports this rule. Does the syntax diagram for the IF statement support this rule?

3. Can the syntax checker guarantee that the expression in an IF statement evaluates to a boolean value? How does it handle a CASE label like 3.2?

4. *Empty statements.* An empty statement is any semicolon not preceded by a statement. For example,

$$\text{BEGIN ; ; END}$$

contains two empty statements. How does our syntax checker handle empty statements?

5. Functions repeat_statement and compound_statement both contain inner loops to consume semicolons between the statements of the statement list. Why not put that loop instead at the end of function statement to consume semicolons after every statement?

6. In some languages like C, the semicolon is a statement terminator, not a separator. How would the statement parsing routines be modified to support such a rule?

7. In some languages like Ada, compound statements are bracketed by statement keywords. For example:

```
IF i < 0 THEN
    i := -i;
    n := n + 1;
END IF;
```

```
IF count > limit THEN
    error_number := 101;
    count := 0;
ELSE
    circumference := 2*pi*r;
    area := pi*r*r;
END IF;
```

```
WHILE count <= limit LOOP
    i := i + 1;
    j := j - 1;
END LOOP;
```

Discuss what general changes are necessary to the statement parsing routines to support such a rule, and whether or not such a rule leads to simpler parsing routines.

8. In FORTRAN, blanks between tokens are not only ignored, but they are unnecessary! For example, the following statement:

```
DO 10 I = 1, 25
```

can also be correctly written as:

```
DO10I=1,25
```

Describe the difficulties of writing a scanner and a parser for FORTRAN. Compare how the previous statement is scanned and parsed with the following statement:

```
DO10I=1.25
```

At what point do the scanner and parser distinguish between the two statements? What sort of backtracking is necessary?

(Cynical compiler writers have said that FORTRAN is a language that must be parsed before it can be scanned.)

CHAPTER 6

Parsing Declarations

Now that we can parse Pascal statements, we are ready to tackle the declarations that precede them in a program: constant definitions, type definitions, and variable declarations. In this chapter, we'll do more than just syntax checking. We will also perform the semantic actions of building the symbol table structures to represent the information in the declarations.

As in the previous chapters, we will develop the necessary skills by writing utility programs. These skills will enable us to:

- parse and analyze Pascal declarations
- enter declaration information into the symbol table
- perform type checking

The first program is a Pascal declarations analyzer that parses declarations, enters the information into the symbol table, and writes out a description of each declaration based on the symbol table information. The second program builds upon the syntax checker of the previous chapter. Not only will this version check the syntax of declarations and statements, but it also will do type checking.

6.1 Pascal declarations

Figure 6-1 shows the syntax diagrams for the Pascal declarations that you will parse. Declarations consist of three parts: constant definition, type definition, and variable declaration. Each part is optional, but they must be in that order, and each part is separated by a semicolon. In this book, you will not do statement label declarations, packed types, pointer types, set types, or variant record types. These constructs are explored in the questions and exercises at the end of this chapter.

The constant definition part consists of the reserved word CONST followed by a list of constant definitions separated by semicolons. Each definition consists of an identifier followed by an equal sign and then a constant. The constant may be a number or a string, or a previously defined constant identifier. A unary + or

---

FIGURE 6-1   Syntax diagrams for Pascal declarations.

declarations

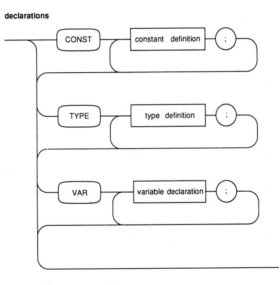

constant definition

type definition

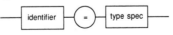

variable declaration

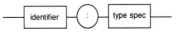

FIGURE 6-1   Continued

type spec

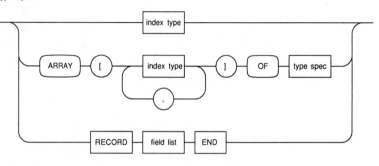

index type

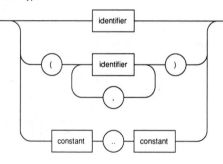

field list

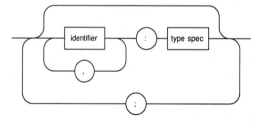

variable declaration

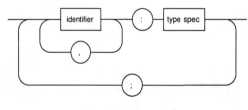

- sign may come before a numeric constant or a constant identifier whose value is a number.

The type definition part consists of the reserved word TYPE followed by a list of type definitions separated by semicolons. Each definition consists of an identifier followed by an equal sign and then a type specification. The specification can be for an enumeration type, a subrange type, an array type, or a record type, or it can simply be a previously-defined type identifier.

The variable declaration part consists of the reserved word VAR followed by a list of variable declarations separated by semicolons. Each declaration consists of a list of identifiers separated by commas, a colon, and then a type specification.

Pascal allows you to define named and unnamed types. The following example defines two names types, the subrange type teens and the array type list. There are also two unnamed types, the subrange type of the values 1..10 and the enumeration type with the values north, south, east, and west.

```
TYPE
    teens = 11..19;
    list  = ARRAY [1..10] OF real;

VAR
    direction : (north, south, east, west);
```

6.2 Changes to the modules

We need to change the parser and symbol table modules to add the ability to parse declarations. Foremost is the addition of the new file decl.c to the parser module:

Parser Module

parser.h	*c*	Parser header file
stmt.c	*c*	Parse statements
expr.c	*c*	Parse expressions
decl.c	*n*	Parse declarations

Scanner Module

scanner.h	*u*	Scanner header file
scanner.c	*u*	Scanner routines

Symbol Table Module

symtab.h	*c*	Symbol table header file
symtab.c	*c*	Symbol table routines

Error Module

| error.h | u | Error header file |
| error.c | u | Error routines |

Miscellaneous

| common.h | u | Common header file |

Where: *u*   file unchanged from the previous chapter
        c   file changed from the previous chapter
        n   new file

New file decl.c contains the routines to parse declarations. We add type checking to the routines in stmt.c and expr.c, and we change symtab.h and symtab.c to add type information to the symbol table. Finally, we make changes to parser.h that are related to type checking.

6.3 Symbol table changes

The key to success in parsing declarations is to design good data structures to represent all the information, and then to build these structures as each declaration is parsed. You should not be too surprised that in order for a compiler or an interpreter to be able to parse data structures it must itself be able to create and manipulate its own data structures!

6.3.1 Symbol table structures and macros

The symbol table that we have built so far contains no type information about each identifier. Figure 6-2 shows the new version of file symtab.h. The new structure type TYPE_STRUCT stores type information about each identifier. The SYMTAB_NODE structure now has a TYPE_STRUCT_PTR field typep that points to a TYPE_STRUCT structure that is allocated for each identifier's symbol table node.

FIGURE 6-2   File symtab.h.

```
/******************************************************/
/*                                                    */
/*      S Y M B O L   T A B L E   (Header)            */
/*                                                    */
/*      FILE:     symtab.h                            */
/*                                                    */
/*      MODULE:   symbol table                        */
/*                                                    */
/******************************************************/

#ifndef symtab_h
#define symtab_h
```

```
#include "common.h"

/*------------------------------------------------------*/
/* Value structure                                      */
/*------------------------------------------------------*/

typedef union {
    int    integer;
    float  real;
    char   character;
    char   *stringp;
} VALUE;
```

```
/*-----------------------------------------------------*/
/*  Definition structure                               */
/*-----------------------------------------------------*/

typedef enum {
    UNDEFINED,
    CONST_DEFN, TYPE_DEFN, VAR_DEFN, FIELD_DEFN,
    VALPARM_DEFN, VARPARM_DEFN,
    PROG_DEFN, PROC_DEFN, FUNC_DEFN,
} DEFN_KEY;

typedef enum {
    DECLARED, FORWARD,
    READ, READLN, WRITE, WRITELN,
    ABS, ARCTAN, CHR, COS, EOFF, EOLN, EXP, LN, ODD, ORD,
    PRED, ROUND, SIN, SQR, SQRT, SUCC, TRUNC,
} ROUTINE_KEY;

typedef struct {
    DEFN_KEY key;
    union {
        struct {
            VALUE value;
        } constant;

        struct {
            ROUTINE_KEY        key;
            int                parm_count;
            int                total_parm_size;
            int                total_local_size;
            struct symtab_node *parms;
            struct symtab_node *locals;
            struct symtab_node *local_symtab;
            char               *code_segment;
        } routine;

        struct {
            int                offset;
            struct symtab_node *record_idp;
        } data;
    } info;
} DEFN_STRUCT;

/*-----------------------------------------------------*/
/*  Type structure                                     */
/*-----------------------------------------------------*/

typedef enum {
    NO_FORM,
    SCALAR_FORM, ENUM_FORM, SUBRANGE_FORM,
    ARRAY_FORM, RECORD_FORM,
} TYPE_FORM;

typedef struct type_struct {
    TYPE_FORM          form;
    int                size;
    struct symtab_node *type_idp;
    union {
        struct {
            struct symtab_node *const_idp;
            int                max;
        } enumeration;

        struct {
            struct type_struct *range_typep;
            int                min, max;
        } subrange;
```

```
        struct {
            struct type_struct *index_typep, *elmt_typep;
            int                min_index, max_index;
            int                elmt_count;
        } array;

        struct {
            struct symtab_node *field_symtab;
        } record;
    } info;
} TYPE_STRUCT, *TYPE_STRUCT_PTR;

/*-----------------------------------------------------*/
/*  Symbol table node                                  */
/*-----------------------------------------------------*/

typedef struct symtab_node {
    struct symtab_node *left, *right;  /* ptrs to subtrees */
    struct symtab_node *next;          /* for chaining nodes */
    char               *name;          /* name string */
    char               *info;          /* ptr to generic info */
    DEFN_STRUCT        defn;           /* definition struct */
    TYPE_STRUCT_PTR    typep;          /* ptr to type struct */
    int                level;          /* nesting level */
    int                label_index;    /* index for code label */
} SYMTAB_NODE, *SYMTAB_NODE_PTR;

/*-----------------------------------------------------*/
/*  Functions                                          */
/*-----------------------------------------------------*/

SYMTAB_NODE_PTR search_symtab();
SYMTAB_NODE_PTR enter_symtab();
TYPE_STRUCT_PTR make_string_typep();

        /***************************************/
        /*                                     */
        /*      Macros to search symbol tables */
        /*                                     */
        /***************************************/

/*-----------------------------------------------------*/
/*  search_this_symtab          Search the given symbol */
/*                              table for the current id */
/*                              name. Set a pointer to the */
/*                              entry if found, else to */
/*                              NULL.                   */
/*-----------------------------------------------------*/

#define search_this_symtab(idp, this_symtab)            \
    idp = search_symtab(word_string, this_symtab)

/*-----------------------------------------------------*/
/*  search_all_symtab           Search the local symbol */
/*                              table for the current id */
/*                              name. Set a pointer to the */
/*                              entry if found, else to */
/*                              NULL.                   */
/*-----------------------------------------------------*/

#define search_all_symtab(idp)                          \
    idp = search_symtab(word_string, symtab_root)

/*-----------------------------------------------------*/
/*  enter_local_symtab          Enter the current id name */
/*                              into the local symbol */
/*                              table, and set a pointer */
```

```
/*                                 to the entry.      */
/*------------------------------------------------------*/

#define enter_local_symtab(idp)                         \
    idp = enter_symtab(word_string, &symtab_root)

/*------------------------------------------------------*/
/*   enter_name_local_symtab      Enter the given name into   */
/*                                the local symbol table, and */
/*                                set a pointer to the entry. */
/*------------------------------------------------------*/

#define enter_name_local_symtab(idp, name)              \
    idp = enter_symtab(name, &symtab_root)

/*------------------------------------------------------*/
/*   search_and_find_all_symtab   Search the local symbol   */
/*                                table for the current id   */
/*                                name. If not found, ID     */
/*                                UNDEFINED error, and enter  */
/*                                into the local symbol table.*/
/*                                Set a pointer to the entry. */
/*------------------------------------------------------*/

#define search_and_find_all_symtab(idp)                 \
    if ((idp = search_symtab(word_string,               \
                    symtab_root)) == NULL) {            \
        error(UNDEFINED_IDENTIFIER);                    \
        idp = enter_symtab(word_string, &symtab_root);  \
        idp->defn.key = UNDEFINED;                      \
        idp->typep = &dummy_type;                       \
    }
```

```
/*------------------------------------------------------*/
/*   search_and_enter_local_symtab   Search the local symbol   */
/*                                table for the current id   */
/*                                name.  Enter the name if   */
/*                                it is not already in there, */
/*                                else ID REDEFINED error.   */
/*                                Set a pointer to the entry. */
/*------------------------------------------------------*/

#define search_and_enter_local_symtab(idp)              \
    if ((idp = search_symtab(word_string,               \
                        symtab_root)) == NULL) {        \
        idp = enter_symtab(word_string, &symtab_root);  \
    }                                                   \
    else error(REDEFINED_IDENTIFIER)

/*------------------------------------------------------*/
/*   search_and_enter_this_symtab   Search the given symbol   */
/*                                table for the current id   */
/*                                name.  Enter the name if   */
/*                                it is not already in there, */
/*                                else ID REDEFINED error.   */
/*                                Set a pointer to the entry. */
/*------------------------------------------------------*/

#define search_and_enter_this_symtab(idp, this_symtab)  \
    if ((idp = search_symtab(word_string,               \
                        this_symtab)) == NULL) {        \
        idp = enter_symtab(word_string, &this_symtab);  \
    }                                                   \
    else error(REDEFINED_IDENTIFIER)

#endif
```

The new enumeration type TYPE_FORM represents the forms of a Pascal type: scalar, enumeration, subrange, array, or record. We set field form of TYPE_STRUCT to one of these constants and field size to the size in bytes of a variable of the type. If the type is named, we point field type_idp to the identifier symbol table node. Otherwise, for an unnamed type, we set the field to NULL. We store particular information for each Pascal type form in the union field info.

We keep information about an enumeration type in info.enumeration. Field const_idp points to the linked list of symbol table nodes for the enumeration constant identifiers, and field max is the maximum enumeration value.

A subrange type uses info.subrange. Field range_typep points to the type structure that represents the range type, and fields min and max are the minimum and maximum values of the subrange.

We store various pieces of information about an array type in info.array. Fields index_typep and elmt_typep point to the type structures that represent the array's index type and element type. Fields min_index and max_index are the minimum and maximum index values, and field elmt_count is the number of elements. Finally, info.record uses field field_symtab to point to a private symbol table for a record type's field identifiers.

Figure 6-3 shows the symbol table nodes and type structures for various type definitions. The multidimensional array type is especially interesting. Both of the following result in the same data structures:

FIGURE 6-3 Symbol table nodes and type structures for sample type definitions. Again, we draw the name strings inside of, instead of pointed to by, the name field of the symbol table nodes.

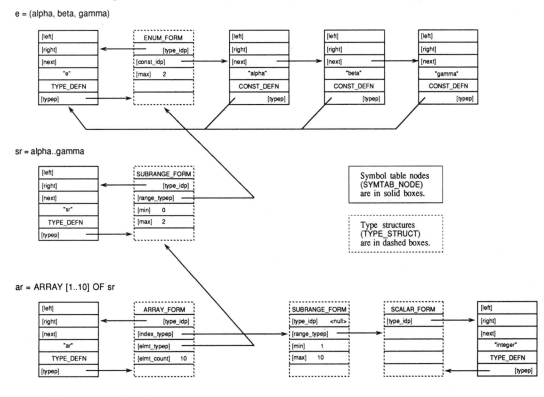

ARRAY [1..10, 3..7] OF integer

ARRAY [1..10] OF ARRAY [3..7] OF integer

Figure 6-4 shows these structures.

    File symtab.h now contains several macros that represent common code sequences for manipulating the symbol table. Their names may not all be meaningful right now; until now, we have used only one symbol table. In this chapter, we will create a private symbol table for each record type, and beginning in the next chapter, we will also create a separate symbol table for each procedure and function. We choose the macro names with all this in mind. In later chapters, we will rewrite some of the macros, but the calls to these macros will not need to change.

    We call macro search_this_symtab to search a particular symbol table for the current identifier name in word_string. If we find it, we point idp to the symbol table node. Otherwise, we set idp to NULL. We call macro search_all_symtab to search all the symbol tables for the current identifier name. For now, we only search the one symbol table pointed to by symtab_root.

FIGURE 6-4   Two equivalent specifications for a multidimensional array type.

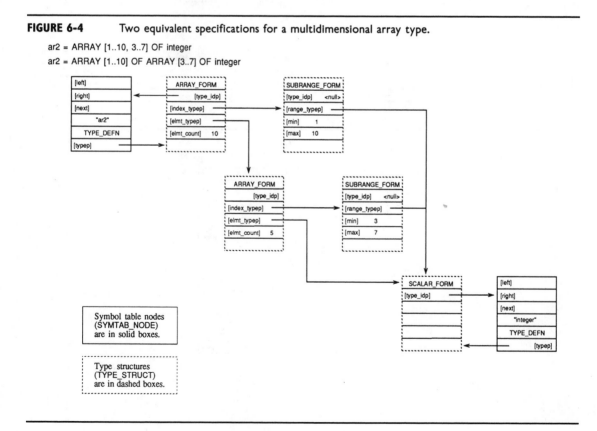

We call macro enter_local_symtab to enter the current identifier name into the local symbol table and to point idp to the new node. For now, the local symbol table is simply the one symbol table pointed to by symtab_root. We call macro enter_name_local_symtab to enter a particular name into the local symbol table.

Whenever we call macro search_and_find_all_symtab, we expect to find the current identifier name. If we find it, we point idp to the symbol table node. Otherwise, we flag the UNDEFINED_IDENTIFIER error, enter the name into the local symbol table, and initialize the new node's defn.key and typep fields to UNDEFINED and dummy_type (explained later). For now, the only symbol table we will work with is the one pointed to by symtab_root.

Whenever we call macro search_and_enter_local_symtab, we expect *not* to find the current identifier name. If the name is not in there, we enter it. Otherwise, we flag the REDEFINED_IDENTIFIER error. In either case, we point idp to the node. For now, the local symbol table is the one pointed to by symtab_root. Macro search_and_enter_this_symtab is similar, except we use a particular symbol table.

6.3.2 Initializing the symbol table

Pascal has four predefined types, integer, real, boolean, and char. Type boolean is an enumeration type with constant identifiers false and true. We must enter all this information into the symbol table before parsing a program.

Figure 6-5 shows the new file symtab.c. There are several new global variables. The four pointer variables integer_typep, real_typep, boolean_typep, and char_typep point to type structures representing the predefined types. Structure dummy_type initializes some symbol table nodes and represents certain errors that the parser will detect.

FIGURE 6-5   File symtab.c.

```
/***************************************************************/
/*                                                             */
/*      S Y M B O L   T A B L E                                */
/*                                                             */
/*      Symbol table routines.                                 */
/*                                                             */
/*      FILE:      symtab.c                                    */
/*                                                             */
/*      MODULE:    symbol table                                */
/*                                                             */
/***************************************************************/

#include <stdio.h>
#include "common.h"
#include "error.h"
#include "symtab.h"

/*-----------------------------------------------------------*/
/* Globals                                                   */
/*-----------------------------------------------------------*/

SYMTAB_NODE_PTR symtab_root = NULL;    /* symbol table root */
```

```
TYPE_STRUCT_PTR integer_typep, real_typep,     /* predefined types */
                boolean_typep, char_typep;

TYPE_STRUCT dummy_type = {        /* for erroneous type definitions */
    NO_FORM,        /* form */
    0,              /* size */
    NULL            /* type_idp */
};

/*-----------------------------------------------------------*/
/* search_symtab     Search for a name in the symbol table.  */
/*                   Return a pointer of the entry if found, */
/*                   or NULL if not.                         */
/*-----------------------------------------------------------*/

    SYMTAB_NODE_PTR
search_symtab(name, np)

    char            *name;      /* name to search for */
    SYMTAB_NODE_PTR np;         /* ptr to symtab root */

    {
```

```
    int cmp;

    /*
    -- Loop to check each node.  Return if the node matches,
    -- else continue search down the left or right subtree.
    */
    while (np != NULL) {
        cmp = strcmp(name, np->name);
        if (cmp == 0) return(np);            /* found */
        np = cmp < 0 ? np->left : np->right; /* continue search */
    }

    return(NULL);                            /* not found */
}

/*--------------------------------------------------------*/
/* enter_symtab     Enter a name into the symbol table,   */
/*                  and return a pointer to the new entry. */
/*--------------------------------------------------------*/

    SYMTAB_NODE_PTR
enter_symtab(name, npp)

    char             *name;    /* name to enter */
    SYMTAB_NODE_PTR  *npp;     /* ptr to ptr to symtab root */

{
    int              cmp;       /* result of strcmp */
    SYMTAB_NODE_PTR  new_nodep; /* ptr to new entry */
    SYMTAB_NODE_PTR  np;        /* ptr to node to test */

    /*
    -- Create the new node for the name.
    */
    new_nodep = alloc_struct(SYMTAB_NODE);
    new_nodep->name = alloc_bytes(strlen(name) + 1);
    strcpy(new_nodep->name, name);
    new_nodep->left = new_nodep->right = new_nodep->next = NULL;
    new_nodep->info = NULL;
    new_nodep->defn.key = UNDEFINED;
    new_nodep->typep = NULL;
    new_nodep->level = new_nodep->label_index = 0;

    /*
    -- Loop to search for the insertion point.
    */
    while ((np = *npp) != NULL) {
        cmp = strcmp(name, np->name);
        npp = cmp < 0 ? &(np->left) : &(np->right);
    }

    *npp = new_nodep;                    /* replace */
    return(new_nodep);
}

/*--------------------------------------------------------*/
/* init_symtab      Initialize the symbol table with      */
```

```
/*                  predefined identifiers and types,     */
/*                  and routines.                         */
/*--------------------------------------------------------*/

init_symtab()

{
    SYMTAB_NODE_PTR integer_idp, real_idp, boolean_idp, char_idp,
                    false_idp, true_idp;

    enter_name_local_symtab(integer_idp, "integer");
    enter_name_local_symtab(real_idp,    "real");
    enter_name_local_symtab(boolean_idp, "boolean");
    enter_name_local_symtab(char_idp,    "char");
    enter_name_local_symtab(false_idp,   "false");
    enter_name_local_symtab(true_idp,    "true");

    integer_typep = alloc_struct(TYPE_STRUCT);
    real_typep    = alloc_struct(TYPE_STRUCT);
    boolean_typep = alloc_struct(TYPE_STRUCT);
    char_typep    = alloc_struct(TYPE_STRUCT);

    integer_idp->defn.key    = TYPE_DEFN;
    integer_idp->typep       = integer_typep;
    integer_typep->form      = SCALAR_FORM;
    integer_typep->size      = sizeof(int);
    integer_typep->type_idp  = integer_idp;

    real_idp->defn.key       = TYPE_DEFN;
    real_idp->typep          = real_typep;
    real_typep->form         = SCALAR_FORM;
    real_typep->size         = sizeof(float);
    real_typep->type_idp     = real_idp;

    boolean_idp->defn.key    = TYPE_DEFN;
    boolean_idp->typep       = boolean_typep;
    boolean_typep->form      = ENUM_FORM;
    boolean_typep->size      = sizeof(int);
    boolean_typep->type_idp  = boolean_idp;

    boolean_typep->info.enumeration.max = 1;
    boolean_idp->typep->info.enumeration.const_idp = false_idp;
    false_idp->defn.key = CONST_DEFN;
    false_idp->defn.info.constant.value.integer = 0;
    false_idp->typep = boolean_typep;

    false_idp->next = true_idp;
    true_idp->defn.key = CONST_DEFN;
    true_idp->defn.info.constant.value.integer = 1;
    true_idp->typep = boolean_typep;

    char_idp->defn.key    = TYPE_DEFN;
    char_idp->typep       = char_typep;
    char_typep->form      = SCALAR_FORM;
    char_typep->size      = sizeof(char);
    char_typep->type_idp  = char_idp;
}
```

In the new function init_symtab, we enter the predefined type names integer, real, boolean, and char, along with false and true, into the symbol table, and then we allocate type structures for the four predefined types. We finish by initializing various fields of the symbol table nodes and type structures. We also chain the nodes for false and true off of the type structure for boolean by pointing boolean_typep->info.enumeration.const_idp to false_idp, and then pointing false_idp->next to true_idp.

6.4 Program 6-1: A Pascal Declarations Analyzer

The routines in file decl.c will be much easier to understand if you can examine the data structures that it builds for each declaration. Therefore, we will study them in the context of the declarations analyzer utility program.

When the parser processes type declarations, it checks the declarations for syntactic correctness. It must also perform the semantic actions of building the data structures and entering the appropriate information into the symbol table. A logical way for a declarations analyzer to work is to examine these data structures and symbol table entries and print out the information in the source listing right after each declaration.

Figure 6-6 shows the main file of the analyzer analyze.c. String arrays defn_ names and form_names contain names that correspond to the DEFN_KEY and TYPE_ FORM enumeration constants. We will write out these names in the analysis.

FIGURE 6-6   File analyze.c.

```
/*****************************************************************/
/*                                                               */
/*      Program 6-1:  Declarations Analyzer                      */
/*                                                               */
/*      Analyze Pascal constant definitions, type definitions,   */
/*      and variable declarations.                               */
/*                                                               */
/*      FILE:       analyze.c                                    */
/*                                                               */
/*      REQUIRES:   Modules symbol table, scanner, error         */
/*                                                               */
/*                  File decl.c                                  */
/*                                                               */
/*      FLAGS:      Macro flag "analyze" must be defined         */
/*                                                               */
/*      USAGE:      analyze sourcefile                           */
/*                                                               */
/*          sourcefile      name of source file containing       */
/*                          declarations to be analyzed          */
/*                                                               */
/*****************************************************************/

#include <stdio.h>
#include "common.h"
#include "error.h"
#include "scanner.h"
#include "symtab.h"

/*-----------------------------------------------------------*/
/* Externals                                                 */
/*-----------------------------------------------------------*/

extern TYPE_STRUCT_PTR integer_typep, real_typep,
```

```
                                    boolean_typep, char_typep;

extern TOKEN_CODE token;
extern int        line_number, error_count;

extern TYPE_STRUCT dummy_type;

/*-----------------------------------------------------------*/
/* Globals                                                   */
/*-----------------------------------------------------------*/

char buffer[MAX_PRINT_LINE_LENGTH];

char *defn_names[] = {"undefined",
                      "constant", "type", "variable",
                      "field", "procedure", "function"};

char *form_names[] = {"no form",
                      "scalar", "enum", "subrange",
                      "array", "record"};

/*-----------------------------------------------------------*/
/* main            Initialize the scanner and the symbol     */
/*                 table, and then call the declarations      */
/*                 routine.                                   */
/*-----------------------------------------------------------*/

main(argc, argv)

    int  argc;
    char *argv[];

{
```

```
SYMTAB_NODE_PTR program_idp;         /* artificial program id */

    /*
    -- Initialize the scanner and the symbol table.
    */
    init_scanner(argv[1]);
    init_symtab();

    /*
    -- Create an artifical program id node.
    */
    program_idp = alloc_struct(SYMTAB_NODE);
    program_idp->defn.key = PROG_DEFN;
    program_idp->defn.info.routine.key = DECLARED;
    program_idp->defn.info.routine.parm_count = 0;
    program_idp->defn.info.routine.total_parm_size = 0;
    program_idp->defn.info.routine.total_local_size = 0;
    program_idp->typep = &dummy_type;
    program_idp->label_index = 0;

    /*
    -- Parse declarations.
    */
    get_token();
    declarations(program_idp);

    /*
    -- Look for the end of file.
    */
    while (token != END_OF_FILE) {
        error(UNEXPECTED_TOKEN);
        get_token();
    }

    quit_scanner();

    /*
    -- Print summary.
    */
    print_line("\n");
    print_line("\n");
    sprintf(buffer, "%20d Source lines.\n", line_number);
    print_line(buffer);
    sprintf(buffer, "%20d Source errors.\n", error_count);
    print_line(buffer);

    exit(0);
}

            /*************************/
            /*                       */
            /*         Analysis      */
            /*                       */
            /*************************/

/*------------------------------------------------------------*/
/* analyze_const_defn      Analyze a constant definition.     */
/*------------------------------------------------------------*/

analyze_const_defn(idp)

    SYMTAB_NODE_PTR idp;         /* constant id */

{
    char *bp;

    /*
```

```
    -- The constant's name ...
    */
    sprintf(buffer, ">> id = %s\n", idp->name);
    print_line(buffer);

    /*
    -- ... definition and value ...
    */
    sprintf(buffer, ">>    defn = %s, value = ",
                    defn_names[idp->defn.key]);
    bp = buffer + strlen(buffer);

    if ((idp->typep == integer_typep) ||
        (idp->typep->form == ENUM_FORM))
        sprintf(bp, "%d\n",
                idp->defn.info.constant.value.integer);
    else if (idp->typep == real_typep)
        sprintf(bp, "%g\n",
                idp->defn.info.constant.value.real);
    else if (idp->typep == char_typep)
        sprintf(bp, "'%c'\n",
                idp->defn.info.constant.value.character);
    else if (idp->typep->form == ARRAY_FORM)
        sprintf(bp, "'%s'\n",
                idp->defn.info.constant.value.stringp);

    print_line(buffer);

    /*
    -- ... and type.  (Don't try to re-analyze an
    -- enumeration type, or an infinite loop will occur.)
    */
    if (idp->typep->form != ENUM_FORM)
        analyze_type(idp->typep, FALSE);
}

/*------------------------------------------------------------*/
/* analyze_type_defn       Analyze a type definition.        */
/*------------------------------------------------------------*/

analyze_type_defn(idp)

    SYMTAB_NODE_PTR idp;         /* type id */

{
    char *bp;

    /*
    -- The type's name, definition ...
    */
    sprintf(buffer, ">> id = %s\n", idp->name);
    print_line(buffer);

    sprintf(buffer, ">>    defn = %s\n",
                    defn_names[idp->defn.key]);
    print_line(buffer);

    /*
    -- ... and type.
    */
    analyze_type(idp->typep, TRUE);
}

/*------------------------------------------------------------*/
/* analyze_type            Analyze a type by calling the     */
/*                         appropriate type analysis routine. */
/*------------------------------------------------------------*/
```

```
analyze_type(tp, verbose_flag)

    TYPE_STRUCT_PTR tp;         /* ptr to type structure */
    BOOLEAN verbose_flag;       /* TRUE for verbose analysis */

{
    char *bp;

    if (tp == NULL) return;

    /*
    -- The form, byte size, and, if named, its type id.
    */
    sprintf(buffer, ">>    form = %s, size = %d bytes, type id = ",
                    form_names[tp->form], tp->size);
    bp = buffer + strlen(buffer);

    if (tp->type_idp != NULL)
        sprintf(bp, "%s\n", tp->type_idp->name);
    else {
        sprintf(bp, "<unnamed type>\n");
        verbose_flag = TRUE;
    }
    print_line(buffer);

    /*
    -- Call the appropriate type analysis routine.
    */
    switch (tp->form) {
        case ENUM_FORM:
            analyze_enum_type(tp, verbose_flag);
            break;

        case SUBRANGE_FORM:
            analyze_subrange_type(tp, verbose_flag);
            break;

        case ARRAY_FORM:
            analyze_array_type(tp, verbose_flag);
            break;

        case RECORD_FORM:
            analyze_record_type(tp, verbose_flag);
            break;
    }
}

/*--------------------------------------------------------------*/
/*  analyze_enum_type       Analyze an enumeration type.        */
/*--------------------------------------------------------------*/

analyze_enum_type(tp, verbose_flag)

    TYPE_STRUCT_PTR tp;         /* ptr to type structure */
    BOOLEAN verbose_flag;       /* TRUE for verbose analysis */

{
    SYMTAB_NODE_PTR idp;

    if (!verbose_flag) return;

    /*
    -- Loop to analyze each enumeration constant
    -- as a constant definition.
    */
    print_line(">>    --- Enum Constants ---\n");
    for (idp = tp->info.enumeration.const_idp;
```

```
              idp != NULL;
              idp = idp->next) analyze_const_defn(idp);
}

/*--------------------------------------------------------------*/
/*  analyze_subrange_type        Analyze a subrange type.       */
/*--------------------------------------------------------------*/

analyze_subrange_type(tp, verbose_flag)

    TYPE_STRUCT_PTR tp;         /* ptr to type structure */
    BOOLEAN verbose_flag;       /* TRUE for verbose analysis */

{
    if (!verbose_flag) return;

    sprintf(buffer, ">>    min value = %d, max value = %d\n",
                    tp->info.subrange.min,
                    tp->info.subrange.max);
    print_line(buffer);

    print_line(">>    --- Range Type ---\n");
    analyze_type(tp->info.subrange.range_typep, FALSE);
}

/*--------------------------------------------------------------*/
/*  analyze_array_type       Analyze an array type.             */
/*--------------------------------------------------------------*/

analyze_array_type(tp, verbose_flag)

    TYPE_STRUCT_PTR tp;         /* ptr to type structure */
    BOOLEAN verbose_flag;       /* TRUE for verbose analysis */

{
    if (!verbose_flag) return;

    sprintf(buffer, ">>    element count = %d\n",
                    tp->info.array.elmt_count);
    print_line(buffer);

    print_line(">>    --- INDEX TYPE ---\n");
    analyze_type(tp->info.array.index_typep, FALSE);

    print_line(">>    --- ELEMENT TYPE ---\n");
    analyze_type(tp->info.array.elmt_typep, FALSE);
}

/*--------------------------------------------------------------*/
/*  analyze_record_type      Analyze a record type.             */
/*--------------------------------------------------------------*/

analyze_record_type(tp, verbose_flag)

    TYPE_STRUCT_PTR tp;         /* ptr to type structure */
    BOOLEAN verbose_flag;       /* TRUE for verbose analysis */

{
    SYMTAB_NODE_PTR idp;

    if (!verbose_flag) return;

    /*
    -- Loop to analyze each record field
    -- as a variable declaration.
    */
    print_line(">>    --- Fields ---\n");
```

```
    for (idp = tp->info.record.field_symtab;        {       sprintf(buffer, ">> id = %s\n", idp->name);
         idp != NULL;                                       print_line(buffer);
         idp = idp->next) analyze_var_decl(idp);
}                                                           sprintf(buffer, ">>    defn = %s, offset = %d\n",
                                                                    defn_names[idp->defn.key],
/*---------------------------------------------------*/             idp->defn.info.data.offset);
/*  analyze_var_decl        Analyze a variable declaration.    */   print_line(buffer);
/*---------------------------------------------------*/
                                                            analyze_type(idp->typep, FALSE);
analyze_var_decl(idp)
                                                        }
    SYMTAB_NODE_PTR idp;        /* variable id */
```

In the main routine, we initialize both the scanner and the symbol table, and then allocate and initialize a dummy symbol table node for the program identifier. This node is needed by function declaration, since the declarations parser will hang information off of this node. In the next chapter, we will actually enter nodes into the symbol table for the program identifier and for each procedure and function identifier.

We call function declarations to parse and analyze declarations. Afterwards, we quit the scanner and print our usual statistics.

All of the analysis routines follow the main routine. We will examine each one in the following sections. We'll first see how to analyze the symbol table and type structure information, and then how the routines in file decl.c build these structures. Figure 6-7 shows a sample input file, and Figure 6-8 shows the listing output of the declarations analyzer.

FIGURE 6-7   Sample input file for the declarations analyzer.

```
CONST                                               ar3 = ARRAY [(fee, fye, foe, fum), ten..hundred] OF
    ten      = 10;                                             ARRAY [ee] OF boolean;
    hundred  = 100;                                 ar4 = ARRAY [boolean, 'm'..'r'] OF char;
    maxlength = 80;
    pi       = 3.1415626;                           rec = RECORD
    ch       = 'x';                                          i  : integer;
    hello    = 'Hello, world.';                             x  : real;
                                                            ch : char;
TYPE                                                        END;
    e  = (alpha, beta, gamma);
    ee = e;                                         VAR
    sr = alpha..gamma;                                  length, width : integer;
    cr = 'a'..ch;                                       radius, circumference : real;
                                                        b      : boolean;
    ar  = ARRAY [1..ten] OF integer;                    letter : 'a'..'z';
    ar1 = ARRAY [1..10] OF integer;                     buffer : ARRAY [1..maxlength] OF char;
    ar2 = ARRAY [e, sr] OF real;                        table  : ARRAY [ee, 1..5] OF rec;
```

FIGURE 6-8   Sample output from the declarations analyzer.

Page 1   analyze.in   Tue Jul 10 02:15:49 1990


```
    1 0: CONST
    2 0:     ten     = 10;
>> id = ten
>>    defn = constant, value = 10
>>    form = scalar, size = 2 bytes, type id = integer
    3 0:     hundred = 100;
>> id = hundred
>>    defn = constant, value = 100
>>    form = scalar, size = 2 bytes, type id = integer
    4 0:     maxlength = 80;
>> id = maxlength
>>    defn = constant, value = 80
>>    form = scalar, size = 2 bytes, type id = integer
    5 0:     pi      = 3.1415626;
>> id = pi
>>    defn = constant, value = 3.14156
>>    form = scalar, size = 4 bytes, type id = real
    6 0:     ch      = 'x';
>> id = ch
>>    defn = constant, value = 'x'
>>    form = scalar, size = 1 bytes, type id = char
    7 0:     hello   = 'Hello, world.';
>> id = hello
>>    defn = constant, value = 'Hello, world.'
>>    form = array, size = 13 bytes, type id = <unnamed type>
>>    element count = 13
>>    --- INDEX TYPE ---
>>    form = subrange, size = 2 bytes, type id = <unnamed type>
>>    min value = 1, max value = 13
>>    --- Range Type ---
>>    form = scalar, size = 2 bytes, type id = integer
>>    --- ELEMENT TYPE ---
>>    form = scalar, size = 1 bytes, type id = char
    8 0:
    9 0: TYPE
   10 0:     e  = (alpha, beta, gamma);
>> id = e
>>    defn = type
>>    form = enum, size = 2 bytes, type id = e
>>    --- Enum Constants ---
>> id = alpha
>>    defn = constant, value = 0
>> id = beta
>>    defn = constant, value = 1
>> id = gamma
>>    defn = constant, value = 2
   11 0:     ee = e;
>> id = ee
>>    defn = type
>>    form = enum, size = 2 bytes, type id = e
```


Page 2   analyze.in   Tue Jul 10 02:15:49 1990


```
>>    --- Enum Constants ---
>> id = alpha
>>    defn = constant, value = 0
>> id = beta
>>    defn = constant, value = 1
```


```
>> id = gamma
>>    defn = constant, value = 2
   12 0:     sr = alpha..gamma;
>> id = sr
>>    defn = type
>>    form = subrange, size = 2 bytes, type id = sr
>>    min value = 0, max value = 2
>>    --- Range Type ---
>>    form = enum, size = 2 bytes, type id = e
   13 0:     cr = 'a'..ch;
>> id = cr
>>    defn = type
>>    form = subrange, size = 1 bytes, type id = cr
>>    min value = 97, max value = 120
>>    --- Range Type ---
>>    form = scalar, size = 1 bytes, type id = char
   14 0:
   15 0:     ar = ARRAY [1..ten] OF integer;
>> id = ar
>>    defn = type
>>    form = array, size = 20 bytes, type id = ar
>>    element count = 10
>>    --- INDEX TYPE ---
>>    form = subrange, size = 2 bytes, type id = <unnamed type>
>>    min value = 1, max value = 10
>>    --- Range Type ---
>>    form = scalar, size = 2 bytes, type id = integer
>>    --- ELEMENT TYPE ---
>>    form = scalar, size = 2 bytes, type id = integer
   16 0:     ar1 = ARRAY [1..10] OF integer;
>> id = ar1
>>    defn = type
>>    form = array, size = 20 bytes, type id = ar1
>>    element count = 10
>>    --- INDEX TYPE ---
>>    form = subrange, size = 2 bytes, type id = <unnamed type>
>>    min value = 1, max value = 10
>>    --- Range Type ---
>>    form = scalar, size = 2 bytes, type id = integer
>>    --- ELEMENT TYPE ---
>>    form = scalar, size = 2 bytes, type id = integer
   17 0:     ar2 = ARRAY [e, sr] OF real;
>> id = ar2
>>    defn = type
>>    form = array, size = 36 bytes, type id = ar2
```


Page 3   analyze.in   Tue Jul 10 02:15:49 1990


```
>>    element count = 3
>>    --- INDEX TYPE ---
>>    form = enum, size = 2 bytes, type id = e
>>    --- ELEMENT TYPE ---
>>    form = array, size = 12 bytes, type id = <unnamed type>
>>    element count = 3
>>    --- INDEX TYPE ---
>>    form = subrange, size = 2 bytes, type id = sr
>>    --- ELEMENT TYPE ---
>>    form = scalar, size = 4 bytes, type id = real
   18 0:     ar3 = ARRAY [(fee, fye, foe, fum), ten..hundred] OF
   19 0:             ARRAY [ee] OF boolean;
>> id = ar3
```

```
>>    defn = type
>>    form = array, size = 2184 bytes, type id = ar3
>>    element count = 4
>>    --- INDEX TYPE ---
>>    form = enum, size = 2 bytes, type id = <unnamed type>
>>    --- Enum Constants ---
>> id = fee
>>    defn = constant, value = 0
>> id = fye
>>    defn = constant, value = 1
>> id = foe
>>    defn = constant, value = 2
>> id = fum
>>    defn = constant, value = 3
>>    --- ELEMENT TYPE ---
>>    form = array, size = 546 bytes, type id = <unnamed type>
>>    element count = 91
>>    --- INDEX TYPE ---
>>    form = subrange, size = 2 bytes, type id = <unnamed type>
>>    min value = 10, max value = 100
>>    --- Range Type ---
>>    form = scalar, size = 2 bytes, type id = integer
>>    --- ELEMENT TYPE ---
>>    form = array, size = 6 bytes, type id = <unnamed type>
>>    element count = 3
>>    --- INDEX TYPE ---
>>    form = enum, size = 2 bytes, type id = e
>>    --- ELEMENT TYPE ---
>>    form = enum, size = 2 bytes, type id = boolean
  20 0:     ar4 = ARRAY [boolean, 'm'..'r'] OF char;
>> id = ar4
>>    defn = type
>>    form = array, size = 12 bytes, type id = ar4
>>    element count = 2
>>    --- INDEX TYPE ---
>>    form = enum, size = 2 bytes, type id = boolean
>>    --- ELEMENT TYPE ---
```

Page 4   analyze.in   Tue Jul 10 02:15:49 1990

```
>>    form = array, size = 6 bytes, type id = <unnamed type>
>>    element count = 6
>>    --- INDEX TYPE ---
>>    form = subrange, size = 1 bytes, type id = <unnamed type>
>>    min value = 109, max value = 114
>>    --- Range Type ---
>>    form = scalar, size = 1 bytes, type id = char
>>    --- ELEMENT TYPE ---
>>    form = scalar, size = 1 bytes, type id = char
  21 0:
  22 0:     rec = RECORD
  23 0:             i  : integer;
  24 0:             x  : real;
  25 0:             ch : char;
  26 0:          END;
>> id = rec
>>    defn = type
>>    form = record, size = 7 bytes, type id = rec
>>    --- Fields ---
>> id = i
>>    defn = field, offset = 0
>>    form = scalar, size = 2 bytes, type id = integer
>> id = x
>>    defn = field, offset = 2
```

```
>>    form = scalar, size = 4 bytes, type id = real
>> id = ch
>>    defn = field, offset = 6
>>    form = scalar, size = 1 bytes, type id = char
  27 0:
  28 0: VAR
  29 0:     length, width : integer;
>> id = length
>>    defn = variable, offset = 0
>>    form = scalar, size = 2 bytes, type id = integer
>> id = width
>>    defn = variable, offset = 1
>>    form = scalar, size = 2 bytes, type id = integer
  30 0:     radius, circumference : real;
>> id = radius
>>    defn = variable, offset = 2
>>    form = scalar, size = 4 bytes, type id = real
>> id = circumference
>>    defn = variable, offset = 3
>>    form = scalar, size = 4 bytes, type id = real
  31 0:     b     : boolean;
>> id = b
>>    defn = variable, offset = 4
>>    form = enum, size = 2 bytes, type id = boolean
  32 0:     letter : 'a'..'z';
>> id = letter
```

Page 5   analyze.in   Tue Jul 10 02:15:49 1990

```
>>    defn = variable, offset = 5
>>    form = subrange, size = 1 bytes, type id = <unnamed type>
>>    min value = 97, max value = 122
>>    --- Range Type ---
>>    form = scalar, size = 1 bytes, type id = char
  33 0:     buffer : ARRAY [1..maxlength] OF char;
>> id = buffer
>>    defn = variable, offset = 6
>>    form = array, size = 80 bytes, type id = <unnamed type>
>>    element count = 80
>>    --- INDEX TYPE ---
>>    form = subrange, size = 2 bytes, type id = <unnamed type>
>>    min value = 1, max value = 80
>>    --- Range Type ---
>>    form = scalar, size = 2 bytes, type id = integer
>>    --- ELEMENT TYPE ---
>>    form = scalar, size = 1 bytes, type id = char
  34 0:     table  : ARRAY [ee, 1..5] OF rec;
>> id = table
>>    defn = variable, offset = 7
>>    form = array, size = 105 bytes, type id = <unnamed type>
>>    element count = 3
>>    --- INDEX TYPE ---
>>    form = enum, size = 2 bytes, type id = e
>>    --- ELEMENT TYPE ---
>>    form = array, size = 35 bytes, type id = <unnamed type>
>>    element count = 5
>>    --- INDEX TYPE ---
>>    form = subrange, size = 2 bytes, type id = <unnamed type>
>>    min value = 1, max value = 5
>>    --- Range Type ---
>>    form = scalar, size = 2 bytes, type id = integer
>>    --- ELEMENT TYPE ---
```

```
>>    form = record, size = 7 bytes, type id = rec                    35 Source lines.
   35 0:                                                                0 Source errors.
```

6.4.1 Analyzing constant definitions

Function `analyze_const_defn` analyzes a constant definition. The analysis includes the constant identifier's name and definition, the constant's value, and the form, size, and identifier of the constant's type. For example, the following definition:

$$pi = 3.1415626$$

produces:

```
>> id = pi
>>    defn = constant, value = 3.14156
>>    form = scalar, size = 4 bytes, type id = real
```

For a string constant, some further information about the array type is desirable. For example, the definition:

$$hello = \text{'Hello, world.'}$$

produces:

```
>> id = hello
>>    defn = constant, value = 'Hello, world.'
>>    form = array, size = 13 bytes, type id = <unnamed type>
>>    element count = 13
>>    --- INDEX TYPE ---
>>    form = subrange, size = 2 bytes, type id = <unnamed type>
>>    min value = 1, max value = 13
>>    --- Range Type ---
>>    form = scalar, size = 2 bytes, type id = integer
>>    --- ELEMENT TYPE ---
>>    form = scalar, size = 1 bytes, type id = char
```

We print the first two lines containing the constant's name, definition, and value in function `analyze_const_defn`. We print the information about the constant's type in function `analyze_type`.

6.4.2 Analyzing type definitions

The analysis of a type definition consists of the type identifier's name and definition, and the type's form, size, and identifier. An enumeration type includes the name, definition, and value of each enumeration constant identifier. A sub-range type includes information about the range type along with the minimum and maximum values. An array type includes information about the index and element types. A record type includes information about each field identifier. Finally, a type that is defined to be equivalent to a previously-defined type includes information about the previously-defined type.

We analyze a type definition in function analyze_type_defn by printing the type identifier's name and definition, and then we call function analyze_type to print the rest of the information, such as a type's form, size, and the type identifier's name. The first argument is a pointer to the type structure to analyze. The second argument is verbose_flag, which controls the amount of information we print. We will use the general rule that we print all type information whenever a new type is being defined, including unnamed types. Otherwise, we print a shorter version of the information. We call the appropriate analysis routine based on the type's form.

We analyze an enumeration type in function analyze_enum_type. We run down the list of the symbol table nodes of the enumeration constant identifiers hanging off of tp->info.enumeration.const_idp. For each identifier, we print the identifier's name, definition, and constant value. For example, the type definition:

$$e = (alpha, beta, gamma)$$

produces:

```
>> id = e
>>    defn = type
>>    form = enum, size = 2 bytes, type id = e
>>    --- Enum Constants ---
>> id = alpha
>>    defn = constant, value = 0
>> id = beta
>>    defn = constant, value = 1
>> id = gamma
>>    defn = constant, value = 2
```

We call function analyze_subrange_type to analyze a subrange type. We print the subrange type's minimum and maximum values, and then recursively call function analyze_type to analyze the range type. For example, the type definition:

$$sr = alpha..gamma$$

produces:

```
>> id = sr
>>    defn = type
```

```
>>      form = subrange, size = 2 bytes, type id = sr
>>      min value = 0, max value = 2
>>      --- Range Type ---
>>      form = enum, size = 2 bytes, type id = e
```

Note that the range type identifier name e is that of the previously-defined enumeration type.

In function analyze_array_type, we analyze an array type. We first print the array's element count, and then recursively call function analyze_type twice, first to analyze the index type and then to analyze the element type. For example, the following type definition:

$$ar1 = ARRAY [1..10] OF integer$$

produces:

```
>> id = ar1
>>      defn = type
>>      form = array, size = 20 bytes, type id = ar1
>>      element count = 10
>>      --- INDEX TYPE ---
>>      form = subrange, size = 2 bytes, type id = <unnamed type>
>>      min value = 1, max value = 10
>>      --- Range Type ---
>>      form = scalar, size = 2 bytes, type id = integer
>>      --- ELEMENT TYPE ---
>>      form = scalar, size = 2 bytes, type id = integer
```

Finally, we use function analyze_record_type, to analyze a record type. We run down the list of the symbol table nodes of the field identifiers hanging off of tp->info.record.field_symtab. For each identifier, we call function analyze_var_decl. For example, the type definition:

```
rec = RECORD
              i  : integer;
              x  : real;
              ch : char;
          END;
```

produces:

```
>> id = rec
>>      defn = type
>>      form = record, size = 7 bytes, type id = rec
```

```
>>      --- Fields ---
>> id = i
>>      defn = field, offset = 0
>>      form = scalar, size = 2 bytes, type id = integer
>> id = x
>>      defn = field, offset = 2
>>      form = scalar, size = 4 bytes, type id = real
>> id = ch
>>      defn = field, offset = 6
>>      form = scalar, size = 1 bytes, type id = char
```

6.4.3 Analyzing variable declarations

Function analyze_var_decl analyzes a record field or a variable declaration. We print the identifier's name and definition, and then call function analyze_type to analyze the identifier's type. For example, the declaration:

b : boolean

produces:

```
>> id = b
>>      defn = variable, offset = 4
>>      form = enum, size = 2 bytes, type id = boolean
```

6.4.4 Parsing declarations

Figure 6-9 shows file decl.c, which contains the declaration parsing routines that build the type structures and enter the symbol table information that we have been analyzing.

FIGURE 6-9   File decl.c.

```
/***************************************************************/
/*                                                             */
/*      D E C L A R A T I O N   P A R S E R                    */
/*                                                             */
/*      Parsing routines for delarations.                      */
/*                                                             */
/*      FILE:     decl.c                                       */
/*                                                             */
/*      MODULE:   parser                                       */
/*                                                             */
/***************************************************************/

#include <stdio.h>
#include "common.h"
#include "error.h"
#include "scanner.h"
#include "symtab.h"
```

```
#include "parser.h"

/*------------------------------------------------------------*/
/* Externals                                                  */
/*------------------------------------------------------------*/

extern TOKEN_CODE     token;
extern char           word_string[];
extern LITERAL        literal;

extern SYMTAB_NODE_PTR  symtab_root;

extern TYPE_STRUCT_PTR  integer_typep, real_typep,
                        boolean_typep, char_typep;

extern TYPE_STRUCT    dummy_type;
```

```
extern TOKEN_CODE          declaration_start_list[],
                           statement_start_list[];

/*----------------------------------------------------------*/
/*  Forwards                                                */
/*----------------------------------------------------------*/

TYPE_STRUCT_PTR do_type(),
                identifier_type(), enumeration_type(),
                subrange_type(), array_type(), record_type();

/*----------------------------------------------------------*/
/*  declarations          Call the routines to process constant   */
/*                        definitions, type definitions, variable */
/*                        declarations, procedure definitions,    */
/*                        and function definitions.               */
/*----------------------------------------------------------*/

declarations(rtn_idp)

    SYMTAB_NODE_PTR rtn_idp;     /* id of program or routine */

{
    if (token == CONST) {
        get_token();
        const_definitions();
    }

    if (token == TYPE) {
        get_token();
        type_definitions();
    }

    if (token == VAR) {
        get_token();
        var_declarations(rtn_idp);
    }
}

                /************************/
                /*                      */
                /*       Constants      */
                /*                      */
                /************************/

/*----------------------------------------------------------*/
/*  const_definitions    Process constant definitions:      */
/*                                                          */
/*                       <id> = <constant>                  */
/*----------------------------------------------------------*/

TOKEN_CODE follow_declaration_list[] = {SEMICOLON, IDENTIFIER,
                                        END_OF_FILE, 0};

const_definitions()

{
    SYMTAB_NODE_PTR const_idp;          /* constant id */

    /*
    -- Loop to process definitions separated by semicolons.
    */
    while (token == IDENTIFIER) {
        search_and_enter_local_symtab(const_idp);
        const_idp->defn.key = CONST_DEFN;

        get_token();
```

```
        if_token_get_else_error(EQUAL, MISSING_EQUAL);

        /*
        -- Process the constant.
        */
        do_const(const_idp);
        analyze_const_defn(const_idp);

        /*
        -- Error synchronization:  Should be ;
        */
        synchronize(follow_declaration_list,
                    declaration_start_list, statement_start_list);
        if_token_get(SEMICOLON);
        else if (token_in(declaration_start_list) ||
                 token_in(statement_start_list))
            error(MISSING_SEMICOLON);
    }
}

/*----------------------------------------------------------*/
/*  do_const          Process the constant of a constant    */
/*                    definition.                           */
/*----------------------------------------------------------*/

do_const(const_idp)

    SYMTAB_NODE_PTR const_idp;           /* constant id */

{
    TOKEN_CODE   sign      = PLUS;      /* unary + or - sign */
    BOOLEAN      saw_sign = FALSE;      /* TRUE iff unary sign */

    /*
    -- Unary + or - sign.
    */
    if ((token == PLUS) || (token == MINUS)) {
        sign     = token;
        saw_sign = TRUE;
        get_token();
    }

    /*
    -- Numeric constant:  Integer or real type.
    */
    if (token == NUMBER) {
        if (literal.type == INTEGER_LIT) {
            const_idp->defn.info.constant.value.integer =
                sign == PLUS ?  literal.value.integer
                             : -literal.value.integer;
            const_idp->typep = integer_typep;
        }
        else {
            const_idp->defn.info.constant.value.real =
                sign == PLUS ?  literal.value.real
                             : -literal.value.real;
            const_idp->typep = real_typep;
        }
    }

    /*
    -- Identifier constant:  Integer, real, character, enumeration,
    --                       or string (character array) type.
    */
    else if (token == IDENTIFIER) {
        SYMTAB_NODE_PTR idp;

        search_all_symtab(idp);
```

```
        if (idp == NULL)
            error(UNDEFINED_IDENTIFIER);
        else if (idp->defn.key != CONST_DEFN)
            error(NOT_A_CONSTANT_IDENTIFIER);

        else if (idp->typep == integer_typep) {
            const_idp->defn.info.constant.value.integer =
                sign == PLUS ?  idp->defn.info.constant.value.integer
                           : -idp->defn.info.constant.value.integer;
            const_idp->typep = integer_typep;
        }
        else if (idp->typep == real_typep) {
            const_idp->defn.info.constant.value.real =
                sign == PLUS ?  idp->defn.info.constant.value.real
                           : -idp->defn.info.constant.value.real;
            const_idp->typep = real_typep;
        }
        else if (idp->typep == char_typep) {
            if (saw_sign) error(INVALID_CONSTANT);

            const_idp->defn.info.constant.value.character =
                            idp->defn.info.constant.value.character;
            const_idp->typep = char_typep;
        }
        else if (idp->typep->form == ENUM_FORM) {
            if (saw_sign) error(INVALID_CONSTANT);

            const_idp->defn.info.constant.value.integer =
                            idp->defn.info.constant.value.integer;
            const_idp->typep = idp->typep;
        }
        else if (idp->typep->form == ARRAY_FORM) {
            if (saw_sign) error(INVALID_CONSTANT);

            const_idp->defn.info.constant.value.stringp =
                            idp->defn.info.constant.value.stringp;
            const_idp->typep = idp->typep;
        }
    }

    /*
    -- String constant:  Character or string (character array) type.
    */
    else if (token == STRING) {
        if (saw_sign) error(INVALID_CONSTANT);

        if (strlen(literal.value.string) == 1) {
            const_idp->defn.info.constant.value.character =
                                    literal.value.string[0];
            const_idp->typep = char_typep;
        }
        else {
            int length = strlen(literal.value.string);

            const_idp->defn.info.constant.value.stringp =
                                    alloc_bytes(length + 1);
            strcpy(const_idp->defn.info.constant.value.stringp,
                literal.value.string);
            const_idp->typep = make_string_typep(length);
        }
    }

    else {
        const_idp->typep = &dummy_type;
        error(INVALID_CONSTANT);
    }
}
```

```
        get_token();
}


                /**************************/
                /*                        */
                /*        Types           */
                /*                        */
                /**************************/

/*----------------------------------------------------------*/
/*  type_definitions     Process type definitions:          */
/*                                                          */
/*                          <id> = <type>                   */
/*----------------------------------------------------------*/

type_definitions()

{
    SYMTAB_NODE_PTR type_idp;            /* type id */

    /*
    -- Loop to process definitions separated by semicolons.
    */
    while (token == IDENTIFIER) {
        search_and_enter_local_symtab(type_idp);
        type_idp->defn.key = TYPE_DEFN;

        get_token();
        if_token_get_else_error(EQUAL, MISSING_EQUAL);

        /*
        -- Process the type specification.
        */
        type_idp->typep = do_type();
        if (type_idp->typep->type_idp == NULL)
            type_idp->typep->type_idp = type_idp;

        analyze_type_defn(type_idp);

        /*
        -- Error synchronization:  Should be ;
        */
        synchronize(follow_declaration_list,
                declaration_start_list, statement_start_list);
        if_token_get(SEMICOLON);
        else if (token_in(declaration_start_list) ||
                token_in(statement_start_list))
            error(MISSING_SEMICOLON);
    }
}

/*----------------------------------------------------------*/
/*  do_type              Process a type specification.  Call the */
/*                       functions that make a type structure    */
/*                       and return a pointer to it.             */
/*----------------------------------------------------------*/

    TYPE_STRUCT_PTR
do_type()

{
    switch (token) {
        case IDENTIFIER: {
            SYMTAB_NODE_PTR idp;

            search_all_symtab(idp);

            if (idp == NULL) {
```

```
                error(UNDEFINED_IDENTIFIER);
                return(&dummy_type);
        }
        else if (idp->defn.key == TYPE_DEFN)
            return(identifier_type(idp));
        else if (idp->defn.key == CONST_DEFN)
            return(subrange_type(idp));
        else {
            error(NOT_A_TYPE_IDENTIFIER);
            return(&dummy_type);
        }
    }

    case LPAREN:    return(enumeration_type());
    case ARRAY:     return(array_type());
    case RECORD:    return(record_type());

    case PLUS:
    case MINUS:
    case NUMBER:
    case STRING:    return(subrange_type(NULL));

    default:        error(INVALID_TYPE);
                    return(&dummy_type);
    }
}

/*-----------------------------------------------------------*/
/*  identifier_type     Process an identifier type, i.e., the  */
/*                      identifier on the right side of a type  */
/*                      equate, and return a pointer to its     */
/*                      type structure.                         */
/*-----------------------------------------------------------*/

    TYPE_STRUCT_PTR
identifier_type(idp)

    SYMTAB_NODE_PTR idp;        /* type id */

{
    TYPE_STRUCT_PTR tp = NULL;

    tp = idp->typep;
    get_token();

    return(tp);
}

/*-----------------------------------------------------------*/
/*  enumeration_type    Process an enumeration type:          */
/*                                                            */
/*                      ( <id1>, <id2>, ..., <idn> )          */
/*                                                            */
/*                      Make a type structure and return a    */
/*                      pointer to it.                         */
/*-----------------------------------------------------------*/

    TYPE_STRUCT_PTR
enumeration_type()

{
    SYMTAB_NODE_PTR const_idp;          /* constant id */
    SYMTAB_NODE_PTR last_idp  = NULL; /* last constant id */
    TYPE_STRUCT_PTR tp        = alloc_struct(TYPE_STRUCT);
    int             const_value = -1;   /* constant value */

    tp->form    = ENUM_FORM;
```

```
    tp->size    = sizeof(int);
    tp->type_idp = NULL;

    get_token();

    /*
    -- Loop to process list of identifiers.
    */
    while (token == IDENTIFIER) {
        search_and_enter_local_symtab(const_idp);
        const_idp->defn.key = CONST_DEFN;
        const_idp->defn.info.constant.value.integer = ++const_value;
        const_idp->typep = tp;

        /*
        -- Link constant ids together.
        */
        if (last_idp == NULL)
            tp->info.enumeration.const_idp = last_idp = const_idp;
        else {
            last_idp->next = const_idp;
            last_idp = const_idp;
        }

        get_token();
        if_token_get(COMMA);
    }

    if_token_get_else_error(RPAREN, MISSING_RPAREN);

    tp->info.enumeration.max = const_value;
    return(tp);
}

/*-----------------------------------------------------------*/
/*  subrange_type       Process a subrange type:             */
/*                                                           */
/*                      <min-const> .. <max-const>           */
/*                                                           */
/*                      Make a type structure and return a   */
/*                      pointer to it.                        */
/*-----------------------------------------------------------*/

TOKEN_CODE follow_min_limit_list[] = {DOTDOT, IDENTIFIER, PLUS, MINUS,
                                      NUMBER, STRING, SEMICOLON,
                                      END_OF_FILE, 0};

    TYPE_STRUCT_PTR
subrange_type(min_idp)

    SYMTAB_NODE_PTR min_idp;    /* min limit const id */

{
    TYPE_STRUCT_PTR max_typep; /* type of max limit */
    TYPE_STRUCT_PTR tp = alloc_struct(TYPE_STRUCT);

    tp->form    = SUBRANGE_FORM;
    tp->type_idp = NULL;

    /*
    -- Minimum constant.
    */
    get_subrange_limit(min_idp,
                &(tp->info.subrange.min),
                &(tp->info.subrange.range_typep));

    /*
```

```
    -- Error synchronization:  Should be ..
    */
    synchronize(follow_min_limit_list, NULL, NULL);
    if_token_get(DOTDOT);
    else if (token_in(follow_min_limit_list) ||
            token_in(declaration_start_list) ||
            token_in(statement_start_list))
        error(MISSING_DOTDOT);

    /*
    -- Maximum constant.
    */
    get_subrange_limit(NULL, &(tp->info.subrange.max), &max_typep);

    /*
    -- Check limits.
    */
    if (max_typep == tp->info.subrange.range_typep) {
        if (tp->info.subrange.min > tp->info.subrange.max)
            error(MIN_GT_MAX);
    }
    else error(INCOMPATIBLE_TYPES);

    tp->size = max_typep == char_typep ? sizeof(char) : sizeof(int);
    return(tp);
}

/*------------------------------------------------------------*/
/*  get_subrange_limit  Process the minimum and maximum limits  */
/*                      of a subrange type.                      */
/*------------------------------------------------------------*/

get_subrange_limit(minmax_idp, minmaxp, typepp)

    SYMTAB_NODE_PTR minmax_idp; /* min const id */
    int             *minmaxp;   /* where to store min or max value */
    TYPE_STRUCT_PTR *typepp;     /* where to store ptr to type struct */

{
    SYMTAB_NODE_PTR idp       = minmax_idp;
    TOKEN_CODE      sign      = PLUS;    /* unary + or - sign */
    BOOLEAN         saw_sign = FALSE;   /* TRUE iff unary sign */

    /*
    -- Unary + or - sign.
    */
    if ((token == PLUS) || (token == MINUS)) {
        sign     = token;
        saw_sign = TRUE;
        get_token();
    }

    /*
    -- Numeric limit:  Integer type only.
    */
    if (token == NUMBER) {
        if (literal.type == INTEGER_LIT) {
            *typepp = integer_typep;
            *minmaxp = (sign == PLUS) ? literal.value.integer
                                      : -literal.value.integer;
        }
        else error(INVALID_SUBRANGE_TYPE);
    }

    /*
    -- Identifier limit:  Value must be integer or character.
    */
```

```
    else if (token == IDENTIFIER) {
        if (idp == NULL) search_all_symtab(idp);

        if (idp == NULL)
            error(UNDEFINED_IDENTIFIER);
        else if (idp->typep == real_typep)
            error(INVALID_SUBRANGE_TYPE);
        else if (idp->defn.key == CONST_DEFN) {
            *typepp  = idp->typep;
            if (idp->typep == char_typep) {
                if (saw_sign) error(INVALID_CONSTANT);
                *minmaxp = idp->defn.info.constant.value.character;
            }
            else if (idp->typep == integer_typep) {
                *minmaxp = idp->defn.info.constant.value.integer;
                if (sign == MINUS) *minmaxp = -(*minmaxp);
            }
            else /* enumeration constant */ {
                if (saw_sign) error(INVALID_CONSTANT);
                *minmaxp = idp->defn.info.constant.value.integer;
            }
        }
        else error(NOT_A_CONSTANT_IDENTIFIER);
    }

    /*
    -- String limit:  Character type only.
    */
    else if (token == STRING) {
        if (saw_sign) error(INVALID_CONSTANT);
        *typepp  = char_typep;
        *minmaxp = literal.value.string[0];

        if (strlen(literal.value.string) != 1)
            error(INVALID_SUBRANGE_TYPE);
    }

    else error(MISSING_CONSTANT);

    get_token();
}

/*------------------------------------------------------------*/
/*  array_type           Process an array type:                */
/*                                                             */
/*                       ARRAY [<index-type-list>]             */
/*                            OF <elmt-type>                   */
/*                                                             */
/*                       Make a type structure and return a    */
/*                       pointer to it.                         */
/*------------------------------------------------------------*/

TOKEN_CODE follow_dimension_list[] = {COMMA, RBRACKET, OF,
                                      SEMICOLON, END_OF_FILE, 0};

TOKEN_CODE index_type_start_list[] = {IDENTIFIER, NUMBER, STRING,
                                      LPAREN, MINUS, PLUS, 0};

TOKEN_CODE follow_indexes_list[] = {OF, IDENTIFIER, LPAREN, ARRAY,
                                    RECORD, PLUS, MINUS, NUMBER,
                                    STRING, SEMICOLON, END_OF_FILE,
                                    0};

    TYPE_STRUCT_PTR
array_type()

{
```

```
TYPE_STRUCT_PTR tp      = alloc_struct(TYPE_STRUCT);
TYPE_STRUCT_PTR index_tp;              /* index type */
TYPE_STRUCT_PTR elmt_tp = tp;          /* element type */
int array_size();

get_token();
if (token != LBRACKET) error(MISSING_LBRACKET);

/*
-- Loop to process index type list.  For each
-- type in the list after the first, create an
-- array element type.
*/
do {
    get_token();

    if (token_in(index_type_start_list)) {
        elmt_tp->form      = ARRAY_FORM;
        elmt_tp->size      = 0;
        elmt_tp->type_idp = NULL;
        elmt_tp->info.array.index_typep = index_tp = do_type();

        switch (index_tp->form) {
            case ENUM_FORM:
                elmt_tp->info.array.elmt_count =
                        index_tp->info.enumeration.max + 1;
                elmt_tp->info.array.min_index = 0;
                elmt_tp->info.array.max_index =
                        index_tp->info.enumeration.max;
                break;

            case SUBRANGE_FORM:
                elmt_tp->info.array.elmt_count =
                        index_tp->info.subrange.max -
                            index_tp->info.subrange.min + 1;
                elmt_tp->info.array.min_index =
                        index_tp->info.subrange.min;
                elmt_tp->info.array.max_index =
                        index_tp->info.subrange.max;
                break;

            default:
                elmt_tp->form      = NO_FORM;
                elmt_tp->size      = 0;
                elmt_tp->type_idp = NULL;
                elmt_tp->info.array.index_typep = &dummy_type;
                error(INVALID_INDEX_TYPE);
                break;
        }
    }
    else {
        elmt_tp->form      = NO_FORM;
        elmt_tp->size      = 0;
        elmt_tp->type_idp = NULL;
        elmt_tp->info.array.index_typep = &dummy_type;
        error(INVALID_INDEX_TYPE);
    }

    /*
    -- Error synchronization:  Should be , or ]
    */
    synchronize(follow_dimension_list, NULL, NULL);

    /*
    -- Create an array element type.
    */
    if (token == COMMA) elmt_tp = elmt_tp->info.array.elmt_typep =
```

```
                                    alloc_struct(TYPE_STRUCT);
} while (token == COMMA);

if_token_get_else_error(RBRACKET, MISSING_RBRACKET);

/*
-- Error synchronization:  Should be OF
*/
synchronize(follow_indexes_list,
            declaration_start_list, statement_start_list);
if_token_get_else_error(OF, MISSING_OF);

/*
-- Element type.
*/
elmt_tp->info.array.elmt_typep = do_type();

tp->size = array_size(tp);
return(tp);
}
```

```
/*------------------------------------------------------------*/
/*  record_type        Process a record type:                 */
/*                                                            */
/*                          RECORD                            */
/*                              <id-list> : <type> ;          */
/*                              ...                           */
/*                          END                               */
/*                                                            */
/*                      Make a type structure and return a    */
/*                      pointer to it.                        */
/*------------------------------------------------------------*/

    TYPE_STRUCT_PTR
record_type()

{
    TYPE_STRUCT_PTR record_tp = alloc_struct(TYPE_STRUCT);

    record_tp->form      = RECORD_FORM;
    record_tp->type_idp = NULL;
    record_tp->info.record.field_symtab = NULL;

    get_token();
    var_or_field_declarations(NULL, record_tp, 0);

    if_token_get_else_error(END, MISSING_END);
    return(record_tp);
}
```

```
/*------------------------------------------------------------*/
/*  make_string_typep   Make a type structure for a string of */
/*                      the given length, and return a pointer*/
/*                      to it.                                 */
/*------------------------------------------------------------*/

    TYPE_STRUCT_PTR
make_string_typep(length)

    int length;                 /* string length */

{
    TYPE_STRUCT_PTR string_tp = alloc_struct(TYPE_STRUCT);
    TYPE_STRUCT_PTR index_tp  = alloc_struct(TYPE_STRUCT);

    /*
    -- Array type.
```

```
        */
        string_tp->form      = ARRAY_FORM;
        string_tp->size      = length;
        string_tp->type_idp = NULL;
        string_tp->info.array.index_typep = index_tp;
        string_tp->info.array.elmt_typep = char_typep;
        string_tp->info.array.elmt_count = length;

        /*
        -- Subrange index type.
        */
        index_tp->form      = SUBRANGE_FORM;
        index_tp->size      = sizeof(int);
        index_tp->type_idp = NULL;
        index_tp->info.subrange.range_typep = integer_typep;
        index_tp->info.subrange.min = 1;
        index_tp->info.subrange.max = length;

        return(string_tp);
}

/*------------------------------------------------------------*/
/*  array_size          Return the size in bytes of an array  */
/*                      type by recursively calculating the   */
/*                      size of each dimension.               */
/*------------------------------------------------------------*/

    int
array_size(tp)

    TYPE_STRUCT_PTR tp;        /* ptr to array type structure */

{
    if (tp->info.array.elmt_typep->size == 0)
        tp->info.array.elmt_typep->size =
                        array_size(tp->info.array.elmt_typep);

    tp->size = tp->info.array.elmt_count *
                tp->info.array.elmt_typep->size;

    return(tp->size);
}

                /************************/
                /*                      */
                /*      Variables       */
                /*                      */
                /************************/

/*------------------------------------------------------------*/
/*  var_declarations    Process variable declarations:        */
/*                                                            */
/*                      <id-list> : <type>                    */
/*------------------------------------------------------------*/

var_declarations(rtn_idp)

    SYMTAB_NODE_PTR rtn_idp;    /* id of program or routine */

{
    var_or_field_declarations(rtn_idp, NULL, 0);
}

/*------------------------------------------------------------*/
/*  var_or_field_declarations   Process variable declarations */
/*                              or record field definitions.  */
/*                              All ids declared with the same */
```

```
/*                      type are linked together into   */
/*                      a sublist, and all the sublists  */
/*                      are then linked together.        */
/*------------------------------------------------------------*/

TOKEN_CODE follow_variables_list[] = {SEMICOLON, IDENTIFIER,
                                      END_OF_FILE, 0};

TOKEN_CODE follow_fields_list[]    = {SEMICOLON, END, IDENTIFIER,
                                      END_OF_FILE, 0};

var_or_field_declarations(rtn_idp, record_tp, offset)

    SYMTAB_NODE_PTR rtn_idp;
    TYPE_STRUCT_PTR record_tp;
    int             offset;

{
    SYMTAB_NODE_PTR idp, first_idp, last_idp;   /* variable or
                                                    field ids */
    SYMTAB_NODE_PTR prev_last_idp = NULL;       /* last id of list */
    TYPE_STRUCT_PTR tp;                          /* type */
    BOOLEAN var_flag = (rtn_idp != NULL);       /* TRUE:  variables */
                                                /* FALSE: fields */
    int size;
    int total_size = 0;

    /*
    -- Loop to process sublist, each of a type.
    */
    while (token == IDENTIFIER) {
        first_idp = NULL;

        /*
        -- Loop process each variable or field id in a sublist.
        */
        while (token == IDENTIFIER) {
            if (var_flag) {
                search_and_enter_local_symtab(idp);
                idp->defn.key = VAR_DEFN;
            }
            else {
                search_and_enter_this_symtab
                    (idp, record_tp->info.record.field_symtab);
                idp->defn.key = FIELD_DEFN;
            }
            idp->label_index = 0;

            /*
            -- Link ids together into a sublist.
            */
            if (first_idp == NULL) {
                first_idp = last_idp = idp;
                if (var_flag &&
                    (rtn_idp->defn.info.routine.locals == NULL))
                    rtn_idp->defn.info.routine.locals = idp;
            }
            else {
                last_idp->next = idp;
                last_idp = idp;
            }

            get_token();
            if_token_get(COMMA);
        }

        /*
```

```
--   Process the sublist's type.                            /*
*/                                                          --  Link this sublist to the previous sublist.
if_token_get_else_error(COLON, MISSING_COLON);              */
tp = do_type();                                             if (prev_last_idp != NULL) prev_last_idp->next = first_idp;
size = tp->size;                                            prev_last_idp = last_idp;

/*                                                          /*
--   Assign the offset and the type to all variable or field  --  Error synchronization:  Should be ; for variable
--   ids in the sublist.                                    --                            declaration, or ; or END for
*/                                                          --                            record type definition.
for (idp = first_idp; idp != NULL; idp = idp->next) {       */
    idp->typep = tp;                                        synchronize(var_flag ? follow_variables_list
                                                                                 : follow_fields_list,
    if (var_flag) {                                                      declaration_start_list, statement_start_list);
        total_size += size;                                if_token_get(SEMICOLON);
        idp->defn.info.data.offset = offset++;             else if (var_flag && ((token_in(declaration_start_list)) ||
        analyze_var_decl(idp);                                                  (token_in(statement_start_list))))
    }                                                          error(MISSING_SEMICOLON);
                                                       }
    else   /* record fields */ {
        idp->defn.info.data.offset = offset;           if (var_flag)
        offset += size;                                    rtn_idp->defn.info.routine.total_local_size = total_size;
    }                                                  else
}                                                          record_tp->size = offset;
                                                       }
```

We called function declarations from the main routine of the declarations analyzer. In it, we successively look for constant definitions, type definitions, and variable declarations, and, as necessary, we call functions const_definitions, type_definitions, and var_declarations. We passed declarations a pointer to the dummy symbol table node for the program identifier. In the next chapter, we will pass in a pointer to the actual symbol table node for the program identifier or for the identifier of a procedure or a function. We pass this pointer on to the other functions.

6.4.5 Parsing constants

We parse constant definitions in function const_definitions, where we loop once for each definition. We first enter the identifier into the symbol table as a constant identifier. Next, we look for the equal sign before we call function do_const to parse the constant, and then we call function analyze_const_defn to analyze the symbol table node and its type structure. After all that, we call function synchronize to resynchronize the parser either at the end of the declaration, at the beginning of the next declaration, or at the beginning of the first statement, in that order of preference. We also check for a missing semicolon.

We do the work of parsing the constant in function do_const. We pass it a pointer to the constant identifier's symbol table node. After taking care of any unary + or - sign, we expect to see either a number, an identifier, or a string. We enter the constant value into the symbol table node in field defn.info.constant. value.

If the constant is numeric, we get the constant value from the scanner's literal variable. We set the constant identifier's typep field to point to the type structure of either the predefined integer or real type.

If the constant is an identifier, we search the symbol table for the identifier, which must already be defined to be a constant. We obtain the identifier's value from its symbol table node. The value may be integer, real, character, enumeration, or string (character array) type. We also set field typep of the constant identifier being defined to point to the type structure of the already-defined identifier.

If the constant is a string, we first check if the string length is one. If so, we have a character constant. We get the character from literal, and we set the constant identifier's typep field to point to the type structure of the predefined character type.

If the string length is greater than one, we make a copy of the string and make defn.info.constant.value.stringp point to the copy. We then call function make_string_typep to create an unnamed character array type. (We'll look at this function later.)

6.4.6 Parsing type definitions

We parse type definitions in function type_definitions, where we loop once for each definition. We first enter the identifier into the symbol table as a type identifier. Next, we look for the equal sign before we call function do_type to parse the type specification, and then we call function analyze_type_defn to analyze the symbol table node and its type structure. After all that, we call function synchronize to resynchronize the parser either at the end of the declaration, at the beginning of the next declaration, or at the beginning of the first statement. We conclude with a check for a missing semicolon.

6.4.7 Parsing type specifications

Function do_type parses a type specification for both named and unnamed types. In it, we call the appropriate parsing function based on the current token, and we return a pointer to a type structure.

If the first token of a type specification is an identifier, we need to check further. We look up the identifier, and if it is an enumeration constant, it must be the lower limit of a subrange type. Otherwise, it must be a previously-defined type identifier.

6.4.8 Parsing identifier types

We call function identifier_type when a type specification is simply a previously-defined type identifier. We return a pointer to the type structure of the identifier.

6.4.9 Parsing enumeration and subrange types

We call function `enumeration_type` to parse an enumeration type specification. First, we allocate a new type structure and set the `form` field to `ENUM_FORM`. We then loop to parse the enumeration constants. We assign each constant identifier its value and enter it into the symbol table. We link the symbol table nodes together via their `next` fields. We point the type structure's `info.enumeration.const_idp` field to the head of this list, and we set its `info.enumeration.max` field to the value of the last enumeration constant. We return a pointer to the type structure.

In function `subrange_type`, we parse a subrange type specification. First, we allocate a new type structure and set the `form` field to `SUBRANGE_FORM`. We call function `get_subrange_limit` twice, first to parse the minimum limit and then to parse the upper limit of the subrange. After the first call, we call function `synchronize` to resynchronize the parser at the `..` token or, if it is missing, at the start of the maximum limit. After the second call, we check to make sure that the types of the minimum and maximum values are the same, and that the maximum value is indeed greater than the minimum value. We store both values and the range type into the type structure, and then we return a pointer to the structure.

A subrange limit may be an integer or character literal, or a constant identifier whose value is an integer or character. We call function `get_subrange_limit` to parse each limit of a subrange type. If a limit is a number, we make sure it is an integer and get its value from the scanner's `literal`. If it is an identifier, we look it up to make sure it is already defined as a constant, and we get the constant value from the symbol table node. Finally, if it is a string, we check that it is a character, and we get its value from `literal`.

6.4.10 Parsing array types

We call function `array_type` to parse an array type specification. First, we allocate a new type structure and set variable `elmt_tp` to point to this structure. We then loop once per index specification.

In the simple case of a single-dimensional array, we execute the index loop only once. At the top of the loop, the token list `index_type_start_list` verifies the start of an index type. We set the array type structure's `form` field to `ARRAY_FORM`. We call function `do_type` to parse the index type, and we point the `info.array.index_typep` field to the index type structure. Then, the `elmt_count`, `min_index`, and `max_index` fields are set according to the index type. After parsing the index, we call function `synchronize` to resynchronize the parser at the comma or] token.

Outside the index loop, we check for a missing] token, and then call `synchronize` again. We want to resynchronize the parser at the `OF`, but if `OF` is missing, we can resynchronize at the start of the element type specification, at the start of the next declaration, or at the start of the first statement. Finally, we call `do_type` to parse the element type, and we point the `info.array.elmt_typep` field to the element type structure.

For a multiple-dimensional array, there can be an index specification for each dimension between the pair of brackets. We need to chain together array type structures, as we saw in Figure 6-4. At the bottom of the loop, we check for a comma. If there is one, another index specification must follow. We allocate new type structure, and we point both elmt_tp and the elmt_typep field of the previous type structure to it. At the top of the next execution of the loop, we set the structure's form field to ARRAY_FORM. Thus, we create a linked list of array type structures, one structure for each dimension. After the loop, we call do_type again to parse the element type, and we point the info.array.elmt_typep field of the last dimension to the element type structure.

To conclude, we call function array_size (explained below) to calculate the byte size of the array. We then return a pointer to the first (or only) array type structure.

6.4.11 Parsing record types

Function record_type parses a record type specification. We allocate a new type structure and set the form field to RECORD_FORM. The info.record.field_symtab field of a record type structure points to a private symbol table that contains the record's field identifiers. They are kept in a private symbol table and not in the global symbol table because of the scope of a field identifier. A field identifier can have the same name as that of a global variable or of another record type's field. (The concept of scope is further explained in the next chapter.)

We call function var_or_field_declarations, passing a pointer to the record type structure. This function parses both record field and variable declarations. For a record type, it enters the field identifiers into the record type's private symbol table. Afterwards, we check for the END, and then we return a pointer to the record type structure.

6.4.12 Creating string types

We call function make_string_typep whenever we need to create a type structure to represent an unnamed string type of a given length. In Pascal, a string type is a one-dimensional array of char. The index type is the subrange of integers from one through the length. We return a pointer to the string type structure.

6.4.13 Sizes of array variables

Function array_size calculates the number of bytes of an array. We call the function recursively for each array element, and then the size of each dimension is the element size times the element count.

6.4.14 Parsing record field and variable declarations

We parse record field or variable declarations in function var_or_field_declarations. We call this function from record_type to parse field declarations, and from var_declarations to parse variable declarations.

A declaration consists of a sublist of one or more identifiers separated by commas, a colon, and then a type specification. We parse one or more declarations separated by semicolons in the outer `while` loop. We parse the identifiers in a sublist in the inner `while` loop.

In the inner `while` loop, each identifier is entered into the symbol table. If we are parsing variables, we use the local symbol table and set the `defn.key` field to `VAR_DEFN`. Otherwise, we are parsing record fields, so we use the record type's private symbol table and set the `defn.key` field to `FIELD_DEFN`. We link the symbol table nodes together into a sublist via their `next` fields.

We also chain the sublists together into one list and set the `defn.info.routine.locals` field of the symbol table node to point to it. This is the node of the program, procedure, or function identifier. In this chapter, it is only the dummy program identifier node.

After the last identifier in a sublist, we look for the colon, and then we call function `do_type`, which parses the type specification and returns a type structure.

In the `for` loop, we set the `typep` field of each node in the sublist to point to the type structure. We calculate the total size of the all the fields or variables being declared, and also set the `defn.info.data.offset` field of each node. (This offset field will be useful in later chapters.) Note that the offset increments by one for variables, but that it increments by the size of each field for record fields.

Now that we are at the end of a declaration, we call function `synchronize` to resynchronize the parser. We want to resynchronize at the point just after the declaration (whether variables or record fields), at the start of the next declaration, or at the start of the first statement. We then check for a missing semicolon.

Finally, we need to set the size fields. If we are parsing variables, we set the `defn.info.routine.total_local_size` field of the symbol table node of the program, procedure, or function identifier. (In this chapter, the dummy program identifier node.) Otherwise, we set the `size` field of the record type structure.

6.4.15 A final detail

Figure 6-10 shows a new version of file `parser.h`. At the end of the file, we now have several new macro definitions. These macros have the same names as the analysis functions that we call from file `decl.c`, and each macro is defined to be the empty string. (The names `analyze_routine_header` and `analyze_block` will be useful in Chapter 8.) The idea is to conditionally remove the calls to the analysis routines when we do *not* want declarations analyzed. Since we bracket the macro definitions with `#ifndef analyze` and `#endif`, the function calls are left in only if we set the macro flag `analyze` before the macro definitions. We need to do this for the declarations analyzer. One way is to insert the following line: `#define analyze` before the `#ifndef analyze` line. Another way is the set the flag with a command-line option when we invoke the C compiler: `/Danalyze`

We add a new enumeration type `USE` whose enumeration constants indicate how a variable is used in a statement, whether it is part of an expression, the

FIGURE 6-10   File `parser.h`.

```
/****************************************************************/          /********************************/
/*                                                  */
/*      P A R S I N G   R O U T I N E S   (Header)  */          /*--------------------------------------------------------*/
/*                                                  */          /*  if_token_get             If token equals token_code, get */
/*    FILE:      parser.h                           */          /*                           the next token.              */
/*                                                  */          /*--------------------------------------------------------*/
/*    MODULE:    parser                             */
/*                                                  */          #define if_token_get(token_code)                \
/****************************************************************/              if (token == token_code) get_token()

#ifndef parser_h                                                /*--------------------------------------------------------*/
#define parser_h                                                /*  if_token_get_else_error   If token equals token_code, get */
                                                                /*                           the next token, else error. */
#include "common.h"                                             /*--------------------------------------------------------*/
#include "symtab.h"
                                                                #define if_token_get_else_error(token_code, error_code) \
/*--------------------------------------------------*/              if (token == token_code) get_token();         \
/*  Uses of a variable                             */              else                      error(error_code)
/*--------------------------------------------------*/
                                                                /*--------------------------------------------------------*/
typedef enum {                                                  /*  Analysis routine calls   Unless the following statements */
    EXPR_USE, TARGET_USE, VARPARM_USE,                          /*                           are preceded by              */
} USE;                                                          /*                                                        */
                                                                /*                                  #define analyze       */
/*--------------------------------------------------*/          /*                                                        */
/*  Functions                                      */          /*                           calls to the analysis routines */
/*--------------------------------------------------*/          /*                           are not compiled.            */
                                                                /*--------------------------------------------------------*/
TYPE_STRUCT_PTR expression();
TYPE_STRUCT_PTR variable();                                     #ifndef analyze
TYPE_STRUCT_PTR routine_call();                                 #define analyze_const_defn(idp)
TYPE_STRUCT_PTR base_type();                                    #define analyze_var_decl(idp)
BOOLEAN         is_assign_type_compatible();                    #define analyze_type_defn(idp)
                                                                #define analyze_routine_header(idp)
          /********************************/                    #define analyze_block(idp)
          /*                          */                        #endif
          /*    Macros for parsing    */
          /*                          */                        #endif
```

target of an assignment, or passed as a VAR parameter. This type will be used in the next utility program. We also specify the return types of functions `expression`, `variable`, `routine_call`, `base_type`, and `is_assign_type_compatible`. These, too, are needed by the next utility program.

6.5 Type checking

Now that we have seen how it parses declarations, we need the parser to perform the semantic action of type checking. Type checking verifies that a program uses types correctly. Three common type checks are:

1. Expressions: whether or not the operands of an operator are of the correct type. For example, the arithmetic operator + requires integer or real operands, and the boolean operator AND requires boolean operands.

2. Assignments: whether or not an expression value of one type can be assigned to a variable of a different type. For example, it is legal to assign an integer value to a real variable, but not vice versa.

3. Statements: whether or not an expression that appears in a statement is of the correct type. For example, the expression in an IF statement must be boolean.

We now add type checking to the parser module. We will see how this checking works with the new version of the Pascal syntax checker utility program.

6.6 Program 6-2: Pascal Syntax Checker II

Our second utility program builds upon the syntax checker of the previous chapter, and the declarations analyzer. Not only does it check the syntax of both declarations and statements, but it also performs the three types checks specified above.

Figure 6-11 shows the main file syntax2.c. In the main routine, we initialize the scanner and the symbol table, and then call function block. In block, we call function declarations to parse declarations, and then call function compound_statement to parse a compound statement. Figure 6-12 shows the syntax diagram for a block.

FIGURE 6-11   File syntax2.c.

```
/*****************************************************************/
/*                                                             */
/*      Program 6-2:  Pascal Syntax Checker II                 */
/*                                                             */
/*      Check the syntax of Pascal declarations and            */
/*      statements.  Perform type checking.                    */
/*                                                             */
/*      FILE:     syntax2.c                                    */
/*                                                             */
/*      REQUIRES:  Modules parser, symbol table, scanner,      */
/*                          error                               */
/*                                                             */
/*      USAGE:     syntax2 sourcefile                          */
/*                                                             */
/*          sourcefile     name of source file containing      */
/*                         statements to be checked            */
/*                                                             */
/*****************************************************************/

#include <stdio.h>
#include "common.h"
#include "error.h"
#include "scanner.h"
#include "parser.h"

/*-------------------------------------------------------------*/
/* Externals                                                   */
/*-------------------------------------------------------------*/
```

```
extern TOKEN_CODE token;
extern int         line_number, error_count;

extern TYPE_STRUCT dummy_type;

/*-------------------------------------------------------------*/
/* Globals                                                     */
/*-------------------------------------------------------------*/

char buffer[MAX_PRINT_LINE_LENGTH];

/*-------------------------------------------------------------*/
/* main                  Initialize the scanner and call the   */
/*                       statement routine.                    */
/*-------------------------------------------------------------*/

main(argc, argv)

    int   argc;
    char *argv[];

{
    SYMTAB_NODE_PTR program_idp;      /* artificial program id */

    /*
    -- Initialize the scanner and the symbol table.
```

```
*/
init_scanner(argv[1]);
init_symtab();

/*
-- Create an artifical program id node.
*/
program_idp = alloc_struct(SYMTAB_NODE);
program_idp->defn.key = PROG_DEFN;
program_idp->defn.info.routine.key = DECLARED;
program_idp->defn.info.routine.parm_count = 0;
program_idp->defn.info.routine.total_parm_size = 0;
program_idp->defn.info.routine.total_local_size = 0;
program_idp->typep = &dummy_type;
program_idp->label_index = 0;

/*
-- Parse a block.
*/
get_token();
block(program_idp);

/*
-- Look for the end of file.
*/
while (token != END_OF_FILE) {
    error(UNEXPECTED_TOKEN);
    get_token();
}

quit_scanner();

/*
-- Print the parser's summary.
*/
```

```
    print_line("\n");
    print_line("\n");
    sprintf(buffer, "%20d Source lines.\n", line_number);
    print_line(buffer);
    sprintf(buffer, "%20d Source errors.\n", error_count);
    print_line(buffer);

    if (error_count == 0) exit(0);
    else                  exit(-SYNTAX_ERROR);
}

/*------------------------------------------------------------*/
/*  block           Process a block, which consists of       */
/*                  declarations followed by a compound       */
/*                  statement.                                */
/*------------------------------------------------------------*/

TOKEN_CODE follow_decls_list[] = {SEMICOLON, BEGIN, END_OF_FILE, 0};

block(rtn_idp)

    SYMTAB_NODE_PTR rtn_idp;      /* id of program or routine */

{
    extern BOOLEAN block_flag;

    declarations(rtn_idp);

    /*
    -- Error synchronization:  Should be ;
    */
    synchronize(follow_decls_list, NULL, NULL);
    if (token != BEGIN) error(MISSING_BEGIN);

    compound_statement();
}
```

FIGURE 6-12   Syntax diagram for a block.

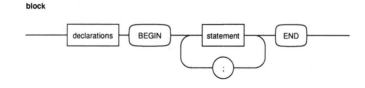

We can use the same file decl.c from the declarations analyzer. Since we do not want to analyze the declarations, we must *not* set the analyze macro flag in file parser.h.

We check the types of expressions and variables in file expr.c, and of statements in file stmt.c. Figure 6-13 shows the new version of file expr.c, and Figure 6-14 shows the new version of file stmt.c.

FIGURE 6-13   File expr.c.

```
/****************************************************************/
/*                                                            */
/*          E X P R E S S I O N   P A R S E R                 */
/*                                                            */
/*          Parsing routines for expressions.                */
/*                                                            */
/*          FILE:       expr.c                                */
/*                                                            */
/*          MODULE:     parser                                */
/*                                                            */
/****************************************************************/

#include <stdio.h>
#include "common.h"
#include "error.h"
#include "scanner.h"
#include "symtab.h"
#include "parser.h"

/*------------------------------------------------------------*/
/* Externals                                                  */
/*------------------------------------------------------------*/

extern TOKEN_CODE token;
extern char       word_string[];
extern LITERAL    literal;

extern SYMTAB_NODE_PTR  symtab_root;

extern TYPE_STRUCT_PTR  integer_typep, real_typep,
                        boolean_typep, char_typep;

extern TYPE_STRUCT      dummy_type;

/*------------------------------------------------------------*/
/* Forwards                                                   */
/*------------------------------------------------------------*/

TYPE_STRUCT_PTR expression(), simple_expression(), term(), factor(),
                function_call();

/*------------------------------------------------------------*/
/* integer_operands    TRUE if both operands are integer,     */
/*                     else FALSE.                            */
/*------------------------------------------------------------*/

#define integer_operands(tp1, tp2)  ((tp1 == integer_typep) && \
                                     (tp2 == integer_typep))

/*------------------------------------------------------------*/
/* real_operands       TRUE if at least one or both operands  */
/*                     are real (and the other integer), else */
/*                     FALSE.                                 */
/*------------------------------------------------------------*/

#define real_operands(tp1, tp2) (((tp1 == real_typep) &&       \
                                  ((tp2 == real_typep) ||      \
                                   (tp2 == integer_typep)))    \
                                 ||                            \
                                 ((tp2 == real_typep) &&       \
                                  ((tp1 == real_typep) ||      \
                                   (tp1 == integer_typep))))

/*------------------------------------------------------------*/
/* boolean_operands    TRUE if both operands are boolean      */
```

```
/*              else FALSE.                                   */
/*------------------------------------------------------------*/

#define boolean_operands(tp1, pt2)  ((tp1 == boolean_typep) && \
                                     (tp2 == boolean_typep))

/*------------------------------------------------------------*/
/* expression          Process an expression consisting of a  */
/*                     simple expression optionally followed  */
/*                     by a relational operator and a second  */
/*                     simple expression.  Return a pointer to*/
/*                     the type structure.                   */
/*------------------------------------------------------------*/

TOKEN_CODE rel_op_list[] = {LT, LE, EQUAL, NE, GE, GT, 0};

    TYPE_STRUCT_PTR
expression()

{
    TOKEN_CODE op;                      /* an operator token */
    TYPE_STRUCT_PTR result_tp, tp2;

    result_tp = simple_expression();    /* first simple expr */

    /*
    -- If there is a relational operator, remember it and
    -- process the second simple expression.
    */
    if (token_in(rel_op_list)) {
        op = token;                     /* remember operator */
        result_tp = base_type(result_tp);

        get_token();
        tp2 = base_type(simple_expression());  /* 2nd simple expr */

        check_rel_op_types(result_tp, tp2);
        result_tp = boolean_typep;
    }

    return(result_tp);
}

/*------------------------------------------------------------*/
/* simple_expression   Process a simple expression consisting */
/*                     of terms separated by +, -, or OR      */
/*                     operators.  There may be a unary + or -*/
/*                     before the first term.  Return a       */
/*                     pointer to the type structure.        */
/*------------------------------------------------------------*/

TOKEN_CODE add_op_list[] = {PLUS, MINUS, OR, 0};

    TYPE_STRUCT_PTR
simple_expression()

{
    TOKEN_CODE op;                      /* an operator token */
    BOOLEAN    saw_unary_op = FALSE;    /* TRUE iff unary operator */
    TOKEN_CODE unary_op = PLUS;         /* a unary operator token */
    TYPE_STRUCT_PTR result_tp, tp2;

    /*
    -- If there is a unary + or -, remember it.
```

```
    */
    if ((token == PLUS) || (token == MINUS)) {
        unary_op = token;
        saw_unary_op = TRUE;
        get_token();
    }

    result_tp = term();        /* first term */

    /*
    -- If there was a unary operator, check that the term
    -- is integer or real.  Negate the top of stack if it
    -- was a unary - either with the NEG instruction or by
    -- calling FLOAT_NEGATE.
    */
    if (saw_unary_op &&
        (base_type(result_tp) != integer_typep) &&
        (result_tp != real_typep)) error(INCOMPATIBLE_TYPES);

    /*
    -- Loop to process subsequent terms separated by operators.
    */
    while (token_in(add_op_list)) {
        op = token;                    /* remember operator */
        result_tp = base_type(result_tp);

        get_token();
        tp2 = base_type(term());       /* subsequent term */

        switch (op) {

            case PLUS:
            case MINUS: {
                /*
                -- integer <op> integer => integer
                */
                if (integer_operands(result_tp, tp2))
                    result_tp = integer_typep;

                /*
                -- Both operands are real, or one is real and the
                -- other is integer.  The result is real.
                */
                else if (real_operands(result_tp, tp2))
                    result_tp = real_typep;

                else {
                error(INCOMPATIBLE_TYPES);
                    result_tp = &dummy_type;
                }

                break;
            }

            case OR: {
                /*
                -- boolean OR boolean => boolean
                */
                if (! boolean_operands(result_tp, tp2))
                    error(INCOMPATIBLE_TYPES);

                result_tp = boolean_typep;
                break;
            }
        }
    }

    return(result_tp);
```

```
    }

    /*------------------------------------------------------------*/
    /*   term              Process a term consisting of factors   */
    /*                     separated by *, /, DIV, MOD, or AND    */
    /*                     operators.  Return a pointer to the    */
    /*                     type structure.                        */
    /*------------------------------------------------------------*/

    TOKEN_CODE mult_op_list[] = {STAR, SLASH, DIV, MOD, AND, 0};

        TYPE_STRUCT_PTR
    term()

    {
        TOKEN_CODE op;                    /* an operator token */
        TYPE_STRUCT_PTR result_tp, tp2;

        result_tp = factor();             /* first factor */

        /*
        -- Loop to process subsequent factors
        -- separated by operators.
        */
        while (token_in(mult_op_list)) {
            op = token;                    /* remember operator */
            result_tp = base_type(result_tp);

            get_token();
            tp2 = base_type(factor());     /* subsequent factor */

            switch (op) {

                case STAR: {
                    /*
                    -- Both operands are integer.
                    */
                    if (integer_operands(result_tp, tp2))
                        result_tp = integer_typep;

                    /*
                    -- Both operands are real, or one is real and the
                    -- other is integer.  The result is real.
                    */
                    else if (real_operands(result_tp, tp2))
                        result_tp = real_typep;

                    else {
                        error(INCOMPATIBLE_TYPES);
                        result_tp = &dummy_type;
                    }

                    break;
                }

                case SLASH: {
                    /*
                    -- Both operands are real, or both are integer, or
                    -- one is real and the other is integer.  The result
                    -- is real.
                    */
                    if ((! real_operands(result_tp, tp2)) &&
                        (! integer_operands(result_tp, tp2)))
                        error(INCOMPATIBLE_TYPES);

                    result_tp = real_typep;
                    break;
```

```
                    }

            case DIV:
            case MOD: {
                /*
                -- integer <op> integer => integer
                */
                if (! integer_operands(result_tp, tp2))
                    error(INCOMPATIBLE_TYPES);

                result_tp = integer_typep;
                break;
            }

            case AND: {
                /*
                -- boolean AND boolean => boolean
                */
                if (! boolean_operands(result_tp, tp2))
                    error(INCOMPATIBLE_TYPES);

                result_tp = boolean_typep;
                break;
            }
        }
    }

    return(result_tp);
}
```

```
/*--------------------------------------------------------------*/
/* factor              Process a factor, which is a variable,   */
/*                     a number, NOT followed by a factor, or   */
/*                     a parenthesized subexpression.  Return   */
/*                     a pointer to the type structure.         */
/*--------------------------------------------------------------*/

    TYPE_STRUCT_PTR
factor()

{
    TYPE_STRUCT_PTR tp;

    switch (token) {

        case IDENTIFIER: {
            SYMTAB_NODE_PTR idp;

            search_and_find_all_symtab(idp);

            if (idp->defn.key == CONST_DEFN) {
                get_token();
                tp = idp->typep;
            }
            else tp = variable(idp, EXPR_USE);

            break;
        }

        case NUMBER:
            tp = literal.type == INTEGER_LIT
                    ? integer_typep
                    : real_typep;
            get_token();
            break;

        case STRING: {
```

```
            int length = strlen(literal.value.string);

            tp = length == 1 ? char_typep
                             : make_string_typep(length);
            get_token();
            break;
        }

        case NOT:
            get_token();
            tp = factor();
            break;

        case LPAREN:
            get_token();
            tp = expression();

            if_token_get_else_error(RPAREN, MISSING_RPAREN);
            break;

        default:
            error(INVALID_EXPRESSION);
            tp = &dummy_type;
            break;
    }

    return(tp);
}
```

```
/*--------------------------------------------------------------*/
/* variable             Process a variable, which can be a      */
/*                      simple identifier, an array identifier  */
/*                      with subscripts, or a record identifier */
/*                      with fields.                            */
/*--------------------------------------------------------------*/

    TYPE_STRUCT_PTR
variable(var_idp, use)

    SYMTAB_NODE_PTR var_idp;    /* variable id */
    USE             use;        /* how variable is used */

{
    TYPE_STRUCT_PTR tp          = var_idp->typep;
    DEFN_KEY        defn_key     = var_idp->defn.key;
    TYPE_STRUCT_PTR array_subscript_list();
    TYPE_STRUCT_PTR record_field();

    /*
    -- Check the variable's definition.
    */
    switch (defn_key) {
        case VAR_DEFN:
        case VALPARM_DEFN:
        case VARPARM_DEFN:
        case FUNC_DEFN:
        case UNDEFINED: break;          /* OK */

        default: {                      /* error */
            tp = &dummy_type;
            error(INVALID_IDENTIFIER_USAGE);
        }
    }

    get_token();

    /*
```

```
    --  Subscripts and/or field designators?
    */
    while ((token == LBRACKET) || (token == PERIOD)) {
        tp = token == LBRACKET ? array_subscript_list(tp)
                               : record_field(tp);
    }

    return(tp);
}

/*-------------------------------------------------*/
/*  array_subscript_list        Process a list of subscripts  */
/*                              following an array identifier: */
/*                                                             */
/*                              [ <expr> , <expr> , ... ]   */
/*-------------------------------------------------*/

    TYPE_STRUCT_PTR
array_subscript_list(tp)

    TYPE_STRUCT_PTR tp;

{
    TYPE_STRUCT_PTR   index_tp, elmt_tp, ss_tp;
    extern TOKEN_CODE statement_end_list[];

    /*
    --  Loop to process a subscript list.
    */
    do {
        if (tp->form == ARRAY_FORM) {
            index_tp = tp->info.array.index_typep;
            elmt_tp  = tp->info.array.elmt_typep;

            get_token();
            ss_tp = expression();

            /*
            --  The subscript expression must be assignment type
            --  compatible with the corresponding subscript type.
            */
            if (!is_assign_type_compatible(index_tp, ss_tp))
                error(INCOMPATIBLE_TYPES);

            tp = elmt_tp;
        }
        else {
            error(TOO_MANY_SUBSCRIPTS);
            while ((token != RBRACKET) &&
                   (! token_in(statement_end_list)))
                get_token();
        }
    } while (token == COMMA);

    if_token_get_else_error(RBRACKET, MISSING_RBRACKET);
    return(tp);
}

/*-------------------------------------------------*/
/*  record_field                 Process a field designation  */
/*                               following a record identifier: */
/*                                                             */
/*                               . <field-variable>          */
/*-------------------------------------------------*/

    TYPE_STRUCT_PTR
record_field(tp)

    TYPE_STRUCT_PTR tp;

{
    SYMTAB_NODE_PTR field_idp;

    get_token();

    if ((token == IDENTIFIER) && (tp->form == RECORD_FORM)) {
        search_this_symtab(field_idp,
                           tp->info.record.field_symtab);

        get_token();

        if (field_idp != NULL) return(field_idp->typep);
        else {
            error(INVALID_FIELD);
            return(&dummy_type);
        }
    }
    else {
        get_token();
        error(INVALID_FIELD);
        return(&dummy_type);
    }
}

            /*******************************/
            /*                             */
            /*        Type compatibility    */
            /*                             */
            /*******************************/

/*-------------------------------------------------*/
/*  check_rel_op_types  Check the operand types for a rela-   */
/*                      tional operator.                      */
/*-------------------------------------------------*/

check_rel_op_types(tp1, tp2)

    TYPE_STRUCT_PTR tp1, tp2;          /* operand types */

{
    /*
    --  Two identical scalar or enumeration types.
    */
    if (   (tp1 == tp2)
        && ((tp1->form == SCALAR_FORM) || (tp1->form == ENUM_FORM)))
        return;

    /*
    --  One integer and one real.
    */
    if (   ((tp1 == integer_typep) && (tp2 == real_typep))
        || ((tp2 == integer_typep) && (tp1 == real_typep))) return;

    /*
    --  Two strings of the same length.
    */
    if ((tp1->form == ARRAY_FORM) &&
        (tp2->form == ARRAY_FORM) &&
        (tp1->info.array.elmt_typep == char_typep) &&
        (tp2->info.array.elmt_typep == char_typep) &&
        (tp1->info.array.elmt_count ==
                        tp2->info.array.elmt_count)) return;

    error(INCOMPATIBLE_TYPES);
}
```

```
/*---------------------------------------------------*/
/* is_assign_type_compatible   Return TRUE iff a value of type */
/*                             tp1 can be assigned to a vari-  */
/*                             able of type tp1.               */
/*---------------------------------------------------*/

    BOOLEAN
is_assign_type_compatible(tp1, tp2)

    TYPE_STRUCT_PTR tp1, tp2;

{
    tp1 = base_type(tp1);
    tp2 = base_type(tp2);

    if (tp1 == tp2) return(TRUE);

    /*
    -- real := integer
    */
    if ((tp1 == real_typep) && (tp2 == integer_typep)) return(TRUE);

    /*
    -- string1 := string2 of the same length
    */
```

```
    if ((tp1->form == ARRAY_FORM) &&
        (tp2->form == ARRAY_FORM) &&
        (tp1->info.array.elmt_typep == char_typep) &&
        (tp2->info.array.elmt_typep == char_typep) &&
        (tp1->info.array.elmt_count ==
                    tp2->info.array.elmt_count)) return(TRUE);

    return(FALSE);
}

/*---------------------------------------------------*/
/* base_type          Return the range type of a subrange  */
/*                    type.                                 */
/*---------------------------------------------------*/

    TYPE_STRUCT_PTR
base_type(tp)

    TYPE_STRUCT_PTR tp;

{
    return((tp->form == SUBRANGE_FORM)
                ? tp->info.subrange.range_typep
                : tp);
}
```

FIGURE 6-14   File stmt.c.

```
/***************************************************************/
/*                                                             */
/*      S T A T E M E N T   P A R S E R                        */
/*                                                             */
/*      Parsing routines for statements.                       */
/*                                                             */
/*      FILE:     stmt.c                                       */
/*                                                             */
/*      MODULE:   parser                                       */
/*                                                             */
/***************************************************************/

#include <stdio.h>
#include "common.h"
#include "error.h"
#include "scanner.h"
#include "symtab.h"
#include "parser.h"

/*---------------------------------------------------*/
/* Externals                                         */
/*---------------------------------------------------*/

extern TOKEN_CODE       token;
extern char             word_string[];
extern LITERAL          literal;
extern TOKEN_CODE       statement_start_list[], statement_end_list[];

extern SYMTAB_NODE_PTR  symtab_root;

extern TYPE_STRUCT_PTR  integer_typep, real_typep,
                        boolean_typep, char_typep;

extern TYPE_STRUCT      dummy_type;
```

```
/*---------------------------------------------------*/
/* statement          Process a statement by calling the   */
/*                    appropriate parsing routine based on */
/*                    the statement's first token.         */
/*---------------------------------------------------*/

statement()

{
    /*
    -- Call the appropriate routine based on the first
    -- token of the statement.
    */
    switch (token) {

        case IDENTIFIER: {
            SYMTAB_NODE_PTR idp;

            /*
            -- Assignment statement.
            */
            search_and_find_all_symtab(idp);
            assignment_statement(idp);

            break;
        }

        case REPEAT:    repeat_statement();     break;
        case WHILE:     while_statement();      break;
        case IF:        if_statement();         break;
        case FOR:       for_statement();        break;
        case CASE:      case_statement();       break;
        case BEGIN:     compound_statement();   break;
    }
```

```
    /*
    -- Error synchronization:  Only a semicolon, END, ELSE, or
    --                         UNTIL may follow a statement.
    --                         Check for a missing semicolon.
    */
    synchronize(statement_end_list, statement_start_list, NULL);
    if (token_in(statement_start_list)) error(MISSING_SEMICOLON);
}

/*-----------------------------------------------------*/
/*  assignment_statement    Process an assignment statement:   */
/*                                                     */
/*                          <id> := <expr>             */
/*-----------------------------------------------------*/

assignment_statement(var_idp)

    SYMTAB_NODE_PTR var_idp;          /* target variable id */

{
    TYPE_STRUCT_PTR var_tp, expr_tp;    /* types of var and expr */

    var_tp = variable(var_idp, TARGET_USE);
    if_token_get_else_error(COLONEQUAL, MISSING_COLONEQUAL);

    expr_tp = expression();

    if (! is_assign_type_compatible(var_tp, expr_tp))
        error(INCOMPATIBLE_ASSIGNMENT);
}

/*-----------------------------------------------------*/
/*  repeat_statement    Process a REPEAT statement:    */
/*                                                     */
/*                       REPEAT <stmt-list> UNTIL <expr>   */
/*-----------------------------------------------------*/

repeat_statement()

{
    TYPE_STRUCT_PTR expr_tp;

    /*
    -- <stmt-list>
    */
    get_token();
    do {
        statement();
        while (token == SEMICOLON) get_token();
    } while (token_in(statement_start_list));

    if_token_get_else_error(UNTIL, MISSING_UNTIL);

    expr_tp = expression();
    if (expr_tp != boolean_typep) error(INCOMPATIBLE_TYPES);
}

/*-----------------------------------------------------*/
/*  while_statement    Process a WHILE statement:      */
/*                                                     */
/*                      WHILE <expr> DO <stmt>         */
/*-----------------------------------------------------*/

while_statement()

{
    TYPE_STRUCT_PTR expr_tp;
```

```
    get_token();

    expr_tp = expression();
    if (expr_tp != boolean_typep) error(INCOMPATIBLE_TYPES);

    if_token_get_else_error(DO, MISSING_DO);
    statement();
}

/*-----------------------------------------------------*/
/*  if_statement         Process an IF statement:      */
/*                                                     */
/*                       IF <expr> THEN <stmt>         */
/*                                                     */
/*                       or:                           */
/*                                                     */
/*                       IF <expr> THEN <stmt> ELSE <stmt>   */
/*-----------------------------------------------------*/

if_statement()

{
    TYPE_STRUCT_PTR expr_tp;

    get_token();

    expr_tp = expression();
    if (expr_tp != boolean_typep) error(INCOMPATIBLE_TYPES);

    if_token_get_else_error(THEN, MISSING_THEN);
    statement();

    /*
    -- ELSE branch?
    */
    if (token == ELSE) {
        get_token();
        statement();
    }
}

/*-----------------------------------------------------*/
/*  for_statement         Process a FOR statement:     */
/*                                                     */
/*                    FOR <id> := <expr> TO|DOWNTO <expr> */
/*                          DO <stmt>                   */
/*-----------------------------------------------------*/

for_statement()

{
    SYMTAB_NODE_PTR for_idp;
    TYPE_STRUCT_PTR for_tp, expr_tp;

    get_token();

    if (token == IDENTIFIER) {
        search_and_find_all_symtab(for_idp);

        for_tp = base_type(for_idp->typep);
        get_token();

        if ((for_tp != integer_typep) &&
            (for_tp != char_typep) &&
            (for_tp->form != ENUM_FORM)) error(INCOMPATIBLE_TYPES);
    }
    else {
```

```
                error(IDENTIFIER, MISSING_IDENTIFIER);
                for_tp = &dummy_type;
        }

        if_token_get_else_error(COLONEQUAL, MISSING_COLONEQUAL);

        expr_tp = expression();
        if (! is_assign_type_compatible(for_tp, expr_tp))
            error(INCOMPATIBLE_TYPES);

        if ((token == TO) || (token == DOWNTO)) get_token();
        else error(MISSING_TO_OR_DOWNTO);

        expr_tp = expression();
        if (! is_assign_type_compatible(for_tp, expr_tp))
            error(INCOMPATIBLE_TYPES);

        if_token_get_else_error(DO, MISSING_DO);
        statement();
}

/*------------------------------------------------------------*/
/*  case_statement       Process a CASE statement:            */
/*                                                            */
/*                          CASE <expr> OF                    */
/*                              <case-branch> ;               */
/*                              ...                           */
/*                              END                           */
/*------------------------------------------------------------*/

TOKEN_CODE follow_expr_list[]      = {OF, SEMICOLON, 0};

TOKEN_CODE case_label_start_list[] = {IDENTIFIER, NUMBER, PLUS,
                                      MINUS, STRING, 0};

case_statement()

{
    BOOLEAN          another_branch;
    TYPE_STRUCT_PTR expr_tp;
    TYPE_STRUCT_PTR case_label();

    get_token();
    expr_tp = expression();

    if (   ((expr_tp->form != SCALAR_FORM) &&
            (expr_tp->form != ENUM_FORM) &&
            (expr_tp->form != SUBRANGE_FORM))
        || (expr_tp == real_typep)) error(INCOMPATIBLE_TYPES);

    /*
    -- Error synchronization:  Should be OF
    */
    synchronize(follow_expr_list, case_label_start_list, NULL);
    if_token_get_else_error(OF, MISSING_OF);

    /*
    -- Loop to process CASE branches.
    */
    another_branch = token_in(case_label_start_list);
    while (another_branch) {
        if (token_in(case_label_start_list)) case_branch(expr_tp);

        if (token == SEMICOLON) {
            get_token();
            another_branch = TRUE;
        }
```

```
        else if (token_in(case_label_start_list)) {
            error(MISSING_SEMICOLON);
            another_branch = TRUE;
        }
        else another_branch = FALSE;
    }

    if_token_get_else_error(END, MISSING_END);
}

/*------------------------------------------------------------*/
/*  case_branch           Process a CASE branch:              */
/*                                                            */
/*                          <case-label-list> : <stmt>        */
/*------------------------------------------------------------*/

TOKEN_CODE follow_case_label_list[] = {COLON, SEMICOLON, 0};

case_branch(expr_tp)

    TYPE_STRUCT_PTR expr_tp;        /* type of CASE expression */

{
    BOOLEAN          another_label;
    TYPE_STRUCT_PTR label_tp;
    TYPE_STRUCT_PTR case_label();

    /*
    -- <case-label-list>
    */
    do {
        label_tp = case_label();
        if (expr_tp != label_tp) error(INCOMPATIBLE_TYPES);

        get_token();
        if (token == COMMA) {
            get_token();
            if (token_in(case_label_start_list)) another_label = TRUE;
            else {
                error(MISSING_CONSTANT);
                another_label = FALSE;
            }
        }
        else another_label = FALSE;
    } while (another_label);

    /*
    -- Error synchronization:  Should be :
    */
    synchronize(follow_case_label_list, statement_start_list, NULL);
    if_token_get_else_error(COLON, MISSING_COLON);

    statement();
}

/*------------------------------------------------------------*/
/*  case_label            Process a CASE label and return a   */
/*                        pointer to its type structure.      */
/*------------------------------------------------------------*/

    TYPE_STRUCT_PTR
case_label()

{
    TOKEN_CODE      sign     = PLUS;   /* unary + or - sign */
    BOOLEAN         saw_sign = FALSE;  /* TRUE iff unary sign */
    TYPE_STRUCT_PTR label_tp;
```

```
/*
-- Unary + or - sign.
*/
if ((token == PLUS) || (token == MINUS)) {
    sign     = token;
    saw_sign = TRUE;
    get_token();
}

/*
-- Numeric constant:  Integer type only.
*/
if (token == NUMBER) {
    if (literal.type == REAL_LIT) error(INVALID_CONSTANT);
    return(integer_typep);
}

/*
-- Identifier constant:  Integer, character, or enumeration
--                       types only.
*/
else if (token == IDENTIFIER) {
    SYMTAB_NODE_PTR idp;

    search_all_symtab(idp);

    if (idp == NULL) {
        error(UNDEFINED_IDENTIFIER);
        return(&dummy_type);
    }

    else if (idp->defn.key != CONST_DEFN) {
        error(NOT_A_CONSTANT_IDENTIFIER);
        return(&dummy_type);
    }

    else if (idp->typep == integer_typep)
        return(integer_typep);

    else if (idp->typep == char_typep) {
        if (saw_sign) error(INVALID_CONSTANT);
        return(char_typep);
    }

    else if (idp->typep->form == ENUM_FORM) {
        if (saw_sign) error(INVALID_CONSTANT);
        return(idp->typep);
    }
```

```
    else return(&dummy_type);
}

/*
-- String constant:  Character type only.
*/
else if (token == STRING) {
    if (saw_sign) error(INVALID_CONSTANT);

    if (strlen(literal.value.string) == 1) return(char_typep);
    else {
        error(INVALID_CONSTANT);
        return(&dummy_type);
    }
}

else {
    error(INVALID_CONSTANT);
    return(&dummy_type);
}
}

/*------------------------------------------------------------*/
/*  compound_statement     Process a compound statement:      */
/*                                                            */
/*                              BEGIN <stmt-list> END         */
/*------------------------------------------------------------*/

compound_statement()

{
    /*
    -- <stmt-list>
    */
    get_token();
    do {
        statement();
        while (token == SEMICOLON) get_token();
        if (token == END) break;

        /*
        -- Error synchronization:  Should be at the start of the
        --                         next statement.
        */
        synchronize(statement_start_list, NULL, NULL);
    } while (token_in(statement_start_list));

    if_token_get_else_error(END, MISSING_END);
}
```

Figure 6-15 shows the output from running the syntax checker on a source file containing syntax and type errors.

FIGURE 6-15   Sample output from the syntax checker II.

```
Page 1   syntax2.in   Tue Jul 10 00:53:14 1990


 1 0: CONST
 2 0:    ten   = 10;
 3 0:    pi    = 3.14159.26;
                         ^
```

```
*** ERROR: Unexpected token.
  4 0:    ch    = 'x';
  5 0:    hello   'Hello, world.';
                                 ^

*** ERROR: Missing = .
  6 0:
  7 0: TYPE
```

```
 8 0:     e  = (alpha, beta, gamma);                32 0:     thing : rec;
 9 0:     ee = e;                                   33 0:
10 0:     sr = alpha..gamma                         34 0: BEGIN
11 0:     cr = 'a'..ch;

*** ERROR: Missing ; .
12 0:                                               Page 2   syntax2.in   Tue Jul 10 00:53:14 1990
13 0:     ar1 = ARRAY [1..ten] OF integer;
14 0:     ar2 = ARRAY [e, sr OF real;
                                  ^                  35 0:     radius := (circumference/pi/2;
*** ERROR: Missing ] .                                                                         ^
15 0:     ar3 = ARRAY [(fee, fye, foe, fum), sr] ARRAY [ee] boolean;
                                                    *** ERROR: Missing right parenthesis.
                                          ^         36 0:     b := ten*radius >= thing.x;
*** ERROR: Missing OF.                              37 0:     greek := thing.a[beta];
                                                    38 0:     a2[alpha, gamma] := a2[beta][alpha];
                                     ^              39 0:     b := a3[foe, alpha, beta] - pi;
*** ERROR: Missing OF.                                                                        ^
16 0:                                               *** ERROR: Incompatible types.
17 0:     rec = RECORD
18 0:             i, j, k : integer;                *** ERROR: Incompatible assignment.
19 0:             x : real;                         40 0:     a3[fye] := a3[7];
20 0:             ch : char;                                            ^
21 0:             a   ARRAY [sr] OF e;              *** ERROR: Incompatible types.
                                                    41 0:     thing.what := list[ten, 7, 3];
*** ERROR: Missing : .                                              ^
22 0:          END;                                 *** ERROR: Invalid field.
23 0:
24 0: VAR                                           *** ERROR: Too many subscripts.
25 0:     radius, circumference : real;                                              ^
26 0:     b      : boolean;                         *** ERROR: Incompatible assignment.
27 0:     letter : 'a'..'z'                         42 0: END
28 0:     greek  : e;
                ^
*** ERROR: Missing ; .
29 0:     list   : ar1;                                            42 Source lines.
30 0:     a2     : ar2;                                            15 Source errors.
31 0:     a3     : ar3;
```

6.6.1 Type checking expressions

In order to type check an expression, we need to know the types of its constituent parts. In file expr.c, we modify the expression parsing functions expression, simple_expression, term, and factor so that each "returns a type"; actually, each function returns pointer to a type structure. In function expression, for example, we return the type of the expression we just parsed.

We add three new macros to check the types of operands. Macro integer_operands and boolean_operands each returns TRUE only if both operands are integer or both are boolean, respectively. Macro real_operands returns TRUE if both operands are real, or if one is real and the other integer.

If we parse only one simple expression in function expression, we return the type of that simple expression. If there is a second simple expression, we return the boolean type. We call function check_rel_op_types to check the types of the operand pairs. We also call function base_type.

In function check_rel_op_typep, we verify the correctness of the two operand types of a relational operator. We check whether both operands have the same scalar or enumeration type, whether one is integer and the other real, or whether both are strings with the same length. If necessary, we flag the INCOMPATIBLE_ TYPES error. In function base_type, we simply return the type that is passed in, or the range type of a subrange type.

If we parse only one term in function simple_expression, we return the type of that term. Otherwise, we update the result type as we parse each subsequent term. If the operator is OR, both operands must be boolean, and the result type is boolean. If both operands are integers, the result type is integer, or if both are real, or one is real and the other is integer, the result type is real.

Function term is similar to simple_expression. We return the type of the factor if there is only a single factor. Otherwise, we update the result type as we parse each subsequent factor. If the operator is DIV or MOD, both operands must be integer, and the result type is integer. If the operator is /, each operand can be either integer or real, and the result type is real. If the operator is AND, both operands must be boolean, and the result type is boolean. If both operands are integer, the result type is integer, or if both are real, or one is real and the other is integer, the result type is real.

Function factor now returns the type of each factor. If the factor is a constant identifier, we return its type. For any other identifier, we call function variable, which returns a type. If the factor is a number, we return either integer or real. If it is a character, we return the character type. If it is string, we call function make_string_typep which returns a string type.

If the token is NOT, we return the type from a recursive call to factor. For a parenthesized expression, we return the type from a recursive call to expression.

6.6.2 Type checking variables

There is a new function variable, in which we parse a variable and return its type. The variable can be a simple identifier, it can be an array variable with subscripts, or a record variable with fields. Whenever we call this function, we pass it a pointer to the variable identifier's symbol table node and the variable's usage. When factor calls variable, the usage is always EXPR_USE, since the variable is used in an expression. We first check the identifier's definition to make sure that we are not using it incorrectly, such as a type identifier in an expression.

A Pascal variable can have a sequence of zero or more subscripts and fields. We parse subscripts and fields in a while loop, where we call functions array_ subscript_list and record_field as appropriate. Each call updates the result type structure pointer tp, which we had initialized to point to the type structure of the variable identifier.

In function array_subscript_list, we loop to parse a list of subscripts between one set of brackets. Argument tp starts out pointing to the type structure of the array identifier. Each time through the loop, we check tp to make sure it is pointing to an array type structure. If so, we call function expression to parse the subscript expression, and then we call is_assignment_compatible to make sure that the type of the subscript is assignment compatible with the corresponding index type. (Assignment compatibility is explained below.) Then, we move tp down to point to the element type structure.

Once we are out of the while loop, tp points to the type structure of an element in the last dimension of the variable. This is the type of the subscripted variable, and it is what we return.

In function record_field, we first make sure that we have a record type and that the current token is an identifier. If so, we look up the identifier in the record type's private symbol table. If we find it there, we return the type of the field identifier.

6.6.3 Assignment compatibility

In Pascal, one type is assignment compatible with another type if an expression of the first type can be assigned to a variable of the second type. We check for assignment compatibility in assignment statements, of course, but also in other places like subscript expressions. Boolean function is_assign_type_compatible is where we make this check. Two types are assignment compatible if they are the same type, or two string types with the same length. We can also assign an integer to a real (but not the other way around). We return TRUE or FALSE, accordingly.

6.6.4 Type checking statements

Now we will see how the statement parsing routines in file stmt.c do type checking. In function assignment_statement, we call function is_assign_type_compatible. In functions while_statement, repeat_statement, and if_statement, we check to make sure that their expressions are boolean.

In function for_statement, we check that the control variable is a scalar but not a real, and we call is_assign_type_compatible twice to check that the initial and final expressions are assignment compatible with the control variable.

In function case_statement, we check that the expression is a scalar but not a real, and in function case_branch, we check that each label is of the same type as the expression. Function case_label now returns the type of the label it parsed.

Now that we can parse declarations and statements, and do type checking, all that remains are procedures and functions. We tackle them in the next chapter.

Questions and exercises

1. *Statement label declarations.* Write the routines to parse statement label declarations. Statement labels can be stored either in the symbol table or in a separate table.

2. *Pointer types and undefined type identifiers.* Write the routines to parse pointer types. Note that it is possible in Pascal to declare a pointer type that points

to a type that is defined later or to a type that is still being defined. For example:

```
TYPE
    recptr = ^rec;
    rec = RECORD
                reclink : ^rec;
                ...
          END;
```

When parsing the definition of recptr, identifier rec is still undefined. When parsing field reclink, the definition of identifier rec is not yet complete. This is the only situation where Pascal allows the use of an undefined identifier. The parser needs to keep track of each such use. When the identifier is finally defined, the parser then must go back and "fix up" each of the previous uses.

3. *Variant records.* Redesign the TYPE_STRUCT for variant records. The structure must keep track of which field, if any, is the tag field, and which fields belong to each value of the tag field type. Write the routines to parse record types that may or may not contain a variant part.

4. *Packed types.* Pascal defines a packed type to be functionally equivalent to an unpacked type, except that a packed type may use less memory. Modify the type parsing routines to accept the reserved word PACKED but otherwise ignore it.

5. *Set types.* Redesign the TYPE_STRUCT for Pascal set types. Write the routines to parse set type specifications, set operations, and set constructors.

6. Extend the cross-referencer utility program from Chapter 3 so that it also prints type information about each identifier.

7. The complete type compatibility rules of Pascal are a bit more complex than we implemented. Look up the complete rules, and rewrite expr.c and stmt.c to implement them.

CHAPTER 7

Parsing Programs, Procedures, and Functions

We can now complete the parser module! In this chapter, we complete the syntax checker from Chapters 5 and 6 to enable it to check the syntax of an entire Pascal program. With this program, we will develop the skills to:

- parse programs, procedures, and functions
- handle scope and nested procedures and functions
- parse calls to both declared and standard procedures and functions

7.1 Changes to the modules

You need to change the parser and symbol table modules. Parser files `routine.c` and `standard.c` are new.

Parser Module

`parser.h`	*u*	Parser header file
`routine.c`	*n*	Parse programs, procedures, and functions
`standard.c`	*n*	Parse standard procedures and functions
`stmt.c`	*c*	Parse statements
`expr.c`	*c*	Parse expressions
`decl.c`	*c*	Parse declarations

Scanner Module

| scanner.h | *u* | Scanner header file |
| scanner.c | *u* | Scanner routines |

Symbol Table Module

| symtab.h | *c* | Symbol table header file |
| symtab.c | *c* | Symbol table routines |

Error Module

| error.h | *u* | Error header file |
| error.c | *u* | Error routines |

Miscellaneous

| common.h | *u* | Common header file |

Where: *u*   file unchanged from the previous chapter
  c   file changed from the previous chapter
  n   new file

File `routine.c` contains routines to parse programs, procedures, and functions. File `standard.c` contains routines to parse the standard predefined procedures and functions like `read` and `sqrt`. Change `symtab.h` and `symtab.c` to accommodate more than one symbol table and to initialize the global table with the names of the standard procedures and functions.

7.2 Program headers

In the previous chapters we have seen how to parse declarations and statements. When we say that we are going to parse programs, procedures, and functions, we really mean we're going to parse their headers and deal with the concept of scope.

Figure 7-1 shows the syntax diagram for a program. As before, our new parsing routines are based on these diagrams. File `routine.c` is shown in Figure 7-2. In its first two functions, `program` and `program_header`, we parse a program and its program header, respectively.

FIGURE 7-1   Syntax diagram for a program.

program

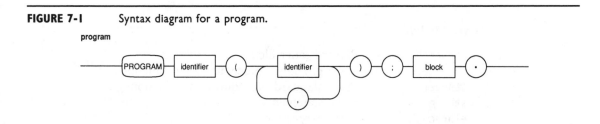

FIGURE 7-2   File routine.c.

```
/******************************************************************/
/*                                                              */
/*      R O U T I N E   P A R S E R                             */
/*                                                              */
/*      Parsing routines for programs and declared             */
/*      procedures and functions.                              */
/*                                                              */
/*      FILE:      routine.c                                   */
/*                                                              */
/*      MODULE:    parser                                      */
/*                                                              */
/******************************************************************/

#include <stdio.h>
#include "common.h"
#include "error.h"
#include "scanner.h"
#include "symtab.h"
#include "parser.h"


/*--------------------------------------------------------------*/
/* Externals                                                    */
/*--------------------------------------------------------------*/

extern int          line_number;
extern int          error_count;

extern TOKEN_CODE    token;
extern char          word_string[];
extern SYMTAB_NODE_PTR symtab_display[];
extern int           level;

extern TYPE_STRUCT   dummy_type;

extern TOKEN_CODE    statement_start_list[],
                     statement_end_list[],
                     declaration_start_list[];

/*--------------------------------------------------------------*/
/* Globals                                                      */
/*--------------------------------------------------------------*/

char buffer[MAX_PRINT_LINE_LENGTH];

/*--------------------------------------------------------------*/
/* Forwards                                                     */
/*--------------------------------------------------------------*/

SYMTAB_NODE_PTR formal_parm_list();
SYMTAB_NODE_PTR program_header(), procedure_header(),
                function_header();

/*--------------------------------------------------------------*/
/* program      Process a program:                             */
/*                                                              */
/*                  <program-header> ; <block> .               */
/*--------------------------------------------------------------*/

TOKEN_CODE follow_header_list[] = {SEMICOLON, END_OF_FILE, 0};

program()

{
    SYMTAB_NODE_PTR program_idp;        /* program id */
```

```
    /*
    --                  PARSE THE PROGRAM
    --
    --
    --  Intialize the symbol table.
    */
    init_symtab();

    /*
    --  Begin parsing with the program header.
    */
    program_idp = program_header();

    /*
    --  Error synchronization:  Should be ;
    */
    synchronize(follow_header_list,
                declaration_start_list, statement_start_list);
    if_token_get(SEMICOLON);
    else if (token_in(declaration_start_list) ||
             token_in(statement_start_list))
        error(MISSING_SEMICOLON);

    analyze_routine_header(program_idp);

    /*
    --  Parse the program's block.
    */
    program_idp->defn.info.routine.locals = NULL;
    block(program_idp);

    program_idp->defn.info.routine.local_symtab = exit_scope();
    program_idp->defn.info.routine.code_segment = NULL;
    analyze_block(program_idp->defn.info.routine.code_segment);

    if_token_get_else_error(PERIOD, MISSING_PERIOD);

    /*
    --  Look for the end of file.
    */
    while (token != END_OF_FILE) {
        error(UNEXPECTED_TOKEN);
        get_token();
    }

    quit_scanner();

    /*
    --  Print the parser's summary.
    */
    print_line("\n");
    print_line("\n");
    sprintf(buffer, "%20d Source lines.\n", line_number);
    print_line(buffer);
    sprintf(buffer, "%20d Source errors.\n", error_count);
    print_line(buffer);

    if (error_count == 0) exit(0);
    else                  exit(-SYNTAX_ERROR);
}

/*--------------------------------------------------------------*/
/* program_header      Process a program header:               */
/*                                                              */
```

```
/*                      PROGRAM <id> ( <id-list> )        */
/*                                                        */
/*                  Return a pointer to the program id    */
/*                  node.                                  */
/*--------------------------------------------------------*/

TOKEN_CODE follow_prog_id_list[] = {LPAREN, SEMICOLON,
                                    END_OF_FILE, 0};

TOKEN_CODE follow_parms_list[]   = {RPAREN, SEMICOLON,
                                    END_OF_FILE, 0};

    SYMTAB_NODE_PTR
program_header()

{
    SYMTAB_NODE_PTR program_idp;          /* program id */
    SYMTAB_NODE_PTR parm_idp;             /* parm id */
    SYMTAB_NODE_PTR prev_parm_idp = NULL;

    if_token_get_else_error(PROGRAM, MISSING_PROGRAM);

    if (token == IDENTIFIER) {
        search_and_enter_local_symtab(program_idp);
        program_idp->defn.key = PROG_DEFN;
        program_idp->defn.info.routine.key = DECLARED;
        program_idp->defn.info.routine.parm_count = 0;
        program_idp->defn.info.routine.total_parm_size = 0;
        program_idp->defn.info.routine.total_local_size = 0;
        program_idp->typep = &dummy_type;
        program_idp->label_index = 0;
        get_token();
    }
    else error(MISSING_IDENTIFIER);

    /*
    -- Error synchronization:  Should be ( or ;
    */
    synchronize(follow_prog_id_list,
                declaration_start_list, statement_start_list);

    enter_scope(NULL);

    /*
    -- Program parameters.
    */
    if (token == LPAREN) {
        /*
        -- <id-list>
        */
        do {
            get_token();
            if (token == IDENTIFIER) {
                search_and_enter_local_symtab(parm_idp);
                parm_idp->defn.key = VARPARM_DEFN;
                parm_idp->typep = &dummy_type;
                get_token();

                /*
                -- Link program parm ids together.
                */
                if (prev_parm_idp == NULL)
                    program_idp->defn.info.routine.parms =
                                    prev_parm_idp = parm_idp;
                else {
                    prev_parm_idp->next = parm_idp;
                    prev_parm_idp = parm_idp;
```

```
            }
        }
        else error(MISSING_IDENTIFIER);
    } while (token == COMMA);

    /*
    -- Error synchronization:  Should be )
    */
    synchronize(follow_parms_list,
                declaration_start_list, statement_start_list);
    if_token_get_else_error(RPAREN, MISSING_RPAREN);
}

    return(program_idp);
}

/*--------------------------------------------------------*/
/* routine          Call the appropriate routine to process */
/*                  a procedure or function definition:   */
/*                                                        */
/*                      <routine-header> ; <block>        */
/*--------------------------------------------------------*/

routine()

{
    SYMTAB_NODE_PTR rtn_idp;      /* routine id */

    rtn_idp = (token == PROCEDURE) ? procedure_header()
                                   : function_header();

    /*
    -- Error synchronization:  Should be ;
    */
    synchronize(follow_header_list,
                declaration_start_list, statement_start_list);
    if_token_get(SEMICOLON);
    else if (token_in(declaration_start_list) ||
             token_in(statement_start_list))
        error(MISSING_SEMICOLON);

    /*
    -- <block> or FORWARD.
    */
    if (strcmp(word_string, "forward") != 0) {
        rtn_idp->defn.info.routine.key = DECLARED;
        analyze_routine_header(rtn_idp);

        rtn_idp->defn.info.routine.locals = NULL;
        block(rtn_idp);

        rtn_idp->defn.info.routine.code_segment = NULL;
        analyze_block(rtn_idp->defn.info.routine.code_segment);
    }
    else {
        get_token();
        rtn_idp->defn.info.routine.key = FORWARD;
        analyze_routine_header(rtn_idp);
    }

    rtn_idp->defn.info.routine.local_symtab = exit_scope();
}

/*--------------------------------------------------------*/
/* procedure_header    Process a procedure header:        */
/*                                                        */
/*                      PROCEDURE <id>                    */
```

```
/*                                         */
/*                  or:                    */
/*                                         */
/*              PROCEDURE <id> ( <parm-list> )   */
/*                                         */
/*              Return a pointer to the procedure id   */
/*              node.                      */
/*-------------------------------------------------*/

TOKEN_CODE follow_proc_id_list[] = {LPAREN, SEMICOLON,
                            END_OF_FILE, 0};


    SYMTAB_NODE_PTR
procedure_header()

{
    SYMTAB_NODE_PTR proc_idp;          /* procedure id */
    SYMTAB_NODE_PTR parm_listp;        /* formal parm list */
    int             parm_count;
    int             total_parm_size;
    BOOLEAN         forward_flag = FALSE;    /* TRUE iff forwarded */

    get_token();

    /*
    -- If the procedure identifier has already been
    -- declared in this scope, it must be a forward.
    */
    if (token == IDENTIFIER) {
        search_local_symtab(proc_idp);
        if (proc_idp == NULL) {
            enter_local_symtab(proc_idp);
            proc_idp->defn.key = PROC_DEFN;
            proc_idp->defn.info.routine.total_local_size = 0;
            proc_idp->typep = &dummy_type;
            proc_idp->label_index = 0;
        }
        else if ((proc_idp->defn.key == PROC_DEFN) &&
                (proc_idp->defn.info.routine.key == FORWARD))
            forward_flag = TRUE;
        else error(REDEFINED_IDENTIFIER);

        get_token();
    }
    else error(MISSING_IDENTIFIER);

    /*
    -- Error synchronization:  Should be ( or ;
    */
    synchronize(follow_proc_id_list,
            declaration_start_list, statement_start_list);

    enter_scope(NULL);

    /*
    -- Optional formal parameters.  If there was a forward,
    -- there must not be any parameters here (but parse them
    -- anyway for error recovery).
    */
    if (token == LPAREN) {
        parm_listp = formal_parm_list(&parm_count, &total_parm_size);

        if (forward_flag) error(ALREADY_FORWARDED);
        else {
            proc_idp->defn.info.routine.parm_count = parm_count;
            proc_idp->defn.info.routine.total_parm_size =
                                        total_parm_size;
```

```
            proc_idp->defn.info.routine.parms = parm_listp;
        }
    }
    else if (!forward_flag) {
        proc_idp->defn.info.routine.parm_count = 0;
        proc_idp->defn.info.routine.total_parm_size = 0;
        proc_idp->defn.info.routine.parms = NULL;
    }

    proc_idp->typep = NULL;
    return(proc_idp);
}

/*-------------------------------------------------------*/
/* function_header    Process a function header:        */
/*                                                      */
/*              FUNCTION <id> : <type-id>               */
/*                                                      */
/*                  or:                                 */
/*                                                      */
/*              FUNCTION <id> ( <parm-list> )           */
/*                  : <type-id>                         */
/*                                                      */
/*              Return a pointer to the function id     */
/*              node.                                   */
/*-------------------------------------------------------*/

TOKEN_CODE follow_func_id_list[] = {LPAREN, COLON, SEMICOLON,
                            END_OF_FILE, 0};


    SYMTAB_NODE_PTR
function_header()

{
    SYMTAB_NODE_PTR func_idp, type_idp;    /* func and type ids*/
    SYMTAB_NODE_PTR parm_listp;            /* formal parm list */
    int             parm_count;
    int             total_parm_size;
    BOOLEAN         forward_flag = FALSE;    /* TRUE iff forwarded */

    get_token();

    /*
    -- If the function identifier has already been
    -- declared in this scope, it must be a forward.
    */
    if (token == IDENTIFIER) {
        search_local_symtab(func_idp);
        if (func_idp == NULL) {
            enter_local_symtab(func_idp);
            func_idp->defn.key = FUNC_DEFN;
            func_idp->defn.info.routine.total_local_size = 0;
            func_idp->typep = &dummy_type;
            func_idp->label_index = 0;
        }
        else if ((func_idp->defn.key == FUNC_DEFN) &&
                (func_idp->defn.info.routine.key == FORWARD))
            forward_flag = TRUE;
        else error(REDEFINED_IDENTIFIER);

        get_token();
    }
    else error(MISSING_IDENTIFIER);

    /*
    -- Error synchronization:  Should be ( or : or ;
    */
```

```
        synchronize(follow_func_id_list,
                    declaration_start_list, statement_start_list);

        enter_scope(NULL);

        /*
        -- Optional formal parameters.  If there was a forward,
        -- there must not be any parameters here (but parse them
        -- anyway for error recovery).
        */
        if (token == LPAREN) {
            parm_listp = formal_parm_list(&parm_count, &total_parm_size);

            if (forward_flag) error(ALREADY_FORWARDED);
            else {
                func_idp->defn.info.routine.parm_count = parm_count;
                func_idp->defn.info.routine.total_parm_size =
                                                total_parm_size;
                func_idp->defn.info.routine.parms = parm_listp;
            }
        }
        else if (!forward_flag) {
            func_idp->defn.info.routine.parm_count = 0;
            func_idp->defn.info.routine.total_parm_size = 0;
            func_idp->defn.info.routine.parms = NULL;
        }

        /*
        -- Function type.  If there was a forward,
        -- there must not be a type here (but parse it
        -- anyway for error recovery).
        */
        if (!forward_flag || (token == COLON)) {
            if_token_get_else_error(COLON, MISSING_COLON);

            if (token == IDENTIFIER) {
                search_and_find_all_symtab(type_idp);
                if (type_idp->defn.key != TYPE_DEFN) error(INVALID_TYPE);
                if (!forward_flag) func_idp->typep = type_idp->typep;
                get_token();
            }
            else {
                error(MISSING_IDENTIFIER);
                func_idp->typep = &dummy_type;
            }

            if (forward_flag) error(ALREADY_FORWARDED);
        }

        return(func_idp);
}

/*------------------------------------------------*/
/*  formal_parm_list    Process a formal parameter list:     */
/*                                                           */
/*                         ( VAR <id-list> : <type> ;        */
/*                           <id-list> : <type> ;            */
/*                              ... )                        */
/*                                                           */
/*                         Return a pointer to the head of the   */
/*                         parameter id list.                */
/*------------------------------------------------*/

    SYMTAB_NODE_PTR
formal_parm_list(countp, total_sizep)

    int *countp;        /* ptr to count of parameters */
```

```
    int *total_sizep;   /* ptr to total byte size of parameters */

{
    SYMTAB_NODE_PTR parm_idp, first_idp, last_idp;    /* parm ids */
    SYMTAB_NODE_PTR prev_last_idp = NULL;        /* last id of list */
    SYMTAB_NODE_PTR parm_listp = NULL;           /* parm list */
    SYMTAB_NODE_PTR type_idp;                    /* type id */
    TYPE_STRUCT_PTR parm_tp;                     /* parm type */
    DEFN_KEY        parm_defn;                   /* parm definition */
    int             parm_count = 0;              /* count of parms */
    int             parm_offset = 0;

    get_token();

    /*
    -- Loop to process parameter declarations separated by ;
    */
    while ((token == IDENTIFIER) || (token == VAR)) {
        first_idp = NULL;

        /*
        -- VAR parms?
        */
        if (token == VAR) {
            parm_defn = VARPARM_DEFN;
            get_token();
        }
        else parm_defn = VALPARM_DEFN;

        /*
        -- <id list>
        */
        while (token == IDENTIFIER) {
            search_and_enter_local_symtab(parm_idp);
            parm_idp->defn.key    = parm_defn;
            parm_idp->label_index = 0;
            ++parm_count;

            if (parm_listp == NULL) parm_listp = parm_idp;

            /*
            -- Link parm ids together.
            */
            if (first_idp == NULL)
                first_idp = last_idp = parm_idp;
            else {
                last_idp->next = parm_idp;
                last_idp = parm_idp;
            }

            get_token();
            if_token_get(COMMA);
        }

        if_token_get_else_error(COLON, MISSING_COLON);

        if (token == IDENTIFIER) {
            search_and_find_all_symtab(type_idp);
            if (type_idp->defn.key != TYPE_DEFN) error(INVALID_TYPE);
            parm_tp = type_idp->typep;
            get_token();
        }
        else {
            error(MISSING_IDENTIFIER);
            parm_tp = &dummy_type;
        }

        /*
```

```
          -- Assign the offset and the type to all parm ids
          -- in the sublist.
          */
          for (parm_idp = first_idp;
               parm_idp != NULL;
               parm_idp = parm_idp->next) {
               parm_idp->typep = parm_tp;
               parm_idp->defn.info.data.offset = parm_offset++;
          }

          /*
          -- Link this list to the list of all parm ids.
          */
          if (prev_last_idp != NULL) prev_last_idp->next = first_idp;
          prev_last_idp = last_idp;

          /*
          -- Error synchronization:  Should be ; or )
          */
          synchronize(follow_parms_list, NULL, NULL);
          if_token_get(SEMICOLON);
     }

     if_token_get_else_error(RPAREN, MISSING_RPAREN);
     *countp = parm_count;
     *total_sizep = parm_offset;

     return(parm_listp);
}

/*------------------------------------------------------------*/
/*  routine_call          Process a call to a declared or     */
/*                        a standard procedure or function.   */
/*                        Return a pointer to the type        */
/*                        structure of the call.              */
/*------------------------------------------------------------*/

     TYPE_STRUCT_PTR
routine_call(rtn_idp, parm_check_flag)

     SYMTAB_NODE_PTR rtn_idp;            /* routine id */
     BOOLEAN         parm_check_flag;    /* if TRUE check parms */

{
     TYPE_STRUCT_PTR declared_routine_call(), standard_routine_call();

     if ((rtn_idp->defn.info.routine.key == DECLARED) ||
         (rtn_idp->defn.info.routine.key == FORWARD) ||
         !parm_check_flag)
          return(declared_routine_call(rtn_idp, parm_check_flag));
     else
          return(standard_routine_call(rtn_idp));
}

/*------------------------------------------------------------*/
/*  declared_routine_call  Process a call to a declared       */
/*                         procedure or function:             */
/*                                                            */
/*                              <id>                          */
/*                                                            */
/*                              or:                           */
/*                                                            */
/*                              <id> ( <parm-list> )          */
/*                                                            */
/*                         The actual parameters are checked  */
/*                         against the formal parameters for  */
/*                         type and number.  Return a pointer */
```

```
/*                        to the type structure of the call.  */
/*------------------------------------------------------------*/

     TYPE_STRUCT_PTR
declared_routine_call(rtn_idp, parm_check_flag)

     SYMTAB_NODE_PTR rtn_idp;            /* routine id */
     BOOLEAN         parm_check_flag;    /* if TRUE check parms */

{
     actual_parm_list(rtn_idp, parm_check_flag);
     return(rtn_idp->defn.key == PROC_DEFN ? NULL : rtn_idp->typep);
}

/*------------------------------------------------------------*/
/*  actual_parm_list     Process an actual parameter list:    */
/*                                                            */
/*                           ( <expr-list> )                  */
/*------------------------------------------------------------*/

TOKEN_CODE follow_parm_list[] = {COMMA, RPAREN, 0};

actual_parm_list(rtn_idp, parm_check_flag)

     SYMTAB_NODE_PTR rtn_idp;            /* routine id */
     BOOLEAN         parm_check_flag;    /* if TRUE check parms */

{
     SYMTAB_NODE_PTR formal_parm_idp;
     DEFN_KEY        formal_parm_defn;
     TYPE_STRUCT_PTR formal_parm_tp, actual_parm_tp;

     if (parm_check_flag)
          formal_parm_idp = rtn_idp->defn.info.routine.parms;

     if (token == LPAREN) {
          /*
          -- Loop to process actual parameter expressions.
          */
          do {
               /*
               -- Obtain info about the corresponding formal parm.
               */
               if (parm_check_flag && (formal_parm_idp != NULL)) {
                    formal_parm_defn = formal_parm_idp->defn.key;
                    formal_parm_tp   = formal_parm_idp->typep;
               }

               get_token();

               /*
               -- Formal value parm:  Actual parm's type must be
               --                     assignment compatible with
               --                     formal parm's type.  Actual
               --                     parm can be an expression.
               */
               if ((formal_parm_idp == NULL) ||
                   (formal_parm_defn == VALPARM_DEFN) ||
                   !parm_check_flag) {
                    actual_parm_tp = expression();
                    if (parm_check_flag && (formal_parm_idp != NULL) &&
                        (! is_assign_type_compatible(formal_parm_tp,
                                                     actual_parm_tp)))
                         error(INCOMPATIBLE_TYPES);
               }

               /*
```

```
    -- Formal VAR parm:  Actual parm's type must be the same
    --                       as formal parm type.  Actual parm
    --                       must be a variable.
    */
    else /* formal_parm_defn == VARPARM_DEFN */ {
        if (token == IDENTIFIER) {
            SYMTAB_NODE_PTR idp;

            search_and_find_all_symtab(idp);
            actual_parm_tp = variable(idp, VARPARM_USE);

            if (formal_parm_tp != actual_parm_tp)
                error(INCOMPATIBLE_TYPES);
        }
        else {
            /*
            -- Not a variable:  Parse an expression anyway
            --                       for error recovery.
            */
            actual_parm_tp = expression();
            error(INVALID_VAR_PARM);
        }
    }

    /*
    -- Check if there are more actual parms
    -- than formal parms.
    */
    if (parm_check_flag) {
        if (formal_parm_idp == NULL)
            error(WRONG_NUMBER_OF_PARMS);
        else formal_parm_idp = formal_parm_idp->next;
    }

    /*
    -- Error synchronization:  Should be , or )
    */
    synchronize(follow_parm_list, statement_end_list, NULL);
    } while (token == COMMA);

    if_token_get_else_error(RPAREN, MISSING_RPAREN);
}

/*
-- Check if there are fewer actual parms than formal parms.
*/
if (parm_check_flag && (formal_parm_idp != NULL))
    error(WRONG_NUMBER_OF_PARMS);
}

/*------------------------------------------------------------*/
/* block              Process a block, which consists of      */
/*                        declarations followed by a compound  */
/*                        statement.                            */
/*------------------------------------------------------------*/

TOKEN_CODE follow_decls_list[] = {SEMICOLON, BEGIN, END_OF_FILE, 0};

block(rtn_idp)

    SYMTAB_NODE_PTR rtn_idp;    /* id of program or routine */

{
    declarations(rtn_idp);

    /*
    -- Error synchronization:  Should be ;
    */
    synchronize(follow_decls_list, NULL, NULL);
    if (token != BEGIN) error(MISSING_BEGIN);

    compound_statement();
}
```

In function program, we first initialize the symbol table. Next, we call function program_header, which parses the header and returns a pointer to the symbol table node of the program identifier. We then call function synchronize and check for a missing semicolon. We want to resynchronize the parser either at the end of the header, at the start of the declarations, or at the start of the first statement, in that order of preference.

In this chapter, ignore the call to analyze_routine_header and to analyze_block (we do *not* define the analyze macro flag in file parser.h). These calls will be useful in the next chapter.

Now we are ready to parse the program's block. We call function block, passing it a pointer to the program identifier's symbol table node. As we saw in the previous chapter, we will enter information into this node when we parse the block's declarations. We'll see what the call to exit_scope does later, and we'll use the defn.info.routine.code_segment field starting in the next chapter. For now, we set the field to NULL. After parsing the program's block, we look for the period and then the end of the file. We finish by quitting the scanner and then printing the statistics.

We parse the program header in function program_header. We enter the program identifier into the local symbol table and initialize the fields of the node. Then, we call function synchronize to resynchronize the parser at the point just after the identifier or at the start of the next declaration or first statement. We call routine enter_scope, which, like exit_scope, is explained later. We enter each program parameter identifier into the local symbol table, and we link the nodes together and hang them off of the defn.info.routine.parms field of the program identifier's symbol table node.

To conclude, we call synchronize and check for a missing right parenthesis. We want to resynchronize the parser either at the end of the parameter list or at the start of the next declaration or first statement.

7.3 Procedure and function declarations

Pascal procedures and functions are declared at the end of a block's declarations. Figure 7-3 shows the complete syntax diagram for declarations. The diagram

FIGURE 7-3   Syntax diagram for declarations.

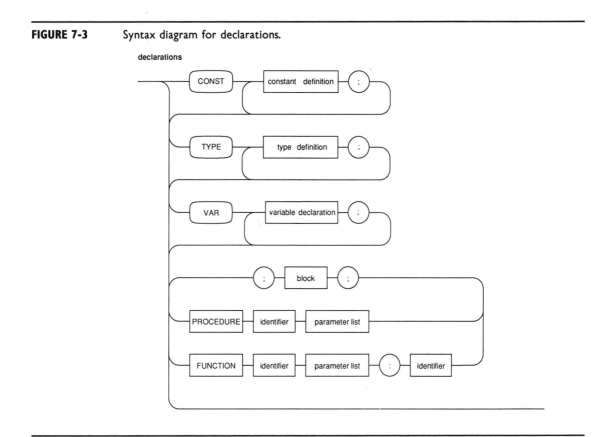

declarations

shows that a procedure or function consists of a header followed by a semicolon, a block, and then another semicolon. Since each procedure or function itself contains a block, they can be nested. Nested routines introduce the problem of dealing with the local variable's scopes.

7.3.1 Scope and the symbol table display stack

The *scope* of a variable is the part of the program where that variable can be used. Pascal allows the same *identifier* in a program to name different *variables* as long the variables are in different scopes. A variable's scope includes every part of the program where its identifier can be used to refer to that particular variable. The scope rules prevent any confusion regarding which variable an identifier refers to.

Not only variables, but any object with a name has a scope. Thus, we can speak of the scope of a constant, type, parameter, procedure, function, or even a program. For example, suppose we declare a global integer variable i in a program that has no procedures or functions. The scope of the variable is the entire program, since we can use identifier i throughout to refer to that integer variable. Now suppose we add a function f to the program, and in f, we declare a local real variable i. The scope of the local real variable i is limited to the function, and now the scope of the global integer variable i is only the part of the program outside of the function. Within f, identifier i refers to the local real variable, and outside f, it refers to the global integer variable.

Since the function is nested within the program, we can say that the scope of its local variables is nested within the scope of the program's global variables. If the function contains a procedure p1 that declares a local character variable i, the scope of the procedure's local variables (including the character i) is nested within the scope of the function's local variables.

So how does scope affect how a parser handles an identifier? Whenever a parser encounters a variable's identifier in the body of a procedure or function, it wants to know which variable the identifier refers to. The parser first checks the variables declared locally by that routine (the local scope). If it cannot find the identifier there, the parser then checks the next enclosing scope. The search continues outward within enclosing scopes towards the outermost, global scope. If the search is successful within any scope, the search stops and the parser uses that declaration. This declaration also hides any other declarations with the same identifier that may appear in any more outer scopes. (In the above example, identifier i within procedure p1 refers to the local character variable, not the real variable of function f or the global integer variable.) Only if the identifier is not found within all enclosing scopes should the parser flag it as undefined. Figure 7-4 shows how a parser can flag scope errors.

FIGURE 7-4   Flagging scope errors.

```
Page 1  scope.pas   Tue Jul 10 03:15:22 1990


  1 0: PROGRAM scope (input, output);
  2 1:
  3 1: VAR
  4 1:     i, j, k : integer;
  5 1:
  6 1: FUNCTION f (j : boolean) : real;
  7 2:
  8 2:     VAR
  9 2:         i : real;
 10 2:
 11 2:     BEGIN {f}
 12 2:         i := 1.0;    {local of f}
 13 2:         j := false;  {parm of f}
 14 2:         k := 3;      {global}
 15 2:
 16 2:         i := 1;  j := 2;  k := 3;
                                ^
*** ERROR: Incompatible assignment.
 17 2:     END {f};
 18 1:
 19 1: PROCEDURE p1 (j : integer);
 20 2:
 21 2:     VAR
 22 2:         i : char;
 23 2:
 24 2:     PROCEDURE p2 (k : boolean);
 25 3:
 26 3:         BEGIN {p2}
 27 3:             i := 'x';    {local of p1}
 28 3:             j := 5;      {parm of p1}
 29 3:             k := true;   {parm of p2}
```

```
 30 3:
 31 3:             i := 1;  j := 2;  k := 3;
                            ^
*** ERROR: Incompatible assignment.

*** ERROR: Incompatible assignment.
 32 3:         END {p2};
 33 2:
 34 2:     BEGIN {p1}
 35 2:         i := 'z';  {local of p1}
 36 2:         j := 7;    {parm of p1}
 37 2:         k := 9;    {global}
 38 2:
 39 2:         i := 1;  j := 2;  k := 3;
                                ^
*** ERROR: Incompatible assignment.
 40 2:     END {p1};
 41 1:
 42 1:


Page 2    scope.pas   Tue Jul 10 03:15:22 1990


 43 1: BEGIN {scope}
 44 1:     i := 1;  {global}
 45 1:     j := 2;  {global}
 46 1:     k := 3;  {global}
 47 1: END {scope}.
 48 0:


                    48 Source lines.
                     4 Source errors.
```

Until now, each of our utility programs has gotten by with a single symbol table. This will no longer suffice, since, as you have seen, an identifier like i can appear in several scopes and refer to different variables. To parse a Pascal program, you need multiple symbol tables: one to contain the global identifiers and one for each procedure and function to contain its local identifiers. In the previous chapter, we saw how the type structure for a record type points field info.record.field_symtab to a private symbol table for the field identifiers. Similarly, each symbol table node for a procedure or function identifier points field defn.info.routine.local_symtab to a private symbol table for the routine's local identifiers.

The best way for the parser to use the private routine symbol tables is to keep them on a stack, with the global symbol table at the bottom and the current routine's symbol table on top. Each time you parse a procedure or function, you push its (initially empty) symbol table onto the top, and when you are finished with the routine, you pop off its symbol table. Then, whenever you search for an identifier, you start with the symbol table at the top of the stack. If the identifier is not found there, the identifier is not defined in the current scope. You look in the next enclosing scope by searching the symbol table just below the top one. This process continues until you find the identifier or until you have searched all the symbol tables on the stack. Each time you move down the symbol table stack, you are in effect searching the next enclosing scope.

This symbol table stack is called a *display*. You increment the *current nesting level* each time the parser enters a routine, and you decrement it as the parser leaves the routine. The nesting level of a program's globals is one. Thus, the globals and the top-level procedures and functions are called level-1 variables and routines. Level zero is reserved for the predefined identifiers such as integer, boolean, true, and false. If you implement the display stack as an array, then you can use the level numbers to index into the array.

To implement a display, we need to make changes throughout files symtab.h and symtab.c. Figure 7-5 shows the new version of symtab.c.

FIGURE 7-5   File symtab.c.

```
/****************************************************************/
/*                                                              */
/*      S Y M B O L   T A B L E                                 */
/*                                                              */
/*      Symbol table routines.                                  */
/*                                                              */
/*      FILE:       symtab.c                                    */
/*                                                              */
/*      MODULE:     symbol table                                */
/*                                                              */
/****************************************************************/

#include <stdio.h>
#include "common.h"
#include "error.h"
#include "symtab.h"

/*--------------------------------------------------------------*/
/* Externals                                                    */
/*--------------------------------------------------------------*/

extern int level;

/*--------------------------------------------------------------*/
/* Globals                                                      */
/*--------------------------------------------------------------*/

SYMTAB_NODE_PTR symtab_display[MAX_NESTING_LEVEL];

TYPE_STRUCT_PTR integer_typep, real_typep,      /* predefined types */
                boolean_typep, char_typep;

TYPE_STRUCT dummy_type = {      /* for erroneous type definitions */
    NO_FORM,        /* form */
    0,              /* size */
    NULL            /* type_idp */
};

/*--------------------------------------------------------------*/
/* search_symtab       Search for a name in the symbol table.   */
/*                     Return a pointer of the entry if found,  */
```

```
/*                            or NULL if not.                   */
/*--------------------------------------------------------------*/

SYMTAB_NODE_PTR
search_symtab(name, np)

    char            *name;      /* name to search for */
    SYMTAB_NODE_PTR np;         /* ptr to symtab root */

{
    int cmp;

    /*
    -- Loop to check each node.  Return if the node matches,
    -- else continue search down the left or right subtree.
    */
    while (np != NULL) {
        cmp = strcmp(name, np->name);
        if (cmp == 0) return(np);               /* found */
        np = cmp < 0 ? np->left : np->right;    /* continue search */
    }

    return(NULL);                               /* not found */
}

/*--------------------------------------------------------------*/
/* search_symtab_display  Search all the symbol tables in the   */
/*                        symbol table display for a name.      */
/*                        Return a pointer to the entry if      */
/*                        found, or NULL if not.                */
/*--------------------------------------------------------------*/

SYMTAB_NODE_PTR
search_symtab_display(name)

    char *name;             /* name to search for */

{
    short i;
    SYMTAB_NODE_PTR np;     /* ptr to symtab node */

    for (i = level; i >= 0; --i) {
```

```
        np = search_symtab(name, symtab_display[i]);
        if (np != NULL) return(np);
    }

    return(NULL);
}

/*------------------------------------------------------------*/
/* enter_symtab        Enter a name into the symbol table,    */
/*                     and return a pointer to the new entry. */
/*------------------------------------------------------------*/

    SYMTAB_NODE_PTR
enter_symtab(name, npp)

    char             *name;       /* name to enter */
    SYMTAB_NODE_PTR *npp;         /* ptr to ptr to symtab root */

{
    int             cmp;          /* result of strcmp */
    SYMTAB_NODE_PTR new_nodep;    /* ptr to new entry */
    SYMTAB_NODE_PTR np;           /* ptr to node to test */

    /*
    -- Create the new node for the name.
    */
    new_nodep = alloc_struct(SYMTAB_NODE);
    new_nodep->name = alloc_bytes(strlen(name) + 1);
    strcpy(new_nodep->name, name);
    new_nodep->left = new_nodep->right = new_nodep->next = NULL;
    new_nodep->info = NULL;
    new_nodep->defn.key = UNDEFINED;
    new_nodep->typep = NULL;
    new_nodep->level = level;
    new_nodep->label_index = 0;

    /*
    -- Loop to search for the insertion point.
    */
    while ((np = *npp) != NULL) {
        cmp = strcmp(name, np->name);
        npp = cmp < 0 ? &(np->left) : &(np->right);
    }

    *npp = new_nodep;                    /* replace */
    return(new_nodep);
}

/*------------------------------------------------------------*/
/* init_symtab         Initialize the symbol table with       */
/*                     predefined identifiers and types,      */
/*                     and routines.                          */
/*------------------------------------------------------------*/

init_symtab()

{
    SYMTAB_NODE_PTR integer_idp, real_idp, boolean_idp, char_idp,
                    false_idp, true_idp;

    /*
    -- Initialize the level-0 symbol table.
    */
    symtab_display[0] = NULL;

    enter_name_local_symtab(integer_idp, "integer");
    enter_name_local_symtab(real_idp,    "real");
```

```
    enter_name_local_symtab(boolean_idp, "boolean");
    enter_name_local_symtab(char_idp,    "char");
    enter_name_local_symtab(false_idp,   "false");
    enter_name_local_symtab(true_idp,    "true");

    integer_typep = alloc_struct(TYPE_STRUCT);
    real_typep    = alloc_struct(TYPE_STRUCT);
    boolean_typep = alloc_struct(TYPE_STRUCT);
    char_typep    = alloc_struct(TYPE_STRUCT);

    integer_idp->defn.key   = TYPE_DEFN;
    integer_idp->typep      = integer_typep;
    integer_typep->form     = SCALAR_FORM;
    integer_typep->size     = sizeof(int);
    integer_typep->type_idp = integer_idp;

    real_idp->defn.key   = TYPE_DEFN;
    real_idp->typep      = real_typep;
    real_typep->form     = SCALAR_FORM;
    real_typep->size     = sizeof(float);
    real_typep->type_idp = real_idp;

    boolean_idp->defn.key   = TYPE_DEFN;
    boolean_idp->typep      = boolean_typep;
    boolean_typep->form     = ENUM_FORM;
    boolean_typep->size     = sizeof(int);
    boolean_typep->type_idp = boolean_idp;

    boolean_typep->info.enumeration.max = 1;
    boolean_idp->typep->info.enumeration.const_idp = false_idp;
    false_idp->defn.key = CONST_DEFN;
    false_idp->defn.info.constant.value.integer = 0;
    false_idp->typep = boolean_typep;

    false_idp->next = true_idp;
    true_idp->defn.key = CONST_DEFN;
    true_idp->defn.info.constant.value.integer = 1;
    true_idp->typep = boolean_typep;

    char_idp->defn.key   = TYPE_DEFN;
    char_idp->typep      = char_typep;
    char_typep->form     = SCALAR_FORM;
    char_typep->size     = sizeof(char);
    char_typep->type_idp = char_idp;

    enter_standard_routine("read",    READ,    PROC_DEFN);
    enter_standard_routine("readln",  READLN,  PROC_DEFN);
    enter_standard_routine("write",   WRITE,   PROC_DEFN);
    enter_standard_routine("writeln", WRITELN, PROC_DEFN);

    enter_standard_routine("abs",    ABS,    FUNC_DEFN);
    enter_standard_routine("arctan", ARCTAN, FUNC_DEFN);
    enter_standard_routine("chr",    CHR,    FUNC_DEFN);
    enter_standard_routine("cos",    COS,    FUNC_DEFN);
    enter_standard_routine("eof",    EOFF,   FUNC_DEFN);
    enter_standard_routine("eoln",   EOLN,   FUNC_DEFN);
    enter_standard_routine("exp",    EXP,    FUNC_DEFN);
    enter_standard_routine("ln",     LN,     FUNC_DEFN);
    enter_standard_routine("odd",    ODD,    FUNC_DEFN);
    enter_standard_routine("ord",    ORD,    FUNC_DEFN);
    enter_standard_routine("pred",   PRED,   FUNC_DEFN);
    enter_standard_routine("round",  ROUND,  FUNC_DEFN);
    enter_standard_routine("sin",    SIN,    FUNC_DEFN);
    enter_standard_routine("sqr",    SQR,    FUNC_DEFN);
    enter_standard_routine("sqrt",   SQRT,   FUNC_DEFN);
    enter_standard_routine("succ",   SUCC,   FUNC_DEFN);
```

```
    enter_standard_routine("trunc",     TRUNC,          FUNC_DEFN);
}

/*----------------------------------------------------------*/
/*  enter_standard_routine      Enter a standard procedure or   */
/*                              function identifier into the    */
/*                              symbol table.                   */
/*----------------------------------------------------------*/

enter_standard_routine(name, routine_key, defn_key)

    char        *name;          /* name string */
    ROUTINE_KEY routine_key;
    DEFN_KEY    defn_key;

{
    SYMTAB_NODE_PTR rtn_idp = enter_name_local_symtab(rtn_idp, name);

    rtn_idp->defn.key                       = defn_key;
    rtn_idp->defn.info.routine.key          = routine_key;
    rtn_idp->defn.info.routine.parms        = NULL;
    rtn_idp->defn.info.routine.local_symtab = NULL;
    rtn_idp->typep                          = NULL;
}

/*----------------------------------------------------------*/
/*  enter_scope       Enter a new nesting level by creating  */
/*                    a new scope.  Push the given symbol    */
/*                    table onto the display stack.          */
/*----------------------------------------------------------*/
```

```
enter_scope(symtab_root)

    SYMTAB_NODE_PTR symtab_root;

{
    if (++level >= MAX_NESTING_LEVEL) {
        error(NESTING_TOO_DEEP);
        exit(-NESTING_TOO_DEEP);
    }

    symtab_display[level] = symtab_root;
}

/*----------------------------------------------------------*/
/*  exit_scope        Exit the current nesting level by      */
/*                    closing the current scope.  Pop the    */
/*                    current symbol table off the display   */
/*                    stack and return a pointer to it.      */
/*----------------------------------------------------------*/

    SYMTAB_NODE_PTR
exit_scope()

{
    SYMTAB_NODE_PTR symtab_root = symtab_display[level--];

    return(symtab_root);
}
```

Now we reference the scanner variable level. (Up until now, it had always been zero.) In function enter_symtab, we set field level to the current value of variable level:

```
            new_nodep->level = level;
```

and we replace the declaration of symtab_root with:

```
            SYMTAB_NODE_PTR symtab_display[MAX_NESTING_LEVEL];
```

From now on, instead of having just one active symbol table, you will have several pointed to by elements of symtab_display. The local symbol table is pointed to by symtab_display[level]. Also, symtab_display[1] points to the table containing the program's global identifier, and symtab_display[0] points to the table containing the predefined identifiers. In the new function search_symtab_display, we search all the active symbol tables pointed to by elements of the display stack from top to bottom.

We call function enter_scope whenever we start to parse a program, procedure, or function. (For example, we previously called it from function program_header.) We increment level and push the pointer to program's or routine's private symbol table onto the display stack.

Conversely, we call function exit_scope whenever we finish parsing a program, procedure, or function. We decrement level to pop the display stack, and we return the pointer to the symbol table that was popped off. This table now contains all the local identifiers, so after we return, we can set the defn.info.routine.local_symtab field of the program or routine identifier's symbol table node to the pointer.

We will look at the rest of the changes in file symtab.c later when we discuss the standard procedures and functions. We will use this version of the file throughout the rest of this book.

Figure 7-6 shows the new version of file symtab.h, which we will also use from now on. Several of the symbol table macros are changed. They must now distinguish between searching just the local symbol table and searching the display stack.

FIGURE 7-6   File symtab.h.

```
/******************************************************************/
/*                                                              */
/*        S Y M B O L   T A B L E   (Header)                    */
/*                                                              */
/*        FILE:      symtab.h                                   */
/*                                                              */
/*        MODULE:    symbol table                               */
/*                                                              */
/******************************************************************/

#ifndef symtab_h
#define symtab_h

#include "common.h"

/*--------------------------------------------------------------*/
/* Value structure                                              */
/*--------------------------------------------------------------*/

typedef union {
    int    integer;
    float  real;
    char   character;
    char  *stringp;
} VALUE;

/*--------------------------------------------------------------*/
/* Definition structure                                         */
/*--------------------------------------------------------------*/

typedef enum {
    UNDEFINED,
    CONST_DEFN, TYPE_DEFN, VAR_DEFN, FIELD_DEFN,
    VALPARM_DEFN, VARPARM_DEFN,
    PROG_DEFN, PROC_DEFN, FUNC_DEFN,
} DEFN_KEY;

typedef enum {
    DECLARED, FORWARD,
    READ, READLN, WRITE, WRITELN,
    ABS, ARCTAN, CHR, COS, EOFF, EOLN, EXP, LN, ODD, ORD,
    PRED, ROUND, SIN, SQR, SQRT, SUCC, TRUNC,
} ROUTINE_KEY;

typedef struct {
```

```
    DEFN_KEY key;
    union {
        struct {
            VALUE value;
        } constant;

        struct {
            ROUTINE_KEY       key;
            int               parm_count;
            int               total_parm_size;
            int               total_local_size;
            struct symtab_node *parms;
            struct symtab_node *locals;
            struct symtab_node *local_symtab;
            char              *code_segment;
        } routine;

        struct {
            int               offset;
            struct symtab_node *record_idp;
        } data;
    } info;
} DEFN_STRUCT;

/*--------------------------------------------------------------*/
/* Type structure                                               */
/*--------------------------------------------------------------*/

typedef enum {
    NO_FORM,
    SCALAR_FORM, ENUM_FORM, SUBRANGE_FORM,
    ARRAY_FORM, RECORD_FORM,
} TYPE_FORM;

typedef struct type_struct {
    TYPE_FORM         form;
    int               size;
    struct symtab_node *type_idp;
    union {
        struct {
            struct symtab_node *const_idp;
            int               max;
        } enumeration;

        struct {
```

```
            struct type_struct *range_typep;
            int             min, max;
        } subrange;

        struct {
            struct type_struct *index_typep, *elmt_typep;
            int             min_index, max_index;
            int             elmt_count;
        } array;

        struct {
            struct symtab_node *field_symtab;
        } record;
    } info;
} TYPE_STRUCT, *TYPE_STRUCT_PTR;

/*-----------------------------------------------*/
/*  Symbol table node                            */
/*-----------------------------------------------*/

typedef struct symtab_node {
    struct symtab_node *left, *right;  /* ptrs to subtrees */
    struct symtab_node *next;          /* for chaining nodes */
    char            *name;             /* name string */
    char            *info;             /* ptr to generic info */
    DEFN_STRUCT     defn;              /* definition struct */
    TYPE_STRUCT_PTR typep;             /* ptr to type struct */
    int             level;             /* nesting level */
    int             label_index;       /* index for code label */
} SYMTAB_NODE, *SYMTAB_NODE_PTR;

/*-------------------------------------------------*/
/*  Functions                                      */
/*-------------------------------------------------*/

SYMTAB_NODE_PTR search_symtab();
SYMTAB_NODE_PTR search_symtab_display();
SYMTAB_NODE_PTR enter_symtab();
SYMTAB_NODE_PTR exit_scope();
TYPE_STRUCT_PTR make_string_typep();

        /***************************************/
        /*                                     */
        /*      Macros to search symbol tables  */
        /*                                     */
        /***************************************/

/*-------------------------------------------------*/
/*  search_local_symtab        Search the local symbol  */
/*                             table for the current id  */
/*                             name. Set a pointer to the */
/*                             entry if found, else to   */
/*                             NULL.                      */
/*-------------------------------------------------*/

#define search_local_symtab(idp)                            \
    idp = search_symtab(word_string, symtab_display[level])

/*-------------------------------------------------*/
/*  search_this_symtab         Search the given symbol   */
/*                             table for the current id  */
/*                             name. Set a pointer to the */
/*                             entry if found, else to   */
/*                             NULL.                      */
/*-------------------------------------------------*/

#define search_this_symtab(idp, this_symtab)                \
    idp = search_symtab(word_string, this_symtab)
```

```
/*-------------------------------------------------*/
/*  search_all_symtab          Search the symbol table   */
/*                             display for the current id */
/*                             name. Set a pointer to the */
/*                             entry if found, else to   */
/*                             NULL.                      */
/*-------------------------------------------------*/
#define search_all_symtab(idp)                              \
    idp = search_symtab_display(word_string)

/*-------------------------------------------------*/
/*  enter_local_symtab         Enter the current id name */
/*                             into the local symbol     */
/*                             table, and set a pointer  */
/*                             to the entry.             */
/*-------------------------------------------------*/

#define enter_local_symtab(idp)                             \
    idp = enter_symtab(word_string, &symtab_display[level])

/*-------------------------------------------------*/
/*  enter_name_local_symtab    Enter the given name into */
/*                             the local symbol table, and */
/*                             set a pointer to the entry. */
/*-------------------------------------------------*/

#define enter_name_local_symtab(idp, name)                  \
    idp = enter_symtab(name, &symtab_display[level])

/*-------------------------------------------------*/
/*  search_and_find_all_symtab  Search the symbol table  */
/*                             display for the current id */
/*                             name. If not found, ID    */
/*                             UNDEFINED error, and enter */
/*                             into the local symbol table. */
/*                             Set a pointer to the entry. */
/*-------------------------------------------------*/

#define search_and_find_all_symtab(idp)                          \
    if ((idp = search_symtab_display(word_string)) == NULL) {    \
        error(UNDEFINED_IDENTIFIER);                             \
        idp = enter_symtab(word_string, &symtab_display[level]); \
        idp->defn.key = UNDEFINED;                               \
        idp->typep = &dummy_type;                                \
    }

/*-------------------------------------------------*/
/*  search_and_enter_local_symtab  Search the local symbol */
/*                             table for the current id  */
/*                             name. Enter the name if   */
/*                             it is not already in there, */
/*                             else ID REDEFINED error.  */
/*                             Set a pointer to the entry. */
/*-------------------------------------------------*/

#define search_and_enter_local_symtab(idp)                       \
    if ((idp = search_symtab(word_string,                        \
                    symtab_display[level])) == NULL) {           \
        idp = enter_symtab(word_string, &symtab_display[level]); \
    }                                                            \
    else error(REDEFINED_IDENTIFIER)

/*-------------------------------------------------*/
/*  search_and_enter_this_symtab  Search the given symbol */
/*                             table for the current id  */
/*                             name. Enter the name if   */
/*                             it is not already in there, */
```

```
/*                          else ID REDEFINED error.    */              this_symtab)) == NULL) {              \
/*                          Set a pointer to the entry. */        idp = enter_symtab(word_string, &this_symtab);    \
/*-----------------------------------------------------------*/          }                                                  \
                                                                    else error(REDEFINED_IDENTIFIER)
#define search_and_enter_this_symtab(idp, this_symtab)     \
    if ((idp = search_symtab(word_string,                  \          #endif
```

Macro `search_local_symtab` is new. We call it to search the local symbol table pointed to by `symtab_display[level]`. Macro `search_all_symtab` now calls function `search_symtab_display` to search the display stack. Macros `enter_local_symtab` and `enter_name_local_symtab` now use the local symbol table pointed to by `symtab_display[level]`.

Macro `search_and_find_all_symtab` now calls function `search_symtab_display` to search the display stack. Macro `search_and_enter_local_symtab` searches the local symbol table pointed to by `symtab_display[level]`. Both macros now enter into the local symbol table.

Macros `search_this_symtab` and `search_and_enter_this_symtab` have not changed.

So from now on, whenever we parse the definition of a new identifier in file `decl.c`, we call `search_and_enter_local_symtab` to make sure the identifier is not already defined in the local scope. Whenever we parse an identifier in an expression, we call `search_and_find_all_symtab` to make sure the identifier is defined in the local or any enclosing scope.

7.3.2 Procedure and function headers

As we have seen, Pascal procedures and functions are declared in the declarations part of a block. Figure 7-7 shows a new version of function `declarations` in file `decl.c`. In the `while` loop, we call function `routine` (in file `routine.c`) to parse a procedure or a function. After parsing each routine, we call function `synchronize` and check for a missing semicolon. We want to resynchronize the parser at the point just after the routine or at the start of the next declaration or first statement. In file `decl.c`, we must also replace the line:

```
extern SYMTAB_NODE_PTR  symtab_root;
```

with the following lines:

```
extern SYMTAB_NODE_PTR  symtab_display[];
extern int              level;
```

FIGURE 7-7   Function declarations in file decl.c.

```
/*-----------------------------------------------------*/
/* declarations        Call the routines to process constant   */
/*                     definitions, type definitions, variable  */
/*                     declarations, procedure definitions,     */
/*                     and function definitions.                */
/*-----------------------------------------------------*/

TOKEN_CODE follow_routine_list[] = {SEMICOLON, END_OF_FILE, 0};

declarations(rtn_idp)

    SYMTAB_NODE_PTR rtn_idp;    /* id of program or routine */

{
    if (token == CONST) {
        get_token();
        const_definitions();
    }

    if (token == TYPE) {
        get_token();
        type_definitions();
    }
```

```
    if (token == VAR) {
        get_token();
        var_declarations(rtn_idp);
    }

    /*
    -- Loop to process routine (procedure and function)
    -- definitions.
    */
    while ((token == PROCEDURE) || (token == FUNCTION)) {
        routine();

        /*
        -- Error synchronization:  Should be ;
        */
        synchronize(follow_routine_list,
                    declaration_start_list, statement_start_list);
        if_token_get(SEMICOLON);
        else if (token_in(declaration_start_list) ||
                 token_in(statement_start_list))
            error(MISSING_SEMICOLON);
    }
}
```

In function routine, we call either function procedure_header or function_header to parse the header. Following the header, we call synchronize and check for a missing semicolon. We want to resynchronize the parser at the point just after the identifier or at the start of the next declaration or first statement.

Then, we parse either the routine's block or the identifier forward. We set the defn.info.routine.key field of the routine identifier's symbol table node either to DECLARED or to FORWARD. If we are declaring the routine, we call function block to parse its block. (Ignore the calls to functions analyze_routine_header and analyze_block.) We conclude with a call to function exit_scope and set the local_symtab field. The routine's private symbol table now contains all of its local identifiers.

In function procedure_header, we first parse the procedure identifier. If the identifier is not already in the local symbol table, we enter it and initialize the node's defn.key field to PROC_DEFN. If the identifier is already in there, it has been previously defined within the same scope. We check whether this previous definition was a forward procedure declaration.

We next call function synchronize to resynchronize the parser at the point after the procedure identifier or at the start of the next declaration or first statement. Then, we call function enter_scope to create the procedure's scope by pushing its private symbol table (initially empty) onto the display stack.

If there is a left parenthesis, we call function formal_parm_list, which parses the formal parameters and returns a pointer to a linked list of symbol table nodes for the parameter identifiers. The function also sets the parameter count and their total byte size. We check to make sure we have not redeclared the parameters if there was a forward declaration. We initialize the parm_count, total_parm_size, and parms fields of the procedure identifier's symbol table node.

If we do not find a formal parameter list, and there was no forward declaration, then the procedure has no parameters. If there was a forward declaration, then we have already parsed the parameters (if any) and initialized the symbol table node fields.

Function function_header is similar, except that we also parse the function type identifier. If there was a forward declaration for the function, neither the formal parameters nor the function type should be redeclared.

7.3.3 Formal parameter lists

In function formal_parm_list, we parse the formal parameter list in a procedure or a function header, and we return a pointer to the linked list of symbol table nodes for the parameter identifiers. Figure 7-8 shows the syntax diagram.

This function is similar to function var_or_field_declarations in file decl.c. We link the symbol table nodes for the parameter identifiers together as we enter them into the local symbol table at the top of the display stack, which is the routine's private symbol table. We set the node's defn.key field to either VARPARM_DEFN or VALPARM_DEFN, depending on whether or not VAR headed the declaration.

We enter all of a routine's local identifiers, including those of its formal parameters and local variables, into its private symbol table, which the defn.info.routine.local_symtab field of its symbol table node points to. As we saw in Chapter 3, the symbol table nodes are linked together into a binary tree via their left and right fields.

In function formal_parm_list, we also link the nodes for parameter identifiers together into a linear linked list via their next fields, and the routine node's parms field points to the head of this list. In file decl.c, we link the nodes for the routine's local variable identifiers together in function var_or_field_declarations, and the routine node's locals field points to the head of this list. Thus, there can be two separate linked lists among the nodes in a routine's private symbol table. We will see how the formal parameter list is useful when we parse actual arguments,

FIGURE 7-8   Syntax diagram for a formal parameter list.

parameter list

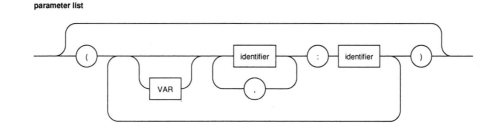

FIGURE 7-9   Syntax diagrams for procedure and function calls.

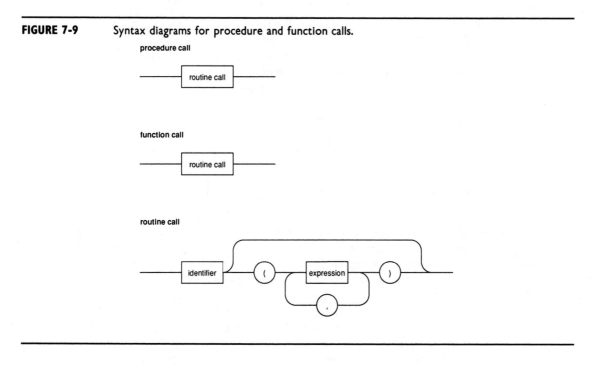

FIGURE 7-10   Syntax diagram for a Pascal statement.

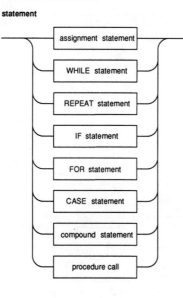

FIGURE 7-11   Syntax diagram for a factor.

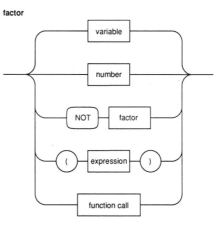

and see how the local variable list is used in later chapters. The offset and total parameter size calculations will become significant in Chapter 9.

7.4 Procedure and function calls

You can see from the syntax diagrams in Figure 7-9 that procedure calls and function calls are syntactically similar. In Figure 7-10, the complete syntax diagram for a Pascal statement shows a procedure call is by itself a statement, and in Figure 7-11, the complete syntax diagram for a factor shows that a function call is a factor.

Figure 7-12 shows the new version of function statement in file stmt.c. If we parse an identifier that leads off a statement, we must check the defn.key field of the identifier's symbol table node to decide whether the statement is an assignment statement or a procedure call. We call function routine_call (in file routine.c) to parse a procedure call.

FIGURE 7-12   Function statement in file stmt.c.

```
/*-----------------------------------------------------------*/
/*  statement            Process a statement by calling the  */
/*                       appropriate parsing routine based on */
/*                       the statement's first token.         */
/*-----------------------------------------------------------*/

statement()

{
    /*
```

```
    --  Call the appropriate routine based on the first
    --  token of the statement.
    */
    switch (token) {

        case IDENTIFIER: {
            SYMTAB_NODE_PTR idp;

            /*
            --  Assignment statement or procedure call?
```

```
*/                                              case IF:      if_statement();       break;
search_and_find_all_symtab(idp);                case FOR:     for_statement();      break;
                                                case CASE:    case_statement();     break;
if (idp->defn.key == PROC_DEFN) {               case BEGIN:   compound_statement(); break;
    get_token();                            }
    routine_call(idp, TRUE);
}                                           /*
else assignment_statement(idp);             -- Error synchronization:  Only a semicolon, END, ELSE, or
                                            --                         UNTIL may follow a statement.
break;                                      --                         Check for a missing semicolon.
}                                           */
                                            synchronize(statement_end_list, statement_start_list, NULL);
                                            if (token_in(statement_start_list)) error(MISSING_SEMICOLON);
case REPEAT:   repeat_statement();  break;
case WHILE:    while_statement();   break;   }
```

Figure 7-13 shows the new version function factor in file expr.c. If we parse an identifier, we must also consider the case that we have a function call. If so, we call routine_call to parse it. (For error handling, if we have a procedure identifier, we go ahead and parse the parameter list.)

FIGURE 7-13   Function factor in file expr.c.

```
/*----------------------------------------------------*/       break;
/*  factor          Process a factor, which is an variable, */
/*                  a number, NOT followed by a factor, or  */    default:
/*                  a parenthesized subexpression.  Return  */        tp = variable(idp, EXPR_USE);
/*                  a pointer to the type structure.        */        break;
/*----------------------------------------------------*/       }

    TYPE_STRUCT_PTR                                       break;
factor()                                              }

{                                                     case NUMBER:
    TYPE_STRUCT_PTR tp;                                   tp = literal.type == INTEGER_LIT
                                                              ? integer_typep
    switch (token) {                                          : real_typep;
                                                         get_token();
        case IDENTIFIER: {                               break;
            SYMTAB_NODE_PTR idp;
                                                      case STRING: {
            search_and_find_all_symtab(idp);             int length = strlen(literal.value.string);

            switch (idp->defn.key) {                     tp = length == 1 ? char_typep
                                                                       : make_string_typep(length);
                case FUNC_DEFN:                          get_token();
                    get_token();                         break;
                    tp = routine_call(idp, TRUE);     }
                    break;
                                                      case NOT:
                case PROC_DEFN:                          get_token();
                    error(INVALID_IDENTIFIER_USAGE);     tp = factor();
                    get_token();                         break;
                    actual_parm_list(idp, FALSE);
                    tp = &dummy_type;                 case LPAREN:
                    break;                               get_token();
                                                         tp = expression();
                case CONST_DEFN:
                    get_token();                         if_token_get_else_error(RPAREN, MISSING_RPAREN);
                    tp = idp->typep;                     break;
```

```
    default:
        error(INVALID_EXPRESSION);
        tp = &dummy_type;
        break;
}

return(tp);
}
```

In both files stmt.c and expr.c, we must replace the line:

```
extern SYMTAB_NODE_PTR  symtab_root;
```

with the following lines:

```
extern SYMTAB_NODE_PTR  symtab_display[];
extern int              level;
```

Back in file routine.c, function routine_call parses procedure calls and function calls. We check the defn.info.routine.key field of the routine identifier's symbol table node to determine whether a call is to a declared (programmer-written) routine or to a standard predefined routine. We call function declared_routine_call for the former and function standard_routine_call (in file standard.c) for the latter, and return the type returned by either of these functions.

Function declared_routine_call parses a call to a declared procedure or function. We call function actual_parm_list to parse the actual parameter list. Then, for a function call, we return the function's type, and for a procedure call, we return NULL.

In function actual_parm_list, we parse the actual parameters and check each parameter's type against the type of the corresponding formal parameter. We also check that the number of parameters is correct. We do neither of these checks if parm_check_flag is FALSE, which is the case if we called the routine to parse an actual parameter list for error recovery (such as parsing a procedure call in a factor). We obtain the list of the symbol table nodes of the formal parameters from the defn.info.routine.parms field of the routine's symbol table node. After parsing each actual parameter, we call function synchronize to resynchronize the parser at the comma or right parenthesis, or at the end of the statement.

An actual parameter corresponding to a formal value parameter may be an expression, and its type must be assignment compatible with that of the formal. An actual parameter corresponding to a formal VAR parameter must be a variable, and its type must be the same as that of the formal. In the latter case, if we find an expression, we parse it anyway for error recovery.

The final function in file routine.c is block, which we take from the main file of the syntax checker in the previous chapter.

7.5 Standard procedures and functions

The standard predefined procedures and functions need special treatment from the parser, since some of them have a variable number of actual parameters of mixed types, and the type of the return value of some of the functions depends on the type of the actual parameter. write and writeln have especially peculiar actual parameters.

We must first enter information about the routines into the level-0 symbol table (the one pointed to by symtab_display[0]). We do this in the new version of function init_symtab and the new function enter_standard_routine in file symtab.c (see Figure 7-5).

File standard.c, shown in Figure 7-14, contains the routines to parse calls to the standard procedures and functions. In function standard_routine_call, we test the defn.info.routine.key field of the standard routine identifier's symbol table node to determine which function to call. We then return the type of a standard function, or NULL if the call was to a standard procedure.

FIGURE 7-14   File standard.c.

```
/***************************************************************/
/*                                                             */
/*        S T A N D A R D   R O U T I N E   P A R S E R        */
/*                                                             */
/*      Parsing routines for calls to standard procedures and  */
/*      functions.                                             */
/*                                                             */
/*      FILE:       standard.c                                 */
/*                                                             */
/*      MODULE:     parser                                     */
/*                                                             */
/***************************************************************/

#include <stdio.h>
#include "common.h"
#include "error.h"
#include "scanner.h"
#include "symtab.h"
#include "parser.h"

#define DEFAULT_NUMERIC_FIELD_WIDTH     10
#define DEFAULT_PRECISION               2

/*------------------------------------------------------------*/
/*  Externals                                                 */
/*------------------------------------------------------------*/

extern TOKEN_CODE       token;
extern char             word_string[];
extern SYMTAB_NODE_PTR  symtab_display[];
extern int              level;
extern TYPE_STRUCT      dummy_type;

extern TYPE_STRUCT_PTR  integer_typep, real_typep,
                        boolean_typep, char_typep;

extern TOKEN_CODE       follow_parm_list[];
```

```
extern TOKEN_CODE       statement_end_list[];

/*------------------------------------------------------------*/
/*  Forwards                                                  */
/*------------------------------------------------------------*/

TYPE_STRUCT_PTR eof_eoln(), abs_sqr(),
                arctan_cos_exp_ln_sin_sqrt(),
                pred_succ(), chr(), odd(), ord(),
                round_trunc();

/*------------------------------------------------------------*/
/*  standard_routine_call   Process a call to a standard      */
/*                          procedure or function.  Return a  */
/*                          pointer to the type structure of  */
/*                          the call.                         */
/*------------------------------------------------------------*/

    TYPE_STRUCT_PTR
standard_routine_call(rtn_idp)

    SYMTAB_NODE_PTR rtn_idp;            /* routine id */

{
    switch (rtn_idp->defn.info.routine.key) {

        case READ:
        case READLN:    read_readln(rtn_idp);       return(NULL);

        case WRITE:
        case WRITELN:   write_writeln(rtn_idp);      return(NULL);

        case EOFF:
        case EOLN:      return(eof_eoln(rtn_idp));

        case ABS:
        case SQR:       return(abs_sqr());
```

```
        case ARCTAN:
        case COS:
        case EXP:
        case LN:
        case SIN:
        case SQRT:      return(arctan_cos_exp_ln_sin_sqrt());

        case PRED:
        case SUCC:      return(pred_succ());

        case CHR:       return(chr());
        case ODD:       return(odd());
        case ORD:       return(ord());

        case ROUND:
        case TRUNC:     return(round_trunc());
    }
}


/*------------------------------------------------------------*/
/*  read_readln           Process a call to read or readln.   */
/*------------------------------------------------------------*/

read_readln(rtn_idp)

    SYMTAB_NODE_PTR rtn_idp;            /* routine id */

{
    TYPE_STRUCT_PTR actual_parm_tp;     /* actual parm type */

    /*
    -- Parameters are optional for readln.
    */
    if (token == LPAREN) {
        /*
        -- <id-list>
        */
        do {
            get_token();

            /*
            -- Actual parms must be variables (but parse
            -- an expression anyway for error recovery).
            */
            if (token == IDENTIFIER) {
                SYMTAB_NODE_PTR idp;

                search_and_find_all_symtab(idp);
                actual_parm_tp = base_type(variable(idp,
                                            VARPARM_USE));

                if (actual_parm_tp->form != SCALAR_FORM)
                    error(INCOMPATIBLE_TYPES);
            }
            else {
                actual_parm_tp = expression();
                error(INVALID_VAR_PARM);
            }

            /*
            -- Error synchronization:  Should be , or )
            */
            synchronize(follow_parm_list, statement_end_list, NULL);

        } while (token == COMMA);

        if_token_get_else_error(RPAREN, MISSING_RPAREN);
```

```
    }
    else if (rtn_idp->defn.info.routine.key == READ)
        error(WRONG_NUMBER_OF_PARMS);
}

/*-----------------------------------------------------------*/
/*  write_writeln        Process a call to write or writeln. */
/*                       Each actual parameter can be:       */
/*                                                           */
/*                               <expr>                      */
/*                                                           */
/*                            or:                            */
/*                                                           */
/*                          <epxr> : <expr>                  */
/*                                                           */
/*                            or:                            */
/*                                                           */
/*                      <expr> : <expr> : <expr>             */
/*-----------------------------------------------------------*/

write_writeln(rtn_idp)

    SYMTAB_NODE_PTR rtn_idp;            /* routine id */

{
    TYPE_STRUCT_PTR actual_parm_tp;     /* actual parm type */
    TYPE_STRUCT_PTR field_width_tp, precision_tp;

    /*
    -- Parameters are optional for writeln.
    */
    if (token == LPAREN) {
        do {
            /*
            -- Value <expr>
            */
            get_token();
            actual_parm_tp = base_type(expression());

            if ((actual_parm_tp->form != SCALAR_FORM) &&
                (actual_parm_tp != boolean_typep) &&
                ((actual_parm_tp->form != ARRAY_FORM) ||
                 (actual_parm_tp->info.array.elmt_typep !=
                                            char_typep)))
                error(INVALID_EXPRESSION);

            /*
            -- Optional field width <expr>
            */
            if (token == COLON) {
                get_token();
                field_width_tp = base_type(expression());

                if (field_width_tp != integer_typep)
                    error(INCOMPATIBLE_TYPES);

                /*
                -- Optional precision <expr>
                */
                if (token == COLON) {
                    get_token();
                    precision_tp = base_type(expression());

                    if (precision_tp != integer_typep)
                        error(INCOMPATIBLE_TYPES);
                }
            }
```

```
        /*
        -- Error synchronization:  Should be , or )
        */
        synchronize(follow_parm_list, statement_end_list, NULL);

    } while (token == COMMA);

    if_token_get_else_error(RPAREN, MISSING_RPAREN);
    }
    else if (rtn_idp->defn.info.routine.key == WRITE)
        error(WRONG_NUMBER_OF_PARMS);
}

/*------------------------------------------------------------*/
/*  eof_eoln            Process a call to eof or to eoln.   */
/*                      No parameters => boolean result.    */
/*------------------------------------------------------------*/

    TYPE_STRUCT_PTR
eof_eoln(rtn_idp)

    SYMTAB_NODE_PTR rtn_idp;        /* routine id */

{
    if (token == LPAREN) {
        error(WRONG_NUMBER_OF_PARMS);
        actual_parm_list(rtn_idp, FALSE);
    }

    return(boolean_typep);
}

/*------------------------------------------------------------*/
/*  abs_sqr             Process a call to abs or to sqr.    */
/*                      integer parm => integer result      */
/*                      real parm    => real result         */
/*------------------------------------------------------------*/

    TYPE_STRUCT_PTR
abs_sqr()

{
    TYPE_STRUCT_PTR parm_tp;        /* actual parameter type */
    TYPE_STRUCT_PTR result_tp;      /* result type */

    if (token == LPAREN) {
        get_token();
        parm_tp = base_type(expression());

        if ((parm_tp != integer_typep) && (parm_tp != real_typep)) {
            error(INCOMPATIBLE_TYPES);
            result_tp = real_typep;
        }
        else result_tp = parm_tp;

        if_token_get_else_error(RPAREN, MISSING_RPAREN);
    }
    else error(WRONG_NUMBER_OF_PARMS);

    return(result_tp);
}

/*------------------------------------------------------------*/
/*  arctan_cos_exp_ln_sin_sqrt  Process a call to arctan, cos, */
/*                              exp, ln, sin, or sqrt.         */
/*                              integer parm => real result    */
/*                              real_parm    => real result     */
/*------------------------------------------------------------*/
```

```
    TYPE_STRUCT_PTR
arctan_cos_exp_ln_sin_sqrt()

{
    TYPE_STRUCT_PTR parm_tp;        /* actual parameter type */

    if (token == LPAREN) {
        get_token();
        parm_tp = base_type(expression());

        if ((parm_tp != integer_typep) && (parm_tp != real_typep))
            error(INCOMPATIBLE_TYPES);

        if_token_get_else_error(RPAREN, MISSING_RPAREN);
    }
    else error(WRONG_NUMBER_OF_PARMS);

    return(real_typep);
}

/*------------------------------------------------------------*/
/*  pred_succ           Process a call to pred or succ.     */
/*                      integer parm => integer result      */
/*                      enum parm    => enum result         */
/*------------------------------------------------------------*/

    TYPE_STRUCT_PTR
pred_succ()

{
    TYPE_STRUCT_PTR parm_tp;        /* actual parameter type */
    TYPE_STRUCT_PTR result_tp;      /* result type */

    if (token == LPAREN) {
        get_token();
        parm_tp = base_type(expression());

        if ((parm_tp != integer_typep) &&
            (parm_tp->form != ENUM_FORM)) {
            error(INCOMPATIBLE_TYPES);
            result_tp = integer_typep;
        }
        else result_tp = parm_tp;

        if_token_get_else_error(RPAREN, MISSING_RPAREN);
    }
    else error(WRONG_NUMBER_OF_PARMS);

    return(result_tp);
}

/*------------------------------------------------------------*/
/*  chr                 Process a call to chr.              */
/*                      integer parm => character result    */
/*------------------------------------------------------------*/

    TYPE_STRUCT_PTR
chr()

{
    TYPE_STRUCT_PTR parm_tp;        /* actual parameter type */

    if (token == LPAREN) {
        get_token();
        parm_tp = base_type(expression());

        if (parm_tp != integer_typep) error(INCOMPATIBLE_TYPES);
        if_token_get_else_error(RPAREN, MISSING_RPAREN);
```

```
    }
    else error(WRONG_NUMBER_OF_PARMS);

    return(char_typep);
}

/*------------------------------------------------*/
/* odd                  Process a call to odd.     */
/*                      integer parm => boolean result */
/*------------------------------------------------*/

    TYPE_STRUCT_PTR
odd()

{
    TYPE_STRUCT_PTR parm_tp;          /* actual parameter type */

    if (token == LPAREN) {
        get_token();
        parm_tp = base_type(expression());

        if (parm_tp != integer_typep) error(INCOMPATIBLE_TYPES);
        if_token_get_else_error(RPAREN, MISSING_RPAREN);
    }
    else error(WRONG_NUMBER_OF_PARMS);

    return(boolean_typep);
}

/*------------------------------------------------*/
/* ord                  Process a call to ord.     */
/*                      enumeration parm => integer result */
/*------------------------------------------------*/

    TYPE_STRUCT_PTR
ord()
```

```
{
    TYPE_STRUCT_PTR parm_tp;          /* actual parameter type */

    if (token == LPAREN) {
        get_token();
        parm_tp = base_type(expression());

        if (parm_tp->form != ENUM_FORM) error(INCOMPATIBLE_TYPES);
        if_token_get_else_error(RPAREN, MISSING_RPAREN);
    }
    else error(WRONG_NUMBER_OF_PARMS);

    return(integer_typep);
}

/*------------------------------------------------*/
/* round_trunc          Process a call to round or trunc. */
/*                      real parm => integer result */
/*------------------------------------------------*/

    TYPE_STRUCT_PTR
round_trunc()

{
    TYPE_STRUCT_PTR parm_tp;          /* actual parameter type */

    if (token == LPAREN) {
        get_token();
        parm_tp = base_type(expression());

        if (parm_tp != real_typep) error(INCOMPATIBLE_TYPES);
        if_token_get_else_error(RPAREN, MISSING_RPAREN);
    }
    else error(WRONG_NUMBER_OF_PARMS);

    return(integer_typep);
}
```

In function read_readln, we parse calls to procedures read and readln. The actual parameters must be variables. We parse calls to procedures write and writeln in function write_writeln. The actual parameters may be expressions, and each parameter may be followed by field width and precision designators, which we check to make sure they are integers.

Function eof_eoln parses calls to the parameterless functions eof and eoln and returns the boolean type. Function abs_sqr parses calls to the single-parameter functions abs and sqr and returns the integer type if the actual parameter is an integer, and the real type if the actual parameter is real.

In function arctan_cos_exp_ln_sin_sqrt, we parse calls to the single-parameter functions arctan, cos, exp, ln, sin, and sqrt. We return the real type, but the actual parameter may be integer or real.

We parse calls to the single-parameter functions pred and succ in function pred_succ, and we return the enumeration type of the actual parameter. In function chr, we parse calls to the single-parameter function chr. We return the character type, but the actual parameter must be integer. In function odd, we parse calls to the single-parameter function odd. We return the boolean type, but the actual parameter must be integer. Finally, in function ord, we parse calls to the single-parameter function ord. We return the integer type, but the actual parameter must be of an enumeration type.

7.6 The FOR statement

Figure 7-15 shows the new version of function for_statement in file stmt.c. We now have a stricter test on the control variable. It must be a local variable or formal parameter, but not a VAR parameter.

FIGURE 7-15   Function for_statement in file stmt.c.

```
/*------------------------------------------------------------*/
/*  for_statement       Process a FOR statement:              */
/*                                                            */
/*                      FOR <id> := <expr> TO|DOWNTO <expr>   */
/*                      DO <stmt>                             */
/*------------------------------------------------------------*/

for_statement()

{
    SYMTAB_NODE_PTR for_idp;
    TYPE_STRUCT_PTR for_tp, expr_tp;

    get_token();

    if (token == IDENTIFIER) {
        search_and_find_all_symtab(for_idp);

        if ((for_idp->level != level) ||
            (for_idp->defn.key != VAR_DEFN))
            error(INVALID_FOR_CONTROL);

        for_tp = base_type(for_idp->typep);
        get_token();


        if ((for_tp != integer_typep) &&
            (for_tp != char_typep) &&
            (for_tp->form != ENUM_FORM)) error(INCOMPATIBLE_TYPES);
    }
    else {
        error(IDENTIFIER, MISSING_IDENTIFIER);
        for_tp = &dummy_type;
    }

    if_token_get_else_error(COLONEQUAL, MISSING_COLONEQUAL);

    expr_tp = expression();
    if (! is_assign_type_compatible(for_tp, expr_tp))
        error(INCOMPATIBLE_TYPES);

    if ((token == TO) || (token == DOWNTO)) get_token();
    else error(MISSING_TO_OR_DOWNTO);

    expr_tp = expression();
    if (! is_assign_type_compatible(for_tp, expr_tp))
        error(INCOMPATIBLE_TYPES);

    if_token_get_else_error(DO, MISSING_DO);
    statement();
}
```

7.7 Program 7-1: Pascal Syntax Checker III

At last, we can put everything together into the third and final version of our syntax checker. Figure 7-16 shows the main file of this utility program, syntax3.c. It initializes the symbol table, fetches the first token, and calls function program.

FIGURE 7-16   File syntax3.c.

```
/****************************************************************/
/*                                                            */
/*      Program 7-1:  Pascal Syntax Checker III               */
/*                                                            */
/*      Read and check the syntax of a Pascal program.        */
/*                                                            */
/*      FILE:       syntax3.c                                 */
/*                                                            */
/*      REQUIRES:   Modules parser, symbol table, scanner,    */
/*                          error                             */
/*                                                            */
/*      USAGE:      syntax3 sourcefile                        */
/*                                                            */
/*          sourcefile    name of source file containing      */
/*                        the program to be checked           */
/*                                                            */
/****************************************************************/

#include <stdio.h>
#include "common.h"
#include "error.h"
#include "scanner.h"
#include "parser.h"
```

```
/*----------------------------------------------------------*/
/*  main            Initialize the scanner and call the    */
/*                  statement routine.                      */
/*----------------------------------------------------------*/

main(argc, argv)

    int argc;
    char *argv[];

{
    /*
    -- Initialize the scanner.
    */
    init_scanner(argv[1]);

    /*
    -- Process a program.
    */
    get_token();
    program();
}
```

This syntax checker can check an entire Pascal program. We saw some sample output from this program in Figure 7-4. Figure 7-17 shows more output that illustrates some of the error checking that it is capable of performing. This program is the foundation for both the interpreter that we will write in the next part of this book, and for the compiler that we will write in the last part of the book.

FIGURE 7-17   Sample output from the syntax checker III.

```
Page 1   rtn.pas   Tue Jul 10 03:13:36 1990

  1 0: PROGRAM rtn(input, output);
  2 1:
  3 1:     VAR
  4 1:         i, j, k   : integer;
  5 1:         p, z      : real;
  6 1:         ch, letter : char;
  7 1:
  8 1:     FUNCTION func(VAR ch : char) : real;
  9 2:         forward;
 10 1:
 11 1:     PROCEDURE proc(b     : boolean;
 12 2:                    VAR x : real;
 13 2:                    y     : real);
 14 2:
 15 2:         CONST
 16 2:             n = 5;
 17 2:
 18 2:         VAR
 19 2:             p, q : boolean;
 20 2:
 21 2:         BEGIN
```

```
 22 2:             p := x + z - n*func(letter);
                                              ^
*** ERROR: Incompatible assignment.
 23 2:             proc(ch);
                        ^
*** ERROR: Incompatible types.
                             ^
*** ERROR: Wrong number of actual parameters.
 24 2:         END;
 25 1:
 26 1:     FUNCTION func(i : integer) : boolean;
                      ^
*** ERROR: Already specified in FORWARD.
                                          ^
*** ERROR: Already specified in FORWARD.
 27 2:
 28 2:         TYPE
 29 2:             stooge = (larry, moe, curly);
 30 2:
 31 2:         VAR
 32 2:             s, t : stooge;
 33 2:
 34 2:         BEGIN
 35 2:             s := pred(t);
```

```
36 2:           proc(s = t, p, j DIV k);              42 1:        j := -3;
37 2:           func(letter) := 'xyz';                43 1:        proc(false, 4.5*z, z);

*** ERROR: Unexpected token.                          *** ERROR: Invalid VAR parameter.
                          ^                            44 1:        z := 3.14 + func(ch, 123) - func + func(p) + func(-3);

                                                       *** ERROR: Wrong number of actual parameters.
                                                                                    ^
Page 2   rtn.pas   Tue Jul 10 03:13:36 1990            *** ERROR: Wrong number of actual parameters.

                                                       *** ERROR: Incompatible types.
*** ERROR: Incompatible assignment.
38 2:           func := round(3.14) - trunc(3);        *** ERROR: Invalid VAR parameter.
                              ^                         45 1:        END.

*** ERROR: Incompatible types.
39 2:       END;                                                    45 Source lines.
40 1:                                                              13 Source errors.
41 1:       BEGIN
```

Questions and exercises

1. In functions program_header, procedure_header, and function_header, we
   call function enter_scope *after* we parse the program or routine identifier and
   before we parse the formal parameters and the block. What does this say
   about the scopes of these elements?

2. Error recovery in function actual_parm_list is awkward if an expression is
   passed as a VAR parameter, and the expression begins with a variable. Improve
   the error recovery in the function.

3. Modify the symbol table and its initialization routines so that the symbol
   table contains enough useful information about the standard procedures and
   functions so that calls to them can be parsed more like calls to the declared
   routines.

4. Upgrade the cross-referencer utility program to list the name of the procedure
   or function in which each identifier is defined.

5. Write a call chart generator utility program that parses an entire source program and then produces a chart showing, for each procedure and function,
   which routines call it and which routines it calls. Show the line number of
   each call.

PART II

Interpreting

CHAPTER 8

An Intermediate Form for Interpretation

In the first part of this book, we wrote a scanner, a parser, and a utility program that can check an entire Pascal program for syntax errors. In the second part of the book, we will build upon our previous programs to write a Pascal interpreter. In this chapter, we see how to translate a source program into an intermediate form that can be interpreted. In the next two chapters, we will write a fully working Pascal interpreter, and in Chapter 11, we will add an interactive debugger.

In this chapter, we will write a pretty-printer utility program to develop our skills to manipulate a source program in its intermediate form. These skills will enable us to:

- convert a Pascal source program into an intermediate form
- interpret the intermediate code to reconstruct the source program

The pretty-printer will work by first translating the source program into the intermediate form. Then, like an interpreter, it will read the intermediate code. Instead of executing it, however, it will reconstruct the source program and write it back out in a neatly-indented format.

8.1 The need for an intermediate form

The calculator utility program in Chapter 4 interpreted expressions and assignment statements directly from the source program—it did the semantic actions as soon as it parsed each statement and expression. Such a scheme is adequate for an interactive calculator that interprets each statement and expression only once, and when speed is not so important.

Speed is more important when interpreting a program. A program can have loops and procedures and functions, so that some statements can be executed many times. It is no longer a good idea to interpret directly from the source, since doing so means that if a statement is in a loop, then each time the interpreter executes the statement it must rescan and reparse the statement and do a symbol table lookup for each identifier in the statement.

The prime motivation for an intermediate form is to do all of the scanning, most of the parsing, and all of symbol table lookups only once. As the interpreter parses the source program, it translates it to this form. The intermediate code for a source statement contains a byte code for each token and a pointer to the symbol table node of each identifier. The scanner provides the token codes, and the parser obtains the symbol table pointers from the symbol table routines as it parses each identifier. We have already seen how all this is happens in our syntax checker.

Therefore, when the interpreter executes a program in the intermediate form, it does not need to do any scanning or symbol table lookups. If an interpreter only executes programs that have no syntax errors, then when it is parsing the intermediate code during execution, it does not need to do any time-consuming syntax and type checking.

You can use a very simple intermediate form for our interpreter, namely, one similar to the crunched form produced by the cruncher utility program in Chapter 3. You only need to convert the executable statements of the source program to this form. As we have done before, you will convert all the declarations into information for the symbol table. Indeed, the symbol table node for each program, procedure, or function identifier will point to a "code segment" containing the intermediate code from the routine's statements.

Other intermediate forms are possible. We will explore some of these in the questions and exercises at the end of the chapter.

8.2 Changes to the modules

We require only a few changes to our modules to generate the intermediate code. There are no new files.

Parser Module

parser.h	*u*	Parser header file
routine.c	*c*	Parse programs, procedures, and functions
standard.c	*u*	Parse standard procedures and functions
stmt.c	*c*	Parse statements
expr.c	*c*	Parse expressions
decl.c	*u*	Parse declarations

Scanner Module

| scanner.h | *u* | Scanner header file |
| scanner.c | *c* | Scanner routines |

Symbol Table Module

| symtab.h | *u* | Symbol table header file |
| symtab.c | *u* | Symbol table routines |

Error Module

| error.h | *u* | Error header file |
| error.c | *u* | Error routines |

Miscellaneous

| common.h | *u* | Common header file |

Where: *u* file unchanged from the previous chapter
        c file changed from the previous chapter

We make a small change to file scanner.c to cause it to output a token code to the intermediate form. We make a few changes to stmt.c and expr.c to enter number and string tokens into the symbol table and to output symbol table pointers to the intermediate form. Finally, we change routine.c to create code segments.

8.3 Program 8-1: A Pascal Source Pretty-Printer

You will see how to translate a source program to its intermediate form in the context of a pretty-printer utility program. This program will also show you how to read the intermediate code. Most of the code for writing and reading the intermediate code will show up in the interpreter.

A pretty-printer reads a source program and rewrites it in a "pretty" format. The rewritten source strictly follows certain coding conventions that govern how to indent statements. Such a utility program is surprisingly easy to write, given all the programs we have written and the skills we have acquired. The output of our pretty-printer may not win any awards for aesthetics, but it does format programs in a consistent manner. The questions and exercises at the end of this chapter will suggest improvements.

You can pretty-print declarations (constant definitions, type definitions, variable declarations, and program, procedure, and function headers) by reconstructing them from information in the symbol table. You can translate a routine's executable statements into the intermediate form and store them in a code segment that you allocate for each routine. You can then pretty-print the statements by reconstructing the statements from the intermediate code. You can continue to pretty-print only while there are no syntax errors.

Besides the modules listed, the pretty-printer has several other files:

pprint.h	header file
pprint.c	main file
ppdecl.c	pretty-print declarations
ppstmt.c	pretty-print statements and expressions

Figure 8-1 shows file pprint.c. In the main routine, we set the scanner variable print_flag to FALSE (since we don't want the usual listing), initialize the scanner, and call routine program to pretty-print the source program.

FIGURE 8-1   File pprint.c.

```
/****************************************************************/
/*                                                              */
/*      Program 8-1:  Pascal Pretty Printer                     */
/*                                                              */
/*      Read and check the syntax of a Pascal program,          */
/*      and then print it out in a nicely-indented format.      */
/*                                                              */
/*      FILE:      pprint.c                                     */
/*                                                              */
/*      REQUIRES:  Modules parser, symbol table, scanner,       */
/*                        error                                 */
/*                                                              */
/*                 Files ppdecl.c, ppstmt.c                     */
/*                                                              */
/*      FLAGS:     Macro flag "analyze" must be defined         */
/*                                                              */
/*      USAGE:     pprint sourcefile                            */
/*                                                              */
/*         sourcefile    name of source file containing         */
/*                       the program to be pretty-printed       */
/*                                                              */
/****************************************************************/

#include <stdio.h>
#include "common.h"
#include "error.h"
#include "scanner.h"
#include "parser.h"
#include "pprint.h"

/*-------------------------------------------------*/
/* Externals                                       */
/*-------------------------------------------------*/

extern BOOLEAN print_flag;

/*-------------------------------------------------*/
/* Globals                                         */
/*-------------------------------------------------*/

char *code_buffer;              /* code buffer */
char *code_bufferp;             /* code buffer ptr */
char *code_segmentp;            /* code segment ptr */
char *code_segment_limit;       /* end of code segment */
```

```
TOKEN_CODE ctoken;                      /* token from code segment */

char pprint_buffer[MAX_PRINT_LINE_LENGTH];   /* print buffer */
int left_margin = 0;                    /* margin in buffer */

/*-------------------------------------------------*/
/* main              Initialize the scanner and call */
/*                   routine program.              */
/*-------------------------------------------------*/

main(argc, argv)

    int  argc;
    char *argv[];

{
    /*
    -- Initialize the scanner.
    */
    print_flag = FALSE;
    init_scanner(argv[1]);

    /*
    -- Process a program.
    */
    get_token();
    program();
    quit_scanner();
}

/*-------------------------------------------------*/
/* emit              Emit a string to the print buffer. */
/*-------------------------------------------------*/

emit(string)

    char *string;

{
    int buffer_length = strlen(pprint_buffer);
    int string_length = strlen(string);

    if (buffer_length + string_length >= MAX_PRINT_LINE_LENGTH - 1) {
```

```
        flush();                                        else
        indent();                                           pprint_buffer[0] = '\0';
    }                                               }

    strcat(pprint_buffer, string);              /*--------------------------------------------------------*/
}                                               /*  flush              Print the print buffer if there is  */
                                                /*                     anything in it.                     */
/*--------------------------------------------------------*/      /*--------------------------------------------------------*/
/*  indent              Indent left_margin spaces in the print  */
/*                      buffer.                           */      flush()
/*--------------------------------------------------------*/

indent()                                        {
                                                    if (pprint_buffer[0] != '\0') {
{                                                       printf("%s\n", pprint_buffer);
    if (left_margin > 0)                                pprint_buffer[0] = '\0';
        sprintf(pprint_buffer, "%*s", left_margin, " ");    }
                                                }
```

We have two new global variables. We construct lines of the pretty-printed program in pprint_buffer before we print them. We keep the current position of the left margin of a pretty-printed line in left_margin. When left_margin is zero, there is no indentation, and when it is four, the line is indented four spaces from the left.

We call function emit to append a string to the end of whatever is already in pprint_buffer. If the string would cause the line to be too long, we print the contents of pprint_buffer and indent the next line by the same amount. In effect, we wrap long lines.

In function indent, we add the correct number of spaces to the beginning of pprint_buffer. We call function flush to print the contents of pprint_buffer if it is not empty.

Figure 8-2 shows the header file pprint.h. It contains several useful macros. Macros advance_left_margin and retreat_left_margin move the left margin forward and back by indent_size spaces. Macro set_left_margin remembers the current position of the left margin and then sets the left margin to the current print position. Macro reset_left_margin puts the left margin back to the remembered position.

FIGURE 8-2   File pprint.h.

```
/****************************************************************/   #define retreat_left_margin() if ((left_margin -= indent_size) < 0) \
/*                                                    */                                          left_margin = 0;
/*      FILE:       pprint.h                          */
/*                                                    */          #define set_left_margin(m)      {m = left_margin; \
/****************************************************************/                                   left_margin = strlen(pprint_buffer);}

#define indent_size 4

#define advance_left_margin() left_margin += indent_size          #define reset_left_margin(m)  left_margin = m
```

8.3.1 Pretty-printing declarations

You can pretty-print each declaration just after you have parsed it and entered its information into the symbol table. You can then pretty-print by analyzing the symbol table information, just as you did for the declarations analyzer in Chapter 6. Therefore, you must reactivate the calls to the functions analyze_const_defn, analyze_type_defn, and analyze_var_decl in file decl.c. As explained in Chapter 6, we accomplish this by making sure the analyze macro flag is defined for file parser.h. Of course, we will write new versions of these functions, along with two new ones, analyze_routine_header and analyze_block.

Figure 8-3 shows the new version of function program, and Figure 8-4 shows the new version of function routine, both in file routine.c. Both functions contain similar calls for pretty-printing. In program, we call function analyze_routine_header (we ignored this call in the previous chapter) to pretty-print the program header. We call function block to parse the program's block. As we will see later, when we are parsing a block's declarations, we pretty-print them, and when we parse a block's statements, we translate them into the internal form.

FIGURE 8-3   Function program in file routine.c.

```
/*------------------------------------------------------------*/
/* program        Process a program:                          */
/*                                                            */
/*                      <program-header> ; <block> .          */
/*------------------------------------------------------------*/

TOKEN_CODE follow_header_list[] = {SEMICOLON, END_OF_FILE, 0};

program()

{
    SYMTAB_NODE_PTR program_idp;        /* program id */

    /*
    --                  PARSE THE PROGRAM
    --
    --
    -- Intialize the symbol table and then allocate
    -- the code buffer.
    */
    init_symtab();
    code_buffer  = alloc_bytes(MAX_CODE_BUFFER_SIZE);
    code_bufferp = code_buffer;

    /*
    -- Begin parsing with the program header.
    */
    program_idp = program_header();

    /*
    -- Error synchronization:  Should be ;
    */
    synchronize(follow_header_list,
                declaration_start_list, statement_start_list);
    if_token_get(SEMICOLON);
    else if (token_in(declaration_start_list) ||
             token_in(statement_start_list))
        error(MISSING_SEMICOLON);

    analyze_routine_header(program_idp);

    /*
    -- Parse the program's block.
    */
    program_idp->defn.info.routine.locals = NULL;
    block(program_idp);

    program_idp->defn.info.routine.local_symtab = exit_scope();
    program_idp->defn.info.routine.code_segment =create_code_segment();
    analyze_block(program_idp->defn.info.routine.code_segment);

    if_token_get_else_error(PERIOD, MISSING_PERIOD);

    /*
    -- Look for the end of file.
    */
    while (token != END_OF_FILE) {
        error(UNEXPECTED_TOKEN);
        get_token();
    }

    quit_scanner();
    free(code_buffer);
    exit(0);
}
```

FIGURE 8-4   Function routine in file routine.c.

```
/*-------------------------------------------------------------*/          error(MISSING_SEMICOLON);
/* routine           Call the appropriate routine to process */
/*                   a procedure or function definition:      */      /*
/*                                                            */      -- <block> or FORWARD.
/*                   <routine-header> ; <block>              */      */
/*-------------------------------------------------------------*/      if (strcmp(word_string, "forward") != 0) {
                                                                           rtn_idp->defn.info.routine.key = DECLARED;
routine()                                                                  analyze_routine_header(rtn_idp);

{                                                                          rtn_idp->defn.info.routine.locals = NULL;
    SYMTAB_NODE_PTR rtn_idp;    /* routine id */                           block(rtn_idp);

    rtn_idp = (token == PROCEDURE) ? procedure_header()                    rtn_idp->defn.info.routine.code_segment = create_code_segment();
                                   : function_header();                    analyze_block(rtn_idp->defn.info.routine.code_segment);
                                                                       }
    /*                                                                 else {
    -- Error synchronization: Should be ;                                  get_token();
    */                                                                     rtn_idp->defn.info.routine.key = FORWARD;
    synchronize(follow_header_list,                                        analyze_routine_header(rtn_idp);
             declaration_start_list, statement_start_list);          }
    if_token_get(SEMICOLON);
    else if (token_in(declaration_start_list) ||                      rtn_idp->defn.info.routine.local_symtab = exit_scope();
           token_in(statement_start_list))
                                                                  }
```

We then call function `create_code_segment`, which allocates a code segment for the program, fills it with the intermediate code from the block's statements, and returns a pointer to a code segment. We point field `defn.info.routine.code_segment` of the program identifier's symbol table node to the code segment. Finally, we call function `analyze_block` (which we also ignored in the previous chapter) to pretty-print the statements. File `ppdecl.c`, shown in Figure 8-5, contains the functions to pretty-print declarations.

FIGURE 8-5   File ppdecl.c.

```
/***************************************************************/      /*-------------------------------------------------------------*/
/*                                                            */      /* Externals                                                  */
/*      Pretty-print declarations and program, procedure, and */      /*-------------------------------------------------------------*/
/*      function headers.                                     */
/*                                                            */      extern TYPE_STRUCT_PTR integer_typep, real_typep,
/*      FILE:      ppdecl.c                                   */                                 boolean_typep, char_typep;
/*                                                            */
/***************************************************************/      extern char pprint_buffer[];
                                                                       extern int  left_margin;
#include <stdio.h>                                                     extern int  error_count;
#include "common.h"
#include "symtab.h"                                                    /*-------------------------------------------------------------*/
#include "pprint.h"                                                    /* Globals                                                    */
                                                                       /*-------------------------------------------------------------*/
```

```
char string[MAX_PRINT_LINE_LENGTH];      /* buffer for literals */
BOOLEAN const_flag, type_flag, var_flag; /* TRUE if keywords
                                            already printed */

/*------------------------------------------------------------*/
/*  analyze_routine_header   Pretty-print a program, procedure, */
/*                           or function header:                */
/*                                                              */
/*                              PROGRAM <id> (<parms>);         */
/*                              PROCEDURE <id> (<parms>);       */
/*                              FUNCTION <id> (<parms>) : <id>  */
/*------------------------------------------------------------*/

analyze_routine_header(rtn_idp)

    SYMTAB_NODE_PTR rtn_idp;

{
    int             save_left_margin;  /* current left margin */
    DEFN_KEY        common_key;        /* defn of parm sublist */
    TYPE_STRUCT_PTR common_tp;         /* type of parm sublist */
    SYMTAB_NODE_PTR parm_idp = rtn_idp->defn.info.routine.parms;

    if (error_count > 0) return;
    const_flag = type_flag = var_flag = FALSE;

    emit(" ");
    flush();
    indent();

    switch (rtn_idp->defn.key) {
        case PROG_DEFN:  emit("PROGRAM ");   break;
        case PROC_DEFN:  emit("PROCEDURE "); break;
        case FUNC_DEFN:  emit("FUNCTION ");  break;
    }

    emit(rtn_idp->name);

    /*
    -- Print the formal parameters if there are any
    -- and the routine was not previously forwarded.
    */
    if ((parm_idp != NULL) &&
        (! (BOOLEAN) rtn_idp->info)) {
        BOOLEAN sublist_done;

        emit(" (");
        set_left_margin(save_left_margin);

        /*
        -- Loop to print the parameter sublists.
        */
        do {
            common_key = parm_idp->defn.key;
            common_tp = parm_idp->typep;
            if ((rtn_idp->defn.key != PROG_DEFN) &&
                (common_key == VARPARM_DEFN)) emit("VAR ");
            emit(parm_idp->name);

            /*
            -- Loop to print the parameters in a sublist.
            */
            do {
                parm_idp = parm_idp->next;
                sublist_done = ((parm_idp == NULL) ||
                            (parm_idp->defn.key != common_key) ||
                            (parm_idp->typep != common_tp));
```

```
                if (!sublist_done) {
                    emit(", ");
                    emit(parm_idp->name);
                }
            } while (!sublist_done);

            if (rtn_idp->defn.key != PROG_DEFN) {
                emit(" : ");
                print_type(common_tp, FALSE);
            }

            if (parm_idp != NULL) {
                emit(";");
                flush();
                indent();
            }
        } while (parm_idp != NULL);

        emit(")");

        if (rtn_idp->defn.key == FUNC_DEFN) {
            emit(" : ");
            print_type(rtn_idp->typep, FALSE);
        }

        reset_left_margin(save_left_margin);
    }

    emit(";");
    flush();

    /*
    -- Print a forward declaration.
    */
    if (rtn_idp->defn.info.routine.key == FORWARD) {
        rtn_idp->info = (char *) TRUE;

        advance_left_margin();
        indent();
        emit("FORWARD;");
        flush();
        retreat_left_margin();
    }

    else advance_left_margin();
}

/*------------------------------------------------------------*/
/*  declaration_keyword    Print the keyword CONST, TYPE, or   */
/*                         VAR in string if flag is FALSE.     */
/*                         Each keyword is printed at most     */
/*                         once per block.                     */
/*------------------------------------------------------------*/

declaration_keyword(flag, string)

    BOOLEAN *flag;      /* TRUE if keyword already printed */
    char    *string;    /* keyword */

{
    if (! *flag) {
        emit(" ");
        flush();

        indent();
        emit(string);
        flush();
```

```
        *flag = TRUE;
    }
}

/*-----------------------------------------------------*/
/*  analyze_const_defn     Pretty-print a constant definition: */
/*                                                     */
/*                         CONST                       */
/*                              <id> = <literal>;      */
/*-----------------------------------------------------*/

analyze_const_defn(const_idp)

    SYMTAB_NODE_PTR const_idp;               /* constant id */

{
    TYPE_STRUCT_PTR const_tp = const_idp->typep;  /* constant type */

    if (error_count > 0) return;

    declaration_keyword(&const_flag, "CONST");
    advance_left_margin();

    indent();
    emit(const_idp->name);
    emit(" = ");

    if (const_tp->form == ARRAY_FORM) {          /* string */
        emit("'");
        emit(const_idp->defn.info.constant.value.stringp);
        emit("'");
    }
    else if (const_tp == integer_typep) {
        sprintf(string, "%d",
                const_idp->defn.info.constant.value.integer);
        emit(string);
    }
    else if (const_tp == real_typep) {
        sprintf(string, "%g",
                const_idp->defn.info.constant.value.real);
        emit(string);
    }
    else if (const_tp == char_typep) {
        sprintf(string, "'%c'",
                const_idp->defn.info.constant.value.character);
        emit(string);
    }

    emit(";");
    flush();
    retreat_left_margin();
}

/*-----------------------------------------------------*/
/*  analyze_type_defn       Pretty-print a type definition:  */
/*                                                     */
/*                         TYPE                        */
/*                              <id> = <type>;         */
/*-----------------------------------------------------*/

analyze_type_defn(type_idp)

    SYMTAB_NODE_PTR type_idp;                /* type id */

{
    if (error_count > 0) return;

    declaration_keyword(&type_flag, "TYPE");
```

```
    advance_left_margin();

    indent();
    emit(type_idp->name);
    emit(" = ");

    print_type(type_idp->typep,
               type_idp == type_idp->typep->type_idp);
    emit(";");
    flush();
    retreat_left_margin();
}

/*-----------------------------------------------------*/
/*  print_type             Pretty-print a type.         */
/*-----------------------------------------------------*/

print_type(tp, defn_flag)

    TYPE_STRUCT_PTR tp;          /* type */
    BOOLEAN         defn_flag;   /* TRUE if named definition */

{
    /*
    -- Identifier type.
    */
    if (!defn_flag && (tp->type_idp != NULL))
        emit(tp->type_idp->name);

    /*
    -- Other type.
    */
    else switch (tp->form) {
        case ENUM_FORM:      print_enum_type(tp);      break;
        case SUBRANGE_FORM:  print_subrange_type(tp);  break;
        case ARRAY_FORM:     print_array_type(tp);     break;
        case RECORD_FORM:    print_record_type(tp);    break;
    }
}

/*-----------------------------------------------------*/
/*  print_enum_type        Pretty-print an enumeration type: */
/*                                                     */
/*                         (<id1>, <id2>, ..., <idn>)  */
/*-----------------------------------------------------*/

print_enum_type(tp)

    TYPE_STRUCT_PTR tp;          /* type */

{
    SYMTAB_NODE_PTR idp = tp->info.enumeration.const_idp;

    emit("(");

    /*
    -- Loop to print the enumeration constant id list.
    */
    while (idp != NULL) {
        emit(idp->name);
        idp = idp->next;
        if (idp != NULL) emit(", ");
    }

    emit(")");
}
```

```
/*-----------------------------------------------*/
/* print_subrange_type    Pretty-print a subrange type:  */
/*                                                */
/*                          (<const1>..<const2>) */
/*-----------------------------------------------*/

print_subrange_type(tp)

    TYPE_STRUCT_PTR tp;          /* type */

{
    print_subrange_limit(tp->info.subrange.min,
                         tp->info.subrange.range_typep);
    emit("..");
    print_subrange_limit(tp->info.subrange.max,
                         tp->info.subrange.range_typep);

}


/*-----------------------------------------------*/
/* print_subrange_limit    Pretty-print a subrange constant */
/*                         limit.                 */
/*-----------------------------------------------*/

print_subrange_limit(limit, range_tp)

    int          limit;
    TYPE_STRUCT_PTR range_tp;

{
    if (range_tp == integer_typep) {
        sprintf(string, "%d", limit);
        emit(string);
    }
    else if (range_tp == char_typep) {
        sprintf(string, "'%c'", limit);
        emit(string);
    }
    else if (range_tp->form == ENUM_FORM) {
        SYMTAB_NODE_PTR idp = range_tp->info.enumeration.const_idp;

        while (limit-- > 0) idp = idp->next;
        emit(idp->name);
    }
}


/*-----------------------------------------------*/
/* print_array_type       Pretty-print an array type:   */
/*                                                */
/*                         ARRAY [<type>] OF       */
/*                         ARRAY [<type>] OF <type> */
/*-----------------------------------------------*/

print_array_type(tp)

    TYPE_STRUCT_PTR tp;            /* type */

{
    int            save_left_margin;  /* current left margin */
    TYPE_STRUCT_PTR index_tp = tp->info.array.index_typep;
    TYPE_STRUCT_PTR elmt_tp  = tp->info.array.elmt_typep;

    set_left_margin(save_left_margin);

    emit("ARRAY [");
    print_type(index_tp, FALSE);
    emit("] OF ");

    if (elmt_tp->type_idp != NULL) print_type(elmt_tp, FALSE);
```

```
    else {
        flush();

        /*
        -- Cascade multidimensional array definitions.
        */
        advance_left_margin();
        indent();
        print_type(elmt_tp, FALSE);
    }

    reset_left_margin(save_left_margin);
}

/*-----------------------------------------------*/
/* print_record_type      Pretty-print a record type:  */
/*                                                */
/*                  RECORD                         */
/*                     <field-list1> : <type>;     */
/*                     <field-list2> : <type>      */
/*                  END                            */
/*-----------------------------------------------*/

print_record_type(tp)

    TYPE_STRUCT_PTR tp;

{
    int            save_left_margin;     /* current left margin */
    BOOLEAN        sublist_done;         /* TRUE iff done */
    SYMTAB_NODE_PTR field_idp = tp->info.record.field_symtab;
    TYPE_STRUCT_PTR common_tp;           /* type of field sublist */

    set_left_margin(save_left_margin);

    emit("RECORD");
    flush();
    advance_left_margin();

    /*
    -- Loop to print field sublists.
    */
    while (field_idp != NULL) {
        indent();
        emit(field_idp->name);
        common_tp = field_idp->typep;

        /*
        -- Loop to print fields of a sublist.
        */
        do {
            field_idp = field_idp->next;
            sublist_done = ((field_idp == NULL) ||
                            (field_idp->typep != common_tp));
            if (!sublist_done) {
                emit(", ");
                emit(field_idp->name);
            }
        } while (!sublist_done);

        emit(" : ");
        print_type(common_tp, FALSE);
        emit(";");
        flush();
    }

    retreat_left_margin();
```

```
        indent();
        emit("END");
        reset_left_margin(save_left_margin);
}

/*------------------------------------------------------*/
/*  analyze_var_decl    Pretty-print a variable declaration: */
/*                                                      */
/*                      VAR                             */
/*                          <id> : <type>;             */
/*------------------------------------------------------*/

analyze_var_decl(var_idp)

    SYMTAB_NODE_PTR var_idp;            /* variable id */

{
    TYPE_STRUCT_PTR common_tp;          /* type of id sublist */
    BOOLEAN         sublist_done;       /* TRUE iff sublist done */
    static SYMTAB_NODE_PTR done_var_idp = NULL;  /* id already
                                            printed */

    if (error_count > 0) return;

    /*
    -- If this variable is part of a sublist that has
    -- already been printed, don't print it again.
    */
    if (var_idp == done_var_idp) {
        done_var_idp = var_idp->next;
```

```
        return;
    }
    else done_var_idp = var_idp->next;

    declaration_keyword(&var_flag, "VAR");
    advance_left_margin();

    indent();
    emit(var_idp->name);
    common_tp = var_idp->typep;

    /*
    -- Loop to print the variables in a sublist.
    */
    do {
        var_idp = var_idp->next;
        sublist_done = (var_idp == NULL);
        if (!sublist_done) {
            emit(", ");
            emit(var_idp->name);
        }
    } while (!sublist_done);

    emit(" : ");
    print_type(common_tp, FALSE);
    emit(";");
    flush();

    retreat_left_margin();
}
```

We pretty-print routine (program, procedure, and function) headers in function analyze_routine_header. We print each header using the current left margin. We print the entire header on one line if there are no formal parameters, if there was a previous forward declaration for the routine, or if the formal parameter lists consists of only one sublist (the parameters all have the same definition and type). This is a "virtual" line, since function emit wraps long lines. Otherwise, we print each parameter sublist on a new line, and we indent the subsequent lines so that they line up just after the opening left parenthesis. If the routine is a function and there wasn't a previous forward declaration for it, we print the function type after the closing right parenthesis. Some examples are:

```
FUNCTION func (VAR ch : char) : real;

PROCEDURE proc (b : boolean;
                VAR x, xx : real;
                y, yy : real);
```

If the header is a forward declaration, we print forward on the line below the header, and indent it from the left margin. Otherwise, we advance the left margin to prepare for pretty-printing the routine's declarations and statements.

We also initialize the global boolean flags const_flag, type_flag, and var_flag to FALSE. These flags make sure that we print the reserved words CONST,

TYPE, and VAR only once for each set of a routine's local declarations. Later, we will call function declaration_keyword to emit one of these reserved words and pass it the corresponding flag to set to TRUE.

We print constant definitions in function analyze_const_defn. Before the first definition, we call declaration_keyword to print CONST on a separate line using the current left margin. We use sprintf to format each constant value. We print definitions on separate lines that we indent from CONST. For example:

```
CONST
    ten = 10;
    pi = 3.14156;
    ch = 'x';
    hello = "Hello, world.";
```

Function analyze_type_defn prints type definitions. Before the first definition, we call declaration_keyword to print TYPE on a separate line using the current left margin. We then print the definitions on the following lines, starting each definition on a new line and indenting it from TYPE. We emit the type identifier followed by =, and then we call function print_type to pretty-print the type specification.

In function print_type, we first check if the type is simply the identifier of a previously-defined type. If so, we emit that identifier. Otherwise, we call the appropriate function to print the type specification.

We print an enumeration type specification on a single line in function print_enum_type. In function print_subrange_type, we print a subrange type specification on a single line, and we call function print_subrange_limit to print each limit of the subrange.

Function print_array_type prints an array type specification. We call print_type recursively to print each index and element type. We print a single-dimensional array type on one line, and multidimensional array types on several lines, one per dimension. We indent the second dimension from the beginning of the ARRAY of the first dimension, and we indent each subsequent dimension similarly from the previous one.

We print a record type specification in function print_record_type. We emit RECORD, print each field sublist starting on a new line, and then call function print_type recursively to print the field type. We indent all the field sublist lines from RECORD. After the last field sublist line, we emit END on a separate line and line it up under RECORD. Examples of pretty-printed type definitions are:

```
TYPE
    e = (alpha, beta, gamma);
    ee = e;
    sr = alpha..gamma;
    cr = 'a'..'x';
    ar1 = ARRAY [1..10] OF integer;
```

```
        ar2 = ARRAY [e] OF
                    ARRAY [sr] OF real;
        ar3 = ARRAY [(fee, fye, foe, fum)] OF
                    ARRAY [sr] OF
                        ARRAY [e] OF boolean;
        rec = RECORD
                    i, j, k : integer;
                    x : real;
                    ch : char;
                    a : ARRAY [sr] OF e;
              END;
```

We call function analyze_var_decl to print a variable declaration. Before the
first definition, we call declaration_keyword to print VAR on a separate line using
the current left margin. We then print the declarations on the following lines,
starting each declaration on a new line and indenting it from VAR.

We call this function once per variable identifier from function var_or_field_
declarations in file decl.c, but we want to print a sublist of variables of the
same type on one line. Therefore, when we call analyze_var_decl for an identifier,
we print not only that identifier, but all the subsequent identifiers in the linked
sublist. To prevent us from printing an identifier in a sublist again, we point static
variable done_var_idp to each identifier. Each time we call the function, we move
done_var_idp to the next identifier in the sublist. If the identifier we pass to the
function is the same as the one done_var_idp points to, we do not print it. Since
done_var_idp is NULL for the first identifier of a sublist, we do print that identifier
and the rest of the sublist. We call print_type recursively to print the type.
Examples of pretty-printed variable declarations are:

```
        VAR
            radius, circumference : real;
            b : boolean;
            letter : 'a'..'z';
            greek : e;
            list : ar1;
```

8.3.2 Pretty-printing statements and expressions

As we discussed before, we only convert the executable statements of a routine's
block to the intermediate form. The scanner does most of the work of converting
a statement's tokens into byte-sized codes, so we need to tell the scanner when
it is scanning the statements. We use a new scanner global, which we now must
declare and initialize at the beginning of file scanner.c:

```
        BOOLEAN block_flag = FALSE;
```

This flag will be TRUE only when we are parsing the statements of a block.

Figure 8-6 shows the new version of function block in file routine.c. We set block_flag to TRUE just before we parse the block's compound statement, and we reset it to FALSE afterwards. We also call function crunch_token to convert the reserved word token BEGIN. (We'll look at this function later.)

FIGURE 8-6   Function block in file routine.c.

```
/*------------------------------------------------------*/        declarations(rtn_idp);
/*  block          Process a block, which consists of    */
/*                 declarations followed by a compound    */        /*
/*                 statement.                             */        -- Error synchronization:  Should be ;
/*------------------------------------------------------*/        */
                                                                   synchronize(follow_decls_list, NULL, NULL);
TOKEN_CODE follow_decls_list[] = {SEMICOLON, BEGIN, END_OF_FILE, 0};    if (token != BEGIN) error(MISSING_BEGIN);

block(rtn_idp)                                                     crunch_token();

    SYMTAB_NODE_PTR rtn_idp;     /* id of program or routine */    block_flag = TRUE;
                                                                   compound_statement();
{                                                                  block_flag = FALSE;
    extern BOOLEAN block_flag;                                 }
```

In the new version of function get_token in file scanner.c shown in Figure 8-7, we test block_flag to decide whether or not to call crunch_token to convert the current token.

FIGURE 8-7   Function get_token in file scanner.c.

```
/*------------------------------------------------------*/        case DIGIT:     get_number();       break;
/*  get_token       Extract the next token from the source */      case QUOTE:     get_string();       break;
/*                  buffer.                                */      case EOF_CODE:  token = END_OF_FILE; break;
/*------------------------------------------------------*/        default:        get_special();      break;
                                                               }
get_token()
                                                                  /*
{                                                                 -- For the interpreter:  While parsing a block, crunch
    skip_blanks();                                                -- the token code and append it to the code buffer.
    tokenp = token_string;                                        */
                                                                  if (block_flag) crunch_token();
    switch (char_code(ch)) {                                   }
        case LETTER:     get_word();            break;
```

Back in Chapter 3, the cruncher utility program entered not only identifiers, but also number and string tokens into the symbol table. We need to do that again here, except that we also enter the literal values. For a number, we set the symbol table node's defn.info.constant.value field to the literal value. We make a copy of a literal string and point the node's info field to the copy. We also set the node's typep field.

When we convert an IDENTIFIER, NUMBER, or STRING token, we want to follow the token code by a pointer to the symbol table node of the token. In this chapter, the pretty-printer only uses the token string from the node's name field. Starting in the next chapter, the literal value will also be useful.

In several functions of the parser module, we now call function crunch_symtab_node_ptr right after we do a symbol table lookup or entry of an identifier, number, or string token. Figures 8-8, 8-9, and 8-10 show new versions of functions statement, for_statement, and case_label, respectively, in file stmt.c. Figures 8-11 and 8-12 show new versions of functions factor and variable, respectively, in file expr.c.

FIGURE 8-8   Function statement in file stmt.c.

```
/*-----------------------------------------------*/
/*  statement       Process a statement by calling the   */
/*                  appropriate parsing routine based on */
/*                  the statement's first token.         */
/*-----------------------------------------------*/

statement()

{
    /*
    -- Call the appropriate routine based on the first
    -- token of the statement.
    */
    switch (token) {

        case IDENTIFIER: {
            SYMTAB_NODE_PTR idp;

            /*
            -- Assignment statement or procedure call?
            */
            search_and_find_all_symtab(idp);

            if (idp->defn.key == PROC_DEFN) {
                crunch_symtab_node_ptr(idp);
                get_token();
                routine_call(idp, TRUE);
            }
            else assignment_statement(idp);

            break;
        }

        case REPEAT:    repeat_statement();     break;
        case WHILE:     while_statement();      break;
        case IF:        if_statement();         break;
        case FOR:       for_statement();        break;
        case CASE:      case_statement();       break;
        case BEGIN:     compound_statement();   break;

    }

    /*
    -- Error synchronization:  Only a semicolon, END, ELSE, or
    --                         UNTIL may follow a statement.
    --                         Check for a missing semicolon.
    */
    synchronize(statement_end_list, statement_start_list, NULL);
    if (token_in(statement_start_list)) error(MISSING_SEMICOLON);
}
```

FIGURE 8-9   Function for_statement in file stmt.c.

```
/*-----------------------------------------------*/
/*  for_statement    Process a FOR statement:          */
/*                                                     */
/*                     FOR <id> := <expr> TO|DOWNTO <expr> */
/*                        DO <stmt>                     */
/*-----------------------------------------------*/

for_statement()

{
    SYMTAB_NODE_PTR for_idp;
    TYPE_STRUCT_PTR for_tp, expr_tp;

    get_token();

    if (token == IDENTIFIER) {
        search_and_find_all_symtab(for_idp);
        crunch_symtab_node_ptr(for_idp);

        if ((for_idp->level != level) ||
            (for_idp->defn.key != VAR_DEFN))
            error(INVALID_FOR_CONTROL);

        for_tp = base_type(for_idp->typep);
        get_token();

        if ((for_tp != integer_typep) &&
            (for_tp != char_typep) &&
```

```
        (for_tp->form != ENUM_FORM)) error(INCOMPATIBLE_TYPES);
}
else {
    error(IDENTIFIER, MISSING_IDENTIFIER);
    for_tp = &dummy_type;
}

if_token_get_else_error(COLONEQUAL, MISSING_COLONEQUAL);

expr_tp = expression();
if (! is_assign_type_compatible(for_tp, expr_tp))
```

```
        error(INCOMPATIBLE_TYPES);

if ((token == TO) || (token == DOWNTO)) get_token();
else error(MISSING_TO_OR_DOWNTO);

expr_tp = expression();
if (! is_assign_type_compatible(for_tp, expr_tp))
    error(INCOMPATIBLE_TYPES);

if_token_get_else_error(DO, MISSING_DO);
statement();
}
```

FIGURE 8-10   Function `case_label` in file `stmt.c`.

```
/*-----------------------------------------------------------*/
/* case_label              Process a CASE label and return a */
/*                         pointer to its type structure.    */
/*-----------------------------------------------------------*/

    TYPE_STRUCT_PTR
case_label()

{
    TOKEN_CODE      sign     = PLUS;    /* unary + or - sign */
    BOOLEAN         saw_sign = FALSE;   /* TRUE iff unary sign */
    TYPE_STRUCT_PTR label_tp;

    /*
    -- Unary + or - sign.
    */
    if ((token == PLUS) || (token == MINUS)) {
        sign     = token;
        saw_sign = TRUE;
        get_token();
    }

    /*
    -- Numeric constant:  Integer type only.
    */
    if (token == NUMBER) {
        SYMTAB_NODE_PTR np = search_symtab(token_string,
                                    symtab_display[1]);

        if (np == NULL) np = enter_symtab(token_string,
                                    symtab_display[1]);
        crunch_symtab_node_ptr(np);

        if (literal.type == REAL_LIT) error(INVALID_CONSTANT);
        return(integer_typep);
    }

    /*
    -- Identifier constant:  Integer, character, or enumeration
    --                       types only.
    */
    else if (token == IDENTIFIER) {
        SYMTAB_NODE_PTR idp;

        search_all_symtab(idp);
        crunch_symtab_node_ptr(idp);

        if (idp == NULL) {
```

```
            error(UNDEFINED_IDENTIFIER);
            return(&dummy_type);
        }

        else if (idp->defn.key != CONST_DEFN) {
            error(NOT_A_CONSTANT_IDENTIFIER);
            return(&dummy_type);
        }

        else if (idp->typep == integer_typep)
            return(integer_typep);

        else if (idp->typep == char_typep) {
            if (saw_sign) error(INVALID_CONSTANT);
            return(char_typep);
        }

        else if (idp->typep->form == ENUM_FORM) {
            if (saw_sign) error(INVALID_CONSTANT);
            return(idp->typep);
        }

        else return(&dummy_type);
    }

    /*
    -- String constant:  Character type only.
    */
    else if (token == STRING) {
        SYMTAB_NODE_PTR np = search_symtab(token_string,
                                        symtab_display[1]);

        if (np == NULL) np = enter_symtab(token_string,
                                        symtab_display[1]);
        crunch_symtab_node_ptr(np);

        if (saw_sign) error(INVALID_CONSTANT);

        if (strlen(literal.value.string) == 1) return(char_typep);
        else {
            error(INVALID_CONSTANT);
            return(&dummy_type);
        }
    }

    else {
```

```
        error(INVALID_CONSTANT);
        return(&dummy_type);
    }
}
```

FIGURE 8-11   Function `factor` in file `expr.c`.

```
/*----------------------------------------------------------*/
/*  factor            Process a factor, which is a variable, */
/*                    a number, NOT followed by a factor, or */
/*                    a parenthesized subexpression.  Return */
/*                    a pointer to the type structure.       */
/*----------------------------------------------------------*/

    TYPE_STRUCT_PTR
factor()

{
    TYPE_STRUCT_PTR tp;

    switch (token) {

        case IDENTIFIER: {
            SYMTAB_NODE_PTR idp;

            search_and_find_all_symtab(idp);

            switch (idp->defn.key) {

                case FUNC_DEFN:
                    crunch_symtab_node_ptr(idp);
                    get_token();
                    tp = routine_call(idp, TRUE);
                    break;

                case PROC_DEFN:
                    error(INVALID_IDENTIFIER_USAGE);
                    get_token();
                    actual_parm_list(idp, FALSE);
                    tp = &dummy_type;
                    break;

                case CONST_DEFN:
                    crunch_symtab_node_ptr(idp);
                    get_token();
                    tp = idp->typep;
                    break;

                default:
                    tp = variable(idp, EXPR_USE);
                    break;
            }

            break;
        }

        case NUMBER: {
            SYMTAB_NODE_PTR np;

            np = search_symtab(token_string, symtab_display[1]);
            if (np == NULL) np = enter_symtab(token_string,
                                              symtab_display[1]);
```

```
            if (literal.type == INTEGER_LIT) {
                tp = np->typep = integer_typep;
                np->defn.info.constant.value.integer =
                    literal.value.integer;
            }
            else {  /* literal.type == REAL_LIT */
                tp = np->typep = real_typep;
                np->defn.info.constant.value.real =
                    literal.value.real;
            }

            crunch_symtab_node_ptr(np);
            get_token();

            break;
        }

        case STRING: {
            SYMTAB_NODE_PTR np;
            int             length = strlen(literal.value.string);

            np = search_symtab(token_string, symtab_display[1]);
            if (np == NULL) np = enter_symtab(token_string,
                                              symtab_display[1]);

            if (length == 1) {
                np->defn.info.constant.value.character =
                    literal.value.string[0];
                tp = char_typep;
            }
            else {
                np->typep = tp = make_string_typep(length);
                np->info  = alloc_bytes(length + 1);
                strcpy(np->info, literal.value.string);
            }

            crunch_symtab_node_ptr(np);

            get_token();
            break;
        }

        case NOT:
            get_token();
            tp = factor();
            break;

        case LPAREN:
            get_token();
            tp = expression();

            if_token_get_else_error(RPAREN, MISSING_RPAREN);
            break;

        default:
```

```
        error(INVALID_EXPRESSION);
        tp = &dummy_type;
        break;

    }

    return(tp);
}
```

FIGURE 8-12   Function `variable` in file `expr.c`.

```
/*-----------------------------------------------*/
/*  variable        Process a variable, which can be a     */
/*                  simple identifier, an array identifier */
/*                  with subscripts, or a record identifier */
/*                  with fields.                           */
/*-----------------------------------------------*/

    TYPE_STRUCT_PTR
variable(var_idp, use)

    SYMTAB_NODE_PTR var_idp;    /* variable id */
    USE             use;        /* how variable is used */

{
    TYPE_STRUCT_PTR tp          = var_idp->typep;
    DEFN_KEY        defn_key     = var_idp->defn.key;
    TYPE_STRUCT_PTR array_subscript_list();
    TYPE_STRUCT_PTR record_field();

    crunch_symtab_node_ptr(var_idp);

    /*
    -- Check the variable's definition.
    */
    switch (defn_key) {
        case VAR_DEFN:
        case VALPARM_DEFN:
        case VARPARM_DEFN:
        case FUNC_DEFN:
```

```
        case UNDEFINED:  break;        /* OK */

        default: {                     /* error */
            tp = &dummy_type;
            error(INVALID_IDENTIFIER_USAGE);
        }

    }

    get_token();

    /*
    -- There must not be a parameter list, but if there is one,
    -- parse it anyway for error recovery.
    */
    if (token == LPAREN) {
        error(UNEXPECTED_TOKEN);
        actual_parm_list(var_idp, FALSE);
        return(tp);
    }

    /*
    -- Subscripts and/or field designators?
    */
    while ((token == LBRACKET) || (token == PERIOD)) {
        tp = token == LBRACKET ? array_subscript_list(tp)
                               : record_field(tp);
    }

    return(tp);
}
```

We manipulate the intermediate form to pretty-print the statements and expressions in file `ppstmt.c`, shown in Figure 8-13. There, we see again the string array `symbol_strings`.

FIGURE 8-13   File `ppstmt.c`.

```
/***************************************************************/
/*                                                             */
/*      Pretty-print statements.                               */
/*                                                             */
/*      FILE:       ppstmt.c                                   */
/*                                                             */
/***************************************************************/

#include <stdio.h>
```

```
#include "common.h"
#include "error.h"
#include "symtab.h"
#include "scanner.h"
#include "pprint.h"

#define MAX_CODE_BUFFER_SIZE 4096
```

```
/*------------------------------------------------*/
/*  Externals                                     */
/*------------------------------------------------*/

extern TOKEN_CODE token;
extern TOKEN_CODE ctoken;

extern int  left_margin;
extern char pprint_buffer[];
extern int  error_count;

extern char *code_buffer;
extern char *code_bufferp;
extern char *code_segmentp;
extern char *code_segment_limit;

/*------------------------------------------------*/
/*  Globals                                       */
/*------------------------------------------------*/

char *symbol_strings[] = {
    "<no token>", "<IDENTIFIER>", "<NUMBER>", "<STRING>",
    "^", "*", "(", ")", "-", "+", "=", "[", "]", ":", ",",
    "<", ">", ";", ".", "/", ":=", "<=", ">=", "<>", "..",
    "<END OF FILE>", "<ERROR>",
    "AND", "ARRAY", "BEGIN", "CASE", "CONST", "DIV", "DO", "DOWNTO",
    "ELSE", "END", "FILE", "FOR", "FUNCTION", "GOTO", "IF", "IN",
    "LABEL", "MOD", "NIL", "NOT", "OF", "OR", "PACKED", "PROCEDURE",
    "PROGRAM", "RECORD", "REPEAT", "SET", "THEN", "TO", "TYPE",
    "UNTIL", "VAR", "WHILE", "WITH",
};

            /********************************/
            /*                              */
            /*      Code segment routines   */
            /*                              */
            /********************************/

/*------------------------------------------------*/
/*  crunch_token        Append the token code to the code   */
/*                      buffer.  Called by the scanner routine  */
/*                      get_token only while parsing a block.   */
/*------------------------------------------------*/

crunch_token()

{
    char token_code = token;    /* byte-sized token code */

    if (code_bufferp >= code_buffer + MAX_CODE_BUFFER_SIZE) {
        error(CODE_SEGMENT_OVERFLOW);
        exit(-CODE_SEGMENT_OVERFLOW);
    }
    else *code_bufferp++ = token_code;
}

/*------------------------------------------------*/
/*  crunch_symtab_node_ptr     Append a symbol table node   */
/*                             pointer to the code buffer.  */
/*------------------------------------------------*/

crunch_symtab_node_ptr(np)

    SYMTAB_NODE_PTR np;         /* pointer to append */

{
    SYMTAB_NODE_PTR *npp = (SYMTAB_NODE_PTR *) code_bufferp;
```

```
    if (code_bufferp >= code_buffer + MAX_CODE_BUFFER_SIZE
                                    - sizeof(SYMTAB_NODE_PTR)) {
        error(CODE_SEGMENT_OVERFLOW);
        exit(-CODE_SEGMENT_OVERFLOW);
    }
    else {
        *npp = np;
        code_bufferp += sizeof(SYMTAB_NODE_PTR);
    }
}

/*------------------------------------------------*/
/*  create_code_segment   Create a code segment and copy in  */
/*                        the contents of the code buffer.   */
/*                        Reset the code buffer pointer.     */
/*                        Return a pointer to the segment.   */
/*------------------------------------------------*/

    char *
create_code_segment()

{
    char *code_segment = alloc_bytes(code_bufferp - code_buffer);

    code_segment_limit = code_segment + (code_bufferp - code_buffer);
    code_bufferp       = code_buffer;
    code_segmentp      = code_segment;

    /*
    -- Copy in the contents of the code buffer.
    */
    while (code_segmentp != code_segment_limit)
        *code_segmentp++ = *code_bufferp++;

    code_bufferp = code_buffer;         /* reset code buffer ptr */
    return(code_segment);
}

/*------------------------------------------------*/
/*  get_ctoken           Extract the next token code from the  */
/*                       current code segment.                 */
/*------------------------------------------------*/

#define get_ctoken()    ctoken = *code_segmentp++

/*------------------------------------------------*/
/*  get_symtab_cptr      Extract a symbol table node pointer   */
/*                       from the current code segment and     */
/*                       return it.                            */
/*------------------------------------------------*/

    SYMTAB_NODE_PTR
get_symtab_cptr()

{
    SYMTAB_NODE_PTR np;
    SYMTAB_NODE_PTR *npp = (SYMTAB_NODE_PTR *) code_segmentp;

    np = *npp;
    code_segmentp += sizeof(SYMTAB_NODE_PTR);
    return(np);
}

            /****************************************/
            /*                                      */
            /*      Pretty-printing routines        */
            /*                                      */
```

```
                    /****************************************/
/*----------------------------------------------------------*/
/*  analyze_block        Pretty-print the code segment of    */
/*                       a block.                            */
/*----------------------------------------------------------*/

analyze_block(code_segment)

    char *code_segment;

{
    if (error_count > 0) return;

    code_segmentp = code_segment;
    emit(" ");
    flush();

    get_ctoken();
    print_statement();        /* should be a compound statement */
    retreat_left_margin();

    /*
    -- Output any trailing semicolons or period.
    */
    while (code_segmentp <= code_segment_limit) {
        indent();
        emit(symbol_strings[token]);
        flush();
        get_ctoken();
    }
}

/*----------------------------------------------------------*/
/*  print_statement     Call the appropriate statement printing */
/*                      routine.                             */
/*----------------------------------------------------------*/

print_statement()

{
    indent();

    switch (ctoken) {
        case IDENTIFIER:  print_assign_or_call_statement();  break;
        case BEGIN:       print_compound_statement();        break;
        case CASE:        print_case_statement();            break;
        case FOR:         print_for_statement();             break;
        case IF:          print_if_statement();              break;
        case REPEAT:      print_repeat_statement();          break;
        case WHILE:       print_while_statement();           break;
    }

    while (ctoken == SEMICOLON) {
        emit(";");
        get_ctoken();
    }

    flush();
}

/*----------------------------------------------------------*/
/*  print_assign_or_call_statement    Pretty-print an assign- */
/*                                    ment or procedure call  */
/*                                    statement:              */
/*                                                            */
/*                                    <variable> := <expr>    */
```

```
/*                             <id>(<parm-list)       */
/*----------------------------------------------------------*/

print_assign_or_call_statement()

{
    print_identifier();

    if (ctoken == COLONEQUAL) {
        emit(" := ");
        get_ctoken();
        print_expression();
    }
}

/*----------------------------------------------------------*/
/*  print_compound_statement     Pretty-print a compound    */
/*                               statement:                 */
/*                                                          */
/*                               BEGIN                      */
/*                                   <stmt-list>            */
/*                               END                        */
/*----------------------------------------------------------*/

print_compound_statement()

{
    emit("BEGIN");
    flush();
    advance_left_margin();

    get_ctoken();
    while (ctoken != END) print_statement();

    retreat_left_margin();
    indent();
    emit("END");
    get_ctoken();
}

/*----------------------------------------------------------*/
/*  print_case_statement     Pretty-print a CASE statement:  */
/*                                                           */
/*                             CASE <expr> OF                */
/*                                 <const-list> : <stmt>     */
/*                                 ...                       */
/*                             END                           */
/*----------------------------------------------------------*/

print_case_statement()

{
    emit("CASE ");

    get_ctoken();
    print_expression();
    emit(" OF ");
    flush();
    advance_left_margin();

    get_ctoken();

    /*
    -- Loop to print CASE branches.
    */
    do {
        indent();
```

```
    /*
    -- Loop to print each constant
    -- in the constant list.
    */
    do {
        print_expression();
        if (ctoken == COMMA) {
            emit(", ");
            get_ctoken();
        }
    } while (ctoken != COLON);

    emit(":");
    flush();
    advance_left_margin();

    get_ctoken();
    print_statement();
    retreat_left_margin();
} while (ctoken != END);

    retreat_left_margin();
    indent();
    emit("END");
    get_ctoken();
}

/*------------------------------------------------------------*/
/*  print_for_statement     Pretty print a FOR statement:     */
/*                                                            */
/*                          FOR <id> := <expr> TO|DOWNTO      */
/*                              <expr> DO <stmt>              */
/*------------------------------------------------------------*/

print_for_statement()

{
    emit("FOR ");

    get_ctoken();
    print_identifier();
    emit(" := ");

    get_ctoken();
    print_expression();
    emit(ctoken == TO ? " TO " : " DOWNTO ");

    get_ctoken();
    print_expression();
    emit(" DO ");
    flush();

    advance_left_margin();
    get_ctoken();
    print_statement();
    retreat_left_margin();
}

/*------------------------------------------------------------*/
/*  print_if_statement        Pretty-print an IF statement:   */
/*                                                            */
/*                            IF <expr> THEN                   */
/*                                <stmt>                       */
/*                                                            */
/*                            IF <expr> THEN                   */
/*                                <stmt>                       */
/*                            ELSE                             */
```

```
/*                          <stmt>                   */
/*------------------------------------------------------------*/

print_if_statement()

{
    emit("IF ");

    get_ctoken();
    print_expression();
    emit(" THEN");
    flush();

    advance_left_margin();
    get_ctoken();
    print_statement();
    retreat_left_margin();

    if (ctoken == ELSE) {
        indent();
        emit("ELSE");
        flush();

        advance_left_margin();
        get_ctoken();
        print_statement();
        retreat_left_margin();
    }
}

/*------------------------------------------------------------*/
/*  print_repeat_statement    Pretty-print a REPEAT           */
/*                            statement:                      */
/*                                                            */
/*                            REPEAT                          */
/*                                <stmt-list>                 */
/*                            UNTIL <expr>                    */
/*------------------------------------------------------------*/

print_repeat_statement()

{
    emit("REPEAT");
    flush();
    advance_left_margin();

    get_ctoken();
    while (ctoken != UNTIL) print_statement();

    retreat_left_margin();
    indent();
    emit("UNTIL ");

    get_ctoken();
    print_expression();
}

/*------------------------------------------------------------*/
/*  print_while_statement    Pretty-print a WHILE statement:  */
/*                                                            */
/*                            WHILE <expr> DO                  */
/*                                <stmt>                       */
/*------------------------------------------------------------*/

print_while_statement()

{
```

```
    emit("WHILE ");

    get_ctoken();
    print_expression();

    emit(" DO");
    flush();
    advance_left_margin();

    get_ctoken();
    print_statement();
    retreat_left_margin();
}

/*------------------------------------------------------------*/
/*  print_expression            Pretty-print an expression.   */
/*------------------------------------------------------------*/

print_expression()

{
    BOOLEAN done = FALSE;        /* TRUE at end of expression */

    do {
        switch (ctoken) {
            case IDENTIFIER:    print_identifier();             break;
            case NUMBER:        print_number();                 break;
            case STRING:        print_string();                 break;

            case PLUS:      emit("+");      get_ctoken();   break;
            case MINUS:     emit("-");      get_ctoken();   break;
            case STAR:      emit("*");      get_ctoken();   break;
            case SLASH:     emit("/");      get_ctoken();   break;
            case DIV:       emit(" DIV ");  get_ctoken();   break;
            case MOD:       emit(" MOD ");  get_ctoken();   break;
            case AND:       emit(" AND ");  get_ctoken();   break;
            case OR:        emit(" OR ");   get_ctoken();   break;
            case EQUAL:     emit(" = ");    get_ctoken();   break;
            case NE:        emit(" <> ");   get_ctoken();   break;
            case LT:        emit(" < ");    get_ctoken();   break;
            case LE:        emit(" <= ");   get_ctoken();   break;
            case GT:        emit(" > ");    get_ctoken();   break;
            case GE:        emit(" >= ");   get_ctoken();   break;
            case NOT:       emit("NOT ");   get_ctoken();   break;

            case LPAREN:
                emit("(");
                get_ctoken();
                print_expression();
                emit(")");
                get_ctoken();
                break;

            default:
                done = TRUE;
                break;
        }
    } while (!done);
}

/*------------------------------------------------------------*/
/*  print_identifier      Pretty-print an identifier, which   */
/*                        can be a variable or a procedure    */
/*                        or function call.                   */
/*------------------------------------------------------------*/
```

```
print_identifier()

{
    SYMTAB_NODE_PTR idp = get_symtab_cptr();

    emit(idp->name);
    get_ctoken();

    /*
    -- Loop to print any following modifiers.
    */
    while ((ctoken == LBRACKET) || (ctoken == LPAREN) ||
           (ctoken == PERIOD)) {
        /*
        -- Subscripts or actual parameters.
        */
        if ((ctoken == LBRACKET) || (ctoken == LPAREN)) {
            emit(ctoken == LBRACKET ? "[" : "(");
            get_ctoken();
            while ((ctoken != RBRACKET) && (ctoken != RPAREN)) {
                print_expression();
                while (ctoken == COLON) {
                    emit(":");
                    get_ctoken();
                    print_expression();
                }
                if (ctoken == COMMA) {
                    emit(", ");
                    get_ctoken();
                }
            }
            emit(ctoken == RBRACKET ? "]" : ")");
            get_ctoken();
        }

        /*
        -- Record fields.
        */
        else /* ctoken == DOT */ {
            emit(".");
            get_ctoken();
            print_identifier();
        }
    }
}

/*------------------------------------------------------------*/
/*  print_number             Pretty-print a number.          */
/*------------------------------------------------------------*/

print_number()

{
    SYMTAB_NODE_PTR idp = get_symtab_cptr();

    emit(idp->name);
    get_ctoken();
}

/*------------------------------------------------------------*/
/*  print_string             Pretty-print a string.          */
/*------------------------------------------------------------*/

print_string()
```

```
{
    SYMTAB_NODE_PTR idp = get_symtab_cptr();
    emit(idp->name);
    get_ctoken();
}
```

Global variable code_buffer contains a block's executable statements in their intermediate form. We reuse this buffer for every block, but after we are done parsing a block (as we saw in functions program and routine), we call function create_code_segment to copy the contents of the code buffer into the routine's code segment. Global pointer variables code_bufferp and code_segmentp point into the code buffer and the code segment, respectively, and code_segment_limit points to the end of the code segment. Global TOKEN_CODE variable ctoken is similar to variable token, except that its value is obtained from the intermediate code in the current code segment.

In functions crunch_token and crunch_symtab_node_ptr, we append a token code and a pointer to a symbol table node to the code buffer, after first checking for an overflow. The byte-sized token code is from the scanner's TOKEN_CODE enumeration type.

As we saw earlier, we call function create_code_segment after we have already parsed and converted a block. We allocate a code segment and copy the contents of the code buffer into the segment. We then reset the code buffer pointer to the beginning and return the pointer to the code segment.

We call macro get_ctoken to set ctoken to the next token code in the current code segment. We call function get_symtab_cptr to retrieve a pointer to a symbol table node.

In function analyze_block, we print the compound statement of a block by calling function print_statement. Afterwards, since we are at the end of a routine, we call retreat_left_margin. We then simply emit any remaining tokens (usually a semicolon or the final period). In function print_statement, we call the appropriate pretty-printing function for the statement, and then we emit any trailing semicolons.

We print an assignment statement or a procedure call in function print_assign_or_call_statement. We call function print_identifier, and then, for an assignment statement, we emit := and call function print_expression.

In function print_compound_statement, we print a compound statement using the format:

```
BEGIN
    <stmt-1>;
    <stmt-2>;
    ...
    <stmt-n>
END
```

In function `print_case_statement`, we print a CASE statement using the format:

```
CASE <expr> OF
    <label-list-1> : <stmt-1>;
    <label-list-2> : <stmt-2>;
    ...
    <label-list-n> : <stmt-n>
END
```

In function `print_for_statement`, we print a FOR statement using the format:

```
FOR <id> := <expr-1> TO <expr-2> DO
    <stmt>
```

(The TO may instead be DOWNTO.)

In function `print_if_statement`, we print an IF statement using either the format:

```
IF <expr> THEN
    <stmt>
```

or the format:

```
IF <expr> THEN
    <stmt-1>
ELSE
    <stmt-2>
```

In function `print_repeat_statement`, we print a REPEAT statement using the format:

```
REPEAT
    <stmt-1>;
    <stmt-2>;
    ...
    <stmt-n>
UNTIL <expr>
```

Finally, in function `print_while_statement`, we print a WHILE statement using the format:

```
WHILE <expr> DO
    <stmt>
```

We print an expression in function print_expression. We simply loop to retrieve tokens from the current code segment that belong to an expression and emit each one. Whenever we retrieve a left parenthesis, we call the function recursively.

In function print_identifier, we print an identifier and any following modifiers, such as array subscripts, record field designators, and actual parameter lists. We call function get_symtab_cptr to retrieve the pointer to the identifier's symbol table node. Here, we also print the field width and precision designators of the actual arguments for calls to write and writeln.

We print a number and a string, respectively, in functions print_number and print_string. In both functions, we call get_symtab_cptr to retrieve the pointer to the token's symbol table node so that we can get back the token string.

The pretty-printer has done almost all of the work of translating a source program into an intermediate form for the interpreter. Figure 8-14 shows sample output. Now we're ready to start executing!

FIGURE 8-14   Sample output from the pretty-printer.

```
PROGRAM graph (output);                                        BEGIN
                                                                   write(' ':n, '*');
    CONST                                                          IF h-n-1 > 0 THEN
        d = 0.0625;                                                    write(' ':h-n-1);
        s = 32;                                                    writeln('|')
        h = 34;                                                END
        c = 6.28318;                                        ELSE
        lim = 32;                                               IF n > h THEN
                                                                   BEGIN
    VAR                                                                write(' ':h, '|');
        x, y : real;                                                  IF n-h-1 > 0 THEN
        i, n : integer;                                                   write(' ':n-h-1);
                                                                      writeln('*')
    BEGIN                                                          END
        i := 0;                                                 ELSE
        WHILE i <= lim DO                                          writeln(' ':n, '*');
            BEGIN                                               i := i+1;
                x := d*i;                                   END;
                y := exp(-x)*sin(c*x);
                n := round(s*y)+h;                      END
                IF n < h THEN
```

Questions and exercises

1. Make the pretty-printer smarter about when to use more than one line. For example, on a single line, it should be able to print the following IF statement:

```
IF p THEN a := b
```

2. Why is it necessary for function `print_expression` to call itself recursively when it encounters a left parenthesis? Why not simply print parentheses like the other expression tokens?

3. The scanner removes all comments. Implement a reasonable algorithm for pretty-printing comments.

4. When two types are equated, as in:

$$\text{TYPE type1 = type2}$$

then, wherever type2 is used in the source program, the pretty-printer replaces it with type1. Fix this problem.

5. Experiment with other intermediate forms, such as a tree-structured form.

CHAPTER 9

Interpreting Procedures, Functions, and Assignment Statements

In this chapter, we finally begin to write the executor module of the interpreter. We will be able to execute assignment statements and calls to procedures and functions, and we'll see how the interpreter manages the resources in its runtime environment. Above all, we will lay a good foundation for the next chapter, where we'll complete the interpreter and then be able to execute entire Pascal programs.

To help us understand how the interpreter executes statements and manages resources, the executor routines in this chapter will print out tracing information as the interpreter executes each statement, fetches and stores data, and enters and exits procedures and functions. In this chapter, we will develop the skills to:

- maintain the runtime stack
- execute procedure and function calls
- execute expressions and assignment statements
- flag runtime errors
- print runtime tracing information

9.1 The runtime stack

In the previous chapters, you saw how to manage various resources like the symbol table and the code segments. When an interpreter executes a program, it manages another major resource, the runtime stack. You were first introduced to this resource by the calculator in Chapter 4.

While the interpreter executes a program, the stack does more than merely provide a place to evaluate expressions. As we will see, at any point during the execution of a program, the stack represents a "snapshot" of the state of the program. The stack contains information about which procedures and functions have been called, their return addresses, the current values of all the parameters and local variables, and which of these values are currently accessible.

9.1.1   Allocating parameters and local variables

In our calculator, we used the runtime stack to store intermediate values as we evaluated an expression. We kept the current value of each variable in its symbol table node. This won't do for a Pascal interpreter because you can call procedures and functions recursively. When you call a procedure recursively, the old set of values for its parameters and local variables must be stored to make way for the new set of values. This new set of values becomes current and is used during the recursive execution of the procedure, while the old set of values is unavailable. When the recursive call returns, the new set of values must be discarded and the old set of values must again become current and available.

It makes sense to keep the current values of parameters and local variables not in the symbol table, but on the runtime stack. Whenever you call a procedure or a function, you can allocate space on top of the stack to store the values. Then when you return from the routine, you pop the values off. If the call is recursive, you allocate a new set of values on top of the old set, and when you return from the call, you pop off those values to uncover the old values. So now, the symbol table node for a parameter or local variable keeps track of where its current value is stored on the stack.

In this scheme, you can consider the global variables to be local to the program itself, so you allocate their values at the bottom of the stack when you start to execute the program.

One further note. We will assume that the stack items for our interpreter's runtime stack are all one size. Each item can contain an integer, real, character, or enumeration value, or an address. Whenever we want to allocate an array or record value, we allocate space for that variable's data area elsewhere and place a pointer to the data area on the stack.

9.1.2 Stack frames

So now you have two uses for the runtime stack: to store the current values of the parameters and local variables of a routine while it is executing, and to store the intermediate results when you evaluate an expression. An interpreter also uses its runtime stack to keep track of where to return to and (for functions) the return values. It also keeps information on the stack that enables it to legitimately access nonlocal values according to Pascal's scope rules. All this information, except for the intermediate results, is arranged in *stack frames*.

You allocate a stack frame for the program itself at the bottom of the runtime stack when you first begin to execute the program. Then you allocate a stack frame on top of the stack each time you call a procedure or function. You can then use the stack space above the topmost stack frame for keeping intermediate results when you evaluate an expression.

Figure 9-1 shows the interpreter's stack frame. The first item is at the *stack frame base*, and it is for the return value of a function. (Procedures allocate the return value item for consistency but do not use it.) This is followed by items for a static link, a dynamic link, and the return address. These four items make up the *stack frame header*. Above the header, you allocate items to store the current value for each of the routine's parameters, and on top of that you allocate items for the values of each of its local variables. The static and dynamic links point back to previous stack frames. (We will explain these links later.)

A routine's stack frame contains the current set of values for its parameters and local variables. If you call a routine recursively, you allocate a new stack frame for each call, and the current set of values is in its topmost stack frame.

The number of items in each stack frame header is constant. The number of parameters and the number of local variables of a procedure or function never

---

FIGURE 9-1   The interpreter's stack frame. The top four items constitute the stack frame header.

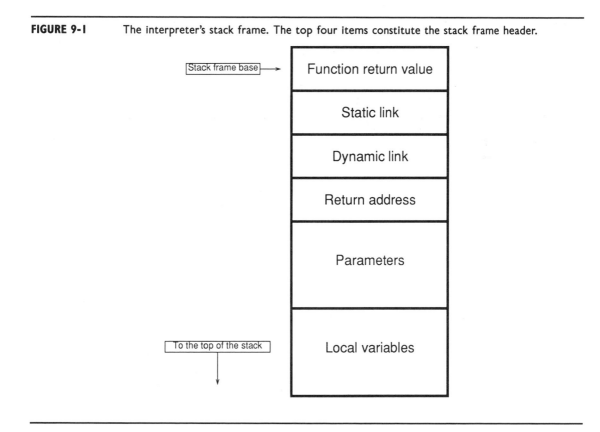

changes. Therefore, if each time you allocate a stack frame for a routine, you allocate the items for the parameters and local variables in the same order (which is reasonable to do), then the offset from the stack frame base to a particular parameter or local variable is always the same. You can store this offset in the symbol table entry so that you can always access the current value of any parameter or local variable. You just get its offset from the symbol table, and the value is in the stack item at that offset from the base of the routine's current stack frame. Figure 9-2 shows the stack frame for a procedure that has several parameters and local variables.

9.1.3 Dynamic links

The dynamic link of a stack frame simply points back to the base of the previous stack frame. In other words, the stack frame of a routine points back to the stack frame of its caller.

When you return from a procedure or a function, the dynamic link enables you to restore the stack to its state when the routine was called. You can pop off the routine's stack frame, so that the stack frame of the caller is again on top.

FIGURE 9-2   The stack frame for a procedure with two parameters p1 and p2, and three local variables i, j, and k. The stack items are all the same size, and the item for each parameter and variable is always at the same offset from the stack frame base. For example, the item for this procedure's local variable i is always at offset +6 from the base.

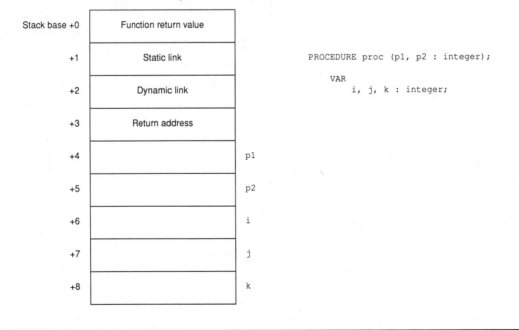

```
PROCEDURE proc (p1, p2 : integer);

    VAR
        i, j, k : integer;
```

When you return from a procedure, you simply reset the top of stack pointer to the item just below the procedure's stack frame base. This puts the pointer back to where it was just before the call. When you return from a function, you reset the top of stack pointer to the item at the base of the function's stack frame. This has the effect of pushing the function return value onto the stack for the caller to use.

9.1.4   Static links

The static link of a routine's stack frame points back to the base of the stack frame of the routine that it is immediately contained in. For example, suppose procedure p1 contains procedure p2 in the source program, and p2 is currently executing. Then, the static link of p2's stack frame points back to the base of p1's stack frame. Thus, while the dynamic links are determined by who *calls* whom at runtime, the static links are determined by who *contains* whom in the source program.

Figure 9-3 shows a program with a nontrivial nesting structure. Figure 9-4 shows how the dynamic and static links change as the program's procedures and functions call each other. As you can see, the dynamic links (drawn on the left) always point back to the stack frame of the caller. The static links are more interesting to watch.

FIGURE 9-3   The outline of a program with nested procedures and functions.

```
PROGRAM main1                                    PROCEDURE proc2

    FUNCTION func2                                   PROCEDURE proc3

        FUNCTION func3                                   BEGIN {proc3}
                                                            ...
            BEGIN {func3}
                ...                                      END

            END                                      BEGIN {proc2}
                                                        ...
        BEGIN {func2}
            ...                                      END

        END                                      BEGIN {main1}
                                                    ...
                                                 END.
```

In Figure 9-4a, when main calls proc2, proc2's static link points back to main's stack frame, since main immediately contains proc2. Similarly, in Figure 9-4b, when proc2 calls proc3, proc3's static link points back to proc2's stack frame, since proc2 immediately contains proc3. Suppose proc3 recursively calls itself. Then, as in Figure 9-4c, the static link in proc3's new stack frame also points back to proc2's stack frame.

FIGURE 9-4   How the runtime stack changes during the execution of the program shown in Figure 9-3. In each stack diagram, we draw the dynamic links on the left and the static links on the right. Each link actually points to the base of a previous stack frame. The stack grows downward in this figure, so the top of the stack is at the bottom of each diagram.

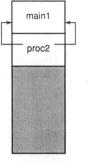

a. main1 > proc2

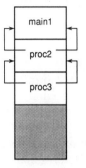

b. main1 > proc2 > proc3

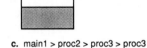

c. main1 > proc2 > proc3 > proc3

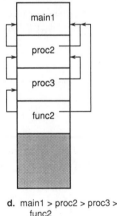

d. main1 > proc2 > proc3 >
        func2

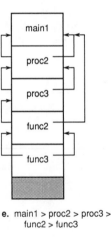

e. main1 > proc2 > proc3 >
        func2 > func3

When proc3 returns from the recursive call, the runtime stack resets to its previous state, as we saw in Figure 9-4b. In Figure 9-4d, proc3 then calls func2, and func2's static link points back to main's stack frame, since main immediately contains func2. Finally, in Figure 9-4e, when func2 calls func3, func3's static link points back to func2's stack frame, since func2 immediately contains func3.

That is a bit of work to keep track of the static links, and what are they good for? The static links enable us to access nonlocal values. In Figure 9-4e, you are executing func3. Certainly, you can access func3's parameter and local variable values, since they are all allocated in func3's stack frame. If you follow the static link back to func2's stack frame, you can also access func2's values. Then if you follow the static link from func2's stack frame back to main's stack frame, you can access main's values. However, from func3, you cannot access any of proc3's or proc2's values. If you look again at Figure 9-3, you see that you are following Pascal's scope rules. Similarly, in Figure 9-4c, from proc3's second invocation, you cannot access the values from its first invocation.

So, you see that accessing nonlocal values is slower than accessing local values, since you have to follow static links to get to them. How much slower depends on how many links you follow.

9.2 Organization of the interpreter

Now we are ready to start writing the routines to do all this. Let's start with a look at the overall organization our interpreter thus far.

Parser Module

parser.h	*u*	Parser header file
routine.c	*c*	Parse programs, procedures, and functions
standard.c	*u*	Parse standard procedures and functions
decl.c	*c*	Parse declarations
stmt.c	*c*	Parse statements
expr.c	*u*	Parse expressions

Scanner Module

scanner.h	*u*	Scanner header file
scanner.c	*u*	Scanner routines

Symbol Table Module

symtab.h	*u*	Symbol table header file
symtab.c	*u*	Symbol table routines

Executor Module

exec.h	*n*	Executor header file
executil.c	*n*	Executor utility routines
execstmt.c	*n*	Execute statements
execexpr.c	*n*	Execute expressions

Error Module

error.h	*c*	Error header file
error.c	*c*	Error routines

Miscellaneous

common.h	*c*	Common header file

Where: *u* file unchanged from the previous chapter
   c file changed from the previous chapter
   n new file

We make a small change in file decl.c to calculate the runtime stack offsets for local variables, and a few changes in stmt.c to add new information to the intermediate form. We change routine.c to calculate stack offsets for parameters and to start the program execution. We add runtime error handling to error.h and error.c. The executor module files are all new. We add two new constants to file common.h:

```
#define MAX_STACK_SIZE          1024
#define STACK_FRAME_HEADER_SIZE 4
```

The first constant is the size (in stack items) of the runtime stack that we will allocate before executing the program. The second constant is the size of the stack frame header. We also define a new type:

```
typedef char *ADDRESS;
```

9.2.1 Runtime error handling

Up until now, the error module has handled only syntax errors that we detect during parsing. An interpreter, as it executes a program, must also detect runtime errors. In file error.h, we add the following enumeration type that represents the runtime errors that our interpreter will be able to detect:

```
typedef enum {
    RUNTIME_STACK_OVERFLOW,
    VALUE_OUT_OF_RANGE,
    INVALID_CASE_VALUE,
    DIVISION_BY_ZERO,
    INVALID_FUNCTION_ARGUMENT,
    UNIMPLEMENTED_RUNTIME_FEATURE,
} RUNTIME_ERROR_CODE;
```

Then, of course, we need to add the corresponding string array to file error.c:

```
char *runtime_error_messages[] = {
    "Runtime stack overflow",
    "Value out of range",
    "Invalid CASE expression value",
    "Division by zero",
```

```
            "Invalid standard function argument",
                        "Unimplemented runtime feature",
                    };
```

Figure 9-5 shows a new function `runtime_error` in `error.c`, which routines in the executor module call to flag runtime errors. The two variables `exec_line_number` and `exec_stmt_count` are defined in the executor module, and they are the line number of the last statement executed (the one that caused the error) and the number of statements executed, respectively. In this version of `runtime_error`, a runtime error aborts the program execution. When we write our debugger in Chapter 11, a new version will enable us to interactively correct the error.

FIGURE 9-5   Function `runtime_error` in file `error.c`.

```
/*------------------------------------------------*/      char      *message = runtime_error_messages[code];
/*  runtime_error      Print a runtime error message and then  */      extern int  exec_line_number;
/*                     abort the program execution.           */      extern long exec_stmt_count;
/*------------------------------------------------*/
                                                          printf("\n*** RUNTIME ERROR in line %d: %s\n",
runtime_error(code)                                               exec_line_number, message);
                                                          printf("\nUnsuccessful completion.  %ld statements executed.\n\n",
    ERROR_CODE code;   /* error code */                           exec_stmt_count);
                                                          exit(-code);
{                                                         }
```

9.2.2 Symbol table changes

Figure 9-6 shows the new version of function `var_declarations` in file `decl.c`. When `var_declarations` calls `var_or_field_declarations`, the third parameter is the runtime stack offset value for the first local variable. This value is the value of `STACK_FRAME_HEADER_SIZE` plus the number of formal parameters, as shown in Figure 9-2. We recall that when function `record_type` calls `var_or_field_declarations`, it passes zero as the initial offset value.

FIGURE 9-6   Function `var_declarations` in file `decl.c`.

```
/*------------------------------------------------*/      SYMTAB_NODE_PTR rtn_idp;    /* id of program or routine */
/*  var_declarations   Process variable declarations:   */
/*                                                 */      {
/*                     <id-list> : <type>          */          var_or_field_declarations(rtn_idp, NULL,
/*------------------------------------------------*/                          STACK_FRAME_HEADER_SIZE
                                                                              + rtn_idp->defn.info.routine
var_declarations(rtn_idp)                                                          .parm_count);
                                                          }
```

Now the reason for the offset field in the symbol table nodes becomes clear. For record fields, the offsets are byte offsets from the beginning of the record. Therefore, we increment parameter offset each time by the size of each field. For variables, the offsets are stack item offsets from the stack frame base, and since the stack items are all one size, we increment offset each time by one.

Figure 9-7 shows a new version of function formal_parm_list in file routine.c, which contains two small changes. We now initialize parm_offset to STACK_FRAME_HEADER_SIZE, since that is the offset of the first parameter (again, see Figure 9-2). As before, we assign the offset to the symbol table node for each parameter, and we increment offset by one each time. The other change is near the end of the function. The total size (in stack items) of all the formal parameters is the final offset value minus STACK_FRAME_HEADER_SIZE.

FIGURE 9-7   Function formal_parm_list in file routine.c.

```
/*----------------------------------------------------------*/
/*  formal_parm_list    Process a formal parameter list:    */
/*                                                          */
/*                         ( VAR <id-list> : <type> ;       */
/*                           <id-list> : <type> ;           */
/*                           ... )                          */
/*                                                          */
/*                         Return a pointer to the head of the  */
/*                         parameter id list.               */
/*----------------------------------------------------------*/

    SYMTAB_NODE_PTR
formal_parm_list(countp, total_sizep)

    int *countp;        /* ptr to count of parameters */
    int *total_sizep;   /* ptr to total byte size of parameters */

{
    SYMTAB_NODE_PTR parm_idp, first_idp, last_idp;    /* parm ids */
    SYMTAB_NODE_PTR prev_last_idp = NULL;      /* last id of list */
    SYMTAB_NODE_PTR parm_listp = NULL;         /* parm list */
    SYMTAB_NODE_PTR type_idp;                  /* type id */
    TYPE_STRUCT_PTR parm_tp;                   /* parm type */
    DEFN_KEY        parm_defn;                 /* parm definition */
    int             parm_count = 0;            /* count of parms */
    int             parm_offset = STACK_FRAME_HEADER_SIZE;

    get_token();

    /*
    -- Loop to process parameter declarations separated by ;
    */
    while ((token == IDENTIFIER) || (token == VAR)) {
        first_idp = NULL;

        /*
        -- VAR parms?
        */
        if (token == VAR) {
            parm_defn = VARPARM_DEFN;
            get_token();
        }
        else parm_defn = VALPARM_DEFN;
```

```
        /*
        -- <id list>
        */
        while (token == IDENTIFIER) {
            search_and_enter_local_symtab(parm_idp);
            parm_idp->defn.key   = parm_defn;
            parm_idp->label_index = 0;
            ++parm_count;

            if (parm_listp == NULL) parm_listp = parm_idp;

            /*
            -- Link parm ids together.
            */
            if (first_idp == NULL)
                first_idp = last_idp = parm_idp;
            else {
                last_idp->next = parm_idp;
                last_idp = parm_idp;
            }

            get_token();
            if_token_get(COMMA);
        }

        if_token_get_else_error(COLON, MISSING_COLON);

        if (token == IDENTIFIER) {
            search_and_find_all_symtab(type_idp);
            if (type_idp->defn.key != TYPE_DEFN) error(INVALID_TYPE);
            parm_tp = type_idp->typep;
            get_token();
        }
        else {
            error(MISSING_IDENTIFIER);
            parm_tp = &dummy_type;
        }

        /*
        -- Assign the offset and the type to all parm ids
        -- in the sublist.
        */
        for (parm_idp = first_idp;
             parm_idp != NULL;
```

```
            parm_idp = parm_idp->next) {                              --  Error synchronization:  Should be ; or )
         parm_idp->typep = parm_tp;                               */
         parm_idp->defn.info.data.offset = parm_offset++;         synchronize(follow_parms_list, NULL, NULL);
      }                                                            if_token_get(SEMICOLON);
                                                                }
      /*
      -- Link this list to the list of all parm ids.          if_token_get_else_error(RPAREN, MISSING_RPAREN);
      */                                                       *countp = parm_count;
      if (prev_last_idp != NULL) prev_last_idp->next = first_idp;  *total_sizep = parm_offset - STACK_FRAME_HEADER_SIZE;
      prev_last_idp = last_idp;
                                                                return(parm_listp);
      /*                                                     }
```

9.2.3 The runtime stack routines

Figure 9-8 shows the header file exec.h of the new executor module. We define two structures for the runtime stack. Union STACK_ITEM shows that each stack item is either an integer, a real, a byte, or an address. Structure STACK_FRAME_ HEADER represents the items that make up the stack frame header.

FIGURE 9-8   File exec.h.

```
/***************************************************************/     /*-------------------------------------------------------------*/
/*                                                           */
/*        E X E C U T O R   (Header)                          */     SYMTAB_NODE_PTR get_symtab_cptr();
/*                                                           */     int             get_statement_cmarker();
/*      FILE:      exec.h                                     */     TYPE_STRUCT_PTR exec_routine_call();
/*                                                           */     TYPE_STRUCT_PTR exec_expression(), exec_variable();
/*      MODULE:    executor                                   */
/*                                                           */                         /***********************/
/***************************************************************/                         /*                     */
                                                                                          /*       Macros        */
#ifndef exec_h                                                                            /*                     */
#define exec_h                                                                            /***********************/

#include "common.h"                                              /*-------------------------------------------------------------*/
                                                                /*  get_ctoken      Extract the next token code from the    */
#define STATEMENT_MARKER 0x70                                    /*                  current code segment.                   */
                                                                /*-------------------------------------------------------------*/
/*------------------------------------------------------*/
/*  Runtime stack                                       */      #define get_ctoken()     ctoken = *code_segmentp++
/*------------------------------------------------------*/
                                                                /*-------------------------------------------------------------*/
typedef union {                                                  /*  pop             Pop the runtime stack.                  */
    int     integer;                                            /*-------------------------------------------------------------*/
    float   real;
    char    byte;                                               #define pop()            --tos
    ADDRESS address;
} STACK_ITEM, *STACK_ITEM_PTR;                                  /*-------------------------------------------------------------*/
                                                                /*  Tracing routine calls   Unless the following statements */
typedef struct {                                                /*                          are preceded by                 */
    STACK_ITEM function_value;                                  /*                                                          */
    STACK_ITEM static_link;                                     /*                              #define trace              */
    STACK_ITEM dynamic_link;                                    /*                                                          */
    STACK_ITEM return_address;                                  /*                          calls to the tracing routines   */
} *STACK_FRAME_HEADER_PTR;                                      /*                          are not compiled.               */
                                                                /*-------------------------------------------------------------*/
/*------------------------------------------------------*/
/*  Functions                                           */      #ifndef trace
```

```
#define trace_routine_entry(idp)                          #define trace_data_fetch(idp, tp, datap)
#define trace_routine_exit(idp)                           #endif
#define trace_statement_execution()
#define trace_data_store(idp, idp_tp, targetp, target_tp)  #endif
```

The significance of the STATEMENT_MARKER constant is explained later. Macros get_ctoken and pop are from the pretty-printer in Chapter 8 and the calculator in Chapter 4, respectively. We will explain the tracing macros at the end of this chapter.

Most of the routines that manipulate the runtime stack are in file executil.c, shown in Figure 9-9. Several important new global variables are declared in this file, namely, the runtime stack, the top of stack pointer tos, and the pointer to the current stack frame base stack_frame_basep. An important old global variable is code_segmentp, which points to a location in the code segment. During program execution, it points to the current token in the intermediate code.

FIGURE 9-9   File executil.c.

```
/****************************************************************/
/*                                                            */
/*         E X E C U T O R   U T I L I T I E S                */
/*                                                            */
/*         Utility routines for the executor module.         */
/*                                                            */
/*         FILE:       executil.c                            */
/*                                                            */
/*         MODULE:     executor                              */
/*                                                            */
/****************************************************************/

#include <stdio.h>
#include "common.h"
#include "error.h"
#include "symtab.h"
#include "scanner.h"
#include "exec.h"

/*----------------------------------------------------------*/
/* Externals                                                */
/*----------------------------------------------------------*/

extern TOKEN_CODE token;
extern int        line_number;
extern int        level;

extern TYPE_STRUCT_PTR integer_typep, real_typep,
                       boolean_typep, char_typep;

/*----------------------------------------------------------*/
/* Globals                                                  */
/*----------------------------------------------------------*/

char *code_buffer;              /* code buffer */
char *code_bufferp;             /* code buffer ptr */
char *code_segmentp;            /* code segment ptr */
char *code_segment_limit;       /* end of code segment */
char *statement_startp;         /* ptr to start of stmt */
```

```
TOKEN_CODE   ctoken;            /* token from code segment */
int          exec_line_number;  /* no. of line executed */
long         exec_stmt_count = 0; /* count of stmts executed */

STACK_ITEM     *stack;          /* runtime stack */
STACK_ITEM_PTR tos;             /* ptr to runtime stack top */
STACK_ITEM_PTR stack_frame_basep; /* ptr to stack frame base */

                /********************************/
                /*                              */
                /*      Code segment routines   */
                /*                              */
                /********************************/

/*----------------------------------------------------------*/
/* crunch_token      Append the token code to the code      */
/*                   buffer.  Called by the scanner routine  */
/*                   get_token only while parsing a block.   */
/*----------------------------------------------------------*/

crunch_token()

{
    char token_code = token;    /* byte-sized token code */

    if (code_bufferp >= code_buffer + MAX_CODE_BUFFER_SIZE) {
        error(CODE_SEGMENT_OVERFLOW);
        exit(-CODE_SEGMENT_OVERFLOW);
    }
    else *code_bufferp++ = token_code;
}

/*----------------------------------------------------------*/
/* crunch_symtab_node_ptr      Append a symbol table node   */
/*                             pointer to the code buffer.   */
/*----------------------------------------------------------*/

crunch_symtab_node_ptr(np)
```

```
    SYMTAB_NODE_PTR np;          /* pointer to append */

{
    SYMTAB_NODE_PTR *npp = (SYMTAB_NODE_PTR *) code_bufferp;

    if (code_bufferp >= code_buffer + MAX_CODE_BUFFER_SIZE
                                 - sizeof(SYMTAB_NODE_PTR)) {
        error(CODE_SEGMENT_OVERFLOW);
        exit(-CODE_SEGMENT_OVERFLOW);
    }
    else {
        *npp = np;
        code_bufferp += sizeof(SYMTAB_NODE_PTR);
    }
}

/*--------------------------------------------------------*/
/*  crunch_statement_marker      Append a statement marker to  */
/*                               the code buffer.              */
/*--------------------------------------------------------*/

crunch_statement_marker()

{
    if (code_bufferp >= code_buffer + MAX_CODE_BUFFER_SIZE
                                 - sizeof(int)) {
        error(CODE_SEGMENT_OVERFLOW);
        exit(-CODE_SEGMENT_OVERFLOW);
    }
    else {
        char save_code = *(--code_bufferp);

        *code_bufferp++ = STATEMENT_MARKER;
        *((int *) code_bufferp) = line_number;
        code_bufferp += sizeof(int);
        *code_bufferp++ = save_code;
    }
}

/*--------------------------------------------------------*/
/*  create_code_segment      Create a code segment and copy in  */
/*                           the contents of the code buffer.   */
/*                           Reset the code buffer pointer.     */
/*                           Return a pointer to the segment.   */
/*--------------------------------------------------------*/

    char *
create_code_segment()

{
    char *code_segment = alloc_bytes(code_bufferp - code_buffer);

    code_segment_limit = code_segment + (code_bufferp - code_buffer);
    code_bufferp       = code_buffer;
    code_segmentp      = code_segment;

    /*
    -- Copy in the contents of the code buffer.
    */
    while (code_segmentp != code_segment_limit)
        *code_segmentp++ = *code_bufferp++;

    code_bufferp = code_buffer;           /* reset code buffer ptr */
    return(code_segment);
}

/*--------------------------------------------------------*/
/*  get_symtab_cptr    Extract a symbol table node pointer   */
```

```
/*                        from the current code segment and     */
/*                        return it.                            */
/*--------------------------------------------------------*/

    SYMTAB_NODE_PTR
get_symtab_cptr()

{
    SYMTAB_NODE_PTR np;
    SYMTAB_NODE_PTR *npp = (SYMTAB_NODE_PTR *) code_segmentp;

    np = *npp;
    code_segmentp += sizeof(SYMTAB_NODE_PTR);
    return(np);
}

/*--------------------------------------------------------*/
/*  get_statement_cmarker   Extract a statement marker from the  */
/*                          current code segment and return its  */
/*                          statement line number.               */
/*--------------------------------------------------------*/

    int
get_statement_cmarker()

{
    int line_num;

    if (ctoken == STATEMENT_MARKER) {
        line_num = *((int *) code_segmentp);
        code_segmentp += sizeof(int);
    }

    return(line_num);
}

            /********************************/
            /*                              */
            /*        Executor utilities    */
            /*                              */
            /********************************/

/*--------------------------------------------------------*/
/*  push_integer       Push an integer onto the runtime stack.  */
/*--------------------------------------------------------*/

push_integer(item_value)

    int item_value;

{
    STACK_ITEM_PTR itemp = ++tos;

    if (itemp >= &stack[MAX_STACK_SIZE])
        runtime_error(RUNTIME_STACK_OVERFLOW);

    itemp->integer = item_value;
}

/*--------------------------------------------------------*/
/*  push_real          Push a real onto the runtime stack.     */
/*--------------------------------------------------------*/

push_real(item_value)

    float item_value;
```

```
{
    STACK_ITEM_PTR itemp = ++tos;

    if (itemp >= &stack[MAX_STACK_SIZE])
        runtime_error(RUNTIME_STACK_OVERFLOW);

    itemp->real = item_value;
}

/*----------------------------------------------------*/
/* push_byte          Push a byte onto the runtime stack.   */
/*----------------------------------------------------*/

push_byte(item_value)

    char item_value;

{
    STACK_ITEM_PTR itemp = ++tos;

    if (itemp >= &stack[MAX_STACK_SIZE])
        runtime_error(RUNTIME_STACK_OVERFLOW);

    itemp->byte = item_value;
}

/*----------------------------------------------------*/
/* push_address       Push an address onto the runtime stack. */
/*----------------------------------------------------*/

push_address(address)

    ADDRESS address;

{
    STACK_ITEM_PTR itemp = ++tos;

    if (itemp >= &stack[MAX_STACK_SIZE])
        runtime_error(RUNTIME_STACK_OVERFLOW);

    itemp->address = address;
}

/*----------------------------------------------------*/
/* execute            Execute a routine's code segment.     */
/*----------------------------------------------------*/

execute(rtn_idp)

    SYMTAB_NODE_PTR rtn_idp;

{
    routine_entry(rtn_idp);

    get_ctoken();
    exec_statement();

    routine_exit(rtn_idp);
}

/*----------------------------------------------------*/
/* routine_entry      Point to the new routine's code      */
/*                    segment, and allocate its locals.    */
/*----------------------------------------------------*/

routine_entry(rtn_idp)
```

```
    SYMTAB_NODE_PTR rtn_idp;    /* new routine's id */

{
    SYMTAB_NODE_PTR var_idp;    /* local variable id */

    trace_routine_entry(rtn_idp);

    /*
    -- Switch to the new code segment.
    */
    code_segmentp = rtn_idp->defn.info.routine.code_segment;

    /*
    -- Allocate local variables.
    */
    for (var_idp = rtn_idp->defn.info.routine.locals;
         var_idp != NULL;
         var_idp = var_idp->next) alloc_local(var_idp->typep);
}

/*----------------------------------------------------*/
/* routine_exit       Deallocate the routine's parameters and */
/*                    locals.  Cut off its stack frame, and   */
/*                    return to the caller's code segment.    */
/*----------------------------------------------------*/

routine_exit(rtn_idp)

    SYMTAB_NODE_PTR rtn_idp;         /* exiting routine's id */

{
    SYMTAB_NODE_PTR        idp;      /* variable or parm id */
    STACK_FRAME_HEADER_PTR hp;       /* ptr to stack frame header */

    trace_routine_exit(rtn_idp);

    /*
    -- Deallocate parameters and local variables.
    */
    for (idp = rtn_idp->defn.info.routine.parms;
         idp != NULL;
         idp = idp->next) free_data(idp);
    for (idp = rtn_idp->defn.info.routine.locals;
         idp != NULL;
         idp = idp->next) free_data(idp);

    /*
    -- Pop off the stack frame and return to the
    -- caller's code segment.
    */
    hp = (STACK_FRAME_HEADER_PTR) stack_frame_basep;
    code_segmentp = hp->return_address.address;
    tos = (rtn_idp->defn.key == PROC_DEFN)
              ? stack_frame_basep - 1
              : stack_frame_basep;
    stack_frame_basep = (STACK_ITEM_PTR) hp->dynamic_link.address;
}

/*----------------------------------------------------*/
/* push_stack_frame_header     Allocate the callee routine's  */
/*                             stack frame.                   */
/*----------------------------------------------------*/

push_stack_frame_header(old_level, new_level)

    int old_level, new_level;   /* levels of caller and callee */

{
```

```
STACK_FRAME_HEADER_PTR hp;

push_integer(0);                           /* return value */
hp = (STACK_FRAME_HEADER_PTR) stack_frame_basep;

/*
-- Static link.
*/
if (new_level == old_level + 1) {
    /*
    -- Calling a routine nested within the caller:
    -- Push pointer to caller's stack frame.
    */
    push_address(hp);
}
else if (new_level == old_level) {
    /*
    -- Calling another routine at the same level:
    -- Push pointer to stack frame of common parent.
    */
    push_address(hp->static_link.address);
}
else  /* new_level < old_level */  {
    /*
    -- Calling a routine at a lesser level (nested less deeply):
    -- Push pointer to stack frame of nearest common ancestor.
    */
    int delta = old_level - new_level;

    while (delta-- >= 0)
        hp = (STACK_FRAME_HEADER_PTR) hp->static_link.address;
    push_address(hp);
}

push_address(stack_frame_basep);           /* dynamic link */
push_address(0);    /* return address to be filled in later */
}

/*------------------------------------------------------------*/
/* alloc_local       Allocate a local variable on the stack. */
/*------------------------------------------------------------*/

alloc_local(tp)

    TYPE_STRUCT_PTR tp;    /* ptr to type of variable */

{
    if      (tp == integer_typep) push_integer(0);
```

```
    else if (tp == real_typep)    push_real(0.0);
    else if (tp == boolean_typep) push_byte(0);
    else if (tp == char_typep)    push_byte(0);

    else switch (tp->form) {
        case ENUM_FORM:
            push_integer(0);
            break;

        case SUBRANGE_FORM:
            alloc_local(tp->info.subrange.range_typep);
            break;

        case ARRAY_FORM: {
            char *ptr = alloc_bytes(tp->size);

            push_address((ADDRESS) ptr);
            break;
        }

        case RECORD_FORM: {
            char *ptr = alloc_bytes(tp->size);

            push_address((ADDRESS) ptr);
            break;
        }
    }
}

/*------------------------------------------------------------*/
/* free_data         Deallocate the data area of an array    */
/*                   or record local variable or value       */
/*                   parameter.                              */
/*------------------------------------------------------------*/

free_data(idp)

    SYMTAB_NODE_PTR idp;              /* parm or variable id */

{
    STACK_ITEM_PTR itemp;             /* ptr to stack item */
    TYPE_STRUCT_PTR tp = idp->typep;  /* ptr to id's type */

    if (   ((tp->form == ARRAY_FORM) || (tp->form == RECORD_FORM))
        && (idp->defn.key != VARPARM_DEFN)) {
        itemp = stack_frame_basep + idp->defn.info.data.offset;
        free(itemp->address);
    }
}
```

You can recognize several of the file's functions from the pretty-printer. New functions include push_integer, push_real, push_byte, and push_address, each of which pushes a stack item of a given type onto the runtime stack. In each function, we first check for a stack overflow, and we call runtime_error if one occurs. The other functions in the file are explained later.

9.3 Interpreting procedure and function calls

Now we are ready to write more of the executor module and to start executing source programs!

9.3.1 Executing programs, procedures, and functions

At the beginning of file `routine.c`, we must add:

```
#include "exec.h"
```

We also need:

```
extern int          line_number;
extern int          error_count;
extern long         exec_stmt_count;

extern STACK_ITEM       *stack;
extern STACK_ITEM_PTR   tos;
extern STACK_ITEM_PTR   stack_frame_basep;
```

Figure 9-10 shows a new version of routine `program` in `routine.c`. We first parse the Pascal source program, as before. With the modifications to the scanner and parser that we made in the previous chapter, we also create code segments containing intermediate code. Now, if there are no syntax errors, we want to execute the source program.

FIGURE 9-10   Function `program` in file `routine.c`.

```
/*-----------------------------------------------------------*/
/* program       Process a program:                          */
/*                                                           */
/*                     <program-header> ; <block> .          */
/*-----------------------------------------------------------*/

TOKEN_CODE follow_header_list[] = {SEMICOLON, END_OF_FILE, 0};

program()

{
    SYMTAB_NODE_PTR program_idp;        /* program id */

    /*
    --                  PARSE THE PROGRAM
    --
    --
    -- Intialize the symbol table and then allocate
    -- the code buffer.
    */
    init_symtab();
    code_buffer  = alloc_bytes(MAX_CODE_BUFFER_SIZE);
    code_bufferp = code_buffer;

    /*
    -- Begin parsing with the program header.
    */
    program_idp = program_header();

    /*
    -- Error synchronization:  Should be ;
```
```
    */
    synchronize(follow_header_list,
                declaration_start_list, statement_start_list);
    if_token_get(SEMICOLON);
    else if (token_in(declaration_start_list) ||
             token_in(statement_start_list))
        error(MISSING_SEMICOLON);

    analyze_routine_header(program_idp);

    /*
    -- Parse the program's block.
    */
    program_idp->defn.info.routine.locals = NULL;
    block(program_idp);

    program_idp->defn.info.routine.local_symtab = exit_scope();
    program_idp->defn.info.routine.code_segment = create_code_segment();
    analyze_block(program_idp->defn.info.routine.code_segment);

    if_token_get_else_error(PERIOD, MISSING_PERIOD);

    /*
    -- Look for the end of file.
    */
    while (token != END_OF_FILE) {
        error(UNEXPECTED_TOKEN);
        get_token();
    }

    quit_scanner();
```

```
free(code_buffer);

/*
-- Print the parser's summary.
*/
print_line("\n");
print_line("\n");
sprintf(buffer, "%20d Source lines.\n", line_number);
print_line(buffer);
sprintf(buffer, "%20d Source errors.\n", error_count);
print_line(buffer);

if (error_count > 0) exit(-SYNTAX_ERROR);
else                printf("%c\n", FORM_FEED_CHAR);

/*
--                  EXECUTE THE PROGRAM
--
--
-- Allocate the runtime stack.
*/
stack = alloc_array(STACK_ITEM, MAX_STACK_SIZE);
```

```
stack_frame_basep = tos = stack;

/*
-- Initialize the program's stack frame.
*/
level = 1;
stack_frame_basep = tos + 1;
push_integer(0);        /* function return value */
push_address(NULL);     /* static link */
push_address(NULL);     /* dynamic link */
push_address(NULL);     /* return address */

/*
-- Go!
*/
execute(program_idp);

free(stack);
printf("\n\nSuccessful completion. %ld statements executed.\n\n",
        exec_stmt_count);
exit(0);
}
```

We begin to execute the source program by allocating the runtime stack. Then, we initialize stack_frame_basep and tos to point to the bottom of the stack. We set level to one, the nesting level of the program's global variables, and then we allocate the program's stack frame header at the bottom of the stack.

We call function execute to execute the source program, passing a pointer to the program identifier's symbol table node. This important function, which we will examine later, can execute the Pascal main program, a procedure, or a function. Like our pretty-printer, it works with the intermediate code in a code segment.

9.3.2 Calling a Pascal procedure or function

Before we study further how we execute a Pascal procedure or function, you need to see how to call such a routine. In the following description, we'll use the term "callee" to refer to the called procedure or function to distinguish it from its caller. First, you allocate the callee's new stack frame on top of the runtime stack (first the stack header, then the parameters followed by the local variables), and then you execute the callee's statements. When you are ready to return to the caller, you pop off the new stack frame.

Figure 9-11 shows file execstmt.c of the executor module. This file is analogous to file stmt.c of the parser module.

FIGURE 9-11   File execstmt.c.

```
/****************************************************************/
/*                                                              */
/*      S T A T E M E N T   E X E C U T O R                     */
/*                                                              */
/*      Execution routines for statements.                      */
/*                                                              */
/*      FILE:       execstmt.c                                  */
/*                                                              */
/*      MODULE:     executor                                    */
/*                                                              */
/****************************************************************/

#include <stdio.h>
#include "common.h"
#include "error.h"
#include "symtab.h"
#include "scanner.h"
#include "parser.h"
#include "exec.h"


/*------------------------------------------------------------*/
/*  Externals                                                 */
/*------------------------------------------------------------*/

extern int          level;
extern int          exec_line_number;
extern long         exec_stmt_count;

extern char         *code_segmentp;
extern char         *statement_startp;
extern TOKEN_CODE   ctoken;

extern STACK_ITEM       *stack;
extern STACK_ITEM_PTR   tos;
extern STACK_ITEM_PTR   stack_frame_basep;

extern TYPE_STRUCT_PTR integer_typep, real_typep,
                       boolean_typep, char_typep;

/*------------------------------------------------------------*/
/*  exec_statement    Execute a statement by calling the      */
/*                    appropriate execution routine.          */
/*------------------------------------------------------------*/

exec_statement()

{
    if (ctoken == STATEMENT_MARKER) {
        exec_line_number = get_statement_cmarker();
        ++exec_stmt_count;

        statement_startp = code_segmentp;
        trace_statement_execution();
        get_ctoken();
    }

    switch (ctoken) {

        case IDENTIFIER: {
            SYMTAB_NODE_PTR idp = get_symtab_cptr();

            if (idp->defn.key == PROC_DEFN)
                exec_routine_call(idp);
            else
```

```
                exec_assignment_statement(idp);

            break;
        }

        case BEGIN:     exec_compound_statement();      break;
        case END:       break;

        default:  runtime_error(UNIMPLEMENTED_RUNTIME_FEATURE);
    }

    while (ctoken == SEMICOLON) get_ctoken();
}

/*------------------------------------------------------------*/
/*  exec_assignment_statement     Execute an assignment       */
/*                                statement.                  */
/*------------------------------------------------------------*/

exec_assignment_statement(idp)

    SYMTAB_NODE_PTR idp;        /* target variable id */

{
    STACK_ITEM_PTR targetp;     /* ptr to assignment target */
    TYPE_STRUCT_PTR target_tp, base_target_tp, expr_tp;

    /*
    -- Assignment to function id:  Target is the first item of
    --                             the appropriate stack frame.
    */

    if (idp->defn.key == FUNC_DEFN) {
        STACK_FRAME_HEADER_PTR hp;
        int                    delta;   /* difference in levels */

        hp    = (STACK_FRAME_HEADER_PTR) stack_frame_basep;
        delta = level - idp->level - 1;
        while (delta-- > 0)
            hp = (STACK_FRAME_HEADER_PTR) hp->static_link.address;

        targetp = (STACK_ITEM_PTR) hp;
        target_tp = idp->typep;
        get_ctoken();
    }

    /*
    -- Assignment to variable:  Routine exec_variable leaves the
    --                          target address on top of stack.
    */
    else {
        target_tp = exec_variable(idp, TARGET_USE);
        targetp   = (STACK_ITEM_PTR) tos->address;

        pop();          /* pop off target address */
    }

    base_target_tp = base_type(target_tp);

    /*
    -- Routine exec_expression leaves the expression value
    -- on top of stack.
    */
    get_ctoken();
```

```
    expr_tp = exec_expression();

    /*
    -- Do the assignment.
    */
    if ((target_tp == real_typep) &&
        (base_type(expr_tp) == integer_typep)) {
        /*
        -- real := integer
        */
        targetp->real = tos->integer;
    }
    else if ((target_tp->form == ARRAY_FORM) ||
             (target_tp->form == RECORD_FORM)) {
        /*
        -- array  := array
        -- record := record
        */
        char *ptr1 = (char *) targetp;
        char *ptr2 = tos->address;
        int  size  = target_tp->size;

        while (size--) *ptr1++ = *ptr2++;
    }
    else if ((base_target_tp == integer_typep) ||
             (target_tp->form == ENUM_FORM)) {
        /*
        -- Range check assignment to integer
        -- or enumeration subrange.
        */
        if (   (target_tp->form == SUBRANGE_FORM)
            && ((tos->integer < target_tp->info.subrange.min) ||
                (tos->integer > target_tp->info.subrange.max)))
            runtime_error(VALUE_OUT_OF_RANGE);
        /*
        -- integer     := integer
        -- enumeration := enumeration
        */
        targetp->integer = tos->integer;
    }
    else if (base_target_tp == char_typep) {
        /*
        -- Range check assigment to character subrange.
        */
        if (   (target_tp->form == SUBRANGE_FORM)
            && ((tos->byte < target_tp->info.subrange.min) ||
                (tos->byte > target_tp->info.subrange.max)))
            runtime_error(VALUE_OUT_OF_RANGE);
        /*
        -- character := character
        */
        targetp->byte = tos->byte;
    }
    else {
        /*
        -- real := real
        */
        targetp->real = tos->real;
    }

    pop();      /* pop off expression value */

    trace_data_store(idp, idp->typep, targetp, target_tp);
}

/*----------------------------------------------------------*/
/* exec_routine_call           Execute a procedure or function */
```

```
/*                             call.  Return a pointer to the  */
/*                             type structure.                 */
/*----------------------------------------------------------*/

    TYPE_STRUCT_PTR
exec_routine_call(rtn_idp)

    SYMTAB_NODE_PTR rtn_idp;    /* routine id */

{
    TYPE_STRUCT_PTR exec_declared_routine_call();
    TYPE_STRUCT_PTR exec_standard_routine_call();

    if (rtn_idp->defn.info.routine.key == DECLARED)
        return(exec_declared_routine_call(rtn_idp));
    else
        return(exec_standard_routine_call(rtn_idp));
}

/*----------------------------------------------------------*/
/* exec_declared_routine_call     Execute a call to a          */
/*                                declared procedure or        */
/*                                function.  Return a pointer  */
/*                                to the type structure.       */
/*----------------------------------------------------------*/

    TYPE_STRUCT_PTR
exec_declared_routine_call(rtn_idp)

    SYMTAB_NODE_PTR rtn_idp;              /* routine id */

{
    int old_level = level;                /* level of caller */
    int new_level = rtn_idp->level + 1;   /* level of callee */
    STACK_ITEM_PTR new_stack_frame_basep;
    STACK_FRAME_HEADER_PTR hp;            /* ptr to frame header */

    /*
    -- Set up stack frame of callee.
    */
    new_stack_frame_basep = tos + 1;
    push_stack_frame_header(old_level, new_level);

    /*
    -- Push parameter values onto the stack.
    */
    get_ctoken();
    if (ctoken == LPAREN) {
        exec_actual_parms(rtn_idp);
        get_ctoken();   /* token after ) */
    }

    /*
    -- Set the return address in the new stack frame,
    -- and execute the callee.
    */
    level = new_level;
    stack_frame_basep = new_stack_frame_basep;
    hp = (STACK_FRAME_HEADER_PTR) stack_frame_basep;
    hp->return_address.address = code_segmentp - 1;
    execute(rtn_idp);

    /*
    -- Return from callee.
    */
    level = old_level;
    get_ctoken();       /* first token after return */
```

```
        return(rtn_idp->defn.key == PROC_DEFN ? NULL : rtn_idp->typep);
}

/*------------------------------------------------------------*/
/*  exec_standard_routine_call     Execute a call to a        */
/*                                 standard procedure or       */
/*                                 function.                   */
/*------------------------------------------------------------*/

    TYPE_STRUCT_PTR
exec_standard_routine_call(rtn_idp)

    SYMTAB_NODE_PTR rtn_idp;    /* routine id */

{
    runtime_error(UNIMPLEMENTED_RUNTIME_FEATURE);
}

/*------------------------------------------------------------*/
/*  exec_actual_parms          Push the values of the actual  */
/*                             parameters onto the stack.      */
/*------------------------------------------------------------*/

exec_actual_parms(rtn_idp)

    SYMTAB_NODE_PTR rtn_idp;        /* id of callee routine */

{
    SYMTAB_NODE_PTR formal_idp;     /* formal parm id */
    TYPE_STRUCT_PTR formal_tp, actual_tp;

    /*
    -- Loop to execute actual parameters.
    */
    for (formal_idp = rtn_idp->defn.info.routine.parms;
         formal_idp != NULL;
         formal_idp = formal_idp->next) {

        formal_tp = formal_idp->typep;
        get_ctoken();

        /*
        -- Value parameter.
        */
        if (formal_idp->defn.key == VALPARM_DEFN) {
            actual_tp = exec_expression();

            /*
            -- Range check for a subrange formal parameter.
            */
            if (formal_tp->form == SUBRANGE_FORM) {
                TYPE_STRUCT_PTR base_formal_tp = base_type(formal_tp);
                int            value;

                value = ((base_formal_tp == integer_typep) ||
```

```
                         (base_formal_tp->form == ENUM_FORM))
                            ? tos->integer
                            : tos->byte;

                if ((value < formal_tp->info.subrange.min) ||
                    (value > formal_tp->info.subrange.max)) {
                    runtime_error(VALUE_OUT_OF_RANGE);
                }
            }

            /*
            -- real formal := integer actual
            */
            else if ((formal_tp == real_typep) &&
                     (base_type(actual_tp) == integer_typep)) {
                tos->real = tos->integer;
            }

            /*
            -- Formal parm is array or record:  Make a copy.
            */
            if ((formal_tp->form == ARRAY_FORM) ||
                (formal_tp->form == RECORD_FORM)) {
                int   size   = formal_tp->size;
                char *ptr1   = alloc_bytes(size);
                char *ptr2   = tos->address;
                char *save_ptr = ptr1;

                while (size--) *ptr1++ = *ptr2++;
                tos->address = save_ptr;
            }
        }

        /*
        -- VAR parameter.
        */
        else {
            SYMTAB_NODE_PTR idp = get_symtab_cptr();

            exec_variable(idp, VARPARM_USE);
        }
    }
}

/*------------------------------------------------------------*/
/*  exec_compound_statement     Execute a compound statement. */
/*------------------------------------------------------------*/

exec_compound_statement()

{
    get_ctoken();
    while (ctoken != END) exec_statement();
    get_ctoken();
}
```

In function exec_statement, we look at the first token of a statement to determine what kind of statement it is. In this chapter, we only know about compound statements, assignment statements, and procedure calls. (STATEMENT_MARKER is explained later.) We call function exec_routine_call if the statement is a procedure call. There, we call either function exec_declared_routine_call or exec_standard_routine_call depending on whether the Pascal routine is programmer-written or standard. Since we won't handle the predefined standard routines until the next chapter, exec_standard_routine_call simply calls runtime_error.

Function exec_declared_routine_call sets up the stack for a Pascal procedure or function call. We set old_level to the current nesting level, which is the level of the caller's parameters and local variables. We set new_level to the nesting level of the parameters and local variables of the callee. Remember that the nesting level of a routine's parameter and local variable identifiers is one greater than the level of the routine's identifier. We also set new_stack_frame_basep to point to the runtime stack item that is one above the top of stack.

Next, we call function push_stack_frame_header to push the stack frame header for the callee onto the stack. We call function exec_actual_parms repeatedly to push the actual parameters (if any) onto the stack on top of the new stack frame header.

Then, we set level and stack_frame_basep to their new values, and we also set the return address into the new stack frame. Now we can call function execute, passing a pointer to the symbol table node of the callee's procedure or function identifier.

Function push_stack_frame_header is defined in file executil.c. We call it from exec_declared_routine_call to push the stack frame header for the callee onto the stack. We first push zero as a placeholder for the return value. Then, we compare the values of old_level (of the caller) and new_level (of the callee) to figure out what to push for the static link.

If new_level equals old_level + 1, then the callee is immediately contained by the caller, so the static link is simply a pointer to the base of the caller's stack frame. (This is still the value of stack_frame_basep, since we haven't yet updated it.)

If new_level equals old_level, then both the caller and the callee are immediately contained by the same routine. The static link is a copy of the caller's static link.

Finally, if new_level is less than old_level, the callee is less deeply nested than the caller. (You see this situation in Figure 9-4d.) The static link must point to the stack frame of the routine that immediately contains the callee. We get to the base of that stack frame by starting with the caller's stack frame and following (old_level - new_level + 1) static links, since each link we follow takes us back one nesting level.

On top of the static link, we push the dynamic link onto the stack. It simply points back to the base of the caller's stack frame. We conclude by pushing another zero, this time as a placeholder for the return address. As we saw before, we set the return address into the stack frame header shortly afterwards in function exec_declared_routine_call. We also saw in that function, that we call function exec_actual_parms to push the values of any actual parameters onto the stack on top of the new stack frame header. In that function, we loop over the formal parameter list of the callee.

For each formal value parameter, we call function exec_expression to push the actual parameter's value onto the stack. If the formal parameter is of a subrange type, we do a runtime range check to make sure the value is not outside of the range. If the formal parameter is real but the actual parameter value is integer, we convert the integer value to real. If the formal parameter is an array or a record, exec_expression leaves a pointer on top of the stack that points to the actual parameter's array or record value. We make a copy of the value and change the pointer at the top of the stack to point to the copy. (We will examine function exec_expression later when we look at how to execute expressions.)

For each formal VAR parameter, we call function exec_variable, passing the VARPARM_USE usage code (from file parser.h), to push the address of the actual parameter (which the parser has guaranteed to be a variable) onto the stack.

We have already seen how, in file executil.c, we call function execute to execute the main program, a procedure, or a function. From there, we call function routine_entry, where we complete the callee's stack frame by calling function alloc_local to allocate the local variables on the stack on top of the allocation for the parameters. We call function trace_routine_entry to print tracing information about entering a Pascal procedure or a function.

In function alloc_local, we call either function push_integer, push_real, or push_byte to push a zero for a scalar or enumeration local variable. We call alloc_local recursively for the range type of a subrange variable. If the local variable is an array or a record, we call alloc_bytes to allocate memory for it, and then we call push_address to push its address onto the stack.

Finally, back in execute, we extract the first token (which should be BEGIN) from the callee's code segment and call routine exec_statement to execute the statements in the callee's block. When we are done doing that, we call function routine_exit.

Let's review the steps involved in calling a Pascal procedure or function:

1. Allocate the callee's stack frame header (done in function push_stack_frame_header).

2. Push the actual arguments onto the stack (exec_actual_parms).

3. Update level and stack_frame_basep (exec_declared_routine_call).

4. Allocate the callee's local variables on the stack (routine_entry).

5. Execute the callee's statements (execute).

9.3.3 Returning from a Pascal procedure or function

Returning from the callee to the caller is simple: You deallocate the callee's parameters and variables, pop off its stack frame, and then resume execution of the caller at the return address.

As soon as the callee's statements are done being executed, function exec_statement returns to function execute. We call function routine_exit, and then call function `trace_routine_exit` to print any tracing information about leaving a Pascal procedure or function. Next, we call function `free_data` to deallocate any memory that we had allocated (in function `exec_actual_parms`) for array and record value parameters, and to deallocate any memory that we had allocated (when function `routine_entry` called `alloc_local`) for any local array and record variables. We set `code_segmentp` to the return address. We pop off the callee's stack frame by resetting `tos` to point to the stack item below the callee's stack frame base if the callee was a procedure, or to the item at the stack frame base (the return value) if the callee was a function. Finally, we use the dynamic link to reset `stack_frame_basep` to point to the base of the caller's stack frame, and then we return to execute.

From function execute, we return to `exec_declared_routine_call` and we are done executing the callee. So now, the stack is back to the way it was (except that a function return value may be on top), and `code_segmentp` points to where we left off in the code segment. We restore `level`, fetch the token from the code segment, and return either the function type if the callee was a function, or `NULL` if it was a procedure.

Let's review the steps involved in returning from a Pascal procedure or function:

1. Deallocate the callee's local variables and value parameters that are arrays or records (done in function `routine_exit`).

2. Reset `code_segmentp` to the return address, pop off the callee's stack frame (but leave a function return value on top), and reset `stack_frame_basep` to point to the base of the caller's stack frame (`routine_exit`).

3. Restore `level` and resume execution of the caller (`exec_declared_routine_call`).

9.4 Interpreting statements and expressions

Now that you have seen how an interpreter calls and returns from a Pascal procedure or function, you may wonder how it executes the callee's statements. The remaining routines of this chapter's executor module execute assignment statements, compound statements, and expressions.

9.4.1 Statement markers

In function `exec_statement`, we test for a `STATEMENT_MARKER`. Each statement marker in the intermediate form marks the beginning of the code of a statement, and it also contains the statement's source line number. A statement marker enables us to update `exec_line_number` and `exec_stmt_count`, and to call function `trace_statement_execution` to print statement tracing information, as we'll see later. As shown in Figure 9-12, we first add statement markers to the code buffer in function statement in file stmt.c. We also have to add the following to the beginning of stmt.c:

```
#include "exec.h"
```

FIGURE 9-12   Function statement in file stmt.c.

```
/*---------------------------------------------------*/                crunch_symtab_node_ptr(idp);
/* statement          Process a statement by calling the   */            get_token();
/*                    appropriate parsing routine based on */            routine_call(idp, TRUE);
/*                    the statement's first token.         */          }
/*---------------------------------------------------*/                else assignment_statement(idp);

statement()                                                              break;
                                                                      }
{
    if (token != BEGIN) crunch_statement_marker();                    case REPEAT:    repeat_statement();      break;
                                                                      case WHILE:     while_statement();       break;
    /*                                                                case IF:        if_statement();          break;
    -- Call the appropriate routine based on the first                case FOR:       for_statement();         break;
    -- token of the statement.                                        case CASE:      case_statement();        break;
    */                                                                case BEGIN:     compound_statement();    break;
    switch (token) {                                                  }

        case IDENTIFIER: {                                        /*
            SYMTAB_NODE_PTR idp;                                  -- Error synchronization:  Only a semicolon, END, ELSE, or
                                                                  --                         UNTIL may follow a statement.
            /*                                                    --                         Check for a missing semicolon.
            -- Assignment statement or procedure call?            */
            */                                                    synchronize(statement_end_list, statement_start_list, NULL);
            search_and_find_all_symtab(idp);                      if (token_in(statement_start_list)) error(MISSING_SEMICOLON);

            if (idp->defn.key == PROC_DEFN) {                 }
```

Function crunch_statement_marker is in file executil.c. We append the statement marker code followed by the current line number to the code buffer. Whenever we call crunch_statement_marker, the first token code of the statement has already been appended to the code buffer, so we must move it after the line number. Later, we call function get_statement_cmarker to retrieve the line number from the code buffer.

9.4.2 Executing assignment statements

Function exec_assignment_statement in file execstmt.c executes assignment statements. We first point targetp to the target of the assignment. The target may be a stack item or a component within a data area allocated for an array or record.

If the assignment is to a function identifier, then we point targetp to the bottom item (the return value) of the function's stack frame. If the assignment statement is not in that function's block (we are assigning a value to a function that contains the current routine), we must follow static links to find the appropriate stack frame.

Otherwise, we call function exec_variable, passing the TARGET_USE usage code, to evaluate and push the addresss of the target onto the stack. We set targetp to this address before we pop it off. We call function exec_expression to evaluate and push the value of the expression onto the stack, and then we can do the assignment.

If the expression value is integer and the target is integer, we convert the value to real. If the target is of an enumeration or a subrange type, we do a runtime range check to make sure the value is not outside of the range.

If the expression evaluates to an array or a record, exec_expression leaves a pointer on top of the stack that points to the value. In this case, targetp must be pointing to a data area that was allocated (when function routine_entry calls alloc_local) for the target array or record. We copy the array or record value. Finally, we call function trace_data_store to print tracing information about storing a value into a variable.

9.4.3 Executing compound statements

Function exec_compound_statement in file execstmt.c executes compound statements. We simply loop and call function exec_statement until we encounter the END token that matches the BEGIN token.

9.4.4 Executing expressions

Figure 9-13 shows file execexpr.c of the executor module. It contains the functions to execute expressions, and is analogous to file expr.c of the parser module. The functions may also remind you of the ones in the calculator utility program of Chapter 4. The main difference is that now the values on the stack may be of several types. The parser guarantees us, however, that there are no type incompatibilities in the expressions.

FIGURE 9-13   File execexpr.c.

```
/*****************************************************************/          #include "exec.h"
/*                                                             */
/*        E X P R E S S I O N   E X E C U T O R                */          /*------------------------------------------------------------*/
/*                                                             */          /*  Externals                                               */
/*        Execution routines for expressions.                 */          /*------------------------------------------------------------*/
/*                                                             */
/*        FILE:     execexpr.c                                 */          extern int          level;
/*                                                             */
/*        MODULE:   executor                                   */          extern char         *code_segmentp;
/*                                                             */          extern TOKEN_CODE   ctoken;
/*****************************************************************/
                                                                           extern STACK_ITEM     *stack;
#include <stdio.h>                                                         extern STACK_ITEM_PTR tos;
#include "common.h"                                                        extern STACK_ITEM_PTR stack_frame_basep;
#include "error.h"
#include "symtab.h"                                                        extern TYPE_STRUCT_PTR integer_typep, real_typep,
#include "scanner.h"                                                                              boolean_typep, char_typep;
#include "parser.h"
```

```
/*------------------------------------------------------------*/
/*  Forwards                                                  */
/*------------------------------------------------------------*/

TYPE_STRUCT_PTR exec_expression(), exec_simple_expression(),
                exec_term(), exec_factor(),
                exec_constant(), exec_variable(),
                exec_subscripts(), exec_field();

/*------------------------------------------------------------*/
/*  exec_expression     Execute an expression consisting of a */
/*                      simple expression optionally followed */
/*                      by a relational operator and a second */
/*                      simple expression.  Return a pointer to*/
/*                      the type structure.                   */
/*------------------------------------------------------------*/

    TYPE_STRUCT_PTR
exec_expression()

{
    STACK_ITEM_PTR   operandp1, operandp2;   /* ptrs to operands */
    TYPE_STRUCT_PTR  result_tp, tp2;         /* ptrs to types */
    TOKEN_CODE       op;                     /* an operator token */
    BOOLEAN          result;

    result_tp = exec_simple_expression();    /* first simple expr */

    /*
    -- If there is a relational operator, remember it and
    -- process the second simple expression.
    */
    if ((ctoken == EQUAL) || (ctoken == LT) || (ctoken == GT) ||
        (ctoken == NE)    || (ctoken == LE) || (ctoken == GE)) {
        op = ctoken;                         /* remember operator */
        result_tp = base_type(result_tp);

        get_ctoken();
        tp2 = base_type(exec_simple_expression()); /* 2nd simp expr */

        operandp1 = tos - 1;
        operandp2 = tos;

        /*
        -- Both operands are integer, boolean, or enumeration.
        */
        if (   ((result_tp == integer_typep) &&
                (tp2       == integer_typep))
            || (result_tp->form == ENUM_FORM)) {
            switch (op) {
                case EQUAL:
                    result = operandp1->integer == operandp2->integer;
                    break;

                case LT:
                    result = operandp1->integer <  operandp2->integer;
                    break;

                case GT:
                    result = operandp1->integer >  operandp2->integer;
                    break;

                case NE:
                    result = operandp1->integer != operandp2->integer;
                    break;

                case LE:
                    result = operandp1->integer <= operandp2->integer;
                    break;

                case GE:
                    result = operandp1->integer >= operandp2->integer;
                    break;
            }
        }

        /*
        -- Both operands are character.
        */
        else if (result_tp == char_typep) {
            switch (op) {
                case EQUAL:
                    result = operandp1->byte == operandp2->byte;
                    break;

                case LT:
                    result = operandp1->byte <  operandp2->byte;
                    break;

                case GT:
                    result = operandp1->byte >  operandp2->byte;
                    break;

                case NE:
                    result = operandp1->byte != operandp2->byte;
                    break;

                case LE:
                    result = operandp1->byte <= operandp2->byte;
                    break;

                case GE:
                    result = operandp1->byte >= operandp2->byte;
                    break;
            }
        }

        /*
        -- Both operands are real, or one is real and the other
        -- is integer.  Convert the integer operand to real.
        */
        else if ((result_tp == real_typep) ||
                 (tp2        == real_typep)) {
            promote_operands_to_real(operandp1, result_tp,
                            operandp2, tp2);

            switch (op) {
                case EQUAL:
                    result = operandp1->real == operandp2->real;
                    break;

                case LT:
                    result = operandp1->real <  operandp2->real;
                    break;

                case GT:
                    result = operandp1->real >  operandp2->real;
                    break;

                case NE:
                    result = operandp1->real != operandp2->real;
                    break;

                case LE:
```

```
                result = operandp1->real <= operandp2->real;
                break;

            case GE:
                result = operandp1->real >= operandp2->real;
                break;
        }
    }

    /*
    -- Both operands are strings.
    */
    else if ((result_tp->form == ARRAY_FORM) &&
             (result_tp->info.array.elmt_typep == char_typep)) {
        int cmp = strncmp(operandp1->address, operandp2->address,
                          result_tp->info.array.elmt_count);

        result = (  (   (cmp < 0)
                    && (    (op == NE)
                        || (op == LE)
                        || (op == LT)))
                 || (   (cmp == 0)
                    && (    (op == EQUAL)
                        || (op == LE)
                        || (op == GE)))
                 || (   (cmp > 0)
                    && (    (op == NE)
                        || (op == GE)
                        || (op == GT))));
    }

    /*
    -- Replace the two operands on the stack with the result.
    */
    operandp1->integer = result ? 1 : 0;
    pop();

    result_tp = boolean_typep;
    }

    return(result_tp);
}

/*------------------------------------------------------------*/
/* exec_simple_expression  Execute a simple expression        */
/*                         consisting of terms separated by +, */
/*                         -, or OR operators.  There may be   */
/*                         a unary + or - before the first     */
/*                         term.  Return a pointer to the      */
/*                         type structure.                     */
/*------------------------------------------------------------*/

    TYPE_STRUCT_PTR
exec_simple_expression()

{
    STACK_ITEM_PTR operandp1, operandp2;    /* ptrs to operands */
    TYPE_STRUCT_PTR result_tp, tp2;         /* ptrs to types */
    TOKEN_CODE op;                          /* an operator token */
    TOKEN_CODE unary_op = PLUS;             /* unary operator token */

    /*
    -- If there is a unary + or -, remember it.
    */
    if ((ctoken == PLUS) || (ctoken == MINUS)) {
        unary_op = ctoken;
        get_ctoken();
```

```
    }

    result_tp = exec_term();      /* first term */

    /*
    -- If there was a unary -, negate the top of stack
    */
    if (unary_op == MINUS) {
        if (result_tp == integer_typep) tos->integer = -tos->integer;
        else                            tos->real    = -tos->real;
    }

    /*
    -- Loop to process subsequent terms
    -- separated by operators.
    */
    while ((ctoken == PLUS) || (ctoken == MINUS) || (ctoken == OR)) {
        op = ctoken;                        /* remember operator */
        result_tp = base_type(result_tp);

        get_ctoken();
        tp2 = base_type(exec_term());   /* subsequent term */

        operandp1 = tos - 1;
        operandp2 = tos;

        /*
        -- OR
        */
        if (op == OR) {
            operandp1->integer = operandp1->integer ||
                                 operandp2->integer;
            result_tp = boolean_typep;
        }

        /*
        -- + or -
        --
        -- Both operands are integer.
        */
        else if ((result_tp == integer_typep) &&
                 (tp2       == integer_typep)) {
            operandp1->integer = (op == PLUS)
                ? operandp1->integer + operandp2->integer
                : operandp1->integer - operandp2->integer;
            result_tp = integer_typep;
        }

        /*
        -- Both operands are real, or one is real and the other
        -- is integer.  Convert the integer operand to real.
        */
        else {
            promote_operands_to_real(operandp1, result_tp,
                                     operandp2, tp2);

            operandp1->real = (op == PLUS)
                ? operandp1->real + operandp2->real
                : operandp1->real - operandp2->real;
            result_tp = real_typep;
        }

        pop();  /* pop off the second operand */
    }

    return(result_tp);
}
```

```
/*-----------------------------------------------------------*/
/* exec_term          Execute a term consisting of factors   */
/*                    separated by *, /, DIV, MOD, or AND     */
/*                    operators.  Return a pointer to the     */
/*                    type structure.                         */
/*-----------------------------------------------------------*/

    TYPE_STRUCT_PTR
exec_term()

{
    STACK_ITEM_PTR operandp1, operandp2;    /* ptrs to operands */
    TYPE_STRUCT_PTR result_tp, tp2;         /* ptrs to types */
    TOKEN_CODE op;                          /* an operator token */

    result_tp = exec_factor();  /* first factor */

    /*
    -- Loop to process subsequent factors
    -- separated by operators.
    */
    while ((ctoken == STAR) || (ctoken == SLASH) || (ctoken == DIV) ||
           (ctoken == MOD)  || (ctoken == AND)) {
        op = ctoken;                        /* remember operator */
        result_tp = base_type(result_tp);

        get_ctoken();
        tp2 = base_type(exec_factor());     /* subsequent factor */

        operandp1 = tos - 1;
        operandp2 = tos;

        /*
        -- AND
        */
        if (op == AND) {
            operandp1->integer = operandp1->integer &&
                            operandp2->integer;
            result_tp = boolean_typep;
        }

        /*
        -- *, /, DIV, or MOD
        */
        else switch (op) {

            case STAR:
                /*
                -- Both operands are integer.
                */
                if (  (result_tp == integer_typep)
                   && (tp2       == integer_typep)) {
                    operandp1->integer =
                        operandp1->integer * operandp2->integer;
                    result_tp = integer_typep;
                }

                /*
                -- Both operands are real, or one is real and the
                -- other is integer.  Convert the integer operand
                -- to real.
                */
                else {
                    promote_operands_to_real(operandp1, result_tp,
                                        operandp2, tp2);

                    operandp1->real =
                        operandp1->real * operandp2->real;
                    result_tp = real_typep;
                }
                break;

            case SLASH:
                /*
                -- Both operands are real, or one is real and the
                -- other is integer.  Convert the integer operand
                -- to real.
                */
                promote_operands_to_real(operandp1, result_tp,
                                    operandp2, tp2);

                if (operandp2->real == 0.0)
                    runtime_error(DIVISION_BY_ZERO);
                else
                    operandp1->real = operandp1->real/operandp2->real;

                result_tp = real_typep;
                break;

            case DIV:
            case MOD:
                /*
                -- Both operands are integer.
                */
                if (operandp2->integer == 0)
                    runtime_error(DIVISION_BY_ZERO);
                else
                    operandp1->integer = (op == DIV)
                        ? operandp1->integer / operandp2->integer
                        : operandp1->integer % operandp2->integer;

                result_tp = integer_typep;
                break;
        }

        pop();  /* pop off the second operand */
    }

    return(result_tp);
}

/*-----------------------------------------------------------*/
/* exec_factor        Execute a factor, which is a variable, */
/*                    a number, NOT followed by a factor, or  */
/*                    a parenthesized subexpression.  Return  */
/*                    a pointer to the type structure.        */
/*-----------------------------------------------------------*/

    TYPE_STRUCT_PTR
exec_factor()

{
    TYPE_STRUCT_PTR result_tp;          /* type pointer */

    switch (ctoken) {

        case IDENTIFIER: {
            SYMTAB_NODE_PTR idp = get_symtab_cptr();

            /*
            -- Function call or constant or variable.
            */
            if (idp->defn.key == FUNC_DEFN)
                result_tp = exec_routine_call(idp);
```

```
        else if (idp->defn.key == CONST_DEFN)
            result_tp = exec_constant(idp);
        else
            result_tp = exec_variable(idp, EXPR_USE);

        break;
}

case NUMBER: {
    SYMTAB_NODE_PTR np = get_symtab_cptr();

    /*
    -- Obtain the integer or real value from the
    -- symbol table entry and push it onto the stack.
    */
    if (np->typep == integer_typep) {
        push_integer(np->defn.info.constant.value.integer);
        result_tp = integer_typep;
    }
    else {
        push_real(np->defn.info.constant.value.real);
        result_tp = real_typep;
    }

    get_ctoken();
    break;
}

case STRING: {
    SYMTAB_NODE_PTR np     = get_symtab_cptr();
    int             length = strlen(np->name);

    /*
    -- Obtain the character or string from the symbol
    -- table entry.  Note that the quotes were included,
    -- so the string lengths need to be decreased by 2.
    */
    if (length > 3) {
        /*
        -- String:  Push its address onto the stack.
        */
        push_address(np->info);
        result_tp = np->typep;
    }
    else {
        /*
        -- Character:  Push its value onto the stack.
        */
        push_byte(np->name[1]);
        result_tp = char_typep;
    }

    get_ctoken();
    break;
}

case NOT:
    get_ctoken();
    result_tp = exec_factor();
    tos->integer = 1 - tos->integer;    /* 0 => 1, 1 => 0 */
    break;

case LPAREN:
    get_ctoken();
    result_tp = exec_expression();
    get_ctoken();        /* token after ) */
    break;
```

```
    }

    return(result_tp);
}
```

```
/*--------------------------------------------------------------*/
/*  exec_constant       Push the value of a non-string constant */
/*                      identifier, or the address of the value */
/*                      of a string constant identifier onto    */
/*                      the stack.  Return a pointer to the     */
/*                      type structure.                         */
/*--------------------------------------------------------------*/

    TYPE_STRUCT_PTR
exec_constant(idp)

    SYMTAB_NODE_PTR idp;        /* constant id */

{
    TYPE_STRUCT_PTR tp = idp->typep;

    if ((base_type(tp) == integer_typep) || (tp->form == ENUM_FORM))
        push_integer(idp->defn.info.constant.value.integer);
    else if (tp == real_typep)
        push_real(idp->defn.info.constant.value.real);
    else if (tp == char_typep)
        push_integer(idp->defn.info.constant.value.integer);
    else if (tp->form == ARRAY_FORM)
        push_address(idp->defn.info.constant.value.stringp);

    trace_data_fetch(idp, tp, tos);
    get_ctoken();

    return(tp);
}

/*--------------------------------------------------------------*/
/*  exec_variable       Push either the variable's address or   */
/*                      its value onto the stack.  Return a     */
/*                      pointer to the type structure.          */
/*--------------------------------------------------------------*/

    TYPE_STRUCT_PTR
exec_variable(idp, use)

    SYMTAB_NODE_PTR idp;        /* variable id */
    USE             use;        /* how variable is used */

{
    int             delta;          /* difference in levels */
    TYPE_STRUCT_PTR tp = idp->typep;
    TYPE_STRUCT_PTR base_tp;
    STACK_ITEM_PTR  datap;          /* ptr to data area */
    STACK_FRAME_HEADER_PTR hp;

    /*
    -- Point to the variable's stack item.  If the variable's level
    -- is less than the current level, follow the static links to
    -- the appropriate stack frame base.
    */
    hp = (STACK_FRAME_HEADER_PTR) stack_frame_basep;
    delta = level - idp->level;
    while (delta-- > 0)
        hp = (STACK_FRAME_HEADER_PTR) hp->static_link.address;
    datap = (STACK_ITEM_PTR) hp + idp->defn.info.data.offset;

    /*
```

```
    --  If a scalar or enumeration VAR parm, that item
    --  points to the actual item.
    */
    if ((idp->defn.key == VARPARM_DEFN) &&
        (tp->form != ARRAY_FORM) &&
        (tp->form != RECORD_FORM))
        datap = (STACK_ITEM_PTR) datap->address;


    /*
    --  Push the address of the variable's data area.
    */
    if ((tp->form == ARRAY_FORM) ||
        (tp->form == RECORD_FORM))
        push_address((ADDRESS) datap->address);
    else
        push_address((ADDRESS) datap);


    /*
    --  If there are subscripts or field designators,
    --  modify the address to point to the array element
    --  record field.
    */
    get_ctoken();
    while ((ctoken == LBRACKET) || (ctoken == PERIOD)) {
        if      (ctoken == LBRACKET) tp = exec_subscripts(tp);
        else if (ctoken == PERIOD)   tp = exec_field();
    }


    base_tp = base_type(tp);


    /*
    --  Leave the modified address on top of the stack if:
    --      it is an assignment target, or
    --      it represents a parameter passed by reference, or
    --      it is the address of an array or record.
    --  Otherwise, replace the address with the value that it
    --  points to.
    */
    if ((use != TARGET_USE) && (use != VARPARM_USE) &&
        (tp->form != ARRAY_FORM) && (tp->form != RECORD_FORM)) {

        if ((base_tp == integer_typep) || (tp->form == ENUM_FORM))
            tos->integer = *((int *) tos->address);
        else if (base_tp == char_typep)
            tos->byte = *((char *) tos->address);
        else
            tos->real = *((float *) tos->address);
    }


    if ((use != TARGET_USE) && (use != VARPARM_USE))
        trace_data_fetch(idp, tp,
                         (tp->form == ARRAY_FORM) ||
                         (tp->form == RECORD_FORM)
                            ? tos->address
                            : tos);


    return(tp);
}

/*-----------------------------------------------------------*/
/*  exec_subscripts    Execute subscripts to modify the array */
/*                     data area address on the top of the    */
/*                     stack.  Return a pointer to the type of */
/*                     the array element.                      */
/*-----------------------------------------------------------*/

    TYPE_STRUCT_PTR
```

```
exec_subscripts(tp)

    TYPE_STRUCT_PTR tp;         /* ptr to type structure */

{
    int subscript_value;

    /*
    --  Loop to execute bracketed subscripts.
    */
    while (ctoken == LBRACKET) {
        /*
        --  Loop to execute a subscript list.
        */
        do {
            get_ctoken();
            exec_expression();

            subscript_value = tos->integer;
            pop();

            /*
            --  Range check.
            */
            if ((subscript_value < tp->info.array.min_index) ||
                (subscript_value > tp->info.array.max_index))
                runtime_error(VALUE_OUT_OF_RANGE);

            /*
            --  Modify the data area address.
            */
            tos->address +=
                (subscript_value - tp->info.array.min_index) *
                                 tp->info.array.elmt_typep->size;

            if (ctoken == COMMA) tp = tp->info.array.elmt_typep;
        } while (ctoken == COMMA);

        get_ctoken();
        if (ctoken == LBRACKET) tp = tp->info.array.elmt_typep;
    }

    return(tp->info.array.elmt_typep);
}

/*-----------------------------------------------------------*/
/*  exec_field         Execute a field designator to modify   */
/*                     the record data area address on the    */
/*                     top of the stack.  Return a pointer to  */
/*                     the type of the record field.          */
/*-----------------------------------------------------------*/

    TYPE_STRUCT_PTR
exec_field()

{
    SYMTAB_NODE_PTR field_idp;

    get_ctoken();
    field_idp = get_symtab_cptr();

    tos->address += field_idp->defn.info.data.offset;

    get_ctoken();
    return(field_idp->typep);
}
```

```
/*-------------------------------------------------------------*/        TYPE_STRUCT_PTR tp1, tp2;              /* ptrs to types */
/*  promote_operands_to_real    If either operand is integer,  */
/*                         convert it to real.                 */
/*-------------------------------------------------------------*/   {

promote_operands_to_real(operandp1, tp1, operandp2, tp2)             if (tp1 == integer_typep) operandp1->real = operandp1->integer;
                                                                    if (tp2 == integer_typep) operandp2->real = operandp2->integer;
    STACK_ITEM_PTR operandp1, operandp2;    /* ptrs to operands */  }
```

In function exec_expression, we execute an expression to evaluate it and leave the result value on the top of the stack. We also return the type (that is, a pointer to the type structure) of the result. We can compare two integer, two real, two character (byte), or two string values, and we compare two enumeration values as integers. Before we compare two real values or an integer value to a real value, we call function promote_operands_to_real, where we check both operands and convert any integer value to real.

Function exec_simple_expression executes a simple expression and leaves the result value on the top of the stack. For the OR operator, we operate on two boolean values. For the + and - operators, we operate on two integer values. We call promote_operands_to_real before we operate on the values if both are real, or if one is integer and the other is real. We return the type of the result.

We execute a term in function exec_term and leave the result value on the top of the stack. For the AND operator, we operate on two boolean values. For the * operator, we operate on two integer values. We call promote_operands_to_real before we operate on the values if both are real, or if one is integer and the other is real. For the / operator, we operate on integer or real values, but we call promote_operands_to_real first to convert any integer values to real. We only operate on two integer values for the DIV and MOD operators. We return the type of the result.

Function exec_factor executes a factor and leaves the result value on the top of the stack, and then returns its type. If the factor is an identifier, a number, or a string, we call function get_symtab_cptr to retrieve the pointer to its symbol table node. If it's an identifier, we check the node's defn.key field to decide whether to call function exec_routine_call (to execute a function call), exec_constant, or exec_variable. If the factor is a number, we push the value in the node's defn.info.constant.value field. We call either function push_integer or push_real.

If the factor is a string, we obtain the string that the node's info field points to, and we check its length. If the string is a single character, we call function push_byte. Otherwise, we call push_address to push the address of the string.

In function exec_constant, we push the value that we obtain from the symbol table, and then we return its type.

9.4.5 Evaluating variables

Function exec_variable pushes either the value or the address of a variable or a formal parameter onto the runtime stack. Whether we push a value or an address depends on the type of the variable or parameter and how it is used. We also return the type of the variable or parameter. In the following description, anything we say about a variable also applies to a formal parameter, unless we say otherwise.

We first compare level to the variable's level and point hp to the appropriate stack frame. We want datap to point to the stack item that was allocated for the variable, so we point it to the item that is the variable's stack offset away from the base of the stack frame.

If we are evaluating a VAR parameter that is a scalar or an enumeration, datap now points to the stack item that contains the address of the actual stack item. We set datap to datap->address to point it to the actual stack item.

Next, we want to push the address of the variable's data. If the variable is a scalar, datap points to the stack item containing the variable's value so we just push the value of datap. If the variable is an array or variable, the stack item that datap points to contains the *address* of the variable's data area (which we allocated in function alloc_local) so we push the value of datap->address.

So now we have the address of the variable's data on top of the stack. If the variable is subscripted, we call function exec_subscripts to modify that address. If the variable is a record field, we call function exec_field to modify the address.

Then it is time to decide whether to leave the address on top of the stack or to replace the address with the value that it points to. We leave the address alone if the variable is used as the target of an assignment statement (usage is TARGET_USE), if it is being passed as an actual parameter that corresponds to a formal VAR parameter (usage is VARPARM_USE), or if the variable is an array or record. In all other cases, we replace the address with the value. Finally, we call function trace_data_fetch to print tracing information about fetching the value of a variable.

Note that we never put array and record values on the stack. Instead, we always put the address of the data area on the stack. (That's what function alloc_local does too.)

In function exec_subscripts, we loop to execute array subscript expressions to modify the array data address that is on top of the stack. To modify the address for each subscript, we first subtract the array's minimum subscript value from the subscript expression value, multiply this by the element size, and add the product to the address. We also do a range check of the subscript value. After the last subscript, we return the type of the array element.

We modify the record data address that is on top of the stack in function exec_field by adding the field's byte offset. Then we return the type of the record field.

9.4.6 Range checking

Range checking is a runtime error check that is possible because of Pascal's subrange types. This check ensures that a value is not outside the permissible range of values.

You have seen three places where we do a range check. One is in function exec_assignment_statement to check the assignment of a value to a subrange variable. Another is in exec_actual_parms to check the value of an actual parameter against a formal subrange parameter. The third is in function exec_subscripts to check a subscript value against the index subrange.

9.5 Program 9-1: Pascal Interpreter I

Now we are all set to put everything together into an interpreter that can parse and execute Pascal programs that consist of procedures and functions, calls to these routines, and assignment statements.

Figure 9-14 shows the main file of the interpreter run1.c. The main routine is the same as ones we have seen before, but there are also the runtime tracing routines.

FIGURE 9-14   File run1.c.

```
/****************************************************************/
/*                                                            */
/*      Program 9-1:  Pascal Interpreter I                    */
/*                                                            */
/*      Interpret assignment statements in procedures         */
/*      and functions.                                        */
/*                                                            */
/*      FILE:     run1.c                                      */
/*                                                            */
/*      REQUIRES: Modules parser, symbol table, scanner,      */
/*                          executor, error                   */
/*                                                            */
/*      FLAGS:    Macro flag "trace" must be defined          */
/*                                                            */
/*      USAGE:    run1 sourcefile                             */
/*                                                            */
/*         sourcefile    name of source file containing       */
/*                       the statements to interpret          */
/*                                                            */
/****************************************************************/

#include <stdio.h>
#include "symtab.h"
#include "exec.h"

/*-----------------------------------------------------------*/
/* Externals                                                 */
/*-----------------------------------------------------------*/

extern int exec_line_number;

extern TYPE_STRUCT_PTR integer_typep, real_typep,
                       boolean_typep, char_typep;

/*-----------------------------------------------------------*/
/* main              Initialize the scanner and call         */
/*                   routine program.                        */
/*-----------------------------------------------------------*/

main(argc, argv)

    int  argc;
```

```
    char *argv[];

{
    /*
    -- Initialize the scanner.
    */
    init_scanner(argv[1]);

    /*
    -- Process a program.
    */
    get_token();
    program();
}

/*-----------------------------------------------------------*/
/* trace_routine_entry      Trace the entry into a routine. */
/*-----------------------------------------------------------*/

trace_routine_entry(idp)

    SYMTAB_NODE_PTR idp;        /* routine id */

{
    printf(">> Entering routine %s\n", idp->name);
}

/*-----------------------------------------------------------*/
/* trace_routine_exit       Trace the exit from a routine.  */
/*-----------------------------------------------------------*/

trace_routine_exit(idp)

    SYMTAB_NODE_PTR idp;        /* routine id */

{
    printf(">> Exiting routine %s\n", idp->name);
}

/*-----------------------------------------------------------*/
/* trace_statement_execution  Trace the execution of a      */
```

```
/*                        statement.               */
/*------------------------------------------------*/

trace_statement_execution()

{
    printf(">>  Stmt %d\n", exec_line_number);
}

/*------------------------------------------------*/
/*  trace_data_store       Trace the storing of data into */
/*                         a variable.            */
/*------------------------------------------------*/

trace_data_store(idp, idp_tp, targetp, target_tp)

    SYMTAB_NODE_PTR idp;          /* id of target variable */
    TYPE_STRUCT_PTR idp_tp;       /* ptr to id's type */
    STACK_ITEM_PTR targetp;       /* ptr to target location */
    TYPE_STRUCT_PTR target_tp;    /* ptr to target's type */

{
    printf(">>  %s", idp->name);
    if      (idp_tp->form == ARRAY_FORM)  printf("[*]");
    else if (idp_tp->form == RECORD_FORM) printf(".*");
    print_data_value(targetp, target_tp, ":=");
}

/*------------------------------------------------*/
/*  trace_data_fetch       Trace the fetching of data from */
/*                         a variable.            */
/*------------------------------------------------*/

trace_data_fetch(idp, tp, datap)

    SYMTAB_NODE_PTR idp;          /* id of target variable */
    TYPE_STRUCT_PTR tp;           /* ptr to id's type */
    STACK_ITEM_PTR  datap;        /* ptr to data */

{
    printf(">>  %s", idp->name);
    if      (tp->form == ARRAY_FORM)  printf("[*]");
    else if (tp->form == RECORD_FORM) printf(".*");
    print_data_value(datap, tp, "=");
}
```

```
/*------------------------------------------------*/
/*  print_data_value        Print a data value.        */
/*------------------------------------------------*/

print_data_value(datap, tp, str)

    STACK_ITEM_PTR  datap;     /* ptr to data value to print */
    TYPE_STRUCT_PTR tp;        /* ptr to type of stack item */
    char           *str;       /* " = " or " := " */

{
    /*
    -- Reduce a subrange type to its range type.
    -- Convert a non-boolean enumeration type to integer.
    */
    if (tp->form == SUBRANGE_FORM)
        tp = tp->info.subrange.range_typep;
    if ((tp->form == ENUM_FORM) && (tp != boolean_typep))
        tp = integer_typep;

    if (tp == integer_typep)
        printf(" %s %d\n", str, datap->integer);
    else if (tp == real_typep)
        printf(" %s %0.6g\n", str, datap->real);
    else if (tp == boolean_typep)
        printf(" %s %s\n", str, datap->integer == 1
                                ? "true" : "false");
    else if (tp == char_typep)
        printf(" %s '%c'\n", str, datap->byte);

    else if (tp->form == ARRAY_FORM) {
        if (tp->info.array.elmt_typep == char_typep) {
            char *chp = (char *) datap;
            int  size = tp->info.array.elmt_count;

            printf(" %s '", str);
            while (size--) printf("%c", *chp++);
            printf("'\n");
        }
        else printf(" %s <array>\n", str);
    }
    else if (tp->form == RECORD_FORM)
        printf(" %s <record>\n", str);
}
```

We call function `trace_routine_entry` from function `routine_entry`, and function `trace_routine_exit` from `routine_exit`. In both tracing functions, we print the name of the procedure or function. We call function `trace_statement_execution` from `exec_statement`. There, we print the line number of the statement that we are about to execute.

We call function `trace_data_fetch` from functions `exec_constant` and `exec_variable`, and function `trace_data_store` from `exec_assignment_statement`. In both tracing functions, we print the name of the constant or variable identifier and the value that we fetch or store. If the variable is an array, we print [*] after its name, and if it's a record, we print .* . We call function `print_data_value` to print the value. It prints either a scalar value, a string value, or, for arrays and records, <array> or <record>.

In Chapter 10, we will want to remove the calls to the tracing routines. In file exec.h, we see that the calls are left in only if we first define the macro flag trace. This is similar to the macro flag analyze that we defined in Chapter 6 for the declarations analyzer and in Chapter 8 for the pretty-printer. We will define trace again in Chapter 11 for the debugger.

Figure 9-15 shows sample interpreter output from a Pascal program containing various assignment statements. Figure 9-16 shows the effect of value and VAR parameters. Figure 9-17 shows output from nested procedures and functions. Figure 9-18 shows a runtime range error.

FIGURE 9-15   Sample interpreter output from a Pascal program containing various assignment statements.

```
Page 1   assign.pas   Wed Jul 11 00:15:10 1990


   1 0: PROGRAM assign (output);
   2 1:
   3 1: CONST
   4 1:     ten = 10;
   5 1:     pi  = 3.14159;
   6 1:
   7 1: TYPE
   8 1:     subrange = 5..ten;
   9 1:     enum = (zero, one, two, three, four, five);
  10 1:     arr = ARRAY [enum] OF real;
  11 1:     rec = RECORD
  12 1:              i : integer;
  13 1:              z : RECORD
  14 1:                     x  : real;
  15 1:                     al : arr;
  16 1:                  END;
  17 1:           END;
  18 1:     arc = ARRAY [12..15] OF rec;
  19 1:
  20 1: VAR
  21 1:     i, j, k : subrange;
  22 1:     el, e2  : enum;
  23 1:     x, y, z : real;
  24 1:     p, q    : boolean;
  25 1:     ch      : char;
  26 1:     r       : rec;
  27 1:     a       : arc;
  28 1:     string1, string2 : ARRAY [1..ten] OF char;
  29 1:
  30 1: BEGIN
  31 1:     i := 7;
  32 1:     j := ten DIV 2;
  33 1:     k := 4*(i - j);
  34 1:     el := three;
  35 1:     e2 := el;
  36 1:     x := pi/7.2;
  37 1:     y := x + 3;
  38 1:     z := x - ten + y;
  39 1:     p := true;
  40 1:     q := NOT (x = y) AND p;
  41 1:
  42 1:     r.i := 7;
  43 1:     r.z.x := 3.14;
  44 1:     r.z.al[two] := +2.2;
  45 1:     i := r.i;
```

```
  46 1:     x := r.z.x;
  47 1:     x := r.z.al[two];
  48 1:
  49 1:     a[14].i := 7;
  50 1:     a[14].z.x := 3.14;


Page 2   assign.pas   Wed Jul 11 00:15:10 1990


  51 1:     a[14].z.al[two] := +2.2;
  52 1:     i := a[14].i;
  53 1:     x := a[14].z.x;
  54 1:     x := a[14].z.al[two];
  55 1:
  56 1:     ch := 'x';
  57 1:     string1 := 'Hello, you';
  58 1:     string2 := string1;
  59 1:     p := string1 = string2;
  60 1:     string1[ten] := ch;
  61 1:     ch := string1[1];
  62 1:     p := string1 = string2;
  63 1:     p := string1 > string2;
  64 1: END.
  65 0:
  66 0:


                     66 Source lines.
                      0 Source errors.


>> Entering routine assign
>>   Stmt 31
>>     i := 7
>>   Stmt 32
>>     ten = 10
>>     j := 5
>>   Stmt 33
>>     i = 7
>>     j = 5
>>     k := 8
>>   Stmt 34
>>     three = 3
>>     el := 3
>>   Stmt 35
```

```
>>  e1 = 3                          >>  two = 2
>>  e2 := 3                         >>  a[*] := 2.2
>>  Stmt 36                         >>  Stmt 52
>>  pi = 3.14159                    >>  a = 7
>>  x := 0.436332                   >>  i := 7
>>  Stmt 37                         >>  Stmt 53
>>  x = 0.436332                    >>  a = 3.14
>>  y := 3.43633                    >>  x := 3.14
>>  Stmt 38                         >>  Stmt 54
>>  x = 0.436332                    >>  two = 2
>>  ten = 10                        >>  a = 2.2
>>  y := 3.43633                    >>  x := 2.2
>>  z := -6.12734                   >>  Stmt 56
>>  Stmt 39                         >>  ch := 'x'
>>  true = true                     >>  Stmt 57
>>  p := true                       >>  string1[*] := 'Hello, you'
>>  Stmt 40                         >>  Stmt 58
>>  x = 0.436332                    >>  string1[*] = 'Hello, you'
>>  y = 3.43633                     >>  string2[*] = 'Hello, you'
>>  p = true                        >>  Stmt 59
>>  q := true                       >>  string1[*] = 'Hello, you'
>>  Stmt 42                         >>  string2[*] = 'Hello, you'
>>  r.* := 7                        >>  p := true
>>  Stmt 43                         >>  Stmt 60
>>  r.* := 3.14                     >>  ten = 10
>>  Stmt 44                         >>  ch = 'x'
>>  two = 2                         >>  string1[*] := 'x'
>>  r.* := 2.2                      >>  Stmt 61
>>  Stmt 45                         >>  string1 = 'H'
>>  r = 7                           >>  ch := 'H'
>>  i := 7                          >>  Stmt 62
>>  Stmt 46                         >>  string1[*] := 'Hello, yox'
>>  r = 3.14                        >>  string2[*] = 'Hello, you'
>>  x := 3.14                       >>  p := false
>>  Stmt 47                         >>  Stmt 63
>>  two = 2                         >>  string1[*] = 'Hello, yox'
>>  r = 2.2                         >>  string2[*] = 'Hello, you'
>>  x := 2.2                        >>  p := true
>>  Stmt 49                         >> Exiting routine assign
>>  a[*] := 7
>>  Stmt 50
>>  a[*] := 3.14                    Successful completion.  30 statements executed.
>>  Stmt 51
```

FIGURE 9-16   Sample interpreter output showing the effects of value and VAR parameters.

```
Page 1   arrparms.pas   Wed Jul 11 00:15:43 1990      14 2:        j : integer;
                                                      15 2:
                                                      16 2:    PROCEDURE proc3 (    ppm1 : matrix;
 1 0: PROGRAM arrparms (output);                      17 3:                    VAR ppm2 : matrix);
 2 1:                                                 18 3:
 3 1: TYPE                                            19 3:        VAR
 4 1:     matrix = ARRAY [1..2, 1..3] OF integer;     20 3:            j : integer;
 5 1:                                                 21 3:
 6 1: VAR                                             22 3:        BEGIN
 7 1:     i    : integer;                             23 3:            ppm1[1,1] := 99;      {99}
 8 1:     m1, m2 : matrix;                            24 3:            ppm2[1,1] := -99;     {-99}
 9 1:                                                 25 3:            j := ppm1[1,1];       {99}
10 1: PROCEDURE proc2 (    pm1 : matrix;              26 3:            j := ppm2[1,1];       {-99}
11 2:                   VAR pm2 : matrix);            27 3:            j := m1[1,1];         {11}
12 2:                                                 28 3:            j := m2[1,1];         {-99}
13 2:     VAR                                         29 3:        END;
```

```
30 2:
31 2:         BEGIN
32 2:             pm1[2,2] := 77;      {77}
33 2:             pm2[2,2] := -77;     {-77}
34 2:             j := pm1[2,2];       {77}
35 2:             j := pm2[2,2];       {-77}
36 2:             j := m1[2,2];        {22}
37 2:             j := m2[2,2];        {-77}
38 2:
39 2:             proc3(pm1, pm2);
40 2:         END;
41 1:
42 1: BEGIN
43 1:     m1[1,1] := 11;  m1[1,2] := 12;  m1[1,3] := 13;
44 1:     m1[2,1] := 21;  m1[2,2] := 22;  m1[2,3] := 23;
45 1:
46 1:     m2[1,1] := -11;  m2[1,2] := -12;  m2[1,3] := -13;
47 1:     m2[2,1] := -21;  m2[2,2] := -22;  m2[2,3] := -23;
48 1:
49 1:     i := m1[1,1];        {11}
50 1:     i := m2[1,1];        {-11}
```

Page 2   arrparms.pas   Wed Jul 11 00:15:43 1990

```
51 1:     i := m1[2,2];        {22}
52 1:     i := m2[2,2];        {-22}
53 1:
54 1:     proc2(m1, m2);
55 1:
56 1:     i := m1[1,1];        {11}
57 1:     i := m2[1,1];        {-99}
58 1:     i := m1[2,2];        {22}
59 1:     i := m2[2,2];        {-77}
60 1: END.
61 0:
```

                    61 Source lines.
                     0 Source errors.

```
>> Entering routine arrparms
>> Stmt 43
>>    m1[*] := 11
>> Stmt 43
>>    m1[*] := 12
>> Stmt 43
>>    m1[*] := 13
>> Stmt 44
>>    m1[*] := 21
>> Stmt 44
>>    m1[*] := 22
>> Stmt 44
>>    m1[*] := 23
>> Stmt 46
>>    m2[*] := -11
>> Stmt 46
>>    m2[*] := -12
>> Stmt 46
>>    m2[*] := -13
```

```
>> Stmt 47
>>    m2[*] := -21
>> Stmt 47
>>    m2[*] := -22
>> Stmt 47
>>    m2[*] := -23
>> Stmt 49
>>    m1 = 11
>>    i := 11
>> Stmt 50
>>    m2 = -11
>>    i := -11
>> Stmt 51
>>    m1 = 22
>>    i := 22
>> Stmt 52
>>    m2 = -22
>>    i := -22
>> Stmt 54
>>    m1[*] = <array>
>> Entering routine proc2
>> Stmt 32
>>    pm1[*] := 77
>> Stmt 33
>>    pm2[*] := -77
>> Stmt 34
>>    pm1 = 77
>>    j := 77
>> Stmt 35
>>    pm2 = -77
>>    j := -77
>> Stmt 36
>>    m1 = 22
>>    j := 22
>> Stmt 37
>>    m2 = -77
>>    j := -77
>> Stmt 39
>>    pm1[*] = <array>
>> Entering routine proc3
>> Stmt 23
>>    ppm1[*] := 99
>> Stmt 24
>>    ppm2[*] := -99
>> Stmt 25
>>    ppm1 = 99
>>    j := 99
>> Stmt 26
>>    ppm2 = -99
>>    j := -99
>> Stmt 27
>>    m1 = 11
>>    j := 11
>> Stmt 28
>>    m2 = -99
>>    j := -99
>> Exiting routine proc3
>> Exiting routine proc2
>> Stmt 56
>>    m1 = 11
>>    i := 11
>> Stmt 57
>>    m2 = -99
>>    i := -99
```

```
>>  Stmt 58                              >>   i := -77
>>   m1 = 22                             >> Exiting routine arrparms
>>   i := 22
>>  Stmt 59
>>   m2 = -77                            Successful completion.  34 statements executed.
```

FIGURE 9-17   Sample interpreter output from nested procedures and functions.

Page 1   nested.pas   Wed Jul 11 00:16:25 1990   Page 2   nested.pas   Wed Jul 11 00:16:25 1990

```
  1 0: PROGRAM main1 (output);                51 1:       i := 1;     {1}
  2 1:                                        52 1:       proc2;
  3 1:     VAR                                53 1:       j := i;     {1}
  4 1:         i, j : integer;                54 1:  END.
  5 1:                                        55 0:
  6 1:     FUNCTION func2 : integer;          56 0:
  7 2:                                        57 0:
  8 2:         VAR
  9 2:             i, j : integer;
 10 2:
 11 2:         FUNCTION func3 : integer;                     57 Source lines.
 12 3:                                                        0 Source errors.
 13 3:             VAR
 14 3:                 i, j : integer;
 15 3:
 16 3:             BEGIN                      >> Entering routine main1
 17 3:                 i := 123;     {123}    >>  Stmt 51
 18 3:                 func3 := 0;   {0}      >>   i := 1
 19 3:                 j := i;       {123}    >>  Stmt 52
 20 3:             END;                       >> Entering routine proc2
 21 2:                                        >>  Stmt 45
 22 2:         BEGIN                          >>   i := -12
 23 2:             i := 12;          {12}     >>  Stmt 46
 24 2:             func2 := func3;   {0}      >> Entering routine proc3
 25 2:             j := i;           {12}     >>  Stmt 39
 26 2:         END;                           >>   i := -123
 27 1:                                        >>  Stmt 40
 28 1:     PROCEDURE proc2;                   >> Entering routine func2
 29 2:                                        >>  Stmt 23
 30 2:         VAR                            >>   i := 12
 31 2:             i, j : integer;            >>  Stmt 24
 32 2:                                        >> Entering routine func3
 33 2:         PROCEDURE proc3;               >>  Stmt 17
 34 3:                                        >>   i := 123
 35 3:             VAR                        >>  Stmt 18
 36 3:                 i, j : integer;        >>   func3 := 0
 37 3:                                        >>  Stmt 19
 38 3:             BEGIN                      >>   i = 123
 39 3:                 i := -123;    {-123}   >>   j := 123
 40 3:                 j := func2;   {0}      >> Exiting routine func3
 41 3:                 j := i;       {-123}   >>   func2 := 0
 42 3:             END;                       >>  Stmt 25
 43 2:                                        >>   i = 12
 44 2:         BEGIN                          >>   j := 12
 45 2:             i := -12;   {-12}          >> Exiting routine func2
 46 2:             proc3;                     >>   j := 0
 47 2:             j := i;     {-12}          >>  Stmt 41
 48 2:         END;                           >>   i = -123
 49 1:                                        >>   j := -123
 50 1:     BEGIN                              >> Exiting routine proc3
                                              >>  Stmt 47
                                              >>   i = -12
```

```
>>    j := -12
>> Exiting routine proc2
>>   Stmt 53
>>    i = 1
>>    j := 1
>> Exiting routine main1


Successful completion.  15 statements executed.
```

FIGURE 9-18   Sample interpreter output showing a runtime range error.

```
Page 1   range1.pas   Wed Jul 11 00:16:48 1990                              13 Source lines.
                                                                            0 Source errors.

  1 0: PROGRAM range1 (output);
  2 1:
  3 1: VAR
  4 1:    i : 1..10;                                        >> Entering routine range1
  5 1:    j : integer;                                      >> Stmt 8
  6 1:                                                      >> j := 0
  7 1: BEGIN                                                >> Stmt 9
  8 1:    j := 0;                                           >> j = 0
  9 1:    i := j;      {range error!}
 10 1: END.                                                 *** RUNTIME ERROR in line 9: Value out of range
 11 0:
 12 0:                                                      Unsuccessful completion.  2 statements executed.
 13 0:
```

In the next chapter, we will complete this interpreter so that it can execute all Pascal statements and the standard predefined procedures and functions.

Questions and exercises

1. Experiment with different stack frame formats. Try allocating array and record data on the stack.

2. In most Pascal programs, we make many references to the program's global variables. We allocate them at the bottom of the runtime stack and if we are in a deeply-nested procedure or function we must follow several static links to get to a global value. Improve this situation by taking advantage of the fact that we know the global values are on the bottom of the stack.

3. Improve the data fetch and store tracing routines to print the values of subscripts and the names of record fields.

4. Improve the parser to do range checking while it is parsing constants and literals.

CHAPTER 10

Interpreting Control Statements

In this chapter, we will complete the executor module by adding execution routines for Pascal control statements and predefined standard procedures and functions. When we finish, we will have reached a major milestone: a fully functional Pascal interpreter. Then in the next chapter, we will enhance the interpreter further by adding interactive debugging capabilities. This chapter develops the skills to:

- use address markers to support executing control statements
- execute calls to the standard procedures and functions
- interpret entire Pascal programs

10.1 Interpreter organization

To execute Pascal control statements, we need to add new files execstmt.c and execstd.c to the executor module, and change several old files.

Parser Module

parser.h	*u*	Parser header file
routine.c	*u*	Parse programs, procedures, and functions
standard.c	*u*	Parse standard procedures and functions
decl.c	*u*	Parse declarations

| stmt.c | *c* | Parse statements |
| expr.c | *u* | Parse expressions |

Scanner Module

| scanner.h | *u* | Scanner header file |
| scanner.c | *u* | Scanner routines |

Symbol Table Module

| symtab.h | *u* | Symbol table header file |
| symtab.c | *u* | Symbol table routines |

Executor Module

exec.h	*c*	Executor header file
executil.c	*c*	Executor utility routines
execstmt.c	*c*	Execute statements
execexpr.c	*u*	Execute expressions
execstd.c	*n*	Execute standard procedures and functions

Error Module

| error.h | *u* | Error header file |
| error.c | *u* | Error routines |

Miscellaneous

| common.h | *u* | Common header file |

Where: *u* file unchanged from the previous chapter
       c file changed from the previous chapter
       n new file

File execstmt.c contains the routines to execute control statements, and execstd.c contains the routines to execute calls to the standard procedures and functions. We add a few new support routines in executil.c. In stmt.c, we modify some of the statement parsing routines to insert address markers into the code buffer. In file exec.h, we add the new constant:

```
#define ADDRESS_MARKER    0x71
```

and the function types:

```
char *crunch_address_marker();
char *fixup_address_marker();
char *get_address_cmarker();
int  get_cinteger();
char *get_caddress();
```

10.2 Executing control statements

The interpreter executes Pascal control statements in essentially the same way that it executes expressions, assignment statements, and calls to procedure and function. As we saw in Chapter 9, the interpreter extracts tokens from the current code segment and then decides what to do based on what the tokens are.

Control statements require a bit more work. For example, you may need to skip part of the intermediate code for an IF statement, and you need to repeatedly execute the intermediate code for a REPEAT statement. We will see later what we can add to the intermediate code to make skipping and looping more efficient.

Figure 10-1 shows a new version of function exec_statement in file execstmt.c. Depending on the value of ctoken, the function can now call the appropriate function to execute the various control statements. Figure 10-2 shows these new functions.

FIGURE 10-1   Function exec_statement in file execstmt.c.

```
/*--------------------------------------------------------*/
/* exec_statement     Execute a statement by calling the  */
/*                    appropriate execution routine.      */
/*--------------------------------------------------------*/

exec_statement()

{
  if (ctoken == STATEMENT_MARKER) {
      exec_line_number = get_statement_cmarker();
      ++exec_stmt_count;

      statement_startp = code_segmentp;
      trace_statement_execution();
      get_ctoken();
  }

  switch (ctoken) {

      case IDENTIFIER: {
          SYMTAB_NODE_PTR idp = get_symtab_cptr();

          if (idp->defn.key == PROC_DEFN)
```

```
              exec_routine_call(idp);
          else
              exec_assignment_statement(idp);

          break;
      }

      case BEGIN:    exec_compound_statement();    break;
      case CASE:     exec_case_statement();        break;
      case FOR:      exec_for_statement();         break;
      case IF:       exec_if_statement();          break;
      case REPEAT:   exec_repeat_statement();      break;
      case WHILE:    exec_while_statement();        break;

      case SEMICOLON:
      case END:
      case ELSE:
      case UNTIL:                                  break;

      default:  runtime_error(UNIMPLEMENTED_RUNTIME_FEATURE);
  }

  while (ctoken == SEMICOLON) get_ctoken();
}
```

FIGURE 10-2   Functions in file execstmt.c that execute the Pascal control statements.

```
/*--------------------------------------------------------*/
/* exec_case_statement      Execute a CASE statement:     */
/*                                                        */
/*                          CASE <expr> OF                */
/*                              <case-branch> ;           */
/*                              ...                        */
/*                          END                           */
/*--------------------------------------------------------*/
```

```
exec_case_statement()

{
  int     case_expr_value;         /* CASE expr value */
  int     case_label_count;        /* CASE label count */
  int     case_label_value;        /* CASE label value */
  char    *branch_table_location;  /* branch table addr */
  char    *case_branch_location;   /* CASE branch addr */
```

```
TYPE_STRUCT_PTR case_expr_tp;              /* CASE expr type */
BOOLEAN         done = FALSE;

get_ctoken();        /* token after CASE */
branch_table_location = get_address_cmarker();

/*
-- Evaluate the CASE expression.
*/
get_ctoken();
case_expr_tp = exec_expression();
case_expr_value = (case_expr_tp == integer_typep) ||
                  (case_expr_tp->form == ENUM_FORM)
                      ? tos->integer
                      : tos->byte;
pop();       /* expression value */

/*
-- Search the branch table for the expression value.
*/
code_segmentp = branch_table_location;
get_ctoken();
case_label_count = get_cinteger();
while (!done && case_label_count--) {
    case_label_value    = get_cinteger();
    case_branch_location = get_caddress();
    done = case_label_value == case_expr_value;
}

/*
-- If found, go to the appropriate CASE branch.
*/
if (case_label_count >= 0) {
    code_segmentp = case_branch_location;
    get_ctoken();
    exec_statement();

    code_segmentp = get_address_cmarker();
    get_ctoken();
}
else runtime_error(INVALID_CASE_VALUE);
}

/*------------------------------------------------------------*/
/* exec_for_statement       Execute a FOR statement:         */
/*                                                           */
/*                          FOR <id> := <expr>               */
/*                              TO|DOWNTO <expr>             */
/*                              DO <stmt>                     */
/*------------------------------------------------------------*/

exec_for_statement()

{
    SYMTAB_NODE_PTR control_idp;         /* control var id */
    TYPE_STRUCT_PTR control_tp;          /* control var type */
    STACK_ITEM_PTR  targetp;             /* ptr to control target */
    char            *loop_start_location; /* addr of start of loop */
    char            *loop_end_location;   /* addr of end of loop */
    int             control_value;        /* value of control var */
    int             initial_value, final_value, delta_value;

    get_ctoken();        /* token after FOR */
    loop_end_location = get_address_cmarker();

    /*
    -- Get the address of the control variable's stack item.
```

```
    */
    get_ctoken();
    control_idp = get_symtab_cptr();
    control_tp = exec_variable(control_idp, TARGET_USE);
    targetp    = (STACK_ITEM_PTR) tos->address;
    pop();        /* control variable address */

    /*
    -- Evaluate the initial expression.
    */
    get_ctoken();
    exec_expression();
    initial_value = (control_tp == integer_typep)
                        ? tos->integer
                        : tos->byte;
    pop();        /* initial value */

    delta_value = (ctoken == TO) ? 1 : -1;

    /*
    -- Evaluate the final expression.
    */
    get_ctoken();
    exec_expression();
    final_value = (control_tp == integer_typep)
                        ? tos->integer
                        : tos->byte;
    pop();        /* final value */

    loop_start_location = code_segmentp;
    control_value = initial_value;

    /*
    -- Execute the FOR loop.
    */
    while (   ((delta_value == 1) &&
               (control_value <= final_value))
           || ((delta_value == -1) &&
               (control_value >= final_value))) {
        if (control_tp == integer_typep)
            targetp->integer = control_value;
        else
            targetp->byte = control_value;

        get_ctoken();            /* token after DO */
        exec_statement();

        control_value += delta_value;
        code_segmentp = loop_start_location;
    }

    code_segmentp = loop_end_location;
    get_ctoken();        /* token after FOR statement */
}

/*------------------------------------------------------------*/
/* exec_if_statement   Execute an IF statement:              */
/*                                                           */
/*                     IF <expr> THEN <stmt>                 */
/*                                                           */
/*                     or:                                   */
/*                                                           */
/*                     IF <expr> THEN <stmt> ELSE <stmt>     */
/*------------------------------------------------------------*/

exec_if_statement()

{
```

```
char          *false_location;     /* address of false branch */
BOOLEAN       test;

get_ctoken();        /* token after IF */
false_location = get_address_cmarker();

/*
-- Evaluate the boolean expression.
*/
get_ctoken();
exec_expression();
test = tos->integer == 1;
pop();       /* boolean value */

if (test) {
    /*
    -- True:  Execute the true branch.
    */
    get_ctoken();    /* token after THEN */
    exec_statement();

    if (ctoken == ELSE) {
        get_ctoken();                /* token after ELSE */
        code_segmentp = get_address_cmarker();
        get_ctoken();                /* token after false stmt */
    }
}
else {
    /*
    -- False:  Execute the false branch if there is one.
    */
    code_segmentp = false_location;
    get_ctoken();

    if (ctoken == ELSE) {
        get_ctoken();                /* token after ELSE */
        get_address_cmarker();       /* skip address marker */

        get_ctoken();
        exec_statement();
    }
}
}

/*------------------------------------------------------------*/
/* exec_repeat_statement      Execute a REPEAT statement:     */
/*                                                            */
/*                            REPEAT <stmt-list>              */
/*                            UNTIL <expr>                     */
/*------------------------------------------------------------*/

exec_repeat_statement()

{
    char *loop_start_location = code_segmentp;  /* addr of
                                                   loop start */

    do {
        get_ctoken();        /* token after REPEAT */
```

```
        /*
        -- Execute the statement list.
        */
        do {
            exec_statement();
        } while (ctoken != UNTIL);

        /*
        -- Evaluate the boolean expression.
        */
        get_ctoken();
        exec_expression();
        if (tos->integer == 0) code_segmentp = loop_start_location;
        pop();               /* boolean value */
    } while (code_segmentp == loop_start_location);
}

/*------------------------------------------------------------*/
/* exec_while_statement        Process a WHILE statement:     */
/*                                                            */
/*                             WHILE <expr> DO <stmt>         */
/*------------------------------------------------------------*/

exec_while_statement()

{
    char    *loop_end_location;        /* addr of end of loop */
    char    *test_location;            /* addr of boolean expr */
    BOOLEAN loop_done = FALSE;

    get_ctoken();        /* token after WHILE */
    loop_end_location = get_address_cmarker();
    test_location     = code_segmentp;

    do {
        /*
        -- Evaluate the boolean expression.
        */
        get_ctoken();
        exec_expression();
        if (tos->integer == 0) {
            code_segmentp = loop_end_location;
            loop_done = TRUE;
        }
        pop();           /* boolean value */

        /*
        -- If true, execute the statement.
        */
        if (!loop_done) {
            get_ctoken();
            exec_statement();
            code_segmentp = test_location;
        }
    } while (!loop_done);

    get_ctoken();        /* token after WHILE statement */
}
```

10.2.1 Executing the REPEAT statement

We begin with the simplest control statement, the REPEAT statement. Figure 10-3 shows the intermediate *code diagram* for the statement. A code diagram is similar to a syntax diagram, except that it represents how the parser lays out the intermediate code in the code buffer (which we later copy into a code segment where we execute it). The code starts with the single token (represented with an oval) for REPEAT, which is then followed by all the intermediate code (represented by a rectangle) for the statements in the statement list. After that comes the single token for UNTIL followed by the intermediate code for the boolean expression.

FIGURE 10-3   The intermediate code diagram for the REPEAT statement.

When we call the new function exec_repeat_statement in file execstmt.c, the code segment pointer code_segmentp points to the first token code of the first statement in the statement list. Since this statement list is in a loop, we point loop_start_location to this token. We call function exec_statement to execute each statement in the list, and then we call exec_expression to evaluate the boolean expression. If the expression value is zero (false), we must execute the statement list again, so we reset code_segmentp to the value of loop_start_location. Otherwise, we leave code_segmentp pointing to the first token after the REPEAT statement.

10.2.2 Executing the WHILE statement with an address marker

Figure 10-4 shows the intermediate code diagram for the WHILE statement that represents what the parser has been producing up until now. As with the REPEAT statement, you need to remember the location of the first token after the WHILE token. This is the start of the boolean expression, which you evaluate before each time through the loop.

FIGURE 10-4   The original intermediate code diagram for the WHILE statement.

If the expression is true, you execute the statement part, loop back, and re-evaluate the expression. But what happens if the expression is false? You can imagine going into a "skipping mode," when you extract statements from the code segment but do not execute them. Then, you must go back into "execution mode" when you reach the first statement after the WHILE statement.

A cleaner and much more efficient solution is to place an *address marker* into the intermediate code, as shown in Figure 10-5. The addresss marker points to the first token after the WHILE statement, which is where you want to go if the boolean expression is false.

FIGURE 10-5   The intermediate code diagram for the WHILE statement with an address marker.

The parser emits these address markers into the intermediate code in the code buffer. Figure 10-6 shows new versions of some of the statement parsing functions in file stmt.c. In the new version of function while_statement, we call function crunch_address_marker to insert the address marker into the code buffer after the WHILE token. Function crunch_address_marker is one of several new functions in file executil.c that insert new information into the code buffer. They are all shown in Figure 10-7.

FIGURE 10-6   Control statement parsing functions in file stmt.c that insert address markers into the intermediate code.

```
/*--------------------------------------------------------*/
/*  while_statement     Process a WHILE statement:        */
/*                                                        */
/*                           WHILE <expr> DO <stmt>       */
/*--------------------------------------------------------*/

while_statement()

{
    TYPE_STRUCT_PTR expr_tp;
    char            *loop_end_location;

    get_token();
    loop_end_location = crunch_address_marker(NULL);

    expr_tp = expression();
    if (expr_tp != boolean_typep) error(INCOMPATIBLE_TYPES);

    if_token_get_else_error(DO, MISSING_DO);
    statement();

    fixup_address_marker(loop_end_location);
}
```

```
/*----------------------------------------------------------------*/
/*  if_statement       Process an IF statement:                   */
/*                                                                */
/*                          IF <expr> THEN <stmt>                 */
/*                                                                */
/*                       or:                                      */
/*                                                                */
/*                          IF <expr> THEN <stmt> ELSE <stmt>     */
/*----------------------------------------------------------------*/

if_statement()

{
    TYPE_STRUCT_PTR expr_tp;
    char            *false_location;
    char            *if_end_location;

    get_token();
    false_location = crunch_address_marker(NULL);

    expr_tp = expression();
    if (expr_tp != boolean_typep) error(INCOMPATIBLE_TYPES);

    if_token_get_else_error(THEN, MISSING_THEN);
```

```
        statement();

        fixup_address_marker(false_location);

        /*
        -- ELSE branch?
        */
        if (token == ELSE) {
            get_token();
            if_end_location = crunch_address_marker(NULL);

            statement();

            fixup_address_marker(if_end_location);
        }
}

/*------------------------------------------------------------*/
/* for_statement       Process a FOR statement:               */
/*                                                            */
/*                     FOR <id> := <expr> TO|DOWNTO <expr>    */
/*                     DO <stmt>                              */
/*------------------------------------------------------------*/

for_statement()

{
    SYMTAB_NODE_PTR for_idp;
    TYPE_STRUCT_PTR for_tp, expr_tp;
    char            *loop_end_location;

    get_token();
    loop_end_location = crunch_address_marker(NULL);

    if (token == IDENTIFIER) {
        search_and_find_all_symtab(for_idp);
        crunch_symtab_node_ptr(for_idp);

        if ((for_idp->level != level) ||
            (for_idp->defn.key != VAR_DEFN))
            error(INVALID_FOR_CONTROL);

        for_tp = base_type(for_idp->typep);
        get_token();

        if ((for_tp != integer_typep) &&
            (for_tp != char_typep) &&
            (for_tp->form != ENUM_FORM)) error(INCOMPATIBLE_TYPES);
    }
    else {
        error(IDENTIFIER, MISSING_IDENTIFIER);
        for_tp = &dummy_type;
    }

    if_token_get_else_error(COLONEQUAL, MISSING_COLONEQUAL);

    expr_tp = expression();
    if (! is_assign_type_compatible(for_tp, expr_tp))
        error(INCOMPATIBLE_TYPES);

    if ((token == TO) || (token == DOWNTO)) get_token();
    else error(MISSING_TO_OR_DOWNTO);

    expr_tp = expression();
    if (! is_assign_type_compatible(for_tp, expr_tp))
        error(INCOMPATIBLE_TYPES);
```

```
        if_token_get_else_error(DO, MISSING_DO);
        statement();

        fixup_address_marker(loop_end_location);
}

/*------------------------------------------------------------*/
/* CASE statement globals                                     */
/*------------------------------------------------------------*/

typedef struct case_item {
    int             label_value;
    char            *branch_location;
    struct case_item *next;
} CASE_ITEM, *CASE_ITEM_PTR;

CASE_ITEM_PTR case_item_head, case_item_tail;
int           case_label_count;

/*------------------------------------------------------------*/
/* case_statement      Process a CASE statement:              */
/*                                                            */
/*                     CASE <expr> OF                         */
/*                         <case-branch> ;                    */
/*                         ...                                */
/*                     END                                    */
/*------------------------------------------------------------*/

TOKEN_CODE follow_expr_list[]       = {OF, SEMICOLON, 0};

TOKEN_CODE case_label_start_list[] = {IDENTIFIER, NUMBER, PLUS,
                                      MINUS, STRING, 0};

case_statement()

{
    BOOLEAN        another_branch;
    TYPE_STRUCT_PTR expr_tp;
    TYPE_STRUCT_PTR case_label();
    CASE_ITEM_PTR  case_itemp, next_case_itemp;
    char           *branch_table_location;
    char           *case_end_chain = NULL;

    /*
    -- Initializations for the branch table.
    */
    get_token();
    branch_table_location = crunch_address_marker(NULL);
    case_item_head = case_item_tail = NULL;
    case_label_count = 0;

    expr_tp = expression();

    if (  ((expr_tp->form != SCALAR_FORM) &&
           (expr_tp->form != ENUM_FORM) &&
           (expr_tp->form != SUBRANGE_FORM))
        || (expr_tp == real_typep)) error(INCOMPATIBLE_TYPES);

    /*
    -- Error synchronization:  Should be OF
    */
    synchronize(follow_expr_list, case_label_start_list, NULL);
    if_token_get_else_error(OF, MISSING_OF);

    /*
    -- Loop to process CASE branches.
    */
```

```
    another_branch = token_in(case_label_start_list);
    while (another_branch) {
        if (token_in(case_label_start_list)) case_branch(expr_tp);

        /*
        -- Link another address marker at the end of
        -- the CASE branch to point to the end of
        -- the CASE statement.
        */
        case_end_chain = crunch_address_marker(case_end_chain);

        if (token == SEMICOLON) {
            get_token();
            another_branch = TRUE;
        }
        else if (token_in(case_label_start_list)) {
            error(MISSING_SEMICOLON);
            another_branch = TRUE;
        }
        else another_branch = FALSE;
    }

    /*
    -- Emit the branch table.
    */
    fixup_address_marker(branch_table_location);
    crunch_integer(case_label_count);
    case_itemp = case_item_head;
    while (case_itemp != NULL) {
        crunch_integer(case_itemp->label_value);
        crunch_offset(case_itemp->branch_location);
        next_case_itemp = case_itemp->next;
        free(case_itemp);
        case_itemp = next_case_itemp;
    }

    if_token_get_else_error(END, MISSING_END);

    /*
    -- Patch the CASE branch address markers.
    */
    while (case_end_chain != NULL)
        case_end_chain = fixup_address_marker(case_end_chain);
}

/*------------------------------------------------------------*/
/* case_branch              Process a CASE branch:            */
/*                                                            */
/*                              <case-label-list> : <stmt>    */
/*------------------------------------------------------------*/

TOKEN_CODE follow_case_label_list[] = {COLON, SEMICOLON, 0};

case_branch(expr_tp)

    TYPE_STRUCT_PTR expr_tp;            /* type of CASE expression */

{
    BOOLEAN          another_label;
    TYPE_STRUCT_PTR  label_tp;
    CASE_ITEM_PTR    case_itemp;
    CASE_ITEM_PTR    old_case_item_tail = case_item_tail;
    TYPE_STRUCT_PTR  case_label();

    /*
    -- <case-label-list>
    */
    do {
        label_tp = case_label();
        if (expr_tp != label_tp) error(INCOMPATIBLE_TYPES);

        get_token();
        if (token == COMMA) {
            get_token();
            if (token_in(case_label_start_list)) another_label = TRUE;
            else {
                error(MISSING_CONSTANT);
                another_label = FALSE;
            }
        }
        else another_label = FALSE;
    } while (another_label);

    /*
    -- Error synchronization:  Should be :
    */
    synchronize(follow_case_label_list, statement_start_list, NULL);
    if_token_get_else_error(COLON, MISSING_COLON);

    /*
    -- Loop to fill in the branch_location field of
    -- each CASE_ITEM item for this branch.
    */
    case_itemp = old_case_item_tail == NULL
                    ? case_item_head
                    : old_case_item_tail->next;
    while (case_itemp != NULL) {
        case_itemp->branch_location = code_bufferp;
        case_itemp = case_itemp->next;
    }

    statement();
}

/*------------------------------------------------------------*/
/* case_label              Process a CASE label and return a  */
/*                          pointer to its type structure.    */
/*------------------------------------------------------------*/

    TYPE_STRUCT_PTR
case_label()

{
    TOKEN_CODE      sign    = PLUS;   /* unary + or - sign */
    BOOLEAN         saw_sign = FALSE;  /* TRUE iff unary sign */
    TYPE_STRUCT_PTR label_tp;
    CASE_ITEM_PTR   case_itemp = alloc_struct(CASE_ITEM);

    /*
    -- Link in a CASE_ITEM item for this label.
    */
    if (case_item_head != NULL) {
        case_item_tail->next = case_itemp;
        case_item_tail = case_itemp;
    }
    else {
        case_item_head = case_item_tail = case_itemp;
    }
    case_itemp->next = NULL;
    ++case_label_count;

    /*
    -- Unary + or - sign.
    */
```

```
    if ((token == PLUS) || (token == MINUS)) {                                      : -idp->defn.info.constant
        sign     = token;                                                                        .value.integer;
        saw_sign = TRUE;                                            return(integer_typep);
        get_token();                                           }
    }
                                                               else if (idp->typep == char_typep) {
    /*                                                             if (saw_sign) error(INVALID_CONSTANT);
    -- Numeric constant:  Integer type only.                       case_itemp->label_value = idp->defn.info.constant
    */                                                                                      .value.character;
    if (token == NUMBER) {                                         return(char_typep);
        SYMTAB_NODE_PTR np = search_symtab(token_string,       }
                                 symtab_display[1]);
                                                               else if (idp->typep->form == ENUM_FORM) {
        if (np == NULL) np = enter_symtab(token_string,            if (saw_sign) error(INVALID_CONSTANT);
                                   symtab_display[1]);             case_itemp->label_value = idp->defn.info.constant
        crunch_symtab_node_ptr(np);                                                         .value.integer;
                                                                   return(idp->typep);
        if (literal.type == INTEGER_LIT)                       }
            case_itemp->label_value = sign == PLUS
                                    ? literal.value.integer    else return(&dummy_type);
                                    : -literal.value.integer;
        else error(INVALID_CONSTANT);                      }
        return(integer_typep);
    }                                                      /*
                                                           -- String constant:  Character type only.
    /*                                                     */
    -- Identifier constant:  Integer, character, or enumeration    else if (token == STRING) {
    --                       types only.                       SYMTAB_NODE_PTR np = search_symtab(token_string,
    */                                                                                        symtab_display[1]);
    else if (token == IDENTIFIER) {
        SYMTAB_NODE_PTR idp;                                   if (np == NULL) np = enter_symtab(token_string,
                                                                                        symtab_display[1]);
        search_all_symtab(idp);                                crunch_symtab_node_ptr(np);
        crunch_symtab_node_ptr(idp);
                                                               if (saw_sign) error(INVALID_CONSTANT);
        if (idp == NULL) {
            error(UNDEFINED_IDENTIFIER);                       if (strlen(literal.value.string) == 1) {
            return(&dummy_type);                                   case_itemp->label_value = literal.value.string[0];
        }                                                          return(char_typep);
                                                               }
        else if (idp->defn.key != CONST_DEFN) {                else {
            error(NOT_A_CONSTANT_IDENTIFIER);                      error(INVALID_CONSTANT);
            return(&dummy_type);                                   return(&dummy_type);
        }                                                      }
                                                           }
        else if (idp->typep == integer_typep) {
            case_itemp->label_value = sign == PLUS         else {
                                    ? idp->defn.info.constant     error(INVALID_CONSTANT);
                                        .value.integer            return(&dummy_type);
                                                           }
                                                       }
```

FIGURE 10-7   Functions in file `executil.c` that insert new information into the code buffer.

```
/*----------------------------------------------------------*/        {
/* crunch_address_marker     Append a code address to the   */
/*                           code buffer.  Return the        */            char *save_code_bufferp;
/*                           addesss of the address.         */
/*----------------------------------------------------------*/            if (code_bufferp >= code_buffer + MAX_CODE_BUFFER_SIZE
                                                                                                  - sizeof(ADDRESS)) {
    char *                                                                    error(CODE_SEGMENT_OVERFLOW);
crunch_address_marker(address)                                                exit(-CODE_SEGMENT_OVERFLOW);
                                                                         }
    ADDRESS address;    /* address value to append */                    else {
```

```
    char save_code = *(--code_bufferp);

    *code_bufferp++ = ADDRESS_MARKER;
    save_code_bufferp = code_bufferp;
    *((ADDRESS *) code_bufferp) = address;
    code_bufferp += sizeof(ADDRESS);
    *code_bufferp++ = save_code;

    return(save_code_bufferp);
    }
}

/*------------------------------------------------*/
/*  fixup_address_marker    Fix up an address marker with   */
/*                          the offset from the address     */
/*                          marker to the current code      */
/*                          buffer address.  Return the old */
/*                          value of the address marker.    */
/*------------------------------------------------*/

    char *
fixup_address_marker(address)

    ADDRESS address;     /* address of address marker to be fixed up */

{
    char *old_address = *((ADDRESS *) address);

    *((int *) address) = code_bufferp - address;
    return(old_address);
}

/*------------------------------------------------*/
/*  crunch_integer    Append an integer value to the code   */
/*                    buffer.                                */
/*------------------------------------------------*/

crunch_integer(value)
```

```
    int value;          /* value to append */

{
    if (code_bufferp >= code_buffer + MAX_CODE_BUFFER_SIZE
                                        - sizeof(int)) {
        error(CODE_SEGMENT_OVERFLOW);
        exit(-CODE_SEGMENT_OVERFLOW);
    }
    else {
        *((int *) code_bufferp) = value;
        code_bufferp += sizeof(int);
    }
}

/*------------------------------------------------*/
/*  crunch_offset     Append an integer value to the code   */
/*                    that represents the offset from the   */
/*                    given address to the current code     */
/*                    buffer address.                       */
/*------------------------------------------------*/

crunch_offset(address)

    ADDRESS address;     /* address from which to offset */

{
    if (code_bufferp >= code_buffer + MAX_CODE_BUFFER_SIZE
                                        - sizeof(int)) {
        error(CODE_SEGMENT_OVERFLOW);
        exit(-CODE_SEGMENT_OVERFLOW);
    }
    else {
        *((int *) code_bufferp) = address - code_bufferp;
        code_bufferp += sizeof(int);
    }
}
```

Function crunch_address_marker is similar to function crunch_statement_
marker. When we call this function, we pass it an address of a location in the
code buffer. First, we insert the ADDRESS_MARKER code followed by the address
value into the code buffer behind the last token code. Then we return the code
buffer address of that address value.

In function while_statement, when we first call crunch_address_marker, we
do not yet know the address of the end of the WHILE statement. Therefore, we
pass NULL so the address marker is initially just a place holder. We store the address
of this NULL value in loop_end_location. Later, when we finish parsing the WHILE
statement, we pass loop_end_location to function fixup_address_marker to patch
the address marker with the current code buffer address, which by then is the
address of the first token after the WHILE statement.

So what should function fixup_address_marker do? Your first thought might
be that it should just replace the placeholder NULL value with the current code
buffer address. Then, you should have the intermediate code shown in Figure 10-
5, with the address marker containing the address of the first token in the code
buffer after the WHILE statement. Unfortunately, that won't work. You execute the

intermediate code after it has been copied into a code segment, not in the code buffer. So, what you want is a code *segment* address. To solve this dilemma, you can calculate the byte offset between the address of the placeholder NULL value and the current code buffer address, and then you replace the NULL value with this offset. Later, when you are executing the intermediate code, you can calculate the code segment address by adding the offset to the current code segment address.

When we are finished in fixup_address_marker, we return the previous value of the address marker. Only parser function case_statement uses this value, so most of the time we ignore it.

Figure 10-8 shows the other new functions in file executil.c, the ones that retrieve the new information from the code segment. One new function is get_address_cmarker, which we call when we encounter an address marker in a code segment as we are executing a statement. It extracts the offset from the code segment, adds the current code segment address, and then subtracts one to calculate the desired code segment address. Subtracting one compensates for the fact that code_segmentp always points one byte ahead of the current token in ctoken. We return the address.

FIGURE 10-8   Functions in file executil.c that retrieve the new information from a code segment.

```
/*-----------------------------------------------------*/
/*  get_address_cmarker    Extract an address marker from the  */
/*                         current code segment.  Add its      */
/*                         offset value to the code segment    */
/*                         address and return the new address. */
/*-----------------------------------------------------*/

    char *
get_address_cmarker()

{
    ADDRESS address;     /* address to return */

    if (ctoken == ADDRESS_MARKER) {
        address = *((int *) code_segmentp) + code_segmentp - 1;
        code_segmentp += sizeof(ADDRESS);
    }

    return(address);
}

/*-----------------------------------------------------*/
/*  get_cinteger      Extract an integer value from the      */
/*                    current code segment and return the    */
/*                    value.                                 */
/*-----------------------------------------------------*/

    int
```

```
get_cinteger()

{
    int value;          /* value to extract and return */

    value = *((int *) code_segmentp);
    code_segmentp += sizeof(int);

    return(value);
}

/*-----------------------------------------------------------*/
/*  get_caddress      Extract an offset from the current code */
/*                    segment and add it to the code segment  */
/*                    address.  Return the new address.       */
/*-----------------------------------------------------------*/

    char *
get_caddress()

{
    ADDRESS address;     /* address to return */

    address = *((int *) code_segmentp) + code_segmentp - 1;
    code_segmentp += sizeof(int);

    return(address);
}
```

In the new function exec_while_statement, we call get_address_cmarker to obtain the address of the first token after the WHILE statement, and we store this address in loop_end_location. Then we store the address of the first token of the boolean expression in test_location. We call exec_expression to evaluate the expression.

If the expression is false, we set code_segmentp to the value of loop_end_location to point it to the first token after the WHILE statement, and we are done. Otherwise, if the expression is true, we call exec_statement to execute the statement part. Afterwards, we reset code_segmentp to the value of test_location in order to loop back and re-evaluate the boolean expression.

10.2.3 Executing the FOR statement

Figure 10-9 shows the intermediate code diagram for the FOR statement. Like the WHILE statement, an address marker points to the first token after the statement.

FIGURE 10-9   The intermediate code diagram for the FOR statement.

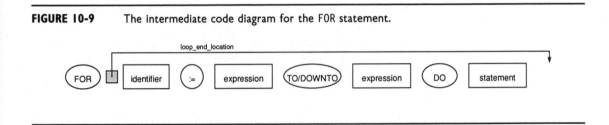

In the new version of function for_statement, we point loop_end_location to the first token after the statement. We create an address marker at the beginning and patch it at the end.

In the new function exec_for_statement, we first call get_address_cmarker to obtain the address of the first token after the FOR statement and store the address in loop_end_location. Next, we call exec_variable, passing usage code TARGET_USE, to obtain the address of the stack item of the control variable. We then evaluate the initial and final expressions with calls to exec_expression. In the while loop, we check and set the value of the control variable, call exec_statement to execute the statement part, and increment or decrement the control variable. Once we reach the final value, we set code_segmentp to the value of loop_end_location. We leave the control variable with the final value.

10.2.4 Executing the IF statement

Figures 10-10 and 10-11 show the intermediate code diagrams of the IF statement without and with the ELSE part, respectively. The former requires one address marker, and the latter requires two.

FIGURE 10-10   The intermediate code diagram for the IF statement without the ELSE part.

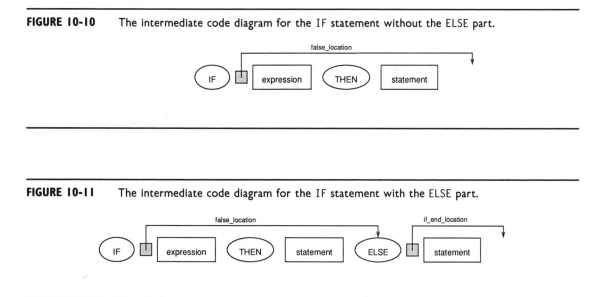

FIGURE 10-11   The intermediate code diagram for the IF statement with the ELSE part.

In the new version of function if_statement, we create an addresss marker at the beginning and store its address in false_location. After we have parsed the THEN part, we patch the address marker. Thus, the false_location address marker either points to the first token after the IF statement if there is no ELSE part (Figure 10-10), or to the ELSE token if there is an ELSE part (Figure 10-11).

If there is an ELSE part, we insert an address marker after the ELSE token, and we store its address in if_end_location. We patch this address marker after we've parsed the ELSE part. Thus, the if_end_location marker points to the first token after the IF statement.

In the new function exec_if_statement, we first call get_address_cmarker to obtain the address of the end of the THEN part and store the address in false_location. Then, we call exec_expression to evaluate the boolean expression.

If the expression is true, we call exec_statement to execute the THEN part. If the next token is not ELSE we are done, since there is no ELSE part and code_segmentp now points to the first token after the IF statement. However, if the next token is ELSE then we must call get_address_cmarker to point code_segmentp to the first token after the ELSE part, and then we are done.

If the boolean expression is false, we set code_segmentp to false_location. If the token at that location is not ELSE then we are done, since there is no ELSE part, and code_segmentp now points to the first token after the IF statement. If the token is ELSE, the function must call get_address_cmarker to skip over the address marker after the ELSE. code_segmentp then points to the first token of the ELSE part. We call exec_statement to execute that statement, and then we are done.

10.2.5 Executing the CASE statement

The CASE statement is the most challenging Pascal control statement. Figure 10-12 shows the intermediate code diagram for a sample statement. At the beginning, just after the CASE token, an address marker points to the CASE *branch table* which is located just after the last CASE branch. At the end of each CASE branch, an address marker points to the first token after the CASE statement.

The branch table begins with the number of entries in the table. There is one entry per CASE label. Each entry consists of the value of its label and the address of the first token of the branch statement corresponding to that label value. We output the branch table to the code buffer after the code for the last branch statement because not until then do we know the addresses of all the branch statements.

We insert these addresss markers and output the branch table in the new version of function case_statement. We need to patch all the address markers at the ends of the CASE branches with the address of the first token after the CASE statement, so we need to keep track of the address markers. We do this by linking the address markers themselves together. Figure 10-13 shows how each address marker initially points to the previous one. At the end of the CASE statement, we

FIGURE 10-12   The intermediate code diagram for a sample CASE statement.

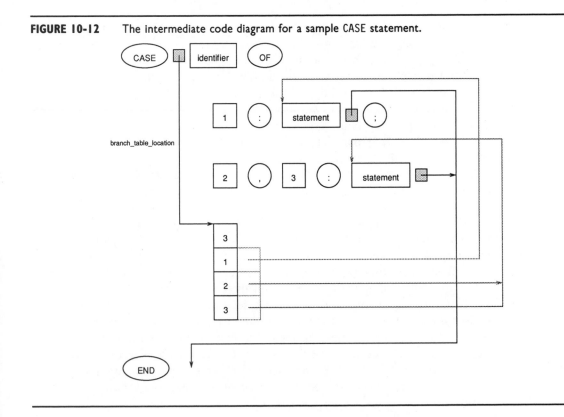

FIGURE 10-13   How each address marker for a CASE statement initially points to the previous one.

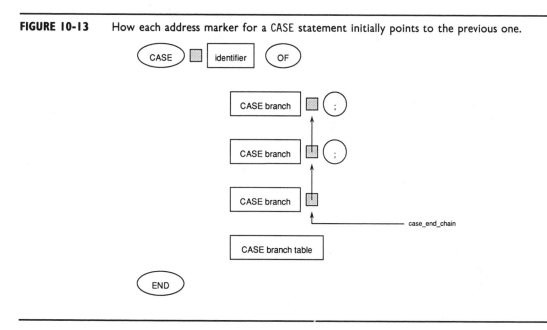

merely run down this list and patch each address marker to point to the first token after the statement.

We keep the data for the branch table in a separate linked list of CASE_ITEM items. We build the list in functions case_branch and case_label, and at the end of function case_statement, we run down the list to emit the branch table.

In case_statement, we begin by creating an address marker and storing its address in branch_table_location. We patch this address marker after we've parsed the last CASE branch. Then we emit the branch table.

We also create an address marker after we have parsed each CASE branch. We link them together by passing the address of the previous marker to crunch_address_marker, and we point case_end_chain to the head of the list. At the end of the CASE statement, we call fixup_address_marker in a loop that runs down the linked list. This is the only call to fixup_address_marker that makes use of the function's return value.

In function case_label, we increment case_label_count and allocate a CASE_ITEM item for each CASE label, which we then link to the end of the list. The new global variables case_item_head and case_item_tail point to the head and tail of this list. We set the label_value field and return to function case_branch.

Back in case_branch, after parsing the colon, we point the branch_location field of each of the branch items to the first token of the CASE branch statement.

When we emit the branch table in function case_statement we call two new functions in file emitutil.c, functions crunch_integer and crunch_offset. Whenever we call crunch_integer, we pass an integer which we append to the code buffer. Whenever we call crunch_offset, we pass a code buffer address. We compute the offset between that address and the current code buffer address, and we append the offset to the code buffer. So each branch table entry contains the offset between the offset itself and the start of the branch statement.

We also have new functions get_cinteger and get_caddress in file execu-til.c. Function get_cinteger extracts and returns an integer value from the current code segment. In function get_caddress, we return a code segment address that we calculate by extracting an offset value from the code segment, adding the current code segment address, and then subtracting one (to compensate for code_segmentp being one byte ahead of ctoken).

In the new function exec_case_statement, we first call function get_address_cmarker to obtain the address of the branch table, which we store in branch_table_location. We call exec_expression to evaluate the expression, and we store the value in case_expr_value.

We set code_segmentp to the value of branch_table_location to jump down to the branch table. We call get_cinteger to obtain the number of branch table entries. Then in a while loop, we call get_cinteger and get_caddress to obtain the CASE label value and the address of the corresponding CASE branch statement.

We compare case_expr_value to the label value of each branch table entry. If there is a match, we set code_segmentp to the corresponding branch statement address and call exec_statement to execute the branch statement at that address. After we execute the branch statement, we call get_address_cmarker to set code_segmentp to the address of the first token after the CASE statement, and we are done. If there was no match, we abort the program execution with the INVALID_CASE_VALUE error.

10.3 Executing calls to standard procedures and functions

Now we can execute all the Pascal control statements. To complete our interpreter, we need to execute calls to Pascal's standard predefined procedures and functions.

Figure 10-14 shows the new file execstd.c of the executor module. Its routines are analogous to those in file standard.c of the parser module.

FIGURE 10-14   File execstd.c.

```
/**************************************************/
/*                                                */
/*    S T A N D A R D   R O U T I N E   E X E C U T O R    */
/*                                                */
/*    Execution routines for statements.          */
/*                                                */
/*    FILE:      execstd.c                         */
/*                                                */
/*    MODULE:    executor                          */
/*                                                */
/**************************************************/

#include <stdio.h>
#include <math.h>
```

```
#include "common.h"
#include "error.h"
#include "symtab.h"
#include "scanner.h"
#include "parser.h"
#include "exec.h"

#define EOF_CHAR                    '\x7f'

#define DEFAULT_NUMERIC_FIELD_WIDTH    10
#define DEFAULT_PRECISION               2

/*----------------------------------------------*/
/* Externals                                    */
/*----------------------------------------------*/
```

```
extern int              level;
extern int              exec_line_number;

extern char             *code_segmentp;
extern TOKEN_CODE       ctoken;

extern STACK_ITEM       *stack;
extern STACK_ITEM_PTR tos;
extern STACK_ITEM_PTR stack_frame_basep;
extern STACK_ITEM_PTR stack_display[];

extern TYPE_STRUCT_PTR integer_typep, real_typep,
                        boolean_typep, char_typep;

/*----------------------------------------------------*/
/* Forwards                                           */
/*----------------------------------------------------*/

TYPE_STRUCT_PTR exec_eof_eoln(), exec_abs_sqr(),
                exec_arctan_cos_exp_ln_sin_sqrt(),
                exec_pred_succ(), exec_chr(),
                exec_odd(), exec_ord(), exec_round_trunc();

/*----------------------------------------------------*/
/* Globals                                            */
/*----------------------------------------------------*/

BOOLEAN eof_flag = FALSE;

/*----------------------------------------------------*/
/* exec_standard_routine_call  Execute a call to a standard */
/*                             procedure or function. Return */
/*                             a pointer to the type structure */
/*                             of the call.            */
/*----------------------------------------------------*/

    TYPE_STRUCT_PTR
exec_standard_routine_call(rtn_idp)

    SYMTAB_NODE_PTR rtn_idp;            /* routine id */

{
    switch (rtn_idp->defn.info.routine.key) {

        case READ:
        case READLN:    exec_read_readln(rtn_idp);      return(NULL);

        case WRITE:
        case WRITELN:   exec_write_writeln(rtn_idp);    return(NULL);

        case EOFF:
        case EOLN:      return(exec_eof_eoln(rtn_idp));

        case ABS:
        case SQR:       return(exec_abs_sqr(rtn_idp));

        case ARCTAN:
        case COS:
        case EXP:
        case LN:
        case SIN:
        case SQRT:      return(exec_arctan_cos_exp_ln_sin_sqrt
                                (rtn_idp));

        case PRED:
        case SUCC:      return(exec_pred_succ(rtn_idp));
```

```
        case CHR:       return(exec_chr());
        case ODD:       return(exec_odd());
        case ORD:       return(exec_ord());

        case ROUND:
        case TRUNC:     return(exec_round_trunc(rtn_idp));
    }
}

/*----------------------------------------------------*/
/* exec_read_readln      Execute a call to read or readln.  */
/*----------------------------------------------------*/

exec_read_readln(rtn_idp)

    SYMTAB_NODE_PTR rtn_idp;            /* routine id */

{
    SYMTAB_NODE_PTR parm_idp;           /* parm id */
    TYPE_STRUCT_PTR parm_tp;            /* parm type */
    STACK_ITEM_PTR  targetp;            /* ptr to read target */

    /*
    -- Parameters are optional for readln.
    */
    get_ctoken();
    if (ctoken == LPAREN) {
        /*
        -- <id-list>
        */
        do {
            get_ctoken();
            parm_idp = get_symtab_cptr();
            parm_tp = base_type(exec_variable(parm_idp,
                                        VARPARM_USE));
            targetp = (STACK_ITEM_PTR) tos->address;

            pop();      /* pop off address */

            if (parm_tp == integer_typep)
                scanf("%d", &targetp->integer);
            else if (parm_tp == real_typep)
                scanf("%g", &targetp->real);

            else if (parm_tp == char_typep) {
                scanf("%c", &targetp->byte);
                if (eof_flag ||
                    (targetp->byte == '\n')) targetp->byte = ' ';
            }

            trace_data_store(parm_idp, parm_idp->typep,
                            targetp, parm_tp);
        } while (ctoken == COMMA);

        get_ctoken();   /* token after ) */
    }

    if (rtn_idp->defn.info.routine.key == READLN) {
        char ch;

        do {
            ch = getchar();
        } while(!eof_flag && (ch != '\n'));
    }
}

/*----------------------------------------------------*/
/* exec_write_writeln    Execute a call to write or writeln. */
```

```
/*                        Each actual parameter can be:      */
/*                                                           */
/*                             <expr>                        */
/*                                                           */
/*                             or:                           */
/*                                                           */
/*                        <epxr> : <expr>                    */
/*                                                           */
/*                             or:                           */
/*                                                           */
/*                   <expr> : <expr> : <ex  >                */
/*-------------------------------------------- -----------*/

exec_write_writeln(rtn_idp)

    SYMTAB_NODE_PTR rtn_idp;            /* routine id */

{
    TYPE_STRUCT_PTR parm_tp;           /* parm type */
    int             field_width;
    int             precision;

    /*
    -- Parameters are optional for writeln.
    */
    get_ctoken();
    if (ctoken == LPAREN) {
        do {
            /*
            -- Push value
            */
            get_ctoken();
            parm_tp = base_type(exec_expression());

            if (parm_tp == integer_typep)
                field_width = DEFAULT_NUMERIC_FIELD_WIDTH;
            else if (parm_tp == real_typep) {
                field_width = DEFAULT_NUMERIC_FIELD_WIDTH;
                precision   = DEFAULT_PRECISION;
            }
            else field_width = 0;

            /*
            -- Optional field width <expr>
            */
            if (ctoken == COLON) {
                get_ctoken();
                exec_expression();
                field_width = tos->integer;
                pop();              /* pop off field width */

                /*
                -- Optional decimal places <expr>
                */
                if (ctoken == COLON) {
                    get_ctoken();
                    exec_expression();
                    precision = tos->integer;
                    pop();          /* pop off precision */
                }
            }

            /*
            -- Write value
            */
            if (parm_tp == integer_typep)
                printf("%*d", field_width, tos->integer);
            else if (parm_tp == real_typep)
                printf("%*.*f", field_width, precision, tos->real);
            else if (parm_tp == boolean_typep)
                printf("%*s", field_width, tos->integer == 1
                                            ? "TRUE" : "FALSE");
            else if (parm_tp == char_typep)
                printf("%*c", field_width, tos->byte);

            else if (parm_tp->form == ARRAY_FORM) {
                char buffer[MAX_SOURCE_LINE_LENGTH];

                strncpy(buffer, tos->address,
                                parm_tp->info.array.elmt_count);
                buffer[parm_tp->info.array.elmt_count] = '\0';
                printf("%*s", -field_width, buffer);
            }

            pop();          /* pop off value */
        } while (ctoken == COMMA);

        get_ctoken();       /* token after ) */
    }

    if (rtn_idp->defn.info.routine.key == WRITELN) putchar('\n');
}

/*-----------------------------------------------------------*/
/*  exec_eof_eoln        Execute a call to eof or to eoln.   */
/*                       No parameters => boolean result.    */
/*-----------------------------------------------------------*/

    TYPE_STRUCT_PTR
exec_eof_eoln(rtn_idp)

    SYMTAB_NODE_PTR rtn_idp;            /* routine id */

{
    char ch = getchar();

    switch (rtn_idp->defn.info.routine.key) {

        case EOFF:
            if (eof_flag || feof(stdin)) {
                eof_flag = TRUE;
                push_integer(1);
            }
            else {
                push_integer(0);
                ungetc(ch, stdin);
            }
            break;

        case EOLN:
            if (eof_flag || feof(stdin)) {
                eof_flag = TRUE;
                push_integer(1);
            }
            else {
                push_integer(ch == '\n' ? 1 : 0);
                ungetc(ch, stdin);
            }
            break;
    }

    get_ctoken();           /* token after function name */
    return(boolean_typep);
}
```

```
/*----------------------------------------------------------*/
/*  exec_abs_sqr              Execute a call to abs or to sqr.  */
/*                            integer parm => integer result    */
/*                            real parm   => real result        */
/*----------------------------------------------------------*/

    TYPE_STRUCT_PTR
exec_abs_sqr(rtn_idp)

    SYMTAB_NODE_PTR rtn_idp;              /* routine id */

{
    TYPE_STRUCT_PTR parm_tp;             /* actual parameter type */
    TYPE_STRUCT_PTR result_tp;           /* result type */

    get_ctoken();        /* ( */
    get_ctoken();
    parm_tp = base_type(exec_expression());

    if (parm_tp == integer_typep) {
        tos->integer = rtn_idp->defn.info.routine.key == ABS
                        ? abs(tos->integer)
                        : tos->integer * tos->integer;
        result_tp = integer_typep;
    }
    else {
        tos->real = rtn_idp->defn.info.routine.key == ABS
                        ? fabs(tos->real)
                        : tos->real * tos->real;
        result_tp = real_typep;
    }

    get_ctoken();        /* token after ) */
    return(result_tp);
}

/*----------------------------------------------------------*/
/*  exec_arctan_cos_exp_ln_sin_sqrt Execute a call to arctan,  */
/*                            cos, exp, ln, sin, or sqrt. */
/*                            integer parm => real result */
/*                            real_parm   => real result */
/*----------------------------------------------------------*/

    TYPE_STRUCT_PTR
exec_arctan_cos_exp_ln_sin_sqrt(rtn_idp)

    SYMTAB_NODE_PTR rtn_idp;              /* routine id */

{
    TYPE_STRUCT_PTR parm_tp;             /* actual parameter type */
    int            code = rtn_idp->defn.info.routine.key;

    get_ctoken();        /* ( */
    get_ctoken();
    parm_tp = base_type(exec_expression());
    if (parm_tp == integer_typep) tos->real = tos->integer;

    if (   ((code == LN)   && (tos->real <= 0.0))
        || ((code == SQRT) && (tos->real <  0.0)))
        runtime_error(INVALID_FUNCTION_ARGUMENT);
    else {
        switch (rtn_idp->defn.info.routine.key) {
            case ARCTAN:   tos->real = atan(tos->real);   break;
            case COS:      tos->real = cos(tos->real);    break;
            case EXP:      tos->real = exp(tos->real);    break;
            case LN:       tos->real = log(tos->real);    break;
            case SIN:      tos->real = sin(tos->real);    break;
```

```
            case SQRT:     tos->real = sqrt(tos->real);   break;
        }
    }

    get_ctoken();        /* token after ) */
    return(real_typep);
}

/*----------------------------------------------------------*/
/*  exec_pred_succ           Execute a call to pred or succ.   */
/*                           integer parm => integer result    */
/*                           enum parm   => enum result        */
/*----------------------------------------------------------*/

    TYPE_STRUCT_PTR
exec_pred_succ(rtn_idp)

    SYMTAB_NODE_PTR rtn_idp;              /* routine id */

{
    TYPE_STRUCT_PTR parm_tp;             /* actual parameter type */

    get_ctoken();        /* ( */
    get_ctoken();
    parm_tp = base_type(exec_expression());

    tos->integer = rtn_idp->defn.info.routine.key == PRED
                    ? --tos->integer
                    : ++tos->integer;

    get_ctoken();        /* token after ) */
    return(parm_tp);
}

/*----------------------------------------------------------*/
/*  exec_chr                 Execute a call to chr.            */
/*                           integer parm => character result  */
/*----------------------------------------------------------*/

    TYPE_STRUCT_PTR
exec_chr()

{
    get_ctoken();        /* ( */
    get_ctoken();
    exec_expression();

    tos->byte = tos->integer;

    get_ctoken();        /* token after ) */
    return(char_typep);
}

/*----------------------------------------------------------*/
/*  exec_odd                 Execute a call to odd.           */
/*                           integer parm => boolean result   */
/*----------------------------------------------------------*/

    TYPE_STRUCT_PTR
exec_odd()

{
    get_ctoken();        /* ( */
    get_ctoken();
    exec_expression();

    tos->integer &= 1;
```

```
    get_ctoken();       /* token after ) */
    return(boolean_typep);
}

/*----------------------------------------------*/
/* exec_ord              Execute a call to ord.     */
/*                       enumeration parm => integer result */
/*----------------------------------------------*/

    TYPE_STRUCT_PTR
exec_ord()

{
    get_ctoken();       /* ( */
    get_ctoken();
    exec_expression();

    get_ctoken();       /* token after ) */
    return(integer_typep);
}

/*----------------------------------------------*/
/* exec_round_trunc      Execute a call to round or trunc.  */
```

```
/*                          real parm => integer result       */
/*------------------------------------------------------------*/

    TYPE_STRUCT_PTR
exec_round_trunc(rtn_idp)

    SYMTAB_NODE_PTR rtn_idp;            /* routine id */

{
    get_ctoken();       /* ( */
    get_ctoken();
    exec_expression();

    if (rtn_idp->defn.info.routine.key == ROUND) {
        tos->integer = tos->real > 0.0
                            ? (int) (tos->real + 0.5)
                            : (int) (tos->real - 0.5);
    }
    else tos->integer = (int) tos->real;

    get_ctoken();       /* token after ) */
    return(integer_typep);
}
```

In function `exec_standard_routine_call`, we call the appropriate execution function based on the `defn.info.routine.key` field of the symbol table node of the standard routine's identifier. We return either NULL for a standard procedure, or the type of a standard function.

We execute the standard Pascal procedures `read` and `readln` in function `exec_read_readln`. We call `exec_variable`, passing usage code `VARPARM_USE`, to obtain the address of each actual parameter's stack item to read into, and then we call `scanf` to read in the value. If we are reading a character variable and `eof_flag` is TRUE or the character we read is a carriage return, we use the blank character instead. Ignore the call to `trace_data_store`. (Macro flag trace is *undefined* in file `exec.h`.)

After we have read all the variables in the parameter list, if the standard procedure is `readln`, we skip input characters until we read the carriage return character or we reach the end of the input file.

In function `exec_write_writeln`, we execute the standard Pascal procedures `write` and `writeln`. We call `exec_expression` to evaluate each actual parameter expression and to evaluate any field width and precision expressions. We then call `printf` to output the value in the appropriate format. If the value is a string, we must first copy the string into a buffer and then append the null character. After we have written all the values in the parameter list, if the standard procedure is `writeln`, we output a carriage return.

We execute the standard Pascal functions `eof` and `eoln` in function `exec_eof_eoln`. First we try to read a single character. For `eof`, if the end-of-file condition is true we push one (true) onto the stack; otherwise, we push zero (false). For `eoln`, if the end-of-file condition is true or if the character we read is a carriage return we push one; otherwise, we push zero. Then, unless the end-of-file condition is true, we put the character we read back into the input stream so that the next read or readln will get it. We return a pointer to the boolean type structure.

You can see that the remaining functions are straightforward. They execute the rest of the standard predefined Pascal functions and return the appropriate types. Function exec_arctan_cos_exp_ln_sin_sqrt always requires a real parameter value, so it first converts an integer parameter value to real. It also checks this value for ln and sqrt.

10.4 Program 10-1: Pascal Interpreter II

Figure 10-15 shows the main file for our interpreter, run2.c. The interpreter can parse and execute complete Pascal programs written according to our syntax diagrams.

FIGURE 10-15   File run2.c.

```
/*****************************************************************/
/*                                                               */
/*       Program 10-1:  Pascal Interpreter II                    */
/*                                                               */
/*       Interpret a Pascal program.                             */
/*                                                               */
/*       FILE:     run2.c                                        */
/*                                                               */
/*       REQUIRES:  Modules parser, symbol table, scanner,       */
/*                          executor, error                      */
/*                                                               */
/*       USAGE:     run2 sourcefile                              */
/*                                                               */
/*          sourcefile     name of source file containing        */
/*                          the Pascal program to interpret      */
/*                                                               */
/*****************************************************************/

#include <stdio.h>
#include "symtab.h"
#include "exec.h"

/*--------------------------------------------------------------*/
/* Externals                                                    */
/*--------------------------------------------------------------*/
```

```
extern TYPE_STRUCT_PTR integer_typep, real_typep,
                        boolean_typep, char_typep;

/*--------------------------------------------------------------*/
/* main                    Initialize the scanner and call      */
/*                         routine program.                     */
/*--------------------------------------------------------------*/

main(argc, argv)

    int argc;
    char *argv[];

{
    /*
    -- Initialize the scanner.
    */
    init_scanner(argv[1]);

    /*
    -- Process a program.
    */
    get_token();
    program();
}
```

In the next chapter, we will add interactive debugging capabilities to the interpreter.

Questions and exercises

1. Modify function exec_case_statement so that if the value of the CASE expression is not among the CASE labels, execution resumes with the statement after the CASE statement.

2. Under certain conditions, the CASE branch table can be more efficient if it is not searched linearly but instead is indexed by the value of the CASE expression. Under what conditions is this true?

3. Modify the pretty-printer of Chapter 8 to skip over statement markers, address markers, and branch tables in a code segment.

CHAPTER 11

Interactive Debugging

One of the greatest benefits of using an interpreter is how well it supports interactive debugging. You have already seen how an interpreter retains full control as it executes a source program, and how it maintains the runtime resources. You would indeed have a very powerful tool for program development if you could interact with the interpreter as it executes a program.

In this chapter, we take the Pascal interpreter we completed in the previous chapter and develop it further by adding an interactive debugger. With this debugger, you will be able to monitor the interpreter as it executes a program by setting breakpoints, watching the values of variables, printing the values of arbitrary expressions, assigning new values to variables, tracing, and executing statements in single-step mode. In this chapter, you will develop the skills to:

- monitor the execution of a Pascal program
- manipulate the program's resources that are maintained by the interpreter
- interpret a simple interactive debugger command language

11.1 Source-level debugging

Two types of software debuggers are used by programmers, *machine-level* and *source-level*. Machine-level debuggers allow you to debug a program at a low level that is close to the machine language. With such a debugger, you can execute a program one machine instruction at a time and monitor such activity as data moving in and out of the machine registers. Machine-level debuggers may have little or no knowledge of the statements or data structures of the original source program. They are often used to debug compiled programs.

Source-level debuggers, on the other hand, allow you to debug at the same level as the high-level language the program is written in. It knows about the statements and data structures of the language, and when you use one, you can think in terms of the programming language, not the machine instructions. A Pascal source-level debugger, for example, allows you to execute a program a statement at a time and monitor the values of the program's variables. You refer to the statements by their line numbers and to variables by their names (hence, source-level debuggers are also called *symbolic debuggers*). Source-level debuggers are often used to debug interpreted programs, although source-level debugging of compiled programs is possible if the compiler can generate special debugging information along with the machine code.

The rest of this chapter shows how we can build a credible source-level debugger on top of the interpreter we completed in the previous chapter. As you will see, we only need to add some debugging routines to the executor module.

11.1.1 Debugger command language

Our debugger will be interactive, so we must implement a command language. Examples of commands you can give to the debugger are "Set a breakpoint at line 17" and "Show me the current value of `table[index].word`."

A command language can range in sophistication from one with a very simple and rigid format to one that is as flexible and expressive as a programming language. For our debugger, we will implement a command language that is simple and yet retains a Pascal flavor. It has a small vocabulary of commands, but it uses Pascal syntax for variables, expressions, and assignment statements. Like Pascal, it is insensitive to whether you use uppercase or lowercase letters. Figure 11-1 shows a sample interactive session using the debugger command language.

FIGURE 11-1   A sample session with the interactive debugger.

```
C:\BOOK\CHAP11>run3 newton.pas


Page 1   newton.pas   Tue Feb 13 00:35:56 1990

  1 0: PROGRAM newton (input, output);
  2 1:
  3 1: CONST
  4 1:     epsilon = 1e-6;
  5 1:
  6 1: VAR
  7 1:     number, root, sqroot : real;
  8 1:
  9 1: BEGIN
 10 1:    REPEAT
```

```
11 1:        writeln;
12 1:        write('Enter new number (0 to quit): ');
13 1:        read(number);
14 1:
15 1:        IF number = 0 THEN BEGIN
16 1:            writeln(number:12:6, 0.0:12:6);
17 1:        END
18 1:        ELSE IF number < 0 THEN BEGIN
19 1:            writeln('*** ERROR:  number < 0');
20 1:        END
21 1:        ELSE BEGIN
22 1:            sqroot := sqrt(number);
23 1:            writeln(number:12:6, sqroot:12:6);
24 1:            writeln;

26 1:            root := 1;
27 1:        REPEAT
```

```
28 1:                     root := (number/root + root)/2;
29 1:                     writeln(root:24:6,
30 1:                           100*abs(root - sqroot)/sqroot:12:2,
31 1:                           '%')
32 1:              UNTIL abs(number/sqr(root) - 1) < epsilon;
33 1:         END
34 1:      UNTIL number = 0
35 1: END.

                35 Source lines.
                 0 Source errors.


Command? break 15


Command?


Enter new number (0 to quit): 9


Breakpoint
At  15: IF number = 0


Command?
    9.000000    3.000000

                       5.000000      66.67%
                       3.400000      13.33%
                       3.023530       0.78%
                       3.000092       0.00%
                       3.000000       0.00%


Enter new number (0 to quit): 12


Breakpoint
At  15: IF number = 0


Command? assign number := 16


Command? show sqrt(number)
    4


Command? show pi/number
            ^
 *** ERROR: Undefined identifier.
                  ^
 *** ERROR: Incompatible types.


Command? where


At  15: IF number = 0


Command? step


Command?


At  15: IF number = 0


Command?


At  18: IF number < 0


Command?
```

```
At  22: sqroot := sqrt ( number )


Command?


At  23: writeln ( number : 12 : 6 , sqroot : 12 : 6 )
    16.000000    4.000000


Command?


At  24: writeln


Command?


At  26: root := 1


Command? unstep


Command? trace


Command?
<27><28><29>                    8.500000     112.50%
<28><29>                        5.191176      29.78%
<28><29>                        4.136665       3.42%
<28><29>                        4.002257       0.06%
<28><29>                        4.000000       0.00%
<11>
<12>Enter new number (0 to quit): <13>36


Breakpoint
At  15: IF number = 0


Command? untrace


Command? store root


Command? watch
Variables being watched:
        root    (store)


Command? break
Statement breakpoints at:
  15


Command?
    36.000000    6.000000


At 26:  Store root := 1


At 28:  Store root := 18.5
                18.500000     208.33%


At 28:  Store root := 10.2229729
                10.222973      70.38%


At 28:  Store root := 6.87222672
                 6.872227      14.54%


At 28:  Store root := 6.05535173
                 6.055352       0.92%
```

```
At 28:  Store root := 6.00025272              Breakpoint
            6.000253        0.00%             At  15: IF number = 0

At 28:  Store root := 6                       Command? kill
            6.000000        0.00%             Program killed.

Enter new number (0 to quit): 0
```

11.1.2 Breakpoints

A breakpoint is a special tag placed on an executable statement that tells the debugger to temporarily halt the execution of the program just before that statement is to be executed. When the debugger reaches a statement with a breakpoint, it prints the statement's line number followed by the text of the statement, and then it reads a debugging command.

Command: break *number*

Place a breakpoint at the statement beginning on line *number*. For example, break 14. If there are several statements that begin on that line, place a breakpoint at each one of them.

Command: break

Print the line numbers of all the breakpoints.

Command: unbreak *number*

Remove the breakpoint from the statement beginning on line *number*. For example, unbreak 14. If several statements begin on that line, remove all their breakpoints.

Command: unbreak

Remove all breakpoints from all statements.

11.1.3 Statement and routine tracing

Tracing program execution enables you to know which statements and which procedures and functions have been executed, and in what order. Our debugger traces statements by printing the line number of each statement just before executing that statement. It traces procedures and functions by printing a message that a routine has just been entered or is just about to be exited.

Command: trace

Turn on statement tracing.

Command: `untrace`

Turn off statement tracing.

Command: `entry`

Turn on tracing of procedure and function entries.

Command: `unentry`

Turn off tracing of procedure and function entries.

Command: `exit`

Turn on tracing of procedure and function exits.

Command: `unexit`

Turn off tracing of procedure and function exits.

11.1.4 Single-stepping

Single-stepping is running the program one statement at a time. When the debugger executes a program in single-step mode, it operates as though a breakpoint were placed at every statement. Thus, you have an opportunity to enter a debugger command before each statement is executed.

Command: `step`

Turn on single-stepping.

Command: `unstep`

Turn off single-stepping.

The debugger does not allow single-stepping and tracing both to be turned on at the same time. Turning one on automatically turns the other one off.

During single-stepping mode, the debugger prints out the current line number and the text of the statement it is about to execute.

11.1.5 Watching variables

Chapter 9 introduced the useful feature of printing the value of a variable each time it is used (a data fetch) and its new value each time it is assigned one (a data store). The debugger allows you to turn this feature on and off for individual variables. You can watch data fetches, data stores, or both.

Command: `fetch` *variable*
             `store` *variable*
             `watch` *variable*

You can print each data fetch, or each data store, or both fetches and stores of *variable*, respectively. The variable may only be an identifier; it may not be followed by any subscripts or field designators. If you watch an array or record identifier, then you watch all of its elements or fields.

Examples: `fetch alpha`
                `store beta`
                `watch gamma`

Command: `watch`
Print the names of all the variables being watched.

Command: `unwatch` *variable*
Remove the watch from *variable*. For example, `unwatch beta`.

Command: `unwatch`
Remove the watches from all the variables.

Whenever you enter an identifier, the debugger checks to make sure that it is a validly defined identifier. It makes this check in the current scope context of the program. In other words, when you enter a `watch` command, the debugger has stopped program execution before a certain statement. Any identifier that you enter must be valid for the program at that point.

11.1.6 Evaluating expressions

A very useful feature of the debugger is printing the value of an arbitrary Pascal expression. The debugger checks the expression both for syntactic correctness and to ensure that all its identifiers are valid with respect to the current program context.

Command: `show` *expression*
Print the value of *expression*.

Examples: `show table[index].word`
                `show (1.0 - sqrt(rho))/(pi*sqr(sigma))`

11.1.7 Assigning values to variables

When you are debugging a program, you may want to change the value of a variable. You can use the command language to do this with a standard Pascal assignment statement, which the debugger checks for validity.

Command: assign *variable* := *expression*

Here, *variable* is any valid Pascal variable, and it may be followed by subscripts and field designators. The *expression* is, as before, any valid Pascal expression.

Example: assign table[3].count := table[3].count + 1

11.1.8 Where am I?

Sometimes, especially during an intensive debugging session, you can forget where you are in the program.

Command: where

Print the line number followed by the text of the statement to be executed next.

11.1.9 Killing the program

The kill command terminates the program execution.

Command: kill

11.2 Debugger organization

Since we have created a new command language, someone must parse, syntax check, and execute the commands. Yet despite all this, adding interactive debugging capabilities to our interpreter is actually quite straightforward. Because we kept the command language simple, syntax checking will not be a problem. As for parsing and executing, we simply make use of the interpreter's existing modules!

This chapter adds only one new file, debug.c, to the executor module, and modifies files routine.c and error.c.

Parser Module

parser.h	*u*	Parser header file
routine.c	*c*	Parse programs, procedures, and functions
standard.c	*u*	Parse standard procedures and functions
decl.c	*u*	Parse declarations
stmt.c	*u*	Parse statements
expr.c	*u*	Parse expressions

Scanner Module

scanner.h	*u*	Scanner header file
scanner.c	*u*	Scanner routines

Symbol Table Module

symtab.h	*u*	Symbol table header file
symtab.c	*u*	Symbol table routines

Executor Module

exec.h	*u*	Executor header file
executil.c	*u*	Executor utility routines
execstmt.c	*u*	Execute statements
execexpr.c	*u*	Execute expressions
execstd.c	*u*	Execute standard procedures and functions
debug.c	*n*	Interactive debugger

Error Module

error.h	*u*	Error header file
error.c	*c*	Error routines

Miscellaneous

common.h	*u*	Common header file

Where: *u* file unchanged from the previous chapter
        c file changed from the previous chapter
        n new file

Once again, we will need to activate the calls to the tracing routines that we used in the first version of the interpreter that we wrote in Chapter 9. Therefore, we must make sure that the trace macro flag is *defined* for file exec.h.

11.3 Debugger implementation

In file routine.c, we make one simple change near the end of function program to initialize the debugger. Just before it calls function execute, we add the lines:

```
/*
-- Initialize the debugger.
*/
init_debugger();
```

Figure 11-2 shows the new file, debug.c, of the executor module. It contains all of the routines that make up the interactive debugger.

FIGURE 11-2   File debug.c.

```
/*****************************************************************/
/*                                                             */
/*        I N T E R A C T I V E   D E B U G G E R              */
/*                                                             */
/*        Interactive debugging routines.                      */
/*                                                             */
/*        FILE:      debug.c                                   */
/*                                                             */
/*        MODULE:    executor                                  */
/*                                                             */
/*****************************************************************/

#include <stdio.h>
#include "common.h"
#include "error.h"
#include "scanner.h"
#include "symtab.h"
#include "exec.h"

#define MAX_BREAKS     16
#define MAX_WATCHES    16
#define COMMAND_QUERY  "Command? "

/*------------------------------------------------------------*/
/* Externals                                                  */
/*------------------------------------------------------------*/

extern TYPE_STRUCT_PTR  integer_typep, real_typep,
                        boolean_typep, char_typep;

extern TYPE_STRUCT      dummy_type;

extern int              level;
extern SYMTAB_NODE_PTR  symtab_display[];
extern STACK_ITEM_PTR   tos;

extern int       line_number;
extern int       buffer_offset;
extern BOOLEAN   print_flag;

extern char      *code_segmentp;
extern char      *statement_startp;
extern int       ctoken;
extern int       exec_line_number;
extern int       error_count;

extern char      *bufferp;
extern char      ch;
extern char      source_buffer[];
extern char      word_string[];
extern int       token;
extern LITERAL   literal;
extern BOOLEAN   block_flag;

extern char      *code_buffer;
extern char      *code_bufferp;
extern char      *code_segmentp;

/*------------------------------------------------------------*/
/* Globals                                                    */
/*------------------------------------------------------------*/

FILE    *console;
```

```
BOOLEAN debugger_command_flag,  /* TRUE during debug command */
        halt_flag,              /* TRUE to pause for debug command */
        trace_flag,             /* TRUE to trace statement */
        step_flag,              /* TRUE to single-step */
        entry_flag,             /* TRUE to trace routine entry */
        exit_flag;              /* TRUE to trace routine exit */

int     break_count;                 /* count of breakpoints */
int     break_list[MAX_BREAKS];      /* list of breakpoints */

int              watch_count;        /* count of watches */
SYMTAB_NODE_PTR watch_list[MAX_WATCHES];   /* list of watches */

typedef struct {                     /* watch structure */
    SYMTAB_NODE_PTR watch_idp;       /* id node watched variable */
    BOOLEAN         store_flag;      /* TRUE to trace stores */
    BOOLEAN         fetch_flag;      /* TRUE to trace fetches */
} WATCH_STRUCT, *WATCH_STRUCT_PTR;

char *symbol_strings[] = {
    "<no token>", "<IDENTIFIER>", "<NUMBER>", "<STRING>",
    "^", "*", "(", ")", "-", "+", "=", "[", "]", ":", ";",
    "<", ">", ",", ".", "/", ":=", "<=", ">=", "<>", "..",
    "<END OF FILE>", "<ERROR>",
    "AND", "ARRAY", "BEGIN", "CASE", "CONST", "DIV", "DO", "DOWNTO",
    "ELSE", "END", "FILE", "FOR", "FUNCTION", "GOTO", "IF", "IN",
    "LABEL", "MOD", "NIL", "NOT", "OF", "OR", "PACKED", "PROCEDURE",
    "PROGRAM", "RECORD", "REPEAT", "SET", "THEN", "TO", "TYPE",
    "UNTIL", "VAR", "WHILE", "WITH",
};

/*------------------------------------------------------------*/
/* init_debugger      Initialize the interactive debugger.   */
/*------------------------------------------------------------*/

init_debugger()

{
    int i;

    /*
    -- Initialize the debugger's globals.
    */
    console = fopen("CON", "r");
    code_buffer = alloc_bytes(MAX_SOURCE_LINE_LENGTH + 1);

    print_flag = FALSE;
    halt_flag  = block_flag = TRUE;
    debugger_command_flag = trace_flag = step_flag
                          = entry_flag = exit_flag
                          = FALSE;

    break_count = 0;
    for (i = 0; i < MAX_BREAKS; ++i) break_list[i] = 0;

    watch_count = 0;
    for (i = 0; i < MAX_WATCHES; ++i) watch_list[i] = NULL;
}

/*------------------------------------------------------------*/
/* read_debugger_command    Read and process a debugging     */
/*                          command typed in by the user.    */
/*------------------------------------------------------------*/
```

```
read_debugger_command()

{
    BOOLEAN done = FALSE;

    debugger_command_flag = TRUE;

    do {
        printf("\n%s", COMMAND_QUERY);

        /*
        -- Read in a debugging command and replace the
        -- final \n\0 with ;;\0
        */
        bufferp = fgets(source_buffer, MAX_SOURCE_LINE_LENGTH,
                        console);
        strcpy(&source_buffer[strlen(source_buffer) - 1], ";;");

        ch = *bufferp++;
        buffer_offset = sizeof(COMMAND_QUERY);
        code_bufferp  = code_buffer;
        error_count   = 0;

        get_token();

        /*
        -- Process the command.
        */
        switch (token) {
            case SEMICOLON:     done = TRUE;                 break;
            case IDENTIFIER:    execute_debugger_command(); break;
        }

        if (token != SEMICOLON) error(UNEXPECTED_TOKEN);
    } while (!done);

    debugger_command_flag = FALSE;
}

/*--------------------------------------------------------------*/
/* execute_debugger_command      Execute a debugger command.  */
/*--------------------------------------------------------------*/

execute_debugger_command()

{
    WATCH_STRUCT_PTR wp;
    WATCH_STRUCT_PTR allocate_watch();

    if (strcmp(word_string, "trace") == 0) {
        trace_flag = TRUE;
        step_flag  = FALSE;
        get_token();
    }
    else if (strcmp(word_string, "untrace") == 0) {
        trace_flag = FALSE;
        get_token();
    }

    else if (strcmp(word_string, "step") == 0) {
        step_flag  = TRUE;
        trace_flag = FALSE;
        get_token();
    }
    else if (strcmp(word_string, "unstep") == 0) {
        step_flag = FALSE;
        get_token();
    }

    else if (strcmp(word_string, "break") == 0)
        set_breakpoint();
    else if (strcmp(word_string, "unbreak") == 0)
        remove_breakpoint();

    else if (strcmp(word_string, "entry") == 0) {
        entry_flag = TRUE;
        get_token();
    }
    else if (strcmp(word_string, "unentry") == 0) {
        entry_flag = FALSE;
        get_token();
    }

    else if (strcmp(word_string, "exit") == 0) {
        exit_flag = TRUE;
        get_token();
    }
    else if (strcmp(word_string, "unexit") == 0) {
        exit_flag = FALSE;
        get_token();
    }

    else if (strcmp(word_string, "watch") == 0) {
        wp = allocate_watch();
        if (wp != NULL) {
            wp->store_flag = TRUE;
            wp->fetch_flag = TRUE;
        }
    }
    else if (strcmp(word_string, "unwatch") == 0)
        remove_watch();

    else if (strcmp(word_string, "store") == 0) {
        wp = allocate_watch();
        if (wp != NULL) wp->store_flag = TRUE;
    }
    else if (strcmp(word_string, "fetch") == 0) {
        wp = allocate_watch();
        if (wp != NULL) wp->fetch_flag = TRUE;
    }

    else if (strcmp(word_string, "show") == 0)
        show_value();
    else if (strcmp(word_string, "assign") == 0)
        assign_variable();

    else if (strcmp(word_string, "where") == 0) {
        print_statement();
        get_token();
    }
    else if (strcmp(word_string, "kill") == 0) {
        printf("Program killed.\n");
        exit(0);
    }
}
```

```
/********************************/
/*                              */
/*      Tracing routines        */
/*                              */
/********************************/
```

```
/*--------------------------------------------------------------*/
/* trace_statement_execution   Called just before the        */
```

```
/*                       execution of each statement.   */
/*-------------------------------------------------------*/

trace_statement_execution()

{
    if (break_count > 0) {
        int i;

        /*
        -- Check if the statement is a breakpoint.
        */
        for (i = 0; i < break_count; ++i) {
            if (exec_line_number == break_list[i]) {
                printf("\nBreakpoint");
                print_statement();
                halt_flag = TRUE;
                break;
            }
        }
    }

    /*
    -- Pause if necessary to read a debugger command.
    */
    if (halt_flag) {
        read_debugger_command();
        halt_flag = step_flag;
    }

    /*
    -- If single-stepping, print the current statement.
    -- If tracing, print the current line number.
    */
    if (step_flag)  print_statement();
    if (trace_flag) print_line_number();
}

/*-------------------------------------------------------*/
/* trace_routine_entry       Called upon entry into a    */
/*                           procedure or a function.    */
/*-------------------------------------------------------*/

trace_routine_entry(idp)

    SYMTAB_NODE_PTR idp;        /* routine id */

{
    if (entry_flag) printf("\nEntering %s\n", idp->name);
}

/*-------------------------------------------------------*/
/* trace_routine_exit        Called upon exit from a     */
/*                           procedure or a function.    */
/*-------------------------------------------------------*/

trace_routine_exit(idp)

    SYMTAB_NODE_PTR idp;        /* routine id */

{
    if (exit_flag) printf("\nExiting %s\n", idp->name);
}

/*-------------------------------------------------------*/
/* trace_data_store          Called just before a variable */
/*                           is stored into.             */
/*-------------------------------------------------------*/
```

```
trace_data_store(idp, idp_tp, targetp, target_tp)

    SYMTAB_NODE_PTR idp;         /* id of target variable */
    TYPE_STRUCT_PTR idp_tp;      /* ptr to id's type */
    STACK_ITEM_PTR  targetp;     /* ptr to target location */
    TYPE_STRUCT_PTR target_tp;   /* ptr to target's type */

{
    /*
    -- Check if the variable is being watched for stores.
    */
    if ((idp->info != NULL) &&
        ((WATCH_STRUCT_PTR) idp->info)->store_flag) {
        printf("\nAt %d:  Store %s", exec_line_number, idp->name);
        if      (idp_tp->form == ARRAY_FORM)  printf("[*]");
        else if (idp_tp->form == RECORD_FORM) printf(".*");
        print_data_value(targetp, target_tp, ":=");
    }
}

/*-------------------------------------------------------*/
/* trace_data_fetch          Called just before a variable */
/*                           is fetched from.            */
/*-------------------------------------------------------*/

trace_data_fetch(idp, tp, datap)

    SYMTAB_NODE_PTR idp;         /* id of target variable */
    TYPE_STRUCT_PTR tp;          /* ptr to id's type */
    STACK_ITEM_PTR  datap;       /* ptr to data */

{
    TYPE_STRUCT_PTR idp_tp = idp->typep;

    /*
    -- Check if the variable is being watched for fetches.
    */
    if (   (idp->info != NULL)
        && ((WATCH_STRUCT_PTR) idp->info)->fetch_flag) {
        printf("\nAt %d: Fetch %s", exec_line_number, idp->name);
        if      (idp_tp-> form == ARRAY_FORM)  printf("[*]");
        else if (idp_tp->form == RECORD_FORM) printf(".*");
        print_data_value(datap, tp, "=");
    }
}

                /********************************/
                /*                              */
                /*      Printing routines       */
                /*                              */
                /********************************/

/*-------------------------------------------------------*/
/* print_statement           Uncrunch and print a statement. */
/*-------------------------------------------------------*/

print_statement()

{
    int     tk;                 /* token code */
    BOOLEAN done = FALSE;
    char    *csp = statement_startp;

    printf("\nAt %3d:", exec_line_number);

    do {
        switch (tk = *csp++) {
```

```
                case SEMICOLON:
                case END:
                case ELSE:
                case THEN:
                case UNTIL:
                case BEGIN:
                case OF:
                case STATEMENT_MARKER:      done = TRUE;
                                            break;

                default:
                    done = FALSE;

                    switch (tk) {

                        case ADDRESS_MARKER:
                            csp += sizeof(ADDRESS);
                            break;

                        case IDENTIFIER:
                        case NUMBER:
                        case STRING: {
                            SYMTAB_NODE_PTR np = *((SYMTAB_NODE_PTR *) csp);

                            printf(" %s", np->name);
                            csp += sizeof(SYMTAB_NODE_PTR);
                            break;
                        }

                        default:
                            printf(" %s", symbol_strings[tk]);
                            break;
                    }
            }
    } while (!done);

    printf("\n");
}

/*--------------------------------------------------------*/
/* print_line_number          Print the current line number. */
/*--------------------------------------------------------*/

print_line_number()

{
    printf("<%d>", exec_line_number);
}

/*--------------------------------------------------------*/
/* print_data_value            Print a data value.        */
/*--------------------------------------------------------*/

print_data_value(datap, tp, str)

    STACK_ITEM_PTR  datap;      /* ptr to data value to print */
    TYPE_STRUCT_PTR tp;         /* ptr to type of stack item */
    char            *str;       /* " = " or " := " */

{
    /*
    -- Reduce a subrange type to its range type.
    -- Convert a non-boolean enumeration type to integer.
    */
    if (tp->form == SUBRANGE_FORM)
        tp = tp->info.subrange.range_typep;
    if ((tp->form == ENUM_FORM) && (tp != boolean_typep))
```

```
        tp = integer_typep;

    if (tp == integer_typep)
        printf(" %s %d\n", str, datap->integer);
    else if (tp == real_typep)
        printf(" %s %0.6g\n", str, datap->real);
    else if (tp == boolean_typep)
        printf(" %s %s\n", str, datap->integer == 1 ? "true"
                                                     : "false");
    else if (tp == char_typep)
        printf(" %s '%c'\n", str, datap->byte);
    else if (tp->form == ARRAY_FORM) {
        if (tp->info.array.elmt_typep == char_typep) {
            char *chp = (char *) datap;
            int  size = tp->info.array.elmt_count;

            printf(" %s '", str);
            while (size--) printf("%c", *chp++);
            printf("'\n");
        }
        else printf(" %s <array>\n", str);
    }
    else if (tp->form == RECORD_FORM)
        printf(" %s <record>\n", str);
}

        /****************************************/
        /*                                      */
        /*      Breakpoints and watches         */
        /*                                      */
        /****************************************/

/*--------------------------------------------------------*/
/* set_breakpoint      Set a breakpoint, or print all     */
/*                     breakpoints in the break list.     */
/*--------------------------------------------------------*/

set_breakpoint()

{
    get_token();

    switch (token) {

        case SEMICOLON: {
            /*
            -- No line number:  List all breakpoints.
            */
            int i;

            printf("Statement breakpoints at:\n");

            for (i = 0; i < break_count; ++i)
                printf("%5d\n", break_list[i]);

            break;
        }

        case NUMBER: {
            /*
            -- Set a breakpoint by appending it to
            -- the break list.
            */
            int number;

            if (literal.type == INTEGER_LIT) {
                number = literal.value.integer;
```

```
                 if ((number > 0) && (number <= line_number)) {
                     if (break_count < MAX_BREAKS) {
                         break_list[break_count] = number;
                         ++break_count;
                     }
                     else printf("Break list is full.\n");
                 }
                 else error(VALUE_OUT_OF_RANGE);
             }
             else error(UNEXPECTED_TOKEN);

             get_token();
             break;
         }
     }
}

/*------------------------------------------------------*/
/*  remove_breakpoint   Remove a specific breakpoint, or remove */
/*                      all breakpoints.                */
/*------------------------------------------------------*/

remove_breakpoint()

{
    int i, j, number;

    get_token();

    switch (token) {

        case SEMICOLON: {
            /*
            -- No line number:  Remove all breakpoints.
            */
            for (i = 0; i < break_count; ++i) break_list[i] = 0;
            break_count = 0;
            break;
        }

        case NUMBER: {
            /*
            -- Remove a breakpoint from the break list.
            -- Move the following breakpoints up one in the
            -- list to fill in the gap.
            */
            if (literal.type == INTEGER_LIT) {
                number = literal.value.integer;
                if (number > 0) {
                    for (i = 0; i < break_count; ++i) {
                        if (break_list[i] == number) {
                            break_list[i] = 0;
                            --break_count;

                            for (j = i; j < break_count; ++j)
                                break_list[j] = break_list[j+1];

                            break;
                        }
                    }
                }
                else error(VALUE_OUT_OF_RANGE);
            }

            get_token();
            break;
        }
}
```

```
     }
 }
/*------------------------------------------------------*/
/*  allocate_watch       Return a pointer to a watch structure, */
/*                       or print all variables being watched.  */
/*------------------------------------------------------*/

    WATCH_STRUCT_PTR
allocate_watch()

{
    int              i;
    SYMTAB_NODE_PTR  idp;
    WATCH_STRUCT_PTR wp;

    get_token();

    switch (token) {

        case SEMICOLON: {
            /*
            -- No variable:  Print all variables being watched.
            */
            printf("Variables being watched:\n");

            for (i = 0; i < watch_count; ++i) {
                idp = watch_list[i];
                if (idp != NULL) {
                    wp = (WATCH_STRUCT_PTR) idp->info;
                    printf ("%16s  ", idp->name);
                    if (wp->store_flag) printf(" (store)");
                    if (wp->fetch_flag) printf(" (fetch)");
                    printf("\n");
                }
            }

            return(NULL);
        }

        case IDENTIFIER: {
            search_and_find_all_symtab(idp);
            get_token();

            switch (idp->defn.key) {

                case UNDEFINED:
                    return(NULL);

                case CONST_DEFN:
                case VAR_DEFN:
                case FIELD_DEFN:
                case VALPARM_DEFN:
                case VARPARM_DEFN: {
                    /*
                    -- Return a pointer to the variable's watch
                    -- structure if it is already being watched.
                    -- Otherwise, allocate and return a pointer
                    -- to a new watch structure.
                    */
                    if (idp->info != NULL)
                        return((WATCH_STRUCT_PTR) idp->info);
                    else if (watch_count < MAX_WATCHES) {
                        wp = alloc_struct(WATCH_STRUCT);
                        wp->store_flag = FALSE;
                        wp->fetch_flag = FALSE;

                        idp->info = (char *) wp;
```

```
                    watch_list[watch_count] = idp;
                    ++watch_count;

                    return(wp);
                }
                else {
                    printf("Watch list is full.\n");
                    return(NULL);
                }
            }

            default: {
                error(INVALID_IDENTIFIER_USAGE);
                return(NULL);
            }
        }
    }
}
```

```
/*------------------------------------------------------*/
/*  remove_watch        Remove a specific variable from being   */
/*                      watched, or remove all variables from   */
/*                      the watch list.                  */
/*------------------------------------------------------*/

remove_watch()

{
    int             i, j;
    SYMTAB_NODE_PTR idp;
    WATCH_STRUCT_PTR wp;

    get_token();

    switch (token) {

        case SEMICOLON: {
            /*
            -- No variable:  Remove all variables from watch list.
            */
            for (i = 0; i < watch_count; ++i) {
                if ((idp = watch_list[i]) != NULL) {
                    wp = (WATCH_STRUCT_PTR) idp->info;
                    watch_list[i] = NULL;
                    idp->info = NULL;
                    free(wp);
                }
            }
            watch_count = 0;
            break;
        }

        case IDENTIFIER: {
            /*
            -- Remove a variable from the watch list.
            -- Move the following watches up one in the
            -- list to fill in the gap.
            */
            search_and_find_all_symtab(idp);
            get_token();

            if ((idp != NULL) && (idp->info != NULL)) {
                wp = (WATCH_STRUCT_PTR) idp->info;
                for (i = 0; i < watch_count; ++i) {
                    if (watch_list[i] == idp) {
                        watch_list[i] = NULL;
```

```
                        idp->info = NULL;
                        free(wp);
                        --watch_count;

                        for (j = i; j < watch_count; ++j)
                            watch_list[j] = watch_list[j+1];

                        break;
                    }
                }
            }
            break;
        }
    }
}
```

```
/********************************/
/*                              */
/*        Show and assign       */
/*                              */
/********************************/
```

```
/*------------------------------------------------------*/
/*  show_value          Print the value of an expression.       */
/*------------------------------------------------------*/

show_value()

{
    get_token();

    switch (token) {

        case SEMICOLON: {
            error(INVALID_EXPRESSION);
            break;
        }

        default: {
            /*
            -- First parse, then execute the expression
            -- from the code buffer.
            */
            TYPE_STRUCT_PTR expression();
            TYPE_STRUCT_PTR tp     = expression();    /* parse */
            char *save_code_segmentp = code_segmentp;
            int   save_ctoken        = ctoken;

            if (error_count > 0) break;

            /*
            -- Switch to the code buffer.
            */
            code_segmentp = code_buffer + 1;
            get_ctoken();
            exec_expression();                        /* execute */

            /*
            -- Print, then pop off the value.
            */
            if ((tp->form == ARRAY_FORM) ||
                (tp->form == RECORD_FORM))
                print_data_value(tos->address, tp, " ");
            else
                print_data_value(tos, tp, " ");

            pop();
```

```
        /*                                              -- First parse, then execute the assignment statement
        -- Resume the code segment.                     -- from the code buffer.
        */                                              */
        code_segmentp = save_code_segmentp;             SYMTAB_NODE_PTR idp;
        ctoken = save_ctoken;                           char *save_code_segmentp = code_segmentp;
        break;                                          int  save_ctoken       = ctoken;
    }
  }                                                     search_and_find_all_symtab(idp);
}
                                                        assignment_statement(idp);          /* parse */
/*------------------------------------------------*/    if (error_count > 0) break;
/* assign_variable    Execute an assignment statement.  */
/*------------------------------------------------*/    /*
                                                        -- Switch to the code buffer.
assign_variable()                                       */
                                                        code_segmentp = code_buffer + 1;
{                                                       get_ctoken();
    get_token();                                        idp = get_symtab_cptr();
                                                        exec_assignment_statement(idp);     /* execute */
    switch (token) {
                                                        /*
        case SEMICOLON: {                               -- Resume the code segment.
            error(MISSING_VARIABLE);                    */
            break;                                      code_segmentp = save_code_segmentp;
        }                                               ctoken = save_ctoken;
                                                        break;
        case IDENTIFIER: {                          }
            /*                                      }
                                                }
```

Function init_debugger initializes the debugger. We open the console from which we will read the debugger commands, and we allocate a new code_buffer to store the commands in their intermediate form. Then we initialize break_list and watch_list, which will keep track of breakpoints and watched variables, respectively.

11.3.1 Tracing

The key to running a program under control of the debugger is function trace_statement_execution. As we first saw in Chapter 9, this function is called by function exec_statement in file execstmt.c just before each statement is executed. In its new version, it allows the debugger to assume control before each statement.

In trace_statement_execution, we first check to see if the statement is in the break_list. If so, we print the statement by calling function print_statement and set halt_flag to TRUE. Whenever halt_flag is TRUE, we read a debugger command. We then reset halt_flag to the value of step_flag, which is set by the step and unstep commands. Finally, we call function print_statement if step_flag is TRUE, or function print_line_number if trace_flag is TRUE. trace_flag is set by the trace and untrace commands.

Functions trace_routine_entry and trace_routine_exit are called by functions routine_entry and routine_exit, respectively, in file executil.c (as we saw in Chapter 9). We print their messages if entry_flag and exit_flag are TRUE. These flags are set by the entry and exit debugger commands.

We have already seen calls to function `trace_data_store` from function `exec_assignment_statement` in file `execstmt.c` and from function `exec_read_readln` in file `execstd.c`, and calls to function `trace_data_fetch` from functions `exec_constant` and `exec_variable` in file `execexpr.c`.

Variables that we want to watch have a watch structure pointed to by the `info` field of their identifier's symbol table node. This is done by the `fetch`, `store`, `watch`, and `unwatch` debugger commands. Function `trace_data_store` prints only if the `store_flag` of the watch structure is TRUE, and function `trace_data_fetch` prints only if the structure's `fetch_flag` is TRUE.

11.3.2 Printing

Function `print_statement` "uncrunches" a statement from its intermediate form with the aid of the string array `symbol_strings`. This is an operation that we have seen several times in previous utility programs. This version is very simple; we make no attempt to make the output pretty. We do know to skip over any address markers, however.

Function `print_line_number` prints the current line number during statement tracing. Function `print_data_value` is the same function we first saw in Chapter 9.

11.3.3 Reading and interpreting debugger commands

Function `read_debugger_command` prompts for and reads a debugger command from the console. Since we read the command into the scanner's `source_buffer`, we can let our existing scanner module do the scanning.

We replace the line feed character \n with two semicolons to mark the end of the command. Two are necessary because after `get_token` has gotten the first semicolon, the second one keeps the scanner from trying to read another source line.

We reset `code_bufferp` to point to the beginning of the `code_buffer`, which will contain the current debugger command in its intermediate form. We decide what to do based on the first token of the command. An empty command causes the debugger to resume executing the source program.

Note that boolean variable `debugger_command_flag` is TRUE only during the execution of function `read_debugger_command`. We will see later how function `runtime_error` uses this flag.

Function `execute_debugger_command` executes the debugger command. We decide what to do based on the command keyword.

11.3.4 Breakpoints and watches

Function `set_breakpoint` executes the `break` command. If the command does not include a line number, we print the line numbers in the `break_list`. If there is a line number, we append the number to the end of the `break_list`. We check to see if the line number is positive and not greater than the number of the last program line. We do not check, however, that an executable statement starts on the line with that number.

Function `remove_breakpoint` executes the unbreak command. If there is no line number in the command, we clear the `break_list`. If there is a line number, we remove that line number from the `break_list`, and move any following numbers in the list up to fill in the gap. This makes searching the `break_list` faster in function `trace_statement_execution`.

We call function `allocate_watch` for the fetch, store, or watch debugger command. If the command does not include a variable identifier, we print the identifiers in the `watch_list`, along with whether each variable is being watched for fetches, stores, or both.

If the command does include a variable identifier, we search the symbol table for the identifier. We do this with the current state of the symbol table display so the current scope context is maintained. If the identifier is already being watched, we return a pointer to its watch structure. Otherwise, we add the variable to the `watch_list`, allocate a new watch structure, and return a pointer to it.

Function `remove_watch` executes the unwatch debugger command. If there was no variable identifier in the command, we clear the `watch_list`. Otherwise, we look up the identifier, remove it from the `watch_list`, and then fill in the gap.

11.3.5 Expressions and assignments

Function `show_value` executes the show debugger command. Since we must parse, check, and evaluate a Pascal expression, we make use of existing functions in the interpreter. First, we call the parser function `expression` to parse and check the expression, and then we call the executor function `exec_expression` to execute it. But before making this latter call, we temporarily divert `code_segmentp` to point to the `code_buffer`, so that `exec_expression` executes the debugger command's intermediate code in the code buffer instead of the Pascal routine's intermediate code in the current code segment. The expression value is left on top of the runtime stack, where we can print it and then pop it off. At the end, we reset `code_segmentp` to point into the current code segment so the program execution can resume from where it was halted.

Function `assign_variable` executes the assign debugger command. Again, we make use of existing interpreter functions. We call the parser function `assignment_statement` to parse and check the assignment, and then we call the executor function `exec_assignment_statement` to execute the intermediate code in the `code_buffer`.

11.3.6 Runtime error handling

As we saw in Chapter 10, whenever the interpreter encounters a runtime error, it calls function `runtime_error` which then prints an error message and terminates the program execution. With an interactive debugger, a more reasonable action is to halt the program execution and then read a debugger command. You may be able to correct or repair the error before resuming program execution.

Figure 11-3 shows a new version of function runtime_error in file error.c. Normally, it calls read_debugger_command. However, if debugger_command_flag is TRUE, that means that the runtime error was caused by a debugger command, not by the program. In that case, the debugger will itself prompt for and read another command.

FIGURE 11-3   Function runtime_error in file error.c.

```
/*----------------------------------------------------------*/
/*  runtime_error       Print a runtime error message and then  */
/*                      abort the program execution.         */
/*----------------------------------------------------------*/

runtime_error(code)

    ERROR_CODE code;    /* error code */

{
    char            *message = runtime_error_messages[code];
```

```
    extern int      exec_line_number;
    extern BOOLEAN debugger_command_flag;

    if (debugger_command_flag) printf("%s\n", message);
    else {
        printf("\n*** RUNTIME ERROR in line %d: %s\n",
               exec_line_number, message);
        read_debugger_command();
    }
}
```

11.4 Program 11-1: Interactive Debugger

Figure 11-4 shows the main file, run3.c, of the interactive Pascal debugger. This debugger is the culmination of all the programs we have written so far.

FIGURE 11-4   File run3.c.

```
/***************************************************************/
/*                                                             */
/*      Program 11-1:  Interactive Pascal Debugger             */
/*                                                             */
/*      Interpret a Pascal program under the control of an     */
/*      interactive debugger.                                  */
/*                                                             */
/*      FILE:     run3.c                                       */
/*                                                             */
/*      REQUIRES:  Modules parser, symbol table, scanner,      */
/*                      executor, error                        */
/*                                                             */
/*      FLAGS:     Macro flag "trace" must be defined          */
/*                                                             */
/*      USAGE:     run3 sourcefile                             */
/*                                                             */
/*         sourcefile    name of source file containing        */
/*                       the Pascal program to interpret       */
/*                                                             */
/***************************************************************/
```

```
#include <stdio.h>

/*----------------------------------------------------------*/
/*  main                Initialize the scanner and call      */
/*                      routine program.                     */
/*----------------------------------------------------------*/

main(argc, argv)

    int  argc;
    char *argv[];

{
    /*
    -- Initialize the scanner.
    */
    init_scanner(argv[1]);
```

```
/*                                                  get_token();
-- Process a program.                               program();
*/                                              }
```

The next chapter begins the third and final part of this book, where we write a Pascal compiler.

Questions and exercises

1. *Execution profiler.* An execution profiler is a very useful tool to use if you want to rewrite a program to make it run faster. A profiler keeps track of how many times each statement has executed, and when the program is finished, it prints this information. Then, you can tell where the program spends most of its time, and you can concentrate on rewriting just those parts. Modify the debugger to maintain and print profiling information.

2. *Conditional breakpoints.* The breakpoints implemented in this chapter are unconditional: the debugger always halts the program execution whenever it encounters one. A conditional breakpoint has a boolean expression attached to it. When the debugger encounters such a breakpoint, it evaluates the expression and halts the execution only if the expression is true. For example, the following debugger command can set a conditional breakpoint:

```
break 14 if number > 7
```

Implement conditional breakpoints.

3. Rewrite the variable tracing routines to enable a specific array element or a specific record field to be watched. Implement conditional watches. For example:

```
watch table[index].count if index > 100
```

4. *Nonlocal references.* Examine the following program fragment:

```
PROGRAM example (input, output);
    VAR i : integer;

    PROCEDURE proc;
        VAR i : real;

        FUNCTION func : real;
            VAR i : char;
```

```
                             BEGIN {func}
                                 {*** BREAKPOINT HERE ***}
                             END {func};

                         BEGIN {proc}
                             {call func}
                         END {proc};

                     BEGIN {example}
                         {call proc}
                     END {example}.
```

At the breakpoint, three variables named i are active: the global integer i, the real i local to proc, and the character i local to func. The debugger command language implemented in this chapter only allows access to the character i. Implement the ability for the debugger to access the other nonlocal variables named i. For example, the new command language notation might be:

```
                    example'i
                    proc'i
                example'proc'i
```

where the first references the integer i and the second and third both reference the real i.

5. *Call stack.* Sometimes, you want to know more than just where you are in the program, but you also want to know how you got there. As you know, the interpreter's runtime stack contains information about who called whom. Implement a debugger command that prints the current list of calls. Do you need to add more information into each stack frame?

6. Design and implement a better debugger command language. Will you still be able to parse and execute this language using the existing functions?

PART III

Compiling

CHAPTER 12

Emitting 8086 Assembly Language Code

In the third part of the book, we will write a compiler for Pascal programs. This chapter sets the stage with overviews of the 8086 processor architecture and assembly language. We examine both the new code module, which emits the object code, and a runtime library. In the next chapter, we will modify the parser module to make calls to the code module in order to compile procedures, functions, and assignment statements. Then, in Chapter 14, we will complete the compiler so that it can compile entire Pascal programs.

Our compiler will translate a Pascal source program into assembly language code instead of directly into machine language code. Thus, our object language is assembly language. In order for us to see what the compiler is generating, we must be able to read what it emits. Reading assembly code is much easier than deciphering a hexadecimal dump of machine code. Also, an assembler does much useful work. The individual bits of a machine language instruction must be set correctly. Besides the actual code itself, the machine code file must contain various tables and other pieces of information to allow the code to be loaded into memory for execution. Producing a machine language file is difficult, and the assembler does a very nice job for us.

12.1 The 8086 processor architecture

We start with a brief look at the architecture of the 8086 processor. We will examine the processor only enough for us to write the compiler, not in any great detail or thoroughness. This simplified overview also applies to the 80286 and the 80386 processors. Our compiler does not generate code that relies on any features unique to either the 80286 or the 80386.

12.1.1 Machine registers and memory

As shown in Figure 12-1, the 8086 processor has several hardware registers. The 16-bit general-purpose registers are named AX, BX, CX, and DX. Register AX (accumulator) is used for most arithmetic and logic operations. Register DX (data) can also participate in these operations. Register BX (base) is used to contain an address in order to access memory indirectly. Register CX (count) is used as a counter in certain iterative instructions.

FIGURE 12-1   Registers of the 8086 processor.

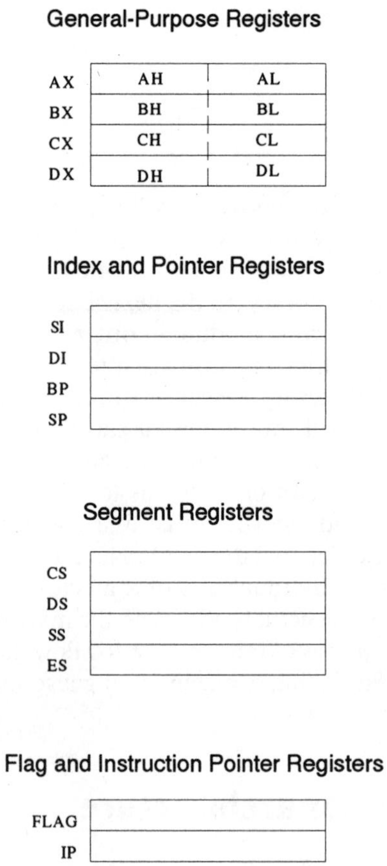

General-Purpose Registers

AX	AH	AL
BX	BH	BL
CX	CH	CL
DX	DH	DL

Index and Pointer Registers

SI	
DI	
BP	
SP	

Segment Registers

CS	
DS	
SS	
ES	

Flag and Instruction Pointer Registers

FLAG	
IP	

Each of the general-purpose registers can also be used as two separate 8-bit registers. For example, you can use the AX register as register AH (A-high) and register AL (A-low).

The index and pointer registers are SI, DI, BP, and SP. Registers SI (source index) and DI (destination index) point to bytes in the source and destination areas of memory for certain string and block operations, such as a string compare and a block move. Register BP (base pointer) points to the current stack frame. Register SP (stack pointer) points to the top of the stack.

The segment registers are CS (code segment), DS (data segment), SS (stack segment), and ES (extra segment). These registers point to the start of the various memory segments.

The IP (instruction pointer) register points to the current instruction. You cannot access it directly from a program; it is implicitly set as instructions are executed. The flag register contains 1-bit flags that record the status of certain conditions, such as the result of a comparison. Conditional jump instructions are affected by bits in the flag register.

A word in memory is 16 bits wide, and a doubleword is 32. The 8086 stores word and doubleword data in memory with their bytes in reversed order. In Figure 12-2, the hexadecimal word value at the memory location labeled WORD is 1234. The hexadecimal doubleword value at the memory location labeled DWORD is 89ABCDEF. Thus, the high-order half of the doubleword value is at DWORD+2.

A word value is usually loaded into register AX to be operated upon, and sometimes into register DX. A doubleword value is loaded into registers with its high-order half in DX and its low-order half in AX (known as the DX:AX register pair). A byte value is usually loaded into register AL.

12.1.2 Code and data segments

The 8086 processor supports a segmented memory architecture. The segment registers point to the start of segments, each one of which can be up to 64K bytes. Segments are a particularly complex feature of the 8086. To keep things simple for our compiler, we use only two segments, a code segment and a data segment, as shown in Figure 12-3. We make the stack segment the same as the data segment

---

FIGURE 12-2 Data are stored in memory with their bytes in reverse order. In the first example, WORD is the address of the word value 1234 (hexadecimal). In the second example, DWORD is the address of the doubleword value 89ABCDEF (hexadecimal). DWORD+2 is the address of the high-order half.

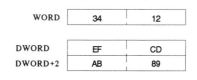

FIGURE 12-3   The code and data segments. The stack segment is the same as the data segment, and the stack grows upward from the bottom of the segment. (These diagrams are drawn so that the lowest address of the segment is at the top.)

Register IP points to the current instruction. Register SP points to the top of the stack, and register BP points to the current stack frame.

Code segment

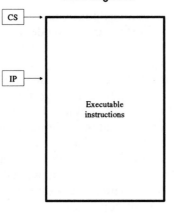

Data segment

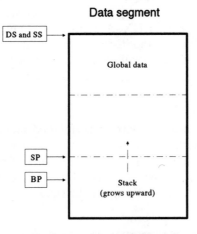

by setting DS and SS to the same value. Our compiler makes very limited use of ES, but when it does, it also sets it to the value of DS.

We allocate global data in the data segment starting from the segment's lowest address and the stack starting at the segment's highest address. Since we drew the segments in the figure with their lowest addresses at the top, the stack begins at the bottom of the data segment and grows upwards to the lower addresses. Register SP always points to the topmost word of the stack. Only word values can be pushed and popped, so pushing a doubleword value onto the stack requires two pushes, first the high-order half followed by the low-order half.

12.1.3 The runtime stack

Just like the software stack of our interpreter, the runtime stack maintained by the 8086 processor is used to store both intermediate results during expression evaluation and the stack frames of active routines.

Figure 12-4 shows the stack frame that is standard for the most popular Pascal compilers on the IBM PC, such as those by Microsoft and Borland. It has the same components as the stack frame we used in our interpreter, only arranged differently. Also, the stack frame base pointer register BP actually points to a word within the frame, instead of to the base of the frame. Thus, both positive and negative offsets off of register BP are needed to access all the items of the stack frame.

FIGURE 12-4   Stack frames from Pascal procedures and functions. These diagrams assume that each routine has two word-sized parameters and two word-sized local variables. Remember that the stack grows upward in these diagrams.

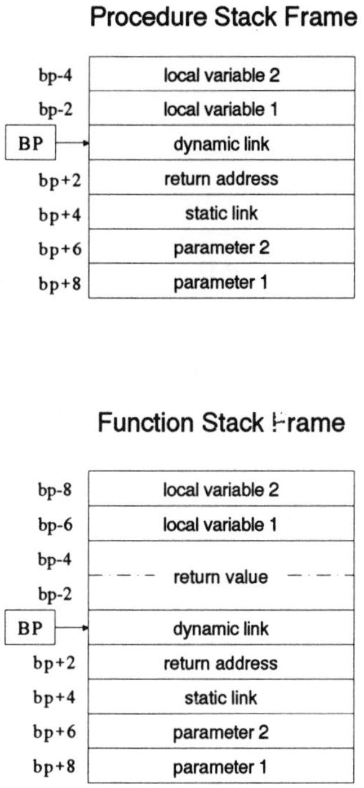

Procedure Stack Frame

bp-4	local variable 2
bp-2	local variable 1
BP →	dynamic link
bp+2	return address
bp+4	static link
bp+6	parameter 2
bp+8	parameter 1

Function Stack Frame

bp-8	local variable 2
bp-6	local variable 1
bp-4	
	— — — return value — — —
bp-2	
BP →	dynamic link
bp+2	return address
bp+4	static link
bp+6	parameter 2
bp+8	parameter 1

Because the stack grows towards the lower address of the data segment, pushing values onto the stack decreases the top of stack pointer register SP, and popping values off increases SP.

12.2 The 8086 assembly language

The instruction set of a processor is largely determined by the processor's architecture. Assembly language is one step above the machine language, and there is a one-to-one correspondence between assembly instructions and the machine language instructions.

12.2.1 Assembly language instructions

The following is a list of the instructions that the compiler generates, along with a brief description of each.

mov	*destination,source*	Move a word or a byte from *source* to *destination*.
rep	movsb	Move a block of contiguous bytes. The source address is in register SI, and the destination address is in register DI. The number of bytes to move is in register CX.
lea	*destination,source*	Load the effective address of *source* into *destination*.
cmp	*value1,value2*	Compare *value1* to *value2*.
repe	cmpsb	Compare *string1* to *string2*. The source (*string1*) address is in register SI, and the destination (*string2*) address is in register DI. The number of bytes to compare is in register CX.
push	*source*	Push the *source* word onto the stack.
pop	*destination*	Pop a word from the stack into *destination*.
not	*destination*	*destination* = ˜*destination*
and	*destination,source*	*destination* = *destination* & *source*
or	*destination,source*	*destination* = *destination* | *source*
add	*destination,source*	*destination* = *destination* + *source*
sub	*destination,source*	*destination* = *destination* − *source*
imul	*source*	DX:AX = AX * *source*
idiv	*source*	AX = DX:AX / *source* DX = DX:AX % *source*

call *target*	Call routine *target*.
ret *n*	Return from the current routine and cut the stack back by *n* bytes (by adding *n* to register SP).
jmp *target*	Unconditional jump to *target*.
jl *target*	Jump to *target* if $<$
jle *target*	Jump to *target* if $<=$
je *target*	Jump to *target* if $==$
jne *target*	Jump to *target* if $!=$
jge *target*	Jump to *target* if $>=$
jg *target*	Jump to *target* if $>$

12.2.2 Assembly language operands

An operand of an assembly instruction is either a memory reference, a register, or an immediate value. In an instruction that requires two operands, at most one of the operands can be a memory reference. A memory reference can either be direct, or it can be indirect through register BX or register BP. The data that are referenced are either bytes or words. The compiler always generates the type operator BYTE PTR or WORD PTR before a memory reference to indicate the type of the operand. Some examples are:

mov ax,3	Move the immediate value 3 into register AX.
mov ax,dx	Move the contents of register DX into register AX.
mov ax,WORD PTR avg mov dx,WORD PTR avg+2	Move the doubleword real value at the memory location labelled avg directly into registers AX (low-order half) and DX (high-order half).
mov al,BYTE PTR [bx]	Move the byte data pointed to by register BX (indirect reference) into register AL.
mov dx,WORD PTR [bp+8]	Move into register DX the word data located 8 bytes from the location pointed to by register BP (based on the stack frame format, this is a parameter passed to a routine).

12.3 Using a runtime library

Some operations, such as input and output, real arthmetic, and the standard Pascal functions, are difficult for the compiler to generate code to do. You can take care of such operations with a runtime library. The compiler then generates calls to the library routines whenever necessary. After you assemble the compiler's output, you must link and load the library routines along with the assembled code.

Since the runtime library is separate from the compiler, you have several options for how you can write its routines. In an actual development environment, these routines should be as small and fast as possible, so you would probably write them in C or assembly language.

For our compiler, we will strive instead for simplicity. Figure 12-5 shows file paslib.c, which contains all of our runtime library routines written as C functions. We also make use of C library functions such as printf which, unfortunately, will cause the final object code to be larger than it otherwise would be. Using C functions also introduces a few other perverse features.

FIGURE 12-5   File paslib.c.

```
/*****************************************************************/
/*                                                             */
/*        P A S C A L   R U N T I M E   L I B R A R Y          */
/*                                                             */
/*        Note that all formal parameters are reversed to      */
/*        accomodate the Pascal calling convention of the      */
/*        compiled code.                                       */
/*                                                             */
/*        All floating point parameters are passed in as longs */
/*        to bypass unwanted type conversions.  Floating point */
/*        function values are also returned as longs.          */
/*                                                             */
/*****************************************************************/

#include <stdio.h>
#include <math.h>

#define MAX_SOURCE_LINE_LENGTH  256

typedef enum {
    FALSE, TRUE
} BOOLEAN;

union {
    float real;
    long  dword;
} value;

/*-------------------------------------------------------------*/
/* Globals                                                     */
/*-------------------------------------------------------------*/

BOOLEAN eof_flag  = FALSE;
BOOLEAN eoln_flag = FALSE;

/*-------------------------------------------------------------*/
/* main            The main routine, which calls              */
/*                 pascal_main, the "main" of the compiled    */
/*                 program.                                    */
/*-------------------------------------------------------------*/

main(argc, argv)

    int  argc;
    char *argv[];

{
    pascal_main();
    exit(0);
}

        /********************************/
        /*                              */
        /*          Read routines       */
        /*                              */
        /********************************/

/*-------------------------------------------------------------*/
/* read_integer        Read an integer value.                 */
/*-------------------------------------------------------------*/

    int
read_integer()

{
    int i;

    scanf("%d", &i);
    return(i);
}

/*-------------------------------------------------------------*/
/* read_real           Read a real value.                     */
/*-------------------------------------------------------------*/

    long
read_real()

{
    scanf("%g", &value.real);
    return(value.dword);
}

/*-------------------------------------------------------------*/
/* read_char           Read a character value.                */
/*-------------------------------------------------------------*/

    char
read_char()

{
```

```
    char ch;

    scanf("%c", &ch);
    if (eof_flag || (ch == '\n')) ch = ' ';

    return(ch);
}

/*------------------------------------------------------*/
/* read_line         Skip the rest of the input record. */
/*------------------------------------------------------*/

read_line()

{
    char ch;

    do {
        ch = getchar();
    } while(!eof_flag && (ch != '\n'));
}

                    /*******************************/
                    /*                             */
                    /*       Write routines        */
                    /*                             */
                    /*******************************/

/*------------------------------------------------------*/
/* write_integer        Write an integer value.         */
/*------------------------------------------------------*/

write_integer(field_width, i)

    int i;
    int field_width;

{
    printf("%*d", field_width, i);
}

/*------------------------------------------------------*/
/* write_real        Write a real value.                */
/*------------------------------------------------------*/

write_real(precision, field_width, i)

    long i;
    int  field_width;
    int  precision;

{
    value.dword = i;
    printf("%*.*f", field_width, precision, value.real);
}

/*------------------------------------------------------*/
/* write_boolean        Write a boolean value.          */
/*------------------------------------------------------*/

write_boolean(field_width, b)

    int b;
    int field_width;

{
    printf("%*s", field_width, b == 0 ? "FALSE" : "TRUE");
}
```

```
}

/*------------------------------------------------------*/
/* write_char        Write a character value.           */
/*------------------------------------------------------*/

write_char(field_width, ch)

    int ch;
    int field_width;

{
    printf("%*c", field_width, ch);
}

/*------------------------------------------------------*/
/* write_string        Write a string value.            */
/*------------------------------------------------------*/

write_string(length, field_width, value)

    char *value;
    int  field_width;
    int  length;

{
    char buffer[MAX_SOURCE_LINE_LENGTH];

    strncpy(buffer, value, length);
    buffer[length] = '\0';

    printf("%*s", -field_width, buffer);
}

/*------------------------------------------------------*/
/* write_line        Write a carriage return.           */
/*------------------------------------------------------*/

write_line()

{
    putchar('\n');
}

                    /*******************************/
                    /*                             */
                    /*      Other I/O routines     */
                    /*                             */
                    /*******************************/

/*------------------------------------------------------*/
/* std_end_of_file    Return 1 if at end of file, else 0. */
/*------------------------------------------------------*/

    BOOLEAN
std_end_of_file()

{
    char ch = getchar();

    if (eof_flag || feof(stdin)) eof_flag = TRUE;
    else                         ungetc(ch, stdin);

    return(eof_flag);
}
```

```
/*------------------------------------------------*/
/* std_end_of_line     Return 1 if at end of line, else 0.    */
/*------------------------------------------------*/

    BOOLEAN
std_end_of_line()

{
    char ch = getchar();

    if (eof_flag || feof(stdin))
        eoln_flag = eof_flag = TRUE;
    else {
        eoln_flag = ch == '\n';
        ungetc(ch, stdin);
    }

    return(eoln_flag);
}


            /**********************************************/
            /*                                            */
            /*          Floating point arithmetic routines    */
            /*                                            */
            /**********************************************/

/*------------------------------------------------*/
/* float_negate        Return the negated value.         */
/*------------------------------------------------*/

    long
float_negate(i)

    long i;

{
    value.dword = i;

    value.real = -value.real;
    return(value.dword);
}

/*------------------------------------------------*/
/* float_add           Return the sum x + y.             */
/*------------------------------------------------*/

    long
float_add(j, i)

    long i, j;

{
    float x, y;

    value.dword = i;   x = value.real;
    value.dword = j;   y = value.real;

    value.real = x + y;
    return(value.dword);
}

/*------------------------------------------------*/
/* float_subtract      Return the difference x - y.      */
/*------------------------------------------------*/

    long
float_subtract(j, i)
```

```
    long i, j;
}

    float x, y;

    value.dword = i;   x = value.real;
    value.dword = j;   y = value.real;

    value.real = x - y;
    return(value.dword);
}

/*------------------------------------------------*/
/* float_multiply      Return the product x*y.           */
/*------------------------------------------------*/

    long
float_multiply(j, i)

    long i, j;

{
    float x, y;

    value.dword = i;   x = value.real;
    value.dword = j;   y = value.real;

    value.real = x*y;
    return(value.dword);
}

/*------------------------------------------------*/
/* float_divide        Return the quotient x/y.          */
/*------------------------------------------------*/

    long
float_divide(j, i)

    long i, j;

{
    float x, y;

    value.dword = i;   x = value.real;
    value.dword = j;   y = value.real;

    value.real = x/y;
    return(value.dword);
}

/*------------------------------------------------*/
/* float_convert       Convert an integer value to real and   */
/*                     return the converted value.       */
/*------------------------------------------------*/

    long
float_convert(i)

    int i;

{
    value.real = i;
    return(value.dword);
}

/*------------------------------------------------*/
/* float_compare       Return -1 if x <  y               */
```

```
/*                              0 if x == y                  */
/*                              +1 if x >  y                 */
/*---------------------------------------------------------*/

float_compare(j, i)

   long i, j;

{
   int   comp;
   float x, y;

   value.dword = i;  x = value.real;
   value.dword = j;  y = value.real;

   if (x < y)         comp = -1;
   else if (x == y)   comp =  0;
   else               comp = +1;

   return(comp);
}


            /***********************************************/
            /*                                             */
            /*        Standard floating point functions    */
            /*                                             */
            /***********************************************/


/*---------------------------------------------------------*/
/*  std_abs          Return abs of parameter.              */
/*---------------------------------------------------------*/

   long
std_abs(i)

   long i;

{
   value.dword = i;

   value.real = fabs(value.real);
   return(value.dword);
}


/*---------------------------------------------------------*/
/*  std_arctan        Return arctan of parameter.          */
/*---------------------------------------------------------*/

   long
std_arctan(i)

   long i;

{
   value.dword = i;

   value.real = atan(value.real);
   return(value.dword);
}


/*---------------------------------------------------------*/
/*  std_cos          Return cos of parameter.              */
/*---------------------------------------------------------*/

   long
std_cos(i)
```

```
   long i;

{
   value.dword = i;

   value.real = cos(value.real);
   return(value.dword);
}


/*---------------------------------------------------------*/
/*  std_exp           Return exp of parameter.             */
/*---------------------------------------------------------*/

   long
std_exp(i)

   long i;

{
   value.dword = i;

   value.real = exp(value.real);
   return(value.dword);
}


/*---------------------------------------------------------*/
/*  std_ln            Return ln of parameter.              */
/*---------------------------------------------------------*/

   long
std_ln(i)

   long i;

{
   value.dword = i;

   value.real = log(value.real);
   return(value.dword);
}


/*---------------------------------------------------------*/
/*  std_sin           Return sin of parameter.             */
/*---------------------------------------------------------*/

   long
std_sin(i)

   long i;

{
   value.dword = i;

   value.real = sin(value.real);
   return(value.dword);
}


/*---------------------------------------------------------*/
/*  std_sqrt          Return sqrt of parameter.            */
/*---------------------------------------------------------*/

   long
std_sqrt(i)

   long i;

{
```

```
    value.dword = i;

    value.real = sqrt(value.real);
    return(value.dword);
}

/*----------------------------------------------*/
/* std_round        Return round of parameter.       */
/*----------------------------------------------*/

    int
std_round(i)

    long i;

{
    value.dword = i;

    value.dword = (int) (value.real + 0.5);
```

```
    return((int) value.dword);
}

/*--------------------------------------------------------------*/
/* std_trunc        Return trunc of parameter.              */
/*--------------------------------------------------------------*/

    int
std_trunc(i)

    long i;

{
    value.dword = i;

    value.dword = (int) value.real;
    return((int) value.dword);
}
```

The library routines that have more than one formal parameter point out a major difference between how C routines and Pascal routines expect their parameters. Pascal routines expect parameters to be pushed onto the stack in the order that they are written in the source program, so that the last parameter value is on top of the others on the stack. C functions expect the parameters to be pushed in reverse order, so that the first parameter value is on top of the others.

You can get around this difference with a kludge: simply list the formal parameters of the library routines in reverse order. This way, the compiler can use the same code module routines to emit code to pass parameters both to Pascal routines and to the library routines.

Another difference between C and Pascal routines is the code to return from a routine. (This is explained in the next chapter.)

A library function that takes real parameters must receive them as long integers, and one that returns a real value must return it as a long integer. When the C compiler compiles a function with real parameters or that returns a real value, it generates code that expects the caller to convert these real values to a form suitable for a numeric coprocessor or for floating-point emulation routines. This is beyond the scope of these chapters, so we bypass these conversions by dealing only with integers.

Finally, to simplify matters further, we compile the main routine of the Pascal source program as though it were a procedure, and we always give it the name pascal_main. Then, one of the library routines is the main routine that calls pascal_main. Starting the execution of a compiled Pascal program with a main routine written in C ensures us that the various initializations required by C functions are done. Then, the library routines will work properly when they are called by the compiled Pascal program.

Functions read_integer, read_real, read_char, and read_line are extracted from the runtime library of the interpreter (function exec_read_readln in file execstd.c). Functions std_end_of_file and std_end_of_line are also taken from the interpreter (function exec_eof_eoln).

The functions to execute the standard functions are std_abs, std_arctan, std_cos, std_exp, std_ln, std_sin, std_sqrt, and std_trunc. Each function contains a call to the corresponding function in the C library.

12.4 The code module

Now that we have had our overview of the 8086 architecture and its assembly language, we can examine some of the files and routines of the new code module. As we will see in the next two chapters, these routines are called from the parser module to emit assembly code as the compiler parses a Pascal program.

Code Module

code.h	n	Code generator header file
emitasm.c	n	Emit assembly language statements

Where: *n* new file

Figure 12-6 shows the new header file code.h. It defines various useful constants, types, and macros used by the code generation routines.

FIGURE 12-6   File code.h.

```
/****************************************************************/
/*                                                            */
/*      C O D E   G E N E R A T O R   (Header)               */
/*                                                            */
/*      FILE:      code.h                                     */
/*                                                            */
/*      MODULE:    code                                       */
/*                                                            */
/****************************************************************/

#ifndef code_h
#define code_h

#include "common.h"

/*----------------------------------------------------------*/
/*  Assembly label prefixes                                 */
/*----------------------------------------------------------*/

#define STMT_LABEL_PREFIX        "$L"
#define FLOAT_LABEL_PREFIX       "$F"
#define STRING_LABEL_PREFIX      "$S"

/*----------------------------------------------------------*/
/*  Names of library routines                               */
/*----------------------------------------------------------*/

#define FLOAT_NEGATE      "_float_negate"
#define FLOAT_ADD         "_float_add"
#define FLOAT_SUBTRACT    "_float_subtract"
#define FLOAT_MULTIPLY    "_float_multiply"
```

```
#define FLOAT_DIVIDE     "_float_divide"
#define FLOAT_COMPARE    "_float_compare"
#define FLOAT_CONVERT    "_float_convert"

#define WRITE_INTEGER    "_write_integer"
#define WRITE_REAL       "_write_real"
#define WRITE_BOOLEAN    "_write_boolean"
#define WRITE_CHAR       "_write_char"
#define WRITE_STRING     "_write_string"
#define WRITE_LINE       "_write_line"

#define READ_INTEGER     "_read_integer"
#define READ_REAL        "_read_real"
#define READ_CHAR        "_read_char"
#define READ_LINE        "_read_line"

#define STD_END_OF_FILE "_std_end_of_file"
#define STD_END_OF_LINE "_std_end_of_line"

#define STD_ABS          "_std_abs"

#define STD_ARCTAN       "_std_arctan"
#define STD_COS          "_std_cos"
#define STD_EXP          "_std_exp"
#define STD_LN           "_std_ln"
#define STD_SIN          "_std_sin"
#define STD_SQRT         "_std_sqrt"

#define STD_ROUND        "_std_round"
#define STD_TRUNC        "_std_trunc"
```

```
/*-----------------------------------------------------*/
/* Stack frame                                        */
/*-----------------------------------------------------*/

#define PROC_LOCALS_STACK_FRAME_OFFSET   0
#define FUNC_LOCALS_STACK_FRAME_OFFSET  -4
#define PARAMETERS_STACK_FRAME_OFFSET   +6

#define STATIC_LINK          "$STATIC_LINK"         /* EQU <bp+4> */
#define RETURN_VALUE         "$RETURN_VALUE"        /* EQU <bp-4> */
#define HIGH_RETURN_VALUE    "$HIGH_RETURN_VALUE"   /* EQU <bp-2> */

/*-----------------------------------------------------*/
/* Registers and instruction op codes                 */
/*-----------------------------------------------------*/

typedef enum {
    AX, AH, AL, BX, BH, BL, CX, CH, CL, DX, DH, DL,
    CS, DS, ES, SS, SP, BP, SI, DI,
} REGISTER;

typedef enum {
    MOVE, MOVE_BLOCK, LOAD_ADDRESS, EXCHANGE,
    COMPARE, COMPARE_STRINGS, POP, PUSH, AND_BITS, OR_BITS, XOR_BITS,
    NEGATE, INCREMENT, DECREMENT, ADD, SUBTRACT, MULTIPLY, DIVIDE,
    CLEAR_DIRECTION, CALL, RETURN,
    JUMP, JUMP_LT, JUMP_LE, JUMP_EQ, JUMP_NE, JUMP_GE, JUMP_GT,
} INSTRUCTION;

        /**********************************************/
        /*                                            */
        /*         Macros to emit assembly statements */
        /*                                            */
        /**********************************************/

/*-----------------------------------------------------*/
/* emit            Emit a no-operand instruction.     */
/*-----------------------------------------------------*/

#define emit(opcode)                          \
{                                             \
    operator(opcode);                         \
    fprintf(code_file, "%s\n", asm_buffer);   \
    asm_bufferp = asm_buffer;                 \
}

/*-----------------------------------------------------*/
/* emit_1           Emit a one-operand instruction.   */
/*-----------------------------------------------------*/

#define emit_1(opcode, operand1)              \
{                                             \
    operator(opcode);                         \
    *asm_bufferp++ = '\t';                    \
    operand1;                                 \
    fprintf(code_file, "%s\n", asm_buffer);   \
    asm_bufferp = asm_buffer;                 \
}

/*-----------------------------------------------------*/
/* emit_2           Emit a two-operand instruction.   */
/*-----------------------------------------------------*/

#define emit_2(opcode, operand1, operand2)    \
{                                             \
    operator(opcode);                         \
    *asm_bufferp++ = '\t';                    \
    operand1;                                 \
    *asm_bufferp++ = ',';                     \
    operand2;                                 \
    fprintf(code_file, "%s\n", asm_buffer);   \
    asm_bufferp = asm_buffer;                 \
}

/*-----------------------------------------------------*/
/* emit_label       Emit a statement label.           */
/*-----------------------------------------------------*/

#define emit_label(prefix, index)  fprintf(code_file,  \
                                    "%s_%03d:\n",      \
                                    prefix, index);

/*-----------------------------------------------------*/
/* advance_asm_bufferp    Advance asm_bufferp to the end */
/*                        of the assembly statement.    */
/*-----------------------------------------------------*/

#define advance_asm_bufferp()   while (*asm_bufferp != '\0') \
                                    ++asm_bufferp;

/*-----------------------------------------------------*/
/* new_label_index            Return a new label index. */
/*-----------------------------------------------------*/

#define new_label_index()       ++label_index

#endif
```

The constants STMT_LABEL_PREFIX, FLOAT_LABEL_PREFIX, and STRING_LABEL_PREFIX are prefixes for labels in the assembly code. For example, $L_007 is a statement label and $S_014 is a string label.

Next, we define constants that represent the names of the library routines in paslib.c. By convention, we preface the names of external routines in assembly language programs with an underscore.

We then define several constants for the stack frame. As we will see in the next chapter, constants PROC_LOCALS_STACK_FRAME_OFFSET, FUNC_LOCALS_STACK_FRAME_OFFSET, and PARAMETERS_STACK_FRAME_OFFSET will be used as initial offset values in function var_declarations, of file decl.c, and in function formal_parm_

list, of file routine.c. The constants STATIC_LINK, RETURN_VALUE, and HIGH_RE-
TURN_VALUE define assembly code labels that will be equated in the object program
to items in the stack frame.

Type REGISTER defines enumeration constants for the machine's registers.
Type INSTRUCTION defines enumeration constants for the assembly language instructions that the compiler can generate.

Macros emit, emit_1, and emit_2 are called by the code module to write
assembly language instructions with zero, one, or two operands, respectively, into
the character buffer asm_buffer. Variable asm_bufferp points into this buffer. (asm_
buffer and asm_bufferp are defined in file emitasm.c.) Parameter opcode must
be one of the INSTRUCTION constants. (We will see later that function operator
writes the instruction mnemonic into asm_buffer.)

Parameters operand1 and operand2 must be calls to functions that write into
asm_buffer. (These functions are also defined in file emitasm.c.) emit_1 and emit_
2 place a tab between parts of the instruction. Each macro prints the complete
instruction in asm_buffer to the object code file and points asm_bufferp to the
beginning of the buffer. (We will see examples of macros emit, emit_1, and emit_
2 later.)

Macro emit_label writes a statement label to the object code file. A statement
label consists of a prefix followed by an underscore, an index, and a colon. For
example, $L_003: Macro advance_asm_bufferp advances asm_bufferp to the end
of the contents of asm_buffer so that *asm_bufferp is the null character. Macro
new_label_index returns a label index by incrementing label_index, defined in
file emitasm.c. Figure 12-7 shows the new file emitasm.c, which contains functions
that write parts of an assembly language statement, such as a label or an operand,
to asm_buffer.

FIGURE 12-7   File emitasm.c.

```
/******************************************************************/
/*                                                                */
/*      E M I T   A S S E M B L Y   S T A T E M E N T S           */
/*                                                                */
/*      Routines for generating and emitting                      */
/*      language statements.                                      */
/*                                                                */
/*      FILE:       emitasm.c                                     */
/*                                                                */
/*      MODULE:     code                                          */
/*                                                                */
/******************************************************************/

#include <stdio.h>
#include "symtab.h"
#include "code.h"


/*--------------------------------------------------------*/
/* Globals                                                */
/*--------------------------------------------------------*/

int label_index = 0;
```

```
char asm_buffer[MAX_PRINT_LINE_LENGTH];      /* assembly stmt buffer */
char *asm_bufferp = asm_buffer;              /* ptr into asm buffer */

char *register_strings[] = {
    "ax", "ah", "al", "bx", "bh", "bl", "cx", "ch", "cl",
    "dx", "dh", "dl", "cs", "ds", "es", "ss",
    "sp", "bp", "si", "di",
};

char *instruction_strings[] = {
    "mov", "rep\tmovsb", "lea", "xchg", "cmp", "repe\tcmpsb",
    "pop", "push", "and", "or", "xor",
    "neg", "inc", "dec", "add", "sub", "imul", "idiv",
    "cld", "call", "ret",
    "jmp", "jl", "jle", "je", "jne", "jge", "jg",
};

/***********************************************/
/*                                             */
/*      Write parts of assembly statements     */
/*                                             */
/***********************************************/
```

```
/*-------------------------------------------------*/
/* label              Write a generic label constructed from  */
/*                    the prefix and the label index.         */
/*                                                            */
/*                    Example:      $L_007                    */
/*-------------------------------------------------*/

label(prefix, index)

    char *prefix;
    int  index;

{
    sprintf(asm_bufferp, "%s_%03d", prefix, index);
    advance_asm_bufferp();
}


/*-------------------------------------------------*/
/* word_label         Write a word label constructed from     */
/*                    the prefix and the label index.         */
/*                                                            */
/*                    Example:      WORD PTR $F_007           */
/*-------------------------------------------------*/

word_label(prefix, index)

    char *prefix;
    int  index;

{
    sprintf(asm_bufferp, "WORD PTR %s_%03d", prefix, index);
    advance_asm_bufferp();
}


/*-------------------------------------------------*/
/* high_dword_label   Write a word label constructed from     */
/*                    the prefix and the label index and      */
/*                    offset by 2 to point to the high word   */
/*                    of a double word.                       */
/*                                                            */
/*                    Example:      WORD PTR $F_007+2         */
/*-------------------------------------------------*/

high_dword_label(prefix, index)

    char *prefix;
    int  index;

{
    sprintf(asm_bufferp, "WORD PTR %s_%03d+2", prefix, index);
    advance_asm_bufferp();
}


/*-------------------------------------------------*/
/* reg                Write a register name. Example: ax      */
/*-------------------------------------------------*/

reg(r)

    REGISTER r;

{
    sprintf(asm_bufferp, "%s", register_strings[r]);
    advance_asm_bufferp();
}
```

```
/*-------------------------------------------------*/
/* operator           Write an opcode. Example: add          */
/*-------------------------------------------------*/

operator(opcode)

    INSTRUCTION opcode;

{
    sprintf(asm_bufferp, "\t%s", instruction_strings[opcode]);
    advance_asm_bufferp();
}


/*-------------------------------------------------*/
/* byte               Write a byte label constructed from     */
/*                    the id name and its label index.        */
/*                                                            */
/*                    Example:      BYTE_PTR ch_007           */
/*-------------------------------------------------*/

byte(idp)

    SYMTAB_NODE_PTR idp;

{
    sprintf(asm_bufferp, "BYTE PTR %s_%03d",
                          idp->name, idp->label_index);
    advance_asm_bufferp();
}


/*-------------------------------------------------*/
/* byte_indirect      Write an indirect reference to a byte   */
/*                    via a register.                         */
/*                                                            */
/*                    Example:      BYTE PTR [bx]             */
/*-------------------------------------------------*/

byte_indirect(r)

    REGISTER r;

{
    sprintf(asm_bufferp, "BYTE PTR [%s]", register_strings[r]);
    advance_asm_bufferp();
}


/*-------------------------------------------------*/
/* word               Write a word label constructed from     */
/*                    the id name and its label index.        */
/*                                                            */
/*                    Example:      WORD_PTR sum_007          */
/*-------------------------------------------------*/

word(idp)

    SYMTAB_NODE_PTR idp;

{
    sprintf(asm_bufferp, "WORD PTR %s_%03d",
                          idp->name, idp->label_index);
    advance_asm_bufferp();
}


/*-------------------------------------------------*/
/* high_dword         Write a word label constructed from     */
/*                    the id name and its label index and     */
/*                    offset by 2 to point to the high word   */
```

```
/*                          of a double word.             */
/*                                                        */
/*                  Example:        WORD_PTR sum_007+2     */
/*--------------------------------------------------------*/

high_dword(idp)

    SYMTAB_NODE_PTR idp;

{
    sprintf(asm_bufferp, "WORD PTR %s_%03d+2",
                    idp->name, idp->label_index);
    advance_asm_bufferp();
}

/*--------------------------------------------------------*/
/*  word_indirect     Write an indirect reference to a word */
/*                    via a register.                     */
/*                                                        */
/*                  Example:        WORD PTR [bx]         */
/*--------------------------------------------------------*/

word_indirect(r)

    REGISTER r;

{
    sprintf(asm_bufferp, "WORD PTR [%s]", register_strings[r]);
    advance_asm_bufferp();
}

/*--------------------------------------------------------*/
/*  high_dword_indirect   Write an indirect reference to the */
/*                        high word of a double word via a */
/*                        register.                       */
/*                                                        */
/*                  Example:        WORD PTR [bx+2]       */
/*--------------------------------------------------------*/

high_dword_indirect(r)

    REGISTER r;

{
    sprintf(asm_bufferp, "WORD PTR [%s+2]", register_strings[r]);
    advance_asm_bufferp();
}

/*--------------------------------------------------------*/
/*  tagged_name       Write an id name tagged with the id's */
/*                    label index.                        */
/*                                                        */
```

```
/*                  Example:        x_007                 */
/*--------------------------------------------------------*/

tagged_name(idp)

    SYMTAB_NODE_PTR idp;

{
    sprintf(asm_buffer, "%s_%03d", idp->name, idp->label_index);
    advance_asm_bufferp();
}

/*--------------------------------------------------------*/
/*  name_lit          Write a literal name.              */
/*                                                        */
/*                  Example:        _float_convert        */
/*--------------------------------------------------------*/

name_lit(name)

    char *name;

{
    sprintf(asm_bufferp, "%s", name);
    advance_asm_bufferp();
}

/*--------------------------------------------------------*/
/*  integer_lit       Write an integer as a string.      */
/*--------------------------------------------------------*/

integer_lit(n)

    int n;

{
    sprintf(asm_bufferp, "%d", n);
    advance_asm_bufferp();
}

/*--------------------------------------------------------*/
/*  char_lit          Write a character surrounded by single */
/*                    quotes.                             */
/*--------------------------------------------------------*/

char_lit(ch)

    char ch;

{
    sprintf(asm_bufferp, "'%c'", ch);
    advance_asm_bufferp();
}
```

First, we initialize label_index, which we use to create assembly language labels. We declare asm_buffer, the buffer for an assembly language statement, and asm_bufferp, a pointer into the buffer. The string arrays register_strings and instruction_strings correspond to the enumeration types REGISTER and INSTRUCTION.

Whenever we emit references to memory data, we can use names derived from the original names in the Pascal source program to make it easier for us to read the generated code. Because assembly programs do not have the scope rules of Pascal, we must tag each name in the generated code with a unique integer. We store this integer in the label_index field of the identifier's symbol table node.

For example, suppose a procedure in a Pascal program has a local variable count, and a function in the same program also has a local variable count. When we compile the Pascal program into assembly language, we can use names like count_007 and count_014.

Function label writes a label consisting of a label prefix, an underscore, and a label index, such as $L_003. Function word_label is similar, except that we also add WORD PTR before the label, such as WORD PTR $F_009. Such a label is used as an instruction operand. Function high_dword_label writes a label for the high-order half of a doubleword, such as WORD PTR $F_009+2.

Function reg simply writes a register name from register_strings, such as ax, and function operator writes an instruction mnemonic from instruction_strings.

Function byte writes a label to a byte value. This label is used as an instruction operand and consists of a name from the Pascal source tagged with a label index, such as BYTE PTR ch_014. Function byte_indirect writes an indirect reference to byte data, such as BYTE PTR [bx]. Functions word and word_indirect are similar, except that they use WORD_PTR. Function high_dword writes a label that references the high-order half of a doubleword, such as WORD PTR sum_017+2. Function high_dword_indirect writes an indirect reference to the high-order half of a doubleword, such as WORD PTR [bx+2].

Function tagged_name writes a name from the Pascal source tagged with its label index, such as x_021. Function literal_name writes the name without a tag. Finally, functions integer_lit and char_lit write integers and characters as strings. Examples are -453 and 'x'.

Now for some examples of how we use macros emit, emit_1, and emit_2 with the functions in file emitasm.c. The macro call emit(RETURN); writes the assembly instruction ret to the code file. The macro call emit_1(PUSH, reg(AX)); writes push ax and the macro call emit_2(MOVE, reg(AX), word(var_idp)); writes mov ax,WORD PTR gamma_003 if we assume that var_idp->name is gamma and var_idp->label_index is 3.

Questions and exercises

1. Calling C runtime library functions in file paslib.c causes our final executable files to be large, since portions of the C runtime library end up being linked with our programs. Rewrite paslib.c so that it does not call any C library functions.

CHAPTER 13

Compiling Procedures, Functions, and Assignment Statements

In this chapter and the next one, we will write a compiler based on the work we have done so far. The previous chapter introduced some of the routines of the code module that emit assembly language code. We now look at the remaining files and routines of the code module and add calls from the parser module.

Many of the things we considered and did in the interpreter carry over to the compiler. For example, we still check types and perform type conversions in expressions. The difference is that instead of actually performing some of these operations, we now generate the code to perform them. So even though the compiler does not have an executor module, many of that module's semantic actions reappear in the parser module.

Another difference between our interpreter and our compiler is that the compiler does its job with only one pass over the source code. It does not use an intermediate form, which is another reason we make calls to the code generation routines directly from the parser module. We will take a brief look at multipass compilers in Chapter 15.

Our interpreter operated on an idealized stack machine architecture that it maintained within itself. Our compiler, on the other hand, generates code for an actual IBM PC, that is, for the 8086 processor. We therefore must deal with the processor's features and idiosyncrasies.

In this chapter, we write the parts of the compiler to generate code for procedures, functions, and assignment statements. We will complete the compiler in the next chapter. This chapter develops the skills to:

• compile calls and returns and assignment statements

- make calls from the parser to code generation routines
- generate calls to a runtime library

This chapter covers much ground in detail; however, it is not as complex as it may seem. Keep in mind that the code the compiler emits for Pascal statements is designed to do what the interpreter did at run time for the same statements.

13.1 Organization of the compiler

The syntax checker we wrote in Chapter 7 is the basis for the compiler. You can also compare it to the interpreter: it lacks the executor module but gains the code module that we began in the previous chapter.

Parser Module

parser.h	*c*	Parser header file
routine.c	*c*	Parse programs, procedures, and functions
standard.c	*c*	Parse standard procedures and functions
decl.c	*c*	Parse declarations
stmt.c	*c*	Parse statements
expr.c	*c*	Parse expressions

Scanner Module

scanner.h	*u*	Scanner header file
scanner.c	*c*	Scanner routines

Symbol Table Module

symtab.h	*u*	Symbol table header file
symtab.c	*u*	Symbol table routines

Code Module

code.h	*u*	Code generator header file
emitasm.c	*u*	Emit assembly language statements
emitcode.c	*n*	Emit sequences of assembly code

Error Module

error.h	*c*	Error header file
error.c	*c*	Error routines

Miscellaneous

common.h	*c*	Common header file

Where: *u*   file unchanged from the previous chapter
        c   file changed from the previous chapter
        n   new file

We modify the parser module to make calls to the code generation routines. Files error.h and error.c revert to the way they were in Chapter 7. We no longer need all the runtime error messages and routines that were used by the interpreter's executor module. File common.h also reverts to what it was in Chapter 7.

In Figure 13-1, the routines of the new file emitcode.c emit sequences of assembly code. We will examine each function later.

FIGURE 13-1   File emitcode.c.

```
/****************************************************************/
/*                                                              */
/*      E M I T   C O D E   S E Q U E N C E S                   */
/*                                                              */
/*      Routines for emitting standard                          */
/*      assembly code sequences.                                */
/*                                                              */
/*      FILE:      emitcode.c                                   */
/*                                                              */
/*      MODULE:    code                                         */
/*                                                              */
/****************************************************************/

#include <stdio.h>
#include "symtab.h"
#include "code.h"


/*------------------------------------------------------------*/
/* Externals                                                  */
/*------------------------------------------------------------*/

extern TYPE_STRUCT_PTR  integer_typep, real_typep,
                        boolean_typep, char_typep;

extern int level;

extern char     asm_buffer[];
extern char     *asm_bufferp;
extern FILE     *code_file;

/*------------------------------------------------------------*/
/* Globals                                                    */
/*------------------------------------------------------------*/

SYMTAB_NODE_PTR  float_literal_list  = NULL;
SYMTAB_NODE_PTR  string_literal_list = NULL;

                /***************************************/
                /*                                     */
                /*    Emit prologues and epilogues     */
                /*                                     */
                /***************************************/

/*------------------------------------------------------------*/
/* emit_program_prologue    Emit the program prologue.        */
/*------------------------------------------------------------*/
```

```
emit_program_prologue()

{
    fprintf(code_file, "\tDOSSEG\n");
    fprintf(code_file, "\t.MODEL  small\n");
    fprintf(code_file, "\t.STACK  1024\n");
    fprintf(code_file, "\n");
    fprintf(code_file, "\t.CODE\n");
    fprintf(code_file, "\n");
    fprintf(code_file, "\tPUBLIC\t_pascal_main\n");
    fprintf(code_file, "\tINCLUDE\ttpasextrn.inc\n");
    fprintf(code_file, "\n");

    /*
    -- Equates for stack frame components.
    */
    fprintf(code_file, "%s\t\tEQU\t<WORD PTR [bp+4]>\n",
                       STATIC_LINK);
    fprintf(code_file, "%s\t\tEQU\t<WORD PTR [bp-4]>\n",
                       RETURN_VALUE);
    fprintf(code_file, "%s\t\tEQU\t<WORD PTR [bp-2]>\n",
                       HIGH_RETURN_VALUE);
    fprintf(code_file, "\n");
}

/*------------------------------------------------------------*/
/* emit_program_epilogue        Emit the program epilogue,    */
/*                              which includes the data       */
/*                              segment.                      */
/*------------------------------------------------------------*/

emit_program_epilogue(prog_idp)

    SYMTAB_NODE_PTR prog_idp;   /* id of program */

{
    SYMTAB_NODE_PTR np;
    int             i, length;

    fprintf(code_file, "\n");
    fprintf(code_file, "\t.DATA\n");
    fprintf(code_file, "\n");

    /*
    -- Emit declarations for the program's global variables.
    */
    for (np = prog_idp->defn.info.routine.locals;
```

```
        np != NULL;
        np = np->next) {
        fprintf(code_file, "%s_%03d\t", np->name, np->label_index);
        if (np->typep == char_typep)
            fprintf(code_file, "DB\t0\n");
        else if (np->typep == real_typep)
            fprintf(code_file, "DD\t0.0\n");
        else if (np->typep->form == ARRAY_FORM)
            fprintf(code_file, "DB\t%d DUP(0)\n", np->typep->size);
        else if (np->typep->form == RECORD_FORM)
            fprintf(code_file, "DB\t%d DUP(0)\n", np->typep->size);
        else
            fprintf(code_file, "DW\t0\n");
    }

    /*
    -- Emit declarations for the program's floating point literals.
    */
    for (np = float_literal_list; np != NULL; np = np->next)
        fprintf(code_file, "%s_%03d\tDD\t%e\n", FLOAT_LABEL_PREFIX,
                            np->label_index,
                            np->defn.info.constant.value.real);

    /*
    -- Emit declarations for the program's string literals.
    */
    for (np = string_literal_list; np != NULL; np = np->next) {
        fprintf(code_file, "%s_%03d\tDB\t\"", STRING_LABEL_PREFIX,
                            np->label_index);

        length = strlen(np->name) - 2;
        for (i = 1; i <= length; ++i) fputc(np->name[i], code_file);

        fprintf(code_file, "\"\n");
    }

    fprintf(code_file, "\n");
    fprintf(code_file, "\tEND\n");
}

/*--------------------------------------------------------------*/
/* emit_main_prologue        Emit the prologue for the main     */
/*                           routine _pascal_main.              */
/*--------------------------------------------------------------*/

emit_main_prologue()

{
    fprintf(code_file, "\n");
    fprintf(code_file, "_pascal_main\tPROC\n");
    fprintf(code_file, "\n");

    emit_1(PUSH, reg(BP));              /* dynamic link */
    emit_2(MOVE, reg(BP), reg(SP));     /* new stack frame base */
}

/*--------------------------------------------------------------*/
/* emit_main_epilogue        Emit the epilogue for the main     */
/*                           routine _pascal_main.              */
/*--------------------------------------------------------------*/

emit_main_epilogue()

{
    emit_1(POP, reg(BP));       /* restore caller's stack frame */
    emit(RETURN);               /* return */

    fprintf(code_file, "\n");
```

```
    fprintf(code_file, "_pascal_main\tENDP\n");
}

/*--------------------------------------------------------------*/
/* emit_routine_prologue        Emit the prologue for a proce-  */
/*                              dure or a function.             */
/*------- -----------------------------------------------------*/

emit_routine_prologue(rtn_idp)

    SYMTAB_NODE_PTR rtn_idp;

{
    fprintf(code_file, "\n");
    fprintf(code_file, "%s_%03d\tPROC\n",
                        rtn_idp->name, rtn_idp->label_index);
    fprintf(code_file, "\n");

    emit_1(PUSH, reg(BP));              /* dynamic link */
    emit_2(MOVE, reg(BP), reg(SP));     /* new stack frame base */

    /*
    -- Allocate stack space for a function's return value.
    */
    if (rtn_idp->defn.key == FUNC_DEFN) emit_2(SUBTRACT, reg(SP),
                                               integer_lit(4));

    /*
    -- Allocate stack space for the local variables.
    */
    if (rtn_idp->defn.info.routine.total_local_size > 0)
        emit_2(SUBTRACT, reg(SP),
               integer_lit(rtn_idp->defn.info.routine
                                    .total_local_size));
}

/*--------------------------------------------------------------*/
/* emit_routine_epilogue        Emit the epilogue for a proce-  */
/*                              dure or a function.             */
/*--------------------------------------------------------------*/

emit_routine_epilogue(rtn_idp)

    SYMTAB_NODE_PTR rtn_idp;

{
    /*
    -- Load a function's return value into the ax or dx:ax registers.
    */
    if (rtn_idp->defn.key == FUNC_DEFN) {
        emit_2(MOVE, reg(AX), name_lit(RETURN_VALUE));
        if (rtn_idp->typep == real_typep)
            emit_2(MOVE, reg(DX), name_lit(HIGH_RETURN_VALUE));
    }

    emit_2(MOVE, reg(SP), reg(BP)); /* cut back to caller's stack */
    emit_1(POP, reg(BP));           /* restore caller's stack frame */

    emit_1(RETURN, integer_lit(rtn_idp->defn.info.routine
                                       .total_parm_size + 2));
                                    /* return and cut back stack */

    fprintf(code_file, "\n");
    fprintf(code_file, "%s_%03d\tENDP\n",
                        rtn_idp->name, rtn_idp->label_index);
}
```

```
/********************************/
/*                              */
/*       Emit equates and data  */
/*                              */
/********************************/

/*-----------------------------------------------------------*/
/*  emit_declarations    Emit the parameter and local variable */
/*                       declarations for a procedure or a   */
/*                       function.                           */
/*-----------------------------------------------------------*/

emit_declarations(rtn_idp)

    SYMTAB_NODE_PTR rtn_idp;

{
    SYMTAB_NODE_PTR parm_idp = rtn_idp->defn.info.routine.parms;
    SYMTAB_NODE_PTR var_idp  = rtn_idp->defn.info.routine.locals;

    fprintf(code_file, "\n");

    /*
    -- Parameters.
    */
    while (parm_idp != NULL) {
        emit_text_equate(parm_idp);
        parm_idp = parm_idp->next;
    }

    /*
    -- Local variables.
    */
    while (var_idp != NULL) {
        emit_text_equate(var_idp);
        var_idp = var_idp->next;
    }
}

/*-----------------------------------------------------------*/
/*  emit_numeric_equate  Emit a numeric equate for a field   */
/*                       id and its offset.                  */
/*                                                           */
/*                       Example:   field_007 EQU 3          */
/*-----------------------------------------------------------*/

emit_numeric_equate(idp)

    SYMTAB_NODE_PTR idp;

{
    fprintf(code_file, "%s_%03d\tEQU\t%d\n",
                       idp->name, idp->label_index,
                       idp->defn.info.data.offset);
}

/*-----------------------------------------------------------*/
/*  emit_numeric_equate  Emit a numeric equate for a para-   */
/*                       meter or a local variable id and    */
/*                       its stack frame offset.             */
/*                                                           */
/*                       Examples:  parm_007   EQU <bp+6>    */
/*                                  var_008    EQU <bp-10>   */
/*                                  dword_010  EQU <bp-14>   */
/*                                  dword_010h EQU <bp-14+2> */
/*-----------------------------------------------------------*/

emit_text_equate(idp)
```

```
    SYMTAB_NODE_PTR idp;

{
    char *name       = idp->name;
    int  label_index = idp->label_index;
    int  offset      = idp->defn.info.data.offset;

    if (idp->typep == char_typep)
        fprintf(code_file, "%s_%03d\tEQU\t<BYTE PTR [bp%+d]>\n",
                           name, label_index, offset);
    else if (idp->typep == real_typep)
        fprintf(code_file, "%s_%03d\tEQU\t<WORD PTR [bp%+d]>\n",
                           name, label_index, offset);
    else
        fprintf(code_file, "%s_%03d\tEQU\t<WORD PTR [bp%+d]>\n",
                           name, label_index, offset);
}

/********************************/
/*                              */
/*       Emit loads and pushes  */
/*                              */
/********************************/

/*-----------------------------------------------------------*/
/*  emit_load_value     Emit code to load a scalar value     */
/*                      into AX or DX:AX.                     */
/*-----------------------------------------------------------*/

emit_load_value(var_idp, var_tp)

    SYMTAB_NODE_PTR var_idp;
    TYPE_STRUCT_PTR var_tp;

{
    int     var_level    = var_idp->level;
    BOOLEAN varparm_flag = var_idp->defn.key == VARPARM_DEFN;

    if (varparm_flag) {
        /*
        -- VAR formal parameter.
        -- AX or DX:AX = value the address points to
        */
        emit_2(MOVE, reg(BX), word(var_idp));
        if (var_tp == char_typep) {
            emit_2(SUBTRACT, reg(AX), reg(AX));
            emit_2(MOVE, reg(AL), byte_indirect(BX));
        }
        else if (var_tp == real_typep) {
            emit_2(MOVE, reg(AX), word_indirect(BX));
            emit_2(MOVE, reg(AX), high_dword_indirect(BX));
        }
        else emit_2(MOVE, reg(AX), word_indirect(BX));
    }
    else if ((var_level == level) || (var_level == 1)) {
        /*
        -- Global or local parameter or variable:
        -- AX or DX:AX = value
        */
        if (var_tp == char_typep) {
            emit_2(SUBTRACT, reg(AX), reg(AX));
            emit_2(MOVE, reg(AL), byte(var_idp));
        }
        else if (var_tp == real_typep) {
            emit_2(MOVE, reg(AX), word(var_idp));
            emit_2(MOVE, reg(DX), high_dword(var_idp));
```

```
        }
        else emit_2(MOVE, reg(AX), word(var_idp));
    }
    else    /* var_level < level */  {
        /*
        -- Nonlocal parameter or variable.
        -- First locate the appropriate stack frame, then:
        -- AX or DX:AX = value
        */
        int lev = var_level;

        emit_2(MOVE, reg(BX), reg(BP));
        do {
            emit_2(MOVE, reg(BP), name_lit(STATIC_LINK));
        } while (++lev < level);

        if (var_tp == char_typep) {
            emit_2(SUBTRACT, reg(AX), reg(AX));
            emit_2(MOVE, reg(AL), byte(var_idp));
        }
        else if (var_tp == real_typep) {
            emit_2(MOVE, reg(AX), word(var_idp));
            emit_2(MOVE, reg(DX), high_dword(var_idp));
        }
        else emit_2(MOVE, reg(AX), word(var_idp));

        emit_2(MOVE, reg(BP), reg(BX));
    }
}

/*------------------------------------------------------------*/
/*  emit_push_operand   Emit code to push a scalar operand    */
/*                      value onto the stack.                 */
/*------------------------------------------------------------*/

emit_push_operand(tp)

    TYPE_STRUCT_PTR tp;

{
    if ((tp->form == ARRAY_FORM) || (tp->form == RECORD_FORM)) return;

    if (tp == real_typep) emit_1(PUSH, reg(DX));
    emit_1(PUSH, reg(AX));
}

/*------------------------------------------------------------*/
/*  emit_push_address   Emit code to push an address onto the */
/*                      stack.                                 */
/*------------------------------------------------------------*/

emit_push_address(var_idp)

    SYMTAB_NODE_PTR var_idp;

{
    int     var_level    = var_idp->level;
    BOOLEAN varparm_flag = var_idp->defn.key == VARPARM_DEFN;

    if ((var_level == level) || (var_level == 1))
        emit_2(varparm_flag ? MOVE : LOAD_ADDRESS,
            reg(AX), word(var_idp))

    else    /* var_level < level */  {
        int lev = var_level;

        emit_2(MOVE, reg(BX), reg(BP));
```

```
        do {
            emit_2(MOVE, reg(BP), name_lit(STATIC_LINK));
        } while (++lev < level);
        emit_2(varparm_flag ? MOVE : LOAD_ADDRESS,
            reg(AX), word(var_idp));
        emit_2(MOVE, reg(BP), reg(BX));
    }

    emit_1(PUSH, reg(AX));
}

/*------------------------------------------------------------*/
/*  emit_push_return_value_address      Emit code to push the */
/*                                   address of the function  */
/*                                   return value in the      */
/*                                   stack frame.             */
/*------------------------------------------------------------*/

emit_push_return_value_address(var_idp)

    SYMTAB_NODE_PTR var_idp;

{
    int lev = var_idp->level + 1;

    if (lev < level) {
        /*
        -- Find the appropriate stack frame.
        */
        emit_2(MOVE, reg(BX), reg(BP));
        do {
            emit_2(MOVE, reg(BP), name_lit(STATIC_LINK));
        } while (++lev < level);
        emit_2(LOAD_ADDRESS, reg(AX), name_lit(RETURN_VALUE));
        emit_2(MOVE, reg(BP), reg(BX));
    }
    else emit_2(LOAD_ADDRESS, reg(AX), name_lit(RETURN_VALUE));

    emit_1(PUSH, reg(AX));
}

        /***************************************/
        /*                                     */
        /*        Emit miscellaneous code      */
        /*                                     */
        /***************************************/

/*------------------------------------------------------------*/
/*  emit_promote_to_real    Emit code to convert integer      */
/*                          operands to real.                 */
/*------------------------------------------------------------*/

emit_promote_to_real(tp1, tp2)

    TYPE_STRUCT_PTR tp1, tp2;

{
    if (tp2 == integer_typep) {
        emit_1(CALL, name_lit(FLOAT_CONVERT));
        emit_2(ADD, reg(SP), integer_lit(2));
        emit_1(PUSH, reg(DX));
        emit_1(PUSH, reg(AX));                  /* ???_1 real_2 */
    }

    if (tp1 == integer_typep) {
        emit_1(POP, reg(AX));
        emit_1(POP, reg(DX));
```

```
emit_1(POP,  reg(BX));                                              emit_1(POP,  reg(BX));
emit_1(PUSH, reg(DX));                                              emit_1(POP,  reg(CX));
emit_1(PUSH, reg(AX));                                              emit_1(PUSH, reg(DX));
emit_1(PUSH, reg(BX));            /* real_2 integer_1 */            emit_1(PUSH, reg(AX));
                                                                    emit_1(PUSH, reg(CX));
                                                                    emit_1(PUSH, reg(BX));            /* real_1 real_2 */
emit_1(CALL, name_lit(FLOAT_CONVERT));                         }
emit_2(ADD,  reg(SP), integer_lit(2));  /* real_2 real_1 */    }
```

Figure 13-2 shows the new version of function get_source_line in file scan-ner.c. This version outputs each source line to the object code file code_file as an assembly language comment line. This will help us match the emitted code with the original source lines.

FIGURE 13-2   Function get_source_line in file scanner.c.

```
/*---------------------------------------------------------*/                                        source_file)) != NULL) {
/*  get_source_line   Read the next line from the source  */             ++line_number;
/*                    file.  If there is one, print it out */
/*                    and return TRUE.  Else return FALSE. */             if (print_flag) {
/*                    for the end of file.                 */                 sprintf(print_buffer, "%4d %d: %s",
/*---------------------------------------------------------*/                                line_number, level, source_buffer);
                                                                             print_line(print_buffer);
    BOOLEAN                                                               }
get_source_line()
                                                                         fprintf(code_file, "; %4d: %s", line_number, source_buffer);
{                                                                        return(TRUE);
    char print_buffer[MAX_SOURCE_LINE_LENGTH + 9];                   }
    extern FILE *code_file;                                         else return(FALSE);

    if ((fgets(source_buffer, MAX_SOURCE_LINE_LENGTH,            }
```

13.2 Procedures and functions

In the previous chapter, we saw how the functions in file emitasm.c emit assembly statements. Now we will look at the code the compiler actually generates for Pascal procedures and functions.

13.2.1 Managing the runtime stack

Like the interpreter, the code generated by the compiler must manage the runtime stack during calls to and returns from Pascal procedures and functions. The only significant difference is the stack frame format, as we saw in Figure 12-4. To call a procedure or function, the *caller* must perform these steps:

1. Push the actual parameter values onto the stack. The last parameter value ends up on top of the stack.

2. Push the static link onto the stack.

3. Push the return address onto the stack.

   Then, the *callee* must perform these steps:

4. Push the dynamic link onto the stack.

5. Set register BP to point to the callee's stack frame.

6. Function only: Allocate space on top of the stack for the return value.

7. Allocate space on top of the stack for local variables.

   Just before the callee returns to its caller, it must perform these steps:

8. Function only: Load the return value from the stack frame into register AX or the DX:AX register pair.

9. Cut the stack back to remove the callee's local variables and, for a function, the return value.

10. Use the dynamic link to restore register BP to point to the caller's stack frame.

11. Pop off the return address.

12. Cut the stack back to remove the actual parameters and the static link.

We will refer to these steps by number when we describe the code emitted by the compiler.

13.2.2 Memory data and symbol table changes

In the previous chapter, you saw that parameters and local variables are allocated on the runtime stack, just as they were in the interpreter. The code generated by the compiler has one major difference: the program's global variables are allocated in the data segment instead of at the bottom of the stack. We do this for efficiency, since data allocated in the data segment can be accessed directly, whereas data allocated on the stack must be accessed indirectly through register BP.

You also saw how the compiler uses names taken from the Pascal source when it generates assembly code. These names are tagged with a label index. For example, variable length in the Pascal program becomes length_009 in the assembly code, assuming a label index value of 9. We store the label index in the label_index field of the identifier's symbol table node. Figure 13-3 shows a new version of routine var_or_field_declarations in file decl.c. This version calls macro new_label_index in file emitasm.c to assign a unique label index to each identifier.

FIGURE 13-3   Function var_or_field_declarations in file decl.c.

```
/*--------------------------------------------------------------*/          /*                          a sublist, and all the sublists */
/* var_or_field_declarations  Process variable declarations   */          /*                          are then linked together.      */
/*                            or record field definitions.    */          /*--------------------------------------------------------------*/
/*                            All ids declared with the same   */
/*                            type are linked together into    */          TOKEN_CODE follow_variables_list[] = {SEMICOLON, IDENTIFIER,
```

```
                                    END_OF_FILE, 0};

TOKEN_CODE follow_fields_list[]    = {SEMICOLON, END, IDENTIFIER,
                                    END_OF_FILE, 0};

var_or_field_declarations(rtn_idp, record_tp, offset)

    SYMTAB_NODE_PTR rtn_idp;
    TYPE_STRUCT_PTR record_tp;
    int             offset;

{

    SYMTAB_NODE_PTR idp, first_idp, last_idp;  /* variable or
                                                  field ids */

    SYMTAB_NODE_PTR prev_last_idp = NULL;      /* last id of list */
    TYPE_STRUCT_PTR tp;                        /* type */
    BOOLEAN var_flag = (rtn_idp != NULL);      /* TRUE:  variables */
                                               /* FALSE: fields */

    int size;
    int total_size = 0;

    /*
    -- Loop to process sublist, each of a type.
    */
    while (token == IDENTIFIER) {
        first_idp = NULL;

        /*
        -- Loop process each variable or field id in a sublist.
        */
        while (token == IDENTIFIER) {
            if (var_flag) {
                search_and_enter_local_symtab(idp);
                idp->defn.key = VAR_DEFN;
            }
            else {
                search_and_enter_this_symtab
                    (idp, record_tp->info.record.field_symtab);
                idp->defn.key = FIELD_DEFN;
            }
            idp->label_index = new_label_index();

            /*
            -- Link ids together into a sublist.
            */
            if (first_idp == NULL) {
                first_idp = last_idp = idp;
                if (var_flag &&
                    (rtn_idp->defn.info.routine.locals == NULL))
                    rtn_idp->defn.info.routine.locals = idp;
            }
            else {
                last_idp->next = idp;
                last_idp = idp;
            }

            get_token();
            if_token_get(COMMA);
        }
```

```
        /*
        -- Process the sublist's type.
        */
        if_token_get_else_error(COLON, MISSING_COLON);
        tp = do_type();
        size = tp->size;
        if (size & 1) ++size;   /* round up to even */

        /*
        -- Assign the offset and the type to all variable or field
        -- ids in the sublist.
        */
        for (idp = first_idp; idp != NULL; idp = idp->next) {
            idp->typep = tp;

            if (var_flag) {
                offset -= size;
                total_size += size;
                idp->defn.info.data.offset = offset;
                analyze_var_decl(idp);
            }

            else  /* record fields */ {
                idp->defn.info.data.offset = offset;
                offset += size;

                /*
                -- Emit numeric equate for the field id's
                -- name and offset.
                */
                emit_numeric_equate(idp);
            }
        }

        /*
        -- Link this sublist to the previous sublist.
        */
        if (prev_last_idp != NULL) prev_last_idp->next = first_idp;
        prev_last_idp = last_idp;

        /*
        -- Error synchronization:  Should be ; for variable
        --                         declaration, or ; or END for
        --                         record type definition.
        */
        synchronize(var_flag ? follow_variables_list
                    : follow_fields_list,
                    declaration_start_list, statement_start_list);
        if_token_get(SEMICOLON);
        else if (var_flag && ((token_in(declaration_start_list)) ||
                            (token_in(statement_start_list))))
            error(MISSING_SEMICOLON);
    }

if (var_flag)
    rtn_idp->defn.info.routine.total_local_size = total_size;
else
    record_tp->size = offset;
}
```

Function `var_or_field_declarations` allocates stack offsets for local variables differently from how they were allocated for the interpreter. For the compiled code, the offsets must be negative (see Figure 12-4). We decrement variable `offset` each time by the size of the variable. As always, we keep track of the total byte size of all the local variables in `total_size`, and at the end, we set this value in the `total_local_size` field of the symbol table node of the procedure or function identifier.

For each record field, `var_or_field_declarations` calls function `emit_numeric_equate` in file `emitcode.c` to equate the tagged field name with its offset. As we will see later, these names are used in the generated code to calculate record field addresses. For example, the record definition:

```
RECORD
    i : integer;
    x : real;
    b : boolean;
END
```

results in the equates:

```
i_003 EQU 0
x_004 EQU 2
b_005 EQU 6
```

The new version of routine `var_declarations` in file `decl.c` (shown in Figure 13-4) now passes a different initial offset value depending on whether the Pascal routine is a procedure or a function. As we saw in Chapter 12, a function allocates two words on the stack frame for its return value.

FIGURE 13-4   Function `var_declarations` in file `decl.c`.

```
/*-----------------------------------------------------------*/        SYMTAB_NODE_PTR rtn_idp;   /* id of program or routine */
/*  var_declarations   Process variable declarations:        */
/*                                                            */        {
/*                     <id-list> : <type>                     */        var_or_field_declarations(rtn_idp, NULL,
/*-----------------------------------------------------------*/                                  rtn_idp->defn.key == PROC_DEFN
                                                                                                  ? PROC_LOCALS_STACK_FRAME_OFFSET
                                                                                                  : FUNC_LOCALS_STACK_FRAME_OFFSET);
var_declarations(rtn_idp)                                               }
```

Figure 13-5 shows a new version of function `formal_parm_list` in file `routine.c`. We access formal parameter values with positive offsets from the stack frame location pointed to by register BP (see Figure 12-4). However, we must assign the offsets in reverse order, the last parameter gets the smallest offset, and the first parameter gets the largest offset.

FIGURE 13-5   Function `formal_parm_list` in file `routine.c`.

```
/*------------------------------------------------------------*/
/*  formal_parm_list    Process a formal parameter list:      */
/*                                                            */
/*                          ( VAR <id-list> : <type> ;        */
/*                                <id-list> : <type> ;        */
/*                                  ... )                     */
/*                                                            */
/*                      Return a pointer to the head of the   */
/*                      parameter id list.                    */
/*------------------------------------------------------------*/

    SYMTAB_NODE_PTR
formal_parm_list(countp, total_sizep)

    int *countp;        /* ptr to count of parameters */
    int *total_sizep;   /* ptr to total byte size of parameters */

{
    SYMTAB_NODE_PTR parm_idp, first_idp, last_idp;   /* parm ids */
    SYMTAB_NODE_PTR prev_last_idp = NULL;         /* last id of list */
    SYMTAB_NODE_PTR parm_listp = NULL;            /* parm list */
    SYMTAB_NODE_PTR type_idp;                     /* type id */
    TYPE_STRUCT_PTR parm_tp;                      /* parm type */
    DEFN_KEY        parm_defn;                    /* parm definition */
    int             parm_count = 0;               /* count of parms */
    int             parm_offset = PARAMETERS_STACK_FRAME_OFFSET;

    get_token();

    /*
    -- Loop to process parameter declarations separated by ;
    */
    while ((token == IDENTIFIER) || (token == VAR)) {
        first_idp = NULL;

        /*
        -- VAR parms?
        */
        if (token == VAR) {
            parm_defn = VARPARM_DEFN;
            get_token();
        }
        else parm_defn = VALPARM_DEFN;

        /*
        -- <id list>
        */
        while (token == IDENTIFIER) {
            search_and_enter_local_symtab(parm_idp);
            parm_idp->defn.key   = parm_defn;
            parm_idp->label_index = new_label_index();
            ++parm_count;

            if (parm_listp == NULL) parm_listp = parm_idp;

            /*
            -- Link parm ids together.
            */
```

```
            if (first_idp == NULL)
                first_idp = last_idp = parm_idp;
            else {
                last_idp->next = parm_idp;
                last_idp = parm_idp;
            }

            get_token();
            if_token_get(COMMA);
        }

        if_token_get_else_error(COLON, MISSING_COLON);

        if (token == IDENTIFIER) {
            search_and_find_all_symtab(type_idp);
            if (type_idp->defn.key != TYPE_DEFN) error(INVALID_TYPE);
            parm_tp = type_idp->typep;
            get_token();
        }
        else {
            error(MISSING_IDENTIFIER);
            parm_tp = &dummy_type;
        }

        /*
        -- Assign the type to all parm ids in the sublist.
        */
        for (parm_idp = first_idp;
             parm_idp != NULL;
             parm_idp = parm_idp->next) parm_idp->typep = parm_tp;

        /*
        -- Link this list to the list of all parm ids.
        */
        if (prev_last_idp != NULL) prev_last_idp->next = first_idp;
        prev_last_idp = last_idp;

        /*
        -- Error synchronization:  Should be ; or )
        */
        synchronize(follow_parms_list, NULL, NULL);
        if_token_get(SEMICOLON);
    }

    /*
    -- Assign the offset to all parm ids in reverse order.
    */
    reverse_list(&parm_listp);
    for (parm_idp = parm_listp;
         parm_idp != NULL;
         parm_idp = parm_idp->next) {
        parm_idp->defn.info.data.offset = parm_offset;
        parm_offset += parm_idp->defn.key == VALPARM_DEFN
                            ? parm_idp->typep->size
                            : sizeof(char *);
        if (parm_offset & 1) ++parm_offset;   /* round up to even */
    }
```

```
reverse_list(&parm_listp);                                    *total_sizep = parm_offset - PARAMETERS_STACK_FRAME_OFFSET;

if_token_get_else_error(RPAREN, MISSING_RPAREN);              return(parm_listp);
*countp = parm_count;                                      }
```

To assign the offsets, we first call function reverse_list to reverse the order of the formal parameter list. We increment variable offset by the size of each parameter. Then we call reverse_list a second time to restore the original order of the parameter list. This new function is also defined in routine.c, and it is shown in Figure 13-6.

FIGURE 13-6   Function reverse_list in file routine.c.

```
/*----------------------------------------------------*/         -- Reverse the list in place.
/*  reverse_list        Reverse a list of symbol table nodes.  */         */
/*----------------------------------------------------*/         while (thisp != NULL) {
                                                                     nextp = thisp->next;
reverse_list(listpp)                                                 thisp->next = prevp;
                                                                     prevp = thisp;
    SYMTAB_NODE_PTR *listpp;     /* ptr to ptr to node list head */   thisp = nextp;
                                                                 }
{
    SYMTAB_NODE_PTR prevp = NULL;                                /*
    SYMTAB_NODE_PTR thisp = *listpp;                            -- Point to the new head (former tail) of the list.
    SYMTAB_NODE_PTR nextp;                                       */
                                                                *listpp = prevp;
    /*                                                       }
```

As before, we keep track of the total byte size of all the formal parameters in function formal_parm_list. Functions procedure_header and function_header set this value in the total_parm_size field of the symbol table node for the procedure or function identifier.

13.2.3 Program prologue and epilogue code

The new version of function program in file routine.c is shown in Figure 13-7. We call function emit_program_prologue, defined in file emitcode.c, which emits the following directives that appear at the start of every assembly program produced by the compiler:

```
DOSSEG
.MODEL   small
.STACK   1024


.CODE
```

```
                        PUBLIC   _pascal_main
                        INCLUDE  pasextrn.inc

         $STATIC_LINK           EQU   <WORD PTR [bp+4]>
         $RETURN_VALUE          EQU   <WORD PTR [bp-4]>
         $HIGH_RETURN_VALUE     EQU   <WORD PTR [bp-2]>
```

FIGURE 13-7   Function program in file routine.c.

```
/*-----------------------------------------------------*/      -- Parse the program's block.
/* program      Process a program:                 */          */
/*                                                 */           program_idp->defn.info.routine.locals = NULL;
/*             <program-header> ; <block> .        */           block(program_idp);
/*-----------------------------------------------------*/       program_idp->defn.info.routine.local_symtab = exit_scope();

TOKEN_CODE follow_header_list[] = {SEMICOLON, END_OF_FILE, 0};   if_token_get_else_error(PERIOD, MISSING_PERIOD);

program()                                                       /*
                                                                -- Emit the main routine's epilogue code
{                                                               -- followed by the program's epilogue code.
    SYMTAB_NODE_PTR program_idp;        /* program id */        */
                                                                emit_main_epilogue();
    /*                                                          emit_program_epilogue(program_idp);
    -- Intialize the symbol table and then emit
    -- the program prologue code.                               /*
    */                                                          -- Look for the end of file.
    init_symtab();                                              */
    emit_program_prologue();                                    while (token != END_OF_FILE) {
                                                                    error(UNEXPECTED_TOKEN);
    /*                                                              get_token();
    -- Begin parsing with the program header.                   }
    */
    program_idp = program_header();                             quit_scanner();

    /*                                                          /*
    -- Error synchronization:  Should be ;                     -- Print the parser's summary.
    */                                                          */
    synchronize(follow_header_list,                             print_line("\n");
            declaration_start_list, statement_start_list);      print_line("\n");
    if_token_get(SEMICOLON);                                    sprintf(buffer, "%20d Source lines.\n", line_number);
    else if (token_in(declaration_start_list) ||               print_line(buffer);
            token_in(statement_start_list))                     sprintf(buffer, "%20d Source errors.\n", error_count);
        error(MISSING_SEMICOLON);                               print_line(buffer);

    analyze_routine_header(program_idp);                        if (error_count == 0) exit(0);
                                                                else            exit(-SYNTAX_ERROR);
    /*                                                      }
```

These directives give the assembler useful information. DOSSEG tells the assembler to place the segments in the object file in the conventional order, and .MODEL specifies that the program will use the "small" memory model, which is one code segment and one data segment (see Figure 12-3). The size of the stack at bottom of the data segment is specified by .STACK while .CODE specifies the start of the code segment. PUBLIC makes the name _pascal_main available to the main library routine (by convention, the assembler adds an underscore in front of each public name). INCLUDE is similar to #include in a C program; it causes the file pasextrn.inc to be included. Each EQU directive is similar to a #define in a C program and the < and > are string delimiters. These statements give names to certain components of the stack frame.

File pasextrn.inc, shown in Figure 13-8, contains EXTRN directives. Each specifies that a library routine is defined elsewhere.

FIGURE 13-8   File pasextrn.inc.

```
EXTRN   _float_negate:PROC          EXTRN   _read_char:PROC
EXTRN   _float_add:PROC             EXTRN   _read_line:PROC
EXTRN   _float_subtract:PROC
EXTRN   _float_multiply:PROC        EXTRN   _std_end_of_file:PROC
EXTRN   _float_divide:PROC          EXTRN   _std_end_of_line:PROC
EXTRN   _float_compare:PROC
EXTRN   _float_convert:PROC         EXTRN   _std_abs:PROC

EXTRN   _write_integer:PROC         EXTRN   _std_arctan:PROC
EXTRN   _write_real:PROC            EXTRN   _std_cos:PROC
EXTRN   _write_boolean:PROC         EXTRN   _std_exp:PROC
EXTRN   _write_char:PROC            EXTRN   _std_ln:PROC
EXTRN   _write_string:PROC          EXTRN   _std_sin:PROC
EXTRN   _write_line:PROC            EXTRN   _std_sqrt:PROC

EXTRN   _read_integer:PROC          EXTRN   _std_round:PROC
EXTRN   _read_real:PROC             EXTRN   _std_trunc:PROC
```

Near the end of function program, we call function emit_program_epilogue, defined in file emitcode.c, where we emit code that appears at the end of every assembly program produced by the compiler. The first line of the code is the directive .DATA which specifies the start of the data segment. Then, we emit the declarations for the program's global variables. Examples of scalar declarations are:

```
ch_012     DB  0
sides_015  DW  0
beta_017   DD  0.0
```

These declare a character, integer, and a real value, respectively. We initialize all values to 0 or 0.0. Following is an example of an array or record declaration which declares a block of 144 bytes, all initialized to 0:

```
vector_020   DB  144 DUP(0)
```

The program epilogue code also declares any floating point and string literals that appeared in the Pascal program. These literals must be declared in the data segment because floating point and string literals cannot be used as immediate operands to assembly instructions. As we will see later, these literals must be entered into the symbol table just like in the interpreter. All the floating point literal symbol table entries are linked together, and pointer variable `float_literal_list`, declared in file `emitcode.c`, points to the head of this list. Similarly, the string literal symbol table entries are linked together, and pointer variable `string_literal_list` points to the head of the list. So after emitting the global variable declarations, we emit the declarations for any floating point and string literals. Examples of such declarations are:

```
$F_021   DD   3.141590e+000
$S_026   DB   "Hello, world."
```

Recall that in file `code.h` (see Figure 12-6), we defined the label prefixes for floating point literals and for string literals to be $F and $S, respectively.

13.2.4 Main routine prologue and epilogue code

Figure 13-9 shows a new version of function `block` in file `routine.c`. For the main Pascal routine, we call function `emit_main_prologue`. Function `program` (Figure 13-7) also calls function `emit_main_epilogue`. These new routines are defined in file `emitcode.c` and emit the prologue and epilogue code for the main Pascal routine.

FIGURE 13-9   Function `block` in file `routine.c`.

```
/*----------------------------------------------------------*/
/* block              Process a block, which consists of    */
/*                    declarations followed by a compound    */
/*                    statement.                             */
/*----------------------------------------------------------*/

TOKEN_CODE follow_decls_list[] = {SEMICOLON, BEGIN, END_OF_FILE, 0};

block(rtn_idp)

    SYMTAB_NODE_PTR rtn_idp;     /* id of program or routine */

{
    extern BOOLEAN block_flag;

    declarations(rtn_idp);

    /*
    -- Emit the prologue code for the main routine
    -- or for a procedure or function.
    */
    if (rtn_idp->defn.key == PROG_DEFN)
        emit_main_prologue();
    else
        emit_routine_prologue(rtn_idp);

    /*
    -- Error synchronization:  Should be ;
    */
    synchronize(follow_decls_list, NULL, NULL);
    if (token != BEGIN) error(MISSING_BEGIN);

    block_flag = TRUE;
    compound_statement();
    block_flag = FALSE;
}
```

The prologue code consists of the following:

```
_pascal_main PROC

        push bp
        mov  bp,sp
```

The push bp pushes the dynamic link onto the stack, and the mov bp,sp points register BP to the new stack frame (steps 4 and 5 of 13.2.1 Managing the runtime stack). Since the global variables are allocated in the data segment, no data are allocated on the stack for the Pascal main routine (step 7).

The epilogue code consists of the following:

```
pop bp
ret


_pascal_main  ENDP
```

The pop bp restores register BP (step 10) to point to the caller's stack frame (that of routine main in the runtime library). ret pops off the return address (step 11). The other steps are not necessary for the main Pascal routine.

13.2.5 Procedure and function prologue and epilogue code

Function block calls function emit_routine_prologue for a Pascal procedure or function. In the new version of function routine in file routine.c (shown in Figure 13-10), we call function emit_routine_epilogue at the end. These new routines are defined in file emitcode.c and emit the prologue and epilogue code, respectively, for Pascal routines.

FIGURE 13-10   Function routine in file routine.c.

```
/*----------------------------------------------------*/
/*  routine           Call the appropriate routine to process */
/*                    a procedure or function definition:     */
/*                                                      */
/*                        <routine-header> ; <block>    */
/*----------------------------------------------------*/

routine()

{
    SYMTAB_NODE_PTR rtn_idp;     /* routine id */

    rtn_idp = (token == PROCEDURE) ? procedure_header()
                                   : function_header();

    /*
    -- Error synchronization:  Should be ;
    */
    synchronize(follow_header_list,
            declaration_start_list, statement_start_list);
    if_token_get(SEMICOLON);
    else if (token_in(declaration_start_list) ||
            token_in(statement_start_list))
        error(MISSING_SEMICOLON);

    /*
    -- <block> or FORWARD.
    */
    if (strcmp(word_string, "forward") != 0) {
        rtn_idp->defn.info.routine.key = DECLARED;
        analyze_routine_header(rtn_idp);

        rtn_idp->defn.info.routine.locals = NULL;
        block(rtn_idp);
    }
    else {
        get_token();
        rtn_idp->defn.info.routine.key = FORWARD;
        analyze_routine_header(rtn_idp);
    }

    /*
    -- Exit the current scope and emit the
    -- routine's epilogue code.
    */
    rtn_idp->defn.info.routine.local_symtab = exit_scope();
    emit_routine_epilogue(rtn_idp);
}
```

The prologue code for a Pascal function consists of the following:

```
push bp
mov  bp,sp
sub  sp,4
sub  sp,var_size
```

The push bp pushes the dynamic link onto the stack, and the mov bp,sp points register BP to the new stack frame (steps 4 and 5). The sub sp,4 allocates stack space for the return value (step 6), and the sub sp, var_size allocates stack space for the local variables (step 7). The total byte size of all of the function's local variables is var_size. The prologue code for a Pascal procedure is similar, except we do not emit the sub sp,4.

The epilogue code for a Pascal function consists of:

```
mov  ax,$RETURN_VALUE
mov  sp,bp
pop  bp
ret  parm_size+2
```

The mov ax,$RETURN_VALUE moves the return value into register AX (step 8). ($RETURN_VALUE was equated to WORD PTR [bp-4] in the program prologue.) If the function returns a real value, that statement is followed by mov dx,$HIGH_RETURN_VALUE (equated to WORD PTR [bp-2]) to move the high-order half of the return value into register DX. The mov sp,bp cuts the stack back to remove the function's local variables and the return value (step 9). The pop bp retrieves the dynamic link and restores register BP to point to the caller's stack frame (step 10). Finally, the ret parm_size+2 pops off the return address (step 11) and cuts the stack back by parm_size+2 bytes to remove the static link and the actual parameters (step 12). parm_size is the total byte size of all of the function's formal parameters. (Of course, the ret instruction also causes a return to the caller.)

The epilogue code for a Pascal procedure is similar, except we do not emit mov ax,$RETURN_VALUE or mov dx,$HIGH_RETURN_VALUE.

13.2.6 Declarations

In order to make the generated assembly code easier to read, the compiler emits text equates for all of a Pascal procedure's or function's formal parameters and local variables, which are allocated in the stack frame. For example, if a procedure has formal parameters p1 and p2 (both type integer) and local variable var (type real), the compiler emits:

```
p1_008    EQU <WORD PTR [bp+8]>
p2_009    EQU <WORD PTR [bp+6]>
var_010   EQU <WORD PTR [bp-4]>
```

The compiler then uses the tagged names in the generated code.

These equates are emitted by function emit_declarations, defined in file emitcode.c. This function calls function emit_text_equate, defined in the same file. Figure 13-11 shows a new version of function declarations in file decl.c. It makes a call to emit_declarations after it has parsed a routine's variable declarations.

FIGURE 13-11   Function declarations in file decl.c.

```
/*----------------------------------------------------------*/              var_declarations(rtn_idp);
/*  declarations       Call the routines to process constant   */        }
/*                     definitions, type definitions, variable */
/*                     declarations, procedure definitions,    */        /*
/*                     and function definitions.               */        -- Emit declarations for parameters and local variables.
/*----------------------------------------------------------*/            */
                                                                          if (rtn_idp->defn.key != PROG_DEFN) emit_declarations(rtn_idp);
TOKEN_CODE follow_routine_list[] = {SEMICOLON, END_OF_FILE, 0};
                                                                          /*
declarations(rtn_idp)                                                     -- Loop to process routine (procedure and function)
                                                                          -- definitions.
    SYMTAB_NODE_PTR rtn_idp;      /* id of program or routine */          */
                                                                          while ((token == PROCEDURE) || (token == FUNCTION)) {
{                                                                             routine();
    if (token == CONST) {
        get_token();                                                          /*
        const_definitions();                                                  -- Error synchronization:  Should be ;
    }                                                                         */
                                                                              synchronize(follow_routine_list,
    if (token == TYPE) {                                                               declaration_start_list, statement_start_list);
        get_token();                                                          if_token_get(SEMICOLON);
        type_definitions();                                                   else if (token_in(declaration_start_list) ||
    }                                                                                 token_in(statement_start_list))
                                                                                      error(MISSING_SEMICOLON);
    if (token == VAR) {                                                   }
        get_token();                                                  }
```

Note that in the case of nested Pascal routines, we emit the declarations for all of the routines together before any of their executable code. This does not cause any problems for the assembler.

13.2.7 Calls to procedures and functions

Now we will look at the code the compiler generates to call a Pascal procedure or function. We emit this code in functions declared_routine_call and actual_parm_list in file routine.c. Figures 13-12 and 13-13 show new versions of these functions.

FIGURE 13-12 Function `declared_routine_call` in file `routine.c`.

```
/*------------------------------------------------------------*/
/* declared_routine_call    Process a call to a declared      */
/*                          procedure or function:            */
/*                                                            */
/*                                 <id>                       */
/*                                                            */
/*                          or:                               */
/*                                                            */
/*                                 <id> ( <parm-list> )       */
/*                                                            */
/*                          The actual parameters are checked */
/*                          against the formal parameters for */
/*                          type and number.  Return a pointer*/
/*                          to the type structure of the call.*/
/*------------------------------------------------------------*/

    TYPE_STRUCT_PTR
declared_routine_call(rtn_idp, parm_check_flag)

    SYMTAB_NODE_PTR rtn_idp;          /* routine id */
    BOOLEAN         parm_check_flag;  /* if TRUE check parms */

{
    int old_level = level;               /* level of caller */
    int new_level = rtn_idp->level + 1;  /* level of callee */

    actual_parm_list(rtn_idp, parm_check_flag);

    /*
    -- Push the static link onto the stack.
    */

    if (new_level == old_level + 1) {
        /*
        -- Calling a routine nested within the caller:
        -- Push pointer to caller's stack frame.
        */
        emit_1(PUSH, reg(BP));
    }
    else if (new_level == old_level) {
        /*
        -- Calling another routine at the same level:
        -- Push pointer to stack frame of common parent.
        */
        emit_1(PUSH, name_lit(STATIC_LINK));
    }
    else  /* new_level < old_level */ {
        /*
        -- Calling a routine at a lesser level (nested less deeply):
        -- Push pointer to stack frame of nearest common ancestor.
        */
        int lev;

        emit_2(MOVE, reg(BX), reg(BP));
        for (lev = old_level; lev >= new_level; --lev)
            emit_2(MOVE, reg(BP), name_lit(STATIC_LINK));
        emit_1(PUSH, reg(BP));
        emit_2(MOVE, reg(BP), reg(BX));
    }

    emit_1(CALL, tagged_name(rtn_idp));

    return(rtn_idp->defn.key == PROC_DEFN ? NULL : rtn_idp->typep);
}
```

FIGURE 13-13 Function `actual_parm_list` in file `routine.c`.

```
/*------------------------------------------------------------*/
/* actual_parm_list    Process an actual parameter list:      */
/*                                                            */
/*                          ( <expr-list> )                   */
/*------------------------------------------------------------*/

TOKEN_CODE follow_parm_list[] = {COMMA, RPAREN, 0};

actual_parm_list(rtn_idp, parm_check_flag)

    SYMTAB_NODE_PTR rtn_idp;          /* routine id */
    BOOLEAN         parm_check_flag;  /* if TRUE check parms */

{
    SYMTAB_NODE_PTR formal_parm_idp;
    DEFN_KEY        formal_parm_defn;
    TYPE_STRUCT_PTR formal_parm_tp, actual_parm_tp;

    if (parm_check_flag)
        formal_parm_idp = rtn_idp->defn.info.routine.parms;

    if (token == LPAREN) {
        /*
        -- Loop to process actual parameter expressions.
```

```
        */
        do {
            /*
            -- Obtain info about the corresponding formal parm.
            */
            if (parm_check_flag && (formal_parm_idp != NULL)) {
                formal_parm_defn = formal_parm_idp->defn.key;
                formal_parm_tp   = formal_parm_idp->typep;
            }

            get_token();

            /*
            -- Check the actual parm's type against the formal parm.
            -- An actual parm's type must be the same as the type of
            -- a formal VAR parm and assignment compatible with the
            -- type of a formal value parm.
            */
            if ((formal_parm_idp == NULL) ||
                (formal_parm_defn == VALPARM_DEFN) ||
                !parm_check_flag) {
                actual_parm_tp = expression();
                if (parm_check_flag && (formal_parm_idp != NULL) &&
                    (! is_assign_type_compatible(formal_parm_tp,
```

```
                              actual_parm_tp)))              if (token == IDENTIFIER) {
        error(INCOMPATIBLE_TYPES);                               SYMTAB_NODE_PTR idp;

    /*                                                           search_and_find_all_symtab(idp);
    -- Push the argument value onto the stack.                   actual_parm_tp = variable(idp, VARPARM_USE);
    */
    if (formal_parm_tp == real_typep) {                          if (formal_parm_tp != actual_parm_tp)
        /*                                                           error(INCOMPATIBLE_TYPES);
        -- Real formal parm.                                 }
        */                                                   else {
        if (actual_parm_tp == integer_typep) {                   actual_parm_tp = expression();
            emit_1(PUSH, reg(AX));                               error(INVALID_VAR_PARM);
            emit_1(CALL, name_lit(FLOAT_CONVERT));           }
            emit_2(ADD,  reg(SP), integer_lit(2));       }
        }
        emit_1(PUSH, reg(DX));                           /*
        emit_1(PUSH, reg(AX));                           -- Check if there are more actual parms
    }                                                    -- than formal parms.
    else if ((actual_parm_tp->form == ARRAY_FORM) ||     */
             (actual_parm_tp->form == RECORD_FORM)) {    if (parm_check_flag) {
                                                             if (formal_parm_idp == NULL)
        /*                                                       error(WRONG_NUMBER_OF_PARMS);
        -- Block move onto the stack.                        else formal_parm_idp = formal_parm_idp->next;
        */                                               }
        int size = actual_parm_tp->size;
        int offset = size%2 == 0 ? size : size + 1;      /*
                                                         -- Error synchronization:  Should be , or )
        emit(CLEAR_DIRECTION);                           */
        emit_1(POP, reg(SI));                            synchronize(follow_parm_list, statement_end_list, NULL);
        emit_2(SUBTRACT, reg(SP), integer_lit(offset));
        emit_2(MOVE, reg(DI), reg(SP));              } while (token == COMMA);
        emit_2(MOVE, reg(CX), integer_lit(size));
        emit_2(MOVE, reg(AX), reg(DS));                  if_token_get_else_error(RPAREN, MISSING_RPAREN);
        emit_2(MOVE, reg(ES), reg(AX));              }
        emit(MOVE_BLOCK);
    }                                                /*
    else {                                           -- Check if there are fewer actual parms than formal parms.
        emit_1(PUSH, reg(AX));                       */
    }                                                if (parm_check_flag && (formal_parm_idp != NULL))
}                                                        error(WRONG_NUMBER_OF_PARMS);
else  /* formal_parm_defn == VARPARM_DEFN */ {   }
```

First, declared_routine_call calls actual_parm_list, where we handle the actual parameters of a call (step 1). As we did in the interpreter, we call function expression to process each actual parameter passed by value, and function variable to process each actual parameter passed by reference (corresponding to a formal VAR parameter). These two functions are defined in file expr.c and we will examine them in detail later. All you need to know for now is that function expression generates code that leaves a scalar word value in register AX, a scalar doubleword value in the DX:AX register pair, or the address of an array or record value on the top of the runtime stack. Function variable, when called with VARPARM_USE, always generates code that leaves the address of the variable on top of the stack.

In function actual_parm_list, we want to emit code that pushes the value of a parameter passed by value. Therefore, after calling expression, we emit the assembly instruction push ax if the expression type is integer, enumeration, or character. Or, if the expression type and the formal parameter type are real, we emit:

```
push dx
push ax
```

to push the high-order half of the doubleword followed by the low-order half. If the expression type is integer but the formal parameter type is real, we must emit code to convert the expression value. Therefore, we emit:

```
push ax
call _float_convert
add  sp,2
push dx
push ax
```

Library function _float_convert is defined in paslib.c. And note the add sp,2. C functions, by convention, do not remove the actual parameters off of the stack; it is the responsibility of the caller. A static link is not pushed onto the stack when calling a C routine.

   If the parameter value is an array or a record, the emitted code must allocate and make a copy of the value on the stack. We first obtain the byte size of the value and store this in variable size. Since only words are ever pushed or allocated on the stack, we set variable offset to the smallest even number of bytes that can contain the value. The following code pops off the address of the value and copies the value onto the stack:

```
cld                    ; clear direction flag
pop  si                ; SI = source address
sub  sp,offset         ; allocate stack space
mov  di,sp             ; DI = destination address
mov  cx,size           ; CX = number of bytes to move
mov  ax,ds             ; AX = DS
mov  es,ax             ; ES = AX
rep  movsb             ; block move
```

   cld clears the direction flag to indicate that the block move is to proceed forward. Registers SI and DI are set to point the source and destination, respectively. The source address is popped off the stack, and the destination is space allocated on the stack by subtracting the value of *offset* from register SP (remember that the stack grows towards lower addresses). Register CX is set to *size*, the number of consecutive bytes to move (actually, copy).

   Register SI normally points to a location in the "extra" segment. We get around this by setting register ES to point to the data segment. The 8086 processor does not allow the contents of register DS to be moved directly into register ES, so the generated code uses register AX as an intermediary. Finally, `rep movsb` does a block move.

After function `actual_parm_list` returns to function `declared_routine_call`, we emit code to push the static link onto the stack (step 2). This code will do what the interpreter did. If the callee is nested in the caller (the nesting level of the callee is one greater than the level of the caller), the static link must point to the caller's stack frame: `push bp`.

If the callee is at the same nesting level as the caller routine (both routines have the same parent routine), the static link must point to the parent's stack frame: `push $STATIC_LINK`.

In all other cases (the nesting level of the callee routine is less than the level of the caller routine), the code must search the chain of static links to find the one that points to the nearest common ancestor routine of the caller and the callee. As we saw in the interpreter, this ancestor is the parent of the callee, and its stack frame pointer is found by following `old_level - new_level + 1` static links. For example, if the caller is at level 5 and the callee is at level 3, the ancestor must be at level 2, and the code to push a pointer to its stack frame is:

```
mov   bx,bp                ; save current BP in BX
mov   bp,$STATIC_LINK      ; BP -> level 4 stack frame
mov   bp,$STATIC_LINK      ; BP -> level 3 stack frame
mov   bp,$STATIC_LINK      ; BP -> level 2 stack frame
push  bp                   ; push static link
mov   bp,bx                ; restore current BP
```

Finally, we emit code to push the return address onto the stack (step 3). The `call` instruction automatically does this, for example: `call proc_032`.

13.3 Assignment statements

Now that we have code to enter and exit procedures and functions, we can look at the code to execute the statements contained in these routines. Figure 13-14 shows the new version of file `stmt.c`. In this chapter, the only statements the compiler can handle are procedure calls, assignment statements, and compound statements. (We will tackle the other statements in the next chapter.)

FIGURE 13-14   File `stmt.c`.

```
/***************************************************************/     /*     MODULE:     parser                      */
/*                                                     */     /*                                             */
/*     S T A T E M E N T   P A R S E R                 */     /***************************************************************/
/*                                                     */
/*     Parsing routines for statements.                */     #include <stdio.h>
/*                                                     */     #include "common.h"
/*     FILE:      stmt.c                               */     #include "error.h"
/*                                                     */     #include "scanner.h"
```

```
#include "symtab.h"
#include "parser.h"
#include "code.h"

/*--------------------------------------------------------*/
/*  Externals                                             */
/*--------------------------------------------------------*/

extern TOKEN_CODE       token;
extern char             word_string[];
extern LITERAL          literal;
extern TOKEN_CODE       statement_start_list[], statement_end_list[];

extern SYMTAB_NODE_PTR  symtab_display[];
extern int              level;

extern TYPE_STRUCT_PTR  integer_typep, real_typep,
                        boolean_typep, char_typep;

extern TYPE_STRUCT      dummy_type;

extern int              label_index;
extern char             asm_buffer[];
extern char             *asm_bufferp;
extern FILE             *code_file;

/*--------------------------------------------------------*/
/*  statement       Process a statement by calling the    */
/*                  appropriate parsing routine based on   */
/*                  the statement's first token.           */
/*--------------------------------------------------------*/

statement()

{
    /*
    -- Call the appropriate routine based on the first
    -- token of the statement.
    */
    switch (token) {

        case IDENTIFIER: {
            SYMTAB_NODE_PTR idp;

            /*
            -- Assignment statement or procedure call?
            */
            search_and_find_all_symtab(idp);

            if (idp->defn.key == PROC_DEFN) {
                get_token();
                routine_call(idp, TRUE);
            }
            else assignment_statement(idp);

            break;
        }

        case BEGIN:     compound_statement();   break;

        case WHILE:
        case REPEAT:
        case IF:
        case FOR:
        case CASE: {
            error(UNIMPLEMENTED_FEATURE);
            exit(-UNIMPLEMENTED_FEATURE);
```

```
    }
}

/*
-- Error synchronization: Only a semicolon, END, ELSE, or
--                         UNTIL may follow a statement.
--                         Check for a missing semicolon.
*/
synchronize(statement_end_list, statement_start_list, NULL);
if (token_in(statement_start_list)) error(MISSING_SEMICOLON);
}

/*--------------------------------------------------------*/
/*  assignment_statement    Process an assignment statement: */
/*                                                        */
/*                      <id> := <expr>                    */
/*--------------------------------------------------------*/

assignment_statement(var_idp)

    SYMTAB_NODE_PTR var_idp;        /* target variable id */

{
    TYPE_STRUCT_PTR var_tp, expr_tp;    /* types of var and expr */
    BOOLEAN         stacked_flag;       /* TRUE iff target address
                                           was pushed on stack */

    var_tp = variable(var_idp, TARGET_USE);
    stacked_flag = (var_idp->defn.key == VARPARM_DEFN) ||
                   (var_idp->defn.key == FUNC_DEFN) ||
                   (var_idp->typep->form == ARRAY_FORM) ||
                   (var_idp->typep->form == RECORD_FORM) ||
                   ((var_idp->level > 1) && (var_idp->level < level));

    if_token_get_else_error(COLONEQUAL, MISSING_COLONEQUAL);
    expr_tp = expression();

    if (! is_assign_type_compatible(var_tp, expr_tp))
        error(INCOMPATIBLE_ASSIGNMENT);

    var_tp  = base_type(var_tp);
    expr_tp = base_type(expr_tp);

    /*
    -- Emit code to do the assignment.
    */
    if (var_tp == char_typep) {
        /*
        -- char := char
        */
        if (stacked_flag) {
            emit_1(POP, reg(BX));
            emit_2(MOVE, byte_indirect(BX), reg(AL));
        }
        else emit_2(MOVE, byte(var_idp), reg(AL));
    }
    else if (var_tp == real_typep) {
        /*
        -- real := ...
        */
        if (expr_tp == integer_typep) {
            /*
            -- ... integer
            */
            emit_1(PUSH, reg(AX));
            emit_1(CALL, name_lit(FLOAT_CONVERT));
            emit_2(ADD, reg(SP), integer_lit(2));
```

```
        }
        /*
        -- ... real
        */
        if (stacked_flag) {
            emit_1(POP, reg(BX));
            emit_2(MOVE, word_indirect(BX), reg(AX));
            emit_2(MOVE, high_dword_indirect(BX), reg(DX));
        }
        else {
            emit_2(MOVE, word(var_idp), reg(AX));
            emit_2(MOVE, high_dword(var_idp), reg(DX));
        }
    }
    else if ((var_tp->form == ARRAY_FORM) ||
             (var_tp->form == RECORD_FORM)) {
        /*
        -- array  := array
        -- record := record
        */
        emit_2(MOVE, reg(CX), integer_lit(var_tp->size));
        emit_1(POP,  reg(SI));
        emit_1(POP,  reg(DI));
        emit_2(MOVE, reg(AX), reg(DS));
        emit_2(MOVE, reg(ES), reg(AX));
        emit(CLEAR_DIRECTION);
        emit(MOVE_BLOCK);
    }
    else {
        /*
        -- integer := integer
        -- enum    := enum
        */
        if (stacked_flag) {
```

```
            emit_1(POP, reg(BX));
            emit_2(MOVE, word_indirect(BX), reg(AX));
        }
        else emit_2(MOVE, word(var_idp), reg(AX));
    }
}

/*----------------------------------------------------------------*/
/* compound_statement       Process a compound statement:        */
/*                                                                */
/*                          BEGIN <stmt-list> END                 */
/*----------------------------------------------------------------*/

compound_statement()

{
    /*
    -- <stmt-list>
    */
    get_token();
    do {
        statement();
        while (token == SEMICOLON) get_token();
        if (token == END) break;

        /*
        -- Error synchronization:  Should be at the start of the
        --                         next statement.
        */
        synchronize(statement_start_list, NULL, NULL);
    } while (token_in(statement_start_list));

    if_token_get_else_error(END, MISSING_END);
}
```

The compiler-generated code for an assignment statement behaves very similarly to how the interpreter executed an assignment statement. We emit the code in function `assignment_statement`, which calls function `variable` for the assignment target, and function `expression` for the expression.

When the interpreter called function `variable` with TARGET_USE, the function pushed the address of the assignment target onto the stack. The code generated by the compiler does the same, except when the assignment target is one of the following:

- a simple global scalar variable (one that is not subscripted or a record field)
- a simple local scalar variable
- a simple local value parameter

In these cases, function `expression` emits code to leave the scalar value in register AX or in the DX:AX register pair, and this value can be moved directly into the target. For example:

```
mov   WORD PTR width_011,ax
```

assigns a word value. We do this to make the object code a bit more efficient. In all other cases, function variable generates code to push the target address onto the stack. Then, for example:

```
pop  bx
mov  WORD PTR [bx],ax
```

moves a word value to the target.

In function assignment_statement, boolean variable stacked_flag is TRUE whenever the target address is pushed onto the stack, and FALSE otherwise. The following are examples of the code we emit for a direct assignment when stacked_flag is FALSE:

```
mov  BYTE PTR ch_003,al

mov  WORD_PTR count_007,ax

mov  WORD_PTR average_009,ax
mov  WORD_PTR average_009+2,dx
```

These statements assign a byte (character), a word (integer or enumeration), and a doubleword (real), respectively.

If an integer value is assigned to a real target, an example of the code we emit is:

```
push ax
call _float_convert
add  sp,2
mov  WORD PTR average_009,ax
mov  WORD PTR average_009+2,dx
```

If the target address is on the stack (stacked_flag is TRUE), examples of the code we emit are:

```
pop  bx
mov  BYTE PTR [bx],al

pop  bx
mov  WORD PTR [bx],ax

pop  bx
mov  WORD PTR [bx],ax
mov  WORD PTR [bx+2],dx
```

```
push ax
call _float_convert
add  sp,2
pop  bx
mov  WORD PTR [bx],ax
mov  WORD PTR [bx+2],dx
```

These statements assign a byte (character), a word (integer or enumeration), a doubleword (real), and a real value converted from an integer value, respectively.

If the expression value is an array or a record, an example of the code we emit is:

```
mov cx,size          ; CX = number of bytes to move
pop si               ; SI = source address
pop di               ; DI = destination address
mov ax,ds            ; AX = DS
mov es,ax            ; ES = AX
cld                  ; clear direction flag
rep movsb            ; block move
```

where *size* is the structure size in bytes.

13.4 Expressions

Figure 13-15 shows the new version of file expr.c. Routines in this file now call the code generation routines to emit code that evaluates expressions.

FIGURE 13-15   File expr.c.

```
*/****************************************************************/
/*                                                          */
/*       E X P R E S S I O N   P A R S E R                  */
/*                                                          */
/*       Parsing routines for expressions.                 */
/*                                                          */
/*       FILE:     expr.c                                   */
/*                                                          */
/*       MODULE:   parser                                   */
/*                                                          */
/*****************************************************************/

#include <stdio.h>
#include "common.h"
#include "error.h"
#include "scanner.h"
#include "symtab.h"
#include "parser.h"
#include "code.h"

/*-----------------------------------------------------------*/
/* Externals                                                 */
/*-----------------------------------------------------------*/
```

```
extern TOKEN_CODE token;
extern char       token_string[];
extern char       word_string[];
extern LITERAL    literal;

extern SYMTAB_NODE_PTR symtab_display[];
extern int             level;

extern TYPE_STRUCT_PTR integer_typep, real_typep,
                       boolean_typep, char_typep;

extern TYPE_STRUCT     dummy_type;

extern SYMTAB_NODE_PTR float_literal_list;
extern SYMTAB_NODE_PTR string_literal_list;

extern int             label_index;
extern char            asm_buffer[];
extern char            *asm_bufferp;
extern FILE            *code_file;
```

```
/*------------------------------------------------------*/
/* Forwards                                             */
/*------------------------------------------------------*/

TYPE_STRUCT_PTR expression(), simple_expression(), term(), factor(),
                constant_identifier(), function_call();

TYPE_STRUCT_PTR float_literal(), string_literal();

/*------------------------------------------------------*/
/* integer_operands    TRUE if both operands are integer,  */
/*                     else FALSE.                         */
/*------------------------------------------------------*/

#define integer_operands(tp1, tp2) ((tp1 == integer_typep) && \
                                    (tp2 == integer_typep))

/*------------------------------------------------------*/
/* real_operands      TRUE if at least one or both operands */
/*                    are real (and the other integer), else */
/*                    FALSE.                                 */
/*------------------------------------------------------*/

#define real_operands(tp1, tp2) (((tp1 == real_typep) &&        \
                                 ((tp2 == real_typep) ||        \
                                  (tp2 == integer_typep)))      \
                                             ||                 \
                                 ((tp2 == real_typep) &&        \
                                  ((tp1 == real_typep) ||       \
                                   (tp1 == integer_typep))))

/*------------------------------------------------------*/
/* boolean_operands   TRUE if both operands are boolean    */
/*                    else FALSE.                          */
/*------------------------------------------------------*/

#define boolean_operands(tp1, pt2) ((tp1 == boolean_typep) && \
                                    (tp2 == boolean_typep))

/*------------------------------------------------------*/
/* expression         Process an expression consisting of a  */
/*                    simple expression optionally followed  */
/*                    by a relational operator and a second  */
/*                    simple expression.  Return a pointer to */
/*                    the type structure.                    */
/*------------------------------------------------------*/

TOKEN_CODE rel_op_list[] = {LT, LE, EQUAL, NE, GE, GT, 0};

    TYPE_STRUCT_PTR
expression()

{
    TOKEN_CODE      op;             /* an operator token */
    TYPE_STRUCT_PTR result_tp, tp2;
    int             jump_label_index;  /* jump target label index */
    INSTRUCTION     jump_opcode;       /* opcode for cond. jump */

    result_tp = simple_expression();   /* first simple expr */

    /*
    -- If there is a relational operator, remember it and
    -- process the second simple expression.
    */
    if (token_in(rel_op_list)) {
        op = token;                 /* remember operator */

        result_tp = base_type(result_tp);
```

```
    emit_push_operand(result_tp);

    get_token();
    tp2 = base_type(simple_expression());   /* 2nd simple expr */

    check_rel_op_types(result_tp, tp2);

    /*
    -- Both operands are integer, character, boolean, or
    -- the same enumeration type.  Compare DX (operand 1)
    -- to AX (operand 2).
    */
    if (integer_operands(result_tp, tp2) ||
        (result_tp == char_typep) ||
        (result_tp->form == ENUM_FORM)) {
        emit_1(POP, reg(DX));
        emit_2(COMPARE, reg(DX), reg(AX));
    }

    /*
    -- Both operands are real, or one is real and the other
    -- is integer.  Convert the integer operand to real.
    -- Call FLOAT_COMPARE to do the comparison, which returns
    -- -1 (less), 0 (equal), or +1 (greater).
    */
    else if ((result_tp == real_typep) || (tp2 == real_typep)) {
        emit_push_operand(tp2);
        emit_promote_to_real(result_tp, tp2);

        emit_1(CALL, name_lit(FLOAT_COMPARE));
        emit_2(ADD, reg(SP), integer_lit(8));
        emit_2(COMPARE, reg(AX), integer_lit(0));
    }

    /*
    -- Both operands are strings.  Compare the string pointed
    -- to by SI (operand 1) to the string pointed to by DI
    -- (operand 2).
    */
    else if (result_tp->form == ARRAY_FORM) {
        emit_1(POP,  reg(DI));
        emit_1(POP,  reg(SI));
        emit_2(MOVE, reg(AX), reg(DS));
        emit_2(MOVE, reg(ES), reg(AX));
        emit(CLEAR_DIRECTION);
        emit_2(MOVE, reg(CX),
               integer_lit(result_tp->info.array.elmt_count));
        emit(COMPARE_STRINGS);
    }

    emit_2(MOVE, reg(AX), integer_lit(1));  /* default: load 1 */

    switch (op) {
        case LT:    jump_opcode = JUMP_LT;  break;
        case LE:    jump_opcode = JUMP_LE;  break;
        case EQUAL: jump_opcode = JUMP_EQ;  break;
        case NE:    jump_opcode = JUMP_NE;  break;
        case GE:    jump_opcode = JUMP_GE;  break;
        case GT:    jump_opcode = JUMP_GT;  break;
    }

    jump_label_index = new_label_index();
    emit_1(jump_opcode, label(STMT_LABEL_PREFIX,
           jump_label_index));

    emit_2(SUBTRACT, reg(AX), reg(AX));     /* load 0 if false */
    emit_label(STMT_LABEL_PREFIX, jump_label_index);
```

```
            result_tp = boolean_typep;
      }

      return(result_tp);
}

/*-------------------------------------------------------------*/
/*  simple_expression   Process a simple expression consisting */
/*                      of terms separated by +, -, or OR      */
/*                      operators.  There may be a unary + or - */
/*                      before the first term.  Return a       */
/*                      pointer to the type structure.         */
/*-------------------------------------------------------------*/

TOKEN_CODE add_op_list[] = {PLUS, MINUS, OR, 0};

    TYPE_STRUCT_PTR
simple_expression()

{
    TOKEN_CODE op;                      /* an operator token */
    BOOLEAN    saw_unary_op = FALSE;    /* TRUE iff unary operator */
    TOKEN_CODE unary_op = PLUS;         /* a unary operator token */
    TYPE_STRUCT_PTR result_tp, tp2;

    /*
    -- If there is a unary + or -, remember it.
    */
    if ((token == PLUS) || (token == MINUS)) {
        unary_op = token;
        saw_unary_op = TRUE;
        get_token();
    }

    result_tp = term();        /* first term */

    /*
    -- If there was a unary operator, check that the term
    -- is integer or real.  Negate the top of stack if it
    -- was a unary - either with the NEG instruction or by
    -- calling FLOAT_NEGATE.
    */
    if (saw_unary_op) {
        if (base_type(result_tp) == integer_typep) {
            if (unary_op == MINUS) emit_1(NEGATE, reg(AX));
        }
        else if (result_tp == real_typep) {
            if (unary_op == MINUS) {
                emit_push_operand(result_tp);
                emit_1(CALL, name_lit(FLOAT_NEGATE));
                emit_2(ADD, reg(SP), integer_lit(4));
            }
        }
        else error(INCOMPATIBLE_TYPES);
    }

    /*
    -- Loop to process subsequent terms separated by operators.
    */
    while (token_in(add_op_list)) {
        op = token;                     /* remember operator */

        result_tp = base_type(result_tp);
        emit_push_operand(result_tp);

        get_token();
        tp2 = base_type(term());        /* subsequent term */

        switch (op) {

            case PLUS:
            case MINUS: {
                /*
                -- integer <op> integer => integer
                -- AX = AX +|- DX
                */
                if (integer_operands(result_tp, tp2)) {
                    emit_1(POP, reg(DX));
                    if (op == PLUS) emit_2(ADD, reg(AX), reg(DX))
                    else {
                        emit_2(SUBTRACT, reg(DX), reg(AX));
                        emit_2(MOVE, reg(AX), reg(DX));
                    }
                    result_tp = integer_typep;
                }

                /*
                -- Both operands are real, or one is real and the
                -- other is integer.  Convert the integer operand
                -- to real.  The result is real.  Call FLOAT_ADDor
                -- FLOAT_SUBTRACT.
                */
                else if (real_operands(result_tp, tp2)) {
                    emit_push_operand(tp2);
                    emit_promote_to_real(result_tp, tp2);

                    emit_1(CALL, name_lit(op == PLUS
                                        ? FLOAT_ADD
                                        : FLOAT_SUBTRACT));
                    emit_2(ADD, reg(SP), integer_lit(8));

                    result_tp = real_typep;
                }

                else {
                    error(INCOMPATIBLE_TYPES);
                    result_tp = &dummy_type;
                }

                break;
            }

            case OR: {
                /*
                -- boolean OR boolean => boolean
                -- AX = AX OR DX
                */
                if (boolean_operands(result_tp, tp2)) {
                    emit_1(POP, reg(DX));
                    emit_2(OR_BITS, reg(AX), reg(DX));
                }
                else error(INCOMPATIBLE_TYPES);

                result_tp = boolean_typep;
                break;
            }
        }
    }

    return(result_tp);
}

/*-------------------------------------------------------------*/
/*  term              Process a term consisting of factors     */
/*                    separated by *, /, DIV, MOD, or AND       */
```

```
/*                      operators.  Return a pointer to the      */
/*                      type structure.                          */
/*----------------------------------------------------------------*/

TOKEN_CODE mult_op_list[] = {STAR, SLASH, DIV, MOD, AND, 0};

    TYPE_STRUCT_PTR
term()

{
    TOKEN_CODE op;                      /* an operator token */
    TYPE_STRUCT_PTR result_tp, tp2;

    result_tp = factor();               /* first factor */

    /*
    -- Loop to process subsequent factors
    -- separated by operators.
    */
    while (token_in(mult_op_list)) {
        op = token;                     /* remember operator */

        result_tp = base_type(result_tp);
        emit_push_operand(result_tp);

        get_token();
        tp2 = base_type(factor());      /* subsequent factor */

        switch (op) {

            case STAR: {
                /*
                -- Both operands are integer.
                -- AX = AX*DX
                */
                if (integer_operands(result_tp, tp2)) {
                    emit_1(POP, reg(DX));
                    emit_1(MULTIPLY, reg(DX));

                    result_tp = integer_typep;
                }

                /*
                -- Both operands are real, or one is real and the
                -- other is integer.  Convert the integer operand
                -- to real.  The result is real.
                -- Call FLOAT_MULTIPLY.
                */
                else if (real_operands(result_tp, tp2)) {
                    emit_push_operand(tp2);
                    emit_promote_to_real(result_tp, tp2);

                    emit_1(CALL, name_lit(FLOAT_MULTIPLY));
                    emit_2(ADD, reg(SP), integer_lit(8));

                    result_tp = real_typep;
                }

                else {
                    error(INCOMPATIBLE_TYPES);
                    result_tp = &dummy_type;
                }

                break;
            }

            case SLASH: {
```

```
            /*
            -- Both operands are real, or both are integer, or
            -- one is real and the other is integer.  Convert
            -- any integer operand to real.  The result is real.
            -- Call FLOAT_DIVIDE.
            */
            if (real_operands(result_tp, tp2) ||
                integer_operands(result_tp, tp2)) {
                emit_push_operand(tp2);
                emit_promote_to_real(result_tp, tp2);

                emit_1(CALL, name_lit(FLOAT_DIVIDE));
                emit_2(ADD, reg(SP), integer_lit(8));
            }
            else error(INCOMPATIBLE_TYPES);

            result_tp = real_typep;
            break;
        }

        case DIV:
        case MOD: {
            /*
            -- integer <op> integer => integer
            -- AX = AX IDIV CX
            */
            if (integer_operands(result_tp, tp2)) {
                emit_2(MOVE, reg(CX), reg(AX));
                emit_1(POP, reg(AX));
                emit_2(SUBTRACT, reg(DX), reg(DX));
                emit_1(DIVIDE, reg(CX));
                if (op == MOD) emit_2(MOVE, reg(AX), reg(DX));
            }
            else error(INCOMPATIBLE_TYPES);

            result_tp = integer_typep;
            break;
        }

        case AND: {
            /*
            -- boolean AND boolean => boolean
            -- AX = AX AND DX
            */
            if (boolean_operands(result_tp, tp2)) {
                emit_1(POP, reg(DX));
                emit_2(AND_BITS, reg(AX), reg(DX));
            }
            else error(INCOMPATIBLE_TYPES);

            result_tp = boolean_typep;
            break;
        }
    }
}

return(result_tp);
}

/*----------------------------------------------------------------*/
/*  factor            Process a factor, which is a variable,      */
/*                    a number, NOT followed by a factor, or      */
/*                    a parenthesized subexpression.  Return      */
/*                    a pointer to the type structure.            */
/*----------------------------------------------------------------*/

    TYPE_STRUCT_PTR
```

```
factor()

{
    TYPE_STRUCT_PTR tp;

    switch (token) {

        case IDENTIFIER: {
            SYMTAB_NODE_PTR idp;

            search_and_find_all_symtab(idp);

            switch (idp->defn.key) {

                case FUNC_DEFN:
                    get_token();
                    tp = routine_call(idp, TRUE);
                    break;

                case PROC_DEFN:
                    error(INVALID_IDENTIFIER_USAGE);
                    get_token();
                    actual_parm_list(idp, FALSE);
                    tp = &dummy_type;
                    break;

                case CONST_DEFN:
                    tp = constant_identifier(idp);
                    break;

                default:
                    tp = variable(idp, EXPR_USE);
                    break;
            }

            break;
        }

        case NUMBER: {
            if (literal.type == INTEGER_LIT) {
                /*
                -- AX = value
                */
                emit_2(MOVE, reg(AX),
                        integer_lit(literal.value.integer));
                tp = integer_typep;
            }

            else { /* literal.type == REAL_LIT */
                /*
                -- DX:AX = value
                */
                tp = float_literal(token_string, literal.value.real);
            }

            get_token();
            break;
        }

        case STRING: {
            int length = strlen(literal.value.string);

            if (length == 1) {
                /*
                -- AH = 0
                -- AL = value
                */
```

```
                emit_2(MOVE, reg(AX),
                        char_lit(literal.value.string[0]));
                tp = char_typep;
            }
            else {
                /*
                -- AX = address of string
                */
                tp = string_literal(literal.value.string, length);
            }

            get_token();
            break;
        }

        case NOT:
            /*
            -- AX = NOT AX
            */
            get_token();
            tp = factor();
            emit_2(XOR_BITS, reg(AX), integer_lit(1));
            break;

        case LPAREN:
            get_token();
            tp = expression();

            if_token_get_else_error(RPAREN, MISSING_RPAREN);
            break;

        default:
            error(INVALID_EXPRESSION);
            tp = &dummy_type;
            break;
    }

    return(tp);
}

/*------------------------------------------------------------*/
/* float_literal        Process a floating point literal.    */
/*------------------------------------------------------------*/

    TYPE_STRUCT_PTR
float_literal(string, value)

    char  string[];
    float value;

{
    SYMTAB_NODE_PTR np = search_symtab(string, symtab_display[1]);

    /*
    -- Enter the literal into the symbol table
    -- if it isn't already in there.
    */
    if (np == NULL) {
        np = enter_symtab(string, symtab_display[1]);
        np->defn.key = CONST_DEFN;
        np->defn.info.constant.value.real  = value;
        np->label_index = new_label_index();
        np->next = float_literal_list;
        float_literal_list = np;
    }

    /*
```

```
    --  DX:AX = value
    */
    emit_2(MOVE, reg(AX), word_label(FLOAT_LABEL_PREFIX,
                                     np->label_index));
    emit_2(MOVE, reg(DX), high_dword_label(FLOAT_LABEL_PREFIX,
                                     np->label_index));

    return(real_typep);
}

/*-------------------------------------------------------------*/
/*  string_literal        Process a string_literal.           */
/*-------------------------------------------------------------*/

    TYPE_STRUCT_PTR
string_literal(string, length)

    char  string[];
    int   length;

{
    SYMTAB_NODE_PTR np;
    TYPE_STRUCT_PTR tp = make_string_typep(length);
    char            buffer[MAX_SOURCE_LINE_LENGTH];

    sprintf(buffer, "'%s'", string);
    np = search_symtab(buffer, symtab_display[1]);

    /*
    --  Enter the literal into the symbol table
    --  if it isn't already in there.
    */
    if (np == NULL) {
        np = enter_symtab(buffer, symtab_display[1]);
        np->defn.key = CONST_DEFN;
        np->label_index = new_label_index();
        np->next = string_literal_list;
        string_literal_list = np;
    }

    /*
    --  AX = address of string
    */
    emit_2(LOAD_ADDRESS, reg(AX),
           word_label(STRING_LABEL_PREFIX, np->label_index));
    emit_1(PUSH, reg(AX));
    return(tp);
}

/*-------------------------------------------------------------*/
/*  constant_identifier      Process a constant identifier.   */
/*-------------------------------------------------------------*/

    TYPE_STRUCT_PTR
constant_identifier(idp)

    SYMTAB_NODE_PTR idp;               /* id of constant */

{
    TYPE_STRUCT_PTR tp = idp->typep;   /* type of constant */

    get_token();

    if ((tp == integer_typep) || (tp->form == ENUM_FORM)) {
        /*
        --  AX = value
        */
```

```
        emit_2(MOVE, reg(AX),
               integer_lit(idp->defn.info.constant.value.integer));
    }
    else if (tp == char_typep) {
        /*
        --  AX = value
        */
        emit_2(MOVE, reg(AX),
               char_lit(idp->defn.info.constant.value.character));
    }
    else if (tp == real_typep) {
        /*
        --  Create a literal and then call float_literal.
        */
        float value = idp->defn.info.constant.value.real;
        char  string[MAX_SOURCE_LINE_LENGTH];

        sprintf(string, "%e", value);
        float_literal(string, value);
    }
    else  /* string constant */ {
        string_literal(idp->defn.info.constant.value.stringp,
                    strlen(idp->defn.info.constant.value.stringp));
    }

    return(tp);
}

/*-------------------------------------------------------------*/
/*  variable           Process a variable, which can be a      */
/*                     simple identifier, an array identifier  */
/*                     with subscripts, or a record identifier */
/*                     with fields.                            */
/*-------------------------------------------------------------*/

    TYPE_STRUCT_PTR
variable(var_idp, use)

    SYMTAB_NODE_PTR var_idp;   /* variable id */
    USE             use;       /* how variable is used */

{
    TYPE_STRUCT_PTR tp           = var_idp->typep;
    DEFN_KEY        defn_key     = var_idp->defn.key;
    BOOLEAN         varparm_flag = defn_key == VARPARM_DEFN;
    TYPE_STRUCT_PTR array_subscript_list();
    TYPE_STRUCT_PTR record_field();

    /*
    --  Check the variable's definition.
    */
    switch (defn_key) {
        case VAR_DEFN:
        case VALPARM_DEFN:
        case VARPARM_DEFN:
        case FUNC_DEFN:
        case UNDEFINED:  break;      /* OK */

        default: {                   /* error */
            tp = &dummy_type;
            error(INVALID_IDENTIFIER_USAGE);
        }
    }

    get_token();

    /*
```

```
--  There must not be a parameter list, but if there is one,
--  parse it anyway for error recovery.
*/
if (token == LPAREN) {
    error(UNEXPECTED_TOKEN);
    actual_parm_list(var_idp, FALSE);
    return(tp);
}


/*
--  Subscripts and/or field designators?
*/
if ((token == LBRACKET) || (token == PERIOD)) {
    /*
    --  Push the address of the array or record onto the
    --  stack, where it is then modified by code generated
    --  in array_subscript_list and record_field.
    */
    emit_push_address(var_idp);

    while ((token == LBRACKET) || (token == PERIOD)) {
        tp = token == LBRACKET ? array_subscript_list(tp)
                               : record_field(tp);
    }

    /*
    --  Leave the modified address on top of the stack if:
    --      it is an assignment target,
    --      it represents a parameter passed by reference, or
    --      it is the address of an array or record.
    --  Otherwise, load AX with the value that the modified
    --  address points to.
    */
    if ((use != TARGET_USE) && (use != VARPARM_USE) &&
        (tp->form != ARRAY_FORM) && (tp->form != RECORD_FORM)) {
        emit_1(POP, reg(BX));
        if (tp == char_typep) {
            emit_2(SUBTRACT, reg(AX), reg(AX));
            emit_2(MOVE, reg(AL), byte_indirect(BX));
        }
        else if (tp == real_typep) {
            emit_2(MOVE, reg(AX), word_indirect(BX));
            emit_2(MOVE, reg(DX), high_dword_indirect(BX));
        }
        else emit_2(MOVE, reg(AX), word_indirect(BX));
    }
}

else if (use == TARGET_USE) {
    /*
    --  Push the address of an assignment target onto the stack,
    --  unless it is a local or global scalar parameter or
    --  variable.
    */
    if (defn_key == FUNC_DEFN)
        emit_push_return_value_address(var_idp);
    else if (varparm_flag || (tp->form == ARRAY_FORM) ||
             (tp->form == RECORD_FORM) ||
             ((var_idp->level > 1) && (var_idp->level < level)))
        emit_push_address(var_idp);
}
else if (use == VARPARM_USE) {
    /*
    --  Push the address of a variable
    --  being passed as a VAR parameter.
    */
    emit_push_address(var_idp);
```

```
}
else if ((tp->form == ARRAY_FORM) || (tp->form == RECORD_FORM)) {
    /*
    --  Push the address of an array or record value.
    */
    emit_push_address(var_idp);
}
else {
    /*
    --  AX = scalar value
    */
    emit_load_value(var_idp, base_type(tp));
}

return(tp);
}

/*------------------------------------------------------------*/
/*  array_subscript_list      Process a list of subscripts    */
/*                            following an array identifier:   */
/*                                                            */
/*                            [ <expr> , <expr> , ... ]       */
/*------------------------------------------------------------*/

    TYPE_STRUCT_PTR
array_subscript_list(tp)

    TYPE_STRUCT_PTR tp;

{
    TYPE_STRUCT_PTR   index_tp, elmt_tp, ss_tp;
    int               min_index, elmt_size;
    extern TOKEN_CODE statement_end_list[];

    /*
    --  Loop to process a subscript list.
    */
    do {
        if (tp->form == ARRAY_FORM) {
            index_tp = tp->info.array.index_typep;
            elmt_tp  = tp->info.array.elmt_typep;

            get_token();
            ss_tp = expression();

            /*
            --  The subscript expression must be assignment type
            --  compatible with the corresponding subscript type.
            */
            if (!is_assign_type_compatible(index_tp, ss_tp))
                error(INCOMPATIBLE_TYPES);

            min_index = tp->info.array.min_index;
            elmt_size = tp->info.array.elmt_typep->size;

            /*
            --  Convert the subscript into an offset by subracting
            --  the mininum index from it and then multiplying the
            --  result by the element size.   Add the offset to the
            --  address at the top of the stack.
            */
            if (min_index != 0) emit_2(SUBTRACT, reg(AX),
                                        integer_lit(min_index));
            if (elmt_size > 1) {
                emit_2(MOVE, reg(DX), integer_lit(elmt_size));
                emit_1(MULTIPLY, reg(DX));
            }
```

```
            emit_1(POP,  reg(DX));
            emit_2(ADD,  reg(DX), reg(AX));
            emit_1(PUSH, reg(DX));

            tp = elmt_tp;
        }
        else {
            error(TOO_MANY_SUBSCRIPTS);
            while ((token != RBRACKET) &&
                   (! token_in(statement_end_list)))
                get_token();
        }
    } while (token == COMMA);

    if_token_get_else_error(RBRACKET, MISSING_RBRACKET);
    return(tp);
}


/*-----------------------------------------------------*/
/* record_field            Process a field designation */
/*                         following a record identifier: */
/*                                                     */
/*                         . <field-variable>          */
/*-----------------------------------------------------*/

    TYPE_STRUCT_PTR
record_field(tp)

    TYPE_STRUCT_PTR tp;

{
    SYMTAB_NODE_PTR field_idp;

    get_token();

    if ((token == IDENTIFIER) && (tp->form == RECORD_FORM)) {
        search_this_symtab(field_idp,
                        tp->info.record.field_symtab);
        get_token();

        /*
        -- Add the field's offset (using the numeric equate)
        -- to the address at the top of the stack.
        */
        if (field_idp != NULL) {
            emit_1(POP,  reg(AX));
            emit_2(ADD,  reg(AX), tagged_name(field_idp));
            emit_1(PUSH, reg(AX));
            return(field_idp->typep);
        }
        else {
            error(INVALID_FIELD);
            return(&dummy_type);
        }
    }
    else {
        get_token();
        error(INVALID_FIELD);
        return(&dummy_type);
    }
}

            /*******************************/
            /*                             */
            /*      Type compatibility     */
            /*                             */
            /*******************************/
```

```
/*-----------------------------------------------------*/
/* check_rel_op_types  Check the operand types for a rela- */
/*                     tional operator.                */
/*-----------------------------------------------------*/

check_rel_op_types(tp1, tp2)

    TYPE_STRUCT_PTR tp1, tp2;          /* operand types */

{
    /*
    -- Two identical scalar or enumeration types.
    */
    if (   (tp1 == tp2)
        && ((tp1->form == SCALAR_FORM) || (tp1->form == ENUM_FORM)))
        return;

    /*
    -- One integer and one real.
    */
    if (   ((tp1 == integer_typep) && (tp2 == real_typep))
        || ((tp2 == integer_typep) && (tp1 == real_typep))) return;

    /*
    -- Two strings of the same length.
    */
    if ((tp1->form == ARRAY_FORM) &&
        (tp2->form == ARRAY_FORM) &&
        (tp1->info.array.elmt_typep == char_typep) &&
        (tp2->info.array.elmt_typep == char_typep) &&
        (tp1->info.array.elmt_count ==
                        tp2->info.array.elmt_count)) return;

    error(INCOMPATIBLE_TYPES);
}

/*-----------------------------------------------------*/
/* is_assign_type_compatible  Return TRUE iff a value of type */
/*                            tp1 can be assigned to a vari- */
/*                            able of type tp1.        */
/*-----------------------------------------------------*/

    BOOLEAN
is_assign_type_compatible(tp1, tp2)

    TYPE_STRUCT_PTR tp1, tp2;

{
    tp1 = base_type(tp1);
    tp2 = base_type(tp2);

    if (tp1 == tp2) return(TRUE);

    /*
    -- real := integer
    */
    if ((tp1 == real_typep) && (tp2 == integer_typep)) return(TRUE);

    /*
    -- string1 := string2 of the same length
    */
    if ((tp1->form == ARRAY_FORM) &&
        (tp2->form == ARRAY_FORM) &&
        (tp1->info.array.elmt_typep == char_typep) &&
        (tp2->info.array.elmt_typep == char_typep) &&
        (tp1->info.array.elmt_count ==
                    tp2->info.array.elmt_count)) return(TRUE);
```

```
   return(FALSE);                                          base_type(tp)
}
                                                               TYPE_STRUCT_PTR tp;

/*-------------------------------------------------*/
/* base_type          Return the range type of a subrange  */      {
/*                    type.                          */
/*-------------------------------------------------*/                 return((tp->form == SUBRANGE_FORM)
                                                                            ? tp->info.subrange.range_typep
    TYPE_STRUCT_PTR                                                          : tp);

                                                               }
```

The emitted code, when executed, always leaves scalar values in register AX or in the DX:AX register pair. Array or record values are always allocated on top of the stack. Addresses, such as for assignment targets or the address of variables being passed by reference, are pushed onto the stack.

13.4.1 Variables

Function variable emits code to process a variable. It handles several cases. If the variable is subscripted or followed by a field name, we first call function emit_push_address (defined in file emitcode.c). It emits code to push the address of the variable onto the stack. Next, we call functions array_subscript_list and record_field to emit code that modifies this address. Then, if the variable is not an assignment target and the value that is being accessed is a scalar, we emit code to load the value into register AX or the DX:AX register pair:

```
        pop  bx                    ; BX = modified address
        sub  ax,ax                 ; AX = 0
        mov  al,BYTE PTR [bx]      ; AL = character
```

(loads a character value into register AL)

```
        pop  bx                    ; BX = modified address
        mov  ax,WORD PTR [bx]      ; AX = low-order half
        mov  dx,WORD PTR [bx+2]    ; DX = high-order half
```

(loads a real value into the DX:AX register pair)

```
        pop  bx                    ; BX = modified address
        mov  ax,WORD PTR [bx]      ; AX = value
```

(loads an integer or enumeration value into register AX).

If the variable is an assignment target, we emit code to push the variable's address onto the stack, unless the variable matches one of the three cases described for assignment targets. If we are assigning a value to a Pascal function, we call function emit_push_return_value to emit code to push the address of the return value slot in the appropriate stack frame. Otherwise, we call function emit_push_ address to emit code to push the address of the variable. These code-emitting functions are all defined in file emitcode.c and are described later.

If the variable is being passed by reference to a Pascal procedure or function (the corresponding formal parameter is a VAR parameter), or if the variable is an array or a record, we call function emit_push_address to emit code to push its address onto the stack.

Finally, if the variable is a simple scalar, we call function emit_load_value to load the value into register AX or into the DX:AX register pair.

Function array_subscript_list emits code to calculate the byte offset represented by a subscript value, and adds this offset to the address on top of the stack. This calculation is similar to the one done by the interpreter. We first call function expression which emits code to evaluate a subscript expression and leave the value in register AX. Then we emit the code:

```
sub   ax,min           ; subtract minimum subscript value
mov   dx,size          ; DX = dimension size
imul  dx               ; AX = offset
pop   dx               ; DX = array address
add   dx,ax            ; DX = address + offset
push  dx               ; push modified address
```

where *min* is the minimum subscript value for its dimension, and *size* is the size in bytes of that dimension. We do not emit the initial sub instruction if *min* is zero.

Function record_field emits code to simply add the field's offset to the address on top of the stack. The code uses the tagged equate name of the field, for example:

```
pop   ax               ; AX = record address
add   ax,x_004         ; AX = address + offset
push  ax               ; push modified address
```

where x_004 is the name that was equated (by code emitted by function var_or_field_declarations) to its numeric offset.

File emitcode.c (see Figure 13-1) defines several functions that emit code to push and load values and addresses. (We saw previously how we call some of them.)

Function emit_load_value emits code to load the value of a variable into register AX or into the DX:AX register pair. If the variable is global or local, the code is simple:

```
sub   ax,ax
mov   al,BYTE PTR ch_016    ; AX = character value

mov   ax,WORD PTR ip_021    ; AX = integer value
```

```
mov   ax,WORD PTR d_025
mov   dx,WORD PTR d_025+2          ; DX:AX = real value
```

If the variable is nonglobal and nonlocal (it is declared in an enclosing procedure or function), the emitted code must establish the appropriate stack frame before loading the value. This is done by following the static links from the current stack frame up to the appropriate one. The number of links to follow is the difference between the current nesting level and the level of the variable. For example, the code to load the integer value of a variable declared in the current routine's "grandparent" (two nesting levels lower) is:

```
mov   bx,bp                       ; save current BP in BX
mov   bp,$STATIC_LINK             ; BP -> parent's stack frame
mov   bp,$STATIC_LINK             ; BP -> grandparent's stack frame
mov   ax,WORD PTR rows_026        ; AX = integer value
mov   bp,bx                       ; restore current BP
```

where $STATIC_LINK is equated in the program prologue to WORD PTR [bp+4].

Finally, if the variable is a formal VAR parameter, we must access the value indirectly though the parameter's address value. For example:

```
mov   bx,WORD PTR parm_029        ; BX = address of value
mov   ax,WORD PTR [bx]            ; AX = integer value
```

Function emit_push_address emits code to push a variable's address onto the stack. If the variable is global or local, an example of the emitted code is:

```
lea   ax,WORD PTR i_030           ; AX = address
push ax                           ; push address
```

If the variable is nonglobal and nonlocal, we must follow the static links up to the appropriate stack frame. For example:

```
mov   bx,bp                       ; save current BP in BX
mov   bp,$STATIC_LINK             ; BP -> parent's stack frame
lea   ax,WORD PTR k_031           ; AX = address
mov   bp,bx                       ; restore current BP
push ax                           ; push address
```

If the variable is actually a formal VAR parameter, its value is an address. In that case, the emitted code is the same, except that the lea instruction is replaced by a mov instruction.

Function emit_push_return_value_address emits code to push the address of the function return value slot in the appropriate stack frame. If the value of the current function is being set, the code is simply:

```
lea  ax,$RETURN_VALUE          ; AX = address
push ax                        ; push address
```

where $RETURN_VALUE is equated in the program prologue to WORD PTR [bp-4]. However, if the value of an enclosing function is being set, the code must follow static links up to the appropriate stack frame, for example:

```
mov  bx,bp                     ; save current BP in BX
mov  bp,$STATIC_LINK           ; BP -> parent's stack frame
mov  bp,$STATIC_LINK           ; BP -> grandparent's stack frame
lea  ax,$RETURN_VALUE          ; AX = address
mov  bp,bx                     ; restore current BP
push ax                        ; push address
```

13.4.2 Arithmetic and logical operations

The remaining functions in file expr.c parse expressions and emit code to evaluate them. Each of the functions emits code to leave either a scalar value in register AX or in the DX:AX register pair, or an address on top of the stack. Functions expression, simple_expression, and term each calls emit_push_operand to emit code to push a scalar operand onto the stack before emitting code to evaluate a subsequent operand.

Function expression emits code to do a comparison. If the operands are integer, character, boolean, or other enumeration, we emit:

```
pop  dx                        ; DX = operand 1 value
cmp  dx,ax                     ; compare DX to AX
```

If the operands are real, or real and integer, we call function emit_push_operand to push the current operand value onto the stack (so both operands are on the stack). We also call function promote_operands_to_real to convert any integer operand to real, and then we emit:

```
call _float_compare
add  sp,8                      ; pop off operands
cmp  ax,0                      ; check result of float compare
```

where _float_compare is a library routine (see Figure 12-5) that returns 0 if the two operands are equal, −1 if the first operand is less than the second operand, or 1 if the first operand is greater than the second operand.

If the operands are two strings, both string addresses are on the stack, and so we emit:

```
pop  di                        ; DI = string 2 address
pop  si                        ; SI = string 1 address
```

```
mov   ax,ds                    ; AX = DS
mov   es,ax                    ; ES = AX
cld                            ; clear direction flag
mov   cx,length                ; CX = string length
repe  cmpsb                    ; compare strings
```

where *length* is the string length. Following any of the those code sequences, we then emit:

```
mov   ax,1                     ; AX = TRUE (1)
jump  $L_nnn
sub   ax,ax                    ; AX = FALSE (0)
$L_nnn:
```

where *jump* is either jl, jle, je, jne, jge, or jg, depending on whether the comparison operator in the Pascal source was <, <=, =, <>, >, or >=, respectively, and *nnn* is the label index.

Function simple_expression emits the code:

```
neg   ax
```

to negate an integer value that was preceded by a unary minus. If a real value must be negated, we call function push_operand to push the value onto the stack, and then we emit:

```
call  _float_negate
add   sp,4                     ; pop off operand
```

to call the library routine to negate the value.

With integer operands and the + operator, we emit:

```
pop   dx                       ; DX = operand 1 value
add   ax,dx                    ; AX = AX + DX
```

If the operator is -, we emit instead:

```
pop   dx                       ; DX = operand 1 value
sub   dx,ax                    ; DX = DX − AX
mov   ax,dx                    ; AX = DX
```

With real operands, or integer and real operands, and the + operator, we call emit_push_operand to push the current operand value onto the stack (so both operands are on the stack). Next, we call function promote_operands_to_real to convert any integer operand to real, and then we emit:

```
        call  _float_add
        add   sp,8                    ; pop off operands
```

to call the library routine to do the addition. If the operator is -, we emit a call to _float_subtract instead. Finally, if the operator is OR, we emit:

```
        pop   dx                      ; DX = operand 1 value
        or    ax,dx                   ; AX = AX|DX
```

With integer operands and the * operator, function term emits the code:

```
        pop   dx                      ; DX = operand 1 value
        imul  dx                      ; DX:AX = AX * DX
```

Subsequent code ignores the value in register DX, so if the product exceeds one word in size, an incorrect value is used. (An exercise at the end of this chapter suggests runtime error checking.) If the operator is div, we emit:

```
        mov   cx,ax                   ; CX = operand 2 value
        pop   ax                      ; AX = operand 1 value
        sub   dx,dx                   ; DX = 0
        idiv  cx                      ; AX = DX:AX / CX
```

If the operator is mod, we follow the previous code sequence with:

```
        mov   ax,dx                   ; AX = DX:AX % CX
```

With real operands, or integer and real operands, and the * operator, we call emit_push_operand to push the current operand value onto the stack (so both operands are on the stack). Next, we call function promote_operands_to_real to convert any integer operand to real, and then we emit:

```
        call  _float_multiply
        add   sp,8                    ; pop off operands
```

to call the library routine to multiply. If the operator is /, we emit a call to _float_divide instead. Finally, if the operator is AND, we emit:

```
        pop   dx                      ; DX = operand 1 value
        and   ax,dx                   ; AX = AX & DX
```

Function factor emits the following code for an integer literal:

```
        mov   ax,n                    ; AX = n
```

where n is the literal. If the literal is a character, we emit:

```
        mov  ax,'c'                      ; AX = character value
```

where *c* is the literal. If the literal is a real number, we call function float_literal, and if the literal is a string, we call function string_literal.

In function float_literal, we enter the token string into the symbol table, assign a label index to the entry, and link the entry to the list headed by pointer variable float_literal_list. We then emit:

```
        mov  ax,WORD PTR $F_nnn         ; AX = low-order half
        mov  dx,WORD PTR $F_nnn+2       ; DX = high-order half
```

where *nnn* is the label index. As described, $F_*nnn* will be declared in the data segment as part of the program epilogue.

Similarly, in function string_literal, we enter the token string into the symbol table, assign a label index to the entry, and link the entry to the list headed by pointer variable string_literal_list. We then emit:

```
        lea  ax,$S_nnn                  ; AX = address of string
        push ax                         ; push address
```

where *nnn* is the label index. $S_*nnn* will also be declared in the data segment as part of the program epilogue.

We call function constant_identifier if the operand is a constant identifier. If the constant is an integer, constant_identifier simply emits:

```
        mov  ax,n                       ; AX = n
```

where *n* is the integer. If the constant is a real number or a string, we write the value into a string buffer and call function float_literal or string_literal, respectively.

For the NOT operator, we emit:

```
        not  ax                         ; AX = ˜AX
```

Function promote_operands_to_real ensures that both stacked operands of a real-valued operation are real. If the second operand (the one on top) is integer, we emit the following code to convert it to real:

```
        call _float_convert
        add  sp,2                       ; pop off operands
        push dx                         ; push high-order half
        push ax                         ; push low-order half
```

The code is a bit more complicated if the first operand is integer, since the second operand is on top of it:

```
pop   ax
pop   dx                    ; DX:AX = operand 2
pop   bx                    ; BX = operand 1
push  dx
push  ax                    ; push operand 2
push  bx                    ; push operand 1
call  _float_convert
add   sp,2                  ; pop off operands
pop   bx
pop   cx                    ; BX:CX = operand 2
push  dx
push  ax                    ; push operand 1 (now real)
push  cx
push  bx                    ; push operand 2
```

13.5 write and writeln

If we are to test the code, the compiler needs to be able to emit code to write out values. Therefore, we modify function write_writeln in file standard.c to emit code for write and writeln (Figure 13-16).

FIGURE 13-16   File standard.c.

```
/*************************************************************/
/*                                                           */
/*        S T A N D A R D   R O U T I N E   P A R S E R      */
/*                                                           */
/*                                                           */
/*      Parsing routines for calls to standard procedures and */
/*      functions.                                           */
/*                                                           */
/*      FILE:      standard.c                                */
/*                                                           */
/*      MODULE:    parser                                    */
/*                                                           */
/*************************************************************/

#include <stdio.h>
#include "common.h"
#include "error.h"
#include "scanner.h"
#include "symtab.h"
#include "parser.h"
#include "code.h"

#define DEFAULT_NUMERIC_FIELD_WIDTH    10
#define DEFAULT_PRECISION              2

/*-----------------------------------------------------------*/
/* Externals                                                 */
/*-----------------------------------------------------------*/

extern TOKEN_CODE    token;
extern char          word_string[];
```

```
extern SYMTAB_NODE_PTR  symtab_display[];
extern int              level;
extern TYPE_STRUCT      dummy_type;

extern TYPE_STRUCT_PTR  integer_typep, real_typep,
                        boolean_typep, char_typep;

extern int              label_index;
extern char             asm_buffer[];
extern char             *asm_bufferp;
extern FILE             *code_file;

extern TOKEN_CODE       follow_parm_list[];
extern TOKEN_CODE       statement_end_list[];

/*-----------------------------------------------------------*/
/* Forwards                                                  */
/*-----------------------------------------------------------*/

TYPE_STRUCT_PTR eof_eoln(), abs_sqr(),
                arctan_cos_exp_ln_sin_sqrt(),
                pred_succ(), chr(), odd(), ord(),
                round_trunc();

/*-----------------------------------------------------------*/
/* standard_routine_call   Process a call to a standard      */
/*                         procedure or function. Return a   */
/*                         pointer to the type structure of  */
/*                         the call.                         */
/*-----------------------------------------------------------*/
```

```
        TYPE_STRUCT_PTR
standard_routine_call(rtn_idp)

    SYMTAB_NODE_PTR rtn_idp;            /* routine id */

{
    switch (rtn_idp->defn.info.routine.key) {

        case WRITE:
        case WRITELN:   write_writeln(rtn_idp);        return(NULL);

        default:
            error(UNIMPLEMENTED_FEATURE);
            exit(-UNIMPLEMENTED_FEATURE);
    }
}


/*------------------------------------------------------------*/
/* write_writeln          Process a call to write or writeln. */
/*                        Each actual parameter can be:       */
/*                                                            */
/*                              <expr>                        */
/*                                                            */
/*                          or:                               */
/*                                                            */
/*                          <epxr> : <expr>                   */
/*                                                            */
/*                          or:                               */
/*                                                            */
/*                          <expr> : <expr> : <expr>          */
/*------------------------------------------------------------*/


write_writeln(rtn_idp)

    SYMTAB_NODE_PTR rtn_idp;            /* routine id */

{

    TYPE_STRUCT_PTR actual_parm_tp;        /* actual parm type */
    TYPE_STRUCT_PTR field_width_tp, precision_tp;

    /*
    -- Parameters are optional for writeln.
    */
    if (token == LPAREN) {
        do {
            /*
            -- Value <expr>
            */
            get_token();
            actual_parm_tp = base_type(expression());

            /*
            -- Push the scalar value to be written onto the stack.
            -- A string value is already on the stack.
            */
            if (actual_parm_tp->form != ARRAY_FORM)
                emit_push_operand(actual_parm_tp);

            if ((actual_parm_tp->form != SCALAR_FORM) &&
                (actual_parm_tp != boolean_typep) &&
                ((actual_parm_tp->form != ARRAY_FORM) ||
                 (actual_parm_tp->info.array.elmt_typep !=
                                            char_typep)))
                error(INVALID_EXPRESSION);

            /*
            -- Optional field width <expr>
```

```
            -- Push onto the stack.
            */
            if (token == COLON) {
                get_token();
                field_width_tp = base_type(expression());
                emit_1(PUSH, reg(AX));

                if (field_width_tp != integer_typep)
                    error(INCOMPATIBLE_TYPES);

                /*
                -- Optional precision <expr>
                -- Push onto the stack if the value to be printed
                -- is of type real.
                */
                if (token == COLON) {
                    get_token();
                    precision_tp = base_type(expression());

                    if (actual_parm_tp == real_typep)
                        emit_1(PUSH, reg(AX));

                    if (precision_tp != integer_typep)
                        error(INCOMPATIBLE_TYPES);
                }
                else if (actual_parm_tp == real_typep) {
                    emit_2(MOVE, reg(AX),
                            integer_lit(DEFAULT_PRECISION));
                    emit_1(PUSH, reg(AX));
                }
            }
            else {
                if (actual_parm_tp == integer_typep) {
                    emit_2(MOVE, reg(AX),
                            integer_lit(DEFAULT_NUMERIC_FIELD_WIDTH));
                    emit_1(PUSH, reg(AX));
                }
                else if (actual_parm_tp == real_typep) {
                    emit_2(MOVE, reg(AX),
                            integer_lit(DEFAULT_NUMERIC_FIELD_WIDTH));
                    emit_1(PUSH, reg(AX));
                    emit_2(MOVE, reg(AX),
                            integer_lit(DEFAULT_PRECISION));
                    emit_1(PUSH, reg(AX));
                }
                else {
                    emit_2(MOVE, reg(AX), integer_lit(0));
                    emit_1(PUSH, reg(AX));
                }
            }

            if (actual_parm_tp == integer_typep) {
                emit_1(CALL, name_lit(WRITE_INTEGER));
                emit_2(ADD, reg(SP), integer_lit(4));
            }
            else if (actual_parm_tp == real_typep) {
                emit_1(CALL, name_lit(WRITE_REAL));
                emit_2(ADD, reg(SP), integer_lit(8));
            }
            else if (actual_parm_tp == boolean_typep) {
                emit_1(CALL, name_lit(WRITE_BOOLEAN));
                emit_2(ADD, reg(SP), integer_lit(4));
            }
            else if (actual_parm_tp == char_typep) {
                emit_1(CALL, name_lit(WRITE_CHAR));
                emit_2(ADD, reg(SP), integer_lit(4));
            }
```

```
else /* string */ {
    /*
    -- Push the string length onto the stack.
    */
    emit_2(MOVE, reg(AX),
            integer_lit(actual_parm_tp->info.array
                                    .elmt_count));

    emit_1(PUSH, reg(AX));
    emit_1(CALL, name_lit(WRITE_STRING));
    emit_2(ADD, reg(SP), integer_lit(6));
}

/*
```

```
                -- Error synchronization:  Should be , or )
                */
                synchronize(follow_parm_list, statement_end_list, NULL);

        } while (token == COMMA);

        if_token_get_else_error(RPAREN, MISSING_RPAREN);
    }
    else if (rtn_idp->defn.info.routine.key == WRITE)
        error(WRONG_NUMBER_OF_PARMS);

    if (rtn_idp->defn.info.routine.key == WRITELN)
        emit_1(CALL, name_lit(WRITE_LINE));
}
```

In function `write_writeln`, we first call function `expression` and then function `push_operand` to emit code that pushes a value onto the stack. If there is a field width specifier, we call `expression` to emit code to evaluate it and then emit `push ax` to push the value onto the stack. If there is a precision specifier, `write_writeln` calls `expression` to emit code to evaluate it, but emits the `push ax` only if the value to be written is real. If any of the field width or precision specifiers are missing, we emit code that pushes default values (based on the type of the value to be written) onto the stack. We then emit calls to the runtime library routines for an integer, real, boolean, character, or string value to be written, respectively:

```
        call _write_integer
        add  sp,4                        ; pop off parameters


        call _write_real
        add  sp,8                        ; pop off parameters


        call _write_boolean
        add  sp,4                        ; pop off parameters


        call _write_char
        add  sp,4                        ; pop off parameters


        mov  ax,length
        push ax                          ; push string length


        call _write_string
        add  sp,6                        ; pop off parameters
```

Note that the length of the string is passed to `_write_string`. This is necessary because Pascal strings are not null-terminated. If the call was to `writeln`, we emit:

```
        call _write_line
```

13.6 Program 13-1: Pascal Compiler I

Figure 13-17 shows file compile1.c, the main file of the compiler for this chapter. Before calling function program, we open the code file code_file for the emitted assembly language code.

FIGURE 13-17   File compile1.c.

```
/*****************************************************************/
/*                                                               */
/*      Program 13-1:  Pascal Compiler I                         */
/*                                                               */
/*      Compile assignement statements in procedures             */
/*      and functions.                                           */
/*                                                               */
/*      FILE:       compile1.c                                   */
/*                                                               */
/*      REQUIRES:   Modules parser, symbol table, scanner,       */
/*                            code, error                        */
/*                                                               */
/*      USAGE:      compile1 sourcefile objectfile               */
/*                                                               */
/*          sourcefile      [input] source file containing the   */
/*                                  the statements to compile    */
/*                                                               */
/*          objectfile      [output] object file to contain the  */
/*                                  generated assembly code       */
/*                                                               */
/*****************************************************************/

#include <stdio.h>

/*-------------------------------------------------------------*/
/* Globals                                                     */
/*-------------------------------------------------------------*/

FILE *code_file;    /* ASCII file for the emitted assembly code */
```

```
/*-------------------------------------------------------------*/
/* main                 Initialize the scanner and call        */
/*                      routine program.                       */
/*-------------------------------------------------------------*/

main(argc, argv)

    int   argc;
    char *argv[];

{
    /*
    -- Open the code file.  If no code file name was given,
    -- use the standard output file.
    */
    code_file = (argc == 3) ? fopen(argv[2], "w")
                            : stdout;

    /*
    -- Initialize the scanner.
    */
    init_scanner(argv[1]);

    /*
    -- Process a program.
    */
    get_token();
    program();
}
```

Figure 13-18 shows a simple Pascal program, and Figure 13-19 shows the emitted assembly code. In the next chapter, we will complete the compiler by generating code for Pascal control statements and calls to the remaining standard procedures and functions.

FIGURE 13-18   A sample Pascal program to be compiled.

```
PROGRAM simple (output);

    VAR
        n : integer;
        x : real;

    PROCEDURE proc (i : integer; VAR j : integer);

        FUNCTION func (y : real) : real;
```

```
        BEGIN {func}
            j := 5;
            func := i + y + 0.5;
        END {func};

    BEGIN {proc}
        j := i DIV 2;
        writeln('In proc, the value of j is', j:3);
```

```
        x := func(3.14);                                                writeln('In simple, the value of n is', n:3);
        writeln('In proc, the value of j is', j:3);                     proc(7, n);
    END {proc};                                                         writeln('In simple, the value of n is', n:3,
                                                                                ' and the value of x is', x:8:4);
  BEGIN {simple}                                                      END {simple}.
    n := 1;
```

FIGURE 13-19   Assembly language object file generated by the compiler for the sample program in Figure 13-18.

```
;   1: PROGRAM simple (output);                                   mov     ax,WORD PTR y_008
        DOSSEG                                                    mov     dx,WORD PTR y_008+2
        .MODEL  small                                            push    dx
        .STACK  1024                                             push    ax
                                                                 pop     ax
        .CODE                                                    pop     dx
                                                                 pop     bx
        PUBLIC  _pascal_main                                     push    dx
        INCLUDE pasextrn.inc                                     push    ax
                                                                 push    bx
$STATIC_LINK        EQU       <WORD PTR [bp+4]>                  call    _float_convert
$RETURN_VALUE       EQU       <WORD PTR [bp-4]>                  add     sp,2
$HIGH_RETURN_VALUE  EQU       <WORD PTR [bp-2]>                  pop     bx
                                                                 pop     cx
;   2:                                                           push    dx
;   3:     VAR                                                   push    ax
;   4:         n : integer;                                      push    cx
;   5:         x : real;                                         push    bx
;   6:                                                           call    float_add
;   7:     PROCEDURE proc (i : integer; VAR j : integer);        add     sp,8
;   8:                                                           push    dx
;   9:         FUNCTION func (y : real) : real;                  push    ax
                                                                 mov     ax,WORD PTR $F_009
i_005    EQU    <WORD PTR [bp+8]>                                mov     dx,WORD PTR $F_009+2
j_006    EQU    <WORD PTR [bp+6]>                                push    dx
;  10:                                                           push    ax
;  11:          BEGIN {func}                                     call    _float_add
                                                                 add     sp,8
y_008    EQU    <WORD PTR [bp+6]>                                pop     bx
                                                                 mov     WORD PTR [bx],ax
func_007        PROC                                             mov     WORD PTR [bx+2],dx
                                                            ;  14:          END {func};
        push    bp                                               mov     ax,$RETURN_VALUE
        mov     bp,sp                                            mov     dx,$HIGH_RETURN_VALUE
        sub     sp,4                                             mov     sp,bp
;  12:          j := 5;                                          pop     bp
        mov     bx,bp                                            ret     6
        mov     bp,$STATIC_LINK
        mov     ax,WORD PTR j_006                           func_007        ENDP
        mov     bp,bx                                       ;  15:
        push    ax                                          ;  16:      BEGIN {proc}
        mov     ax,5
        pop     bx                                          proc_004        PROC
        mov     WORD PTR [bx],ax
;  13:          func := i + y + 0.5;                             push    bp
        lea     ax,$RETURN_VALUE                                 mov     bp,sp
        push    ax                                          ;  17:          j := i DIV 2;
        mov     bx,bp                                            mov     ax,WORD PTR j_006
        mov     bp,$STATIC_LINK                                 push    ax
        mov     ax,WORD PTR i_005                               mov     ax,WORD PTR i_005
        mov     bp,bx                                           push    ax
        push    ax                                              mov     ax,2
```

```
        mov     cx,ax
        pop     ax
        sub     dx,dx
        idiv    cx
        pop     bx
        mov     WORD PTR [bx],ax
;  18:              writeln('In proc, the value of j is', j:3);
        lea     ax,WORD PTR $S_010
        push    ax
        mov     ax,0
        push    ax
        mov     ax,26
        push    ax
        call    _write_string
        add     sp,6
        mov     bx,WORD PTR j_006
        mov     ax,WORD PTR [bx]
        push    ax
        mov     ax,3
        push    ax
        call    _write_integer
        add     sp,4
        call    _write_line
;  19:              x := func(3.14);
        mov     ax,WORD PTR $F_011
        mov     dx,WORD PTR $F_011+2
        push    dx
        push    ax
        push    bp
        call    func_007
        mov     WORD PTR x_003,ax
        mov     WORD PTR x_003+2,dx
;  20:              writeln('In proc, the value of j is', j:3);
        lea     ax,WORD PTR $S_010
        push    ax
        mov     ax,0
        push    ax
        mov     ax,26
        push    ax
        call    _write_string
        add     sp,6
        mov     bx,WORD PTR j_006
        mov     ax,WORD PTR [bx]
        push    ax
        mov     ax,3
        push    ax
        call    _write_integer
        add     sp,4
        call    _write_line
;  21:         END {proc};
        mov     sp,bp
        pop     bp
        ret     6

proc_004        ENDP
;  22:
;  23:      BEGIN {simple}

_pascal_main    PROC

        push    bp
        mov     bp,sp
;  24:      n := 1;
        mov     ax,1
        mov     WORD PTR n_002,ax
;  25:      writeln('In simple, the value of n is', n:3);
        lea     ax,WORD PTR $S_012
```

```
        push    ax
        mov     ax,0
        push    ax
        mov     ax,28
        push    ax
        call    _write_string
        add     sp,6
        mov     ax,WORD PTR n_002
        push    ax
        mov     ax,3
        push    ax
        call    _write_integer
        add     sp,4
        call    _write_line
;  26:      proc(7, n);
        mov     ax,7
        push    ax
        lea     ax,WORD PTR n_002
        push    ax
        push    bp
        call    proc_004
;  27:      writeln('In simple, the value of n is', n:3,
        lea     ax,WORD PTR $S_012
        push    ax
        mov     ax,0
        push    ax
        mov     ax,28
        push    ax
        call    _write_string
        add     sp,6
        mov     ax,WORD PTR n_002
        push    ax
        mov     ax,3
        push    ax
        call    _write_integer
        add     sp,4
;  28:              ' and the value of x is', x:8:4);
        lea     ax,WORD PTR $S_013
        push    ax
        mov     ax,0
        push    ax
        mov     ax,22
        push    ax
        call    _write_string
        add     sp,6
        mov     ax,WORD PTR x_003
        mov     dx,WORD PTR x_003+2
        push    dx
        push    ax
        mov     ax,8
        push    ax
        mov     ax,4
        push    ax
        call    _write_real
        add     sp,8
        call    _write_line
;  29:   END {simple}.
;  30:
;  31:
        pop     bp
        ret

_pascal_main    ENDP

        .DATA

n_002   DW      0
```

```
x_003    DD    0.0                              $S_012   DB    "In simple, the value of n is"
$F_011   DD    3.140000e+000                    $S_010   DB    "In proc, the value of j is"
$F_009   DD    5.000000e-001
$S_013   DB    " and the value of x is"                  END
```

Questions and exercises

1. The interpreter performed several runtime checks, such as checking for values out of range and division by zero. Modify the compiler so that it emits code to do these checks.

2. There are circumstances where the compiler generates unnecessary instructions. For example, for the Pascal statement: n := 7, the compiler currently emits:

   ```
   mov   ax,7
   mov   WORD PTR n_011,ax
   ```

   A better code sequence is simply:

   ```
   mov   WORD PTR n_011,7
   ```

   Find and eliminate as many unnecessary instructions as possible. (More advanced methods of reducing the amount of emitted code are discussed in Chapter 15, where we look at optimization.)

CHAPTER 14

Compiling Control Statements

We can now complete our compiler by adding more calls from the statement parsing routines to the code generation routines. This enables the compiler to generate assembly language code for the Pascal control statements and for calls to the standard procedures and functions. With the experience we gained from implementing the interpreter, the work necessary to complete the compiler and the runtime library is quite straightforward. This chapter develops the skills to:

- emit assembly language code for Pascal control statements
- emit assembly language code for calls to standard Pascal procedures and functions
- compile entire Pascal programs

14.1 Organization of the compiler

We change two files from the previous chapter, stmt.c and standard.c. We modify file stmt.c to compile the control statements, and standard.c to compile calls to the standard procedures and functions.

Parser Module

parser.h	*u*	Parser header file
routine.c	*u*	Parse programs, procedures, and functions

standard.c	*c*	Parse standard procedures and functions
decl.c	*u*	Parse declarations
stmt.c	*c*	Parse statements
expr.c	*u*	Parse expressions

Scanner Module

| scanner.h | *u* | Scanner header file |
| scanner.c | *u* | Scanner routines |

Symbol Table Module

| symtab.h | *u* | Symbol table header file |
| symtab.c | *u* | Symbol table routines |

Code Module

code.h	*u*	Code generator header file
emitasm.c	*u*	Emit assembly language statements
emitcode.c	*u*	Emit sequences of assembly code

Error Module

| error.h | *u* | Error header file |
| error.c | *u* | Error routines |

Miscellaneous

| common.h | *u* | Common header file |

Where: *u*   file unchanged from the previous chapter
        c   file changed from the previous chapter

14.2 Emitting code for the control statements

In Chapter 10, we introduced code diagrams to show how the intermediate code for each statement is laid out. In this chapter, we use code diagrams to show what assembly language code is generated for each statement. We also use *annotated syntax diagrams* to show when the parser emits each statement of the assembly code.

The new complete version of file stmt.c, shown in Figure 14-1, can now generate code for the Pascal control statements.

FIGURE 14-1   File stmt.c.

```
/*****************************************************************/
/*                                                             */
/*       S T A T E M E N T   P A R S E R                       */
/*                                                             */
/*       Parsing routines for statements.                      */
/*                                                             */
/*       FILE:      stmt.c                                     */
/*                                                             */
/*       MODULE:    parser                                     */
/*                                                             */
/*****************************************************************/

#include <stdio.h>
#include "common.h"
#include "error.h"
#include "scanner.h"
#include "symtab.h"
#include "parser.h"
#include "code.h"

/*------------------------------------------------------------*/
/* Externals                                                  */
/*------------------------------------------------------------*/

extern TOKEN_CODE      token;
extern char            word_string[];
extern LITERAL         literal;
extern TOKEN_CODE      statement_start_list[], statement_end_list[];

extern SYMTAB_NODE_PTR symtab_display[];
extern int             level;

extern TYPE_STRUCT_PTR integer_typep, real_typep,
                       boolean_typep, char_typep;

extern TYPE_STRUCT     dummy_type;

extern int             label_index;
extern char            asm_buffer[];
extern char            *asm_bufferp;
extern FILE            *code_file;

/*------------------------------------------------------------*/
/* statement            Process a statement by calling the    */
/*                      appropriate parsing routine based on  */
/*                      the statement's first token.          */
/*------------------------------------------------------------*/

statement()

{
    /*
    -- Call the appropriate routine based on the first
    -- token of the statement.
    */
    switch (token) {

        case IDENTIFIER: {
            SYMTAB_NODE_PTR idp;

            /*
            -- Assignment statement or procedure call?
            */
            search_and_find_all_symtab(idp);
```

```
            if (idp->defn.key == PROC_DEFN) {
                get_token();
                routine_call(idp, TRUE);
            }
            else assignment_statement(idp);

            break;
        }

        case REPEAT:   repeat_statement();    break;
        case WHILE:    while_statement();     break;
        case IF:       if_statement();        break;
        case FOR:      for_statement();       break;
        case CASE:     case_statement();      break;
        case BEGIN:    compound_statement();  break;
    }

    /*
    -- Error synchronization:  Only a semicolon, END, ELSE, or
    --                         UNTIL may follow a statement.
    --                         Check for a missing semicolon.
    */
    synchronize(statement_end_list, statement_start_list, NULL);
    if (token_in(statement_start_list)) error(MISSING_SEMICOLON);
}

/*------------------------------------------------------------*/
/* assignment_statement    Process an assignment statement:   */
/*                                                            */
/*                              <id> := <expr>                */
/*------------------------------------------------------------*/

assignment_statement(var_idp)

    SYMTAB_NODE_PTR var_idp;          /* target variable id */

{
    TYPE_STRUCT_PTR var_tp, expr_tp;  /* types of var and expr */
    BOOLEAN         stacked_flag;     /* TRUE iff target address
                                         was pushed on stack */

    var_tp = variable(var_idp, TARGET_USE);
    stacked_flag = (var_idp->defn.key == VARPARM_DEFN) ||
                   (var_idp->defn.key == FUNC_DEFN) ||
                   (var_idp->typep->form == ARRAY_FORM) ||
                   (var_idp->typep->form == RECORD_FORM) ||
                   ((var_idp->level > 1) && (var_idp->level < level));

    if_token_get_else_error(COLONEQUAL, MISSING_COLONEQUAL);
    expr_tp = expression();

    if (! is_assign_type_compatible(var_tp, expr_tp))
        error(INCOMPATIBLE_ASSIGNMENT);

    var_tp  = base_type(var_tp);
    expr_tp = base_type(expr_tp);

    /*
    -- Emit code to do the assignment.
    */
    if (var_tp == char_typep) {
        /*
        -- char := char
        */
```

```
        if (stacked_flag) {
            emit_1(POP, reg(BX));
            emit_2(MOVE, byte_indirect(BX), reg(AL));
        }
        else emit_2(MOVE, byte(var_idp), reg(AL));
    }
    else if (var_tp == real_typep) {
        /*
        -- real := ...
        */
        if (expr_tp == integer_typep) {
            /*
            -- ... integer
            */
            emit_1(PUSH, reg(AX));
            emit_1(CALL, name_lit(FLOAT_CONVERT));
            emit_2(ADD, reg(SP), integer_lit(2));
        }
        /*
        -- ... real
        */
        if (stacked_flag) {
            emit_1(POP, reg(BX));
            emit_2(MOVE, word_indirect(BX), reg(AX));
            emit_2(MOVE, high_dword_indirect(BX), reg(DX));
        }
        else {
            emit_2(MOVE, word(var_idp), reg(AX));
            emit_2(MOVE, high_dword(var_idp), reg(DX));
        }
    }
    else if ((var_tp->form == ARRAY_FORM) ||
             (var_tp->form == RECORD_FORM)) {
        /*
        -- array  := array
        -- record := record
        */
        emit_2(MOVE, reg(CX), integer_lit(var_tp->size));
        emit_1(POP,  reg(SI));
        emit_1(POP,  reg(DI));
        emit_2(MOVE, reg(AX), reg(DS));
        emit_2(MOVE, reg(ES), reg(AX));
        emit(CLEAR_DIRECTION);
        emit(MOVE_BLOCK);
    }
    else {
        /*
        -- integer := integer
        -- enum    := enum
        */
        if (stacked_flag) {
            emit_1(POP, reg(BX));
            emit_2(MOVE, word_indirect(BX), reg(AX));
        }
        else emit_2(MOVE, word(var_idp), reg(AX));
    }
}

/*------------------------------------------------------------*/
/* repeat_statement    Process a REPEAT statement:            */
/*                                                            */
/*                     REPEAT <stmt-list> UNTIL <expr>        */
/*------------------------------------------------------------*/

repeat_statement()

{
```

```
    TYPE_STRUCT_PTR expr_tp;
    int             loop_begin_labelx = new_label_index();
    int             loop_exit_labelx  = new_label_index();

    emit_label(STMT_LABEL_PREFIX, loop_begin_labelx);

    /*
    -- <stmt-list>
    */
    get_token();
    do {
        statement();
        while (token == SEMICOLON) get_token();
    } while (token_in(statement_start_list));

    if_token_get_else_error(UNTIL, MISSING_UNTIL);

    expr_tp = expression();
    if (expr_tp != boolean_typep) error(INCOMPATIBLE_TYPES);

    emit_2(COMPARE, reg(AX), integer_lit(1));
    emit_1(JUMP_EQ, label(STMT_LABEL_PREFIX, loop_exit_labelx));
    emit_1(JUMP, label(STMT_LABEL_PREFIX, loop_begin_labelx));
    emit_label(STMT_LABEL_PREFIX, loop_exit_labelx);
}

/*------------------------------------------------------------*/
/* while_statement     Process a WHILE statement:             */
/*                                                            */
/*                     WHILE <expr> DO <stmt>                 */
/*------------------------------------------------------------*/

while_statement()

{
    TYPE_STRUCT_PTR expr_tp;
    int             loop_test_labelx = new_label_index();
    int             loop_stmt_labelx = new_label_index();
    int             loop_exit_labelx = new_label_index();

    emit_label(STMT_LABEL_PREFIX, loop_test_labelx);

    get_token();
    expr_tp = expression();
    if (expr_tp != boolean_typep) error(INCOMPATIBLE_TYPES);

    emit_2(COMPARE, reg(AX), integer_lit(1));
    emit_1(JUMP_EQ, label(STMT_LABEL_PREFIX, loop_stmt_labelx));
    emit_1(JUMP,    label(STMT_LABEL_PREFIX, loop_exit_labelx));
    emit_label(STMT_LABEL_PREFIX, loop_stmt_labelx);

    if_token_get_else_error(DO, MISSING_DO);
    statement();

    emit_1(JUMP, label(STMT_LABEL_PREFIX, loop_test_labelx));
    emit_label(STMT_LABEL_PREFIX, loop_exit_labelx);
}

/*------------------------------------------------------------*/
/* if_statement        Process an IF statement:               */
/*                                                            */
/*                     IF <expr> THEN <stmt>                  */
/*                                                            */
/*                     or:                                    */
/*                                                            */
/*                     IF <expr> THEN <stmt> ELSE <stmt>      */
/*------------------------------------------------------------*/
```

```
if_statement()

{
    TYPE_STRUCT_PTR expr_tp;
    int         true_labelx  = new_label_index();
    int         false_labelx = new_label_index();
    int         if_end_labelx;

    get_token();
    expr_tp = expression();
    if (expr_tp != boolean_typep) error(INCOMPATIBLE_TYPES);

    emit_2(COMPARE, reg(AX), integer_lit(1));
    emit_1(JUMP_EQ, label(STMT_LABEL_PREFIX, true_labelx));
    emit_1(JUMP,    label(STMT_LABEL_PREFIX, false_labelx));
    emit_label(STMT_LABEL_PREFIX, true_labelx);

    if_token_get_else_error(THEN, MISSING_THEN);
    statement();

    /*
    -- ELSE branch?
    */
    if (token == ELSE) {
        if_end_labelx = new_label_index();
        emit_1(JUMP, label(STMT_LABEL_PREFIX, if_end_labelx));
        emit_label(STMT_LABEL_PREFIX, false_labelx);

        get_token();
        statement();

        emit_label(STMT_LABEL_PREFIX, if_end_labelx);
    }
    else emit_label(STMT_LABEL_PREFIX, false_labelx);
}

/*------------------------------------------------------------*/
/*  for_statement       Process a FOR statement:              */
/*                                                            */
/*                       FOR <id> := <expr> TO|DOWNTO <expr>  */
/*                       DO <stmt>                            */
/*------------------------------------------------------------*/

for_statement()

{
    SYMTAB_NODE_PTR for_idp;
    TYPE_STRUCT_PTR for_tp, expr_tp;
    BOOLEAN         to_flag;
    int             loop_test_labelx = new_label_index();
    int             loop_stmt_labelx = new_label_index();
    int             loop_exit_labelx = new_label_index();

    get_token();
    if (token == IDENTIFIER) {
        search_and_find_all_symtab(for_idp);
        if ((for_idp->level != level) ||
            (for_idp->defn.key != VAR_DEFN))
            error(INVALID_FOR_CONTROL);

        for_tp = base_type(for_idp->typep);
        get_token();

        if ((for_tp != integer_typep) &&
            (for_tp != char_typep) &&
            (for_tp->form != ENUM_FORM)) error(INCOMPATIBLE_TYPES);
    }
```

```
    else {
        error(IDENTIFIER, MISSING_IDENTIFIER);
        for_tp = &dummy_type;
    }

    if_token_get_else_error(COLONEQUAL, MISSING_COLONEQUAL);

    expr_tp = expression();
    if (! is_assign_type_compatible(for_tp, expr_tp))
        error(INCOMPATIBLE_TYPES);

    if (for_tp == char_typep) emit_2(MOVE, byte(for_idp), reg(AL))
    else                      emit_2(MOVE, word(for_idp), reg(AX))

    if ((token == TO) || (token == DOWNTO)) {
        to_flag = (token == TO);
        get_token();
    }
    else error(MISSING_TO_OR_DOWNTO);

    emit_label(STMT_LABEL_PREFIX, loop_test_labelx);

    expr_tp = expression();
    if (! is_assign_type_compatible(for_tp, expr_tp))
        error(INCOMPATIBLE_TYPES);

    if (for_tp == char_typep) emit_2(COMPARE, byte(for_idp), reg(AL))
    else                      emit_2(COMPARE, word(for_idp), reg(AX))
    emit_1(to_flag ? JUMP_LE : JUMP_GE,
        label(STMT_LABEL_PREFIX, loop_stmt_labelx));
    emit_1(JUMP, label(STMT_LABEL_PREFIX, loop_exit_labelx));
    emit_label(STMT_LABEL_PREFIX, loop_stmt_labelx);

    if_token_get_else_error(DO, MISSING_DO);
    statement();

    emit_1(to_flag ? INCREMENT : DECREMENT,
        for_tp == char_typep ? byte(for_idp) : word(for_idp));
    emit_1(JUMP, label(STMT_LABEL_PREFIX, loop_test_labelx));

    emit_label(STMT_LABEL_PREFIX, loop_exit_labelx);
    emit_1(to_flag ? DECREMENT : INCREMENT,
        for_tp == char_typep ? byte(for_idp) : word(for_idp));
}

/*------------------------------------------------------------*/
/*  case_statement       Process a CASE statement:            */
/*                                                            */
/*                        CASE <expr> OF                      */
/*                            <case-branch> ;                 */
/*                            ...                             */
/*                        END                                 */
/*------------------------------------------------------------*/

TOKEN_CODE follow_expr_list[]      = {OF, SEMICOLON, 0};

TOKEN_CODE case_label_start_list[] = {IDENTIFIER, NUMBER, PLUS,
                                      MINUS, STRING, 0};

case_statement()

{
    BOOLEAN         another_branch;
    int             case_end_labelx = new_label_index();
    TYPE_STRUCT_PTR expr_tp;

    get_token();
```

```
    expr_tp = expression();

    if (   ((expr_tp->form != SCALAR_FORM) &&
            (expr_tp->form != ENUM_FORM) &&
            (expr_tp->form != SUBRANGE_FORM))
        || (expr_tp == real_typep)) error(INCOMPATIBLE_TYPES);

    /*
    --  Error synchronization:  Should be OF
    */
    synchronize(follow_expr_list, case_label_start_list, NULL);
    if_token_get_else_error(OF, MISSING_OF);

    /*
    --  Loop to process CASE branches.
    */
    another_branch = token_in(case_label_start_list);
    while (another_branch) {
        if (token_in(case_label_start_list))
            case_branch(expr_tp, case_end_labelx);

        if (token == SEMICOLON) {
            get_token();
            another_branch = TRUE;
        }
        else if (token_in(case_label_start_list)) {
            error(MISSING_SEMICOLON);
            another_branch = TRUE;
        }
        else another_branch = FALSE;
    }

    if_token_get_else_error(END, MISSING_END);
    emit_label(STMT_LABEL_PREFIX, case_end_labelx);
}

/*----------------------------------------------------------*/
/* case_branch          Process a CASE branch:              */
/*                                                          */
/*                      <case-label-list> : <stmt>          */
/*----------------------------------------------------------*/

TOKEN_CODE follow_case_label_list[] = {COLON, SEMICOLON, 0};

case_branch(expr_tp, case_end_labelx)

    TYPE_STRUCT_PTR expr_tp;         /* type of CASE expression */
    int             case_end_labelx; /* CASE end label index */

{
    BOOLEAN          another_label;
    int              next_test_labelx;
    int              branch_stmt_labelx = new_label_index();
    TYPE_STRUCT_PTR  label_tp;
    TYPE_STRUCT_PTR  case_label();

    /*
    --  <case-label-list>
    */
    do {
        next_test_labelx = new_label_index();

        label_tp = case_label();
        if (expr_tp != label_tp) error(INCOMPATIBLE_TYPES);

        emit_1(JUMP_NE, label(STMT_LABEL_PREFIX, next_test_labelx));

        get_token();
```

```
        if (token == COMMA) {
            get_token();
            emit_1(JUMP, label(STMT_LABEL_PREFIX, branch_stmt_labelx));

            if (token_in(case_label_start_list)) {
                emit_label(STMT_LABEL_PREFIX, next_test_labelx);
                another_label = TRUE;
            }
            else {
                error(MISSING_CONSTANT);
                another_label = FALSE;
            }
        }
        else another_label = FALSE;
    } while (another_label);

    /*
    --  Error synchronization:  Should be :
    */
    synchronize(follow_case_label_list, statement_start_list, NULL);
    if_token_get_else_error(COLON, MISSING_COLON);

    emit_label(STMT_LABEL_PREFIX, branch_stmt_labelx);
    statement();

    emit_1(JUMP, label(STMT_LABEL_PREFIX, case_end_labelx));
    emit_label(STMT_LABEL_PREFIX, next_test_labelx);
}

/*----------------------------------------------------------*/
/* case_label           Process a CASE label and return a   */
/*                      pointer to its type structure.      */
/*----------------------------------------------------------*/

    TYPE_STRUCT_PTR
case_label()

{
    TOKEN_CODE sign     = PLUS;        /* unary + or - sign */
    BOOLEAN    saw_sign = FALSE;       /* TRUE iff unary sign */

    /*
    --  Unary + or - sign.
    */
    if ((token == PLUS) || (token == MINUS)) {
        sign     = token;
        saw_sign = TRUE;
        get_token();
    }

    /*
    --  Numeric constant:  Integer type only.
    */
    if (token == NUMBER) {
        if (literal.type == INTEGER_LIT)
            emit_2(COMPARE, reg(AX),
                    integer_lit(sign == PLUS
                                    ? literal.value.integer
                                    : -literal.value.integer))
        else error(INVALID_CONSTANT);

        return(integer_typep);
    }

    /*
    --  Identifier constant:  Integer, character, or enumeration
    --                        types only.
    */
```

```
    */
    else if (token == IDENTIFIER) {
        SYMTAB_NODE_PTR idp;

        search_all_symtab(idp);

        if (idp == NULL) {
            error(UNDEFINED_IDENTIFIER);
            return(&dummy_type);
        }

        else if (idp->defn.key != CONST_DEFN) {
            error(NOT_A_CONSTANT_IDENTIFIER);
            return(&dummy_type);
        }

        else if (idp->typep == integer_typep) {
            emit_2(COMPARE, reg(AX),
                integer_lit(sign == PLUS
                                ? idp->defn.info.constant
                                    .value.integer
                                : -idp->defn.info.constant
                                    .value.integer));
            return(integer_typep);
        }

        else if (idp->typep == char_typep) {
            if (saw_sign) error(INVALID_CONSTANT);
            emit_2(COMPARE, reg(AL),
                    char_lit(idp->defn.info.constant
                                    .value.character));
            return(char_typep);
        }

        else if (idp->typep->form == ENUM_FORM) {
            if (saw_sign) error(INVALID_CONSTANT);
            emit_2(COMPARE, reg(AX),
                    integer_lit(idp->defn.info.constant
                                    .value.integer));
            return(idp->typep);
        }

        else return(&dummy_type);
    }

    /*
    -- String constant:  Character type only.
```

```
    */
    else if (token == STRING) {
        if (saw_sign) error(INVALID_CONSTANT);

        if (strlen(literal.value.string) == 1) {
            emit_2(COMPARE, reg(AL), char_lit(literal.value.string[0]));
            return(char_typep);
        }
        else {
            error(INVALID_CONSTANT);
            return(&dummy_type);
        }
    }

    else {
        error(INVALID_CONSTANT);
        return(&dummy_type);
    }
}

/*----------------------------------------------------------*/
/*  compound_statement      Process a compound statement:   */
/*                                                          */
/*                          BEGIN <stmt-list> END           */
/*----------------------------------------------------------*/

compound_statement()

{
    /*
    -- <stmt-list>
    */
    get_token();
    do {
        statement();
        while (token == SEMICOLON) get_token();
        if (token == END) break;

        /*
        -- Error synchronization:  Should be at the start of the
        --                         next statement.
        */
        synchronize(statement_start_list, NULL, NULL);
    } while (token_in(statement_start_list));

    if_token_get_else_error(END, MISSING_END);
}
```

14.2.1   The REPEAT statement

Figure 14-2 shows the annotated syntax diagram and the code diagram for the REPEAT statement. The syntax diagram shows when during the parse of the statement each assembly statement is emitted.

Function repeat_statement generates this code. We first create two statement labels, one with index loop_begin_labelx to mark the beginning of the code for the statements in the loop, and one with index loop_exit_labelx to mark the exit point of the loop. Then we call function statement to emit code for each statement in the loop.

FIGURE 14-2   Annotated syntax diagram and code diagram for the REPEAT statement.

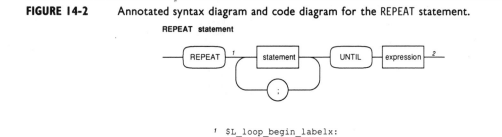

```
¹  $L_loop_begin_labelx:

            ┌─────────────────────┐
            │  code for statements │
            └─────────────────────┘

            ┌─────────────────────┐
            │  code for expression │
            └─────────────────────┘

   2        cmp  ax,1
            jeq  $L_loop_exit_labelx
            j    $L_loop_begin_labelx
        $L_loop_exit_labelx:
```

After the last statement, we call function expression to emit code to evaluate the boolean expression. We then emit the code to test the expression value and to jump based on whether the value is true or false.

We emit the testing code shown in the code diagram instead of the following code, which needs only one label:

```
    cmp  ax,1
    jne  $L_loop_begin_labelx
```

The reason is one of the idiosyncrasies of the 8086 machine architecture. The conditional jump instruction cannot jump 128 or more bytes, while the unconditional jump can jump to any location in the code segment. Thus, the code will fail unless all the code for the statements in the loop is less than 128 bytes long.

Figure 14-3 shows the code generated for a short Pascal program containing a simple REPEAT statement.

FIGURE 14-3   Assembly code generated for a short Pascal program containing a simple REPEAT statement.

```
;   1: PROGRAM exrepeat (output);          $RETURN_VALUE         EQU     <WORD PTR [bp-4]>
    DOSSEG                                 $HIGH_RETURN_VALUE    EQU     <WORD PTR [bp-2]>
    .MODEL  small
    .STACK  1024
                                       ;    2:
    .CODE                              ;    3: VAR
                                       ;    4:    i : integer;
    PUBLIC  _pascal_main               ;    5:
    INCLUDE pasextrn.inc               ;    6: BEGIN

$STATIC_LINK      EQU     <WORD PTR [bp+4]>        _pascal_main    PROC
```

```
        push    bp                              mov     ax,0        •
        mov     bp,sp                           pop     dx
;   7:      i := 10;                            cmp     dx,ax
        mov     ax,10                           mov     ax,1
        mov     WORD PTR i_002,ax               jle     $L_005
;   8:      REPEAT                              sub     ax,ax
$L_003:                                 $L_005:
;   9:          writeln(i);                     cmp     ax,1
        mov     ax,WORD PTR i_002               je      $L_004
        push    ax                              jmp     $L_003
        mov     ax,10                   $L_004:
        push    ax                      ;  12: END.
        call    _write_integer          ;  13:
        add     sp,4                    ;  14:
        call    _write_line
;  10:          i := i - 1;
        mov     ax,WORD PTR i_002               pop     bp
        push    ax                              ret
        mov     ax,1
        pop     dx                      _pascal_main    ENDP
        sub     dx,ax
        mov     ax,dx                           .DATA
        mov     WORD PTR i_002,ax
;  11:      UNTIL i <= 0;               i_002   DW      0
        mov     ax,WORD PTR i_002
        push    ax                              END
```

14.2.2 The WHILE statement

Figure 14-4 shows the annotated syntax diagram and the code diagram for the
WHILE statement, as emitted by function while_statement. We create three state-

FIGURE 14-4   Annotated syntax diagram and code diagram for the WHILE statement.

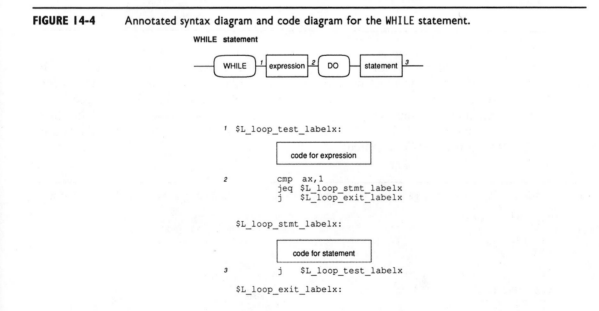

ment labels, one with index loop_stmt_labelx to mark the code for the statement in the loop, one with index loop_exit_labelx to mark the exit point of the loop, and one with index loop_test_labelx to mark the code for the boolean expression.

We first call expression to emit code to evaluate the boolean expression. We next emit code to test the expression value and to jump based on whether the value is true or false, and then we call statement to emit code for the statement in the loop.

The code generated for a short Pascal program containing a simple WHILE statement is shown in Figure 14-5.

FIGURE 14-5   Assembly code generated for a short Pascal program containing a simple WHILE statement.

```
;    1: PROGRAM exwhile (output);            $L_006:
        DOSSEG                                        cmp     ax,1
        .MODEL  small                                je      $L_004
        .STACK  1024                                 jmp     $L_005
                                             $L_004:
        .CODE                                ;    9:           writeln(i);
                                                      mov     ax,WORD PTR i_002
        PUBLIC  _pascal_main                          push    ax
        INCLUDE pasextrn.inc                          mov     ax,10
                                                      push    ax
$STATIC_LINK        EQU    <WORD PTR [bp+4]>          call    _write_integer
$RETURN_VALUE       EQU    <WORD PTR [bp-4]>          add     sp,4
$HIGH_RETURN_VALUE  EQU    <WORD PTR [bp-2]>          call    _write_line
                                             ;   10:           i := i + 1;
;    2:                                               mov     ax,WORD PTR i_002
;    3: VAR                                           push    ax
;    4:    i : integer;                              mov     ax,1
;    5:                                              pop     dx
;    6: BEGIN                                         add     ax,dx
                                                      mov     WORD PTR i_002,ax
_pascal_main    PROC                         ;   11:    END;
                                                      jmp     $L_003
        push    bp                           $L_005:
        mov     bp,sp                        ;   12: END.
;    7:    i := 1;                           ;   13:
        mov     ax,1                         ;   14:
        mov     WORD PTR i_002,ax
;    8:    WHILE i <= 10 DO BEGIN                     pop     bp
$L_003:                                               ret
        mov     ax,WORD PTR i_002
        push    ax                           _pascal_main    ENDP
        mov     ax,10
        pop     dx                                   .DATA
        cmp     dx,ax
        mov     ax,1                         i_002   DW      0
        jle     $L_006
        sub     ax,ax                                END
```

14.2.3 The IF statement

Figure 14-6 shows the annotated syntax diagram and the code diagram for the IF statement, as emitted by function if_statement. We first create two statement labels, one with index `true_labelx` to jump to when the boolean expression is true, and one with index `false_labelx` to jump to when the boolean expression is false. We call `expression` to emit code to evaluate the boolean expression, `statement` to emit code for the true branch statement and, if necessary, `statement` again to emit code for the false branch statement.

FIGURE 14-6   Annotated syntax diagram and code diagram for the IF statement.

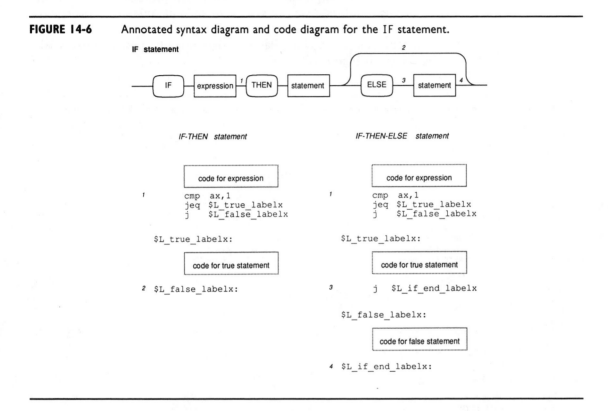

If the IF statement does not have an ELSE branch, the `false_labelx` label marks the code for the statement after the IF statement. If there is an ELSE branch, we create a third label with index `if_end_labelx` to mark the end of the IF statement and emit an unconditional j instruction to jump to that label after the code for the true branch statement. Then, the `false_labelx` label marks the code for the ELSE branch statement. The code generated for a short Pascal program containing simple IF statements is shown in Figure 14-7.

FIGURE 14-7   Assembly code generated for a short Pascal program containing simple IF statements.

```
;   1: PROGRAM exif (output);                    .MODEL  small
       DOSSEG                                    .STACK  1024
```

```
        .CODE

        PUBLIC  _pascal_main
        INCLUDE pasextrn.inc

$STATIC_LINK            EQU     <WORD PTR [bp+4]>
$RETURN_VALUE           EQU     <WORD PTR [bp-4]>
$HIGH_RETURN_VALUE      EQU     <WORD PTR [bp-2]>

;   2:
;   3: CONST
;   4:     one = 1;
;   5:     two = 2;
;   6:
;   7: BEGIN

_pascal_main    PROC

        push    bp
        mov     bp,sp
;   8:     IF one <> two THEN writeln('true');
        mov     ax,1
        push    ax
        mov     ax,2
        pop     dx
        cmp     dx,ax
        mov     ax,1
        jne     $L_004
        sub     ax,ax
$L_004:
        cmp     ax,1
        je      $L_002
        jmp     $L_003
$L_002:
        lea     ax,WORD PTR $S_005
        push    ax
        mov     ax,0
        push    ax
        mov     ax,4
        push    ax
        call    _write_string
        add     sp,6
        call    _write_line
$L_003:
;   9:     IF one = two THEN writeln('true');
        mov     ax,1
        push    ax
        mov     ax,2
        pop     dx
        cmp     dx,ax
        mov     ax,1
        je      $L_008
        sub     ax,ax
$L_008:
        cmp     ax,1
        je      $L_006
        jmp     $L_007
$L_006:
        lea     ax,WORD PTR $S_005
        push    ax
        mov     ax,0
        push    ax
        mov     ax,4
        push    ax
        call    _write_string
        add     sp,6
        call    _write_line
```

```
$L_007:
;  10:
;  11:     IF one <> two THEN writeln('true')
        mov     ax,1
        push    ax
        mov     ax,2
        pop     dx
        cmp     dx,ax
        mov     ax,1
        jne     $L_011
        sub     ax,ax
$L_011:
        cmp     ax,1
        je      $L_009
        jmp     $L_010
$L_009:
        lea     ax,WORD PTR $S_005
        push    ax
        mov     ax,0
        push    ax
        mov     ax,4
        push    ax
        call    _write_string
        add     sp,6
;  12:               ELSE writeln('false');
        call    _write_line
        jmp     $L_012
$L_010:
        lea     ax,WORD PTR $S_013
        push    ax
        mov     ax,0
        push    ax
        mov     ax,5
        push    ax
        call    _write_string
        add     sp,6
        call    _write_line
$L_012:
;  13:     IF one = two THEN writeln('true')
        mov     ax,1
        push    ax
        mov     ax,2
        pop     dx
        cmp     dx,ax
        mov     ax,1
        je      $L_016
        sub     ax,ax
$L_016:
        cmp     ax,1
        je      $L_014
        jmp     $L_015
$L_014:
        lea     ax,WORD PTR $S_005
        push    ax
        mov     ax,0
        push    ax
        mov     ax,4
        push    ax
        call    _write_string
        add     sp,6
;  14:               ELSE writeln('false');
        call    _write_line
        jmp     $L_017
$L_015:
        lea     ax,WORD PTR $S_013
        push    ax
        mov     ax,0
```

```
        push    ax                                          ret
        mov     ax,5
        push    ax                              _pascal_main    ENDP
        call    _write_string
        add     sp,6                                    .DATA
        call    _write_line
$L_017:                                         $S_013  DB      "false"
;   15: END.                                    $S_005  DB      "true"
;   16:
                                                        END
        pop     bp
```

14.2.4 The FOR statement

Figure 14-8 shows the annotated syntax diagram and the code diagram for the FOR statement, as emitted by function for_statement. We first create three statement labels, one with index loop_test_labelx to mark the code to test the control variable, one with index loop_stmt_labelx to mark the code for the statement in the loop, and one with index loop_exit_labelx to mark the exit point of the loop.

FIGURE 14-8   Annotated syntax diagram and code diagram for the FOR statement.

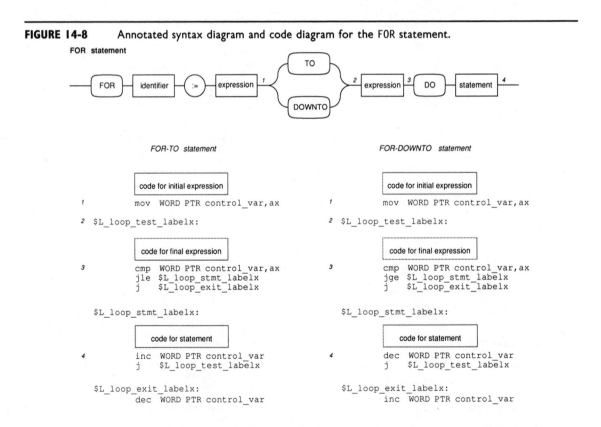

We call expression to emit code to evaluate the initial value expression, and then we emit the appropriate mov instruction to assign the byte or word value to the control variable. We call expression again to emit code to evaluate the final value expression. Then we emit code to compare the control variable's value to the final expression value, followed by code to jump based on the comparison. We emit either a jle or a jge instruction to jump to the code for the statement in the loop depending on whether we saw a TO or DOWNTO, respectively. We follow the jle or jge with an unconditional j instruction to jump to the exit label.

We call function statement to emit code for the statement in the loop. Afterwards, we emit either the inc or the dec instruction to increment or decrement the control variable's value, depending on whether there was a TO or a DOWNTO, respectively.

The code generated for a short Pascal program containing simple FOR statements is shown in Figure 14-9.

FIGURE 14-9 Assembly code generated for a short Pascal program containing simple FOR statements.

```
;   1: PROGRAM exfor (output);                          add      sp,6
        DOSSEG                                          mov      ax,WORD PTR i_002
        .MODEL   small                                 push     ax
        .STACK   1024                                  mov      ax,0
                                                        push     ax
        .CODE                                           call     _write_integer
                                                        add      sp,4
        PUBLIC   _pascal_main                           call     _write_line
        INCLUDE pasextrn.inc                            inc      WORD PTR i_002
                                                        jmp      $L_004
$STATIC_LINK          EQU    <WORD PTR [bp+4]>   $L_006:
$RETURN_VALUE         EQU    <WORD PTR [bp-4]>          dec      WORD PTR i_002
$HIGH_RETURN_VALUE    EQU    <WORD PTR [bp-2]>  ;   9:      writeln;
                                                        call     _write_line
;   2:                                          ;  10:      FOR i := 5 DOWNTO 1 DO writeln('i = ', i:0);
;   3: VAR                                               mov      ax,5
;   4:    i : integer;                                  mov      WORD PTR i_002,ax
;   5:    ch : char;                            $L_008:
;   6:                                                  mov      ax,1
;   7: BEGIN                                            cmp      WORD PTR i_002,ax
                                                        jge      $L_009
_pascal_main    PROC                                    jmp      $L_010
                                                $L_009:
        push     bp                                     lea      ax,WORD PTR $S_007
        mov      bp,sp                                  push     ax
;   8:      FOR i := 1 TO 5 DO writeln('i = ', i:0);    mov      ax,0
        mov      ax,1                                   push     ax
        mov      WORD PTR i_002,ax                      mov      ax,4
$L_004:                                                 push     ax
        mov      ax,5                                   call     _write_string
        cmp      WORD PTR i_002,ax                      add      sp,6
        jle      $L_005                                 mov      ax,WORD PTR i_002
        jmp      $L_006                                 push     ax
$L_005:                                                 mov      ax,0
        lea      ax,WORD PTR $S_007                     push     ax
        push     ax                                     call     _write_integer
        mov      ax,0                                   add      sp,4
        push     ax                                     call     _write_line
        mov      ax,4                                   dec      WORD PTR i_002
        push     ax                                     jmp      $L_008
        call     _write_string                  $L_010:
```

```
        inc     WORD PTR i_002                          push    ax
;   11:    writeln;                                      call    _write_char
        call    _write_line                             add     sp,4
;   12:    FOR ch := 'a' TO 'e' DO writeln('ch = ', ch:0);   call    _write_line
        mov     ax,'a'                                  inc     BYTE PTR ch_003
        mov     BYTE PTR ch_003,al                      jmp     $L_011
$L_011:                                          $L_013:
        mov     ax,'e'                                  dec     BYTE PTR ch_003
        cmp     BYTE PTR ch_003,al              ;   13: END.
        jle     $L_012
        jmp     $L_013                                  pop     bp
$L_012:                                                 ret
        lea     ax,WORD PTR $S_014
        push    ax                              _pascal_main    ENDP
        mov     ax,0
        push    ax                                      .DATA
        mov     ax,5
        push    ax                              i_002   DW      0
        call    _write_string                   ch_003  DB      0
        add     sp,6                            $S_014  DB      "ch = "
        sub     ax,ax                           $S_007  DB      "i = "
        mov     al,BYTE PTR ch_003
        push    ax                                      END
        mov     ax,0
```

14.2.5 The CASE statement

Figure 14-10 shows the annotated syntax diagram and the code diagram for the CASE statement, as emitted by functions case_statement, case_branch, and case_label.

In function case_statement, we create one label with index case_end_labelx to mark the end of the CASE statement. We call expression to evaluate the CASE expression. Then for each CASE branch, we call function case_branch, passing case_end_labelx.

We emit the rest of the code in functions case_branch and case_label. Unlike the interpreter, this code executes the CASE statement as if it were a series of IF statements.

In case_branch, we first create a label with index branch_stmt_labelx to mark the code for the CASE branch statement. Then for each CASE label, we create a label with index next_test_labelx to mark the code to test the next CASE label value. We call case_label, which emits the appropriate cmp instruction to test the label value. We then emit a jne instruction to jump upon inequality to the code to test the next CASE label value. If there is another CASE label in the same CASE branch, we emit an unconditional j instruction to jump to the code for the CASE branch statement, and follow this with the next_test_labelx label that marks the code to test the next CASE label value.

After the last (or only) label of the CASE branch, we emit the branch_stmt_labelx label marking the CASE branch statement, and then we call statement to emit code for that statement. We then emit an unconditional j instruction to jump to the label that was passed from case_branch which marks the end of the CASE statement. Finally, we emit the next_test_labelx label marking the code to test the next CASE label (which, if there is one, is in the next CASE branch).

FIGURE 14-10   Annotated syntax diagram and code diagram for the CASE statement.

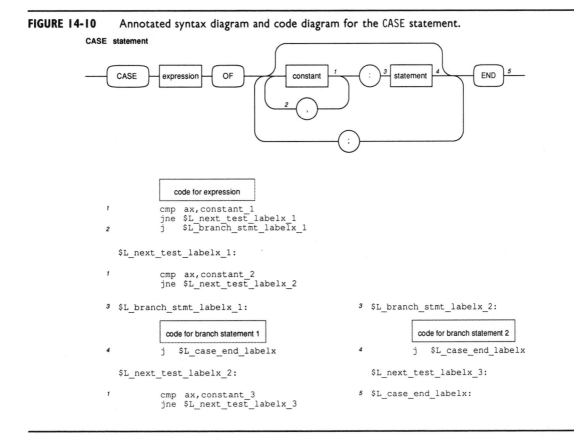

The code generated for a short Pascal program containing a simple CASE statement is shown in Figure 14-11.

FIGURE 14-11   Assembly code generated for a short Pascal program containing a simple CASE statement.

```
;   1: PROGRAM excase (output);          ;    5:
    DOSSEG                               ;    6: VAR
    .MODEL  small                        ;    7:    i : integer;
    .STACK  1024                         ;    8:    ch : char;
                                         ;    9:
    .CODE                                ;   10: BEGIN

    PUBLIC  _pascal_main                 _pascal_main    PROC
    INCLUDE pasextrn.inc
                                                 push    bp
$STATIC_LINK        EQU   <WORD PTR [bp+4]>      mov     bp,sp
$RETURN_VALUE       EQU   <WORD PTR [bp-4]>  ;  11:    FOR i := 1 TO 9 DO BEGIN
$HIGH_RETURN_VALUE  EQU   <WORD PTR [bp-2]>      mov     ax,1
                                                 mov     WORD PTR i_002,ax
;   2:                                   $L_004:
;   3: CONST                                     mov     ax,9
;   4:    six = 6;                               cmp     WORD PTR i_002,ax
```

```
        jle      $L_005
        jmp      $L_006
$L_005:
;   12:          write(i, ' : ');
        mov      ax,WORD PTR i_002
        push     ax
        mov      ax,10
        push     ax
        call     _write_integer
        add      sp,4
        lea      ax,WORD PTR $S_007
        push     ax
        mov      ax,0
        push     ax
        mov      ax,3
        push     ax
        call     _write_string
        add      sp,6
;   13:          CASE i OF
        mov      ax,WORD PTR i_002
;   14:             1:    writeln('one');
        cmp      ax,1
        jne      $L_010
$L_009:
        lea      ax,WORD PTR $S_011
        push     ax
        mov      ax,0
        push     ax
        mov      ax,3
        push     ax
        call     _write_string
        add      sp,6
        call     _write_line
        jmp      $L_008
$L_010:
;   15:             2:    writeln('two');
        cmp      ax,2
        jne      $L_013
$L_012:
        lea      ax,WORD PTR $S_014
        push     ax
        mov      ax,0
        push     ax
        mov      ax,3
        push     ax
        call     _write_string
        add      sp,6
        call     _write_line
        jmp      $L_008
$L_013:
;   16:             3:    writeln('three');
        cmp      ax,3
        jne      $L_016
$L_015:
        lea      ax,WORD PTR $S_017
        push     ax
        mov      ax,0
        push     ax
        mov      ax,5
        push     ax
        call     _write_string
        add      sp,6
        call     _write_line
        jmp      $L_008
$L_016:
;   17:           5,7,4: writeln('four, five, or seven');
        cmp      ax,5
```

```
        jne      $L_019
        jmp      $L_018
$L_019:
        cmp      ax,7
        jne      $L_020
        jmp      $L_018
$L_020:
        cmp      ax,4
        jne      $L_021
$L_018:
        lea      ax,WORD PTR $S_022
        push     ax
        mov      ax,0
        push     ax
        mov      ax,20
        push     ax
        call     _write_string
        add      sp,6
        call     _write_line
        jmp      $L_008
$L_021:
;   18:             six:    writeln('six');
        cmp      ax,6
        jne      $L_024
$L_023:
        lea      ax,WORD PTR $S_025
        push     ax
        mov      ax,0
        push     ax
        mov      ax,3
        push     ax
        call     _write_string
        add      sp,6
        call     _write_line
        jmp      $L_008
$L_024:
;   19:             8:    writeln('eight');
        cmp      ax,8
        jne      $L_027
$L_026:
        lea      ax,WORD PTR $S_028
        push     ax
        mov      ax,0
        push     ax
        mov      ax,5
        push     ax
        call     _write_string
        add      sp,6
        call     _write_line
        jmp      $L_008
$L_027:
;   20:             9:    writeln('nine');
        cmp      ax,9
        jne      $L_030
$L_029:
        lea      ax,WORD PTR $S_031
        push     ax
        mov      ax,0
        push     ax
        mov      ax,4
        push     ax
        call     _write_string
        add      sp,6
        call     _write_line
        jmp      $L_008
$L_030:
;   21:          END;
```

```
$L_008:                                          i_002    DW    0
;   22:    END;                                   ch_003   DB    0
        inc    WORD PTR i_002                     $S_031   DB    "nine"
        jmp    $L_004                             $S_028   DB    "eight"
$L_006:                                           $S_025   DB    "six"
        dec    WORD PTR i_002                     $S_022   DB    "four, five, or seven"
;   23:    END.                                   $S_017   DB    "three"
                                                  $S_014   DB    "two"
        pop    bp                                 $S_011   DB    "one"
        ret                                       $S_007   DB    " : "

_pascal_main    ENDP

        .DATA                                     END
```

14.3 Calling the runtime library routines

Figure 14-12 shows the new complete version of file standard.c, which emits calls to the library routines. Function write_writeln was described in Chapter 13.

FIGURE 14-12   File standard.c.

```
/************************************************************/        boolean_typep, char_typep;
/*                                                        */
/*      S T A N D A R D   R O U T I N E   P A R S E R      */     extern int          label_index;
/*                                                        */     extern char         asm_buffer[];
/*      Parsing routines for calls to standard procedures and */  extern char         *asm_bufferp;
/*      functions.                                        */     extern FILE         *code_file;
/*                                                        */
/*      FILE:     standard.c                              */     extern TOKEN_CODE   follow_parm_list[];
/*                                                        */     extern TOKEN_CODE   statement_end_list[];
/*      MODULE:   parser                                  */
/*                                                        */     /*------------------------------------------------------*/
/************************************************************/     /* Forwards                                             */
                                                                  /*------------------------------------------------------*/
#include <stdio.h>
#include "common.h"                                               TYPE_STRUCT_PTR eof_eoln(), abs_sqr(),
#include "error.h"                                                         arctan_cos_exp_ln_sin_sqrt(),
#include "scanner.h"                                                       pred_succ(), chr(), odd(), ord(),
#include "symtab.h"                                                        round_trunc();
#include "parser.h"
#include "code.h"                                                 /*------------------------------------------------------*/
                                                                  /* standard_routine_call   Process a call to a standard */
#define DEFAULT_NUMERIC_FIELD_WIDTH    10                         /*                         procedure or function. Return a */
#define DEFAULT_PRECISION              2                          /*                         pointer to the type structure of */
                                                                  /*                         the call.                    */
/*------------------------------------------------------*/        /*------------------------------------------------------*/
/* Externals                                            */
/*------------------------------------------------------*/            TYPE_STRUCT_PTR
                                                                  standard_routine_call(rtn_idp)
extern TOKEN_CODE       token;
extern char            word_string[];                                 SYMTAB_NODE_PTR rtn_idp;         /* routine id */
extern SYMTAB_NODE_PTR  symtab_display[];
extern int              level;                                    {
extern TYPE_STRUCT      dummy_type;                                   switch (rtn_idp->defn.info.routine.key) {

extern TYPE_STRUCT_PTR integer_typep, real_typep,                        case READ:
```

```
        case READLN:      read_readln(rtn_idp);       return(NULL);

        case WRITE:
        case WRITELN:     write_writeln(rtn_idp);     return(NULL);

        case EOFF:
        case EOLN:        return(eof_eoln(rtn_idp));

        case ABS:
        case SQR:         return(abs_sqr(rtn_idp));

        case ARCTAN:
        case COS:
        case EXP:
        case LN:
        case SIN:
        case SQRT:        return(arctan_cos_exp_ln_sin_sqrt(rtn_idp));

        case PRED:
        case SUCC:        return(pred_succ(rtn_idp));

        case CHR:         return(chr());
        case ODD:         return(odd());
        case ORD:         return(ord());

        case ROUND:
        case TRUNC:       return(round_trunc(rtn_idp));
    }
}

/*-------------------------------------------------------------*/
/* read_readln           Process a call to read or readln.   */
/*-------------------------------------------------------------*/

read_readln(rtn_idp)

    SYMTAB_NODE_PTR rtn_idp;          /* routine id */

{
    TYPE_STRUCT_PTR actual_parm_tp;     /* actual parm type */

    /*
    -- Parameters are optional for readln.
    */
    if (token == LPAREN) {
        /*
        -- <id-list>
        */
        do {
            get_token();

            /*
            -- Actual parms must be variables (but parse
            -- an expression anyway for error recovery).
            */
            if (token == IDENTIFIER) {
                SYMTAB_NODE_PTR idp;

                search_and_find_all_symtab(idp);
                actual_parm_tp = base_type(variable(idp,
                                            VARPARM_USE));

                if (actual_parm_tp->form != SCALAR_FORM)
                    error(INCOMPATIBLE_TYPES);
                else if (actual_parm_tp == integer_typep) {
                    emit_1(CALL, name_lit(READ_INTEGER));
                    emit_1(POP,  reg(BX));
```

```
                    emit_2(MOVE, word_indirect(BX), reg(AX));
                }
                else if (actual_parm_tp == real_typep) {
                    emit_1(CALL, name_lit(READ_REAL));
                    emit_1(POP,  reg(BX));
                    emit_2(MOVE, word_indirect(BX), reg(AX));
                    emit_2(MOVE, high_dword_indirect(BX), reg(DX));
                }
                else if (actual_parm_tp == char_typep) {
                    emit_1(CALL, name_lit(READ_CHAR));
                    emit_1(POP,  reg(BX));
                    emit_2(MOVE, byte_indirect(BX), reg(AL));
                }
            }
            else {
                actual_parm_tp = expression();
                error(INVALID_VAR_PARM);
            }

            /*
            -- Error synchronization:  Should be , or )
            */
            synchronize(follow_parm_list, statement_end_list, NULL);

        } while (token == COMMA);

        if_token_get_else_error(RPAREN, MISSING_RPAREN);
    }
    else if (rtn_idp->defn.info.routine.key == READ)
        error(WRONG_NUMBER_OF_PARMS);

    if (rtn_idp->defn.info.routine.key == READLN)
        emit_1(CALL, name_lit(READ_LINE));
}

/*-------------------------------------------------------------*/
/* write_writeln          Process a call to write or writeln. */
/*                        Each actual parameter can be:       */
/*                                                            */
/*                            <expr>                          */
/*                                                            */
/*                        or:                                 */
/*                                                            */
/*                            <epxr> : <expr>                 */
/*                                                            */
/*                        or:                                 */
/*                                                            */
/*                            <expr> : <expr> : <expr>        */
/*-------------------------------------------------------------*/

write_writeln(rtn_idp)

    SYMTAB_NODE_PTR rtn_idp;           /* routine id */

{
    TYPE_STRUCT_PTR actual_parm_tp;      /* actual parm type */
    TYPE_STRUCT_PTR field_width_tp, precision_tp;

    /*
    -- Parameters are optional for writeln.
    */
    if (token == LPAREN) {
        do {
            /*
            -- Value <expr>
            */
            get_token();
```

```
actual_parm_tp = base_type(expression());

/*
-- Push the scalar value to be written onto the stack.
-- A string value is already on the stack.
*/
if (actual_parm_tp->form != ARRAY_FORM)
    emit_push_operand(actual_parm_tp);

if ((actual_parm_tp->form != SCALAR_FORM) &&
    (actual_parm_tp != boolean_typep) &&
    ((actual_parm_tp->form != ARRAY_FORM) ||
     (actual_parm_tp->info.array.elmt_typep !=
                                    char_typep)))
    error(INVALID_EXPRESSION);

/*
-- Optional field width <expr>
-- Push onto the stack.
*/
if (token == COLON) {
    get_token();
    field_width_tp = base_type(expression());
    emit_1(PUSH, reg(AX));

    if (field_width_tp != integer_typep)
        error(INCOMPATIBLE_TYPES);

    /*
    -- Optional precision <expr>
    -- Push onto the stack if the value to be printed
    -- is of type real.
    */
    if (token == COLON) {
        get_token();
        precision_tp = base_type(expression());

        if (actual_parm_tp == real_typep)
            emit_1(PUSH, reg(AX));

        if (precision_tp != integer_typep)
            error(INCOMPATIBLE_TYPES);
    }
    else if (actual_parm_tp == real_typep) {
        emit_2(MOVE, reg(AX),
               integer_lit(DEFAULT_PRECISION));
        emit_1(PUSH, reg(AX));
    }
}
else {
    if (actual_parm_tp == integer_typep) {
        emit_2(MOVE, reg(AX),
               integer_lit(DEFAULT_NUMERIC_FIELD_WIDTH));
        emit_1(PUSH, reg(AX));
    }
    else if (actual_parm_tp == real_typep) {
        emit_2(MOVE, reg(AX),
               integer_lit(DEFAULT_NUMERIC_FIELD_WIDTH));
        emit_1(PUSH, reg(AX));
        emit_2(MOVE, reg(AX),
               integer_lit(DEFAULT_PRECISION));
        emit_1(PUSH, reg(AX));
    }
    else {
        emit_2(MOVE, reg(AX), integer_lit(0));
        emit_1(PUSH, reg(AX));
    }
}
```

```
    }
    if (actual_parm_tp == integer_typep) {
        emit_1(CALL, name_lit(WRITE_INTEGER));
        emit_2(ADD, reg(SP), integer_lit(4));
    }
    else if (actual_parm_tp == real_typep) {
        emit_1(CALL, name_lit(WRITE_REAL));
        emit_2(ADD, reg(SP), integer_lit(8));
    }
    else if (actual_parm_tp == boolean_typep) {
        emit_1(CALL, name_lit(WRITE_BOOLEAN));
        emit_2(ADD, reg(SP), integer_lit(4));
    }
    else if (actual_parm_tp == char_typep) {
        emit_1(CALL, name_lit(WRITE_CHAR));
        emit_2(ADD, reg(SP), integer_lit(4));
    }
    else /* string */ {
        /*
        -- Push the string length onto the stack.
        */
        emit_2(MOVE, reg(AX),
               integer_lit(actual_parm_tp->info.array
                                        .elmt_count));

        emit_1(PUSH, reg(AX));
        emit_1(CALL, name_lit(WRITE_STRING));
        emit_2(ADD, reg(SP), integer_lit(6));
    }

    /*
    -- Error synchronization:  Should be , or )
    */
    synchronize(follow_parm_list, statement_end_list, NULL);

} while (token == COMMA);

    if_token_get_else_error(RPAREN, MISSING_RPAREN);
}
else if (rtn_idp->defn.info.routine.key == WRITE)
    error(WRONG_NUMBER_OF_PARMS);

if (rtn_idp->defn.info.routine.key == WRITELN)
    emit_1(CALL, name_lit(WRITE_LINE));
}

/*------------------------------------------------------------*/
/* eof_eoln              Process a call to eof or to eoln.    */
/*                       No parameters => boolean result.     */
/*------------------------------------------------------------*/

    TYPE_STRUCT_PTR
eof_eoln(rtn_idp)

    SYMTAB_NODE_PTR rtn_idp;         /* routine id */

{
    if (token == LPAREN) {
        error(WRONG_NUMBER_OF_PARMS);
        actual_parm_list(rtn_idp, FALSE);
    }

    emit_1(CALL, name_lit(rtn_idp->defn.info.routine.key == EOFF
                          ? STD_END_OF_FILE
                          : STD_END_OF_LINE));

    return(boolean_typep);
```

```
}

/*------------------------------------------------------*/
/* abs_sqr              Process a call to abs or to sqr.  */
/*                      integer parm => integer result    */
/*                      real parm    => real result       */
/*------------------------------------------------------*/

    TYPE_STRUCT_PTR
abs_sqr(rtn_idp)

    SYMTAB_NODE_PTR rtn_idp;          /* routine id */

{
    TYPE_STRUCT_PTR parm_tp;          /* actual parameter type */
    TYPE_STRUCT_PTR result_tp;        /* result type */

    if (token == LPAREN) {
        get_token();
        parm_tp = base_type(expression());

        if ((parm_tp != integer_typep) && (parm_tp != real_typep)) {
            error(INCOMPATIBLE_TYPES);
            result_tp = real_typep;
        }
        else result_tp = parm_tp;

        if_token_get_else_error(RPAREN, MISSING_RPAREN);
    }
    else error(WRONG_NUMBER_OF_PARMS);

    switch (rtn_idp->defn.info.routine.key) {

        case ABS:
            if (parm_tp == integer_typep) {
                int nonnegative_labelx = new_label_index();

                emit_2(COMPARE, reg(AX), integer_lit(0));
                emit_1(JUMP_GE, label(STMT_LABEL_PREFIX,
                                      nonnegative_labelx));
                emit_1(NEGATE, reg(AX));
                emit_label(STMT_LABEL_PREFIX, nonnegative_labelx);
            }
            else {
                emit_push_operand(parm_tp);
                emit_1(CALL, name_lit(STD_ABS));
                emit_2(ADD, reg(SP), integer_lit(4));
            }
            break;

        case SQR:
            if (parm_tp == integer_typep) {
                emit_2(MOVE, reg(DX), reg(AX));
                emit_1(MULTIPLY, reg(DX));
            }
            else {
                emit_push_operand(parm_tp);
                emit_push_operand(parm_tp);
                emit_1(CALL, name_lit(FLOAT_MULTIPLY));
                emit_2(ADD, reg(SP), integer_lit(8));
            }
            break;
    }

    return(result_tp);
}
```

```
/*------------------------------------------------------*/
/* arctan_cos_exp_ln_sin_sqrt  Process a call to arctan, cos,  */
/*                        exp, ln, sin, or sqrt.          */
/*                        integer parm => real result     */
/*                        real_parm    => real result     */
/*------------------------------------------------------*/

    TYPE_STRUCT_PTR
arctan_cos_exp_ln_sin_sqrt(rtn_idp)

    SYMTAB_NODE_PTR rtn_idp;          /* routine id */

{
    TYPE_STRUCT_PTR parm_tp;          /* actual parameter type */
    char           *std_func_name;   /* name of standard func */

    if (token == LPAREN) {
        get_token();
        parm_tp = base_type(expression());

        if ((parm_tp != integer_typep) && (parm_tp != real_typep))
            error(INCOMPATIBLE_TYPES);

        if_token_get_else_error(RPAREN, MISSING_RPAREN);
    }
    else error(WRONG_NUMBER_OF_PARMS);

    if (parm_tp == integer_typep) {
        emit_1(PUSH, reg(AX));
        emit_1(CALL, name_lit(FLOAT_CONVERT));
        emit_2(ADD,  reg(SP), integer_lit(2));
    }

    emit_push_operand(real_typep);

    switch (rtn_idp->defn.info.routine.key) {
        case ARCTAN:    std_func_name = STD_ARCTAN;    break;
        case COS:       std_func_name = STD_COS;       break;
        case EXP:       std_func_name = STD_EXP;       break;
        case LN:        std_func_name = STD_LN;        break;
        case SIN:       std_func_name = STD_SIN;       break;
        case SQRT:      std_func_name = STD_SQRT;      break;
    }

    emit_1(CALL, name_lit(std_func_name));
    emit_2(ADD,  reg(SP), integer_lit(4));

    return(real_typep);
}

/*------------------------------------------------------*/
/* pred_succ            Process a call to pred or succ.   */
/*                      integer parm => integer result    */
/*                      enum parm    => enum result        */
/*------------------------------------------------------*/

    TYPE_STRUCT_PTR
pred_succ(rtn_idp)

    SYMTAB_NODE_PTR rtn_idp;          /* routine id */

{
    TYPE_STRUCT_PTR parm_tp;          /* actual parameter type */
    TYPE_STRUCT_PTR result_tp;        /* result type */

    if (token == LPAREN) {
        get_token();
```

```
        parm_tp = base_type(expression());

        if ((parm_tp != integer_typep) &&
            (parm_tp->form != ENUM_FORM)) {
            error(INCOMPATIBLE_TYPES);
            result_tp = integer_typep;
        }
        else result_tp = parm_tp;

        if_token_get_else_error(RPAREN, MISSING_RPAREN);
    }
    else error(WRONG_NUMBER_OF_PARMS);

    emit_1(rtn_idp->defn.info.routine.key == PRED
               ? DECREMENT : INCREMENT,
           reg(AX));

    return(result_tp);
}

/*-----------------------------------------------------*/
/*  chr                    Process a call to chr.       */
/*                         integer parm => character result  */
/*-----------------------------------------------------*/

    TYPE_STRUCT_PTR
chr()

{
    TYPE_STRUCT_PTR parm_tp;        /* actual parameter type */

    if (token == LPAREN) {
        get_token();
        parm_tp = base_type(expression());

        if (parm_tp != integer_typep) error(INCOMPATIBLE_TYPES);
        if_token_get_else_error(RPAREN, MISSING_RPAREN);
    }
    else error(WRONG_NUMBER_OF_PARMS);

    return(char_typep);
}

/*-----------------------------------------------------*/
/*  odd                    Process a call to odd.       */
/*                         integer parm => boolean result  */
/*-----------------------------------------------------*/

    TYPE_STRUCT_PTR
odd()

{
    TYPE_STRUCT_PTR parm_tp;        /* actual parameter type */

    if (token == LPAREN) {
        get_token();
        parm_tp = base_type(expression());

        if (parm_tp != integer_typep) error(INCOMPATIBLE_TYPES);
        if_token_get_else_error(RPAREN, MISSING_RPAREN);
```

```
    }
    else error(WRONG_NUMBER_OF_PARMS);

    emit_2(AND_BITS, reg(AX), integer_lit(1));
    return(boolean_typep);
}

/*-----------------------------------------------------*/
/*  ord                    Process a call to ord.       */
/*                         enumeration parm => integer result  */
/*-----------------------------------------------------*/

    TYPE_STRUCT_PTR
ord()

{
    TYPE_STRUCT_PTR parm_tp;        /* actual parameter type */

    if (token == LPAREN) {
        get_token();
        parm_tp = base_type(expression());

        if (parm_tp->form != ENUM_FORM) error(INCOMPATIBLE_TYPES);
        if_token_get_else_error(RPAREN, MISSING_RPAREN);
    }
    else error(WRONG_NUMBER_OF_PARMS);

    return(integer_typep);
}

/*-----------------------------------------------------*/
/*  round_trunc            Process a call to round or trunc.  */
/*                         real parm => integer result  */
/*-----------------------------------------------------*/

    TYPE_STRUCT_PTR
round_trunc(rtn_idp)

    SYMTAB_NODE_PTR rtn_idp;        /* routine id */

{
    TYPE_STRUCT_PTR parm_tp;        /* actual parameter type */

    if (token == LPAREN) {
        get_token();
        parm_tp = base_type(expression());

        if (parm_tp != real_typep) error(INCOMPATIBLE_TYPES);
        if_token_get_else_error(RPAREN, MISSING_RPAREN);
    }
    else error(WRONG_NUMBER_OF_PARMS);

    emit_push_operand(parm_tp);
    emit_1(CALL, name_lit(rtn_idp->defn.info.routine.key == ROUND
                             ? STD_ROUND : STD_TRUNC));
    emit_2(ADD, reg(SP), integer_lit(4));

    return(integer_typep);
}
```

Function `read_readln` calls function `variable`, which emits code that leaves the address of the actual parameter of `read` or `readln` on top of the stack. Then, depending on the type of the parameter, we emit a call to the library function read_integer, read_real, or read_char. These routines leave the value that was read in register AX, in register pair DX:AX, or in register AL, respectively. We emit code to pop the address of the actual parameter into register BX and then move the value that was read indirectly into the parameter. Finally, if we saw readln, we emit a call to the library function read_line.

Function eof_eoln emits a call either to the library function std_end_of_file or to the library function std_end_of_line.

Each of the remaining library functions for the standard Pascal functions first calls function expression to emit code to evaluate the actual parameter expression. Some of them then emit more instructions to operate on the expression value in register AX or register pair DX:AX.

In function abs_sqr, if the actual parameter for abs is integer, we create a label with index nonnegative_labelx for the nonnegative case and emit the inline code:

```
        cmp   ax,0                    ; is it negative?
        jge   $L_nonnegative_labelx   ; no
        neg   ax                      ; yes, so negate
$L_nonnegative_labelx:
```

Otherwise, if the parameter is real, we emit:

```
        push dx
        push ax
        call _std_abs
        add  sp,4
```

If the actual parameter for sqr is integer, we emit inline code to multiply the parameter value by itself:

```
        mov   dx,ax
        imul  dx                      ; AX := AX * AX
```

If the actual parameter is real, we emit:

```
        push dx
        push ax                       ; factor on stack
        push dx
        push ax                       ; factor again on stack
        call _float_multiply
        add  sp,8                      ; DX:AX := factor * factor
```

In function arctan_cos_exp_ln_sin_sqrt, if the parameter is integer, we emit code to convert the value to real:

```
push ax
call _float_convert
add  sp,2
```

Then we emit code to call the appropriate library function:

```
push dx
push ax
call routine
add  sp,4
```

where *routine* is either _std_arctan, _std_cos, _std_exp, _std_ln, _std_sin, or _std_sqrt.

Function pred_succ emits either an inc or a dec instruction to increment or decrement the expression value in register AX by 1, depending on whether we saw succ or pred.

Functions chr and ord do not emit any more code beyond what expression emits, since the Pascal functions chr and ord do not change the expression value.

Function odd simply emits:

```
and ax,1
```

When executed, this instruction leaves either a 1 (true) or 0 (false) in register AX, depending on whether the expression value was odd or even.

Finally, function round_trunc emits:

```
push dx
push ax
call routine
add  sp,4
```

where *routine* is either _std_round or _std_trunc, depending on whether the Pascal function was round or trunc.

14.4 Program 14-1: Pascal Compiler II

Figure 14-13 shows the main file of this chapter's program, a Pascal compiler. Figure 14-14 shows a sample Pascal program, and Figure 14-15 shows the assembly language code emitted by the compiler.

FIGURE 14-13   File compile2.c.

```
/******************************************************************/
/*                                                              */
/*      Program 14-1:  Pascal Compiler II                       */
/*                                                              */
/*      Compile Pascal programs.                                */
/*                                                              */
/*      FILE:     compile2.c                                    */
/*                                                              */
/*      REQUIRES: Modules parser, symbol table, scanner,        */
/*                          code, error                         */
/*                                                              */
/*      USAGE:    compile2 sourcefile objectfile                */
/*                                                              */
/*          sourcefile   [input] source file containing the     */
/*                              the statements to compile       */
/*                                                              */
/*          objectfile   [output] object file to contain the    */
/*                              generated assembly code         */
/*                                                              */
/******************************************************************/

#include <stdio.h>

/*----------------------------------------------------------*/
/* Globals                                                  */
/*----------------------------------------------------------*/

FILE *code_file;   /* ASCII file for the emitted assembly code */
```

```
/*----------------------------------------------------------*/
/* main              Initialize the scanner and call        */
/*                   routine program.                       */
/*----------------------------------------------------------*/

main(argc, argv)

    int  argc;
    char *argv[];


{
    /*
    -- Open the code file.  If no code file name was given,
    -- use the standard output file.
    */
    code_file = (argc == 3) ? fopen(argv[2], "w")
                            : stdout;

    /*
    -- Initialize the scanner.
    */
    init_scanner(argv[1]);

    /*
    -- Process a program.
    */
    get_token();
    program();
}
```

FIGURE 14-14   A sample Pascal program to be compiled.

```
PROGRAM newton (input, output);

CONST
    epsilon = 1e-6;

VAR
    number, root, sqroot : real;

BEGIN
    REPEAT
        writeln;
        write('Enter new number (0 to quit): ');
        read(number);

        IF number = 0 THEN BEGIN
            writeln(number:12:6, 0.0:12:6);
        END
        ELSE IF number < 0 THEN BEGIN
            writeln('*** ERROR:  number < 0');
        END
        ELSE BEGIN
            sqroot := sqrt(number);
            writeln(number:12:6, sqroot:12:6);
            writeln;

            root := 1;
            REPEAT
                root := (number/root + root)/2;
                writeln(root:24:6,
                        100*abs(root - sqroot)/sqroot:12:2,
                        '%')
            UNTIL abs(number/sqr(root) - 1) < epsilon;
        END
    UNTIL number = 0
END.
```

FIGURE 14-15   Assembly language object file generated by the compiler for the sample program in
Figure 14-14.

```
;   1: PROGRAM newton (input, output);
       DOSSEG
       .MODEL  small
       .STACK  1024

       .CODE

       PUBLIC  _pascal_main
       INCLUDE pasextrn.inc

$STATIC_LINK         EQU     <WORD PTR [bp+4]>
$RETURN_VALUE        EQU     <WORD PTR [bp-4]>
$HIGH_RETURN_VALUE   EQU     <WORD PTR [bp-2]>

;   2:
;   3: CONST
;   4:     epsilon = 1e-6;
;   5:
;   6: VAR
;   7:     number, root, sqroot : real;
;   8:
;   9: BEGIN

_pascal_main    PROC

       push    bp
       mov     bp,sp
;  10:     REPEAT
$L_005:
;  11:         writeln;
       call    _write_line
;  12:         write('Enter new number (0 to quit): ');
       lea     ax,WORD PTR $S_007
       push    ax
       mov     ax,0
       push    ax
       mov     ax,30
       push    ax
       call    _write_string
       add     sp,6
;  13:         read(number);
       lea     ax,WORD PTR number_002
       push    ax
       call    _read_real
       pop     bx
       mov     WORD PTR [bx],ax
       mov     WORD PTR [bx+2],dx
;  14:
;  15:         IF number = 0 THEN BEGIN
       mov     ax,WORD PTR number_002
       mov     dx,WORD PTR number_002+2
       push    dx
       push    ax
       mov     ax,0
       push    ax
       call    _float_convert
       add     sp,2
       push    dx
       push    ax
       call    _float_compare
       add     sp,8
       cmp     ax,0
       mov     ax,1
```

```
       je      $L_010
       sub     ax,ax
$L_010:
       cmp     ax,1
       je      $L_008
       jmp     $L_009
$L_008:
;  16:             writeln(number:12:6, 0.0:12:6);
       mov     ax,WORD PTR number_002
       mov     dx,WORD PTR number_002+2
       push    dx
       push    ax
       mov     ax,12
       push    ax
       mov     ax,6
       push    ax
       call    _write_real
       add     sp,8
       mov     ax,WORD PTR $F_011
       mov     dx,WORD PTR $F_011+2
       push    dx
       push    ax
       mov     ax,12
       push    ax
       mov     ax,6
       push    ax
       call    _write_real
       add     sp,8
       call    _write_line
;  17:         END
;  18:         ELSE IF number < 0 THEN BEGIN
       jmp     $L_012
$L_009:
       mov     ax,WORD PTR number_002
       mov     dx,WORD PTR number_002+2
       push    dx
       push    ax
       mov     ax,0
       push    ax
       call    _float_convert
       add     sp,2
       push    dx
       push    ax
       call    _float_compare
       add     sp,8
       cmp     ax,0
       mov     ax,1
       jl      $L_015
       sub     ax,ax
$L_015:
       cmp     ax,1
       je      $L_013
       jmp     $L_014
$L_013:
;  19:             writeln('*** ERROR:  number < 0');
       lea     ax,WORD PTR $S_016
       push    ax
       mov     ax,0
       push    ax
       mov     ax,22
       push    ax
       call    _write_string
```

```
        add     sp,6
        call    _write_line
;   20:          END
;   21:          ELSE BEGIN
        jmp     $L_017
$L_014:
;   22:              sqroot := sqrt(number);
        mov     ax,WORD PTR number_002
        mov     dx,WORD PTR number_002+2
        push    dx
        push    ax
        call    _std_sqrt
        add     sp,4
        mov     WORD PTR sqroot_004,ax
        mov     WORD PTR sqroot_004+2,dx
;   23:              writeln(number:12:6, sqroot:12:6);
        mov     ax,WORD PTR number_002
        mov     dx,WORD PTR number_002+2
        push    dx
        push    ax
        mov     ax,12
        push    ax
        mov     ax,6
        push    ax
        call    _write_real
        add     sp,8
        mov     ax,WORD PTR sqroot_004
        mov     dx,WORD PTR sqroot_004+2
        push    dx
        push    ax
        mov     ax,12
        push    ax
        mov     ax,6
        push    ax
        call    _write_real
        add     sp,8
        call    _write_line
;   24:          writeln;
        call    _write_line
;   25:
;   26:          root := 1;
        mov     ax,1
        push    ax
        call    _float_convert
        add     sp,2
        mov     WORD PTR root_003,ax
        mov     WORD PTR root_003+2,dx
;   27:          REPEAT
$L_018:
;   28:              root := (number/root + root)/2;
        mov     ax,WORD PTR number_002
        mov     dx,WORD PTR number_002+2
        push    dx
        push    ax
        mov     ax,WORD PTR root_003
        mov     dx,WORD PTR root_003+2
        push    dx
        push    ax
        call    _float_divide
        add     sp,8
        push    dx
        push    ax
        mov     ax,WORD PTR root_003
        mov     dx,WORD PTR root_003+2
        push    dx
        push    ax
        call    _float_add
```

```
        add     sp,8
        push    dx
        push    ax
        mov     ax,2
        push    ax
        call    _float_convert
        add     sp,2
        push    dx
        push    ax
        call    _float_divide
        add     sp,8
        mov     WORD PTR root_003,ax
        mov     WORD PTR root_003+2,dx
;   29:              writeln(root:24:6,
        mov     ax,WORD PTR root_003
        mov     dx,WORD PTR root_003+2
        push    dx
        push    ax
        mov     ax,24
        push    ax
        mov     ax,6
        push    ax
        call    _write_real
        add     sp,8
;   30:                  100*abs(root - sqroot)/sqroot:12:2,
        mov     ax,100
        push    ax
        mov     ax,WORD PTR root_003
        mov     dx,WORD PTR root_003+2
        push    dx
        push    ax
        mov     ax,WORD PTR sqroot_004
        mov     dx,WORD PTR sqroot_004+2
        push    dx
        push    ax
        call    _float_subtract
        add     sp,8
        push    dx
        push    ax
        call    _std_abs
        add     sp,4
        push    dx
        push    ax
        pop     ax
        pop     dx
        pop     bx
        push    dx
        push    ax
        push    bx
        call    _float_convert
        add     sp,2
        pop     bx
        pop     cx
        push    dx
        push    ax
        push    cx
        push    bx
        call    _float_multiply
        add     sp,8
        push    dx
        push    ax
        mov     ax,WORD PTR sqroot_004
        mov     dx,WORD PTR sqroot_004+2
        push    dx
        push    ax
        call    _float_divide
        add     sp,8
```

```
          push   dx                                        add    sp,8
          push   ax                                        cmp    ax,0
          mov    ax,12                                     mov    ax,1
          push   ax                                        jl     $L_021
          mov    ax,2                                      sub    ax,ax
          push   ax                              $L_021:
          call   _write_real                               cmp    ax,1
          add    sp,8                                      je     $L_019
;   31:                        '%')                        jmp    $L_018
          mov    ax,'%'                          $L_019:
          push   ax                              ;   33:        END
          mov    ax,0                            ;   34:    UNTIL number = 0
          push   ax                              $L_017:
          call   _write_char                     $L_012:
          add    sp,4                                      mov    ax,WORD PTR number_002
;   32:        UNTIL abs(number/sqr(root) - 1) < epsilon;  mov    dx,WORD PTR number_002+2
          call   _write_line                               push   dx
          mov    ax,WORD PTR number_002                     push   ax
          mov    dx,WORD PTR number_002+2                   mov    ax,0
          push   dx                              ;   35: END.
          push   ax                                        push   ax
          mov    ax,WORD PTR root_003                       call   _float_convert
          mov    dx,WORD PTR root_003+2                     add    sp,2
          push   dx                                        push   dx
          push   ax                                        push   ax
          push   dx                                        call   _float_compare
          push   ax                                        add    sp,8
          call   _float_multiply                           cmp    ax,0
          add    sp,8                                      mov    ax,1
          push   dx                                        je     $L_022
          push   ax                                        sub    ax,ax
          call   _float_divide                   $L_022:
          add    sp,8                                      cmp    ax,1
          push   dx                                        je     $L_006
          push   ax                                        jmp    $L_005
          mov    ax,1                            $L_006:
          push   ax
          call   _float_convert                            pop    bp
          add    sp,2                                      ret
          push   dx
          push   ax                              _pascal_main   ENDP
          call   _float_subtract
          add    sp,8                                      .DATA
          push   dx
          push   ax                              number_002    DD       0.0
          call   _std_abs                        root_003      DD       0.0
          add    sp,4                            sqroot_004    DD       0.0
          push   dx                              $F_020   DD    1.000000e-006
          push   ax                              $F_011   DD    0.000000e+000
          mov    ax,WORD PTR $F_020              $S_016   DB    "*** ERROR: number < 0"
          mov    dx,WORD PTR $F_020+2            $S_007   DB    "Enter new number (0 to quit): "
          push   dx
          push   ax                                        END
          call   _float_compare
```

And so, we have reached the second major milestone of this book—a complete, working Pascal compiler. In the next and final chapter of this book, we will briefly look at some advanced topics.

Questions and exercises

1. The code generated for the FOR statement re-evaluates the final expression each time before executing the loop statement. According to the Pascal semantics, both the initial and final expressions should be evaluated only once each time the FOR statement is executed. Modify the generated code accordingly.

2. The interpreter caught the runtime error of the value of a CASE expression not being one of the CASE labels. Modify the generated CASE statement code to make this check.

3. Modify the runtime library code to check for errors such as an attempt to divide by zero.

4. The code to evaluate the boolean expression of a REPEAT, a WHILE, or an IF statement goes through the step of leaving a 0 (false) or a 1 (true) in register AX. Modify the generated code to eliminate this step whenever possible.

CHAPTER 15

Advanced Concepts: An Overview

In this book, we have written a working interpreter, an interactive debugger, and a compiler. These are major accomplishments, and yet, we have examined only the basic concepts of writing compilers and interpreters. This chapter contains a brief overview of some of the advanced concepts that you will encounter if you plan to study and do more work in this field.

15.1 BNF

In this book, we used graphical syntax diagrams to represent the grammar of the source language. A common textual notation is the Backus-Naur Form, or BNF. As an example, we will use this notation to describe the syntax of Pascal expressions.

BNF is a *metalanguage*, a language used to describe another language. Each statement of the metalanguage is called a *production rule*. Compare the following two rules to the first syntax diagram in Figure 4-7:

```
<expression> ::=  <simple expression>
                 | <simple expression> <rel op>
                      <simple expression>

<rel op> ::=  = | < | <= | <> | >= | >
```

The first rule states that an expression is either a single simple expression or two simple expressions separated by a relational operator. The second rules states that a relational operator is one of the six tokens that are listed.

The symbols ::= and | are *metasymbols*. They belong to the BNF metalanguage and not to the Pascal source language. (When the same symbol belongs to both languages, a different font or face can be used to distinguish one use from another.) The metasymbol ::= separates the left-hand side of a rule (a nonterminal symbol) from its right-hand side (the definition). The metasymbol | separates alternate forms in a definition.

In BNF, *nonterminal symbols* are enclosed by the angle brackets < and >. These are symbols that are defined by other rules. *Terminal symbols* are tokens such as >= and IF. In the syntax diagrams, rectangular boxes represent the nonterminal symbols, and rounded boxes represent the terminal symbols. A simple expression is defined by the rules:

```
<simple expression> ::= <term> | <sign> <term>
                      | <simple expression> <add op> <term>

<sign>    ::= - | +

<add op> ::= - | + | OR
```

These rules state that a simple expression is one or more terms separated by adding operators. The first term is optionally preceded by a sign. A sign is either - or +, and an adding operator is either -, +, or the reserved word OR. Notice how BNF uses recursion to specify repetition, in this case multiple terms separated by adding operators. We can now give the rules for a term, a factor, and a (simple) variable:

```
<term>    ::= <factor> | <term> <mult op> <factor>

<mult op> ::= * | / | DIV | MOD | AND

<factor>  ::= <variable> | <unsigned constant>
            | <function call> | NOT <factor>
            | ( <expression> )
```

```
<variable> ::= <identifier>
```

We'll see one of the advantages of using a textual notation like BNF later when we discuss *compiler compilers*.

15.2 Top-down vs. bottom-up parsing

The parser we wrote in this book uses a top-down parsing method known as *recursive descent*. With this method, the parser starts at the topmost nonterminal symbol of the grammar. In our BNF example, that would be <expression>. The parser then proceeds to work its way down to the terminal symbols, such as <expression> to <simple expression> to <term> to <factor> to NOT.

Another way to understand this is to look at the *parse tree* for an expression, as shown in Figure 15-1. The parser starts at the top of the tree and, in effect, constructs the tree downwards to the terminal symbols at the leaves.

You know that a recursive descent parser is implemented by writing a routine to recognize each nonterminal symbol, as defined by the production rule (or syntax diagram) for the symbol. Each routine can contain (possibly recursive) calls to routines to recognize any nonterminal symbols in the definition. You write semantic actions in these routines.

The advantages of a recursive descent parser are that it is easy to write, and once written, it is easy to read and understand. The main disadvantage is that it tends to be large and slow. If the grammar contains many nonterminal symbols, the parser contains many routines. Routine calls and returns can be relatively slow operations.

Another type of parser uses a bottom-up parsing method and is called a *shift-reduce* parser. This parser starts with the terminal symbols and works its way up to the topmost nonterminal symbol. In effect, it starts with the terminal symbols at the bottom of the parse tree and constructs the tree upwards to the topmost nonterminal symbol.

A shift-reduce parser works with a parse stack. The parse stack starts out empty, and during the parse, it contains nonterminal and terminal symbols that

FIGURE 15-1   The parse tree for the expression a + b/c.

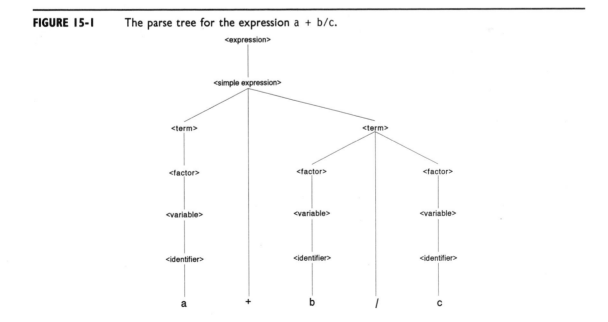

have already been parsed. Each time a token (terminal symbol) is obtained by the scanner, the parser shifts (pushes) the token onto the parse stack. At various times, based on the symbols on top of the stack and the next input token, the parser determines that the symbols on the top of the stack match the right-hand side of a production rule. The matching symbols are then popped off and reduced (replaced) by the nonterminal symbol at the left-hand side of the matching rule. As soon as the stack is reduced to the topmost nonterminal symbol, the parser accepts the input as being syntactically correct.

For example, here is how a shift-reduce parser recognizes the Pascal expression a + b/c. The stack is written horizontally with its bottom at the left, represented by the marker |, and its top at the right. We also show the remaining input at each step with the leftmost token being the next one to be read by the scanner.

Stack	Input	Action
|	a + b/c	shift
| a	+ b/c	reduce
| <identifier>	+ b/c	reduce
| <variable>	+ b/c	reduce
| <factor>	+ b/c	reduce
| <term>	+ b/c	shift
| <term> +	b/c	shift
| <term> + b	/c	reduce
| <term> + <identifier>	/c	reduce
| <term> + <variable>	/c	reduce
| <term> + <factor>	/c	shift
| <term> + <factor> /	c	shift
| <term> + <factor> / c		reduce
| <term> + <factor> / <identifier>		reduce
| <term> + <factor> / <variable>		reduce
| <term> + <factor> / <factor>		reduce
| <term> + <term>		reduce
| <simple expression>		reduce
| <expression>		

A shift-reduce parser uses a parse table which is derived from the grammar. This table determines whether the next action is to shift, reduce, accept, or signal a syntax error. Any semantic actions can also be encoded into this table.

15.3 Compiler compilers

One of the advantages of using a textual metalanguage is that we can feed the description of the syntax of a source language into a *compiler compiler*. A compiler

compiler reads and compiles a syntax description and then generates all or part of a compiler for the source language.

A well-known compiler compiler is Yacc (Yet another compiler-compiler). It reads a syntax description written in a language similar to BNF and generates a shift-reduce parser for the source language. For example, if we described all of Pascal's syntax and fed that into Yacc, it would generate a parser for Pascal. This parser is in the form of a C program. To perform any semantic actions during parsing, we write sequences of C code to perform these operations, and embed these code sequences in the syntax description. When Yacc generates the parser, it includes these code sequences.

For example, suppose we want to write an interpreter for a very simple language consisting of a single expression that has only the add and subtract operators. The following syntax description, along with the embedded semantic code, can be fed into Yacc:

```
%token NUMBER
%left  '+' '-'

expression : expression '+' expression  { $$ = $1 + $3; }
           | expression '-' expression  { $$ = $1 - $3; }
           | '(' expression ')'         { $$ = $2; }
           | NUMBER                     { $$ = $1; }
           ;
```

This description states that NUMBER is a token returned by the scanner, and that the operators + and - are left-associative. In the definition of expression, expression is a nonterminal symbol, and +, -, (,), and NUMBER are terminal symbols. Note that the metasymbol : is used instead of the ::= metasymbol of BNF and that a semicolon terminates each production rule.

Each alternate form in the right-hand side of a rule can have semantic actions attached to it. The C code to perform the semantic actions are enclosed in the { and } braces. Within this code, $$ represents the value of the production rule, and $n represents the value of the nth element of the form. For example, the first semantic action says that the value of parsing and executing an expression plus another expression is the value of the first expression plus the value of the second expression (which is the third element of the form). The fourth semantic action says that whenever the scanner fetches a NUMBER token, the scanner must also specify the token's value (by setting the special variable yylval which is supplied by Yacc).

When Yacc compiles this description, it produces a C routine named yyparse to parse and evaluate an expression. This parser includes the parse stack, a value stack, the parse table, and the semantic code. Within the semantic code, the $$ and $n are replaced by references to the value stack to obtain the appropriate values. The parser calls the scanner, which must be named yylex, whenever it needs the next input token. When it detects a syntax error, the parser calls an error routine named yyerror.

To complete the compiler we must write a C main program that calls yyparse. We must also write the scanner yylex and the error routine yyerror.

A companion to Yacc is Lex, which generates a lexical analyser (a scanner) named yylex. Thus, Yacc and Lex are designed to work together. Lex reads a textual description of the tokens of the source language in order to generate the scanner.

15.4 Intermediate forms for compilers

Our interpreter used an intermediate form to represent the source program, and it executed the program in this form. The intermediate form had a simple linear structure that was interspersed with address markers that pointed off to other parts of the form. Our compiler did not use an intermediate form at all.

There are, however, advantages for a compiler to translate the source program first to an intermediate form. A well-designed intermediate form gives the compiler an opportunity to analyze the program in order to generate better code. When an entire routine (or a substantial portion of a routine) of the source program is available in memory in its intermediate form, the compiler can look at each expression and statement within a greater context. By first examining several parts of an expression or statement, the compiler can generate more optimal code. (We will see examples of this later).

Figure 15-2 shows a tree-structured intermediate form for several Pascal statements. This form can also be used by an interpreter for execution.

15.5 Code optimization

As great a challenge it is for a compiler to generate *correct* code, that is often not enough. You may also want the compiler to generate *optimal* code. Code can be optimal in terms of time (execute as quickly as possible), space (be as small as possible), or both.

A one-pass compiler, such as the one we have written, is not always able to generate optimal code. This is because the parser sees so little of the program at one time, only one or two tokens. For example, for the Pascal assignment statement:

$$count := count + 1$$

our compiler generates code similar to:

```
mov  ax,WORD PTR count
push ax
```

FIGURE 15-2   Tree-structured intermediate forms.

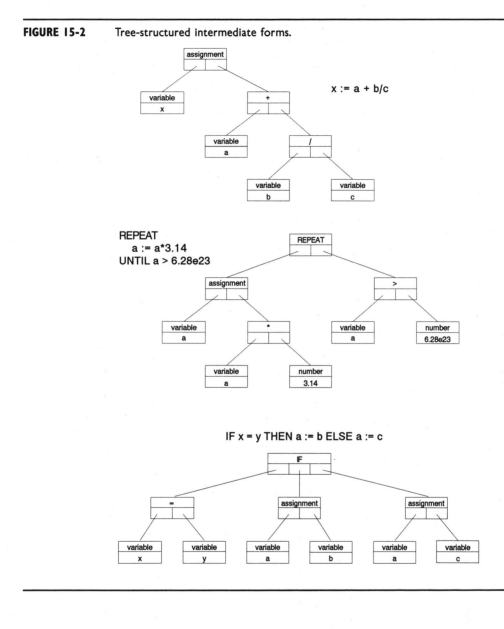

```
        mov   ax,1
        pop   dx
        add   ax,dx
        mov   WORD PTR count,ax
```

This is generic code for an addition that the compiler generates for any addition.

However, if the compiler first translated the statement into an intermediate form and then analyzed the entire statement, it would be able to detect that the constant value 1 is added to the variable count, and that the sum is assigned to the same variable. Such a compiler would then be able to generate much more optimal code:

```
inc count
```

This is an example of a *local optimization* that results from analyzing a small portion of the intermediate form, such as an expression or a statement.

Global optimization requires analysis of larger portions of the intermediate form. Examples of global optimizations include:

- *Dead code elimination.* The compiler simply does not generate code for source statements that can never be reached during execution.
- *In-line calls.* Sometimes when a procedure or a function is short, the expense of a call and a return can be eliminated if the code for the routine itself is inserted in the place of the call.
- *Common subexpressions.* The same subexpression may appear several times in an expression, for example:

$$z := a*(p - q) + b*(p - q) + c*(p - q)$$

To optimize this expression, the compiler can compile the assignment statement as though it were the following two statements:

```
x := p - q;
z := a*x + b*x + c*x
```

It might even be able to compile the second assignment statement as follows:

```
z := x*(a + b + c)
```

to save the cost of two multiplies.

- *Loop-invariant expressions.* An expression in a loop may evaluate to the same value each time through the loop. The compiler can recognize this and move the invariant expression outside of the loop. For example, if the value of limit in the following WHILE loop is not changed within the loop:

```
WHILE i < limit - 1 DO ...
```

the statement can be compiled as though it were written:

```
x := limit - 1;
WHILE i < x DO ...
```

- *Register allocation.* Unlike the 8086 architecture, some machine architectures offer a number of general-purpose registers that can all participate equally in expression evaluation. For faster execution, the compiler generates code that leaves values in the registers as long as possible to save on moves to and from memory. Of course, the compiler must then keep track of which values are in which registers during runtime.

Although optimization is generally desirable, no compiler must ever change the semantics of a program. Rather than risk computing an answer incorrectly (albeit more quickly), most compilers are conservative when it comes to elaborate optimization techniques.

15.6 Common front ends and back ends

Although high-level languages may differ greatly in syntax, they are often alike in semantics. For example, C and Pascal have FOR statements, and FORTRAN has the DO statement. At runtime, these statements behave very similarly.

One of the most efficient ways to write compilers for different languages is to have the compilers share as much as possible. If we design an intermediate form that can represent source programs written in C, Pascal, and FORTRAN, then we only need to write a single compiler "back end" consisting of the optimization and code generation modules. Each language would have its own compiler "front end" consisting of a scanner and a parser. Each front end scans and parses source programs written in the corresponding high-level language and translates the programs to the common intermediate form. Then the common back end takes over to generate the target code.

This scheme also works if we need to write compilers for one source language but for several machine architectures. In this case, we have a single front end but a different back end for each architecture.

15.7 Where to go from here

You may have noticed that we wrote our interpreter and compiler in a very modular fashion. That means that you can substitute routines that work differently but perform the same tasks. For example, you may want to replace the scanner with a faster one, or the parser with one that works bottom-up. The concepts in this chapter might give you some ideas of what you can do to improve what we have written. You should be able to study and understand a more advanced textbook on compiler writing and learn some of the theory behind these concepts.

Of course, you can write a compiler for some high-level language other than Pascal, or improve an existing compiler. A more ambitious project is to invent a new language and then write a compiler or an interpreter (or both) for it.

Whatever it is you want to do from here, go for it!

APPENDIX A

This appendix contains listings of all the source files of the Pascal interpreter with the interactive debugger, as written in Chapter 11.

FIGURE A-I   parser.h

```
/****************************************************************/
/*                                                              */
/*       P A R S I N G   R O U T I N E S   (Header)             */
/*                                                              */
/*       FILE:      parser.h                                    */
/*                                                              */
/*       MODULE:    parser                                      */
/*                                                              */
/****************************************************************/

#ifndef parser_h
#define parser_h

#include "common.h"
#include "symtab.h"

/*------------------------------------------------------------*/
/*  Uses of a variable                                        */
/*------------------------------------------------------------*/

typedef enum {
    EXPR_USE, TARGET_USE, VARPARM_USE,
} USE;

/*------------------------------------------------------------*/
/*  Functions                                                 */
/*------------------------------------------------------------*/

TYPE_STRUCT_PTR expression();
TYPE_STRUCT_PTR variable();
TYPE_STRUCT_PTR routine_call();
TYPE_STRUCT_PTR base_type();
BOOLEAN         is_assign_type_compatible();

        /******************************/
        /*                            */
        /*      Macros for parsing    */
        /*                            */
```

```
        /******************************/

/*------------------------------------------------------------*/
/*  if_token_get            If token equals token_code, get */
/*                          the next token.                 */
/*------------------------------------------------------------*/

#define if_token_get(token_code)                    \
    if (token == token_code) get_token()

/*------------------------------------------------------------*/
/*  if_token_get_else_error   If token equals token_code, get */
/*                            the next token, else error.   */
/*------------------------------------------------------------*/

#define if_token_get_else_error(token_code, error_code) \
    if (token == token_code) get_token();           \
    else                     error(error_code)

/*------------------------------------------------------------*/
/*  Analysis routine calls    Unless the following statements */
/*                            are preceded by               */
/*                                                          */
/*                                  #define analyze         */
/*                                                          */
/*                            calls to the analysis routines */
/*                            are not compiled.             */
/*------------------------------------------------------------*/

#ifndef analyze
#define analyze_const_defn(idp)
#define analyze_var_decl(idp)
#define analyze_type_defn(idp)
#define analyze_routine_header(idp)
#define analyze_block(idp)
#endif

#endif
```

FIGURE A-2   routine.c

```
/****************************************************************/
/*                                                              */
/*       R O U T I N E   P A R S E R                            */
/*                                                              */
/*       Parsing routines for programs and declared            */
/*       procedures and functions.                             */
/*                                                              */
/*       FILE:      routine.c                                   */
/*                                                              */
/*       MODULE:    parser                                      */
/*                                                              */
/****************************************************************/

#include <stdio.h>
#include "common.h"
#include "error.h"
#include "scanner.h"
#include "symtab.h"
```

```
#include "parser.h"
#include "exec.h"

/*------------------------------------------------------------*/
/*  Externals                                                 */
/*------------------------------------------------------------*/

extern int          line_number;
extern int          error_count;
extern long         exec_stmt_count;

extern TOKEN_CODE       token;
extern char             word_string[];
extern SYMTAB_NODE_PTR  symtab_display[];
extern int              level;

extern TYPE_STRUCT      dummy_type;
```

```
extern char          *code_buffer;
extern char          *code_bufferp;
extern STACK_ITEM    *stack;
extern STACK_ITEM_PTR tos;
extern STACK_ITEM_PTR stack_frame_basep;

extern TOKEN_CODE    statement_start_list[],
                     statement_end_list[],
                     declaration_start_list[];

/*------------------------------------------------------------*/
/*  Globals                                                   */
/*------------------------------------------------------------*/

char buffer[MAX_PRINT_LINE_LENGTH];

/*------------------------------------------------------------*/
/*  Forwards                                                  */
/*------------------------------------------------------------*/

SYMTAB_NODE_PTR formal_parm_list();
SYMTAB_NODE_PTR program_header(), procedure_header(),
                function_header();
char            *create_code_segment();

/*------------------------------------------------------------*/
/*  program         Process a program:                        */
/*                                                            */
/*                        <program-header> ; <block> .        */
/*------------------------------------------------------------*/

TOKEN_CODE follow_header_list[] = {SEMICOLON, END_OF_FILE, 0};

program()

{

    SYMTAB_NODE_PTR program_idp;       /* program id */

    /*
    --                PARSE THE PROGRAM
    --
    --
    --  Intialize the symbol table and then allocate
    --  the code buffer.
    */
    init_symtab();
    code_buffer  = alloc_bytes(MAX_CODE_BUFFER_SIZE);
    code_bufferp = code_buffer;

    /*
    --  Begin parsing with the program header.
    */
    program_idp = program_header();

    /*
    --  Error synchronization:  Should be ;
    */
    synchronize(follow_header_list,
                declaration_start_list, statement_start_list);
    if_token_get(SEMICOLON);
    else if (token_in(declaration_start_list) ||
             token_in(statement_start_list))
        error(MISSING_SEMICOLON);

    analyze_routine_header(program_idp);

    /*
```

```
    --  Parse the program's block.
    */
    program_idp->defn.info.routine.locals = NULL;
    block(program_idp);

    program_idp->defn.info.routine.local_symtab = exit_scope();
    program_idp->defn.info.routine.code_segment = create_code_segment();
    analyze_block(program_idp->defn.info.routine.code_segment);

    if_token_get_else_error(PERIOD, MISSING_PERIOD);

    /*
    --  Look for the end of file.
    */
    while (token != END_OF_FILE) {
        error(UNEXPECTED_TOKEN);
        get_token();
    }

    quit_scanner();
    free(code_buffer);

    /*
    --  Print the parser's summary.
    */
    print_line("\n");
    print_line("\n");
    sprintf(buffer, "%20d Source lines.\n", line_number);
    print_line(buffer);
    sprintf(buffer, "%20d Source errors.\n", error_count);
    print_line(buffer);

    if (error_count > 0) exit(-SYNTAX_ERROR);
    else                 printf("%c\n", FORM_FEED_CHAR);

    /*
    --              EXECUTE THE PROGRAM
    --
    --
    --  Allocate the runtime stack.
    */
    stack = alloc_array(STACK_ITEM, MAX_STACK_SIZE);
    stack_frame_basep = tos = stack;

    /*
    --  Initialize the program's stack frame.
    */
    level = 1;
    stack_frame_basep = tos + 1;
    push_integer(0);         /* function return value */
    push_address(NULL);      /* static link */
    push_address(NULL);      /* dynamic link */
    push_address(NULL);      /* return address */

    /*
    --  Initialize the debugger.
    */
    init_debugger();

    /*
    --  Go!
    */
    execute(program_idp);

    free(stack);
    printf("\n\nSuccessful completion.  %ld statements executed.\n\n",
           exec_stmt_count);
```

```
    exit(0);
}

/*------------------------------------------------------*/
/*  program_header      Process a program header:       */
/*                                                       */
/*                      PROGRAM <id> ( <id-list> )       */
/*                                                       */
/*                      Return a pointer to the program id */
/*                      node.                            */
/*------------------------------------------------------*/

TOKEN_CODE follow_prog_id_list[] = {LPAREN, SEMICOLON,
                                    END_OF_FILE, 0};

TOKEN_CODE follow_parms_list[]   = {RPAREN, SEMICOLON,
                                    END_OF_FILE, 0};

    SYMTAB_NODE_PTR
program_header()

{
    SYMTAB_NODE_PTR program_idp;        /* program id */
    SYMTAB_NODE_PTR parm_idp;           /* parm id */
    SYMTAB_NODE_PTR prev_parm_idp = NULL;

    if_token_get_else_error(PROGRAM, MISSING_PROGRAM);

    if (token == IDENTIFIER) {
        search_and_enter_local_symtab(program_idp);
        program_idp->defn.key = PROG_DEFN;
        program_idp->defn.info.routine.key = DECLARED;
        program_idp->defn.info.routine.parm_count = 0;
        program_idp->defn.info.routine.total_parm_size = 0;
        program_idp->defn.info.routine.total_local_size = 0;
        program_idp->typep = &dummy_type;
        program_idp->label_index = 0;
        get_token();
    }
    else error(MISSING_IDENTIFIER);

    /*
    -- Error synchronization:  Should be ( or ;
    */
    synchronize(follow_prog_id_list,
                declaration_start_list, statement_start_list);

    enter_scope(NULL);

    /*
    -- Program parameters.
    */
    if (token == LPAREN) {
        /*
        -- <id-list>
        */
        do {
            get_token();
            if (token == IDENTIFIER) {
                search_and_enter_local_symtab(parm_idp);
                parm_idp->defn.key = VARPARM_DEFN;
                parm_idp->typep = &dummy_type;
                get_token();

                /*
                -- Link program parm ids together.
                */
```

```
                if (prev_parm_idp == NULL)
                    program_idp->defn.info.routine.parms =
                                   prev_parm_idp = parm_idp;
                else {
                    prev_parm_idp->next = parm_idp;
                    prev_parm_idp = parm_idp;
                }
            }
            else error(MISSING_IDENTIFIER);
        } while (token == COMMA);

        /*
        -- Error synchronization:  Should be )
        */
        synchronize(follow_parms_list,
                    declaration_start_list, statement_start_list);
        if_token_get_else_error(RPAREN, MISSING_RPAREN);
    }
    else program_idp->defn.info.routine.parms = NULL;

    return(program_idp);
}

/*------------------------------------------------------*/
/*  routine           Call the appropriate routine to process */
/*                    a procedure or function definition:     */
/*                                                             */
/*                    <routine-header> ; <block>              */
/*------------------------------------------------------*/

routine()

{
    SYMTAB_NODE_PTR rtn_idp;    /* routine id */

    rtn_idp = (token == PROCEDURE) ? procedure_header()
                                   : function_header();

    /*
    -- Error synchronization:  Should be ;
    */
    synchronize(follow_header_list,
                declaration_start_list, statement_start_list);
    if_token_get(SEMICOLON);
    else if (token_in(declaration_start_list) ||
             token_in(statement_start_list))
        error(MISSING_SEMICOLON);

    /*
    -- <block> or FORWARD.
    */
    if (strcmp(word_string, "forward") != 0) {
        rtn_idp->defn.info.routine.key = DECLARED;
        analyze_routine_header(rtn_idp);

        rtn_idp->defn.info.routine.locals = NULL;
        block(rtn_idp);

        rtn_idp->defn.info.routine.code_segment = create_code_segment();
        analyze_block(rtn_idp->defn.info.routine.code_segment);
    }
    else {
        get_token();
        rtn_idp->defn.info.routine.key = FORWARD;
        analyze_routine_header(rtn_idp);
    }

    rtn_idp->defn.info.routine.local_symtab = exit_scope();
```

```
}
/*------------------------------------------------------------*/
/*  procedure_header    Process a procedure header:           */
/*                                                            */
/*                          PROCEDURE <id>                    */
/*                                                            */
/*                      or:                                   */
/*                                                            */
/*                          PROCEDURE <id> ( <parm-list> )    */
/*                                                            */
/*                      Return a pointer to the procedure id  */
/*                      node.                                  */
/*------------------------------------------------------------*/

TOKEN_CODE follow_proc_id_list[] = {LPAREN, SEMICOLON,
                                    END_OF_FILE, 0};

    SYMTAB_NODE_PTR
procedure_header()

{
    SYMTAB_NODE_PTR proc_idp;          /* procedure id */
    SYMTAB_NODE_PTR parm_listp;        /* formal parm list */
    int             parm_count;
    int             total_parm_size;
    BOOLEAN         forward_flag = FALSE;   /* TRUE iff forwarded */

    get_token();

    /*
    -- If the procedure identifier has already been
    -- declared in this scope, it must be a forward.
    */
    if (token == IDENTIFIER) {
        search_local_symtab(proc_idp);
        if (proc_idp == NULL) {
            enter_local_symtab(proc_idp);
            proc_idp->defn.key = PROC_DEFN;
            proc_idp->defn.info.routine.total_local_size = 0;
            proc_idp->typep = &dummy_type;
            proc_idp->label_index = 0;
        }
        else if ((proc_idp->defn.key == PROC_DEFN) &&
                 (proc_idp->defn.info.routine.key == FORWARD))
            forward_flag = TRUE;
        else error(REDEFINED_IDENTIFIER);

        get_token();
    }
    else error(MISSING_IDENTIFIER);

    /*
    -- Error synchronization:  Should be ( or ;
    */
    synchronize(follow_proc_id_list,
                declaration_start_list, statement_start_list);

    enter_scope(NULL);

    /*
    -- Optional formal parameters.  If there was a forward,
    -- there must not be any parameters here (but parse them
    -- anyway for error recovery).
    */
    if (token == LPAREN) {
        parm_listp = formal_parm_list(&parm_count, &total_parm_size);
```

```
        if (forward_flag) error(ALREADY_FORWARDED);
        else {
            proc_idp->defn.info.routine.parm_count = parm_count;
            proc_idp->defn.info.routine.total_parm_size =
                                        total_parm_size;
            proc_idp->defn.info.routine.parms = parm_listp;
        }
    }
    else if (!forward_flag) {
        proc_idp->defn.info.routine.parm_count = 0;
        proc_idp->defn.info.routine.total_parm_size = 0;
        proc_idp->defn.info.routine.parms = NULL;
    }

    proc_idp->typep = NULL;
    return(proc_idp);
}

/*------------------------------------------------------------*/
/*  function_header    Process a function header:             */
/*                                                            */
/*                        FUNCTION <id> : <type-id>           */
/*                                                            */
/*                    or:                                     */
/*                                                            */
/*                        FUNCTION <id> ( <parm-list> )       */
/*                                     : <type-id>            */
/*                                                            */
/*                    Return a pointer to the function id     */
/*                    node.                                   */
/*------------------------------------------------------------*/

TOKEN_CODE follow_func_id_list[] = {LPAREN, COLON, SEMICOLON,
                                    END_OF_FILE, 0};

    SYMTAB_NODE_PTR
function_header()

{
    SYMTAB_NODE_PTR func_idp, type_idp;    /* func and type ids */
    SYMTAB_NODE_PTR parm_listp;            /* formal parm list */
    int             parm_count;
    int             total_parm_size;
    BOOLEAN         forward_flag = FALSE;   /* TRUE iff forwarded */

    get_token();

    /*
    -- If the function identifier has already been
    -- declared in this scope, it must be a forward.
    */
    if (token == IDENTIFIER) {
        search_local_symtab(func_idp);
        if (func_idp == NULL) {
            enter_local_symtab(func_idp);
            func_idp->defn.key = FUNC_DEFN;
            func_idp->defn.info.routine.total_local_size = 0;
            func_idp->typep = &dummy_type;
            func_idp->label_index = 0;
        }
        else if ((func_idp->defn.key == FUNC_DEFN) &&
                 (func_idp->defn.info.routine.key == FORWARD))
            forward_flag = TRUE;
        else error(REDEFINED_IDENTIFIER);

        get_token();
    }
```

```
    else error(MISSING_IDENTIFIER);

    /*
    -- Error synchronization:  Should be ( or : or ;
    */
    synchronize(follow_func_id_list,
                declaration_start_list, statement_start_list);

    enter_scope(NULL);

    /*
    -- Optional formal parameters.  If there was a forward,
    -- there must not be any parameters here (but parse them
    -- anyway for error recovery).
    */
    if (token == LPAREN) {
        parm_listp = formal_parm_list(&parm_count, &total_parm_size);

        if (forward_flag) error(ALREADY_FORWARDED);
        else {
            func_idp->defn.info.routine.parm_count = parm_count;
            func_idp->defn.info.routine.total_parm_size =
                                            total_parm_size;
            func_idp->defn.info.routine.parms = parm_listp;
        }
    }
    else if (!forward_flag) {
        func_idp->defn.info.routine.parm_count = 0;
        func_idp->defn.info.routine.total_parm_size = 0;
        func_idp->defn.info.routine.parms = NULL;
    }

    /*
    -- Function type.  If there was a forward,
    -- there must not be a type here (but parse it
    -- anyway for error recovery).
    */
    if (!forward_flag || (token == COLON)) {
        if_token_get_else_error(COLON, MISSING_COLON);

        if (token == IDENTIFIER) {
            search_and_find_all_symtab(type_idp);
            if (type_idp->defn.key != TYPE_DEFN) error(INVALID_TYPE);
            if (!forward_flag) func_idp->typep = type_idp->typep;
            get_token();
        }
        else {
            error(MISSING_IDENTIFIER);
            func_idp->typep = &dummy_type;
        }

        if (forward_flag) error(ALREADY_FORWARDED);
    }

    return(func_idp);
}

/*-----------------------------------------------------------*/
/*  formal_parm_list    Process a formal parameter list:     */
/*                                                           */
/*                         ( VAR <id-list> : <type> ;        */
/*                           <id-list> : <type> ;            */
/*                              ... )                        */
/*                                                           */
/*                         Return a pointer to the head of the */
/*                         parameter id list.                */
/*-----------------------------------------------------------*/
```

```
    SYMTAB_NODE_PTR
formal_parm_list(countp, total_sizep)

    int *countp;        /* ptr to count of parameters */
    int *total_sizep;   /* ptr to total byte size of parameters */

{
    SYMTAB_NODE_PTR parm_idp, first_idp, last_idp;   /* parm ids */
    SYMTAB_NODE_PTR prev_last_idp = NULL;     /* last id of list */
    SYMTAB_NODE_PTR parm_listp = NULL;        /* parm list */
    SYMTAB_NODE_PTR type_idp;                 /* type id */
    TYPE_STRUCT_PTR parm_tp;                  /* parm type */
    DEFN_KEY        parm_defn;                /* parm definition */
    int             parm_count = 0;           /* count of parms */
    int             parm_offset = STACK_FRAME_HEADER_SIZE;

    get_token();

    /*
    -- Loop to process parameter declarations separated by ;
    */
    while ((token == IDENTIFIER) || (token == VAR)) {
        first_idp = NULL;

        /*
        -- VAR parms?
        */
        if (token == VAR) {
            parm_defn = VARPARM_DEFN;
            get_token();
        }
        else parm_defn = VALPARM_DEFN;

        /*
        -- <id list>
        */
        while (token == IDENTIFIER) {
            search_and_enter_local_symtab(parm_idp);
            parm_idp->defn.key   = parm_defn;
            parm_idp->label_index = 0;
            ++parm_count;

            if (parm_listp == NULL) parm_listp = parm_idp;

            /*
            -- Link parm ids together.
            */
            if (first_idp == NULL)
                first_idp = last_idp = parm_idp;
            else {
                last_idp->next = parm_idp;
                last_idp = parm_idp;
            }

            get_token();
            if_token_get(COMMA);
        }

        if_token_get_else_error(COLON, MISSING_COLON);

        if (token == IDENTIFIER) {
            search_and_find_all_symtab(type_idp);
            if (type_idp->defn.key != TYPE_DEFN) error(INVALID_TYPE);
            parm_tp = type_idp->typep;
            get_token();
        }
        else {
```

```
                error(MISSING_IDENTIFIER);
                parm_tp = &dummy_type;
        }

        /*
        -- Assign the offset and the type to all parm ids
        -- in the sublist.
        */
        for (parm_idp = first_idp;
             parm_idp != NULL;
             parm_idp = parm_idp->next) {
            parm_idp->typep = parm_tp;
            parm_idp->defn.info.data.offset = parm_offset++;
        }

        /*
        -- Link this list to the list of all parm ids.
        */
        if (prev_last_idp != NULL) prev_last_idp->next = first_idp;
        prev_last_idp = last_idp;

        /*
        -- Error synchronization:  Should be ; or )
        */
        synchronize(follow_parms_list, NULL, NULL);
        if_token_get(SEMICOLON);
    }

    if_token_get_else_error(RPAREN, MISSING_RPAREN);
    *countp = parm_count;
    *total_sizep = parm_offset - STACK_FRAME_HEADER_SIZE;

    return(parm_listp);
}

/*----------------------------------------------------------*/
/* routine_call          Process a call to a declared or    */
/*                       a standard procedure or function.  */
/*                       Return a pointer to the type       */
/*                       structure of the call.             */
/*----------------------------------------------------------*/

    TYPE_STRUCT_PTR
routine_call(rtn_idp, parm_check_flag)

    SYMTAB_NODE_PTR rtn_idp;             /* routine id */
    BOOLEAN         parm_check_flag;     /* if TRUE check parms */

{
    TYPE_STRUCT_PTR declared_routine_call(), standard_routine_call();

    if ((rtn_idp->defn.info.routine.key == DECLARED) ||
        (rtn_idp->defn.info.routine.key == FORWARD) ||
        !parm_check_flag)
        return(declared_routine_call(rtn_idp, parm_check_flag));
    else
        return(standard_routine_call(rtn_idp));
}

/*----------------------------------------------------------*/
/* declared_routine_call  Process a call to a declared      */
/*                        procedure or function:            */
/*                                                          */
/*                             <id>                         */
/*                                                          */
/*                        or:                               */
/*                                                          */
/*                             <id> ( <parm-list> )         */
```

```
/*                                                          */
/*              The actual parameters are checked           */
/*              against the formal parameters for           */
/*              type and number.  Return a pointer          */
/*              to the type structure of the call.          */
/*----------------------------------------------------------*/

    TYPE_STRUCT_PTR
declared_routine_call(rtn_idp, parm_check_flag)

    SYMTAB_NODE_PTR rtn_idp;             /* routine id */
    BOOLEAN         parm_check_flag;     /* if TRUE check parms */

{
    actual_parm_list(rtn_idp, parm_check_flag);
    return(rtn_idp->defn.key == PROC_DEFN ? NULL : rtn_idp->typep);
}

/*----------------------------------------------------------*/
/* actual_parm_list    Process an actual parameter list:    */
/*                                                          */
/*                        ( <expr-list> )                   */
/*----------------------------------------------------------*/

TOKEN_CODE follow_parm_list[] = {COMMA, RPAREN, 0};

actual_parm_list(rtn_idp, parm_check_flag)

    SYMTAB_NODE_PTR rtn_idp;             /* routine id */
    BOOLEAN         parm_check_flag;     /* if TRUE check parms */

{
    SYMTAB_NODE_PTR formal_parm_idp;
    DEFN_KEY        formal_parm_defn;
    TYPE_STRUCT_PTR formal_parm_tp, actual_parm_tp;

    if (parm_check_flag)
        formal_parm_idp = rtn_idp->defn.info.routine.parms;

    if (token == LPAREN) {
        /*
        -- Loop to process actual parameter expressions.
        */
        do {
            /*
            -- Obtain info about the corresponding formal parm.
            */
            if (parm_check_flag && (formal_parm_idp != NULL)) {
                formal_parm_defn = formal_parm_idp->defn.key;
                formal_parm_tp   = formal_parm_idp->typep;
            }

            get_token();

            /*
            -- Formal value parm:  Actual parm's type must be
            --                     assignment compatible with
            --                     formal parm's type.  Actual
            --                     parm can be an expression.
            */
            if ((formal_parm_idp == NULL) ||
                (formal_parm_defn == VALPARM_DEFN) ||
                !parm_check_flag) {
                actual_parm_tp = expression();
                if (parm_check_flag && (formal_parm_idp != NULL) &&
                    (! is_assign_type_compatible(formal_parm_tp,
                                                 actual_parm_tp)))
```

```
            error(INCOMPATIBLE_TYPES);                          } while (token == COMMA);
    }
                                                                if_token_get_else_error(RPAREN, MISSING_RPAREN);
    /*                                                      }
    -- Formal VAR parm:  Actual parm's type must be the same
    --                   as formal parm type.  Actual parm     /*
    --                   must be a variable.                    -- Check if there are fewer actual parms than formal parms.
    */                                                          */
    else  /* formal_parm_defn == VARPARM_DEFN */  {            if (parm_check_flag && (formal_parm_idp != NULL))
        if (token == IDENTIFIER) {                                  error(WRONG_NUMBER_OF_PARMS);
            SYMTAB_NODE_PTR idp;                            }

            search_and_find_all_symtab(idp);
            actual_parm_tp = variable(idp, VARPARM_USE);   /*------------------------------------------------------------*/
                                                           /* block           Process a block, which consists of      */
            if (formal_parm_tp != actual_parm_tp)          /*                 declarations followed by a compound     */
                error(INCOMPATIBLE_TYPES);                 /*                 statement.                              */
        }                                                  /*------------------------------------------------------------*/
        else {
            /*                                             TOKEN_CODE follow_decls_list[] = {SEMICOLON, BEGIN, END_OF_FILE, 0};
            -- Not a variable:  Parse an expression anyway
            --                  for error recovery.        block(rtn_idp)
            */
            actual_parm_tp = expression();                     SYMTAB_NODE_PTR rtn_idp;      /* id of program or routine */
            error(INVALID_VAR_PARM);
        }                                                  {
    }
                                                               extern BOOLEAN block_flag;
    /*
    -- Check if there are more actual parms                     declarations(rtn_idp);
    -- than formal parms.
    */                                                         /*
    if (parm_check_flag) {                                      -- Error synchronization:  Should be ;
        if (formal_parm_idp == NULL)                            */
            error(WRONG_NUMBER_OF_PARMS);                       synchronize(follow_decls_list, NULL, NULL);
        else formal_parm_idp = formal_parm_idp->next;           if (token != BEGIN) error(MISSING_BEGIN);
    }
                                                               crunch_token();
    /*
    -- Error synchronization:  Should be , or )                 block_flag = TRUE;
    */                                                         compound_statement();
    synchronize(follow_parm_list, statement_end_list, NULL);    block_flag = FALSE;

}                                                          }
```

FIGURE A-3   standard.c

```
/****************************************************************/     #include "symtab.h"
/*                                                    */              #include "parser.h"
/*      S T A N D A R D   R O U T I N E   P A R S E R   */
/*                                                    */              #define DEFAULT_NUMERIC_FIELD_WIDTH    10
/*      Parsing routines for calls to standard procedures and */      #define DEFAULT_PRECISION               2
/*      functions.                                    */
/*                                                    */              /*------------------------------------------------------------*/
/*      FILE:      standard.c                         */              /* Externals                                                  */
/*                                                    */              /*------------------------------------------------------------*/
/*      MODULE:    parser                             */
/*                                                    */              extern TOKEN_CODE       token;
/****************************************************************/     extern char             word_string[];
                                                                      extern SYMTAB_NODE_PTR  symtab_display[];
#include <stdio.h>                                                    extern int              level;
#include "common.h"                                                   extern TYPE_STRUCT      dummy_type;
#include "error.h"
#include "scanner.h"                                                  extern TYPE_STRUCT_PTR  integer_typep, real_typep,
```

```
                        boolean_typep, char_typep;

extern TOKEN_CODE      follow_parm_list[];
extern TOKEN_CODE      statement_end_list[];

/*------------------------------------------------------------*/
/* Forwards                                                   */
/*------------------------------------------------------------*/

TYPE_STRUCT_PTR eof_eoln(), abs_sqr(),
                arctan_cos_exp_ln_sin_sqrt(),
                pred_succ(), chr(), odd(), ord(),
                round_trunc();

/*------------------------------------------------------------*/
/* standard_routine_call   Process a call to a standard       */
/*                         procedure or function.  Return a   */
/*                         pointer to the type structure of   */
/*                         the call.                          */
/*------------------------------------------------------------*/

    TYPE_STRUCT_PTR
standard_routine_call(rtn_idp)

    SYMTAB_NODE_PTR rtn_idp;          /* routine id */

{
    switch (rtn_idp->defn.info.routine.key) {

        case READ:
        case READLN:    read_readln(rtn_idp);        return(NULL);

        case WRITE:
        case WRITELN:   write_writeln(rtn_idp);      return(NULL);

        case EOFF:
        case EOLN:      return(eof_eoln(rtn_idp));

        case ABS:
        case SQR:       return(abs_sqr());

        case ARCTAN:
        case COS:
        case EXP:
        case LN:
        case SIN:
        case SQRT:      return(arctan_cos_exp_ln_sin_sqrt());

        case PRED:
        case SUCC:      return(pred_succ());

        case CHR:       return(chr());
        case ODD:       return(odd());
        case ORD:       return(ord());

        case ROUND:
        case TRUNC:     return(round_trunc());
    }
}

/*------------------------------------------------------------*/
/* read_readln             Process a call to read or readln.  */
/*------------------------------------------------------------*/

read_readln(rtn_idp)

    SYMTAB_NODE_PTR rtn_idp;          /* routine id */
```

```
{
    TYPE_STRUCT_PTR actual_parm_tp;      /* actual parm type */

    /*
    -- Parameters are optional for readln.
    */
    if (token == LPAREN) {
        /*
        -- <id-list>
        */
        do {
            get_token();

            /*
            -- Actual parms must be variables (but parse
            -- an expression anyway for error recovery).
            */
            if (token == IDENTIFIER) {
                SYMTAB_NODE_PTR idp;

                search_and_find_all_symtab(idp);
                actual_parm_tp = base_type(variable(idp,
                                                VARPARM_USE));

                if (actual_parm_tp->form != SCALAR_FORM)
                    error(INCOMPATIBLE_TYPES);
            }
            else {
                actual_parm_tp = expression();
                error(INVALID_VAR_PARM);
            }

            /*
            -- Error synchronization:  Should be , or )
            */
            synchronize(follow_parm_list, statement_end_list, NULL);

        } while (token == COMMA);

        if_token_get_else_error(RPAREN, MISSING_RPAREN);
    }
    else if (rtn_idp->defn.info.routine.key == READ)
        error(WRONG_NUMBER_OF_PARMS);
}

/*------------------------------------------------------------*/
/* write_writeln          Process a call to write or writeln. */
/*                        Each actual parameter can be:       */
/*                                                            */
/*                              <expr>                        */
/*                                                            */
/*                        or:                                 */
/*                                                            */
/*                              <epxr> : <expr>               */
/*                                                            */
/*                        or:                                 */
/*                                                            */
/*                              <expr> : <expr> : <expr>      */
/*------------------------------------------------------------*/

write_writeln(rtn_idp)

    SYMTAB_NODE_PTR rtn_idp;          /* routine id */

{
    TYPE_STRUCT_PTR actual_parm_tp;      /* actual parm type */
    TYPE_STRUCT_PTR field_width_tp, precision_tp;
```

```
/*
-- Parameters are optional for writeln.
*/
if (token == LPAREN) {
    do {
        /*
        -- Value <expr>
        */
        get_token();
        actual_parm_tp = base_type(expression());

        if ((actual_parm_tp->form != SCALAR_FORM) &&
            (actual_parm_tp != boolean_typep) &&
            ((actual_parm_tp->form != ARRAY_FORM) ||
             (actual_parm_tp->info.array.elmt_typep !=
                                            char_typep)))
            error(INVALID_EXPRESSION);

        /*
        -- Optional field width <expr>
        */
        if (token == COLON) {
            get_token();
            field_width_tp = base_type(expression());

            if (field_width_tp != integer_typep)
                error(INCOMPATIBLE_TYPES);

            /*
            -- Optional precision <expr>
            */
            if (token == COLON) {
                get_token();
                precision_tp = base_type(expression());

                if (precision_tp != integer_typep)
                    error(INCOMPATIBLE_TYPES);
            }
        }

        /*
        -- Error synchronization:  Should be , or )
        */
        synchronize(follow_parm_list, statement_end_list, NULL);

    } while (token == COMMA);

    if_token_get_else_error(RPAREN, MISSING_RPAREN);
}
else if (rtn_idp->defn.info.routine.key == WRITE)
    error(WRONG_NUMBER_OF_PARMS);
}

/*-------------------------------------------------------------*/
/*  eof_eoln              Process a call to eof or to eoln.    */
/*                        No parameters => boolean result.     */
/*-------------------------------------------------------------*/

    TYPE_STRUCT_PTR
eof_eoln(rtn_idp)

    SYMTAB_NODE_PTR rtn_idp;         /* routine id */

{
    if (token == LPAREN) {
        error(WRONG_NUMBER_OF_PARMS);
        actual_parm_list(rtn_idp, FALSE);
```

```
    }

    return(boolean_typep);
}

/*-------------------------------------------------------------*/
/*  abs_sqr               Process a call to abs or to sqr.     */
/*                        integer parm => integer result       */
/*                        real parm   => real result           */
/*-------------------------------------------------------------*/

    TYPE_STRUCT_PTR
abs_sqr()

{
    TYPE_STRUCT_PTR parm_tp;           /* actual parameter type */
    TYPE_STRUCT_PTR result_tp;         /* result type */

    if (token == LPAREN) {
        get_token();
        parm_tp = base_type(expression());

        if ((parm_tp != integer_typep) && (parm_tp != real_typep)) {
            error(INCOMPATIBLE_TYPES);
            result_tp = real_typep;
        }
        else result_tp = parm_tp;

        if_token_get_else_error(RPAREN, MISSING_RPAREN);
    }
    else error(WRONG_NUMBER_OF_PARMS);

    return(result_tp);
}

/*-------------------------------------------------------------*/
/*  arctan_cos_exp_ln_sin_sqrt Process a call to arctan, cos,  */
/*                        exp, ln, sin, or sqrt.               */
/*                        integer parm => real result          */
/*                        real_parm   => real result           */
/*-------------------------------------------------------------*/

    TYPE_STRUCT_PTR
arctan_cos_exp_ln_sin_sqrt()

{
    TYPE_STRUCT_PTR parm_tp;           /* actual parameter type */

    if (token == LPAREN) {
        get_token();
        parm_tp = base_type(expression());

        if ((parm_tp != integer_typep) && (parm_tp != real_typep))
            error(INCOMPATIBLE_TYPES);

        if_token_get_else_error(RPAREN, MISSING_RPAREN);
    }
    else error(WRONG_NUMBER_OF_PARMS);

    return(real_typep);
}

/*-------------------------------------------------------------*/
/*  pred_succ             Process a call to pred or succ.      */
/*                        integer parm => integer result       */
/*                        enum parm   => enum result           */
/*-------------------------------------------------------------*/
```

```
    TYPE_STRUCT_PTR
pred_succ()

{
    TYPE_STRUCT_PTR parm_tp;              /* actual parameter type */
    TYPE_STRUCT_PTR result_tp;           /* result type */

    if (token == LPAREN) {
        get_token();
        parm_tp = base_type(expression());

        if ((parm_tp != integer_typep) &&
            (parm_tp->form != ENUM_FORM)) {
            error(INCOMPATIBLE_TYPES);
            result_tp = integer_typep;
        }
        else result_tp = parm_tp;

        if_token_get_else_error(RPAREN, MISSING_RPAREN);
    }
    else error(WRONG_NUMBER_OF_PARMS);

    return(result_tp);
}

/*----------------------------------------------------------*/
/* chr                      Process a call to chr.          */
/*                          integer parm => character result */
/*----------------------------------------------------------*/

    TYPE_STRUCT_PTR
chr()

{
    TYPE_STRUCT_PTR parm_tp;              /* actual parameter type */

    if (token == LPAREN) {
        get_token();
        parm_tp = base_type(expression());

        if (parm_tp != integer_typep) error(INCOMPATIBLE_TYPES);
        if_token_get_else_error(RPAREN, MISSING_RPAREN);
    }
    else error(WRONG_NUMBER_OF_PARMS);

    return(char_typep);
}

/*----------------------------------------------------------*/
/* odd                      Process a call to odd.          */
/*                          integer parm => boolean result  */
/*----------------------------------------------------------*/

    TYPE_STRUCT_PTR
odd()

{
    TYPE_STRUCT_PTR parm_tp;              /* actual parameter type */
```

```
    if (token == LPAREN) {
        get_token();
        parm_tp = base_type(expression());

        if (parm_tp != integer_typep) error(INCOMPATIBLE_TYPES);
        if_token_get_else_error(RPAREN, MISSING_RPAREN);
    }
    else error(WRONG_NUMBER_OF_PARMS);

    return(boolean_typep);
}

/*----------------------------------------------------------*/
/* ord                      Process a call to ord.          */
/*                          enumeration parm => integer result */
/*----------------------------------------------------------*/

    TYPE_STRUCT_PTR
ord()

{
    TYPE_STRUCT_PTR parm_tp;              /* actual parameter type */

    if (token == LPAREN) {
        get_token();
        parm_tp = base_type(expression());

        if (parm_tp->form != ENUM_FORM) error(INCOMPATIBLE_TYPES);
        if_token_get_else_error(RPAREN, MISSING_RPAREN);
    }
    else error(WRONG_NUMBER_OF_PARMS);

    return(integer_typep);
}

/*----------------------------------------------------------*/
/* round_trunc              Process a call to round or trunc. */
/*                          real parm => integer result     */
/*----------------------------------------------------------*/

    TYPE_STRUCT_PTR
round_trunc()

{
    TYPE_STRUCT_PTR parm_tp;              /* actual parameter type */

    if (token == LPAREN) {
        get_token();
        parm_tp = base_type(expression());

        if (parm_tp != real_typep) error(INCOMPATIBLE_TYPES);
        if_token_get_else_error(RPAREN, MISSING_RPAREN);
    }
    else error(WRONG_NUMBER_OF_PARMS);

    return(integer_typep);
}
```

FIGURE A-4   decl.c

```
/****************************************************************/
/*                                                            */
/*      D E C L A R A T I O N   P A R S E R                   */
/*                                                            */
/*      Parsing routines for delarations.                     */
/*                                                            */
/*      FILE:     decl.c                                       */
/*                                                            */
/*      MODULE:   parser                                       */
/*                                                            */
/****************************************************************/

#include <stdio.h>
#include "common.h"
#include "error.h"
#include "scanner.h"
#include "symtab.h"
#include "parser.h"

/*------------------------------------------------------------*/
/* Externals                                                  */
/*------------------------------------------------------------*/

extern TOKEN_CODE       token;
extern char             word_string[];
extern LITERAL          literal;

extern SYMTAB_NODE_PTR  symtab_display[];
extern int              level;

extern TYPE_STRUCT_PTR  integer_typep, real_typep,
                        boolean_typep, char_typep;

extern TYPE_STRUCT      dummy_type;

extern TOKEN_CODE       declaration_start_list[],
                        statement_start_list[];

/*------------------------------------------------------------*/
/* Forwards                                                   */
/*------------------------------------------------------------*/

TYPE_STRUCT_PTR do_type(),
                identifier_type(), enumeration_type(),
                subrange_type(), array_type(), record_type();

/*------------------------------------------------------------*/
/* declarations      Call the routines to process constant   */
/*                   definitions, type definitions, variable */
/*                   declarations, procedure definitions,    */
/*                   and function definitions.               */
/*------------------------------------------------------------*/

TOKEN_CODE follow_routine_list[] = {SEMICOLON, END_OF_FILE, 0};

declarations(rtn_idp)

    SYMTAB_NODE_PTR rtn_idp;    /* id of program or routine */

{
    if (token == CONST) {
        get_token();
        const_definitions();
    }
```

```
    if (token == TYPE) {
        get_token();
        type_definitions();
    }

    if (token == VAR) {
        get_token();
        var_declarations(rtn_idp);
    }

    /*
    -- Loop to process routine (procedure and function)
    -- definitions.
    */
    while ((token == PROCEDURE) || (token == FUNCTION)) {
        routine();

        /*
        -- Error synchronization:  Should be ;
        */
        synchronize(follow_routine_list,
                    declaration_start_list, statement_start_list);
        if_token_get(SEMICOLON);
        else if (token_in(declaration_start_list) ||
                 token_in(statement_start_list))
            error(MISSING_SEMICOLON);
    }
}
```

```
              /************************/
              /*                      */
              /*       Constants      */
              /*                      */
              /************************/

/*------------------------------------------------------------*/
/* const_definitions   Process constant definitions:         */
/*                                                            */
/*                     <id> = <constant>                      */
/*------------------------------------------------------------*/

TOKEN_CODE follow_declaration_list[] = {SEMICOLON, IDENTIFIER,
                                        END_OF_FILE, 0};

const_definitions()

{
    SYMTAB_NODE_PTR const_idp;         /* constant id */

    /*
    -- Loop to process definitions separated by semicolons.
    */
    while (token == IDENTIFIER) {
        search_and_enter_local_symtab(const_idp);
        const_idp->defn.key = CONST_DEFN;

        get_token();
        if_token_get_else_error(EQUAL, MISSING_EQUAL);

        /*
        -- Process the constant.
        */
        do_const(const_idp);
        analyze_const_defn(const_idp);
```

```
    /*
    -- Error synchronization:  Should be ;
    */
    synchronize(follow_declaration_list,
              declaration_start_list, statement_start_list);
    if_token_get(SEMICOLON);
    else if (token_in(declaration_start_list) ||
            token_in(statement_start_list))
        error(MISSING_SEMICOLON);
    }
}

/*------------------------------------------------------------*/
/*  do_const              Process the constant of a constant  */
/*                        definition.                         */
/*------------------------------------------------------------*/

do_const(const_idp)

    SYMTAB_NODE_PTR const_idp;          /* constant id */

{
    TOKEN_CODE      sign     = PLUS;    /* unary + or - sign */
    BOOLEAN         saw_sign = FALSE;   /* TRUE iff unary sign */

    /*
    -- Unary + or - sign.
    */
    if ((token == PLUS) || (token == MINUS)) {
        sign     = token;
        saw_sign = TRUE;
        get_token();
    }

    /*
    -- Numeric constant:  Integer or real type.
    */
    if (token == NUMBER) {
        if (literal.type == INTEGER_LIT) {
            const_idp->defn.info.constant.value.integer =
                sign == PLUS ?  literal.value.integer
                             : -literal.value.integer;
            const_idp->typep = integer_typep;
        }
        else {
            const_idp->defn.info.constant.value.real =
                sign == PLUS ?  literal.value.real
                             : -literal.value.real;
            const_idp->typep = real_typep;
        }
    }

    /*
    -- Identifier constant:  Integer, real, character, enumeration,
    --                       or string (character array) type.
    */
    else if (token == IDENTIFIER) {
        SYMTAB_NODE_PTR idp;

        search_all_symtab(idp);

        if (idp == NULL)
            error(UNDEFINED_IDENTIFIER);
        else if (idp->defn.key != CONST_DEFN)
            error(NOT_A_CONSTANT_IDENTIFIER);

        else if (idp->typep == integer_typep) {
```

```
            const_idp->defn.info.constant.value.integer =
                sign == PLUS ?  idp->defn.info.constant.value.integer
                             : -idp->defn.info.constant.value.integer;
            const_idp->typep = integer_typep;
        }
        else if (idp->typep == real_typep) {
            const_idp->defn.info.constant.value.real =
                sign == PLUS ?  idp->defn.info.constant.value.real
                             : -idp->defn.info.constant.value.real;
            const_idp->typep = real_typep;
        }
        else if (idp->typep == char_typep) {
            if (saw_sign) error(INVALID_CONSTANT);

            const_idp->defn.info.constant.value.character =
                        idp->defn.info.constant.value.character;
            const_idp->typep = char_typep;
        }
        else if (idp->typep->form == ENUM_FORM) {
            if (saw_sign) error(INVALID_CONSTANT);

            const_idp->defn.info.constant.value.integer =
                        idp->defn.info.constant.value.integer;
            const_idp->typep = idp->typep;
        }
        else if (idp->typep->form == ARRAY_FORM) {
            if (saw_sign) error(INVALID_CONSTANT);

            const_idp->defn.info.constant.value.stringp =
                        idp->defn.info.constant.value.stringp;
            const_idp->typep = idp->typep;
        }
    }

    /*
    -- String constant:  Character or string (character array) type.
    */
    else if (token == STRING) {
        if (saw_sign) error(INVALID_CONSTANT);

        if (strlen(literal.value.string) == 1) {
            const_idp->defn.info.constant.value.character =
                                    literal.value.string[0];
            const_idp->typep = char_typep;
        }
        else {
            int length = strlen(literal.value.string);

            const_idp->defn.info.constant.value.stringp =
                                    alloc_bytes(length + 1);
            strcpy(const_idp->defn.info.constant.value.stringp,
                literal.value.string);
            const_idp->typep = make_string_typep(length);
        }
    }

    else {
        const_idp->typep = &dummy_type;
        error(INVALID_CONSTANT);
    }

    get_token();


                    /***********************/
                    /*                     */
                    /*        Types        */
```

```
                   /*                    */
                   /************************/
```

```
/*-------------------------------------------------------------*/
/* type_definitions     Process type definitions:             */
/*                                                             */
/*                      <id> = <type>                          */
/*-------------------------------------------------------------*/

type_definitions()

{
    SYMTAB_NODE_PTR type_idp;            /* type id */

    /*
    -- Loop to process definitions separated by semicolons.
    */
    while (token == IDENTIFIER) {
        search_and_enter_local_symtab(type_idp);
        type_idp->defn.key = TYPE_DEFN;

        get_token();
        if_token_get_else_error(EQUAL, MISSING_EQUAL);

        /*
        -- Process the type specification.
        */
        type_idp->typep = do_type();
        if (type_idp->typep->type_idp == NULL)
            type_idp->typep->type_idp = type_idp;

        analyze_type_defn(type_idp);

        /*
        -- Error synchronization:  Should be ;
        */
        synchronize(follow_declaration_list,
                    declaration_start_list, statement_start_list);
        if_token_get(SEMICOLON);
        else if (token_in(declaration_start_list) ||
                 token_in(statement_start_list))
            error(MISSING_SEMICOLON);
    }
}

/*-------------------------------------------------------------*/
/* do_type               Process a type specification.  Call the */
/*                       functions that make a type structure   */
/*                       and return a pointer to it.            */
/*-------------------------------------------------------------*/

    TYPE_STRUCT_PTR
do_type()

{
    switch (token) {
        case IDENTIFIER: {
            SYMTAB_NODE_PTR idp;

            search_all_symtab(idp);

            if (idp == NULL) {
                error(UNDEFINED_IDENTIFIER);
                return(&dummy_type);
            }
            else if (idp->defn.key == TYPE_DEFN)
                return(identifier_type(idp));
```

```
            else if (idp->defn.key == CONST_DEFN)
                return(subrange_type(idp));
            else {
                error(NOT_A_TYPE_IDENTIFIER);
                return(&dummy_type);
            }
        }

        case LPAREN:    return(enumeration_type());
        case ARRAY:     return(array_type());
        case RECORD:    return(record_type());

        case PLUS:
        case MINUS:
        case NUMBER:
        case STRING:    return(subrange_type(NULL));

        default:        error(INVALID_TYPE);
                        return(&dummy_type);
    }
}

/*-------------------------------------------------------------*/
/* identifier_type      Process an identifier type, i.e., the  */
/*                      identifier on the right side of a type  */
/*                      equate, and return a pointer to its     */
/*                      type structure.                         */
/*-------------------------------------------------------------*/

    TYPE_STRUCT_PTR
identifier_type(idp)

    SYMTAB_NODE_PTR idp;        /* type id */

{
    TYPE_STRUCT_PTR tp = NULL;

    tp = idp->typep;
    get_token();

    return(tp);
}

/*-------------------------------------------------------------*/
/* enumeration_type     Process an enumeration type:           */
/*                                                             */
/*                      ( <id1>, <id2>, ..., <idn> )           */
/*                                                             */
/*                      Make a type structure and return a     */
/*                      pointer to it.                         */
/*-------------------------------------------------------------*/

    TYPE_STRUCT_PTR
enumeration_type()

{
    SYMTAB_NODE_PTR const_idp;          /* constant id */
    SYMTAB_NODE_PTR last_idp    = NULL; /* last constant id */
    TYPE_STRUCT_PTR tp          = alloc_struct(TYPE_STRUCT);
    int             const_value = -1;   /* constant value */

    tp->form     = ENUM_FORM;
    tp->size     = sizeof(int);
    tp->type_idp = NULL;

    get_token();

    /*
```

```
     --  Loop to process list of identifiers.
     */
     while (token == IDENTIFIER) {
         search_and_enter_local_symtab(const_idp);
         const_idp->defn.key = CONST_DEFN;
         const_idp->defn.info.constant.value.integer = ++const_value;
         const_idp->typep = tp;

         /*
         --  Link constant ids together.
         */
         if (last_idp == NULL)
             tp->info.enumeration.const_idp = last_idp = const_idp;
         else {
             last_idp->next = const_idp;
             last_idp = const_idp;
         }

         get_token();
         if_token_get(COMMA);
     }

     if_token_get_else_error(RPAREN, MISSING_RPAREN);

     tp->info.enumeration.max = const_value;
     return(tp);
}

/*------------------------------------------------------------*/
/*  subrange_type        Process a subrange type:            */
/*                                                            */
/*                           <min-const> .. <max-const>       */
/*                                                            */
/*                           Make a type structure and return a */
/*                           pointer to it.                   */
/*------------------------------------------------------------*/

TOKEN_CODE follow_min_limit_list[] = {DOTDOT, IDENTIFIER, PLUS, MINUS,
                                      NUMBER, STRING, SEMICOLON,
                                      END_OF_FILE, 0};

    TYPE_STRUCT_PTR
subrange_type(min_idp)

    SYMTAB_NODE_PTR min_idp;    /* min limit const id */

{
    TYPE_STRUCT_PTR max_typep;  /* type of max limit */
    TYPE_STRUCT_PTR tp = alloc_struct(TYPE_STRUCT);

    tp->form     = SUBRANGE_FORM;
    tp->type_idp = NULL;

    /*
    --  Minimum constant.
    */
    get_subrange_limit(min_idp,
                  &(tp->info.subrange.min),
                  &(tp->info.subrange.range_typep));

    /*
    --  Error synchronization:  Should be ..
    */
    synchronize(follow_min_limit_list, NULL, NULL);
    if_token_get(DOTDOT);
    else if (token_in(follow_min_limit_list) ||
            token_in(declaration_start_list) ||
```

```
                    token_in(statement_start_list))
             error(MISSING_DOTDOT);

    /*
    --  Maximum constant.
    */
    get_subrange_limit(NULL, &(tp->info.subrange.max), &max_typep);

    /*
    --  Check limits.
    */
    if (max_typep == tp->info.subrange.range_typep) {
        if (tp->info.subrange.min > tp->info.subrange.max)
            error(MIN_GT_MAX);
    }
    else error(INCOMPATIBLE_TYPES);

    tp->size = max_typep == char_typep ? sizeof(char) : sizeof(int);
    return(tp);
}

/*------------------------------------------------------------*/
/*  get_subrange_limit  Process the minimum and maximum limits */
/*                      of a subrange type.                    */
/*------------------------------------------------------------*/

get_subrange_limit(minmax_idp, minmaxp, typepp)

    SYMTAB_NODE_PTR minmax_idp; /* min const id */
    int            *minmaxp;    /* where to store min or max value */
    TYPE_STRUCT_PTR *typepp;     /* where to store ptr to type struct */

{
    SYMTAB_NODE_PTR idp       = minmax_idp;
    TOKEN_CODE      sign      = PLUS;    /* unary + or - sign */
    BOOLEAN         saw_sign  = FALSE;   /* TRUE iff unary sign */

    /*
    --  Unary + or - sign.
    */
    if ((token == PLUS) || (token == MINUS)) {
        sign     = token;
        saw_sign = TRUE;
        get_token();
    }

    /*
    --  Numeric limit:  Integer type only.
    */
    if (token == NUMBER) {
        if (literal.type == INTEGER_LIT) {
            *typepp  = integer_typep;
            *minmaxp = (sign == PLUS) ? literal.value.integer
                                      : -literal.value.integer;
        }
        else error(INVALID_SUBRANGE_TYPE);
    }

    /*
    --  Identifier limit:  Value must be integer or character.
    */
    else if (token == IDENTIFIER) {
        if (idp == NULL) search_all_symtab(idp);

        if (idp == NULL)
            error(UNDEFINED_IDENTIFIER);
        else if (idp->typep == real_typep)
```

```
            error(INVALID_SUBRANGE_TYPE);
        else if (idp->defn.key == CONST_DEFN) {
            *typepp  = idp->typep;
            if (idp->typep == char_typep) {
                if (saw_sign) error(INVALID_CONSTANT);
                *minmaxp = idp->defn.info.constant.value.character;
            }
            else if (idp->typep == integer_typep) {
                *minmaxp = idp->defn.info.constant.value.integer;
                if (sign == MINUS) *minmaxp = -(*minmaxp);
            }
            else /* enumeration constant */ {
                if (saw_sign) error(INVALID_CONSTANT);
                *minmaxp = idp->defn.info.constant.value.integer;
            }
        }
        else error(NOT_A_CONSTANT_IDENTIFIER);
    }

    /*
    -- String limit:  Character type only.
    */
    else if (token == STRING) {
        if (saw_sign) error(INVALID_CONSTANT);
        *typepp  = char_typep;
        *minmaxp = literal.value.string[0];

        if (strlen(literal.value.string) != 1)
            error(INVALID_SUBRANGE_TYPE);
    }

    else error(MISSING_CONSTANT);

    get_token();
}

/*------------------------------------------------------------*/
/*  array_type            Process an array type:             */
/*                                                           */
/*                          ARRAY [<index-type-list>]        */
/*                             OF <elmt-type>                 */
/*                                                           */
/*                          Make a type structure and return a */
/*                          pointer to it.                   */
/*------------------------------------------------------------*/

TOKEN_CODE follow_dimension_list[] = {COMMA, RBRACKET, OF,
                                      SEMICOLON, END_OF_FILE, 0};

TOKEN_CODE index_type_start_list[] = {IDENTIFIER, NUMBER, STRING,
                                      LPAREN, MINUS, PLUS, 0};

TOKEN_CODE follow_indexes_list[]   = {OF, IDENTIFIER, LPAREN, ARRAY,
                                      RECORD, PLUS, MINUS, NUMBER,
                                      STRING, SEMICOLON, END_OF_FILE,
                                      0};

    TYPE_STRUCT_PTR
array_type()

{
    TYPE_STRUCT_PTR tp       = alloc_struct(TYPE_STRUCT);
    TYPE_STRUCT_PTR index_tp;            /* index type */
    TYPE_STRUCT_PTR elmt_tp = tp;        /* element type */
    int array_size();

    get_token();
```

```
    if (token != LBRACKET) error(MISSING_LBRACKET);

    /*
    -- Loop to process index type list.  For each
    -- type in the list after the first, create an
    -- array element type.
    */
    do {
        get_token();

        if (token_in(index_type_start_list)) {
            elmt_tp->form      = ARRAY_FORM;
            elmt_tp->size      = 0;
            elmt_tp->type_idp  = NULL;
            elmt_tp->info.array.index_typep = index_tp = do_type();

            switch (index_tp->form) {
                case ENUM_FORM:
                    elmt_tp->info.array.elmt_count =
                                index_tp->info.enumeration.max + 1;
                    elmt_tp->info.array.min_index = 0;
                    elmt_tp->info.array.max_index =
                                index_tp->info.enumeration.max;
                    break;

                case SUBRANGE_FORM:
                    elmt_tp->info.array.elmt_count =
                                index_tp->info.subrange.max -
                                    index_tp->info.subrange.min + 1;
                    elmt_tp->info.array.min_index =
                                    index_tp->info.subrange.min;
                    elmt_tp->info.array.max_index =
                                    index_tp->info.subrange.max;
                    break;

                default:
                    elmt_tp->form      = NO_FORM;
                    elmt_tp->size      = 0;
                    elmt_tp->type_idp  = NULL;
                    elmt_tp->info.array.index_typep = &dummy_type;
                    error(INVALID_INDEX_TYPE);
                    break;
            }
        }
        else {
            elmt_tp->form      = NO_FORM;
            elmt_tp->size      = 0;
            elmt_tp->type_idp  = NULL;
            elmt_tp->info.array.index_typep = &dummy_type;
            error(INVALID_INDEX_TYPE);
        }

        /*
        -- Error synchronization:  Should be , or ]
        */
        synchronize(follow_dimension_list, NULL, NULL);

        /*
        -- Create an array element type.
        */
        if (token == COMMA) elmt_tp = elmt_tp->info.array.elmt_typep =
                                      alloc_struct(TYPE_STRUCT);
    } while (token == COMMA);

    if_token_get_else_error(RBRACKET, MISSING_RBRACKET);

    /*
```

```
        --  Error synchronization:  Should be OF
        */
        synchronize(follow_indexes_list,
                    declaration_start_list, statement_start_list);
        if_token_get_else_error(OF, MISSING_OF);

        /*
        --  Element type.
        */
        elmt_tp->info.array.elmt_typep = do_type();

        tp->size = array_size(tp);
        return(tp);
}


/*------------------------------------------------------------*/
/*  record_type        Process a record type:                 */
/*                                                            */
/*                          RECORD                             */
/*                              <id-list> : <type> ;           */
/*                              ...                             */
/*                          END                                */
/*                                                            */
/*                      Make a type structure and return a    */
/*                      pointer to it.                         */
/*------------------------------------------------------------*/

    TYPE_STRUCT_PTR
record_type()

{
    TYPE_STRUCT_PTR record_tp = alloc_struct(TYPE_STRUCT);

    record_tp->form     = RECORD_FORM;
    record_tp->type_idp = NULL;
    record_tp->info.record.field_symtab = NULL;

    get_token();
    var_or_field_declarations(NULL, record_tp, 0);

    if_token_get_else_error(END, MISSING_END);
    return(record_tp);
}


/*------------------------------------------------------------*/
/*  make_string_typep  Make a type structure for a string of  */
/*                     the given length, and return a pointer */
/*                     to it.                                  */
/*------------------------------------------------------------*/

    TYPE_STRUCT_PTR
make_string_typep(length)

    int length;                 /* string length */

{
    TYPE_STRUCT_PTR string_tp = alloc_struct(TYPE_STRUCT);
    TYPE_STRUCT_PTR index_tp  = alloc_struct(TYPE_STRUCT);

    /*
    --  Array type.
    */
    string_tp->form     = ARRAY_FORM;
    string_tp->size     = length;
    string_tp->type_idp = NULL;
    string_tp->info.array.index_typep = index_tp;
    string_tp->info.array.elmt_typep  = char_typep;
```

```
        string_tp->info.array.elmt_count  = length;

        /*
        --  Subrange index type.
        */
        index_tp->form      = SUBRANGE_FORM;
        index_tp->size      = sizeof(int);
        index_tp->type_idp = NULL;
        index_tp->info.subrange.range_typep = integer_typep;
        index_tp->info.subrange.min = 1;
        index_tp->info.subrange.max = length;

        return(string_tp);
}

/*------------------------------------------------------------*/
/*  array_size         Return the size in bytes of an array   */
/*                     type by recursively calculating the    */
/*                     size of each dimension.                 */
/*------------------------------------------------------------*/

    int
array_size(tp)

    TYPE_STRUCT_PTR tp;          /* ptr to array type structure */

{
    if (tp->info.array.elmt_typep->size == 0)
        tp->info.array.elmt_typep->size =
                        array_size(tp->info.array.elmt_typep);

    tp->size = tp->info.array.elmt_count *
               tp->info.array.elmt_typep->size;

    return(tp->size);
}

            /************************/
            /*                      */
            /*       Variables      */
            /*                      */
            /************************/

/*------------------------------------------------------------*/
/*  var_declarations   Process variable declarations:         */
/*                                                            */
/*                          <id-list> : <type>                 */
/*------------------------------------------------------------*/

var_declarations(rtn_idp)

    SYMTAB_NODE_PTR rtn_idp;     /* id of program or routine */

{
    var_or_field_declarations(rtn_idp, NULL,
                              STACK_FRAME_HEADER_SIZE
                                + rtn_idp->defn.info.routine
                                         .parm_count);
}

/*------------------------------------------------------------*/
/*  var_or_field_declarations  Process variable declarations  */
/*                             or record field definitions.   */
/*                             All ids declared with the same */
/*                             type are linked together into  */
/*                             a sublist, and all the sublists */
/*                             are then linked together.       */
/*------------------------------------------------------------*/
```

```
TOKEN_CODE follow_variables_list[] = {SEMICOLON, IDENTIFIER,
                                      END_OF_FILE, 0};

TOKEN_CODE follow_fields_list[]    = {SEMICOLON, END, IDENTIFIER,
                                      END_OF_FILE, 0};

var_or_field_declarations(rtn_idp, record_tp, offset)

    SYMTAB_NODE_PTR rtn_idp;
    TYPE_STRUCT_PTR record_tp;
    int            offset;

{
    SYMTAB_NODE_PTR idp, first_idp, last_idp;   /* variable or
                                                     field ids */
    SYMTAB_NODE_PTR prev_last_idp = NULL;       /* last id of list */
    TYPE_STRUCT_PTR tp;                          /* type */
    BOOLEAN var_flag = (rtn_idp != NULL);       /* TRUE:  variables */
                                                /* FALSE: fields */
    int size;
    int total_size = 0;

    /*
    -- Loop to process sublist, each of a type.
    */
    while (token == IDENTIFIER) {
        first_idp = NULL;

        /*
        -- Loop process each variable or field id in a sublist.
        */
        while (token == IDENTIFIER) {
            if (var_flag) {
                search_and_enter_local_symtab(idp);
                idp->defn.key = VAR_DEFN;
            }
            else {
                search_and_enter_this_symtab
                    (idp, record_tp->info.record.field_symtab);
                idp->defn.key = FIELD_DEFN;
            }
            idp->label_index = 0;

            /*
            -- Link ids together into a sublist.
            */
            if (first_idp == NULL) {
                first_idp = last_idp = idp;
                if (var_flag &&
                    (rtn_idp->defn.info.routine.locals == NULL))
                    rtn_idp->defn.info.routine.locals = idp;
            }
            else {
                last_idp->next = idp;
                last_idp = idp;
            }
```

```
            get_token();
            if_token_get(COMMA);
        }

        /*
        -- Process the sublist's type.
        */
        if_token_get_else_error(COLON, MISSING_COLON);
        tp = do_type();
        size = tp->size;

        /*
        -- Assign the offset and the type to all variable or field
        -- ids in the sublist.
        */
        for (idp = first_idp; idp != NULL; idp = idp->next) {
            idp->typep = tp;

            if (var_flag) {
                total_size += size;
                idp->defn.info.data.offset = offset++;
                analyze_var_decl(idp);
            }

            else   /* record fields */ {
                idp->defn.info.data.offset = offset;
                offset += size;
            }
        }

        /*
        -- Link this sublist to the previous sublist.
        */
        if (prev_last_idp != NULL) prev_last_idp->next = first_idp;
        prev_last_idp = last_idp;

        /*
        -- Error synchronization:  Should be ; for variable
        --                         declaration, or ; or END for
        --                         record type definition.
        */
        synchronize(var_flag ? follow_variables_list
                             : follow_fields_list,
                    declaration_start_list, statement_start_list);
        if_token_get(SEMICOLON);
        else if (var_flag && ((token_in(declaration_start_list)) ||
                              (token_in(statement_start_list))))
            error(MISSING_SEMICOLON);
    }

    if (var_flag)
        rtn_idp->defn.info.routine.total_local_size = total_size;
    else
        record_tp->size = offset;
}
```

FIGURE A-5　　　stmt.c

```
/*****************************************************************/    /*    S T A T E M E N T   P A R S E R                */
/*                                                         */    /*                                                   */
                                                                      /*    Parsing routines for statements.              */
```

```
/*                                                      */
/*      FILE:      stmt.c                               */
/*                                                      */
/*      MODULE:    parser                               */
/*                                                      */
/*****************************************************************/

#include <stdio.h>
#include "common.h"
#include "error.h"
#include "scanner.h"
#include "symtab.h"
#include "parser.h"
#include "exec.h"


/*--------------------------------------------------------------*/
/* Externals                                                    */
/*--------------------------------------------------------------*/

extern TOKEN_CODE       token;
extern char             token_string[];
extern char             word_string[];
extern LITERAL          literal;
extern TOKEN_CODE       statement_start_list[], statement_end_list[];

extern SYMTAB_NODE_PTR  symtab_display[];
extern int              level;
extern char             *code_bufferp;

extern TYPE_STRUCT_PTR  integer_typep, real_typep,
                        boolean_typep, char_typep;
extern TYPE_STRUCT      dummy_type;

/*--------------------------------------------------------------*/
/* statement           Process a statement by calling the       */
/*                     appropriate parsing routine based on      */
/*                     the statement's first token.             */
/*--------------------------------------------------------------*/

statement()

{
    if (token != BEGIN) crunch_statement_marker();

    /*
    -- Call the appropriate routine based on the first
    -- token of the statement.
    */
    switch (token) {

        case IDENTIFIER: {
            SYMTAB_NODE_PTR idp;

            /*
            -- Assignment statement or procedure call?
            */
            search_and_find_all_symtab(idp);

            if (idp->defn.key == PROC_DEFN) {
                crunch_symtab_node_ptr(idp);
                get_token();
                routine_call(idp, TRUE);
            }
            else assignment_statement(idp);

            break;
        }

        case REPEAT:    repeat_statement();    break;
        case WHILE:     while_statement();     break;
        case IF:        if_statement();        break;
        case FOR:       for_statement();       break;
        case CASE:      case_statement();      break;
        case BEGIN:     compound_statement();  break;
    }

    /*
    -- Error synchronization:  Only a semicolon, END, ELSE, or
    --                         UNTIL may follow a statement.
    --                         Check for a missing semicolon.
    */
    synchronize(statement_end_list, NULL, NULL);
    if (token_in(statement_start_list)) error(MISSING_SEMICOLON);
}

/*--------------------------------------------------------------*/
/* assignment_statement    Process an assignment statement:     */
/*                                                              */
/*                              <id> := <expr>                   */
/*--------------------------------------------------------------*/

assignment_statement(var_idp)

    SYMTAB_NODE_PTR var_idp;         /* target variable id */

{
    TYPE_STRUCT_PTR var_tp, expr_tp;     /* types of var and expr */

    var_tp = variable(var_idp, TARGET_USE);
    if_token_get_else_error(COLONEQUAL, MISSING_COLONEQUAL);

    expr_tp = expression();

    if (! is_assign_type_compatible(var_tp, expr_tp))
        error(INCOMPATIBLE_ASSIGNMENT);
}

/*--------------------------------------------------------------*/
/* repeat_statement    Process a REPEAT statement:              */
/*                                                              */
/*                         REPEAT <stmt-list> UNTIL <expr>       */
/*--------------------------------------------------------------*/

repeat_statement()

{
    TYPE_STRUCT_PTR expr_tp;

    /*
    -- <stmt-list>
    */
    get_token();
    do {
        statement();
        while (token == SEMICOLON) get_token();
    } while (token_in(statement_start_list));

    if_token_get_else_error(UNTIL, MISSING_UNTIL);

    expr_tp = expression();
    if (expr_tp != boolean_typep) error(INCOMPATIBLE_TYPES);
}

/*--------------------------------------------------------------*/
/* while_statement     Process a WHILE statement:               */
```

```
/*                                                    */
/*                    WHILE <expr> DO <stmt>          */
/*--------------------------------------------------*/

while_statement()

{
    TYPE_STRUCT_PTR  expr_tp;
    char             *loop_end_location;

    get_token();
    loop_end_location = crunch_address_marker(NULL);

    expr_tp = expression();
    if (expr_tp != boolean_typep) error(INCOMPATIBLE_TYPES);

    if_token_get_else_error(DO, MISSING_DO);
    statement();

    fixup_address_marker(loop_end_location);
}


/*--------------------------------------------------*/
/* if_statement      Process an IF statement:       */
/*                                                  */
/*                    IF <expr> THEN <stmt>         */
/*                                                  */
/*              or:                                 */
/*                                                  */
/*              IF <expr> THEN <stmt> ELSE <stmt>   */
/*--------------------------------------------------*/

if_statement()

{
    TYPE_STRUCT_PTR  expr_tp;
    char             *false_location;
    char             *if_end_location;

    get_token();
    false_location = crunch_address_marker(NULL);

    expr_tp = expression();
    if (expr_tp != boolean_typep) error(INCOMPATIBLE_TYPES);

    if_token_get_else_error(THEN, MISSING_THEN);
    statement();

    fixup_address_marker(false_location);

    /*
    -- ELSE branch?
    */
    if (token == ELSE) {
        get_token();
        if_end_location = crunch_address_marker(NULL);

        statement();

        fixup_address_marker(if_end_location);
    }
}

/*--------------------------------------------------*/
/* for_statement     Process a FOR statement:       */
/*                                                  */
/*              FOR <id> := <expr> TO|DOWNTO <expr> */
```

```
/*                    DO <stmt>                     */
/*--------------------------------------------------*/

for_statement()

{
    SYMTAB_NODE_PTR  for_idp;
    TYPE_STRUCT_PTR  for_tp, expr_tp;
    char             *loop_end_location;

    get_token();
    loop_end_location = crunch_address_marker(NULL);

    if (token == IDENTIFIER) {
        search_and_find_all_symtab(for_idp);
        crunch_symtab_node_ptr(for_idp);

        if ((for_idp->level != level) ||
            (for_idp->defn.key != VAR_DEFN))
            error(INVALID_FOR_CONTROL);

        for_tp = base_type(for_idp->typep);
        get_token();

        if ((for_tp != integer_typep) &&
            (for_tp != char_typep) &&
            (for_tp->form != ENUM_FORM)) error(INCOMPATIBLE_TYPES);
    }
    else {
        error(IDENTIFIER, MISSING_IDENTIFIER);
        for_tp = &dummy_type;
    }

    if_token_get_else_error(COLONEQUAL, MISSING_COLONEQUAL);

    expr_tp = expression();
    if (! is_assign_type_compatible(for_tp, expr_tp))
        error(INCOMPATIBLE_TYPES);

    if ((token == TO) || (token == DOWNTO)) get_token();
    else error(MISSING_TO_OR_DOWNTO);

    expr_tp = expression();
    if (! is_assign_type_compatible(for_tp, expr_tp))
        error(INCOMPATIBLE_TYPES);

    if_token_get_else_error(DO, MISSING_DO);
    statement();

    fixup_address_marker(loop_end_location);
}

/*--------------------------------------------------*/
/* CASE statement globals                           */
/*--------------------------------------------------*/

typedef struct case_item {
    int            label_value;
    char           *branch_location;
    struct case_item *next;
} CASE_ITEM, *CASE_ITEM_PTR;

CASE_ITEM_PTR case_item_head, case_item_tail;
int           case_label_count;

/*--------------------------------------------------*/
/* case_statement    Process a CASE statement:      */
```

```
/*                                                  */
/*                    CASE <expr> OF                */
/*                        <case-branch> ;           */
/*                        ...                        */
/*                    END                           */
/*--------------------------------------------------*/

TOKEN_CODE follow_expr_list[]     = {OF, SEMICOLON, 0};

TOKEN_CODE case_label_start_list[] = {IDENTIFIER, NUMBER, PLUS,
                                      MINUS, STRING, 0};


case_statement()

{
    BOOLEAN          another_branch;
    TYPE_STRUCT_PTR  expr_tp;
    TYPE_STRUCT_PTR  case_label();
    CASE_ITEM_PTR    case_itemp, next_case_itemp;
    char             *branch_table_location;
    char             *case_end_chain = NULL;

    /*
    -- Initializations for the branch table.
    */
    get_token();
    branch_table_location = crunch_address_marker(NULL);
    case_item_head = case_item_tail = NULL;
    case_label_count = 0;

    expr_tp = expression();

    if (  ((expr_tp->form != SCALAR_FORM) &&
           (expr_tp->form != ENUM_FORM) &&
           (expr_tp->form != SUBRANGE_FORM))
       || (expr_tp == real_typep)) error(INCOMPATIBLE_TYPES);

    /*
    -- Error synchronization:  Should be OF
    */
    synchronize(follow_expr_list, case_label_start_list, NULL);
    if_token_get_else_error(OF, MISSING_OF);

    /*
    -- Loop to process CASE branches.
    */
    another_branch = token_in(case_label_start_list);
    while (another_branch) {
        if (token_in(case_label_start_list)) case_branch(expr_tp);

        /*
        -- Link another address marker at the end of
        -- the CASE branch to point to the end of
        -- the CASE statement.
        */
        case_end_chain = crunch_address_marker(case_end_chain);

        if (token == SEMICOLON) {
            get_token();
            another_branch = TRUE;
        }
        else if (token_in(case_label_start_list)) {
            error(MISSING_SEMICOLON);
            another_branch = TRUE;
        }
        else another_branch = FALSE;
    }
```

```
    /*
    -- Emit the branch table.
    */
    fixup_address_marker(branch_table_location);
    crunch_integer(case_label_count);
    case_itemp = case_item_head;
    while (case_itemp != NULL) {
        crunch_integer(case_itemp->label_value);
        crunch_offset(case_itemp->branch_location);
        next_case_itemp = case_itemp->next;
        free(case_itemp);
        case_itemp = next_case_itemp;
    }

    if_token_get_else_error(END, MISSING_END);

    /*
    -- Patch the CASE branch address markers.
    */
    while (case_end_chain != NULL)
        case_end_chain = fixup_address_marker(case_end_chain);
}

/*--------------------------------------------------*/
/* case_branch            Process a CASE branch:    */
/*                                                  */
/*                    <case-label-list> : <stmt>    */
/*--------------------------------------------------*/

TOKEN_CODE follow_case_label_list[] = {COLON, SEMICOLON, 0};

case_branch(expr_tp)

    TYPE_STRUCT_PTR expr_tp;         /* type of CASE expression */

{
    BOOLEAN          another_label;
    TYPE_STRUCT_PTR  label_tp;
    CASE_ITEM_PTR    case_itemp;
    CASE_ITEM_PTR    old_case_item_tail = case_item_tail;
    TYPE_STRUCT_PTR  case_label();

    /*
    -- <case-label-list>
    */
    do {
        label_tp = case_label();
        if (expr_tp != label_tp) error(INCOMPATIBLE_TYPES);

        get_token();
        if (token == COMMA) {
            get_token();
            if (token_in(case_label_start_list)) another_label = TRUE;
            else {
                error(MISSING_CONSTANT);
                another_label = FALSE;
            }
        }
        else another_label = FALSE;
    } while (another_label);

    /*
    -- Error synchronization:  Should be :
    */
    synchronize(follow_case_label_list, statement_start_list, NULL);
    if_token_get_else_error(COLON, MISSING_COLON);

    /*
```

```
        --  Loop to fill in the branch_location field of
        --  each CASE_ITEM item for this branch.
        */
        case_itemp = old_case_item_tail == NULL
                          ? case_item_head
                          : old_case_item_tail->next;
        while (case_itemp != NULL) {
            case_itemp->branch_location = code_bufferp;
            case_itemp = case_itemp->next;
        }

        statement();
}

/*-------------------------------------------------------------*/
/*  case_label              Process a CASE label and return a   */
/*                          pointer to its type structure.      */
/*-------------------------------------------------------------*/

    TYPE_STRUCT_PTR
case_label()

{
    TOKEN_CODE      sign     = PLUS;    /* unary + or - sign */
    BOOLEAN         saw_sign = FALSE;   /* TRUE iff unary sign */
    TYPE_STRUCT_PTR label_tp;
    CASE_ITEM_PTR   case_itemp = alloc_struct(CASE_ITEM);

    /*
    --  Link in a CASE_ITEM item for this label.
    */
    if (case_item_head != NULL) {
        case_item_tail->next = case_itemp;
        case_item_tail = case_itemp;
    }
    else {
        case_item_head = case_item_tail = case_itemp;
    }
    case_itemp->next = NULL;
    ++case_label_count;

    /*
    --  Unary + or - sign.
    */
    if ((token == PLUS) || (token == MINUS)) {
        sign     = token;
        saw_sign = TRUE;
        get_token();
    }

    /*
    --  Numeric constant:  Integer type only.
    */
    if (token == NUMBER) {
        SYMTAB_NODE_PTR np = search_symtab(token_string,
                                           symtab_display[1]);

        if (np == NULL) np = enter_symtab(token_string,
                                          symtab_display[1]);
        crunch_symtab_node_ptr(np);

        if (literal.type == INTEGER_LIT)
            case_itemp->label_value = sign == PLUS
                            ? literal.value.integer
                            : -literal.value.integer;
        else error(INVALID_CONSTANT);
        return(integer_typep);
```

```
    }

    /*
    --  Identifier constant:  Integer, character, or enumeration
    --                        types only.
    */
    else if (token == IDENTIFIER) {
        SYMTAB_NODE_PTR idp;

        search_all_symtab(idp);
        crunch_symtab_node_ptr(idp);

        if (idp == NULL) {
            error(UNDEFINED_IDENTIFIER);
            return(&dummy_type);
        }

        else if (idp->defn.key != CONST_DEFN) {
            error(NOT_A_CONSTANT_IDENTIFIER);
            return(&dummy_type);
        }

        else if (idp->typep == integer_typep) {
            case_itemp->label_value = sign == PLUS
                                ? idp->defn.info.constant
                                         .value.integer
                                : -idp->defn.info.constant
                                         .value.integer;
            return(integer_typep);
        }

        else if (idp->typep == char_typep) {
            if (saw_sign) error(INVALID_CONSTANT);
            case_itemp->label_value = idp->defn.info.constant
                                         .value.character;
            return(char_typep);
        }

        else if (idp->typep->form == ENUM_FORM) {
            if (saw_sign) error(INVALID_CONSTANT);
            case_itemp->label_value = idp->defn.info.constant
                                         .value.integer;
            return(idp->typep);
        }

        else return(&dummy_type);
    }

    /*
    --  String constant:  Character type only.
    */
    else if (token == STRING) {
        SYMTAB_NODE_PTR np = search_symtab(token_string,
                                           symtab_display[1]);

        if (np == NULL) np = enter_symtab(token_string,
                                          symtab_display[1]);
        crunch_symtab_node_ptr(np);

        if (saw_sign) error(INVALID_CONSTANT);

        if (strlen(literal.value.string) == 1) {
            case_itemp->label_value = literal.value.string[0];
            return(char_typep);
        }
        else {
            error(INVALID_CONSTANT);
```

```
            return(&dummy_type);
        }
    }

    else {
        error(INVALID_CONSTANT);
        return(&dummy_type);
    }
}

/*-----------------------------------------------------------*/
/*  compound_statement      Process a compound statement:    */
/*                                                           */
/*                              BEGIN <stmt-list> END        */
/*-----------------------------------------------------------*/

compound_statement()

{
```

```
    /*
    -- <stmt-list>
    */
    get_token();
    do {
        statement();
        while (token == SEMICOLON) get_token();
        if (token == END) break;

        /*
        -- Error synchronization:  Should be at the start of the
        --                         next statement.
        */
        synchronize(statement_start_list, NULL, NULL);
    } while (token_in(statement_start_list));

    if_token_get_else_error(END, MISSING_END);
}
```

FIGURE A-6   expr.c

```
/*****************************************************************/
/*                                                             */
/*        E X P R E S S I O N   P A R S E R                    */
/*                                                             */
/*        Parsing routines for expressions.                   */
/*                                                             */
/*        FILE:     expr.c                                     */
/*                                                             */
/*        MODULE:   parser                                     */
/*                                                             */
/*****************************************************************/

#include <stdio.h>
#include "common.h"
#include "error.h"
#include "scanner.h"
#include "symtab.h"
#include "parser.h"

/*-----------------------------------------------------------*/
/*  Externals                                                */
/*-----------------------------------------------------------*/

extern TOKEN_CODE token;
extern char       token_string[];
extern char       word_string[];
extern LITERAL    literal;

extern SYMTAB_NODE_PTR symtab_display[];
extern int             level;

extern TYPE_STRUCT_PTR integer_typep, real_typep,
                       boolean_typep, char_typep;

extern TYPE_STRUCT     dummy_type;

/*-----------------------------------------------------------*/
/*  Forwards                                                 */
/*-----------------------------------------------------------*/

TYPE_STRUCT_PTR expression(), simple_expression(), term(), factor(),
```

```
                function_call();

/*-----------------------------------------------------------*/
/*  integer_operands      TRUE if both operands are integer, */
/*                        else FALSE.                        */
/*-----------------------------------------------------------*/

#define integer_operands(tp1, tp2)  ((tp1 == integer_typep) && \
                                     (tp2 == integer_typep))

/*-----------------------------------------------------------*/
/*  real_operands         TRUE if at least one or both operands */
/*                        operands are real (and the other   */
/*                        integer), else FALSE.              */
/*-----------------------------------------------------------*/

#define real_operands(tp1, tp2) (((tp1 == real_typep) &&      \
                                 ((tp2 == real_typep) ||      \
                                  (tp2 == integer_typep)))    \
                                            ||                \
                                 ((tp2 == real_typep) &&      \
                                  ((tp1 == real_typep) ||     \
                                   (tp1 == integer_typep))))

/*-----------------------------------------------------------*/
/*  boolean_operands      TRUE if both operands are boolean  */
/*                        else FALSE.                        */
/*-----------------------------------------------------------*/

#define boolean_operands(tp1, pt2)  ((tp1 == boolean_typep) && \
                                     (tp2 == boolean_typep))

/*-----------------------------------------------------------*/
/*  expression            Process an expression consisting of a */
/*                        simple expression optionally followed */
/*                        by a relational operator and a second */
/*                        simple expression.  Return a pointer to */
/*                        the type structure.                */
/*-----------------------------------------------------------*/

TOKEN_CODE rel_op_list[] = {LT, LE, EQUAL, NE, GE, GT, 0};
```

```
    TYPE_STRUCT_PTR
expression()

{
    TOKEN_CODE op;                      /* an operator token */
    TYPE_STRUCT_PTR result_tp, tp2;

    result_tp = simple_expression();    /* first simple expr */

    /*
    -- If there is a relational operator, remember it and
    -- process the second simple expression.
    */
    if (token_in(rel_op_list)) {
        op = token;                     /* remember operator */
        result_tp = base_type(result_tp);

        get_token();
        tp2 = base_type(simple_expression());   /* 2nd simple expr */

        check_rel_op_types(result_tp, tp2);
        result_tp = boolean_typep;
    }

    return(result_tp);
}

/*-----------------------------------------------------------*/
/*  simple_expression   Process a simple expression consisting */
/*                      of terms separated by +, -, or OR    */
/*                      operators. There may be a unary + or - */
/*                      before the first term. Return a      */
/*                      pointer to the type structure.       */
/*-----------------------------------------------------------*/

TOKEN_CODE add_op_list[] = {PLUS, MINUS, OR, 0};

    TYPE_STRUCT_PTR
simple_expression()

{
    TOKEN_CODE op;                      /* an operator token */
    BOOLEAN    saw_unary_op = FALSE;    /* TRUE iff unary operator */
    TOKEN_CODE unary_op = PLUS;         /* a unary operator token */
    TYPE_STRUCT_PTR result_tp, tp2;

    /*
    -- If there is a unary + or -, remember it.
    */
    if ((token == PLUS) || (token == MINUS)) {
        unary_op = token;
        saw_unary_op = TRUE;
        get_token();
    }

    result_tp = term();         /* first term */

    /*
    -- If there was a unary operator, check that the term
    -- is integer or real. Negate the top of stack if it
    -- was a unary - either with the NEG instruction or by
    -- calling FLOAT_NEGATE.
    */
    if (saw_unary_op &&
        (base_type(result_tp) != integer_typep) &&
        (result_tp != real_typep)) error(INCOMPATIBLE_TYPES);

    /*
```

```
    -- Loop to process subsequent terms separated by operators.
    */
    while (token_in(add_op_list)) {
        op = token;                     /* remember operator */
        result_tp = base_type(result_tp);

        get_token();
        tp2 = base_type(term());        /* subsequent term */

        switch (op) {

            case PLUS:
            case MINUS: {
                /*
                -- integer <op> integer => integer
                */
                if (integer_operands(result_tp, tp2))
                    result_tp = integer_typep;

                /*
                -- Both operands are real, or one is real and the
                -- other is integer. The result is real.
                */
                else if (real_operands(result_tp, tp2))
                    result_tp = real_typep;

                else {
                    error(INCOMPATIBLE_TYPES);
                    result_tp = &dummy_type;
                }

                break;
            }

            case OR: {
                /*
                -- boolean OR boolean => boolean
                */
                if (! boolean_operands(result_tp, tp2))
                    error(INCOMPATIBLE_TYPES);

                result_tp = boolean_typep;
                break;
            }
        }
    }

    return(result_tp);
}

/*-----------------------------------------------------------*/
/*  term              Process a term consisting of factors   */
/*                    separated by *, /, DIV, MOD, or AND    */
/*                    operators. Return a pointer to the     */
/*                    type structure.                        */
/*-----------------------------------------------------------*/

TOKEN_CODE mult_op_list[] = {STAR, SLASH, DIV, MOD, AND, 0};

    TYPE_STRUCT_PTR
term()

{
    TOKEN_CODE op;                      /* an operator token */
    TYPE_STRUCT_PTR result_tp, tp2;

    result_tp = factor();               /* first factor */
```

```
/*
-- Loop to process subsequent factors
-- separated by operators.
*/
while (token_in(mult_op_list)) {
    op = token;                         /* remember operator */
    result_tp = base_type(result_tp);

    get_token();
    tp2 = base_type(factor());          /* subsequent factor */

    switch (op) {

        case STAR: {
            /*
            -- Both operands are integer.
            */
            if (integer_operands(result_tp, tp2))
                result_tp = integer_typep;

            /*
            -- Both operands are real, or one is real and the
            -- other is integer.  The result is real.
            */
            else if (real_operands(result_tp, tp2))
                result_tp = real_typep;

            else {
                error(INCOMPATIBLE_TYPES);
                result_tp = &dummy_type;
            }

            break;
        }

        case SLASH: {
            /*
            -- Both operands are real, or both are integer, or
            -- one is real and the other is integer.  The result
            -- is real.
            */
            if ((! real_operands(result_tp, tp2)) &&
                (! integer_operands(result_tp, tp2)))
                error(INCOMPATIBLE_TYPES);

            result_tp = real_typep;
            break;
        }

        case DIV:
        case MOD: {
            /*
            -- integer <op> integer => integer
            */
            if (! integer_operands(result_tp, tp2))
                error(INCOMPATIBLE_TYPES);

            result_tp = integer_typep;
            break;
        }

        case AND: {
            /*
            -- boolean AND boolean => boolean
            */
            if (! boolean_operands(result_tp, tp2))
                error(INCOMPATIBLE_TYPES);

            result_tp = boolean_typep;
            break;
        }
    }
}

return(result_tp);
}

/*------------------------------------------------------------*/
/*  factor          Process a factor, which is an variable,  */
/*                  a number, NOT followed by a factor, or    */
/*                  a parenthesized subexpression.  Return    */
/*                  a pointer to the type structure.          */
/*------------------------------------------------------------*/

    TYPE_STRUCT_PTR
factor()

{
    TYPE_STRUCT_PTR tp;

    switch (token) {

        case IDENTIFIER: {
            SYMTAB_NODE_PTR idp;

            search_and_find_all_symtab(idp);

            switch (idp->defn.key) {

                case FUNC_DEFN:
                    crunch_symtab_node_ptr(idp);
                    get_token();
                    tp = routine_call(idp, TRUE);
                    break;

                case PROC_DEFN:
                    error(INVALID_IDENTIFIER_USAGE);
                    get_token();
                    actual_parm_list(idp, FALSE);
                    tp = &dummy_type;
                    break;

                case CONST_DEFN:
                    crunch_symtab_node_ptr(idp);
                    get_token();
                    tp = idp->typep;
                    break;

                default:
                    tp = variable(idp, EXPR_USE);
                    break;
            }

            break;
        }

        case NUMBER: {
            SYMTAB_NODE_PTR np;

            np = search_symtab(token_string, symtab_display[1]);
            if (np == NULL) np = enter_symtab(token_string,
                                              symtab_display[1]);

            if (literal.type == INTEGER_LIT) {
                tp = np->typep = integer_typep;
```

```
            np->defn.info.constant.value.integer =
                literal.value.integer;
        }
        else {  /* literal.type == REAL_LIT */
            tp = np->typep = real_typep;
            np->defn.info.constant.value.real =
                literal.value.real;
        }

        crunch_symtab_node_ptr(np);
        get_token();

        break;
    }

    case STRING: {
        SYMTAB_NODE_PTR np;
        int             length = strlen(literal.value.string);

        np = search_symtab(token_string, symtab_display[1]);
        if (np == NULL) np = enter_symtab(token_string,
                                          symtab_display[1]);

        if (length == 1) {
            np->defn.info.constant.value.character =
                literal.value.string[0];
            tp = char_typep;
        }
        else {
            np->typep = tp = make_string_typep(length);
            np->info  = alloc_bytes(length + 1);
            strcpy(np->info, literal.value.string);
        }

        crunch_symtab_node_ptr(np);

        get_token();
        break;
    }

    case NOT:
        get_token();
        tp = factor();
        break;

    case LPAREN:
        get_token();
        tp = expression();

        if_token_get_else_error(RPAREN, MISSING_RPAREN);
        break;

    default:
        error(INVALID_EXPRESSION);
        tp = &dummy_type;
        break;
    }

    return(tp);
}

/*--------------------------------------------------------------*/
/*  variable          Process a variable, which can be a        */
/*                    simple identifier, an array identifier    */
/*                    with subscripts, or a record identifier   */
/*                    with fields.                              */
/*--------------------------------------------------------------*/
```

```
    TYPE_STRUCT_PTR
variable(var_idp, use)

    SYMTAB_NODE_PTR var_idp;    /* variable id */
    USE             use;        /* how variable is used */

{
    TYPE_STRUCT_PTR tp          = var_idp->typep;
    DEFN_KEY        defn_key    = var_idp->defn.key;
    TYPE_STRUCT_PTR array_subscript_list();
    TYPE_STRUCT_PTR record_field();

    crunch_symtab_node_ptr(var_idp);

    /*
    -- Check the variable's definition.
    */
    switch (defn_key) {
        case VAR_DEFN:
        case VALPARM_DEFN:
        case VARPARM_DEFN:
        case FUNC_DEFN:
        case UNDEFINED: break;          /* OK */

        default: {                      /* error */
            tp = &dummy_type;
            error(INVALID_IDENTIFIER_USAGE);
        }
    }

    get_token();

    /*
    -- There must not be a parameter list, but if there is one,
    -- parse it anyway for error recovery.
    */
    if (token == LPAREN) {
        error(UNEXPECTED_TOKEN);
        actual_parm_list(var_idp, FALSE);
        return(tp);
    }

    /*
    -- Subscripts and/or field designators?
    */
    while ((token == LBRACKET) || (token == PERIOD)) {
        tp = token == LBRACKET ? array_subscript_list(tp)
                               : record_field(tp);
    }

    return(tp);
}

/*--------------------------------------------------------------*/
/*  array_subscript_list    Process a list of subscripts        */
/*                          following an array identifier:      */
/*                                                              */
/*                                [ <expr> , <expr> , ... ]     */
/*--------------------------------------------------------------*/

    TYPE_STRUCT_PTR
array_subscript_list(tp)

    TYPE_STRUCT_PTR tp;

{
    TYPE_STRUCT_PTR   index_tp, elmt_tp, ss_tp;
```

```
extern TOKEN_CODE statement_end_list[];

/*
-- Loop to process a subscript list.
*/
do {
    if (tp->form == ARRAY_FORM) {
        index_tp = tp->info.array.index_typep;
        elmt_tp = tp->info.array.elmt_typep;

        get_token();
        ss_tp = expression();

        /*
        -- The subscript expression must be assignment type
        -- compatible with the corresponding subscript type.
        */
        if (!is_assign_type_compatible(index_tp, ss_tp))
            error(INCOMPATIBLE_TYPES);

        tp = elmt_tp;
    }
    else {
        error(TOO_MANY_SUBSCRIPTS);
        while ((token != RBRACKET) &&
               (! token_in(statement_end_list)))
            get_token();
    }
} while (token == COMMA);

if_token_get_else_error(RBRACKET, MISSING_RBRACKET);
return(tp);
}

/*-----------------------------------------------------------*/
/* record_field            Process a field designation      */
/*                         following a record identifier:   */
/*                                                          */
/*                              . <field-variable>          */
/*-----------------------------------------------------------*/

    TYPE_STRUCT_PTR
record_field(tp)

    TYPE_STRUCT_PTR tp;

{
    SYMTAB_NODE_PTR field_idp;

    get_token();

    if ((token == IDENTIFIER) && (tp->form == RECORD_FORM)) {
        search_this_symtab(field_idp,
                           tp->info.record.field_symtab);

        crunch_symtab_node_ptr(field_idp);
        get_token();

        if (field_idp != NULL) return(field_idp->typep);
        else {
            error(INVALID_FIELD);
            return(&dummy_type);
        }
    }
    else {
        get_token();
        error(INVALID_FIELD);
```

```
        return(&dummy_type);
    }
}

        /********************************/
        /*                              */
        /*        Type compatibility    */
        /*                              */
        /********************************/

/*-----------------------------------------------------------*/
/* check_rel_op_types  Check the operand types for a rela-   */
/*                     tional operator.                      */
/*-----------------------------------------------------------*/

check_rel_op_types(tp1, tp2)

    TYPE_STRUCT_PTR tp1, tp2;          /* operand types */

{
    /*
    -- Two identical scalar or enumeration types.
    */
    if (   (tp1 == tp2)
        && ((tp1->form == SCALAR_FORM) || (tp1->form == ENUM_FORM)))
        return;

    /*
    -- One integer and one real.
    */
    if (   ((tp1 == integer_typep) && (tp2 == real_typep))
        || ((tp2 == integer_typep) && (tp1 == real_typep))) return;

    /*
    -- Two strings of the same length.
    */
    if ((tp1->form == ARRAY_FORM) &&
        (tp2->form == ARRAY_FORM) &&
        (tp1->info.array.elmt_typep == char_typep) &&
        (tp2->info.array.elmt_typep == char_typep) &&
        (tp1->info.array.elmt_count ==
                        tp2->info.array.elmt_count)) return;

    error(INCOMPATIBLE_TYPES);
}

/*-----------------------------------------------------------*/
/* is_assign_type_compatible  Return TRUE iff a value of type */
/*                            tp1 can be assigned to a vari-  */
/*                            able of type tp1.               */
/*-----------------------------------------------------------*/

    BOOLEAN
is_assign_type_compatible(tp1, tp2)

    TYPE_STRUCT_PTR tp1, tp2;

{
    tp1 = base_type(tp1);
    tp2 = base_type(tp2);

    if (tp1 == tp2) return(TRUE);

    /*
    -- real := integer
    */
    if ((tp1 == real_typep) && (tp2 == integer_typep)) return(TRUE);
```

```
    /*
    -- string1 := string2 of the same length
    */
    if ((tp1->form == ARRAY_FORM) &&
        (tp2->form == ARRAY_FORM) &&
        (tp1->info.array.elmt_typep == char_typep) &&
        (tp2->info.array.elmt_typep == char_typep) &&
        (tp1->info.array.elmt_count ==
                    tp2->info.array.elmt_count)) return(TRUE);

    return(FALSE);
}

/*----------------------------------------------------------*/
/* base_type           Return the range type of a subrange      */
```

```
/*                          type.                            */
/*----------------------------------------------------------*/

    TYPE_STRUCT_PTR
base_type(tp)

    TYPE_STRUCT_PTR tp;

{
    return((tp->form == SUBRANGE_FORM)
                ? tp->info.subrange.range_typep
                : tp);
}
```

FIGURE A-7   scanner.h

```
/*****************************************************************/
/*                                                               */
/*      S C A N N E R   (Header)                                 */
/*                                                               */
/*      FILE:       scanner.h                                    */
/*                                                               */
/*      MODULE:     scanner                                      */
/*                                                               */
/*****************************************************************/

#ifndef scanner_h
#define scanner_h

#include "common.h"

/*----------------------------------------------------------*/
/* Token codes                                              */
/*----------------------------------------------------------*/

typedef enum {
    NO_TOKEN, IDENTIFIER, NUMBER, STRING,
    UPARROW, STAR, LPAREN, RPAREN, MINUS, PLUS, EQUAL,
    LBRACKET, RBRACKET, COLON, SEMICOLON, LT, GT, COMMA, PERIOD,
    SLASH, COLONEQUAL, LE, GE, NE, DOTDOT, END_OF_FILE, ERROR,
    AND, ARRAY, BEGIN, CASE, CONST, DIV, DO, DOWNTO, ELSE, END,
    FFILE, FOR, FUNCTION, GOTO, IF, IN, LABEL, MOD, NIL, NOT,
    OF, OR, PACKED, PROCEDURE, PROGRAM, RECORD, REPEAT, SET,
```

```
    THEN, TO, TYPE, UNTIL, VAR, WHILE, WITH,
} TOKEN_CODE;

/*----------------------------------------------------------*/
/* Literal structure                                        */
/*----------------------------------------------------------*/

typedef enum {
    INTEGER_LIT, REAL_LIT, STRING_LIT,
} LITERAL_TYPE;

typedef struct {
    LITERAL_TYPE type;
    union {
        int     integer;
        float   real;
        char    string[MAX_SOURCE_LINE_LENGTH];
    } value;
} LITERAL;

/*----------------------------------------------------------*/
/* Functions                                                */
/*----------------------------------------------------------*/

BOOLEAN token_in();

#endif
```

FIGURE A-8   scanner.c

```
/*****************************************************************/
/*                                                               */
/*      S C A N N E R                                            */
/*                                                               */
/*      Scanner for Pascal tokens.                               */
/*                                                               */
/*      FILE:       scanner.c                                    */
/*                                                               */
```

```
/*      MODULE:     scanner                                      */
/*                                                               */
/*****************************************************************/

#include <stdio.h>
#include <math.h>
#include <sys/types.h>
#include <sys/timeb.h>
```

```c
#include "common.h"
#include "error.h"
#include "scanner.h"

#define EOF_CHAR        '\x7f'
#define TAB_SIZE        8

#define MAX_INTEGER     32767
#define MAX_DIGIT_COUNT 20
#define MAX_EXPONENT    37

#define MIN_RESERVED_WORD_LENGTH   2
#define MAX_RESERVED_WORD_LENGTH   9

/*----------------------------------------------------------------*/
/*  Character codes                                               */
/*----------------------------------------------------------------*/

typedef enum {
    LETTER, DIGIT, QUOTE, SPECIAL, EOF_CODE,
} CHAR_CODE;

/*----------------------------------------------------------------*/
/*  Reserved word tables                                         */
/*----------------------------------------------------------------*/

typedef struct {
    char       *string;
    TOKEN_CODE token_code;
} RW_STRUCT;

RW_STRUCT rw_2[] = {
    {"do", DO}, {"if", IF}, {"in", IN}, {"of", OF}, {"or", OR},
    {"to", TO}, {NULL, 0},
};

RW_STRUCT rw_3[] = {
    {"and", AND}, {"div", DIV}, {"end", END}, {"for", FOR},
    {"mod", MOD}, {"nil", NIL}, {"not", NOT}, {"set", SET},
    {"var", VAR}, {NULL, 0  },
};

RW_STRUCT rw_4[] = {
    {"case", CASE}, {"else", ELSE}, {"file", FFILE},
    {"goto", GOTO}, {"then", THEN}, {"type", TYPE},
    {"with", WITH}, {NULL  , 0  },
};

RW_STRUCT rw_5[] = {
    {"array", ARRAY}, {"begin", BEGIN}, {"const", CONST},
    {"label", LABEL}, {"until", UNTIL}, {"while", WHILE},
    {NULL  , 0  },
};

RW_STRUCT rw_6[] = {
    {"downto", DOWNTO}, {"packed", PACKED}, {"record", RECORD},
    {"repeat", REPEAT}, {NULL  , 0  },
};

RW_STRUCT rw_7[] = {
    {"program", PROGRAM}, {NULL, 0},
};

RW_STRUCT rw_8[] = {
    {"function", FUNCTION}, {NULL, 0},
};

RW_STRUCT rw_9[] = {
    {"procedure", PROCEDURE}, {NULL, 0},
};

RW_STRUCT *rw_table[] = {
    NULL, NULL, rw_2, rw_3, rw_4, rw_5, rw_6, rw_7, rw_8, rw_9,
};

/*----------------------------------------------------------------*/
/*  Token lists                                                  */
/*----------------------------------------------------------------*/

TOKEN_CODE statement_start_list[] = {BEGIN, CASE, FOR, IF, REPEAT,
                                     WHILE, IDENTIFIER, 0};

TOKEN_CODE statement_end_list[]   = {SEMICOLON, END, ELSE, UNTIL,
                                     END_OF_FILE, 0};

TOKEN_CODE declaration_start_list[] = {CONST, TYPE, VAR, PROCEDURE,
                                       FUNCTION, 0};

/*----------------------------------------------------------------*/
/*  Globals                                                      */
/*----------------------------------------------------------------*/

char      ch;            /* current input character */
TOKEN_CODE token;        /* code of current token */
LITERAL   literal;       /* value of literal */
int       buffer_offset; /* char offset into source buffer */
int       level = 0;     /* current nesting level */
int       line_number = 0;  /* current line number */
BOOLEAN   print_flag = TRUE; /* TRUE to print source lines */
BOOLEAN   block_flag = FALSE; /* TRUE only when parsing a block */

char source_buffer[MAX_SOURCE_LINE_LENGTH]; /* source file buffer */
char token_string[MAX_TOKEN_STRING_LENGTH]; /* token string */
char word_string[MAX_TOKEN_STRING_LENGTH];  /* downshifted */
char *bufferp = source_buffer;       /* source buffer ptr */
char *tokenp  = token_string;        /* token string ptr */

int     digit_count;         /* total no. of digits in number */
BOOLEAN count_error;         /* too many digits in number? */

int page_number = 0;
int line_count  = MAX_LINES_PER_PAGE;   /* no. lines on current pg */

char source_name[MAX_FILE_NAME_LENGTH]; /* name of source file */
char date[DATE_STRING_LENGTH];          /* current date and time */

FILE *source_file;

CHAR_CODE char_table[256];

/*----------------------------------------------------------------*/
/*  char_code          Return the character code of ch.          */
/*----------------------------------------------------------------*/

#define char_code(ch)   char_table[ch]

            /********************************/
            /*                              */
            /*        Initialization        */
            /*                              */
            /********************************/

/*----------------------------------------------------------------*/
/*  init_scanner       Initialize the scanner globals            */
/*                     and open the source file.                 */
```

```
/*-----------------------------------------------------*/

init_scanner(name)

    char *name;        /* name of source file */

{
    int ch;

    /*
    -- Initialize character table.
    */
    for (ch = 0;   ch < 256;  ++ch) char_table[ch] = SPECIAL;
    for (ch = '0'; ch <= '9'; ++ch) char_table[ch] = DIGIT;
    for (ch = 'A'; ch <= 'Z'; ++ch) char_table[ch] = LETTER;
    for (ch = 'a'; ch <= 'z'; ++ch) char_table[ch] = LETTER;
    char_table['\''] = QUOTE;
    char_table[EOF_CHAR] = EOF_CODE;

    init_page_header(name);
    open_source_file(name);
}

/*-----------------------------------------------------*/
/* quit_scanner        Terminate the scanner.          */
/*-----------------------------------------------------*/

quit_scanner()

{
    close_source_file();
}

            /*********************************/
            /*                               */
            /*        Character routines     */
            /*                               */
            /*********************************/

/*-----------------------------------------------------*/
/* get_char           Set ch to the next character from the */
/*                    source buffer.                   */
/*-----------------------------------------------------*/

get_char()

{
    BOOLEAN get_source_line();

    /*
    -- If at end of current source line, read another line.
    -- If at end of file, set ch to the EOF character and return.
    */
    if (*bufferp == '\0') {
        if (! get_source_line()) {
            ch = EOF_CHAR;
            return;
        }
        bufferp = source_buffer;
        buffer_offset = 0;
    }

    ch = *bufferp++;    /* next character in the buffer */

    /*
    -- Special character processing:
    --
```

```
    --   tab        Increment buffer_offset up to the next
    --              multiple of TAB_SIZE, and replace ch with
    --              a blank.
    --
    --   new-line   Replace ch with a blank.
    --
    --   {          Start of comment:  Skip over comment and
    --              replace it with a blank.
    */
    switch (ch) {

        case '\t': buffer_offset += TAB_SIZE -
                                    buffer_offset%TAB_SIZE;
                   ch = ' ';
                   break;

        case '\n': ++buffer_offset;
                   ch = ' ';
                   break;

        case '{': ++buffer_offset;
                  skip_comment();
                  ch = ' ';
                  break;

        default:   ++buffer_offset;
    }
}

/*-----------------------------------------------------*/
/* skip_comment        Skip over a comment. Set ch to '}'. */
/*-----------------------------------------------------*/

skip_comment()

{
    do {
        get_char();
    } while ((ch != '}') && (ch != EOF_CHAR));
}

/*-----------------------------------------------------*/
/* skip_blanks         Skip past any blanks at the current */
/*                     location in the source buffer.  Set */
/*                     ch to the next nonblank character.  */
/*-----------------------------------------------------*/

skip_blanks()

{
    while (ch == ' ') get_char();
}

            /*********************************/
            /*                               */
            /*        Token routines         */
            /*                               */
            /*********************************/

    /* Note that after a token has been extracted, */
    /* ch is the first character after the token.   */

/*-----------------------------------------------------*/
/* get_token           Extract the next token from the source */
/*                     buffer.                         */
/*-----------------------------------------------------*/

get_token()
```

```
{
    skip_blanks();
    tokenp = token_string;

    switch (char_code(ch)) {
        case LETTER:    get_word();          break;
        case DIGIT:     get_number();        break;
        case QUOTE:     get_string();        break;
        case EOF_CODE:  token = END_OF_FILE; break;
        default:        get_special();       break;
    }

    /*
    -- For the interpreter:  While parsing a block, crunch
    -- the token code and append it to the code buffer.
    */
    if (block_flag) crunch_token();
}

/*------------------------------------------------------------*/
/* get_word          Extract a word token and downshift its  */
/*                   characters.  Check if it's a reserved   */
/*                   word.  Set token to IDENTIFIER if it's  */
/*                   not.                                     */
/*------------------------------------------------------------*/

get_word()

{
    BOOLEAN is_reserved_word();

    /*
    -- Extract the word.
    */
    while ((char_code(ch) == LETTER) || (char_code(ch) == DIGIT)) {
        *tokenp++ = ch;
        get_char();
    }
    *tokenp = '\0';
    downshift_word();

    if (! is_reserved_word()) token = IDENTIFIER;
}

/*------------------------------------------------------------*/
/* get_number        Extract a number token and set literal  */
/*                   to its value.  Set token to NUMBER.     */
/*------------------------------------------------------------*/

get_number()

{
    int     whole_count    = 0;     /* no. digits in whole part */
    int     decimal_offset = 0;     /* no. digits to move decimal */
    char    exponent_sign  = '+';
    int     exponent       = 0;     /* value of exponent */
    float   nvalue         = 0.0;   /* value of number */
    float   evalue         = 0.0;   /* value of exponent */
    BOOLEAN saw_dotdot     = FALSE; /* TRUE if encounter .. */

    digit_count = 0;
    count_error = FALSE;
    token       = NO_TOKEN;

    literal.type = INTEGER_LIT;     /* assume it's an integer */

    /*
```

```
    -- Extract the whole part of the number by accumulating
    -- the values of its digits into nvalue.  whole_count keeps
    -- track of the number of digits in this part.
    */
    accumulate_value(&nvalue, INVALID_NUMBER);
    if (token == ERROR) return;
    whole_count = digit_count;

    /*
    -- If the current character is a dot, then either we have a
    -- fraction part or we are seeing the first character of a ..
    -- token.  To find out, we must fetch the next character.
    */
    if (ch == '.') {
        get_char();

        if (ch == '.') {
            /*
            -- We have a .. token.  Back up bufferp so that the
            -- token can be extracted next.
            */
            saw_dotdot = TRUE;
            --bufferp;
        }
        else {
            literal.type = REAL_LIT;
            *tokenp++ = '.';

            /*
            -- We have a fraction part.  Accumulate it into nvalue.
            -- decimal_offset keeps track of how many digits to move
            -- the decimal point back.
            */
            accumulate_value(&nvalue, INVALID_FRACTION);
            if (token == ERROR) return;
            decimal_offset = whole_count - digit_count;
        }
    }

    /*
    -- Extract the exponent part, if any. There cannot be an
    -- exponent part if the .. token has been seen.
    */
    if (!saw_dotdot && ((ch == 'E') || (ch == 'e'))) {
        literal.type = REAL_LIT;
        *tokenp++ = ch;
        get_char();

        /*
        -- Fetch the exponent's sign, if any.
        */
        if ((ch == '+') || (ch == '-')) {
            *tokenp++ = exponent_sign = ch;
            get_char();
        }

        /*
        -- Extract the exponent.  Accumulate it into evalue.
        */
        accumulate_value(&evalue, INVALID_EXPONENT);
        if (token == ERROR) return;
        if (exponent_sign == '-') evalue = -evalue;
    }

    /*
    -- Were there too many digits?
    */
```

```
    if (count_error) {
        error(TOO_MANY_DIGITS);
        token = ERROR;
        return;
    }

    /*
    -- Adjust the number's value using
    -- decimal_offset and the exponent.
    */
    exponent = evalue + decimal_offset;
    if ((exponent + whole_count < -MAX_EXPONENT) ||
        (exponent + whole_count >  MAX_EXPONENT)) {
        error(REAL_OUT_OF_RANGE);
        token = ERROR;
        return;
    }
    if (exponent != 0) nvalue *= pow(10, exponent);

    /*
    -- Set the literal's value.
    */
    if (literal.type == INTEGER_LIT) {
        if ((nvalue < -MAX_INTEGER) || (nvalue > MAX_INTEGER)) {
            error(INTEGER_OUT_OF_RANGE);
            token = ERROR;
            return;
        }
        literal.value.integer = nvalue;
    }
    else literal.value.real = nvalue;

    *tokenp = '\0';
    token   = NUMBER;
}

/*------------------------------------------------------------*/
/*  get_string          Extract a string token.  Set token to  */
/*                       STRING.  Note that the quotes are      */
/*                       stored as part of token_string but not */
/*                       literal.value.string.                  */
/*------------------------------------------------------------*/

get_string()

{
    char *sp = literal.value.string;

    *tokenp++ = '\'';
    get_char();

    /*
    --  Extract the string.
    */
    while (ch != EOF_CHAR) {
        /*
        -- Two consecutive single quotes represent
        -- a single quote in the string.
        */
        if (ch == '\'') {
            *tokenp++ = ch;
            get_char();
            if (ch != '\'') break;
        }
        *tokenp++ = ch;
        *sp++     = ch;
        get_char();
```

```
    }

    *tokenp     = '\0';
    *sp         = '\0';
    token       = STRING;
    literal.type = STRING_LIT;
}

/*------------------------------------------------------------*/
/*  get_special          Extract a special token.  Most are     */
/*                        single-character.  Some are double-    */
/*                        character.  Set token appropriately.   */
/*------------------------------------------------------------*/

get_special()

{
    *tokenp++ = ch;
    switch (ch) {
        case '^':  token = UPARROW;    get_char();  break;
        case '*':  token = STAR;       get_char();  break;
        case '(':  token = LPAREN;     get_char();  break;
        case ')':  token = RPAREN;     get_char();  break;
        case '-':  token = MINUS;      get_char();  break;
        case '+':  token = PLUS;       get_char();  break;
        case '=':  token = EQUAL;      get_char();  break;
        case '[':  token = LBRACKET;   get_char();  break;
        case ']':  token = RBRACKET;   get_char();  break;
        case ';':  token = SEMICOLON;  get_char();  break;
        case ',':  token = COMMA;      get_char();  break;
        case '/':  token = SLASH;      get_char();  break;

        case ':':  get_char();          /* : or := */
                   if (ch == '=') {
                       *tokenp++ = '=';
                       token     = COLONEQUAL;
                       get_char();
                   }
                   else token = COLON;
                   break;

        case '<':  get_char();          /* < or <= or <> */
                   if (ch == '=') {
                       *tokenp++ = '=';
                       token     = LE;
                       get_char();
                   }
                   else if (ch == '>') {
                       *tokenp++ = '>';
                       token     = NE;
                       get_char();
                   }
                   else token = LT;
                   break;

        case '>':  get_char();          /* > or >= */
                   if (ch == '=') {
                       *tokenp++ = '=';
                       token     = GE;
                       get_char();
                   }
                   else token = GT;
                   break;

        case '.':  get_char();          /* . or .. */
                   if (ch == '.') {
                       *tokenp++ = '.';
```

```
                    token       = DOTDOT;                      if (++digit_count <= MAX_DIGIT_COUNT)
                    get_char();                                    value = 10*value + (ch - '0');
                }                                          else count_error = TRUE;
                else token = PERIOD;
                break;                                         get_char();
                                                       } while (char_code(ch) == DIGIT);
        default:    token = ERROR;
                    get_char();                            *valuep = value;
                    break;                         }
    }
    *tokenp = '\0';
}                                                         /*******************************/
                                                          /*                             */
/*--------------------------------------------------*/    /*      Token testers          */
/* downshift_word      Copy a word token into word_string */   /*                             */
/*                     with all letters downshifted.   */    /*******************************/
/*--------------------------------------------------*/

downshift_word()                                       /*----------------------------------------------------*/
                                                       /* token_in         Return TRUE if the current token is in */
{                                                      /*                  the token list, else return FALSE.   */
    int  offset = 'a' - 'A';    /* offset to downshift a letter */   /*----------------------------------------------------*/
    char *wp  = word_string;
    char *tp  = token_string;                              BOOLEAN
                                                       token_in(token_list)
    /*
    -- Copy word into word_string.                         TOKEN_CODE token_list[];
    */
    do {                                               {
        *wp++ = (*tp >= 'A') && (*tp <= 'Z')   /* if a letter, */
              ? *tp + offset                   /* then downshift */    TOKEN_CODE *tokenp;
              : *tp;                            /* else just copy */
        ++tp;                                              if (token_list == NULL) return(FALSE);
    } while (*tp != '\0');
                                                           for (tokenp = &token_list[0]; *tokenp; ++tokenp) {
    *wp = '\0';                                                if (token == *tokenp) return(TRUE);
}                                                          }

                                                           return(FALSE);
                                                       }
/*--------------------------------------------------*/
/* accumulate_value    Extract a number part and accumulate */
/*                     its value.  Flag the error if the first */   /*----------------------------------------------------*/
/*                     character is not a digit.        */   /* synchronize      If the current token is not in one of */
/*--------------------------------------------------*/    /*                  the token lists, flag it as an error. */
                                                       /*                  Then skip tokens until one that is in */
accumulate_value(valuep, error_code)                   /*                  one of the token lists.              */
                                                       /*----------------------------------------------------*/
    float      *valuep;
    ERROR_CODE error_code;                             synchronize(token_list1, token_list2, token_list3)

{                                                          TOKEN_CODE token_list1[], token_list2[], token_list3[];
    float value = *valuep;
                                                       {
    /*                                                     BOOLEAN error_flag = (! token_in(token_list1)) &&
    -- Error if the first character is not a digit.                            (! token_in(token_list2)) &&
    */                                                                         (! token_in(token_list3)));
    if (char_code(ch) != DIGIT) {
        error(error_code);                                 if (error_flag) {
        token = ERROR;                                         error(token == END_OF_FILE ? UNEXPECTED_END_OF_FILE
        return;                                                              : UNEXPECTED_TOKEN);
    }
                                                           /*
    /*                                                     -- Skip tokens to resynchronize.
    -- Accumulate the value as long as the total allowable    */
    -- number of digits has not been exceeded.             while ((! token_in(token_list1)) &&
    */                                                            (! token_in(token_list2)) &&
    do {                                                          (! token_in(token_list3)) &&
        *tokenp++ = ch;                                           (token != END_OF_FILE))
                                                               get_token();
                                                       }
```

```
}
```

```
/*-------------------------------------------------*/
/* is_reserved_word   Check to see if a word token is a   */
/*                    reserved word.  If so, set token     */
/*                    appropriately and return TRUE. Else, */
/*                    return FALSE.                        */
/*-------------------------------------------------*/

    BOOLEAN
is_reserved_word()

{
    int      word_length = strlen(word_string);
    RW_STRUCT *rwp;

    /*
    -- Is it the right length?
    */
    if ((word_length >= MIN_RESERVED_WORD_LENGTH) &&
        (word_length <= MAX_RESERVED_WORD_LENGTH)) {
        /*
        -- Yes.  Pick the appropriate reserved word list
        -- and check to see if the word is in there.
        */
        for (rwp = rw_table[word_length];
             rwp->string != NULL;
             ++rwp) {
            if (strcmp(word_string, rwp->string) == 0) {
                token = rwp->token_code;
                return(TRUE);              /* yes, a reserved word */
            }
        }
    }

    return(FALSE);                     /* no, it's not */
}
```

```
            /*******************************/
            /*                             */
            /*      Source file routines   */
            /*                             */
            /*******************************/
```

```
/*-------------------------------------------------*/
/* open_source_file   Open the source file and fetch its  */
/*                    first character.                     */
/*-------------------------------------------------*/

open_source_file(name)

    char *name;        /* name of source file */

{
    if ((name == NULL) ||
        ((source_file = fopen(name, "r")) == NULL)) {
        error(FAILED_SOURCE_FILE_OPEN);
        exit(-FAILED_SOURCE_FILE_OPEN);
    }

    /*
    -- Fetch the first character.
    */
    bufferp = ""      ;
    get_char();
}
```

```
/*-------------------------------------------------*/
/* close_source_file   Close the source file.            */
/*-------------------------------------------------*/

close_source_file()

{
    fclose(source_file);
}
```

```
/*-------------------------------------------------*/
/* get_source_line    Read the next line from the source  */
/*                    file.  If there is one, print it out */
/*                    and return TRUE.  Else return FALSE  */
/*                    for the end of file.                 */
/*-------------------------------------------------*/

    BOOLEAN
get_source_line()

{
    char print_buffer[MAX_SOURCE_LINE_LENGTH + 9];

    if ((fgets(source_buffer, MAX_SOURCE_LINE_LENGTH,
                              source_file)) != NULL) {
        ++line_number;

        if (print_flag) {
            sprintf(print_buffer, "%4d %d: %s",
                        line_number, level, source_buffer);
            print_line(print_buffer);
        }

        return(TRUE);
    }
    else return(FALSE);
}
```

```
            /*******************************/
            /*                             */
            /*      Printout routines      */
            /*                             */
            /*******************************/
```

```
/*-------------------------------------------------*/
/* print_line         Print out a line.  Start a new page if */
/*                    the current page is full.            */
/*-------------------------------------------------*/

print_line(line)

    char line[];       /* line to be printed */

{
    char save_ch;
    char *save_chp = NULL;

    if (++line_count > MAX_LINES_PER_PAGE) {
        print_page_header();
        line_count = 1;
    };

    if (strlen(line) > MAX_PRINT_LINE_LENGTH) {
        save_chp = &line[MAX_PRINT_LINE_LENGTH];
        save_ch  = *save_chp;
        *save_chp = '\0';
    }
```

```
    printf("%s", line);

    if (save_chp) *save_chp = save_ch;
}

/*----------------------------------------------------------*/
/* init_page_header    Initialize the fields of the page    */
/*                     header.                               */
/*----------------------------------------------------------*/

init_page_header(name)

    char *name;         /* name of source file */

{
    time_t timer;

    strncpy(source_name, name, MAX_FILE_NAME_LENGTH - 1);
```

```
    /*
    -- Set the current date and time in the date string.
    */
    time(&timer);
    strcpy(date, asctime(localtime(&timer)));

}

/*----------------------------------------------------------*/
/* print_page_header    Print the page header at the top of */
/*                      the next page.                      */
/*----------------------------------------------------------*/

print_page_header()

{
    putchar(FORM_FEED_CHAR);
    printf("Page %d   %s   %s\n\n", ++page_number, source_name, date);
}
```

FIGURE A-9   symtab.h

```
/****************************************************************/
/*                                                              */
/*      S Y M B O L   T A B L E   (Header)                      */
/*                                                              */
/*      FILE:       symtab.h                                    */
/*                                                              */
/*      MODULE:     symbol table                                */
/*                                                              */
/****************************************************************/

#ifndef symtab_h
#define symtab_h

#include "common.h"

/*----------------------------------------------------------*/
/* Value structure                                          */
/*----------------------------------------------------------*/

typedef union {
    int    integer;
    float  real;
    char   character;
    char   *stringp;
} VALUE;

/*----------------------------------------------------------*/
/* Definition structure                                     */
/*----------------------------------------------------------*/

typedef enum {
    UNDEFINED,
    CONST_DEFN, TYPE_DEFN, VAR_DEFN, FIELD_DEFN,
    VALPARM_DEFN, VARPARM_DEFN,
    PROG_DEFN, PROC_DEFN, FUNC_DEFN,
} DEFN_KEY;

typedef enum {
    DECLARED, FORWARD,
    READ, READLN, WRITE, WRITELN,
    ABS, ARCTAN, CHR, COS, EOFF, EOLN, EXP, LN, ODD, ORD,
```

```
    PRED, ROUND, SIN, SQR, SQRT, SUCC, TRUNC,
} ROUTINE_KEY;

typedef struct {
    DEFN_KEY key;
    union {
        struct {
            VALUE value;
        } constant;

        struct {
            ROUTINE_KEY       key;
            int               parm_count;
            int               total_parm_size;
            int               total_local_size;
            struct symtab_node *parms;
            struct symtab_node *locals;
            struct symtab_node *local_symtab;
            char              *code_segment;
        } routine;

        struct {
            int               offset;
            struct symtab_node *record_idp;
        } data;
    } info;
} DEFN_STRUCT;

/*----------------------------------------------------------*/
/* Type structure                                           */
/*----------------------------------------------------------*/

typedef enum {
    NO_FORM,
    SCALAR_FORM, ENUM_FORM, SUBRANGE_FORM,
    ARRAY_FORM, RECORD_FORM,
} TYPE_FORM;

typedef struct type_struct {
    TYPE_FORM        form;
    int              size;
```

```
        struct symtab_node *type_idp;
        union {
            struct {
                struct symtab_node *const_idp;
                int                 max;
            } enumeration;

            struct {
                struct type_struct *range_typep;
                int                 min, max;
            } subrange;

            struct {
                struct type_struct *index_typep, *elmt_typep;
                int                 min_index, max_index;
                int                 elmt_count;
            } array;

            struct {
                struct symtab_node *field_symtab;
            } record;
        } info;
} TYPE_STRUCT, *TYPE_STRUCT_PTR;

/*------------------------------------------------------*/
/*  Symbol table node                                   */
/*------------------------------------------------------*/

typedef struct symtab_node {
    struct symtab_node *left, *right;  /* ptrs to subtrees */
    struct symtab_node *next;          /* for chaining nodes */
    char               *name;          /* name string */
    char               *info;          /* ptr to generic info */
    DEFN_STRUCT         defn;           /* definition struct */
    TYPE_STRUCT_PTR     typep;          /* ptr to type struct */
    int                 level;          /* nesting level */
    int                 label_index;    /* index for code label */
} SYMTAB_NODE, *SYMTAB_NODE_PTR;

/*------------------------------------------------------*/
/*  Functions                                           */
/*------------------------------------------------------*/

SYMTAB_NODE_PTR search_symtab();
SYMTAB_NODE_PTR search_symtab_display();
SYMTAB_NODE_PTR enter_symtab();
SYMTAB_NODE_PTR exit_scope();
TYPE_STRUCT_PTR make_string_typep();

        /****************************************/
        /*                                      */
        /*      Macros to search symbol tables  */
        /*                                      */
        /****************************************/

/*------------------------------------------------------*/
/*  search_local_symtab         Search the local symbol */
/*                              table for the current id */
/*                              name.  Set a pointer to the */
/*                              entry if found, else to */
/*                              NULL.                    */
/*------------------------------------------------------*/

#define search_local_symtab(idp)                        \
    idp = search_symtab(word_string, symtab_display[level])

/*------------------------------------------------------*/
/*  search_this_symtab          Search the given symbol */
```

```
/*                              table for the current id */
/*                              name.  Set a pointer to the */
/*                              entry if found, else to */
/*                              NULL.                    */
/*------------------------------------------------------*/

#define search_this_symtab(idp, this_symtab)            \
    idp = search_symtab(word_string, this_symtab)

/*------------------------------------------------------*/
/*  search_all_symtab           Search the symbol table */
/*                              display for the current id */
/*                              name.  Set a pointer to the */
/*                              entry if found, else to */
/*                              NULL.                    */
/*------------------------------------------------------*/

#define search_all_symtab(idp)                          \
    idp = search_symtab_display(word_string)

/*------------------------------------------------------*/
/*  enter_local_symtab          Enter the current id name */
/*                              into the local symbol   */
/*                              table, and set a pointer */
/*                              to the entry.           */
/*------------------------------------------------------*/

#define enter_local_symtab(idp)                         \
    idp = enter_symtab(word_string, &symtab_display[level])

/*------------------------------------------------------*/
/*  enter_name_local_symtab     Enter the given name into */
/*                              the local symbol table, and */
/*                              set a pointer to the entry. */
/*------------------------------------------------------*/

#define enter_name_local_symtab(idp, name)              \
    idp = enter_symtab(name, &symtab_display[level])

/*------------------------------------------------------*/
/*  search_and_find_all_symtab  Search the symbol table */
/*                              display for the current id */
/*                              name.  If not found, ID */
/*                              UNDEFINED error, and enter */
/*                              into the local symbol table. */
/*                              Set a pointer to the entry. */
/*------------------------------------------------------*/

#define search_and_find_all_symtab(idp)                         \
    if ((idp = search_symtab_display(word_string)) == NULL) {   \
        error(UNDEFINED_IDENTIFIER);                            \
        idp = enter_symtab(word_string, &symtab_display[level]);\
        idp->defn.key = UNDEFINED;                              \
        idp->typep = &dummy_type;                               \
    }

/*------------------------------------------------------*/
/*  search_and_enter_local_symtab  Search the local symbol */
/*                              table for the current id */
/*                              name.  Enter the name if */
/*                              it is not already in there, */
/*                              else ID REDEFINED error. */
/*                              Set a pointer to the entry. */
/*------------------------------------------------------*/

#define search_and_enter_local_symtab(idp)              \
    if ((idp = search_symtab(word_string,               \
                    symtab_display[level])) == NULL) { \
```

```
        idp = enter_symtab(word_string, &symtab_display[level]);\
    }                                                            \
    else error(REDEFINED_IDENTIFIER)

/*-----------------------------------------------------------*/
/*  search_and_enter_this_symtab     Search the given symbol   */
/*                                   table for the current id  */
/*                                   name.  Enter the name if  */
/*                                   it is not already in there, */
/*                                   else ID REDEFINED error.   */
/*                                   Set a pointer to the entry. */
```

```
/*-------------------------------------------------------------*/

#define search_and_enter_this_symtab(idp, this_symtab)          \
    if ((idp = search_symtab(word_string,                       \
                             this_symtab)) == NULL) {           \
        idp = enter_symtab(word_string, &this_symtab);          \
    }                                                           \
    else error(REDEFINED_IDENTIFIER)

#endif
```

FIGURE A-10   symtab.c

```
/*******************************************************************/
/*                                                                 */
/*           S Y M B O L    T A B L E                              */
/*                                                                 */
/*           Symbol table routines.                                */
/*                                                                 */
/*           FILE:        symtab.c                                 */
/*                                                                 */
/*           MODULE:      symbol table                            */
/*                                                                 */
/*******************************************************************/

#include <stdio.h>
#include "common.h"
#include "error.h"
#include "symtab.h"


/*-----------------------------------------------------------*/
/* Externals                                                 */
/*-----------------------------------------------------------*/

extern int level;


/*-----------------------------------------------------------*/
/* Globals                                                   */
/*-----------------------------------------------------------*/

SYMTAB_NODE_PTR symtab_display[MAX_NESTING_LEVEL];

TYPE_STRUCT_PTR integer_typep, real_typep,       /* predefined types */
                boolean_typep, char_typep;

TYPE_STRUCT dummy_type = {       /* for erroneous type definitions */
    NO_FORM,        /* form */
    0,              /* size */
    NULL            /* type_idp */
};

/*-----------------------------------------------------------*/
/* search_symtab       Search for a name in the symbol table.  */
/*                     Return a pointer of the entry if found, */
/*                     or NULL if not.                         */
/*-----------------------------------------------------------*/

    SYMTAB_NODE_PTR
search_symtab(name, np)

    char        *name;      /* name to search for */
```

```
    SYMTAB_NODE_PTR np;        /* ptr to symtab root */

{
    int cmp;

    /*
    -- Loop to check each node.  Return if the node matches,
    -- else continue search down the left or right subtree.
    */
    while (np != NULL) {
        cmp = strcmp(name, np->name);
        if (cmp == 0) return(np);                  /* found */
        np = cmp < 0 ? np->left : np->right;    /* continue search */
    }

    return(NULL);                              /* not found */
}

/*-----------------------------------------------------------*/
/*  search_symtab_display   Search all the symbol tables in the */
/*                          symbol table display for a name.    */
/*                          Return a pointer to the entry if    */
/*                          found, or NULL if not.              */
/*-----------------------------------------------------------*/

    SYMTAB_NODE_PTR
search_symtab_display(name)

    char *name;                /* name to search for */

{
    short i;
    SYMTAB_NODE_PTR np;        /* ptr to symtab node */

    for (i = level; i >= 0; --i) {
        np = search_symtab(name, symtab_display[i]);
        if (np != NULL) return(np);
    }

    return(NULL);
}

/*-----------------------------------------------------------*/
/*  enter_symtab       Enter a name into the symbol table,      */
/*                     and return a pointer to the new entry.   */
/*-----------------------------------------------------------*/

    SYMTAB_NODE_PTR
```

```
enter_symtab(name, npp)

    char            *name;          /* name to enter */
    SYMTAB_NODE_PTR *npp;           /* ptr to ptr to symtab root */

{
    int             cmp;            /* result of strcmp */
    SYMTAB_NODE_PTR new_nodep;      /* ptr to new entry */
    SYMTAB_NODE_PTR np;             /* ptr to node to test */

    /*
    --  Create the new node for the name.
    */
    new_nodep = alloc_struct(SYMTAB_NODE);
    new_nodep->name = alloc_bytes(strlen(name) + 1);
    strcpy(new_nodep->name, name);
    new_nodep->left = new_nodep->right = new_nodep->next = NULL;
    new_nodep->info = NULL;
    new_nodep->defn.key = UNDEFINED;
    new_nodep->typep = NULL;
    new_nodep->level = level;
    new_nodep->label_index = 0;

    /*
    --  Loop to search for the insertion point.
    */
    while ((np = *npp) != NULL) {
        cmp = strcmp(name, np->name);
        npp = cmp < 0 ? &(np->left) : &(np->right);
    }

    *npp = new_nodep;                   /* replace */
    return(new_nodep);
}

/*-----------------------------------------------------------*/
/*  init_symtab        Initialize the symbol table with      */
/*                     predefined identifiers and types,     */
/*                     and routines.                         */
/*-----------------------------------------------------------*/

init_symtab()

{
    SYMTAB_NODE_PTR integer_idp, real_idp, boolean_idp, char_idp,
                    false_idp, true_idp;

    /*
    --  Initialize the level-0 symbol table.
    */
    symtab_display[0] = NULL;

    enter_name_local_symtab(integer_idp, "integer");
    enter_name_local_symtab(real_idp,    "real");
    enter_name_local_symtab(boolean_idp, "boolean");
    enter_name_local_symtab(char_idp,    "char");
    enter_name_local_symtab(false_idp,   "false");
    enter_name_local_symtab(true_idp,    "true");

    integer_typep = alloc_struct(TYPE_STRUCT);
    real_typep    = alloc_struct(TYPE_STRUCT);
    boolean_typep = alloc_struct(TYPE_STRUCT);
    char_typep    = alloc_struct(TYPE_STRUCT);

    integer_idp->defn.key   = TYPE_DEFN;
    integer_idp->typep      = integer_typep;
    integer_typep->form     = SCALAR_FORM;
```

```
    integer_typep->size     = sizeof(int);
    integer_typep->type_idp = integer_idp;

    real_idp->defn.key      = TYPE_DEFN;
    real_idp->typep         = real_typep;
    real_typep->form        = SCALAR_FORM;
    real_typep->size        = sizeof(float);
    real_typep->type_idp    = real_idp;

    boolean_idp->defn.key   = TYPE_DEFN;
    boolean_idp->typep      = boolean_typep;
    boolean_typep->form     = ENUM_FORM;
    boolean_typep->size     = sizeof(int);
    boolean_typep->type_idp = boolean_idp;

    boolean_typep->info.enumeration.max = 1;
    boolean_idp->typep->info.enumeration.const_idp = false_idp;
    false_idp->defn.key = CONST_DEFN;
    false_idp->defn.info.constant.value.integer = 0;
    false_idp->typep = boolean_typep;

    false_idp->next = true_idp;
    true_idp->defn.key = CONST_DEFN;
    true_idp->defn.info.constant.value.integer = 1;
    true_idp->typep = boolean_typep;

    char_idp->defn.key   = TYPE_DEFN;
    char_idp->typep      = char_typep;
    char_typep->form     = SCALAR_FORM;
    char_typep->size     = sizeof(char);
    char_typep->type_idp = char_idp;

    enter_standard_routine("read",      READ,       PROC_DEFN);
    enter_standard_routine("readln",    READLN,     PROC_DEFN);
    enter_standard_routine("write",     WRITE,      PROC_DEFN);
    enter_standard_routine("writeln",   WRITELN,    PROC_DEFN);

    enter_standard_routine("abs",       ABS,        FUNC_DEFN);
    enter_standard_routine("arctan",    ARCTAN,     FUNC_DEFN);
    enter_standard_routine("chr",       CHR,        FUNC_DEFN);
    enter_standard_routine("cos",       COS,        FUNC_DEFN);
    enter_standard_routine("eof",       EOFF,       FUNC_DEFN);
    enter_standard_routine("eoln",      EOLN,       FUNC_DEFN);
    enter_standard_routine("exp",       EXP,        FUNC_DEFN);
    enter_standard_routine("ln",        LN,         FUNC_DEFN);
    enter_standard_routine("odd",       ODD,        FUNC_DEFN);
    enter_standard_routine("ord",       ORD,        FUNC_DEFN);
    enter_standard_routine("pred",      PRED,       FUNC_DEFN);
    enter_standard_routine("round",     ROUND,      FUNC_DEFN);
    enter_standard_routine("sin",       SIN,        FUNC_DEFN);
    enter_standard_routine("sqr",       SQR,        FUNC_DEFN);
    enter_standard_routine("sqrt",      SQRT,       FUNC_DEFN);
    enter_standard_routine("succ",      SUCC,       FUNC_DEFN);
    enter_standard_routine("trunc",     TRUNC,      FUNC_DEFN);
}

/*-----------------------------------------------------------*/
/*  enter_standard_routine    Enter a standard procedure or  */
/*                            function identifier into the   */
/*                            symbol table.                  */
/*-----------------------------------------------------------*/

enter_standard_routine(name, routine_key, defn_key)

    char        *name;          /* name string */
    ROUTINE_KEY routine_key;
    DEFN_KEY    defn_key;
```

```
{
    SYMTAB_NODE_PTR rtn_idp = enter_name_local_symtab(rtn_idp, name);

    rtn_idp->defn.key                    = defn_key;
    rtn_idp->defn.info.routine.key       = routine_key;
    rtn_idp->defn.info.routine.parms     = NULL;
    rtn_idp->defn.info.routine.local_symtab = NULL;
    rtn_idp->typep                       = NULL;
}


/*------------------------------------------------------------*/
/*  enter_scope          Enter a new nesting level by creating  */
/*                       a new scope.  Push the given symbol    */
/*                       table onto the display stack.          */
/*------------------------------------------------------------*/

enter_scope(symtab_root)

    SYMTAB_NODE_PTR symtab_root;

{
    if (++level >= MAX_NESTING_LEVEL) {
```

```
        error(NESTING_TOO_DEEP);
        exit(-NESTING_TOO_DEEP);
    }

    symtab_display[level] = symtab_root;
}

/*------------------------------------------------------------*/
/*  exit_scope           Exit the current nesting level by    */
/*                       closing the current scope.  Pop the  */
/*                       current symbol table off the display */
/*                       stack and return a pointer to it.    */
/*------------------------------------------------------------*/

    SYMTAB_NODE_PTR
exit_scope()

{
    SYMTAB_NODE_PTR symtab_root = symtab_display[level--];

    return(symtab_root);
}
```

FIGURE A-11   exec.h

```
/****************************************************************/
/*                                                            */
/*          E X E C U T O R   (Header)                        */
/*                                                            */
/*      FILE:      exec.h                                     */
/*                                                            */
/*      MODULE:    executor                                   */
/*                                                            */
/****************************************************************/

#ifndef exec_h
#define exec_h

#include "common.h"

#define STATEMENT_MARKER  0x70
#define ADDRESS_MARKER    0x71


/*------------------------------------------------------------*/
/*  Runtime stack                                             */
/*------------------------------------------------------------*/

typedef union {
    int    integer;
    float  real;
    char   byte;
    ADDRESS address;
} STACK_ITEM, *STACK_ITEM_PTR;

typedef struct {
    STACK_ITEM function_value;
    STACK_ITEM static_link;
    STACK_ITEM dynamic_link;
    STACK_ITEM return_address;
} *STACK_FRAME_HEADER_PTR;
```

```
/*------------------------------------------------------------*/
/*  Functions                                                 */
/*------------------------------------------------------------*/

SYMTAB_NODE_PTR get_symtab_cptr();
TYPE_STRUCT_PTR exec_routine_call();
TYPE_STRUCT_PTR exec_expression(), exec_variable();
char           *crunch_address_marker();
char           *fixup_address_marker();
int            get_statement_cmarker();
char           *get_address_cmarker();
int            get_cinteger();
char           *get_caddress();

                /***********************/
                /*                     */
                /*       Macros        */
                /*                     */
                /***********************/

/*------------------------------------------------------------*/
/*  get_ctoken           Extract the next token code from the */
/*                       current code segment.                */
/*------------------------------------------------------------*/

#define get_ctoken()     ctoken = *code_segmentp++

/*------------------------------------------------------------*/
/*  pop                  Pop the runtime stack.               */
/*------------------------------------------------------------*/

#define pop()            --tos

/*------------------------------------------------------------*/
/*  Tracing routine calls      Unless the following statements */
/*                             are preceded by                 */
/*                                                            */
```

```
/*                              #define trace              */
/*                                                         */
/*                    calls to the tracing routines        */
/*                    are not compiled.                    */
/*-------------------------------------------------------- */
```

```
#ifndef trace
#define trace_routine_entry(idp)
```

```
#define trace_routine_exit(idp)
#define trace_statement_execution()
#define trace_data_store(idp, idp_tp, targetp, target_tp)
#define trace_data_fetch(idp, tp, datap)
#endif
```

```
#endif
```

FIGURE A-12   executil.c

```
/****************************************************************/
/*                                                         */
/*         E X E C U T O R   U T I L I T I E S             */
/*                                                         */
/*         Utility routines for the executor module.      */
/*                                                         */
/*         FILE:      executil.c                           */
/*                                                         */
/*         MODULE:    executor                             */
/*                                                         */
/****************************************************************/
```

```
#include <stdio.h>
#include "common.h"
#include "error.h"
#include "symtab.h"
#include "scanner.h"
#include "exec.h"
```

```
/*--------------------------------------------------------*/
/* Externals                                              */
/*--------------------------------------------------------*/
```

```
extern TOKEN_CODE token;
extern int        line_number;
extern int        level;
```

```
extern TYPE_STRUCT_PTR integer_typep, real_typep,
                       boolean_typep, char_typep;
```

```
/*--------------------------------------------------------*/
/* Globals                                                */
/*--------------------------------------------------------*/
```

```
char *code_buffer;                    /* code buffer */
char *code_bufferp;                   /* code buffer ptr */
char *code_segmentp;                  /* code segment ptr */
char *code_segment_limit;             /* end of code segment */
char *statement_startp;               /* ptr to start of stmt */
```

```
TOKEN_CODE      ctoken;               /* token from code segment */
int             exec_line_number;     /* no. of line executed */
long            exec_stmt_count = 0;  /* count of stmts executed */
```

```
STACK_ITEM      *stack;               /* runtime stack */
STACK_ITEM_PTR  tos;                  /* ptr to runtime stack top */
STACK_ITEM_PTR  stack_frame_basep;    /* ptr to stack frame base */
```

```
/********************************/
/*                              */
/*      Code segment routines   */
```

```
/*                              */
/********************************/
```

```
/*--------------------------------------------------------*/
/* crunch_token         Append the token code to the code */
/*                      buffer.  Called by the scanner routine */
/*                      get_token only while parsing a block.  */
/*--------------------------------------------------------*/
```

```
crunch_token()

{
    char token_code = token;    /* byte-sized token code */

    if (code_bufferp >= code_buffer + MAX_CODE_BUFFER_SIZE) {
        error(CODE_SEGMENT_OVERFLOW);
        exit(-CODE_SEGMENT_OVERFLOW);
    }
    else *code_bufferp++ = token_code;
}
```

```
/*--------------------------------------------------------*/
/* crunch_symtab_node_ptr     Append a symbol table node  */
/*                            pointer to the code buffer.  */
/*--------------------------------------------------------*/
```

```
crunch_symtab_node_ptr(np)

    SYMTAB_NODE_PTR np;         /* pointer to append */

{
    SYMTAB_NODE_PTR *npp = (SYMTAB_NODE_PTR *) code_bufferp;

    if (code_bufferp >= code_buffer + MAX_CODE_BUFFER_SIZE
                              - sizeof(SYMTAB_NODE_PTR)) {
        error(CODE_SEGMENT_OVERFLOW);
        exit(-CODE_SEGMENT_OVERFLOW);
    }
    else {
        *npp = np;
        code_bufferp += sizeof(SYMTAB_NODE_PTR);
    }
}
```

```
/*--------------------------------------------------------*/
/* crunch_statement_marker    Append a statement marker to */
/*                            the code buffer.             */
/*--------------------------------------------------------*/
```

```
crunch_statement_marker()

{
```

```
        if (code_bufferp >= code_buffer + MAX_CODE_BUFFER_SIZE
                                    - sizeof(int)) {
            error(CODE_SEGMENT_OVERFLOW);
            exit(-CODE_SEGMENT_OVERFLOW);
        }
        else {char save_code = *(--code_bufferp);

            *code_bufferp++ = STATEMENT_MARKER;
            *((int *) code_bufferp) = line_number;
            code_bufferp += sizeof(int);
            *code_bufferp++ = save_code;
        }
}


/*--------------------------------------------------------------*/
/*  crunch_address_marker      Append a code address to the     */
/*                             code buffer.  Return the         */
/*                             addesss of the address.          */
/*--------------------------------------------------------------*/

    char *
crunch_address_marker(address)

    ADDRESS address;    /* address value to append */

{
    char *save_code_bufferp;

    if (code_bufferp >= code_buffer + MAX_CODE_BUFFER_SIZE
                                - sizeof(ADDRESS)) {
        error(CODE_SEGMENT_OVERFLOW);
        exit(-CODE_SEGMENT_OVERFLOW);
    }
    else {
        char save_code = *(--code_bufferp);

        *code_bufferp++ = ADDRESS_MARKER;
        save_code_bufferp = code_bufferp;
        *((ADDRESS *) code_bufferp) = address;
        code_bufferp += sizeof(ADDRESS);
        *code_bufferp++ = save_code;

        return(save_code_bufferp);
    }
}


/*--------------------------------------------------------------*/
/*  fixup_address_marker       Fix up an address marker with    */
/*                             the offset from the address      */
/*                             marker to the current code       */
/*                             buffer address.  Return the old  */
/*                             value of the address marker.     */
/*--------------------------------------------------------------*/

    char *
fixup_address_marker(address)

    ADDRESS address;    /* address of address marker to be fixed up */

{
    char *old_address = *((ADDRESS *) address);

    *((int *) address) = code_bufferp - address;
    return(old_address);
}
```

```
/*--------------------------------------------------------------*/
/*  crunch_integer      Append an integer value to the code     */
/*                      buffer.                                  */
/*--------------------------------------------------------------*/

crunch_integer(value)

    int value;          /* value to append */

{
    if (code_bufferp >= code_buffer + MAX_CODE_BUFFER_SIZE
                                    - sizeof(int)) {
        error(CODE_SEGMENT_OVERFLOW);
        exit(-CODE_SEGMENT_OVERFLOW);
    }
    else {
        *((int *) code_bufferp) = value;
        code_bufferp += sizeof(int);
    }
}


/*--------------------------------------------------------------*/
/*  crunch_offset       Append an integer value to the code     */
/*                      that represents the offset from the     */
/*                      given address to the current code       */
/*                      buffer address.                         */
/*--------------------------------------------------------------*/

crunch_offset(address)

    ADDRESS address;    /* address from which to offset */

{
    if (code_bufferp >= code_buffer + MAX_CODE_BUFFER_SIZE
                                - sizeof(int)) {
        error(CODE_SEGMENT_OVERFLOW);
        exit(-CODE_SEGMENT_OVERFLOW);
    }
    else {
        *((int *) code_bufferp) = address - code_bufferp;
        code_bufferp += sizeof(int);
    }
}


/*--------------------------------------------------------------*/
/*  create_code_segment     Create a code segment and copy in   */
/*                          the contents of the code buffer.    */
/*                          Reset the code buffer pointer.      */
/*                          Return a pointer to the segment.    */
/*--------------------------------------------------------------*/

    char *
create_code_segment()

{
    char *code_segment = alloc_bytes(code_bufferp - code_buffer);

    code_segment_limit = code_segment + (code_bufferp - code_buffer);
    code_bufferp       = code_buffer;
    code_segmentp      = code_segment;

    /*
    -- Copy in the contents of the code buffer.
    */
    while (code_segmentp != code_segment_limit)
        *code_segmentp++ = *code_bufferp++;

    code_bufferp = code_buffer;             /* reset code buffer ptr */
```

```
    return(code_segment);
}

/*-----------------------------------------------------*/
/* get_symtab_cptr    Extract a symbol table node pointer   */
/*                    from the current code segment and     */
/*                    return it.                            */
/*-----------------------------------------------------*/

    SYMTAB_NODE_PTR
get_symtab_cptr()

{
    SYMTAB_NODE_PTR np;
    SYMTAB_NODE_PTR *npp = (SYMTAB_NODE_PTR *) code_segmentp;

    np = *npp;
    code_segmentp += sizeof(SYMTAB_NODE_PTR);
    return(np);
}

/*-----------------------------------------------------*/
/* get_statement_cmarker   Extract a statement marker from the  */
/*                         current code segment and return its  */
/*                         statement line number.              */
/*-----------------------------------------------------*/

    int
get_statement_cmarker()

{
    int line_num;

    if (ctoken == STATEMENT_MARKER) {
        line_num = *((int *) code_segmentp);
        code_segmentp += sizeof(int);
    }

    return(line_num);
}

/*-----------------------------------------------------*/
/* get_address_cmarker     Extract an address marker from the   */
/*                         current code segment.  Add its       */
/*                         offset value to the code segment     */
/*                         address and return the new address.  */
/*-----------------------------------------------------*/

    char *
get_address_cmarker()

{
    ADDRESS address;    /* address to return */

    if (ctoken == ADDRESS_MARKER) {
        address = *((int *) code_segmentp) + code_segmentp - 1;
        code_segmentp += sizeof(ADDRESS);
    }

    return(address);
}

/*-----------------------------------------------------*/
/* get_cinteger    Extract an integer value from the    */
/*                 current code segment and return the  */
/*                 value.                               */
/*-----------------------------------------------------*/
```

```
    int
get_cinteger()

{
    int value;        /* value to extract and return */

    value = *((int *) code_segmentp);
    code_segmentp += sizeof(int);

    return(value);
}

/*-----------------------------------------------------*/
/* get_caddress        Extract an offset from the current code */
/*                     segment and add it to the code segment  */
/*                     address.  Return the new address.       */
/*-----------------------------------------------------*/

    char *
get_caddress()

{
    ADDRESS address;    /* address to return */

    address = *((int *) code_segmentp) + code_segmentp - 1;
    code_segmentp += sizeof(int);

    return(address);
}

            /*******************************/
            /*                             */
            /*       Executor utilities    */
            /*                             */
            /*******************************/

/*-----------------------------------------------------*/
/* push_integer       Push an integer onto the runtime stack. */
/*-----------------------------------------------------*/

push_integer(item_value)

    int item_value;

{
    STACK_ITEM_PTR itemp = ++tos;

    if (itemp >= &stack[MAX_STACK_SIZE])
        runtime_error(RUNTIME_STACK_OVERFLOW);

    itemp->integer = item_value;
}

/*-----------------------------------------------------*/
/* push_real          Push a real onto the runtime stack.     */
/*-----------------------------------------------------*/

push_real(item_value)

    float item_value;

{
    STACK_ITEM_PTR itemp = ++tos;

    if (itemp >= &stack[MAX_STACK_SIZE])
        runtime_error(RUNTIME_STACK_OVERFLOW);
```

```
        itemp->real = item_value;
}

/*----------------------------------------------------*/
/* push_byte         Push a byte onto the runtime stack.    */
/*----------------------------------------------------*/

push_byte(item_value)

    char item_value;

{
    STACK_ITEM_PTR itemp = ++tos;

    if (itemp >= &stack[MAX_STACK_SIZE])
        runtime_error(RUNTIME_STACK_OVERFLOW);

    itemp->byte = item_value;
}

/*----------------------------------------------------*/
/* push_address      Push an address onto the runtime stack. */
/*----------------------------------------------------*/

push_address(address)

    ADDRESS address;

{
    STACK_ITEM_PTR itemp = ++tos;

    if (itemp >= &stack[MAX_STACK_SIZE])
        runtime_error(RUNTIME_STACK_OVERFLOW);

    itemp->address = address;
}

/*----------------------------------------------------*/
/* execute           Execute a routine's code segment.      */
/*----------------------------------------------------*/

execute(rtn_idp)

    SYMTAB_NODE_PTR rtn_idp;

{
    routine_entry(rtn_idp);

    get_ctoken();
    exec_statement();

    routine_exit(rtn_idp);
}

/*----------------------------------------------------*/
/* routine_entry     Point to the new routine's code        */
/*                   segment, and allocate its locals.      */
/*----------------------------------------------------*/

routine_entry(rtn_idp)

    SYMTAB_NODE_PTR rtn_idp;       /* new routine's id */

{
    SYMTAB_NODE_PTR var_idp;       /* local variable id */

    trace_routine_entry(rtn_idp);
```

```
    /*
    -- Switch to the new code segment.
    */
    code_segmentp = rtn_idp->defn.info.routine.code_segment;

    /*
    -- Allocate local variables.
    */
    for (var_idp = rtn_idp->defn.info.routine.locals;
         var_idp != NULL;
         var_idp = var_idp->next) alloc_local(var_idp->typep);
}

/*----------------------------------------------------*/
/* routine_exit      Deallocate the routine's parameters and */
/*                   locals. Cut off its stack frame, and    */
/*                   return to the caller's code segment.     */
/*----------------------------------------------------*/

routine_exit(rtn_idp)

    SYMTAB_NODE_PTR rtn_idp;        /* exiting routine's id */

{
    SYMTAB_NODE_PTR        idp;       /* variable or parm id */
    STACK_FRAME_HEADER_PTR hp;        /* ptr to stack frame header */

    trace_routine_exit(rtn_idp);

    /*
    -- Deallocate parameters and local variables.
    */
    for (idp = rtn_idp->defn.info.routine.parms;
         idp != NULL;
         idp = idp->next) free_data(idp);
    for (idp = rtn_idp->defn.info.routine.locals;
         idp != NULL;
         idp = idp->next) free_data(idp);

    /*
    -- Pop off the stack frame and return to the
    -- caller's code segment.
    */
    hp = (STACK_FRAME_HEADER_PTR) stack_frame_basep;
    code_segmentp = hp->return_address.address;
    tos = (rtn_idp->defn.key == PROC_DEFN)
              ? stack_frame_basep - 1
              : stack_frame_basep;
    stack_frame_basep = (STACK_ITEM_PTR) hp->dynamic_link.address;
}

/*----------------------------------------------------*/
/* push_stack_frame_header   Allocate the callee routine's  */
/*                           stack frame.                   */
/*----------------------------------------------------*/

push_stack_frame_header(old_level, new_level)

    int old_level, new_level;  /* levels of caller and callee */

{
    STACK_FRAME_HEADER_PTR hp;

    push_integer(0);                              /* return value */
    hp = (STACK_FRAME_HEADER_PTR) stack_frame_basep;

    /*
```

```
        --  Static link.
        */
        if (new_level == old_level + 1) {
            /*
            --  Calling a routine nested within the caller:
            --  Push pointer to caller's stack frame.
            */
            push_address(hp);
        }
        else if (new_level == old_level) {
            /*
            --  Calling another routine at the same level:
            --  Push pointer to stack frame of common parent.
            */
            push_address(hp->static_link.address);
        }
        else /* new_level < old_level */ {
            /*
            --  Calling a routine at a lesser level (nested less deeply):
            --  Push pointer to stack frame of nearest common ancestor.
            */
            int delta = old_level - new_level;

            while (delta-- >= 0)
                hp = (STACK_FRAME_HEADER_PTR) hp->static_link.address;
            push_address(hp);
        }

        push_address(stack_frame_basep);        /* dynamic link */
        push_address(0);    /* return address to be filled in later */
    }

/*----------------------------------------------------------*/
/*  alloc_local        Allocate a local variable on the stack. */
/*----------------------------------------------------------*/

alloc_local(tp)

    TYPE_STRUCT_PTR tp;     /* ptr to type of variable */

{
    if      (tp == integer_typep) push_integer(0);
    else if (tp == real_typep)    push_real(0.0);
    else if (tp == boolean_typep) push_byte(0);
    else if (tp == char_typep)    push_byte(0);
```

```
    else switch (tp->form) {
        case ENUM_FORM:
            push_integer(0);
            break;

        case SUBRANGE_FORM:
            alloc_local(tp->info.subrange.range_typep);
            break;

        case ARRAY_FORM: {
            char *ptr = alloc_bytes(tp->size);

            push_address((ADDRESS) ptr);
            break;
        }

        case RECORD_FORM: {
            char *ptr = alloc_bytes(tp->size);

            push_address((ADDRESS) ptr);
            break;
        }
    }
}

/*----------------------------------------------------------*/
/*  free_data          Deallocate the data area of an array  */
/*                     or record local variable or value     */
/*                     parameter.                            */
/*----------------------------------------------------------*/

free_data(idp)

    SYMTAB_NODE_PTR idp;                /* parm or variable id */

{
    STACK_ITEM_PTR  itemp;              /* ptr to stack item */
    TYPE_STRUCT_PTR tp = idp->typep;    /* ptr to id's type */

    if (  ((tp->form == ARRAY_FORM) || (tp->form == RECORD_FORM))
        && (idp->defn.key != VARPARM_DEFN)) {
        itemp = stack_frame_basep + idp->defn.info.data.offset;
        free(itemp->address);
    }
}
```

FIGURE A-13   execstmt.c

```
/****************************************************************/
/*                                                              */
/*     S T A T E M E N T   E X E C U T O R                      */
/*                                                              */
/*     Execution routines for statements.                       */
/*                                                              */
/*     FILE:       execstmt.c                                   */
/*                                                              */
/*     MODULE:     executor                                     */
/*                                                              */
/****************************************************************/

#include <stdio.h>
#include "common.h"
```

```
#include "error.h"
#include "symtab.h"
#include "scanner.h"
#include "parser.h"
#include "exec.h"


/*----------------------------------------------------------*/
/*  Externals                                                */
/*----------------------------------------------------------*/


extern int      level;
extern int      exec_line_number;
extern long     exec_stmt_count;
```

```
extern char          *code_segmentp;
extern char          *statement_startp;
extern TOKEN_CODE    ctoken;

extern STACK_ITEM    *stack;
extern STACK_ITEM_PTR tos;
extern STACK_ITEM_PTR stack_frame_basep;

extern TYPE_STRUCT_PTR integer_typep, real_typep,
                       boolean_typep, char_typep;

/*-------------------------------------------------------------*/
/*  exec_statement       Execute a statement by calling the    */
/*                       appropriate execution routine.        */
/*-------------------------------------------------------------*/

exec_statement()

{
    if (ctoken == STATEMENT_MARKER) {
        exec_line_number = get_statement_cmarker();
        ++exec_stmt_count;

        statement_startp = code_segmentp;
        trace_statement_execution();
        get_ctoken();
    }

    switch (ctoken) {

        case IDENTIFIER: {
            SYMTAB_NODE_PTR idp = get_symtab_cptr();

            if (idp->defn.key == PROC_DEFN)
                exec_routine_call(idp);
            else
                exec_assignment_statement(idp);

            break;
        }

        case BEGIN:    exec_compound_statement();    break;
        case CASE:     exec_case_statement();        break;
        case FOR:      exec_for_statement();         break;
        case IF:       exec_if_statement();          break;
        case REPEAT:   exec_repeat_statement();      break;
        case WHILE:    exec_while_statement();       break;

        case SEMICOLON:
        case END:
        case ELSE:
        case UNTIL:                                  break;

        default: runtime_error(UNIMPLEMENTED_RUNTIME_FEATURE);
    }

    while (ctoken == SEMICOLON) get_ctoken();
}

/*-------------------------------------------------------------*/
/*  exec_assignment_statement     Execute an assignment        */
/*                                statement.                   */
/*-------------------------------------------------------------*/

exec_assignment_statement(idp)

    SYMTAB_NODE_PTR idp;        /* target variable id */
```

```
{
    STACK_ITEM_PTR targetp;      /* ptr to assignment target */
    TYPE_STRUCT_PTR target_tp, base_target_tp, expr_tp;

    /*
    -- Assignment to function id:  Target is the first item of
    --                             the appropriate stack frame.
    */

    if (idp->defn.key == FUNC_DEFN) {
        STACK_FRAME_HEADER_PTR hp;
        int                    delta;  /* difference in levels */

        hp    = (STACK_FRAME_HEADER_PTR) stack_frame_basep;
        delta = level - idp->level - 1;
        while (delta-- > 0)
            hp = (STACK_FRAME_HEADER_PTR) hp->static_link.address;

        targetp = (STACK_ITEM_PTR) hp;
        target_tp = idp->typep;
        get_ctoken();
    }

    /*
    -- Assignment to variable:  Routine exec_variable leaves the
    --                          target address on top of stack.
    */
    else {
        target_tp = exec_variable(idp, TARGET_USE);
        targetp = (STACK_ITEM_PTR) tos->address;

        pop();          /* pop off target address */
    }

    base_target_tp = base_type(target_tp);

    /*
    -- Routine exec_expression leaves the expression value
    -- on top of stack.
    */
    get_ctoken();
    expr_tp = exec_expression();

    /*
    -- Do the assignment.
    */
    if ((target_tp == real_typep) &&
        (base_type(expr_tp) == integer_typep)) {
        /*
        -- real := integer
        */
        targetp->real = tos->integer;
    }
    else if ((target_tp->form == ARRAY_FORM) ||
             (target_tp->form == RECORD_FORM)) {
        /*
        -- array  := array
        -- record := record
        */
        char *ptr1 = (char *) targetp;
        char *ptr2 = tos->address;
        int  size  = target_tp->size;

        while (size--) *ptr1++ = *ptr2++;
    }
    else if ((base_target_tp == integer_typep) ||
             (target_tp->form == ENUM_FORM)) {
```

```
    /*
    -- Range check assignment to integer
    -- or enumeration subrange.
    */
    if (  (target_tp->form == SUBRANGE_FORM)
        && ((tos->integer < target_tp->info.subrange.min) ||
            (tos->integer > target_tp->info.subrange.max)))
        runtime_error(VALUE_OUT_OF_RANGE);
    /*
    -- integer     := integer
    -- enumeration := enumeration
    */
    targetp->integer = tos->integer;
}
else if (base_target_tp == char_typep) {
    /*
    -- Range check assigment to character subrange.
    */
    if (  (target_tp->form == SUBRANGE_FORM)
        && ((tos->byte < target_tp->info.subrange.min) ||
            (tos->byte > target_tp->info.subrange.max)))
        runtime_error(VALUE_OUT_OF_RANGE);
    /*
    -- character := character
    */
    targetp->byte = tos->byte;
}
else {
    /*
    -- real := real
    */
    targetp->real = tos->real;
}

pop();        /* pop off expression value */

trace_data_store(idp, idp->typep, targetp, target_tp);
}

/*-------------------------------------------------------------*/
/* exec_routine_call           Execute a procedure or function */
/*                             call.  Return a pointer to the  */
/*                             type structure.                 */
/*-------------------------------------------------------------*/

    TYPE_STRUCT_PTR
exec_routine_call(rtn_idp)

    SYMTAB_NODE_PTR rtn_idp;     /* routine id */

{
    TYPE_STRUCT_PTR exec_declared_routine_call();
    TYPE_STRUCT_PTR exec_standard_routine_call();

    if (rtn_idp->defn.info.routine.key == DECLARED)
        return(exec_declared_routine_call(rtn_idp));
    else
        return(exec_standard_routine_call(rtn_idp));
}

/*-------------------------------------------------------------*/
/* exec_declared_routine_call   Execute a call to a            */
/*                              declared procedure or          */
/*                              function.  Return a pointer    */
/*                              to the type structure.         */
/*-------------------------------------------------------------*/
```

```
    TYPE_STRUCT_PTR
exec_declared_routine_call(rtn_idp)

    SYMTAB_NODE_PTR rtn_idp;              /* routine id */

{
    int old_level = level;               /* level of caller */
    int new_level = rtn_idp->level + 1;  /* level of callee */
    STACK_ITEM_PTR new_stack_frame_basep;
    STACK_FRAME_HEADER_PTR hp;           /* ptr to frame header */

    /*
    -- Set up stack frame of callee.
    */
    new_stack_frame_basep = tos + 1;
    push_stack_frame_header(old_level, new_level);

    /*
    -- Push parameter values onto the stack.
    */
    get_ctoken();
    if (ctoken == LPAREN) {
        exec_actual_parms(rtn_idp);
        get_ctoken();   /* token after ) */
    }

    /*
    -- Set the return address in the new stack frame,
    -- and execute the callee.
    */
    level = new_level;
    stack_frame_basep = new_stack_frame_basep;
    hp = (STACK_FRAME_HEADER_PTR) stack_frame_basep;
    hp->return_address.address = code_segmentp - 1;
    execute(rtn_idp);

    /*
    -- Return from callee.
    */
    level = old_level;
    get_ctoken();        /* first token after return */

    return(rtn_idp->defn.key == PROC_DEFN ? NULL : rtn_idp->typep);
}

/*-------------------------------------------------------------*/
/* exec_actual_parms           Push the values of the actual   */
/*                             parameters onto the stack.      */
/*-------------------------------------------------------------*/

exec_actual_parms(rtn_idp)

    SYMTAB_NODE_PTR rtn_idp;         /* id of callee routine */

{
    SYMTAB_NODE_PTR formal_idp;      /* formal parm id */
    TYPE_STRUCT_PTR formal_tp, actual_tp;

    /*
    -- Loop to execute actual parameters.
    */
    for (formal_idp = rtn_idp->defn.info.routine.parms;
         formal_idp != NULL;
         formal_idp = formal_idp->next) {

        formal_tp = formal_idp->typep;
        get_ctoken();
```

```
        /*
        -- Value parameter.
        */
        if (formal_idp->defn.key == VALPARM_DEFN) {
            actual_tp = exec_expression();

            /*
            -- Range check for a subrange formal parameter.
            */
            if (formal_tp->form == SUBRANGE_FORM) {
                TYPE_STRUCT_PTR base_formal_tp = base_type(formal_tp);
                int            value;

                value = ((base_formal_tp == integer_typep) ||
                         (base_formal_tp->form == ENUM_FORM))
                            ? tos->integer
                            : tos->byte;

                if ((value < formal_tp->info.subrange.min) ||
                    (value > formal_tp->info.subrange.max)) {
                    runtime_error(VALUE_OUT_OF_RANGE);
                }
            }

            /*
            -- real formal := integer actual
            */
            else if ((formal_tp == real_typep) &&
                     (base_type(actual_tp) == integer_typep)) {
                tos->real = tos->integer;
            }

            /*
            -- Formal parm is array or record:  Make a copy.
            */
            if ((formal_tp->form == ARRAY_FORM) ||
                (formal_tp->form == RECORD_FORM)) {
                int size     = formal_tp->size;
                char *ptr1   = alloc_bytes(size);
                char *ptr2   = tos->address;
                char *save_ptr = ptr1;

                while (size--) *ptr1++ = *ptr2++;
                tos->address = save_ptr;
            }
        }

        /*
        -- VAR parameter.
        */
        else {
            SYMTAB_NODE_PTR idp = get_symtab_cptr();

            exec_variable(idp, VARPARM_USE);
        }
    }
}

/*------------------------------------------------------------*/
/* exec_compound_statement    Execute a compound statement.   */
/*------------------------------------------------------------*/

exec_compound_statement()

{
    get_ctoken();
    while (ctoken != END) exec_statement();
```

```
    get_ctoken();
}

/*------------------------------------------------------------*/
/* exec_case_statement       Execute a CASE statement:        */
/*                                                            */
/*                              CASE <expr> OF                 */
/*                                  <case-branch> ;            */
/*                                  ...                        */
/*                                  END                        */
/*------------------------------------------------------------*/

exec_case_statement()

{
    int            case_expr_value;       /* CASE expr value */
    int            case_label_count;      /* CASE label count */
    int            case_label_value;      /* CASE label value */
    char           *branch_table_location; /* branch table addr */
    char           *case_branch_location;  /* CASE branch addr */
    TYPE_STRUCT_PTR case_expr_tp;          /* CASE expr type */
    BOOLEAN        done = FALSE;

    get_ctoken();      /* token after CASE */
    branch_table_location = get_address_cmarker();

    /*
    -- Evaluate the CASE expression.
    */
    get_ctoken();
    case_expr_tp = exec_expression();
    case_expr_value = (case_expr_tp == integer_typep) ||
                      (case_expr_tp->form == ENUM_FORM)
                          ? tos->integer
                          : tos->byte;
    pop();         /* expression value */

    /*
    -- Search the branch table for the expression value.
    */
    code_segmentp = branch_table_location;
    get_ctoken();
    case_label_count = get_cinteger();
    while (!done && case_label_count--) {
        case_label_value    = get_cinteger();
        case_branch_location = get_caddress();
        done = case_label_value == case_expr_value;
    }

    /*
    -- If found, go to the appropriate CASE branch.
    */
    if (case_label_count >= 0) {
        code_segmentp = case_branch_location;
        get_ctoken();
        exec_statement();

        code_segmentp = get_address_cmarker();
        get_ctoken();
    }
    else runtime_error(INVALID_CASE_VALUE);
}

/*------------------------------------------------------------*/
/* exec_for_statement        Execute a FOR statement:         */
/*                                                            */
/*                              FOR <id> := <expr>            */
```

```
/*                              TO|DOWNTO <expr>        */
/*                              DO <stmt>               */
/*--------------------------------------------------------*/

exec_for_statement()

{
    SYMTAB_NODE_PTR control_idp;            /* control var id */
    TYPE_STRUCT_PTR control_tp;             /* control var type */
    STACK_ITEM_PTR  targetp;                /* ptr to control target */
    char            *loop_start_location;   /* addr of start of loop */
    char            *loop_end_location;     /* addr of end of loop */
    int             control_value;          /* value of control var */
    int             initial_value, final_value, delta_value;

    get_ctoken();       /* token after FOR */
    loop_end_location = get_address_cmarker();

    /*
    -- Get the address of the control variable's stack item.
    */
    get_ctoken();
    control_idp = get_symtab_cptr();
    control_tp  = exec_variable(control_idp, TARGET_USE);
    targetp     = (STACK_ITEM_PTR) tos->address;
    pop();        /* control variable address */

    /*
    -- Evaluate the initial expression.
    */
    get_ctoken();
    exec_expression();
    initial_value = (control_tp == integer_typep)
                        ? tos->integer
                        : tos->byte;
    pop();        /* initial value */

    delta_value = (ctoken == TO) ? 1 : -1;

    /*
    -- Evaluate the final expression.
    */
    get_ctoken();
    exec_expression();
    final_value = (control_tp == integer_typep)
                        ? tos->integer
                        : tos->byte;
    pop();        /* final value */

    loop_start_location = code_segmentp;
    control_value = initial_value;

    /*
    -- Execute the FOR loop.
    */
    while (  ((delta_value == 1) &&
              (control_value <= final_value))
          || ((delta_value == -1) &&
              (control_value >= final_value))) {
        if (control_tp == integer_typep)
            targetp->integer = control_value;
        else
            targetp->byte = control_value;

        get_ctoken();          /* token after DO */
        exec_statement();

        control_value += delta_value;
```

```
        code_segmentp = loop_start_location;
    }

    code_segmentp = loop_end_location;
    get_ctoken();          /* token after FOR statement */
}

/*------------------------------------------------------------*/
/*  exec_if_statement    Execute an IF statement:            */
/*                                                           */
/*                      IF <expr> THEN <stmt>                */
/*                                                           */
/*                  or:                                      */
/*                                                           */
/*                      IF <expr> THEN <stmt> ELSE <stmt>    */
/*------------------------------------------------------------*/

exec_if_statement()

{
    char        *false_location;    /* address of false branch */
    BOOLEAN     test;

    get_ctoken();          /* token after IF */
    false_location = get_address_cmarker();

    /*
    -- Evaluate the boolean expression.
    */
    get_ctoken();
    exec_expression();
    test = tos->integer == 1;
    pop();       /* boolean value */

    if (test) {
        /*
        -- True:  Execute the true branch.
        */
        get_ctoken();    /* token after THEN */
        exec_statement();

        if (ctoken == ELSE) {
            get_ctoken();                 /* token after ELSE */
            code_segmentp = get_address_cmarker();
            get_ctoken();                 /* token after false stmt */
        }
    }
    else {
        /*
        -- False:  Execute the false branch if there is one.
        */
        code_segmentp = false_location;
        get_ctoken();

        if (ctoken == ELSE) {
            get_ctoken();                 /* token after ELSE */
            get_address_cmarker();        /* skip address marker */

            get_ctoken();
            exec_statement();
        }
    }
}

/*------------------------------------------------------------*/
/*  exec_repeat_statement      Execute a REPEAT statement:   */
/*                                                           */
```

```
/*                      REPEAT <stmt-list>      */
/*                      UNTIL <expr>            */
/*------------------------------------------------*/

exec_repeat_statement()

{
    char *loop_start_location = code_segmentp;  /* addr of
                                                   loop start */

    do {
        get_ctoken();        /* token after REPEAT */

        /*
        -- Execute the statement list.
        */
        do {
            exec_statement();
        } while (ctoken != UNTIL);

        /*
        -- Evaluate the boolean expression.
        */
        get_ctoken();
        exec_expression();
        if (tos->integer == 0) code_segmentp = loop_start_location;
        pop();               /* boolean value */
    } while (code_segmentp == loop_start_location);
}

/*------------------------------------------------*/
/* exec_while_statement      Process a WHILE statement:  */
/*                                                       */
/*                           WHILE <expr> DO <stmt>      */
/*------------------------------------------------*/
```

```
exec_while_statement()

{
    char    *loop_end_location;      /* addr of end of loop */
    char    *test_location;          /* addr of boolean expr */
    BOOLEAN loop_done = FALSE;

    get_ctoken();           /* token after WHILE */
    loop_end_location = get_address_cmarker();
    test_location     = code_segmentp;

    do {
        /*
        -- Evaluate the boolean expression.
        */
        get_ctoken();
        exec_expression();
        if (tos->integer == 0) {
            code_segmentp = loop_end_location;
            loop_done = TRUE;
        }
        pop();          /* boolean value */

        /*
        -- If true, execute the statement.
        */
        if (!loop_done) {
            get_ctoken();
            exec_statement();
            code_segmentp = test_location;
        }
    } while (!loop_done);

    get_ctoken();           /* token after WHILE statement */
}
```

FIGURE A-14   execexpr.c

```
/*****************************************************************/
/*                                                               */
/*      E X P R E S S I O N   E X E C U T O R                     */
/*                                                               */
/*      Execution routines for expressions.                      */
/*                                                               */
/*      FILE:       execexpr.c                                   */
/*                                                               */
/*      MODULE:     executor                                     */
/*                                                               */
/*****************************************************************/

#include <stdio.h>
#include "common.h"
#include "error.h"
#include "symtab.h"
#include "scanner.h"
#include "parser.h"
#include "exec.h"


/*------------------------------------------------*/
/* Externals                                      */
/*------------------------------------------------*/
```

```
extern int          level;

extern char         *code_segmentp;
extern TOKEN_CODE    ctoken;

extern STACK_ITEM      *stack;
extern STACK_ITEM_PTR  tos;
extern STACK_ITEM_PTR  stack_frame_basep;

extern TYPE_STRUCT_PTR integer_typep, real_typep,
                       boolean_typep, char_typep;

/*------------------------------------------------*/
/* Forwards                                       */
/*------------------------------------------------*/

TYPE_STRUCT_PTR exec_expression(), exec_simple_expression(),
                exec_term(), exec_factor(),
                exec_constant(), exec_variable(),
                exec_subscripts(), exec_field();

/*------------------------------------------------*/
/* exec_expression     Execute an expression consisting of a  */
/*                     simple expression optionally followed  */
```

```
/*                      by a relational operator and a second    */
/*                      simple expression.  Return a pointer to  */
/*                      the type structure.                      */
/*-------------------------------------------------------------*/

    TYPE_STRUCT_PTR
exec_expression()

{
    STACK_ITEM_PTR  operandp1, operandp2;   /* ptrs to operands */
    TYPE_STRUCT_PTR result_tp, tp2;         /* ptrs to types */
    TOKEN_CODE      op;                      /* an operator token */
    BOOLEAN         result;

    result_tp = exec_simple_expression();   /* first simple expr */

    /*
    -- If there is a relational operator, remember it and
    -- process the second simple expression.
    */
    if ((ctoken == EQUAL) || (ctoken == LT) || (ctoken == GT) ||
        (ctoken == NE)    || (ctoken == LE) || (ctoken == GE)) {
        op = ctoken;                         /* remember operator */
        result_tp = base_type(result_tp);

        get_ctoken();
        tp2 = base_type(exec_simple_expression()); /* 2nd simp expr */

        operandp1 = tos - 1;
        operandp2 = tos;

        /*
        -- Both operands are integer, boolean, or enumeration.
        */
        if (  ((result_tp == integer_typep) &&
               (tp2       == integer_typep))
           || (result_tp->form == ENUM_FORM)) {
            switch (op) {
                case EQUAL:
                    result = operandp1->integer == operandp2->integer;
                    break;

                case LT:
                    result = operandp1->integer <  operandp2->integer;
                    break;

                case GT:
                    result = operandp1->integer >  operandp2->integer;
                    break;

                case NE:
                    result = operandp1->integer != operandp2->integer;
                    break;

                case LE:
                    result = operandp1->integer <= operandp2->integer;
                    break;

                case GE:
                    result = operandp1->integer >= operandp2->integer;
                    break;
            }
        }

        /*
        -- Both operands are character.
        */
        else if (result_tp == char_typep) {
            switch (op) {
                case EQUAL:
                    result = operandp1->byte == operandp2->byte;
                    break;

                case LT:
                    result = operandp1->byte <  operandp2->byte;
                    break;

                case GT:
                    result = operandp1->byte >  operandp2->byte;
                    break;

                case NE:
                    result = operandp1->byte != operandp2->byte;
                    break;

                case LE:
                    result = operandp1->byte <= operandp2->byte;
                    break;

                case GE:
                    result = operandp1->byte >= operandp2->byte;
                    break;
            }
        }

        /*
        -- Both operands are real, or one is real and the other
        -- is integer.  Convert the integer operand to real.
        */
        else if ((result_tp == real_typep) ||
                 (tp2        == real_typep)) {
            promote_operands_to_real(operandp1, result_tp,
                                     operandp2, tp2);

            switch (op) {
                case EQUAL:
                    result = operandp1->real == operandp2->real;
                    break;

                case LT:
                    result = operandp1->real <  operandp2->real;
                    break;

                case GT:
                    result = operandp1->real >  operandp2->real;
                    break;

                case NE:
                    result = operandp1->real != operandp2->real;
                    break;

                case LE:
                    result = operandp1->real <= operandp2->real;
                    break;

                case GE:
                    result = operandp1->real >= operandp2->real;
                    break;
            }
        }

        /*
        -- Both operands are strings.
        */
```

```
        else if ((result_tp->form == ARRAY_FORM) &&
                 (result_tp->info.array.elmt_typep == char_typep)) {
            int cmp = strncmp(operandp1->address, operandp2->address,
                              result_tp->info.array.elmt_count);

            result = (    (   (cmp < 0)
                           && (   (op == NE)
                               || (op == LE)
                               || (op == LT)))
                       || (   (cmp == 0)
                           && (   (op == EQUAL)
                               || (op == LE)
                               || (op == GE)))
                       || (   (cmp > 0)
                           && (   (op == NE)
                               || (op == GE)
                               || (op == GT))));
        }

        /*
        -- Replace the two operands on the stack with the result.
        */
        operandp1->integer = result ? 1 : 0;
        pop();

        result_tp = boolean_typep;
    }

    return(result_tp);
}

/*----------------------------------------------------------*/
/* exec_simple_expression   Execute a simple expression     */
/*                          consisting of terms separated by +, */
/*                          -, or OR operators.  There may be */
/*                          a unary + or - before the first */
/*                          term.  Return a pointer to the  */
/*                          type structure.                 */
/*----------------------------------------------------------*/

    TYPE_STRUCT_PTR
exec_simple_expression()

{
    STACK_ITEM_PTR operandp1, operandp2;   /* ptrs to operands */
    TYPE_STRUCT_PTR result_tp, tp2;        /* ptrs to types */
    TOKEN_CODE op;                         /* an operator token */
    TOKEN_CODE unary_op = PLUS;            /* unary operator token */

    /*
    -- If there is a unary + or -, remember it.
    */
    if ((ctoken == PLUS) || (ctoken == MINUS)) {
        unary_op = ctoken;
        get_ctoken();
    }

    result_tp = exec_term();    /* first term */

    /*
    -- If there was a unary -, negate the top of stack
    */
    if (unary_op == MINUS) {
        if (result_tp == integer_typep) tos->integer = -tos->integer;
        else                            tos->real    = -tos->real;
    }

    /*
```

```
    -- Loop to process subsequent terms
    -- separated by operators.
    */
    while ((ctoken == PLUS) || (ctoken == MINUS) || (ctoken == OR)) {
        op = ctoken;                    /* remember operator */
        result_tp = base_type(result_tp);

        get_ctoken();
        tp2 = base_type(exec_term());   /* subsequent term */

        operandp1 = tos - 1;
        operandp2 = tos;

        /*
        -- OR
        */
        if (op == OR) {
            operandp1->integer = operandp1->integer ||
                                 operandp2->integer;
            result_tp = boolean_typep;
        }

        /*
        -- + or -
        --
        -- Both operands are integer.
        */
        else if ((result_tp == integer_typep) &&
                 (tp2        == integer_typep)) {
            operandp1->integer = (op == PLUS)
                ? operandp1->integer + operandp2->integer
                : operandp1->integer - operandp2->integer;
            result_tp = integer_typep;
        }

        /*
        -- Both operands are real, or one is real and the other
        -- is integer.  Convert the integer operand to real.
        */
        else {
            promote_operands_to_real(operandp1, result_tp,
                                     operandp2, tp2);

            operandp1->real = (op == PLUS)
                ? operandp1->real + operandp2->real
                : operandp1->real - operandp2->real;
            result_tp = real_typep;
        }

        pop();  /* pop off the second operand */
    }

    return(result_tp);
}

/*----------------------------------------------------------*/
/* exec_term           Execute a term consisting of factors */
/*                     separated by *, /, DIV, MOD, or AND  */
/*                     operators.  Return a pointer to the  */
/*                     type structure.                      */
/*----------------------------------------------------------*/

    TYPE_STRUCT_PTR
exec_term()

{
    STACK_ITEM_PTR operandp1, operandp2;   /* ptrs to operands */
    TYPE_STRUCT_PTR result_tp, tp2;        /* ptrs to types */
```

```
TOKEN_CODE op;                      /* an operator token */

result_tp = exec_factor();  /* first factor */

/*
-- Loop to process subsequent factors
-- separated by operators.
*/
while ((ctoken == STAR) || (ctoken == SLASH) || (ctoken == DIV) ||
       (ctoken == MOD) || (ctoken == AND)) {
    op = ctoken;                      /* remember operator */
    result_tp = base_type(result_tp);

    get_ctoken();
    tp2 = base_type(exec_factor());    /* subsequent factor */

    operandp1 = tos - 1;
    operandp2 = tos;

    /*
    -- AND
    */
    if (op == AND) {
        operandp1->integer = operandp1->integer &&
                             operandp2->integer;
        result_tp = boolean_typep;
    }

    /*
    -- *, /, DIV, or MOD
    */
    else switch (op) {

        case STAR:
            /*
            -- Both operands are integer.
            */
            if (   (result_tp == integer_typep)
                && (tp2       == integer_typep)) {
                operandp1->integer =
                    operandp1->integer * operandp2->integer;
                result_tp = integer_typep;
            }

            /*
            -- Both operands are real, or one is real and the
            -- other is integer.  Convert the integer operand
            -- to real.
            */
            else {
                promote_operands_to_real(operandp1, result_tp,
                                    operandp2, tp2);

                operandp1->real =
                    operandp1->real * operandp2->real;
                result_tp = real_typep;
            }
            break;

        case SLASH:
            /*
            -- Both operands are real, or one is real and the
            -- other is integer.  Convert the integer operand
            -- to real.
            */
            promote_operands_to_real(operandp1, result_tp,
                                operandp2, tp2);
```

```
            if (operandp2->real == 0.0)
                runtime_error(DIVISION_BY_ZERO);
            else
                operandp1->real = operandp1->real/operandp2->real;

            result_tp = real_typep;
            break;

        case DIV:
        case MOD:
            /*
            -- Both operands are integer.
            */
            if (operandp2->integer == 0)
                runtime_error(DIVISION_BY_ZERO);
            else
                operandp1->integer = (op == DIV)
                    ? operandp1->integer / operandp2->integer
                    : operandp1->integer % operandp2->integer;

            result_tp = integer_typep;
            break;
    }

    pop();  /* pop off the second operand */
}

return(result_tp);
}

/*-----------------------------------------------------------*/
/* exec_factor        Execute a factor, which is a variable, */
/*                    a number, NOT followed by a factor, or */
/*                    a parenthesized subexpression.  Return */
/*                    a pointer to the type structure.       */
/*-----------------------------------------------------------*/

    TYPE_STRUCT_PTR
exec_factor()

{
    TYPE_STRUCT_PTR result_tp;      /* type pointer */

    switch (ctoken) {

        case IDENTIFIER: {
            SYMTAB_NODE_PTR idp = get_symtab_cptr();

            /*
            -- Function call or constant or variable.
            */
            if (idp->defn.key == FUNC_DEFN)
                result_tp = exec_routine_call(idp);
            else if (idp->defn.key == CONST_DEFN)
                result_tp = exec_constant(idp);
            else
                result_tp = exec_variable(idp, EXPR_USE);

            break;
        }

        case NUMBER: {
            SYMTAB_NODE_PTR np = get_symtab_cptr();

            /*
            -- Obtain the integer or real value from the
            -- symbol table entry and push it onto the stack.
```

```
        */
        if (np->typep == integer_typep) {
            push_integer(np->defn.info.constant.value.integer);
            result_tp = integer_typep;
        }
        else {
            push_real(np->defn.info.constant.value.real);
            result_tp = real_typep;
        }

        get_ctoken();
        break;
    }

    case STRING: {
        SYMTAB_NODE_PTR np     = get_symtab_cptr();
        int             length = strlen(np->name);

        /*
        -- Obtain the character or string from the symbol
        -- table entry.  Note that the quotes were included,
        -- so the string lengths need to be decreased by 2.
        */
        if (length > 3) {
            /*
            -- String:  Push its address onto the stack.
            */
            push_address(np->info);
            result_tp = np->typep;
        }
        else {
            /*
            -- Character:  Push its value onto the stack.
            */
            push_byte(np->name[1]);
            result_tp = char_typep;
        }

        get_ctoken();
        break;
    }

    case NOT:
        get_ctoken();
        result_tp = exec_factor();
        tos->integer = 1 - tos->integer;    /* 0 => 1, 1 => 0 */
        break;

    case LPAREN:
        get_ctoken();
        result_tp = exec_expression();
        get_ctoken();        /* token after ) */
        break;
    }

    return(result_tp);
}

/*-----------------------------------------------------*/
/* exec_constant      Push the value of a non-string constant */
/*                    identifier, or the address of the value */
/*                    a string constant identifier onto the   */
/*                    stack.  Return a pointer to the type     */
/*                    structure.                               */
/*-----------------------------------------------------*/

    TYPE_STRUCT_PTR
```

```
exec_constant(idp)

    SYMTAB_NODE_PTR idp;         /* constant id */

{
    TYPE_STRUCT_PTR tp = idp->typep;

    if ((base_type(tp) == integer_typep) || (tp->form == ENUM_FORM))
        push_integer(idp->defn.info.constant.value.integer);
    else if (tp == real_typep)
        push_real(idp->defn.info.constant.value.real);
    else if (tp == char_typep)
        push_integer(idp->defn.info.constant.value.integer);
    else if (tp->form == ARRAY_FORM)
        push_address(idp->defn.info.constant.value.stringp);

    trace_data_fetch(idp, tp, tos);
    get_ctoken();

    return(tp);
}

/*-----------------------------------------------------*/
/* exec_variable      Push either the variable's address or  */
/*                    its value onto the stack.  Return a    */
/*                    pointer to the type structure.         */
/*-----------------------------------------------------*/

    TYPE_STRUCT_PTR
exec_variable(idp, use)

    SYMTAB_NODE_PTR idp;     /* variable id */
    USE             use;     /* how variable is used */

{
    int             delta;        /* difference in levels */
    TYPE_STRUCT_PTR tp = idp->typep;
    TYPE_STRUCT_PTR base_tp;
    STACK_ITEM_PTR  datap;        /* ptr to data area */
    STACK_FRAME_HEADER_PTR hp;

    /*
    -- Point to the variable's stack item.  If the variable's level
    -- is less than the current level, follow the static links to
    -- the appropriate stack frame base.
    */
    hp = (STACK_FRAME_HEADER_PTR) stack_frame_basep;
    delta = level - idp->level;
    while (delta-- > 0)
        hp = (STACK_FRAME_HEADER_PTR) hp->static_link.address;
    datap = (STACK_ITEM_PTR) hp + idp->defn.info.data.offset;

    /*
    -- If a scalar or enumeration VAR parm, that item
    -- points to the actual item.
    */
    if ((idp->defn.key == VARPARM_DEFN) &&
        (tp->form != ARRAY_FORM) &&
        (tp->form != RECORD_FORM))
        datap = (STACK_ITEM_PTR) datap->address;

    /*
    -- Push the address of the variable's data area.
    */
    if ((tp->form == ARRAY_FORM) ||
        (tp->form == RECORD_FORM))
        push_address((ADDRESS) datap->address);
```

```
    else
        push_address((ADDRESS) datap);


    /*
    -- If there are subscripts or field designators,
    -- modify the address to point to the array element
    -- record field.
    */
    get_ctoken();
    while ((ctoken == LBRACKET) || (ctoken == PERIOD)) {
        if      (ctoken == LBRACKET) tp = exec_subscripts(tp);
        else if (ctoken == PERIOD)   tp = exec_field();
    }


    base_tp = base_type(tp);


    /*
    -- Leave the modified address on top of the stack if:
    --     it is an assignment target, or
    --     it represents a parameter passed by reference, or
    --     it is the address of an array or record.
    -- Otherwise, replace the address with the value that it
    -- points to.
    */
    if ((use != TARGET_USE) && (use != VARPARM_USE) &&
        (tp->form != ARRAY_FORM) && (tp->form != RECORD_FORM)) {

        if ((base_tp == integer_typep) || (tp->form == ENUM_FORM))
            tos->integer = *((int *) tos->address);
        else if (base_tp == char_typep)
            tos->byte = *((char *) tos->address);
        else
            tos->real = *((float *) tos->address);
    }


    if ((use != TARGET_USE) && (use != VARPARM_USE))
        trace_data_fetch(idp, tp,
                         (tp->form == ARRAY_FORM) ||
                         (tp->form == RECORD_FORM)
                             ? tos->address
                             : tos);


    return(tp);
}


/*------------------------------------------------------------*/
/* exec_subscripts      Execute subscripts to modify the array */
/*                      data area address on the top of stack. */
/*                      Return a pointer to the type of the    */
/*                      array element.                         */
/*------------------------------------------------------------*/

    TYPE_STRUCT_PTR
exec_subscripts(tp)

    TYPE_STRUCT_PTR tp;          /* ptr to type structure */

{
    int subscript_value;

    /*
    -- Loop to execute bracketed subscripts.
    */
```

```
    while (ctoken == LBRACKET) {
        /*
        -- Loop to execute a subscript list.
        */
        do {
            get_ctoken();
            exec_expression();

            subscript_value = tos->integer;
            pop();


            /*
            -- Range check.
            */
            if ((subscript_value < tp->info.array.min_index) ||
                (subscript_value > tp->info.array.max_index))
                runtime_error(VALUE_OUT_OF_RANGE);


            /*
            -- Modify the data area address.
            */
            tos->address +=
                (subscript_value - tp->info.array.min_index) *
                                tp->info.array.elmt_typep->size;


            if (ctoken == COMMA) tp = tp->info.array.elmt_typep;
        } while (ctoken == COMMA);


        get_ctoken();
        if (ctoken == LBRACKET) tp = tp->info.array.elmt_typep;
    }


    return(tp->info.array.elmt_typep);
}


/*------------------------------------------------------------*/
/* exec_field           Execute a field designator to modify  */
/*                      the record data area address on the   */
/*                      top of stack.  Return a pointer to the */
/*                      type of the record field.             */
/*------------------------------------------------------------*/


    TYPE_STRUCT_PTR
exec_field()


{

    SYMTAB_NODE_PTR field_idp;


    get_ctoken();
    field_idp = get_symtab_cptr();


    tos->address += field_idp->defn.info.data.offset;


    get_ctoken();
    return(field_idp->typep);
}


/*------------------------------------------------------------*/
/* promote_operands_to_real   If either operand is integer,   */
/*                            convert it to real.             */
/*------------------------------------------------------------*/
```

```
promote_operands_to_real(operandp1, tp1, operandp2, tp2)          {

    STACK_ITEM_PTR operandp1, operandp2;    /* ptrs to operands */         if (tp1 == integer_typep) operandp1->real = operandp1->integer;
    TYPE_STRUCT_PTR tp1, tp2;               /* ptrs to types */            if (tp2 == integer_typep) operandp2->real = operandp2->integer;
                                                                      }
```

FIGURE A-15   execstd.c

```
/***************************************************************/      BOOLEAN eof_flag = FALSE;
/*                                                           */
/*        S T A N D A R D   R O U T I N E   E X E C U T O R   */      /*----------------------------------------------------------*/
/*                                                           */      /* exec_standard_routine_call   Execute a call to a standard  */
/*        Execution routines for statements.                 */      /*                              procedure or function.  Return */
/*                                                           */      /*                              a pointer to the type structure */
/*        FILE:      execstd.c                                */      /*                              of the call.                 */
/*                                                           */      /*----------------------------------------------------------*/
/*        MODULE:    executor                                 */
/*                                                           */          TYPE_STRUCT_PTR
/***************************************************************/      exec_standard_routine_call(rtn_idp)

#include <stdio.h>                                                        SYMTAB_NODE_PTR rtn_idp;          /* routine id */
#include <math.h>
#include "common.h"                                                   {
#include "error.h"                                                        switch (rtn_idp->defn.info.routine.key) {
#include "symtab.h"
#include "scanner.h"                                                          case READ:
#include "parser.h"                                                          case READLN:     exec_read_readln(rtn_idp);      return(NULL);
#include "exec.h"
                                                                             case WRITE:
#define EOF_CHAR                '\x7f'                                        case WRITELN:    exec_write_writeln(rtn_idp);    return(NULL);

#define DEFAULT_NUMERIC_FIELD_WIDTH    10                                    case EOFF:
#define DEFAULT_PRECISION              2                                     case EOLN:       return(exec_eof_eoln(rtn_idp));

/*----------------------------------------------------------*/               case ABS:
/* Externals                                                */               case SQR:        return(exec_abs_sqr(rtn_idp));
/*----------------------------------------------------------*/
                                                                             case ARCTAN:
extern int        level;                                                     case COS:
extern int        exec_line_number;                                          case EXP:
                                                                             case LN:
extern char       *code_segmentp;                                            case SIN:
extern TOKEN_CODE ctoken;                                                    case SQRT:       return(exec_arctan_cos_exp_ln_sin_sqrt
                                                                                                        (rtn_idp));
extern STACK_ITEM     *stack;
extern STACK_ITEM_PTR tos;                                                   case PRED:
extern STACK_ITEM_PTR stack_frame_basep;                                     case SUCC:       return(exec_pred_succ(rtn_idp));
extern STACK_ITEM_PTR stack_display[];
                                                                             case CHR:        return(exec_chr());
extern TYPE_STRUCT_PTR integer_typep, real_typep,                            case ODD:        return(exec_odd());
                       boolean_typep, char_typep;                            case ORD:        return(exec_ord());

/*----------------------------------------------------------*/               case ROUND:
/* Forwards                                                 */               case TRUNC:      return(exec_round_trunc(rtn_idp));
/*----------------------------------------------------------*/           }
                                                                      }
TYPE_STRUCT_PTR exec_eof_eoln(), exec_abs_sqr(),
                exec_arctan_cos_exp_ln_sin_sqrt(),                    /*----------------------------------------------------------*/
                exec_pred_succ(), exec_chr(),                         /* exec_read_readln     Execute a call to read or readln.   */
                exec_odd(), exec_ord(), exec_round_trunc();           /*----------------------------------------------------------*/

/*----------------------------------------------------------*/
/* Globals                                                  */        exec_read_readln(rtn_idp)
/*----------------------------------------------------------*/
```

```
    SYMTAB_NODE_PTR rtn_idp;            /* routine id */


{

    SYMTAB_NODE_PTR parm_idp;          /* parm id */
    TYPE_STRUCT_PTR parm_tp;           /* parm type */
    STACK_ITEM_PTR targetp;            /* ptr to read target */

    /*
    -- Parameters are optional for readln.
    */
    get_ctoken();
    if (ctoken == LPAREN) {
        /*
        -- <id-list>
        */
        do {
            get_ctoken();
            parm_idp = get_symtab_cptr();
            parm_tp  = base_type(exec_variable(parm_idp,
                                        VARPARM_USE));
            targetp  = (STACK_ITEM_PTR) tos->address;

            pop();       /* pop off address */

            if (parm_tp == integer_typep)
                scanf("%d", &targetp->integer);
            else if (parm_tp == real_typep)
                scanf("%g", &targetp->real);

            else if (parm_tp == char_typep) {
                scanf("%c", &targetp->byte);
                if (eof_flag ||
                    (targetp->byte == '\n')) targetp->byte = ' ';
            }

            trace_data_store(parm_idp, parm_idp->typep,
                            targetp, parm_tp);
        } while (ctoken == COMMA);

        get_ctoken();   /* token after ) */
    }

    if (rtn_idp->defn.info.routine.key == READLN) {
        char ch;

        do {
            ch = getchar();
        } while (!eof_flag && (ch != '\n'));
    }
}


/*------------------------------------------------------*/
/* exec_write_writeln      Execute a call to write or writeln. */
/*                         Each actual parameter can be:       */
/*                                                             */
/*                                                             */
/*                               <expr>                        */
/*                                                             */
/*                       or:                                   */
/*                                                             */
/*                               <epxr> : <expr>               */
/*                                                             */
/*                       or:                                   */
/*                                                             */
/*                               <expr> : <expr> : <expr>      */
/*------------------------------------------------------*/

exec_write_writeln(rtn_idp)
```

```
    SYMTAB_NODE_PTR rtn_idp;            /* routine id */


{

    TYPE_STRUCT_PTR parm_tp;           /* parm type */
    int             field_width;
    int             precision;

    /*
    -- Parameters are optional for writeln.
    */
    get_ctoken();
    if (ctoken == LPAREN) {
        do {
            /*
            -- Push value
            */
            get_ctoken();
            parm_tp = base_type(exec_expression());

            if (parm_tp == integer_typep)
                field_width = DEFAULT_NUMERIC_FIELD_WIDTH;
            else if (parm_tp == real_typep) {
                field_width = DEFAULT_NUMERIC_FIELD_WIDTH;
                precision   = DEFAULT_PRECISION;
            }
            else field_width = 0;

            /*
            -- Optional field width <expr>
            */
            if (ctoken == COLON) {
                get_ctoken();
                exec_expression();
                field_width = tos->integer;
                pop();          /* pop off field width */

                /*
                -- Optional decimal places <expr>
                */
                if (ctoken == COLON) {
                    get_ctoken();
                    exec_expression();
                    precision = tos->integer;
                    pop();      /* pop off precision */
                }
            }

            /*
            -- Write value
            */
            if (parm_tp == integer_typep)
                printf("%*d", field_width, tos->integer);
            else if (parm_tp == real_typep)
                printf("%*.*f", field_width, precision, tos->real);
            else if (parm_tp == boolean_typep)
                printf("%*s", field_width, tos->integer == 1
                                    ? "TRUE" : "FALSE");
            else if (parm_tp == char_typep)
                printf("%*c", field_width, tos->byte);

            else if (parm_tp->form == ARRAY_FORM) {
                char buffer[MAX_SOURCE_LINE_LENGTH];

                strncpy(buffer, tos->address,
                            parm_tp->info.array.elmt_count);
                buffer[parm_tp->info.array.elmt_count] = '\0';
                printf("%*s", -field_width, buffer);
```

```
            }

                pop();        /* pop off value */
        } while (ctoken == COMMA);

        get_ctoken();    /* token after ) */
    }

    if (rtn_idp->defn.info.routine.key == WRITELN) putchar('\n');
}

/*------------------------------------------------------------*/
/* exec_eof_eoln        Execute a call to eof or to eoln.  */
/*                      No parameters => boolean result.   */
/*------------------------------------------------------------*/

    TYPE_STRUCT_PTR
exec_eof_eoln(rtn_idp)

    SYMTAB_NODE_PTR rtn_idp;        /* routine id */

{
    char ch = getchar();

    switch (rtn_idp->defn.info.routine.key) {

        case EOFF:
            if (eof_flag || feof(stdin)) {
                eof_flag = TRUE;
                push_integer(1);
            }
            else {
                push_integer(0);
                ungetc(ch, stdin);
            }
            break;

        case EOLN:
            if (eof_flag || feof(stdin)) {
                eof_flag = TRUE;
                push_integer(1);
            }
            else {
                push_integer(ch == '\n' ? 1 : 0);
                ungetc(ch, stdin);
            }
            break;
    }

    get_ctoken();        /* token after function name */
    return(boolean_typep);
}

/*------------------------------------------------------------*/
/* exec_abs_sqr        Execute a call to abs or to sqr.    */
/*                     integer parm => integer result      */
/*                     real parm    => real result         */
/*------------------------------------------------------------*/

    TYPE_STRUCT_PTR
exec_abs_sqr(rtn_idp)

    SYMTAB_NODE_PTR rtn_idp;        /* routine id */

{
    TYPE_STRUCT_PTR parm_tp;        /* actual parameter type */
    TYPE_STRUCT_PTR result_tp;      /* result type */
```

```
    get_ctoken();        /* ( */
    get_ctoken();
    parm_tp = base_type(exec_expression());

    if (parm_tp == integer_typep) {
        tos->integer = rtn_idp->defn.info.routine.key == ABS
                        ? abs(tos->integer)
                        : tos->integer * tos->integer;
        result_tp = integer_typep;
    }
    else {
        tos->real = rtn_idp->defn.info.routine.key == ABS
                        ? fabs(tos->real)
                        : tos->real * tos->real;
        result_tp = real_typep;
    }

    get_ctoken();        /* token after ) */
    return(result_tp);
}

/*------------------------------------------------------------*/
/* exec_arctan_cos_exp_ln_sin_sqrt Execute a call to arctan,  */
/*                          cos, exp, ln, sin, or sqrt. */
/*                          integer parm => real result */
/*                          real_parm    => real result */
/*------------------------------------------------------------*/

    TYPE_STRUCT_PTR
exec_arctan_cos_exp_ln_sin_sqrt(rtn_idp)

    SYMTAB_NODE_PTR rtn_idp;        /* routine id */

{
    TYPE_STRUCT_PTR parm_tp;        /* actual parameter type */
    int            code = rtn_idp->defn.info.routine.key;

    get_ctoken();        /* ( */
    get_ctoken();
    parm_tp = base_type(exec_expression());
    if (parm_tp == integer_typep) tos->real = tos->integer;

    if (   ((code == LN)   && (tos->real <= 0.0))
        || ((code == SQRT) && (tos->real <  0.0)))
        runtime_error(INVALID_FUNCTION_ARGUMENT);
    else {
        switch (rtn_idp->defn.info.routine.key) {
            case ARCTAN:    tos->real = atan(tos->real);    break;
            case COS:       tos->real = cos(tos->real);     break;
            case EXP:       tos->real = exp(tos->real);     break;
            case LN:        tos->real = log(tos->real);     break;
            case SIN:       tos->real = sin(tos->real);     break;
            case SQRT:      tos->real = sqrt(tos->real);    break;
        }
    }

    get_ctoken();        /* token after ) */
    return(real_typep);
}

/*------------------------------------------------------------*/
/* exec_pred_succ      Execute a call to pred or succ.     */
/*                     integer parm => integer result      */
/*                     enum parm    => enum result         */
/*------------------------------------------------------------*/

    TYPE_STRUCT_PTR
```

```
exec_pred_succ(rtn_idp)

    SYMTAB_NODE_PTR rtn_idp;          /* routine id */

{
    TYPE_STRUCT_PTR parm_tp;          /* actual parameter type */

    get_ctoken();       /* ( */
    get_ctoken();
    parm_tp = base_type(exec_expression());

    tos->integer = rtn_idp->defn.info.routine.key == PRED
                     ? --tos->integer
                     : ++tos->integer;

    get_ctoken();       /* token after ) */
    return(parm_tp);
}

/*-----------------------------------------------------*/
/* exec_chr            Execute a call to chr.          */
/*                     integer parm => character result */
/*-----------------------------------------------------*/

    TYPE_STRUCT_PTR
exec_chr()

{
    get_ctoken();       /* ( */
    get_ctoken();
    exec_expression();

    tos->byte = tos->integer;

    get_ctoken();       /* token after ) */
    return(char_typep);
}

/*-----------------------------------------------------*/
/* exec_odd            Execute a call to odd.          */
/*                     integer parm => boolean result  */
/*-----------------------------------------------------*/

    TYPE_STRUCT_PTR
exec_odd()

{
    get_ctoken();       /* ( */
    get_ctoken();
```

```
    exec_expression();

    tos->integer &= 1;

    get_ctoken();       /* token after ) */
    return(boolean_typep);
}

/*-----------------------------------------------------*/
/* exec_ord            Execute a call to ord.          */
/*                     enumeration parm => integer result */
/*-----------------------------------------------------*/

    TYPE_STRUCT_PTR
exec_ord()

{
    get_ctoken();       /* ( */
    get_ctoken();
    exec_expression();

    get_ctoken();       /* token after ) */
    return(integer_typep);
}

/*-----------------------------------------------------*/
/* exec_round_trunc    Execute a call to round or trunc. */
/*                     real parm => integer result     */
/*-----------------------------------------------------*/

    TYPE_STRUCT_PTR
exec_round_trunc(rtn_idp)

    SYMTAB_NODE_PTR rtn_idp;          /* routine id */

{
    get_ctoken();       /* ( */
    get_ctoken();
    exec_expression();

    if (rtn_idp->defn.info.routine.key == ROUND) {
        tos->integer = tos->real > 0.0
                         ? (int) (tos->real + 0.5)
                         : (int) (tos->real - 0.5);
    }
    else tos->integer = (int) tos->real;

    get_ctoken();       /* token after ) */
    return(integer_typep);
}
```

FIGURE A-16   debug.c

```
/****************************************************/    /*    MODULE:    executor                    */
/*                                              */    /*                                           */
/*    I N T E R A C T I V E   D E B U G G E R   */    /****************************************************/
/*                                              */
/*    Interactive debugging routines.           */    #include <stdio.h>
/*                                              */    #include "common.h"
/*    FILE:    debug.c                           */    #include "error.h"
/*                                              */    #include "scanner.h"
```

```c
#include "symtab.h"
#include "exec.h"

#define MAX_BREAKS      16
#define MAX_WATCHES     16
#define COMMAND_QUERY   "Command? "

/*----------------------------------------------------------*/
/* Externals                                                */
/*----------------------------------------------------------*/

extern TYPE_STRUCT_PTR  integer_typep, real_typep,
                        boolean_typep, char_typep;

extern TYPE_STRUCT      dummy_type;

extern int              level;
extern SYMTAB_NODE_PTR  symtab_display[];
extern STACK_ITEM_PTR   tos;

extern int          line_number;
extern int          buffer_offset;
extern BOOLEAN      print_flag;

extern char         *code_segmentp;
extern char         *statement_startp;
extern int          ctoken;
extern int          exec_line_number;
extern int          error_count;

extern char         *bufferp;
extern char         ch;
extern char         source_buffer[];
extern char         word_string[];
extern int          token;
extern LITERAL      literal;
extern BOOLEAN      block_flag;

extern char         *code_buffer;
extern char         *code_bufferp;
extern char         *code_segmentp;

/*----------------------------------------------------------*/
/* Globals                                                  */
/*----------------------------------------------------------*/

FILE    *console;

BOOLEAN debugger_command_flag,  /* TRUE during debug command */
        halt_flag,              /* TRUE to pause for debug command */
        trace_flag,             /* TRUE to trace statement */
        step_flag,              /* TRUE to single-step */
        entry_flag,             /* TRUE to trace routine entry */
        exit_flag;              /* TRUE to trace routine exit */

int     break_count;                    /* count of breakpoints */
int     break_list[MAX_BREAKS];         /* list of breakpoints */

int                 watch_count;        /* count of watches */
SYMTAB_NODE_PTR watch_list[MAX_WATCHES];    /* list of watches */

typedef struct {                        /* watch structure */
    SYMTAB_NODE_PTR watch_idp;          /* id node watched variable */
    BOOLEAN         store_flag;         /* TRUE to trace stores */
    BOOLEAN         fetch_flag;         /* TRUE to trace fetches */
} WATCH_STRUCT, *WATCH_STRUCT_PTR;

char *symbol_strings[] = {
    "<no token>", "<IDENTIFIER>", "<NUMBER>", "<STRING>",
    "^", "*", "(", ")", "-", "+", "=", "[", "]", ":", ";",
    "<", ">", ",", ".", "/", ":=", "<=", ">=", "<>", "..",
    "<END OF FILE>", "<ERROR>",
    "AND", "ARRAY", "BEGIN", "CASE", "CONST", "DIV", "DO", "DOWNTO",
    "ELSE", "END", "FILE", "FOR", "FUNCTION", "GOTO", "IF", "IN",
    "LABEL", "MOD", "NIL", "NOT", "OF", "OR", "PACKED", "PROCEDURE",
    "PROGRAM", "RECORD", "REPEAT", "SET", "THEN", "TO", "TYPE",
    "UNTIL", "VAR", "WHILE", "WITH",
};

/*----------------------------------------------------------*/
/* init_debugger        Initialize the interactive debugger. */
/*----------------------------------------------------------*/

init_debugger()

{
    int i;

    /*
    --  Initialize the debugger's globals.
    */
    console = fopen("CON", "r");
    code_buffer = alloc_bytes(MAX_SOURCE_LINE_LENGTH + 1);

    print_flag = FALSE;
    halt_flag = block_flag = TRUE;
    debugger_command_flag = trace_flag = step_flag
                = entry_flag = exit_flag
                = FALSE;

    break_count = 0;
    for (i = 0; i < MAX_BREAKS; ++i) break_list[i] = 0;

    watch_count = 0;
    for (i = 0; i < MAX_WATCHES; ++i) watch_list[i] = NULL;
}

/*----------------------------------------------------------*/
/* read_debugger_command        Read and process a debugging */
/*                              command typed in by the user. */
/*----------------------------------------------------------*/

read_debugger_command()

{
    BOOLEAN done = FALSE;

    debugger_command_flag = TRUE;

    do {
        printf("\n%s", COMMAND_QUERY);

        /*
        --  Read in a debugging command and replace the
        --  final \n\0 with ;;\0
        */
        bufferp = fgets(source_buffer, MAX_SOURCE_LINE_LENGTH,
                    console);
        strcpy(&source_buffer[strlen(source_buffer) - 1], ";;");

        ch = *bufferp++;
        buffer_offset = sizeof(COMMAND_QUERY);
        code_bufferp = code_buffer;
        error_count  = 0;
```

```
    get_token();

    /*
    -- Process the command.
    */
    switch (token) {
        case SEMICOLON:    done = TRUE;                  break;
        case IDENTIFIER:   execute_debugger_command(); break;
    }

    if (token != SEMICOLON) error(UNEXPECTED_TOKEN);
} while (!done);

    debugger_command_flag = FALSE;
}

/*------------------------------------------------------------*/
/* execute_debugger_command     Execute a debugger command.  */
/*------------------------------------------------------------*/

execute_debugger_command()

{
    WATCH_STRUCT_PTR wp;
    WATCH_STRUCT_PTR allocate_watch();

    if (strcmp(word_string, "trace") == 0) {
        trace_flag = TRUE;
        step_flag  = FALSE;
        get_token();
    }
    else if (strcmp(word_string, "untrace") == 0) {
        trace_flag = FALSE;
        get_token();
    }

    else if (strcmp(word_string, "step") == 0) {
        step_flag = TRUE;
        trace_flag = FALSE;
        get_token();
    }
    else if (strcmp(word_string, "unstep") == 0) {
        step_flag = FALSE;
        get_token();
    }

    else if (strcmp(word_string, "break") == 0)
        set_breakpoint();
    else if (strcmp(word_string, "unbreak") == 0)
        remove_breakpoint();

    else if (strcmp(word_string, "entry") == 0) {
        entry_flag = TRUE;
        get_token();
    }
    else if (strcmp(word_string, "unentry") == 0) {
        entry_flag = FALSE;
        get_token();
    }

    else if (strcmp(word_string, "exit") == 0) {
        exit_flag = TRUE;
        get_token();
    }
    else if (strcmp(word_string, "unexit") == 0) {
        exit_flag = FALSE;
        get_token();
    }
```

```
    }
    else if (strcmp(word_string, "watch") == 0) {
        wp = allocate_watch();
        if (wp != NULL) {
            wp->store_flag = TRUE;
            wp->fetch_flag = TRUE;
        }
    }
    else if (strcmp(word_string, "unwatch") == 0)
        remove_watch();

    else if (strcmp(word_string, "store") == 0) {
        wp = allocate_watch();
        if (wp != NULL) wp->store_flag = TRUE;
    }
    else if (strcmp(word_string, "fetch") == 0) {
        wp = allocate_watch();
        if (wp != NULL) wp->fetch_flag = TRUE;
    }

    else if (strcmp(word_string, "show") == 0)
        show_value();
    else if (strcmp(word_string, "assign") == 0)
        assign_variable();

    else if (strcmp(word_string, "where") == 0) {
        print_statement();
        get_token();
    }
    else if (strcmp(word_string, "kill") == 0) {
        printf("Program killed.\n");
        exit(0);
    }
}

                /*******************************/
                /*                             */
                /*      Tracing routines       */
                /*                             */
                /*******************************/

/*------------------------------------------------------------*/
/* trace_statement_execution    Called just before the       */
/*                              execution of each statement.  */
/*------------------------------------------------------------*/

trace_statement_execution()

{
    if (break_count > 0) {
        int i;

        /*
        -- Check if the statement is a breakpoint.
        */
        for (i = 0; i < break_count; ++i) {
            if (exec_line_number == break_list[i]) {
                printf("\nBreakpoint");
                print_statement();
                halt_flag = TRUE;
                break;
            }
        }
    }

    /*
```

```
    --  Pause if necessary to read a debugger command.
    */
    if (halt_flag) {
        read_debugger_command();
        halt_flag = step_flag;
    }

    /*
    --  If single-stepping, print the current statement.
    --  If tracing, print the current line number.
    */
    if (step_flag)  print_statement();
    if (trace_flag) print_line_number();
}

/*-----------------------------------------------------------*/
/*  trace_routine_entry       Called upon entry into a       */
/*                            procedure or a function.       */
/*-----------------------------------------------------------*/

trace_routine_entry(idp)

    SYMTAB_NODE_PTR idp;        /* routine id */

{
    if (entry_flag) printf("\nEntering %s\n", idp->name);
}

/*-----------------------------------------------------------*/
/*  trace_routine_exit        Called upon exit from a        */
/*                            procedure or a function.       */
/*-----------------------------------------------------------*/

trace_routine_exit(idp)

    SYMTAB_NODE_PTR idp;        /* routine id */

{
    if (exit_flag) printf("\nExiting %s\n", idp->name);
}

/*-----------------------------------------------------------*/
/*  trace_data_store          Called just before a variable  */
/*                            is stored into.                */
/*-----------------------------------------------------------*/

trace_data_store(idp, idp_tp, targetp, target_tp)

    SYMTAB_NODE_PTR idp;            /* id of target variable */
    TYPE_STRUCT_PTR idp_tp;         /* ptr to id's type */
    STACK_ITEM_PTR  targetp;        /* ptr to target location */
    TYPE_STRUCT_PTR target_tp;      /* ptr to target's type */

{
    /*
    --  Check if the variable is being watched for stores.
    */
    if ((idp->info != NULL) &&
        ((WATCH_STRUCT_PTR) idp->info)->store_flag) {
        printf("\nAt %d:  Store %s", exec_line_number, idp->name);
        if      (idp_tp->form == ARRAY_FORM)  printf("[*]");
        else if (idp_tp->form == RECORD_FORM) printf(".*");
        print_data_value(targetp, target_tp, ":=");
    }
}

/*-----------------------------------------------------------*/
/*  trace_data_fetch          Called just before a variable  */
```

```
/*                            is fetched from.               */
/*-----------------------------------------------------------*/

trace_data_fetch(idp, tp, datap)

    SYMTAB_NODE_PTR idp;            /* id of target variable */
    TYPE_STRUCT_PTR tp;             /* ptr to id's type */
    STACK_ITEM_PTR  datap;          /* ptr to data */

{
    TYPE_STRUCT_PTR idp_tp = idp->typep;

    /*
    --  Check if the variable is being watched for fetches.
    */
    if (   (idp->info != NULL)
        && ((WATCH_STRUCT_PTR) idp->info)->fetch_flag) {
        printf("\nAt %d:  Fetch %s", exec_line_number, idp->name);
        if      (idp_tp-> form == ARRAY_FORM) printf("[*]");
        else if (idp_tp->form == RECORD_FORM) printf(".*");
        print_data_value(datap, tp, "=");
    }
}

        /********************************/
        /*                              */
        /*        Printing routines     */
        /*                              */
        /********************************/

/*-----------------------------------------------------------*/
/*  print_statement           Uncrunch and print a statement. */
/*-----------------------------------------------------------*/

print_statement()

{
    int     tk;                 /* token code */
    BOOLEAN done = FALSE;
    char    *csp = statement_startp;

    printf("\nAt %3d:", exec_line_number);

    do {
        switch (tk = *csp++) {

            case SEMICOLON:
            case END:
            case ELSE:
            case THEN:
            case UNTIL:
            case BEGIN:
            case OF:
            case STATEMENT_MARKER:       done = TRUE;
                                         break;

            default:
                done = FALSE;

                switch (tk) {

                    case ADDRESS_MARKER:
                        csp += sizeof(ADDRESS);
                        break;

                    case IDENTIFIER:
                    case NUMBER:
```

```
                case STRING: {
                    SYMTAB_NODE_PTR np = *((SYMTAB_NODE_PTR *) csp);

                    printf(" %s", np->name);
                    csp += sizeof(SYMTAB_NODE_PTR);
                    break;
                }

                default:
                    printf(" %s", symbol_strings[tk]);
                    break;
            }
        }
    } while (!done);

    printf("\n");
}

/*-----------------------------------------------------------*/
/*  print_line_number          Print the current line number.  */
/*-----------------------------------------------------------*/

print_line_number()

{
    printf("<%d>", exec_line_number);
}

/*-----------------------------------------------------------*/
/*  print_data_value           Print a data value.            */
/*-----------------------------------------------------------*/

print_data_value(datap, tp, str)

    STACK_ITEM_PTR  datap;      /* ptr to data value to print */
    TYPE_STRUCT_PTR tp;         /* ptr to type of stack item */
    char            *str;       /* " = " or " := " */

{
    /*
    -- Reduce a subrange type to its range type.
    -- Convert a non-boolean enumeration type to integer.
    */
    if (tp->form == SUBRANGE_FORM)
        tp = tp->info.subrange.range_typep;
    if ((tp->form == ENUM_FORM) && (tp != boolean_typep))
        tp = integer_typep;

    if (tp == integer_typep)
        printf(" %s %d\n", str, datap->integer);
    else if (tp == real_typep)
        printf(" %s %0.6g\n", str, datap->real);
    else if (tp == boolean_typep)
        printf(" %s %s\n", str, datap->integer == 1 ? "true"
                                                     : "false");
    else if (tp == char_typep)
        printf(" %s '%c'\n", str, datap->byte);
    else if (tp->form == ARRAY_FORM) {
        if (tp->info.array.elmt_typep == char_typep) {
            char *chp = (char *) datap;
            int  size = tp->info.array.elmt_count;

            printf(" %s '", str);
            while (size--) printf("%c", *chp++);
            printf("'\n");
        }
        else printf(" %s <array>\n", str);
```

```
    }
    else if (tp->form == RECORD_FORM)
        printf(" %s <record>\n", str);
}

            /*****************************************/
            /*                                       */
            /*         Breakpoints and watches       */
            /*                                       */
            /*****************************************/

/*-----------------------------------------------------------*/
/*  set_breakpoint       Set a breakpoint, or print all       */
/*                       breakpoints in the break list.       */
/*-----------------------------------------------------------*/

set_breakpoint()

{
    get_token();

    switch (token) {

        case SEMICOLON: {
            /*
            -- No line number:  List all breakpoints.
            */
            int i;

            printf("Statement breakpoints at:\n");

            for (i = 0; i < break_count; ++i)
                printf("%5d\n", break_list[i]);

            break;
        }

        case NUMBER: {
            /*
            -- Set a breakpoint by appending it to
            -- the break list.
            */
            int number;

            if (literal.type == INTEGER_LIT) {
                number = literal.value.integer;
                if ((number > 0) && (number <= line_number)) {
                    if (break_count < MAX_BREAKS) {
                        break_list[break_count] = number;
                        ++break_count;
                    }
                    else printf("Break list is full.\n");
                }
                else error(VALUE_OUT_OF_RANGE);
            }
            else error(UNEXPECTED_TOKEN);

            get_token();
            break;
        }
    }
}

/*-----------------------------------------------------------*/
/*  remove_breakpoint    Remove a specific breakpoint, or remove */
/*                       all breakpoints.                     */
/*-----------------------------------------------------------*/
```

```
remove_breakpoint()

{
    int i, j, number;

    get_token();

    switch (token) {

        case SEMICOLON: {
            /*
            -- No line number:  Remove all breakpoints.
            */
            for (i = 0; i < break_count; ++i) break_list[i] = 0;
            break_count = 0;
            break;
        }

        case NUMBER: {
            /*
            -- Remove a breakpoint from the break list.
            -- Move the following breakpoints up one in the
            -- list to fill in the gap.
            */
            if (literal.type == INTEGER_LIT) {
                number = literal.value.integer;
                if (number > 0) {
                    for (i = 0; i < break_count; ++i) {
                        if (break_list[i] == number) {
                            break_list[i] = 0;
                            --break_count;

                            for (j = i; j < break_count; ++j)
                                break_list[j] = break_list[j+1];

                            break;
                        }
                    }
                }
                else error(VALUE_OUT_OF_RANGE);
            }

            get_token();
            break;
        }
    }
}

/*------------------------------------------------------*/
/* allocate_watch       Return a pointer to a watch structure,  */
/*                      or print all variables being watched.   */
/*------------------------------------------------------*/

    WATCH_STRUCT_PTR
allocate_watch()

{
    int             i;
    SYMTAB_NODE_PTR idp;
    WATCH_STRUCT_PTR wp;

    get_token();

    switch (token) {

        case SEMICOLON: {
            /*
```

```
            -- No variable:  Print all variables being watched.
            */
            printf("Variables being watched:\n");

            for (i = 0; i < watch_count; ++i) {
                idp = watch_list[i];
                if (idp != NULL) {
                    wp = (WATCH_STRUCT_PTR) idp->info;
                    printf ("%16s  ", idp->name);
                    if (wp->store_flag) printf(" (store)");
                    if (wp->fetch_flag) printf(" (fetch)");
                    printf("\n");
                }
            }

            return(NULL);
        }

        case IDENTIFIER: {
            search_and_find_all_symtab(idp);
            get_token();

            switch (idp->defn.key) {

                case UNDEFINED:
                    return(NULL);

                case CONST_DEFN:
                case VAR_DEFN:
                case FIELD_DEFN:
                case VALPARM_DEFN:
                case VARPARM_DEFN: {
                    /*
                    -- Return a pointer to the variable's watch
                    -- structure if it is already being watched.
                    -- Otherwise, allocate and return a pointer
                    -- to a new watch structure.
                    */
                    if (idp->info != NULL)
                        return((WATCH_STRUCT_PTR) idp->info);
                    else if (watch_count < MAX_WATCHES) {
                        wp = alloc_struct(WATCH_STRUCT);
                        wp->store_flag = FALSE;
                        wp->fetch_flag = FALSE;

                        idp->info = (char *) wp;

                        watch_list[watch_count] = idp;
                        ++watch_count;

                        return(wp);
                    }
                    else {
                        printf("Watch list is full.\n");
                        return(NULL);
                    }
                }

                default: {
                    error(INVALID_IDENTIFIER_USAGE);
                    return(NULL);
                }
            }
        }
    }
}
```

```
/*--------------------------------------------------------*/
/* remove_watch        Remove a specific variable from being  */
/*                     watched, or remove all variables from  */
/*                     the watch list.                        */
/*--------------------------------------------------------*/

remove_watch()

{
    int             i, j;
    SYMTAB_NODE_PTR idp;
    WATCH_STRUCT_PTR wp;

    get_token();

    switch (token) {

        case SEMICOLON: {
            /*
            -- No variable:  Remove all variables from watch list.
            */
            for (i = 0; i < watch_count; ++i) {
                if ((idp = watch_list[i]) != NULL) {
                    wp = (WATCH_STRUCT_PTR) idp->info;
                    watch_list[i] = NULL;
                    idp->info = NULL;
                    free(wp);
                }
            }
            watch_count = 0;
            break;
        }

        case IDENTIFIER: {
            /*
            -- Remove a variable from the watch list.
            -- Move the following watches up one in the
            -- list to fill in the gap.
            */
            search_and_find_all_symtab(idp);
            get_token();

            if ((idp != NULL) && (idp->info != NULL)) {
                wp = (WATCH_STRUCT_PTR) idp->info;
                for (i = 0; i < watch_count; ++i) {
                    if (watch_list[i] == idp) {
                        watch_list[i] = NULL;
                        idp->info = NULL;
                        free(wp);
                        --watch_count;

                        for (j = i; j < watch_count; ++j)
                            watch_list[j] = watch_list[j+1];

                        break;
                    }
                }
            }
            break;
        }
    }
}
```

```
/********************************/
/*                              */
/*       Show and assign        */
/*                              */
```

```
/********************************/
```

```
/*--------------------------------------------------------*/
/* show_value          Print the value of an expression.   */
/*--------------------------------------------------------*/

show_value()

{
    get_token();

    switch (token) {

        case SEMICOLON: {
            error(INVALID_EXPRESSION);
            break;
        }

        default: {
            /*
            -- First parse, then execute the expression
            -- from the code buffer.
            */
            TYPE_STRUCT_PTR expression();
            TYPE_STRUCT_PTR tp       = expression();    /* parse */
            char *save_code_segmentp = code_segmentp;
            int   save_ctoken        = ctoken;

            if (error_count > 0) break;

            /*
            -- Switch to the code buffer.
            */
            code_segmentp = code_buffer + 1;
            get_ctoken();
            exec_expression();                          /* execute */

            /*
            -- Print, then pop off the value.
            */
            if ((tp->form == ARRAY_FORM) ||
                (tp->form == RECORD_FORM))
                print_data_value(tos->address, tp, " ");
            else
                print_data_value(tos, tp, " ");

            pop();

            /*
            -- Resume the code segment.
            */
            code_segmentp = save_code_segmentp;
            ctoken = save_ctoken;
            break;
        }
    }
}
```

```
/*--------------------------------------------------------*/
/* assign_variable     Execute an assignment statement.    */
/*--------------------------------------------------------*/

assign_variable()

{
    get_token();

    switch (token) {
```

```
case SEMICOLON: {
    error(MISSING_VARIABLE);
    break;
}

case IDENTIFIER: {
    /*
    -- First parse, then execute the assignment statement
    -- from the code buffer.
    */
    SYMTAB_NODE_PTR idp;
    char *save_code_segmentp = code_segmentp;
    int  save_ctoken        = ctoken;

    search_and_find_all_symtab(idp);

    assignment_statement(idp);            /* parse */
    if (error_count > 0) break;
```

```
    /*
    -- Switch to the code buffer.
    */
    code_segmentp = code_buffer + 1;
    get_ctoken();
    idp = get_symtab_cptr();
    exec_assignment_statement(idp);       /* execute */

    /*
    -- Resume the code segment.
    */
    code_segmentp = save_code_segmentp;
    ctoken = save_ctoken;
    break;
    }
}
}
```

FIGURE A-17   error.h

```
/*******************************************************************/
/*                                                                 */
/*      E R R O R   R O U T I N E S   (Header)                     */
/*                                                                 */
/*      FILE:      error.h                                         */
/*                                                                 */
/*      MODULE:    error                                           */
/*                                                                 */
/*******************************************************************/

#ifndef error_h
#define error_h

#define MAX_SYNTAX_ERRORS 25

/*----------------------------------------------------------------*/
/* Error codes                                                    */
/*----------------------------------------------------------------*/

typedef enum {
    NO_ERROR,
    SYNTAX_ERROR,
    TOO_MANY_SYNTAX_ERRORS,
    FAILED_SOURCE_FILE_OPEN,
    UNEXPECTED_END_OF_FILE,
    INVALID_NUMBER,
    INVALID_FRACTION,
    INVALID_EXPONENT,
    TOO_MANY_DIGITS,
    REAL_OUT_OF_RANGE,
    INTEGER_OUT_OF_RANGE,
    MISSING_RPAREN,
    INVALID_EXPRESSION,
    INVALID_ASSIGNMENT,
    MISSING_IDENTIFIER,
    MISSING_COLONEQUAL,
    UNDEFINED_IDENTIFIER,
    STACK_OVERFLOW,
    INVALID_STATEMENT,
    UNEXPECTED_TOKEN,
    MISSING_SEMICOLON,
    MISSING_DO,
    MISSING_UNTIL,
    MISSING_THEN,
    INVALID_FOR_CONTROL,
    MISSING_OF,
    INVALID_CONSTANT,
    MISSING_CONSTANT,
    MISSING_COLON,
    MISSING_END,
    MISSING_TO_OR_DOWNTO,
    REDEFINED_IDENTIFIER,
    MISSING_EQUAL,
    INVALID_TYPE,
    NOT_A_TYPE_IDENTIFIER,
    INVALID_SUBRANGE_TYPE,
    NOT_A_CONSTANT_IDENTIFIER,
    MISSING_DOTDOT,
    INCOMPATIBLE_TYPES,
    INVALID_TARGET,
    INVALID_IDENTIFIER_USAGE,
    INCOMPATIBLE_ASSIGNMENT,
    MIN_GT_MAX,
    MISSING_LBRACKET,
    MISSING_RBRACKET,
    INVALID_INDEX_TYPE,
    MISSING_BEGIN,
    MISSING_PERIOD,
    TOO_MANY_SUBSCRIPTS,
    INVALID_FIELD,
    NESTING_TOO_DEEP,
    MISSING_PROGRAM,
    ALREADY_FORWARDED,
    WRONG_NUMBER_OF_PARMS,
    INVALID_VAR_PARM,
    NOT_A_RECORD_VARIABLE,
    MISSING_VARIABLE,
    CODE_SEGMENT_OVERFLOW,
    UNIMPLEMENTED_FEATURE,
} ERROR_CODE;

typedef enum {
```

```
      RUNTIME_STACK_OVERFLOW,                              UNIMPLEMENTED_RUNTIME_FEATURE,
      VALUE_OUT_OF_RANGE,                              } RUNTIME_ERROR_CODE;
      INVALID_CASE_VALUE,
      DIVISION_BY_ZERO,
      INVALID_FUNCTION_ARGUMENT,                      #endif
```

FIGURE A-18   error.c

```
/******************************************************/
/*                                                    */
/*      E R R O R   R O U T I N E S                   */
/*                                                    */
/*      Error messages and routines to print them.    */
/*                                                    */
/*      FILE:      error.c                             */
/*                                                    */
/*      MODULE:    error                               */
/*                                                    */
/******************************************************/

#include <stdio.h>
#include "common.h"
#include "error.h"

/*--------------------------------------------------*/
/* Externals                                        */
/*--------------------------------------------------*/

extern char     *tokenp;
extern BOOLEAN  print_flag;
extern char     source_buffer[];
extern char     *bufferp;

/*--------------------------------------------------*/
/* Error messages    Keyed to enumeration type ERROR_CODE */
/*                   in file error.h.               */
/*--------------------------------------------------*/

char *error_messages[] = {
    "No error",
    "Syntax error",
    "Too many syntax errors",
    "Failed to open source file",
    "Unexpected end of file",
    "Invalid number",
    "Invalid fraction",
    "Invalid exponent",
    "Too many digits",
    "Real literal out of range",
    "Integer literal out of range",
    "Missing right parenthesis",
    "Invalid expression",
    "Invalid assignment statement",
    "Missing identifier",
    "Missing := ",
    "Undefined identifier",
    "Stack overflow",
    "Invalid statement",
    "Unexpected token",
    "Missing ; ",
    "Missing DO",
    "Missing UNTIL",
    "Missing THEN",
    "Invalid FOR control variable",
    "Missing OF",
    "Invalid constant",
    "Missing constant",
    "Missing : ",
    "Missing END",
    "Missing TO or DOWNTO",
    "Redefined identifier",
    "Missing = ",
    "Invalid type",
    "Not a type identifier",
    "Invalid subrangetype",
    "Not a constant identifier",
    "Missing .. ",
    "Incompatible types",
    "Invalid assignment target",
    "Invalid identifier usage",
    "Incompatible assignment",
    "Min limit greater than max limit",
    "Missing [ ",
    "Missing ] ",
    "Invalid index type",
    "Missing BEGIN",
    "Missing period",
    "Too many subscripts",
    "Invalid field",
    "Nesting too deep",
    "Missing PROGRAM",
    "Already specified in FORWARD",
    "Wrong number of actual parameters",
    "Invalid VAR parameter",
    "Not a record variable",
    "Missing variable",
    "Code segment overflow",
    "Unimplemented feature",
};

char *runtime_error_messages[] = {
    "Runtime stack overflow",
    "Value out of range",
    "Invalid CASE expression value",
    "Division by zero",
    "Invalid standard function argument",
    "Unimplemented runtime feature",
};

/*--------------------------------------------------*/
/* Globals                                          */
/*--------------------------------------------------*/

int error_count = 0;     /* number of syntax errors */

            /******************************/
```

```
                /*                         */
                /*      Error routines      */
                /*                         */
                /***************************/
```

```
/*----------------------------------------------------------*/
/* error            Print an arrow under the error and then */
/*                  print the error message.                */
/*----------------------------------------------------------*/

error(code)

    ERROR_CODE code;    /* error code */

{
    extern int buffer_offset;
    char message_buffer[MAX_PRINT_LINE_LENGTH];
    char *message = error_messages[code];
    int  offset  = buffer_offset - 2;

    /*
    -- Print the arrow pointing to the token just scanned.
    */
    if (print_flag) offset += 8;
    sprintf(message_buffer, "%*s^\n", offset, " ");
    if (print_flag) print_line(message_buffer);
    else            printf(message_buffer);

    /*
    -- Print the error message.
    */
    sprintf(message_buffer, " *** ERROR: %s.\n", message);
    if (print_flag) print_line(message_buffer);
    else            printf(message_buffer);
```

```
    *tokenp = '\0';
    ++error_count;

    if (error_count > MAX_SYNTAX_ERRORS) {
        sprintf(message_buffer,
                "Too many syntax errors.  Aborted.\n");
        if (print_flag) print_line(message_buffer);
        else            printf(message_buffer);

        exit(-TOO_MANY_SYNTAX_ERRORS);
    }
}
```

```
/*----------------------------------------------------------*/
/* runtime_error      Print a runtime error message and then */
/*                    abort the program execution.           */
/*----------------------------------------------------------*/

runtime_error(code)

    ERROR_CODE code;    /* error code */

{
    char         *message = runtime_error_messages[code];
    extern int    exec_line_number;
    extern BOOLEAN debugger_command_flag;

    if (debugger_command_flag) printf("%s\n", message);
    else {
        printf("\n*** RUNTIME ERROR in line %d: %s\n",
               exec_line_number, message);
        read_debugger_command();
    }
}
```

FIGURE A-19   common.h

```
/****************************************************************/
/*                                                              */
/*      C O M M O N   R O U T I N E S   (Header)                */
/*                                                              */
/*      FILE:     common.h                                      */
/*                                                              */
/*      MODULE:   common                                        */
/*                                                              */
/****************************************************************/

#ifndef common_h
#define common_h

#define FORM_FEED_CHAR          '\f'

#define MAX_FILE_NAME_LENGTH     32
#define MAX_SOURCE_LINE_LENGTH   256
#define MAX_PRINT_LINE_LENGTH    80
```

```
#define MAX_LINES_PER_PAGE       50
#define DATE_STRING_LENGTH       26
#define MAX_TOKEN_STRING_LENGTH  MAX_SOURCE_LINE_LENGTH
#define MAX_CODE_BUFFER_SIZE     4096
#define MAX_NESTING_LEVEL        16
#define MAX_STACK_SIZE           1024
#define STACK_FRAME_HEADER_SIZE  4

typedef enum {
    FALSE, TRUE,
} BOOLEAN;

typedef char *ADDRESS;

                /***************************************/
                /*                                     */
                /*      Macros for memory allocation   */
                /*                                     */
                /***************************************/
```

```
#define alloc_struct(type)          (type *) malloc(sizeof(type))        #define alloc_bytes(length)          (char *) malloc(length)
#define alloc_array(type, count)    (type *) malloc(count*sizeof(type))
                                                                         #endif
```

FIGURE A-20   run3.c

```
/******************************************************************/         /*----------------------------------------------------------------*/
/*                                                                */         /* main              Initialize the scanner and call              */
/*      Program 11-1:  Interactive Pascal Debugger                */         /*                   routine program.                             */
/*                                                                */         /*----------------------------------------------------------------*/
/*      Interpret a Pascal program under the control of an        */
/*      interactive debugger.                                     */         main(argc, argv)
/*                                                                */
/*      FILE:     run3.c                                          */             int  argc;
/*                                                                */             char *argv[];
/*      REQUIRES: Modules parser, symbol table, scanner,          */
/*                     executor, error                            */         {
/*                                                                */             /*
/*      FLAGS:    Macro flag "trace" must be defined              */             --  Initialize the scanner.
/*                                                                */             */
/*      USAGE:    run3 sourcefile                                 */             init_scanner(argv[1]);
/*                                                                */
/*          sourcefile      name of source file containing        */             /*
/*                          the Pascal program to interpret       */             --  Process a program.
/*                                                                */             */
/******************************************************************/             get_token();
                                                                                 program();
#include <stdio.h>                                                           }
```

APPENDIX B

This appendix contains listings of all the source files of the Pascal compiler and the runtime library, as written in Chapter 14.

Parser Module

Scanner Module

Symbol Table Module

Code Module

Error Module

Miscellaneous

FIGURE B-1   parser.h

```
/*****************************************************************/          /********************************/
/*                                                             */
/*      P A R S I N G   R O U T I N E S   (Header)             */          /*--------------------------------------------------------*/
/*                                                             */          /*  if_token_get              If token equals token_code, get */
/*      FILE:      parser.h                                    */          /*                            the next token.              */
/*                                                             */          /*--------------------------------------------------------*/
/*      MODULE:    parser                                      */
/*                                                             */          #define if_token_get(token_code)                 \
/*****************************************************************/              if (token == token_code) get_token()

#ifndef parser_h                                                            /*--------------------------------------------------------*/
#define parser_h                                                            /*  if_token_get_else_error    If token equals token_code, get */
                                                                            /*                             the next token, else error.  */
#include "common.h"                                                         /*--------------------------------------------------------*/
#include "symtab.h"
                                                                            #define if_token_get_else_error(token_code, error_code) \
/*--------------------------------------------------------*/                    if (token == token_code) get_token();          \
/*  Uses of a variable                                    */                    else                     error(error_code)
/*--------------------------------------------------------*/
                                                                            /*--------------------------------------------------------*/
typedef enum {                                                              /*  Analysis routine calls      Unless the following statements */
    EXPR_USE, TARGET_USE, VARPARM_USE,                                      /*                              are preceded by              */
} USE;                                                                      /*                                                          */
                                                                            /*                                   #define analyze          */
/*--------------------------------------------------------*/                /*                                                          */
/*  Functions                                             */                /*                              calls to the analysis routines */
/*--------------------------------------------------------*/                /*                              are not compiled.            */
                                                                            /*--------------------------------------------------------*/
TYPE_STRUCT_PTR  expression();
TYPE_STRUCT_PTR  variable();                                                #ifndef analyze
TYPE_STRUCT_PTR  routine_call();                                            #define analyze_const_defn(idp)
TYPE_STRUCT_PTR  base_type();                                               #define analyze_var_decl(idp)
BOOLEAN         is_assign_type_compatible();                                #define analyze_type_defn(idp)
                                                                            #define analyze_routine_header(idp)
              /********************************/                            #define analyze_block(idp)
              /*                            */                              #endif
              /*      Macros for parsing    */
              /*                            */                              #endif
```

FIGURE B-2   routine.c

```
/*****************************************************************/          #include "parser.h"
/*                                                             */          #include "code.h"
/*      R O U T I N E   P A R S E R                            */
/*                                                             */          /*--------------------------------------------------------*/
/*      Parsing routines for programs and declared            */          /*  Externals                                             */
/*      procedures and functions.                             */          /*--------------------------------------------------------*/
/*                                                             */
/*      FILE:      routine.c                                   */          extern int            line_number;
/*                                                             */          extern int            error_count;
/*      MODULE:    parser                                      */          extern long           exec_stmt_count;
/*                                                             */
/*****************************************************************/          extern TOKEN_CODE     token;
                                                                            extern char           word_string[];
#include <stdio.h>                                                          extern SYMTAB_NODE_PTR symtab_display[];
#include "common.h"                                                         extern int            level;
#include "error.h"
#include "scanner.h"                                                        extern TYPE_STRUCT_PTR integer_typep, real_typep;
#include "symtab.h"                                                         extern TYPE_STRUCT    dummy_type;
```

```
extern int              label_index;
extern char             asm_buffer[];
extern char             *asm_bufferp;
extern FILE             *code_file;

extern TOKEN_CODE       statement_start_list[],
                        statement_end_list[],
                        declaration_start_list[];

/*----------------------------------------------------------*/
/* Globals                                                  */
/*----------------------------------------------------------*/

char buffer[MAX_PRINT_LINE_LENGTH];

/*----------------------------------------------------------*/
/* Forwards                                                 */
/*----------------------------------------------------------*/

SYMTAB_NODE_PTR formal_parm_list();
SYMTAB_NODE_PTR program_header(), procedure_header(),
                function_header();

/*----------------------------------------------------------*/
/*  program        Process a program:                       */
/*                                                          */
/*                      <program-header> ; <block> .        */
/*----------------------------------------------------------*/

TOKEN_CODE follow_header_list[] = {SEMICOLON, END_OF_FILE, 0};

program()

{
    SYMTAB_NODE_PTR program_idp;        /* program id */

    /*
    -- Intialize the symbol table and then emit
    -- the program prologue code.
    */
    init_symtab();
    emit_program_prologue();

    /*
    -- Begin parsing with the program header.
    */
    program_idp = program_header();

    /*
    -- Error synchronization:  Should be ;
    */
    synchronize(follow_header_list,
            declaration_start_list, statement_start_list);
    if_token_get(SEMICOLON);
    else if (token_in(declaration_start_list) ||
            token_in(statement_start_list))
        error(MISSING_SEMICOLON);

    analyze_routine_header(program_idp);

    /*
    -- Parse the program's block.
    */
    program_idp->defn.info.routine.locals = NULL;
    block(program_idp);
    program_idp->defn.info.routine.local_symtab = exit_scope();

    if_token_get_else_error(PERIOD, MISSING_PERIOD);
```

```
    /*
    -- Emit the main routine's epilogue code
    -- followed by the program's epilogue code.
    */
    emit_main_epilogue();
    emit_program_epilogue(program_idp);

    /*
    -- Look for the end of file.
    */
    while (token != END_OF_FILE) {
        error(UNEXPECTED_TOKEN);
        get_token();
    }

    quit_scanner();

    /*
    -- Print the parser's summary.
    */
    print_line("\n");
    print_line("\n");
    sprintf(buffer, "%20d Source lines.\n", line_number);
    print_line(buffer);
    sprintf(buffer, "%20d Source errors.\n", error_count);
    print_line(buffer);

    if (error_count == 0) exit(0);
    else                exit(-SYNTAX_ERROR);
}

/*----------------------------------------------------------*/
/*  program_header    Process a program header:             */
/*                                                          */
/*                    PROGRAM <id> ( <id-list> )            */
/*                                                          */
/*                    Return a pointer to the program id    */
/*                    node.                                  */
/*----------------------------------------------------------*/

TOKEN_CODE follow_prog_id_list[] = {LPAREN, SEMICOLON,
                                    END_OF_FILE, 0};

TOKEN_CODE follow_parms_list[]   = {RPAREN, SEMICOLON,
                                    END_OF_FILE, 0};

    SYMTAB_NODE_PTR
program_header()

{
    SYMTAB_NODE_PTR program_idp;        /* program id */
    SYMTAB_NODE_PTR parm_idp;           /* parm id */
    SYMTAB_NODE_PTR prev_parm_idp = NULL;

    if_token_get_else_error(PROGRAM, MISSING_PROGRAM);

    if (token == IDENTIFIER) {
        search_and_enter_local_symtab(program_idp);
        program_idp->defn.key = PROG_DEFN;
        program_idp->defn.info.routine.key = DECLARED;
        program_idp->defn.info.routine.parm_count = 0;
        program_idp->defn.info.routine.total_parm_size = 0;
        program_idp->defn.info.routine.total_local_size = 0;
        program_idp->typep = &dummy_type;
        program_idp->label_index = new_label_index();
        get_token();
    }
```

```
        else error(MISSING_IDENTIFIER);

    /*
    -- Error synchronization:  Should be ( or ;
    */
    synchronize(follow_prog_id_list,
                declaration_start_list, statement_start_list);

    enter_scope(NULL);

    /*
    -- Program parameters.
    */
    if (token == LPAREN) {
        /*
        -- <id-list>
        */
        do {
            get_token();
            if (token == IDENTIFIER) {
                search_and_enter_local_symtab(parm_idp);
                parm_idp->defn.key = VARPARM_DEFN;
                parm_idp->typep = &dummy_type;
                get_token();

                /*
                -- Link program parm ids together.
                */
                if (prev_parm_idp == NULL)
                    program_idp->defn.info.routine.parms =
                                    prev_parm_idp = parm_idp;
                else {
                    prev_parm_idp->next = parm_idp;
                    prev_parm_idp = parm_idp;
                }
            }
            else error(MISSING_IDENTIFIER);
        } while (token == COMMA);

        /*
        -- Error synchronization:  Should be )
        */
        synchronize(follow_parms_list,
                    declaration_start_list, statement_start_list);
        if_token_get_else_error(RPAREN, MISSING_RPAREN);
    }
    else program_idp->defn.info.routine.parms = NULL;

    return(program_idp);
}

/*-------------------------------------------------------------*/
/* routine             Call the appropriate routine to process */
/*                     a procedure or function definition:     */
/*                                                             */
/*                         <routine-header> ; <block>          */
/*-------------------------------------------------------------*/

routine()

{
    SYMTAB_NODE_PTR rtn_idp;    /* routine id */

    rtn_idp = (token == PROCEDURE) ? procedure_header()
                                   : function_header();

    /*
```

```
    -- Error synchronization:  Should be ;
    */
    synchronize(follow_header_list,
                declaration_start_list, statement_start_list);
    if_token_get(SEMICOLON);
    else if (token_in(declaration_start_list) ||
             token_in(statement_start_list))
        error(MISSING_SEMICOLON);

    /*
    -- <block> or FORWARD.
    */
    if (strcmp(word_string, "forward") != 0) {
        rtn_idp->defn.info.routine.key = DECLARED;
        analyze_routine_header(rtn_idp);

        rtn_idp->defn.info.routine.locals = NULL;
        block(rtn_idp);
    }
    else {
        get_token();
        rtn_idp->defn.info.routine.key = FORWARD;
        analyze_routine_header(rtn_idp);
    }

    /*
    -- Exit the current scope and emit the
    -- routine's epilogue code.
    */
    rtn_idp->defn.info.routine.local_symtab = exit_scope();
    emit_routine_epilogue(rtn_idp);
}

/*-------------------------------------------------------------*/
/* procedure_header     Process a procedure header:            */
/*                                                             */
/*                         PROCEDURE <id>                      */
/*                                                             */
/*                     or:                                     */
/*                                                             */
/*                         PROCEDURE <id> ( <parm-list> )      */
/*                                                             */
/*                     Return a pointer to the procedure id    */
/*                     node.                                    */
/*-------------------------------------------------------------*/

TOKEN_CODE follow_proc_id_list[] = {LPAREN, SEMICOLON,
                                    END_OF_FILE, 0};

    SYMTAB_NODE_PTR
procedure_header()

{
    SYMTAB_NODE_PTR proc_idp;        /* procedure id */
    SYMTAB_NODE_PTR parm_listp;      /* formal parm list */
    int             parm_count;
    int             total_parm_size;
    BOOLEAN         forward_flag = FALSE;   /* TRUE iff forwarded */

    get_token();

    /*
    -- If the procedure identifier has already been
    -- declared in this scope, it must be a forward.
    */
    if (token == IDENTIFIER) {
        search_local_symtab(proc_idp);
```

```
        if (proc_idp == NULL) {
            enter_local_symtab(proc_idp);
            proc_idp->defn.key = PROC_DEFN;
            proc_idp->defn.info.routine.total_local_size = 0;
            proc_idp->typep = &dummy_type;
            proc_idp->label_index = new_label_index();
        }
        else if ((proc_idp->defn.key == PROC_DEFN) &&
                (proc_idp->defn.info.routine.key == FORWARD))
            forward_flag = TRUE;
        else error(REDEFINED_IDENTIFIER);

        get_token();
    }
    else error(MISSING_IDENTIFIER);

    /*
    -- Error synchronization:  Should be ( or ;
    */
    synchronize(follow_proc_id_list,
            declaration_start_list, statement_start_list);

    enter_scope(NULL);

    /*
    -- Optional formal parameters.  If there was a forward,
    -- there must not be any parameters here (but parse them
    -- anyway for error recovery).
    */
    if (token == LPAREN) {
        parm_listp = formal_parm_list(&parm_count, &total_parm_size);

        if (forward_flag) error(ALREADY_FORWARDED);
        else {
            proc_idp->defn.info.routine.parm_count = parm_count;
            proc_idp->defn.info.routine.total_parm_size =
                                            total_parm_size;
            proc_idp->defn.info.routine.parms = parm_listp;
        }
    }
    else if (!forward_flag) {
        proc_idp->defn.info.routine.parm_count = 0;
        proc_idp->defn.info.routine.total_parm_size = 0;
        proc_idp->defn.info.routine.parms = NULL;
    }

    proc_idp->typep = NULL;
    return(proc_idp);
}

/*--------------------------------------------------*/
/* function_header     Process a function header:   */
/*                                                  */
/*                        FUNCTION <id> : <type-id> */
/*                                                  */
/*                 or:                              */
/*                                                  */
/*                        FUNCTION <id> ( <parm-list> ) */
/*                            : <type-id>           */
/*                                                  */
/*                     Return a pointer to the function id */
/*                     node.                        */
/*--------------------------------------------------*/

TOKEN_CODE follow_func_id_list[] = {LPAREN, COLON, SEMICOLON,
                        END_OF_FILE, 0};

    SYMTAB_NODE_PTR
function_header()

{
    SYMTAB_NODE_PTR func_idp, type_idp;    /* func and type ids */
    SYMTAB_NODE_PTR parm_listp;            /* formal parm list */
    int             parm_count;
    int             total_parm_size;
    BOOLEAN         forward_flag = FALSE;  /* TRUE iff forwarded */

    get_token();

    /*
    -- If the function identifier has already been
    -- declared in this scope, it must be a forward.
    */
    if (token == IDENTIFIER) {
        search_local_symtab(func_idp);
        if (func_idp == NULL) {
            enter_local_symtab(func_idp);
            func_idp->defn.key = FUNC_DEFN;
            func_idp->defn.info.routine.total_local_size = 0;
            func_idp->typep = &dummy_type;
            func_idp->label_index = new_label_index();
        }
        else if ((func_idp->defn.key == FUNC_DEFN) &&
                (func_idp->defn.info.routine.key == FORWARD))
            forward_flag = TRUE;
        else error(REDEFINED_IDENTIFIER);

        get_token();
    }
    else error(MISSING_IDENTIFIER);

    /*
    -- Error synchronization:  Should be ( or : or ;
    */
    synchronize(follow_func_id_list,
            declaration_start_list, statement_start_list);

    enter_scope(NULL);

    /*
    -- Optional formal parameters.  If there was a forward,
    -- there must not be any parameters here (but parse them
    -- anyway for error recovery).
    */
    if (token == LPAREN) {
        parm_listp = formal_parm_list(&parm_count, &total_parm_size);

        if (forward_flag) error(ALREADY_FORWARDED);
        else {
            func_idp->defn.info.routine.parm_count = parm_count;
            func_idp->defn.info.routine.total_parm_size =
                                            total_parm_size;
            func_idp->defn.info.routine.parms = parm_listp;
        }
    }
    else if (!forward_flag) {
        func_idp->defn.info.routine.parm_count = 0;
        func_idp->defn.info.routine.total_parm_size = 0;
        func_idp->defn.info.routine.parms = NULL;
    }

    /*
    -- Function type.  If there was a forward,
    -- there must not be a type here (but parse it
```

```
    --  anyway for error recovery).
    */
    if (!forward_flag || (token == COLON)) {
        if_token_get_else_error(COLON, MISSING_COLON);

        if (token == IDENTIFIER) {
            search_and_find_all_symtab(type_idp);
            if (type_idp->defn.key != TYPE_DEFN) error(INVALID_TYPE);
            if (!forward_flag) func_idp->typep = type_idp->typep;
            get_token();
        }
        else {
            error(MISSING_IDENTIFIER);
            func_idp->typep = &dummy_type;
        }

        if (forward_flag) error(ALREADY_FORWARDED);
    }

    return(func_idp);
}

/*------------------------------------------------------------*/
/*  formal_parm_list    Process a formal parameter list:      */
/*                                                            */
/*                          ( VAR <id-list> : <type> ;        */
/*                            <id-list> : <type> ;            */
/*                            ... )                           */
/*                                                            */
/*                          Return a pointer to the head of the */
/*                          parameter id list.                */
/*------------------------------------------------------------*/

    SYMTAB_NODE_PTR
formal_parm_list(countp, total_sizep)

    int *countp;        /* ptr to count of parameters */
    int *total_sizep;   /* ptr to total byte size of parameters */

{
    SYMTAB_NODE_PTR parm_idp, first_idp, last_idp;    /* parm ids */
    SYMTAB_NODE_PTR prev_last_idp = NULL;        /* last id of list */
    SYMTAB_NODE_PTR parm_listp = NULL;           /* parm list */
    SYMTAB_NODE_PTR type_idp;                    /* type id */
    TYPE_STRUCT_PTR parm_tp;                     /* parm type */
    DEFN_KEY        parm_defn;                   /* parm definition */
    int             parm_count = 0;              /* count of parms */
    int             parm_offset = PARAMETERS_STACK_FRAME_OFFSET;

    get_token();

    /*
    --  Loop to process parameter declarations separated by ;
    */
    while ((token == IDENTIFIER) || (token == VAR)) {
        first_idp = NULL;

        /*
        --  VAR parms?
        */
        if (token == VAR) {
            parm_defn = VARPARM_DEFN;
            get_token();
        }
        else parm_defn = VALPARM_DEFN;

        /*
```

```
        --  <id list>
        */
        while (token == IDENTIFIER) {
            search_and_enter_local_symtab(parm_idp);
            parm_idp->defn.key    = parm_defn;
            parm_idp->label_index = new_label_index();
            ++parm_count;

            if (parm_listp == NULL) parm_listp = parm_idp;

            /*
            --  Link parm ids together.
            */
            if (first_idp == NULL)
                first_idp = last_idp = parm_idp;
            else {
                last_idp->next = parm_idp;
                last_idp = parm_idp;
            }

            get_token();
            if_token_get(COMMA);
        }

        if_token_get_else_error(COLON, MISSING_COLON);

        if (token == IDENTIFIER) {
            search_and_find_all_symtab(type_idp);
            if (type_idp->defn.key != TYPE_DEFN) error(INVALID_TYPE);
            parm_tp = type_idp->typep;
            get_token();
        }
        else {
            error(MISSING_IDENTIFIER);
            parm_tp = &dummy_type;
        }

        /*
        --  Assign the type to all parm ids in the sublist.
        */
        for (parm_idp = first_idp;
             parm_idp != NULL;
             parm_idp = parm_idp->next) parm_idp->typep = parm_tp;

        /*
        --  Link this list to the list of all parm ids.
        */
        if (prev_last_idp != NULL) prev_last_idp->next = first_idp;
        prev_last_idp = last_idp;

        /*
        --  Error synchronization:  Should be ; or )
        */
        synchronize(follow_parms_list, NULL, NULL);
        if_token_get(SEMICOLON);
    }

    /*
    --  Assign the offset to all parm ids in reverse order.
    */
    reverse_list(&parm_listp);
    for (parm_idp = parm_listp;
         parm_idp != NULL;
         parm_idp = parm_idp->next) {
        parm_idp->defn.info.data.offset = parm_offset;
        parm_offset += parm_idp->defn.key == VALPARM_DEFN
                            ? parm_idp->typep->size
```

```
                         : sizeof(char *);
        if (parm_offset & 1) ++parm_offset;    /* round up to even */
    }
    reverse_list(&parm_listp);

    if_token_get_else_error(RPAREN, MISSING_RPAREN);
    *countp = parm_count;
    *total_sizep = parm_offset - PARAMETERS_STACK_FRAME_OFFSET;

    return(parm_listp);
}

/*-------------------------------------------------------------*/
/*  reverse_list        Reverse a list of symbol table nodes.  */
/*-------------------------------------------------------------*/

reverse_list(listpp)

    SYMTAB_NODE_PTR *listpp;      /* ptr to ptr to node list head */

{
    SYMTAB_NODE_PTR prevp = NULL;
    SYMTAB_NODE_PTR thisp = *listpp;
    SYMTAB_NODE_PTR nextp;

    /*
    --  Reverse the list in place.
    */
    while (thisp != NULL) {
        nextp = thisp->next;
        thisp->next = prevp;
        prevp = thisp;
        thisp = nextp;
    }

    /*
    --  Point to the new head (former tail) of the list.
    */
    *listpp = prevp;
}

/*-------------------------------------------------------------*/
/*  routine_call        Process a call to a declared or        */
/*                      a standard procedure or function.      */
/*                      Return a pointer to the type           */
/*                      structure of the call.                 */
/*-------------------------------------------------------------*/

    TYPE_STRUCT_PTR
routine_call(rtn_idp, parm_check_flag)

    SYMTAB_NODE_PTR rtn_idp;            /* routine id */
    BOOLEAN         parm_check_flag;    /* if TRUE check parms */

{
    TYPE_STRUCT_PTR declared_routine_call(), standard_routine_call();

    if ((rtn_idp->defn.info.routine.key == DECLARED) ||
        (rtn_idp->defn.info.routine.key == FORWARD) ||
        !parm_check_flag)
        return(declared_routine_call(rtn_idp, parm_check_flag));
    else
        return(standard_routine_call(rtn_idp));
}

/*-------------------------------------------------------------*/
/*  declared_routine_call   Process a call to a declared       */
```

```
/*                      procedure or function:                 */
/*                                                             */
/*                              <id>                           */
/*                                                             */
/*                          or:                                */
/*                                                             */
/*                          <id> ( <parm-list> )               */
/*                                                             */
/*                      The actual parameters are checked      */
/*                      against the formal parameters for      */
/*                      type and number.  Return a pointer     */
/*                      to the type structure of the call.     */
/*-------------------------------------------------------------*/

    TYPE_STRUCT_PTR
declared_routine_call(rtn_idp, parm_check_flag)

    SYMTAB_NODE_PTR rtn_idp;            /* routine id */
    BOOLEAN         parm_check_flag;    /* if TRUE check parms */

{
    int old_level = level;              /* level of caller */
    int new_level = rtn_idp->level + 1; /* level of callee */

    actual_parm_list(rtn_idp, parm_check_flag);

    /*
    --  Push the static link onto the stack.
    */
    if (new_level == old_level + 1) {
        /*
        --  Calling a routine nested within the caller:
        --  Push pointer to caller's stack frame.
        */
        emit_1(PUSH, reg(BP));
    }
    else if (new_level == old_level) {
        /*
        --  Calling another routine at the same level:
        --  Push pointer to stack frame of common parent.
        */
        emit_1(PUSH, name_lit(STATIC_LINK));
    }
    else  /* new_level < old_level */ {
        /*
        --  Calling a routine at a lesser level (nested less deeply):
        --  Push pointer to stack frame of nearest common ancestor.
        */
        int lev;

        emit_2(MOVE, reg(BX), reg(BP));
        for (lev = old_level; lev >= new_level; --lev)
            emit_2(MOVE, reg(BP), name_lit(STATIC_LINK));
        emit_1(PUSH, reg(BP));
        emit_2(MOVE, reg(BP), reg(BX));
    }

    emit_1(CALL, tagged_name(rtn_idp));

    return(rtn_idp->defn.key == PROC_DEFN ? NULL : rtn_idp->typep);
}

/*-------------------------------------------------------------*/
/*  actual_parm_list    Process an actual parameter list:      */
/*                                                             */
/*                          ( <expr-list> )                    */
/*-------------------------------------------------------------*/
```

```
TOKEN_CODE follow_parm_list[] = {COMMA, RPAREN, 0};

actual_parm_list(rtn_idp, parm_check_flag)

    SYMTAB_NODE_PTR rtn_idp;              /* routine id */
    BOOLEAN         parm_check_flag;      /* if TRUE check parms */

{
    SYMTAB_NODE_PTR formal_parm_idp;
    DEFN_KEY        formal_parm_defn;
    TYPE_STRUCT_PTR formal_parm_tp, actual_parm_tp;

    if (parm_check_flag)
        formal_parm_idp = rtn_idp->defn.info.routine.parms;

    if (token == LPAREN) {
        /*
        -- Loop to process actual parameter expressions.
        */
        do {
            /*
            -- Obtain info about the corresponding formal parm.
            */
            if (parm_check_flag && (formal_parm_idp != NULL)) {
                formal_parm_defn = formal_parm_idp->defn.key;
                formal_parm_tp   = formal_parm_idp->typep;
            }

            get_token();

            /*
            -- Check the actual parm's type against the formal parm.
            -- An actual parm's type must be the same as the type of
            -- a formal VAR parm and assignment compatible with the
            -- type of a formal value parm.
            */
            if ((formal_parm_idp == NULL) ||
                (formal_parm_defn == VALPARM_DEFN) ||
                !parm_check_flag) {
                actual_parm_tp = expression();
                if (parm_check_flag && (formal_parm_idp != NULL) &&
                    (! is_assign_type_compatible(formal_parm_tp,
                                                 actual_parm_tp)))
                    error(INCOMPATIBLE_TYPES);

                /*
                -- Push the argument value onto the stack.
                */
                if (formal_parm_tp == real_typep) {
                    /*
                    -- Real formal parm.
                    */
                    if (actual_parm_tp == integer_typep) {
                        emit_1(PUSH, reg(AX));
                        emit_1(CALL, name_lit(FLOAT_CONVERT));
                        emit_2(ADD,  reg(SP), integer_lit(2));
                    }
                    emit_1(PUSH, reg(DX));
                    emit_1(PUSH, reg(AX));
                }
                else if ((actual_parm_tp->form == ARRAY_FORM) ||
                         (actual_parm_tp->form == RECORD_FORM)) {

                    /*
                    -- Block move onto the stack.
                    */
                    int size = actual_parm_tp->size;
```

```
                    int offset = size%2 == 0 ? size : size + 1;

                    emit(CLEAR_DIRECTION);
                    emit_1(POP,  reg(SI));
                    emit_2(SUBTRACT, reg(SP), integer_lit(offset));
                    emit_2(MOVE, reg(DI), reg(SP));
                    emit_2(MOVE, reg(CX), integer_lit(size));
                    emit_2(MOVE, reg(AX), reg(DS));
                    emit_2(MOVE, reg(ES), reg(AX));
                    emit(MOVE_BLOCK);
                }
                else {
                    emit_1(PUSH, reg(AX));
                }
            }

            else  /* formal_parm_defn == VARPARM_DEFN */  {
                if (token == IDENTIFIER) {
                    SYMTAB_NODE_PTR idp;

                    search_and_find_all_symtab(idp);
                    actual_parm_tp = variable(idp, VARPARM_USE);

                    if (formal_parm_tp != actual_parm_tp)
                        error(INCOMPATIBLE_TYPES);
                }
                else {
                    actual_parm_tp = expression();
                    error(INVALID_VAR_PARM);
                }
            }

            /*
            -- Check if there are more actual parms
            -- than formal parms.
            */
            if (parm_check_flag) {
                if (formal_parm_idp == NULL)
                    error(WRONG_NUMBER_OF_PARMS);
                else formal_parm_idp = formal_parm_idp->next;
            }

            /*
            -- Error synchronization:  Should be , or )
            */
            synchronize(follow_parm_list, statement_end_list, NULL);

        } while (token == COMMA);

        if_token_get_else_error(RPAREN, MISSING_RPAREN);
    }

    /*
    -- Check if there are fewer actual parms than formal parms.
    */
    if (parm_check_flag && (formal_parm_idp != NULL))
        error(WRONG_NUMBER_OF_PARMS);
}

/*------------------------------------------------------------*/
/* block              Process a block, which consists of      */
/*                    declarations followed by a compound      */
/*                    statement.                               */
/*------------------------------------------------------------*/

TOKEN_CODE follow_decls_list[] = {SEMICOLON, BEGIN, END_OF_FILE, 0};

block(rtn_idp)
```

```
    SYMTAB_NODE_PTR rtn_idp;      /* id of program or routine */

{
    extern BOOLEAN block_flag;

    declarations(rtn_idp);

    /*
    -- Emit the prologue code for the main routine
    -- or for a procedure or function.
    */
    if (rtn_idp->defn.key == PROG_DEFN)
        emit_main_prologue();
```

```
    else
        emit_routine_prologue(rtn_idp);

    /*
    -- Error synchronization:  Should be ;
    */
    synchronize(follow_decls_list, NULL, NULL);
    if (token != BEGIN) error(MISSING_BEGIN);

    block_flag = TRUE;
    compound_statement();
    block_flag = FALSE;
}
```

FIGURE B-3   standard.c

```c
/* Figure 14-12 */

/****************************************************************/
/*                                                              */
/*              S T A N D A R D   R O U T I N E   P A R S E R   */
/*                                                              */
/*      Parsing routines for calls to standard procedures and   */
/*      functions.                                              */
/*                                                              */
/*      FILE:       standard.c                                  */
/*                                                              */
/*      MODULE:     parser                                      */
/*                                                              */
/****************************************************************/

#include <stdio.h>
#include "common.h"
#include "error.h"
#include "scanner.h"
#include "symtab.h"
#include "parser.h"
#include "code.h"

#define DEFAULT_NUMERIC_FIELD_WIDTH    10
#define DEFAULT_PRECISION               2

/*------------------------------------------------------------*/
/* Externals                                                  */
/*------------------------------------------------------------*/

extern TOKEN_CODE       token;
extern char             word_string[];
extern SYMTAB_NODE_PTR  symtab_display[];
extern int              level;
extern TYPE_STRUCT      dummy_type;

extern TYPE_STRUCT_PTR  integer_typep, real_typep,
                        boolean_typep, char_typep;

extern int              label_index;
extern char             asm_buffer[];
extern char             *asm_bufferp;
extern FILE             *code_file;

extern TOKEN_CODE       follow_parm_list[];
extern TOKEN_CODE       statement_end_list[];
```

```c
/*------------------------------------------------------------*/
/* Forwards                                                   */
/*------------------------------------------------------------*/

TYPE_STRUCT_PTR eof_eoln(), abs_sqr(),
                arctan_cos_exp_ln_sin_sqrt(),
                pred_succ(), chr(), odd(), ord(),
                round_trunc();

/*------------------------------------------------------------*/
/* standard_routine_call   Process a call to a standard       */
/*                         procedure or function.  Return a   */
/*                         pointer to the type structure of   */
/*                         the call.                          */
/*------------------------------------------------------------*/

    TYPE_STRUCT_PTR
standard_routine_call(rtn_idp)

    SYMTAB_NODE_PTR rtn_idp;           /* routine id */

{
    switch (rtn_idp->defn.info.routine.key) {

        case READ:
        case READLN:    read_readln(rtn_idp);       return(NULL);

        case WRITE:
        case WRITELN:   write_writeln(rtn_idp);     return(NULL);

        case EOFF:
        case EOLN:      return(eof_eoln(rtn_idp));

        case ABS:
        case SQR:       return(abs_sqr(rtn_idp));

        case ARCTAN:
        case COS:
        case EXP:
        case LN:
        case SIN:
        case SQRT:      return(arctan_cos_exp_ln_sin_sqrt(rtn_idp));

        case PRED:
        case SUCC:      return(pred_succ(rtn_idp));
```

```
        case CHR:       return(chr());
        case ODD:       return(odd());
        case ORD:       return(ord());

        case ROUND:
        case TRUNC:     return(round_trunc(rtn_idp));
    }
}

/*------------------------------------------------------------*/
/*  read_readln               Process a call to read or readln.  */
/*------------------------------------------------------------*/

read_readln(rtn_idp)

    SYMTAB_NODE_PTR rtn_idp;            /* routine id */

{

    TYPE_STRUCT_PTR actual_parm_tp;     /* actual parm type */

    /*
    -- Parameters are optional for readln.
    */
    if (token == LPAREN) {
        /*
        -- <id-list>
        */
        do {
            get_token();

            /*
            -- Actual parms must be variables (but parse
            -- an expression anyway for error recovery).
            */
            if (token == IDENTIFIER) {
                SYMTAB_NODE_PTR idp;

                search_and_find_all_symtab(idp);
                actual_parm_tp = base_type(variable(idp,
                                            VARPARM_USE));

                if (actual_parm_tp->form != SCALAR_FORM)
                    error(INCOMPATIBLE_TYPES);
                else if (actual_parm_tp == integer_typep) {
                    emit_1(CALL, name_lit(READ_INTEGER));
                    emit_1(POP,  reg(BX));
                    emit_2(MOVE, word_indirect(BX), reg(AX));
                }
                else if (actual_parm_tp == real_typep) {
                    emit_1(CALL, name_lit(READ_REAL));
                    emit_1(POP,  reg(BX));
                    emit_2(MOVE, word_indirect(BX), reg(AX));
                    emit_2(MOVE, high_dword_indirect(BX), reg(DX));
                }
                else if (actual_parm_tp == char_typep) {
                    emit_1(CALL, name_lit(READ_CHAR));
                    emit_1(POP,  reg(BX));
                    emit_2(MOVE, byte_indirect(BX), reg(AL));
                }
            }
            else {
                actual_parm_tp = expression();
                error(INVALID_VAR_PARM);
            }

            /*
            -- Error synchronization:  Should be , or )
```

```
            */
            synchronize(follow_parm_list, statement_end_list, NULL);

        } while (token == COMMA);

        if_token_get_else_error(RPAREN, MISSING_RPAREN);
    }
    else if (rtn_idp->defn.info.routine.key == READ)
        error(WRONG_NUMBER_OF_PARMS);

    if (rtn_idp->defn.info.routine.key == READLN)
        emit_1(CALL, name_lit(READ_LINE));
}

/*------------------------------------------------------------*/
/*  write_writeln            Process a call to write or writeln. */
/*                           Each actual parameter can be:       */
/*                                                               */
/*                               <expr>                          */
/*                                                               */
/*                           or:                                 */
/*                                                               */
/*                               <epxr> : <expr>                 */
/*                                                               */
/*                           or:                                 */
/*                                                               */
/*                               <expr> : <expr> : <expr>        */
/*------------------------------------------------------------*/

write_writeln(rtn_idp)

    SYMTAB_NODE_PTR rtn_idp;            /* routine id */

{

    TYPE_STRUCT_PTR actual_parm_tp;     /* actual parm type */
    TYPE_STRUCT_PTR field_width_tp, precision_tp;

    /*
    -- Parameters are optional for writeln.
    */
    if (token == LPAREN) {
        do {
            /*
            -- Value <expr>
            */
            get_token();
            actual_parm_tp = base_type(expression());

            /*
            -- Push the scalar value to be written onto the stack.
            -- A string value is already on the stack.
            */
            if (actual_parm_tp->form != ARRAY_FORM)
                emit_push_operand(actual_parm_tp);

            if ((actual_parm_tp->form != SCALAR_FORM) &&
                (actual_parm_tp != boolean_typep) &&
                ((actual_parm_tp->form != ARRAY_FORM) ||
                 (actual_parm_tp->info.array.elmt_typep !=
                                            char_typep)))

                error(INVALID_EXPRESSION);

            /*
            -- Optional field width <expr>
            -- Push onto the stack.
            */
            if (token == COLON) {
```

```
    get_token();
    field_width_tp = base_type(expression());
    emit_1(PUSH, reg(AX));

    if (field_width_tp != integer_typep)
        error(INCOMPATIBLE_TYPES);

    /*
    -- Optional precision <expr>
    -- Push onto the stack if the value to be printed
    -- is of type real.
    */
    if (token == COLON) {
        get_token();
        precision_tp = base_type(expression());

        if (actual_parm_tp == real_typep)
            emit_1(PUSH, reg(AX));

        if (precision_tp != integer_typep)
            error(INCOMPATIBLE_TYPES);
    }
    else if (actual_parm_tp == real_typep) {
        emit_2(MOVE, reg(AX),
               integer_lit(DEFAULT_PRECISION));
        emit_1(PUSH, reg(AX));
    }
}
else {
    if (actual_parm_tp == integer_typep) {
        emit_2(MOVE, reg(AX),
               integer_lit(DEFAULT_NUMERIC_FIELD_WIDTH));
        emit_1(PUSH, reg(AX));
    }
    else if (actual_parm_tp == real_typep) {
        emit_2(MOVE, reg(AX),
               integer_lit(DEFAULT_NUMERIC_FIELD_WIDTH));
        emit_1(PUSH, reg(AX));
        emit_2(MOVE, reg(AX),
               integer_lit(DEFAULT_PRECISION));
        emit_1(PUSH, reg(AX));
    }
    else {
        emit_2(MOVE, reg(AX), integer_lit(0));
        emit_1(PUSH, reg(AX));
    }
}

if (actual_parm_tp == integer_typep) {
    emit_1(CALL, name_lit(WRITE_INTEGER));
    emit_2(ADD, reg(SP), integer_lit(4));
}
else if (actual_parm_tp == real_typep) {
    emit_1(CALL, name_lit(WRITE_REAL));
    emit_2(ADD, reg(SP), integer_lit(8));
}
else if (actual_parm_tp == boolean_typep) {
    emit_1(CALL, name_lit(WRITE_BOOLEAN));
    emit_2(ADD, reg(SP), integer_lit(4));
}
else if (actual_parm_tp == char_typep) {
    emit_1(CALL, name_lit(WRITE_CHAR));
    emit_2(ADD, reg(SP), integer_lit(4));
}
else /* string */ {
    /*
    -- Push the string length onto the stack.
```

```
    */
    emit_2(MOVE, reg(AX),
           integer_lit(actual_parm_tp->info.array
                                    .elmt_count));

    emit_1(PUSH, reg(AX));
    emit_1(CALL, name_lit(WRITE_STRING));
    emit_2(ADD, reg(SP), integer_lit(6));
}

/*
-- Error synchronization:  Should be , or )
*/
synchronize(follow_parm_list, statement_end_list, NULL);

} while (token == COMMA);

if_token_get_else_error(RPAREN, MISSING_RPAREN);
}
else if (rtn_idp->defn.info.routine.key == WRITE)
    error(WRONG_NUMBER_OF_PARMS);

if (rtn_idp->defn.info.routine.key == WRITELN)
    emit_1(CALL, name_lit(WRITE_LINE));
}

/*------------------------------------------------------------*/
/*  eof_eoln              Process a call to eof or to eoln.  */
/*                        No parameters => boolean result.   */
/*------------------------------------------------------------*/

    TYPE_STRUCT_PTR
eof_eoln(rtn_idp)

    SYMTAB_NODE_PTR rtn_idp;         /* routine id */

{
    if (token == LPAREN) {
        error(WRONG_NUMBER_OF_PARMS);
        actual_parm_list(rtn_idp, FALSE);
    }

    emit_1(CALL, name_lit(rtn_idp->defn.info.routine.key == EOFF
                          ? STD_END_OF_FILE
                          : STD_END_OF_LINE));

    return(boolean_typep);
}

/*------------------------------------------------------------*/
/*  abs_sqr               Process a call to abs or to sqr.   */
/*                        integer parm => integer result     */
/*                        real parm    => real result        */
/*------------------------------------------------------------*/

    TYPE_STRUCT_PTR
abs_sqr(rtn_idp)

    SYMTAB_NODE_PTR rtn_idp;         /* routine id */

{
    TYPE_STRUCT_PTR parm_tp;         /* actual parameter type */
    TYPE_STRUCT_PTR result_tp;       /* result type */

    if (token == LPAREN) {
        get_token();
        parm_tp = base_type(expression());
```

```
        if ((parm_tp != integer_typep) && (parm_tp != real_typep)) {
            error(INCOMPATIBLE_TYPES);
            result_tp = real_typep;
        }
        else result_tp = parm_tp;

        if_token_get_else_error(RPAREN, MISSING_RPAREN);
    }
    else error(WRONG_NUMBER_OF_PARMS);

    switch (rtn_idp->defn.info.routine.key) {

        case ABS:
            if (parm_tp == integer_typep) {
                int nonnegative_labelx = new_label_index();

                emit_2(COMPARE, reg(AX), integer_lit(0));
                emit_1(JUMP_GE, label(STMT_LABEL_PREFIX,
                                      nonnegative_labelx));
                emit_1(NEGATE, reg(AX));
                emit_label(STMT_LABEL_PREFIX, nonnegative_labelx);
            }
            else {
                emit_push_operand(parm_tp);
                emit_1(CALL, name_lit(STD_ABS));
                emit_2(ADD, reg(SP), integer_lit(4));
            }
            break;

        case SQR:
            if (parm_tp == integer_typep) {
                emit_2(MOVE, reg(DX), reg(AX));
                emit_1(MULTIPLY, reg(DX));
            }
            else {
                emit_push_operand(parm_tp);
                emit_push_operand(parm_tp);
                emit_1(CALL, name_lit(FLOAT_MULTIPLY));
                emit_2(ADD, reg(SP), integer_lit(8));
            }
            break;
    }

    return(result_tp);
}

/*----------------------------------------------------------------*/
/* arctan_cos_exp_ln_sin_sqrt   Process a call to arctan, cos,   */
/*                              exp, ln, sin, or sqrt.           */
/*                              integer parm => real result      */
/*                              real_parm    => real result      */
/*----------------------------------------------------------------*/

    TYPE_STRUCT_PTR
arctan_cos_exp_ln_sin_sqrt(rtn_idp)

    SYMTAB_NODE_PTR rtn_idp;         /* routine id */

{
    TYPE_STRUCT_PTR parm_tp;         /* actual parameter type */
    char            *std_func_name;  /* name of standard func */

    if (token == LPAREN) {
        get_token();
        parm_tp = base_type(expression());

        if ((parm_tp != integer_typep) && (parm_tp != real_typep))
            error(INCOMPATIBLE_TYPES);
```

```
        if_token_get_else_error(RPAREN, MISSING_RPAREN);
    }
    else error(WRONG_NUMBER_OF_PARMS);

    if (parm_tp == integer_typep) {
        emit_1(PUSH, reg(AX));
        emit_1(CALL, name_lit(FLOAT_CONVERT));
        emit_2(ADD,  reg(SP), integer_lit(2));
    }

    emit_push_operand(real_typep);

    switch (rtn_idp->defn.info.routine.key) {
        case ARCTAN:    std_func_name = STD_ARCTAN;    break;
        case COS:       std_func_name = STD_COS;       break;
        case EXP:       std_func_name = STD_EXP;       break;
        case LN:        std_func_name = STD_LN;        break;
        case SIN:       std_func_name = STD_SIN;       break;
        case SQRT:      std_func_name = STD_SQRT;      break;
    }

    emit_1(CALL, name_lit(std_func_name));
    emit_2(ADD,  reg(SP), integer_lit(4));

    return(real_typep);
}

/*----------------------------------------------------------------*/
/* pred_succ            Process a call to pred or succ.          */
/*                      integer parm => integer result          */
/*                      enum parm    => enum result             */
/*----------------------------------------------------------------*/

    TYPE_STRUCT_PTR
pred_succ(rtn_idp)

    SYMTAB_NODE_PTR rtn_idp;         /* routine id */

{
    TYPE_STRUCT_PTR parm_tp;         /* actual parameter type */
    TYPE_STRUCT_PTR result_tp;       /* result type */

    if (token == LPAREN) {
        get_token();
        parm_tp = base_type(expression());

        if ((parm_tp != integer_typep) &&
            (parm_tp->form != ENUM_FORM)) {
            error(INCOMPATIBLE_TYPES);
            result_tp = integer_typep;
        }
        else result_tp = parm_tp;

        if_token_get_else_error(RPAREN, MISSING_RPAREN);
    }
    else error(WRONG_NUMBER_OF_PARMS);

    emit_1(rtn_idp->defn.info.routine.key == PRED
               ? DECREMENT : INCREMENT,
           reg(AX));

    return(result_tp);
}

/*----------------------------------------------------------------*/
/* chr                  Process a call to chr.                   */
```

```
/*                        integer parm => character result    */
/*----------------------------------------------------------*/

    TYPE_STRUCT_PTR
chr()

{
    TYPE_STRUCT_PTR parm_tp;           /* actual parameter type */

    if (token == LPAREN) {
        get_token();
        parm_tp = base_type(expression());

        if (parm_tp != integer_typep) error(INCOMPATIBLE_TYPES);
        if_token_get_else_error(RPAREN, MISSING_RPAREN);
    }
    else error(WRONG_NUMBER_OF_PARMS);

    return(char_typep);
}


/*----------------------------------------------------------*/
/* odd                     Process a call to odd.           */
/*                         integer parm => boolean result   */
/*----------------------------------------------------------*/

    TYPE_STRUCT_PTR
odd()

{
    TYPE_STRUCT_PTR parm_tp;           /* actual parameter type */

    if (token == LPAREN) {
        get_token();
        parm_tp = base_type(expression());

        if (parm_tp != integer_typep) error(INCOMPATIBLE_TYPES);
        if_token_get_else_error(RPAREN, MISSING_RPAREN);
    }
    else error(WRONG_NUMBER_OF_PARMS);

    emit_2(AND_BITS, reg(AX), integer_lit(1));
    return(boolean_typep);
}

/*----------------------------------------------------------*/
/* ord                     Process a call to ord.           */
/*                         enumeration parm => integer result */
/*----------------------------------------------------------*/
```

```
    TYPE_STRUCT_PTR
ord()

{
    TYPE_STRUCT_PTR parm_tp;           /* actual parameter type */

    if (token == LPAREN) {
        get_token();
        parm_tp = base_type(expression());

        if (parm_tp->form != ENUM_FORM) error(INCOMPATIBLE_TYPES);
        if_token_get_else_error(RPAREN, MISSING_RPAREN);
    }
    else error(WRONG_NUMBER_OF_PARMS);

    return(integer_typep);
}


/*----------------------------------------------------------*/
/* round_trunc             Process a call to round or trunc. */
/*                         real parm => integer result      */
/*----------------------------------------------------------*/

    TYPE_STRUCT_PTR
round_trunc(rtn_idp)

    SYMTAB_NODE_PTR rtn_idp;            /* routine id */

{
    TYPE_STRUCT_PTR parm_tp;           /* actual parameter type */

    if (token == LPAREN) {
        get_token();
        parm_tp = base_type(expression());

        if (parm_tp != real_typep) error(INCOMPATIBLE_TYPES);
        if_token_get_else_error(RPAREN, MISSING_RPAREN);
    }
    else error(WRONG_NUMBER_OF_PARMS);

    emit_push_operand(parm_tp);
    emit_1(CALL, name_lit(rtn_idp->defn.info.routine.key == ROUND
                          ? STD_ROUND : STD_TRUNC));
    emit_2(ADD, reg(SP), integer_lit(4));

    return(integer_typep);
}
```

FIGURE B-4   decl.c

```
/************************************************************/
/*                                                          */
/*      D E C L A R A T I O N   P A R S E R                 */
/*                                                          */
/*      Parsing routines for delarations.                   */
/*                                                          */
/*      FILE:      decl.c                                    */
/*                                                          */
/*      MODULE:    parser                                   */
/*                                                          */
/************************************************************/
```

```
#include <stdio.h>
#include "common.h"
#include "error.h"
#include "scanner.h"
#include "symtab.h"
#include "parser.h"
#include "code.h"

/*----------------------------------------------------------*/
/* Externals                                                */
/*----------------------------------------------------------*/
```

```
extern TOKEN_CODE       token;
extern char             word_string[];
extern LITERAL          literal;

extern SYMTAB_NODE_PTR  symtab_display[];
extern int              level;

extern TYPE_STRUCT_PTR  integer_typep, real_typep,
                        boolean_typep, char_typep;

extern TYPE_STRUCT      dummy_type;

extern int              label_index;

extern TOKEN_CODE       declaration_start_list[],
                        statement_start_list[];

/*------------------------------------------------------------*/
/* Forwards                                                   */
/*------------------------------------------------------------*/

TYPE_STRUCT_PTR do_type(),
            identifier_type(), enumeration_type(),
            subrange_type(), array_type(), record_type();

/*------------------------------------------------------------*/
/* delarations         Call the routines to process constant */
/*                     definitions, type definitions, variable*/
/*                     declarations, procedure definitions,   */
/*                     and function definitions.              */
/*------------------------------------------------------------*/

TOKEN_CODE follow_routine_list[] = {SEMICOLON, END_OF_FILE, 0};

declarations(rtn_idp)

    SYMTAB_NODE_PTR rtn_idp;    /* id of program or routine */

{
    if (token == CONST) {
        get_token();
        const_definitions();
    }

    if (token == TYPE) {
        get_token();
        type_definitions();
    }

    if (token == VAR) {
        get_token();
        var_declarations(rtn_idp);
    }

    /*
    -- Emit declarations for parameters and local variables.
    */
    if (rtn_idp->defn.key != PROG_DEFN) emit_declarations(rtn_idp);

    /*
    -- Loop to process routine (procedure and function)
    -- definitions.
    */
    while ((token == PROCEDURE) || (token == FUNCTION)) {
        routine();

        /*
```

```
        -- Error synchronization:  Should be ;
        */
        synchronize(follow_routine_list,
                    declaration_start_list, statement_start_list);
        if_token_get(SEMICOLON);
        else if (token_in(declaration_start_list) ||
                 token_in(statement_start_list))
            error(MISSING_SEMICOLON);
    }
}


                    /***********************/
                    /*                     */
                    /*       Constants     */
                    /*                     */
                    /***********************/

/*------------------------------------------------------------*/
/* const_definitions   Process constant definitions:         */
/*                                                            */
/*                        <id> = <constant>                   */
/*------------------------------------------------------------*/

TOKEN_CODE follow_declaration_list[] = {SEMICOLON, IDENTIFIER,
                                        END_OF_FILE, 0};

const_definitions()

{
    SYMTAB_NODE_PTR const_idp;          /* constant id */

    /*
    -- Loop to process definitions separated by semicolons.
    */
    while (token == IDENTIFIER) {
        search_and_enter_local_symtab(const_idp);
        const_idp->defn.key = CONST_DEFN;

        get_token();
        if_token_get_else_error(EQUAL, MISSING_EQUAL);

        /*
        -- Process the constant.
        */
        do_const(const_idp);
        analyze_const_defn(const_idp);

        /*
        -- Error synchronization:  Should be ;
        */
        synchronize(follow_declaration_list,
                    declaration_start_list, statement_start_list);
        if_token_get(SEMICOLON);
        else if (token_in(declaration_start_list) ||
                 token_in(statement_start_list))
            error(MISSING_SEMICOLON);
    }
}

/*------------------------------------------------------------*/
/* do_const             Process the constant of a constant   */
/*                      definition.                          */
/*------------------------------------------------------------*/

do_const(const_idp)

    SYMTAB_NODE_PTR const_idp;          /* constant id */
```

```
{
    TOKEN_CODE    sign     = PLUS;     /* unary + or - sign */
    BOOLEAN       saw_sign = FALSE;    /* TRUE iff unary sign */

    /*
    -- Unary + or - sign.
    */
    if ((token == PLUS) || (token == MINUS)) {
        sign     = token;
        saw_sign = TRUE;
        get_token();
    }

    /*
    -- Numeric constant:  Integer or real type.
    */
    if (token == NUMBER) {
        if (literal.type == INTEGER_LIT) {
            const_idp->defn.info.constant.value.integer =
                sign == PLUS ?  literal.value.integer
                             : -literal.value.integer;
            const_idp->typep = integer_typep;
        }
        else {
            const_idp->defn.info.constant.value.real =
                sign == PLUS ?  literal.value.real
                             : -literal.value.real;
            const_idp->typep = real_typep;
        }
    }

    /*
    -- Identifier constant:  Integer, real, character, enumeration,
    --                       or string (character array) type.
    */
    else if (token == IDENTIFIER) {
        SYMTAB_NODE_PTR idp;

        search_all_symtab(idp);

        if (idp == NULL)
            error(UNDEFINED_IDENTIFIER);
        else if (idp->defn.key != CONST_DEFN)
            error(NOT_A_CONSTANT_IDENTIFIER);

        else if (idp->typep == integer_typep) {
            const_idp->defn.info.constant.value.integer =
                sign == PLUS ?  idp->defn.info.constant.value.integer
                             : -idp->defn.info.constant.value.integer;
            const_idp->typep = integer_typep;
        }
        else if (idp->typep == real_typep) {
            const_idp->defn.info.constant.value.real =
                sign == PLUS ?  idp->defn.info.constant.value.real
                             : -idp->defn.info.constant.value.real;
            const_idp->typep = real_typep;
        }
        else if (idp->typep == char_typep) {
            if (saw_sign) error(INVALID_CONSTANT);

            const_idp->defn.info.constant.value.character =
                            idp->defn.info.constant.value.character;
            const_idp->typep = char_typep;
        }
        else if (idp->typep->form == ENUM_FORM) {
            if (saw_sign) error(INVALID_CONSTANT);

            const_idp->defn.info.constant.value.integer =
                            idp->defn.info.constant.value.integer;
            const_idp->typep = idp->typep;
        }
        else if (idp->typep->form == ARRAY_FORM) {
            if (saw_sign) error(INVALID_CONSTANT);

            const_idp->defn.info.constant.value.stringp =
                            idp->defn.info.constant.value.stringp;
            const_idp->typep = idp->typep;
        }
    }

    /*
    -- String constant:  Character or string (character array) type.
    */
    else if (token == STRING) {
        if (saw_sign) error(INVALID_CONSTANT);

        if (strlen(literal.value.string) == 1) {
            const_idp->defn.info.constant.value.character =
                                        literal.value.string[0];
            const_idp->typep = char_typep;
        }
        else {
            int length = strlen(literal.value.string);

            const_idp->defn.info.constant.value.stringp =
                                alloc_bytes(length + 1);
            strcpy(const_idp->defn.info.constant.value.stringp,
                   literal.value.string);
            const_idp->typep = make_string_typep(length);
        }
    }

    else {
        const_idp->typep = &dummy_type;
        error(INVALID_CONSTANT);
    }

    get_token();
}

                /*************************/
                /*                       */
                /*        Types          */
                /*                       */
                /*************************/

/*--------------------------------------------------------------*/
/* type_definitions    Process type definitions:                */
/*                                                              */
/*                    <id> = <type>                             */
/*--------------------------------------------------------------*/

type_definitions()

{
    SYMTAB_NODE_PTR type_idp;          /* type id */

    /*
    -- Loop to process definitions separated by semicolons.
    */
    while (token == IDENTIFIER) {
        search_and_enter_local_symtab(type_idp);
        type_idp->defn.key = TYPE_DEFN;

        get_token();
```

```
            if_token_get_else_error(EQUAL, MISSING_EQUAL);

            /*
            -- Process the type specification.
            */
            type_idp->typep = do_type();
            if (type_idp->typep->type_idp == NULL)
                type_idp->typep->type_idp = type_idp;

            analyze_type_defn(type_idp);

            /*
            -- Error synchronization:  Should be ;
            */
            synchronize(follow_declaration_list,
                        declaration_start_list, statement_start_list);
            if_token_get(SEMICOLON);
            else if (token_in(declaration_start_list) ||
                     token_in(statement_start_list))
                error(MISSING_SEMICOLON);
        }
}


/*------------------------------------------------------------*/
/*  do_type              Process a type specification. Call the */
/*                       functions that make a type structure   */
/*                       and return a pointer to it.            */
/*------------------------------------------------------------*/

    TYPE_STRUCT_PTR
do_type()

{
    switch (token) {
        case IDENTIFIER: {
            SYMTAB_NODE_PTR idp;

            search_all_symtab(idp);

            if (idp == NULL) {
                error(UNDEFINED_IDENTIFIER);
                return(&dummy_type);
            }
            else if (idp->defn.key == TYPE_DEFN)
                return(identifier_type(idp));
            else if (idp->defn.key == CONST_DEFN)
                return(subrange_type(idp));
            else {
                error(NOT_A_TYPE_IDENTIFIER);
                return(&dummy_type);
            }
        }

        case LPAREN:    return(enumeration_type());
        case ARRAY:     return(array_type());
        case RECORD:    return(record_type());

        case PLUS:
        case MINUS:
        case NUMBER:
        case STRING:    return(subrange_type(NULL));

        default:        error(INVALID_TYPE);
                        return(&dummy_type);
    }
}
```

```
/*------------------------------------------------------------*/
/*  identifier_type      Process an identifier type, i.e., the  */
/*                       identifier on the right side of a type */
/*                       equate, and return a pointer to its    */
/*                       type structure.                        */
/*------------------------------------------------------------*/

    TYPE_STRUCT_PTR
identifier_type(idp)

    SYMTAB_NODE_PTR idp;        /* type id */

{
    TYPE_STRUCT_PTR tp = NULL;

    tp = idp->typep;
    get_token();

    return(tp);
}


/*------------------------------------------------------------*/
/*  enumeration_type     Process an enumeration type:           */
/*                                                              */
/*                         ( <id1>, <id2>, ..., <idn> )         */
/*                                                              */
/*                       Make a type structure and return a     */
/*                       pointer to it.                         */
/*------------------------------------------------------------*/

    TYPE_STRUCT_PTR
enumeration_type()

{
    SYMTAB_NODE_PTR const_idp;          /* constant id */
    SYMTAB_NODE_PTR last_idp    = NULL; /* last constant id */
    TYPE_STRUCT_PTR tp          = alloc_struct(TYPE_STRUCT);
    int             const_value = -1;   /* constant value */

    tp->form     = ENUM_FORM;
    tp->size     = sizeof(int);
    tp->type_idp = NULL;

    get_token();

    /*
    -- Loop to process list of identifiers.
    */
    while (token == IDENTIFIER) {
        search_and_enter_local_symtab(const_idp);
        const_idp->defn.key = CONST_DEFN;
        const_idp->defn.info.constant.value.integer = ++const_value;
        const_idp->typep = tp;

        /*
        -- Link constant ids together.
        */
        if (last_idp == NULL)
            tp->info.enumeration.const_idp = last_idp = const_idp;
        else {
            last_idp->next = const_idp;
            last_idp = const_idp;
        }

        get_token();
        if_token_get(COMMA);
    }
```

```
        if_token_get_else_error(RPAREN, MISSING_RPAREN);

        tp->info.enumeration.max = const_value;
        return(tp);
}

/*-----------------------------------------------------------*/
/*  subrange_type        Process a subrange type:            */
/*                                                           */
/*                       <min-const> .. <max-const>          */
/*                                                           */
/*                       Make a type structure and return a  */
/*                       pointer to it.                      */
/*-----------------------------------------------------------*/

TOKEN_CODE follow_min_limit_list[] = {DOTDOT, IDENTIFIER, PLUS, MINUS,
                                      NUMBER, STRING, SEMICOLON,
                                      END_OF_FILE, 0};

    TYPE_STRUCT_PTR
subrange_type(min_idp)

    SYMTAB_NODE_PTR min_idp;    /* min limit const id */

{
    TYPE_STRUCT_PTR max_typep;  /* type of max limit */
    TYPE_STRUCT_PTR tp = alloc_struct(TYPE_STRUCT);

    tp->form     = SUBRANGE_FORM;
    tp->type_idp = NULL;

    /*
    -- Minimum constant.
    */
    get_subrange_limit(min_idp,
                    &(tp->info.subrange.min),
                    &(tp->info.subrange.range_typep));

    /*
    -- Error synchronization:  Should be ..
    */
    synchronize(follow_min_limit_list, NULL, NULL);
    if_token_get(DOTDOT);
    else if (token_in(follow_min_limit_list) ||
             token_in(declaration_start_list) ||
             token_in(statement_start_list))
        error(MISSING_DOTDOT);

    /*
    -- Maximum constant.
    */
    get_subrange_limit(NULL, &(tp->info.subrange.max), &max_typep);

    /*
    -- Check limits.
    */
    if (max_typep == tp->info.subrange.range_typep) {
        if (tp->info.subrange.min > tp->info.subrange.max)
            error(MIN_GT_MAX);
    }
    else error(INCOMPATIBLE_TYPES);

    tp->size = max_typep == char_typep ? sizeof(char) : sizeof(int);
    return(tp);
}

/*-----------------------------------------------------------*/
/*  get_subrange_limit  Process the minimum and maximum limits  */
```

```
/*                       of a subrange type.                 */
/*-----------------------------------------------------------*/

get_subrange_limit(minmax_idp, minmaxp, typepp)

    SYMTAB_NODE_PTR minmax_idp; /* min const id */
    int             *minmaxp;   /* where to store min or max value */
    TYPE_STRUCT_PTR *typepp;     /* where to store ptr to type struct */

{
    SYMTAB_NODE_PTR idp       = minmax_idp;
    TOKEN_CODE      sign      = PLUS;   /* unary + or - sign */
    BOOLEAN         saw_sign = FALSE;  /* TRUE iff unary sign */

    /*
    -- Unary + or - sign.
    */
    if ((token == PLUS) || (token == MINUS)) {
        sign     = token;
        saw_sign = TRUE;
        get_token();
    }

    /*
    -- Numeric limit:  Integer type only.
    */
    if (token == NUMBER) {
        if (literal.type == INTEGER_LIT) {
            *typepp  = integer_typep;
            *minmaxp = (sign == PLUS) ? literal.value.integer
                                      : -literal.value.integer;
        }
        else error(INVALID_SUBRANGE_TYPE);
    }

    /*
    -- Identifier limit:  Value must be integer or character.
    */
    else if (token == IDENTIFIER) {
        if (idp == NULL) search_all_symtab(idp);

        if (idp == NULL)
            error(UNDEFINED_IDENTIFIER);
        else if (idp->typep == real_typep)
            error(INVALID_SUBRANGE_TYPE);
        else if (idp->defn.key == CONST_DEFN) {
            *typepp = idp->typep;
            if (idp->typep == char_typep) {
                if (saw_sign) error(INVALID_CONSTANT);
                *minmaxp = idp->defn.info.constant.value.character;
            }
            else if (idp->typep == integer_typep) {
                *minmaxp = idp->defn.info.constant.value.integer;
                if (sign == MINUS) *minmaxp = -(*minmaxp);
            }
            else /* enumeration constant */ {
                if (saw_sign) error(INVALID_CONSTANT);
                *minmaxp = idp->defn.info.constant.value.integer;
            }
        }
        else error(NOT_A_CONSTANT_IDENTIFIER);
    }

    /*
    -- String limit:  Character type only.
    */
    else if (token == STRING) {
```

```
        if (saw_sign) error(INVALID_CONSTANT);
        *typepp = char_typep;
        *minmaxp = literal.value.string[0];

        if (strlen(literal.value.string) != 1)
            error(INVALID_SUBRANGE_TYPE);
    }

    else error(MISSING_CONSTANT);

    get_token();
}

/*------------------------------------------------------------*/
/*  array_type          Process an array type:              */
/*                                                           */
/*                          ARRAY [<index-type-list>]        */
/*                              OF <elmt-type>               */
/*                                                           */
/*                          Make a type structure and return a */
/*                          pointer to it.                   */
/*------------------------------------------------------------*/

TOKEN_CODE follow_dimension_list[] = {COMMA, RBRACKET, OF,
                                SEMICOLON, END_OF_FILE, 0};

TOKEN_CODE index_type_start_list[] = {IDENTIFIER, NUMBER, STRING,
                                LPAREN, MINUS, PLUS, 0};

TOKEN_CODE follow_indexes_list[] = {OF, IDENTIFIER, LPAREN, ARRAY,
                                RECORD, PLUS, MINUS, NUMBER,
                                STRING, SEMICOLON, END_OF_FILE,
                                0};

    TYPE_STRUCT_PTR
array_type()

{
    TYPE_STRUCT_PTR tp        = alloc_struct(TYPE_STRUCT);
    TYPE_STRUCT_PTR index_tp;          /* index type */
    TYPE_STRUCT_PTR elmt_tp = tp;      /* element type */
    int array_size();

    get_token();
    if (token != LBRACKET) error(MISSING_LBRACKET);

    /*
    -- Loop to process index type list. For each
    -- type in the list after the first, create an
    -- array element type.
    */
    do {
        get_token();

        if (token_in(index_type_start_list)) {
            elmt_tp->form      = ARRAY_FORM;
            elmt_tp->size      = 0;
            elmt_tp->type_idp = NULL;
            elmt_tp->info.array.index_typep = index_tp = do_type();

            switch (index_tp->form) {
                case ENUM_FORM:
                    elmt_tp->info.array.elmt_count =
                                index_tp->info.enumeration.max + 1;
                    elmt_tp->info.array.min_index = 0;
                    elmt_tp->info.array.max_index =
                                index_tp->info.enumeration.max;
```

```
                    break;

                case SUBRANGE_FORM:
                    elmt_tp->info.array.elmt_count =
                                index_tp->info.subrange.max -
                                    index_tp->info.subrange.min + 1;
                    elmt_tp->info.array.min_index =
                                    index_tp->info.subrange.min;
                    elmt_tp->info.array.max_index =
                                    index_tp->info.subrange.max;
                    break;

                default:
                    elmt_tp->form      = NO_FORM;
                    elmt_tp->size      = 0;
                    elmt_tp->type_idp = NULL;
                    elmt_tp->info.array.index_typep = &dummy_type;
                    error(INVALID_INDEX_TYPE);
                    break;
            }
        }
        else {
            elmt_tp->form      = NO_FORM;
            elmt_tp->size      = 0;
            elmt_tp->type_idp = NULL;
            elmt_tp->info.array.index_typep = &dummy_type;
            error(INVALID_INDEX_TYPE);
        }

        /*
        -- Error synchronization:  Should be , or ]
        */
        synchronize(follow_dimension_list, NULL, NULL);

        /*
        -- Create an array element type.
        */
        if (token == COMMA) elmt_tp = elmt_tp->info.array.elmt_typep =
                                    alloc_struct(TYPE_STRUCT);
    } while (token == COMMA);

    if_token_get_else_error(RBRACKET, MISSING_RBRACKET);

    /*
    -- Error synchronization:  Should be OF
    */
    synchronize(follow_indexes_list,
                declaration_start_list, statement_start_list);
    if_token_get_else_error(OF, MISSING_OF);

    /*
    -- Element type.
    */
    elmt_tp->info.array.elmt_typep = do_type();

    tp->size = array_size(tp);
    return(tp);
}

/*------------------------------------------------------------*/
/*  record_type         Process a record type:              */
/*                                                           */
/*                          RECORD                            */
/*                              <id-list> : <type> ;         */
/*                                  ...                       */
/*                              END                           */
```

```
/*                                                   */
/*                   Make a type structure and return a  */
/*                   pointer to it.                   */
/*----------------------------------------------------*/

    TYPE_STRUCT_PTR
record_type()

{
    TYPE_STRUCT_PTR record_tp = alloc_struct(TYPE_STRUCT);

    record_tp->form       = RECORD_FORM;
    record_tp->type_idp = NULL;
    record_tp->info.record.field_symtab = NULL;

    get_token();
    var_or_field_declarations(NULL, record_tp, 0);

    if_token_get_else_error(END, MISSING_END);
    return(record_tp);
}

/*----------------------------------------------------*/
/*  make_string_typep  Make a type structure for a string of  */
/*                     the given length, and return a pointer  */
/*                     to it.                         */
/*----------------------------------------------------*/

    TYPE_STRUCT_PTR
make_string_typep(length)

    int length;              /* string length */

{
    TYPE_STRUCT_PTR string_tp = alloc_struct(TYPE_STRUCT);
    TYPE_STRUCT_PTR index_tp  = alloc_struct(TYPE_STRUCT);

    /*
    -- Array type.
    */
    string_tp->form       = ARRAY_FORM;
    string_tp->size       = length;
    string_tp->type_idp = NULL;
    string_tp->info.array.index_typep = index_tp;
    string_tp->info.array.elmt_typep = char_typep;
    string_tp->info.array.elmt_count = length;

    /*
    -- Subrange index type.
    */
    index_tp->form       = SUBRANGE_FORM;
    index_tp->size       = sizeof(int);
    index_tp->type_idp = NULL;
    index_tp->info.subrange.range_typep = integer_typep;
    index_tp->info.subrange.min = 1;
    index_tp->info.subrange.max = length;

    return(string_tp);
}

/*----------------------------------------------------*/
/*  array_size          Return the size in bytes of an array  */
/*                      type by recursively calculating the  */
/*                      size of each dimension.       */
/*----------------------------------------------------*/

    int
```

```
array_size(tp)

    TYPE_STRUCT_PTR tp;        /* ptr to array type structure */

{
    if (tp->info.array.elmt_typep->size == 0)
        tp->info.array.elmt_typep->size =
                        array_size(tp->info.array.elmt_typep);

    tp->size = tp->info.array.elmt_count *
               tp->info.array.elmt_typep->size;

    return(tp->size);
}

            /*************************/
            /*                       */
            /*        Variables      */
            /*                       */
            /*************************/

/*----------------------------------------------------*/
/*  var_declarations     Process variable declarations:  */
/*                                                    */
/*                       <id-list> : <type>          */
/*----------------------------------------------------*/

var_declarations(rtn_idp)

    SYMTAB_NODE_PTR rtn_idp;    /* id of program or routine */

{
    var_or_field_declarations(rtn_idp, NULL,
                        rtn_idp->defn.key == PROC_DEFN
                            ? PROC_LOCALS_STACK_FRAME_OFFSET
                            : FUNC_LOCALS_STACK_FRAME_OFFSET);
}

/*----------------------------------------------------*/
/*  var_or_field_declarations  Process variable declarations  */
/*                        or record field definitions.  */
/*                        All ids declared with the same  */
/*                        type are linked together into  */
/*                        a sublist, and all the sublists  */
/*                        are then linked together.  */
/*----------------------------------------------------*/

TOKEN_CODE follow_variables_list[] = {SEMICOLON, IDENTIFIER,
                                      END_OF_FILE, 0};

TOKEN_CODE follow_fields_list[]    = {SEMICOLON, END, IDENTIFIER,
                                      END_OF_FILE, 0};

var_or_field_declarations(rtn_idp, record_tp, offset)

    SYMTAB_NODE_PTR rtn_idp;
    TYPE_STRUCT_PTR record_tp;
    int             offset;

{
    SYMTAB_NODE_PTR idp, first_idp, last_idp;  /* variable or
                                                  field ids */

    SYMTAB_NODE_PTR prev_last_idp = NULL;      /* last id of list */
    TYPE_STRUCT_PTR tp;                         /* type */
    BOOLEAN var_flag = (rtn_idp != NULL);      /* TRUE:  variables */
                                               /* FALSE: fields */

    int size;
```

```
    int total_size = 0;

    /*
    -- Loop to process sublist, each of a type.
    */
    while (token == IDENTIFIER) {
        first_idp = NULL;

        /*
        -- Loop process each variable or field id in a sublist.
        */
        while (token == IDENTIFIER) {
            if (var_flag) {
                search_and_enter_local_symtab(idp);
                idp->defn.key = VAR_DEFN;
            }
            else {
                search_and_enter_this_symtab
                    (idp, record_tp->info.record.field_symtab);
                idp->defn.key = FIELD_DEFN;
            }
            idp->label_index = new_label_index();

            /*
            -- Link ids together into a sublist.
            */
            if (first_idp == NULL) {
                first_idp = last_idp = idp;
                if (var_flag &&
                    (rtn_idp->defn.info.routine.locals == NULL))
                    rtn_idp->defn.info.routine.locals = idp;
            }
            else {
                last_idp->next = idp;
                last_idp = idp;
            }

            get_token();
            if_token_get(COMMA);
        }

        /*
        -- Process the sublist's type.
        */
        if_token_get_else_error(COLON, MISSING_COLON);
        tp = do_type();
        size = tp->size;
        if (size & 1) ++size;   /* round up to even */

        /*
```

```
        -- Assign the offset and the type to all variable or field
        -- ids in the sublist.
        */
        for (idp = first_idp; idp != NULL; idp = idp->next) {
            idp->typep = tp;

            if (var_flag) {
                offset -= size;
                total_size += size;
                idp->defn.info.data.offset = offset;
                analyze_var_decl(idp);
            }

            else   /* record fields */ {
                idp->defn.info.data.offset = offset;
                offset += size;

                /*
                -- Emit numeric equate for the field id's
                -- name and offset.
                */
                emit_numeric_equate(idp);
            }
        }

        /*
        -- Link this sublist to the previous sublist.
        */
        if (prev_last_idp != NULL) prev_last_idp->next = first_idp;
        prev_last_idp = last_idp;

        /*
        -- Error synchronization:  Should be ; for variable
        --                         declaration, or ; or END for
        --                         record type definition.
        */
        synchronize(var_flag ? follow_variables_list
                             : follow_fields_list,
                    declaration_start_list, statement_start_list);
        if_token_get(SEMICOLON);
        else if (var_flag && ((token_in(declaration_start_list)) ||
                              (token_in(statement_start_list))))
                error(MISSING_SEMICOLON);
    }

    if (var_flag)
        rtn_idp->defn.info.routine.total_local_size = total_size;
    else
        record_tp->size = offset;
}
```

FIGURE B-5   stmt.c

```
/* Figure 14-1 */

/****************************************************************/
/*                                                              */
/*      S T A T E M E N T   P A R S E R                         */
/*                                                              */
/*      Parsing routines for statements.                        */
/*                                                              */
/*      FILE:     stmt.c                                        */
/*                                                              */
```

```
/*      MODULE:     parser                                      */
/*                                                              */
/****************************************************************/

#include <stdio.h>
#include "common.h"
#include "error.h"
#include "scanner.h"
#include "symtab.h"
#include "parser.h"
```

```
#include "code.h"

/*-----------------------------------------------------------*/
/*  Externals                                                */
/*-----------------------------------------------------------*/


extern TOKEN_CODE       token;
extern char             word_string[];
extern LITERAL          literal;
extern TOKEN_CODE       statement_start_list[], statement_end_list[];

extern SYMTAB_NODE_PTR  symtab_display[];
extern int              level;

extern TYPE_STRUCT_PTR  integer_typep, real_typep,
                        boolean_typep, char_typep;

extern TYPE_STRUCT      dummy_type;

extern int              label_index;
extern char             asm_buffer[];
extern char             *asm_bufferp;
extern FILE             *code_file;

/*-----------------------------------------------------------*/
/*  statement          Process a statement by calling the    */
/*                     appropriate parsing routine based on  */
/*                     the statement's first token.          */
/*-----------------------------------------------------------*/

statement()

{
    /*
    -- Call the appropriate routine based on the first
    -- token of the statement.
    */
    switch (token) {

        case IDENTIFIER: {
            SYMTAB_NODE_PTR idp;

            /*
            -- Assignment statement or procedure call?
            */
            search_and_find_all_symtab(idp);

            if (idp->defn.key == PROC_DEFN) {
                get_token();
                routine_call(idp, TRUE);
            }
            else assignment_statement(idp);

            break;
        }

        case REPEAT:    repeat_statement();     break;
        case WHILE:     while_statement();      break;
        case IF:        if_statement();         break;
        case FOR:       for_statement();        break;
        case CASE:      case_statement();       break;
        case BEGIN:     compound_statement();   break;
    }

    /*
    -- Error synchronization:  Only a semicolon, END, ELSE, or
    --                         UNTIL may follow a statement.
```

```
    --                         Check for a missing semicolon.
    */
    synchronize(statement_end_list, statement_start_list, NULL);
    if (token_in(statement_start_list)) error(MISSING_SEMICOLON);
}

/*-----------------------------------------------------------*/
/*  assignment_statement    Process an assignment statement: */
/*                                                           */
/*                          <id> := <expr>                   */
/*-----------------------------------------------------------*/

assignment_statement(var_idp)

    SYMTAB_NODE_PTR var_idp;            /* target variable id */

{
    TYPE_STRUCT_PTR var_tp, expr_tp;    /* types of var and expr */
    BOOLEAN         stacked_flag;       /* TRUE iff target address
                                           was pushed on stack */

    var_tp = variable(var_idp, TARGET_USE);
    stacked_flag = (var_idp->defn.key == VARPARM_DEFN) ||
                   (var_idp->defn.key == FUNC_DEFN) ||
                   (var_idp->typep->form == ARRAY_FORM) ||
                   (var_idp->typep->form == RECORD_FORM) ||
                   ((var_idp->level > 1) && (var_idp->level < level));

    if_token_get_else_error(COLONEQUAL, MISSING_COLONEQUAL);
    expr_tp = expression();

    if (! is_assign_type_compatible(var_tp, expr_tp))
        error(INCOMPATIBLE_ASSIGNMENT);

    var_tp  = base_type(var_tp);
    expr_tp = base_type(expr_tp);

    /*
    -- Emit code to do the assignment.
    */
    if (var_tp == char_typep) {
        /*
        -- char := char
        */
        if (stacked_flag) {
            emit_1(POP, reg(BX));
            emit_2(MOVE, byte_indirect(BX), reg(AL));
        }
        else emit_2(MOVE, byte(var_tp), reg(AL));
    }
    else if (var_tp == real_typep) {
        /*
        -- real := ...
        */
        if (expr_tp == integer_typep) {
            /*
            -- ... integer
            */
            emit_1(PUSH, reg(AX));
            emit_1(CALL, name_lit(FLOAT_CONVERT));
            emit_2(ADD, reg(SP), integer_lit(2));
        }
        /*
        -- ... real
        */
        if (stacked_flag) {
            emit_1(POP, reg(BX));
```

```
            emit_2(MOVE, word_indirect(BX), reg(AX));
            emit_2(MOVE, high_dword_indirect(BX), reg(DX));
        }
        else {
            emit_2(MOVE, word(var_idp), reg(AX));
            emit_2(MOVE, high_dword(var_idp), reg(DX));
        }
    }
    else if ((var_tp->form == ARRAY_FORM) ||
             (var_tp->form == RECORD_FORM)) {
        /*
        -- array  := array
        -- record := record
        */
        emit_2(MOVE, reg(CX), integer_lit(var_tp->size));
        emit_1(POP,  reg(SI));
        emit_1(POP,  reg(DI));
        emit_2(MOVE, reg(AX), reg(DS));
        emit_2(MOVE, reg(ES), reg(AX));
        emit(CLEAR_DIRECTION);
        emit(MOVE_BLOCK);
    }
    else {
        /*
        -- integer := integer
        -- enum    := enum
        */
        if (stacked_flag) {
            emit_1(POP, reg(BX));
            emit_2(MOVE, word_indirect(BX), reg(AX));
        }
        else emit_2(MOVE, word(var_idp), reg(AX));
    }
}


/*------------------------------------------------------------*/
/* repeat_statement    Process a REPEAT statement:            */
/*                                                            */
/*                     REPEAT <stmt-list> UNTIL <expr>        */
/*------------------------------------------------------------*/

repeat_statement()

{
    TYPE_STRUCT_PTR expr_tp;
    int            loop_begin_labelx = new_label_index();
    int            loop_exit_labelx  = new_label_index();

    emit_label(STMT_LABEL_PREFIX, loop_begin_labelx);

    /*
    -- <stmt-list>
    */
    get_token();
    do {
        statement();
        while (token == SEMICOLON) get_token();
    } while (token_in(statement_start_list));

    if_token_get_else_error(UNTIL, MISSING_UNTIL);

    expr_tp = expression();
    if (expr_tp != boolean_typep) error(INCOMPATIBLE_TYPES);

    emit_2(COMPARE, reg(AX), integer_lit(1));
    emit_1(JUMP_EQ, label(STMT_LABEL_PREFIX, loop_exit_labelx));
    emit_1(JUMP, label(STMT_LABEL_PREFIX, loop_begin_labelx));
```

```
    emit_label(STMT_LABEL_PREFIX, loop_exit_labelx);
}

/*------------------------------------------------------------*/
/* while_statement     Process a WHILE statement:             */
/*                                                            */
/*                     WHILE <expr> DO <stmt>                 */
/*------------------------------------------------------------*/

while_statement()

{
    TYPE_STRUCT_PTR expr_tp;
    int            loop_test_labelx = new_label_index();
    int            loop_stmt_labelx = new_label_index();
    int            loop_exit_labelx = new_label_index();

    emit_label(STMT_LABEL_PREFIX, loop_test_labelx);

    get_token();
    expr_tp = expression();
    if (expr_tp != boolean_typep) error(INCOMPATIBLE_TYPES);

    emit_2(COMPARE, reg(AX), integer_lit(1));
    emit_1(JUMP_EQ, label(STMT_LABEL_PREFIX, loop_stmt_labelx));
    emit_1(JUMP,    label(STMT_LABEL_PREFIX, loop_exit_labelx));
    emit_label(STMT_LABEL_PREFIX, loop_stmt_labelx);

    if_token_get_else_error(DO, MISSING_DO);
    statement();

    emit_1(JUMP, label(STMT_LABEL_PREFIX, loop_test_labelx));
    emit_label(STMT_LABEL_PREFIX, loop_exit_labelx);
}

/*------------------------------------------------------------*/
/* if_statement        Process an IF statement:               */
/*                                                            */
/*                     IF <expr> THEN <stmt>                  */
/*                                                            */
/*                     or:                                    */
/*                                                            */
/*                     IF <expr> THEN <stmt> ELSE <stmt>      */
/*------------------------------------------------------------*/

if_statement()

{
    TYPE_STRUCT_PTR expr_tp;
    int            true_labelx  = new_label_index();
    int            false_labelx = new_label_index();
    int            if_end_labelx;

    get_token();
    expr_tp = expression();
    if (expr_tp != boolean_typep) error(INCOMPATIBLE_TYPES);

    emit_2(COMPARE, reg(AX), integer_lit(1));
    emit_1(JUMP_EQ, label(STMT_LABEL_PREFIX, true_labelx));
    emit_1(JUMP,    label(STMT_LABEL_PREFIX, false_labelx));
    emit_label(STMT_LABEL_PREFIX, true_labelx);

    if_token_get_else_error(THEN, MISSING_THEN);
    statement();

    /*
    -- ELSE branch?
```

```
            */
        if (token == ELSE) {
            if_end_labelx = new_label_index();
            emit_1(JUMP, label(STMT_LABEL_PREFIX, if_end_labelx));
            emit_label(STMT_LABEL_PREFIX, false_labelx);

            get_token();
            statement();

            emit_label(STMT_LABEL_PREFIX, if_end_labelx);
        }
        else emit_label(STMT_LABEL_PREFIX, false_labelx);
}

/*------------------------------------------------------------*/
/*  for_statement       Process a FOR statement:              */
/*                                                            */
/*                          FOR <id> := <expr> TO|DOWNTO <expr> */
/*                          DO <stmt>                         */
/*------------------------------------------------------------*/

for_statement()

{
    SYMTAB_NODE_PTR for_idp;
    TYPE_STRUCT_PTR for_tp, expr_tp;
    BOOLEAN         to_flag;
    int             loop_test_labelx = new_label_index();
    int             loop_stmt_labelx = new_label_index();
    int             loop_exit_labelx = new_label_index();

    get_token();
    if (token == IDENTIFIER) {
        search_and_find_all_symtab(for_idp);
        if ((for_idp->level != level) ||
            (for_idp->defn.key != VAR_DEFN))
            error(INVALID_FOR_CONTROL);

        for_tp = base_type(for_idp->typep);
        get_token();

        if ((for_tp != integer_typep) &&
            (for_tp != char_typep) &&
            (for_tp->form != ENUM_FORM)) error(INCOMPATIBLE_TYPES);
    }
    else {
        error(IDENTIFIER, MISSING_IDENTIFIER);
        for_tp = &dummy_type;
    }

    if_token_get_else_error(COLONEQUAL, MISSING_COLONEQUAL);

    expr_tp = expression();
    if (! is_assign_type_compatible(for_tp, expr_tp))
        error(INCOMPATIBLE_TYPES);

    if (for_tp == char_typep) emit_2(MOVE, byte(for_idp), reg(AL))
    else                      emit_2(MOVE, word(for_idp), reg(AX))

    if ((token == TO) || (token == DOWNTO)) {
        to_flag = (token == TO);
        get_token();
    }
    else error(MISSING_TO_OR_DOWNTO);

    emit_label(STMT_LABEL_PREFIX, loop_test_labelx);

    expr_tp = expression();
```

```
        if (! is_assign_type_compatible(for_tp, expr_tp))
            error(INCOMPATIBLE_TYPES);

    if (for_tp == char_typep) emit_2(COMPARE, byte(for_idp), reg(AL))
    else                      emit_2(COMPARE, word(for_idp), reg(AX))
    emit_1(to_flag ? JUMP_LE : JUMP_GE,
            label(STMT_LABEL_PREFIX, loop_stmt_labelx));
    emit_1(JUMP, label(STMT_LABEL_PREFIX, loop_exit_labelx));
    emit_label(STMT_LABEL_PREFIX, loop_stmt_labelx);

    if_token_get_else_error(DO, MISSING_DO);
    statement();

    emit_1(to_flag ? INCREMENT : DECREMENT,
            for_tp == char_typep ? byte(for_idp) : word(for_idp));
    emit_1(JUMP, label(STMT_LABEL_PREFIX, loop_test_labelx));

    emit_label(STMT_LABEL_PREFIX, loop_exit_labelx);
    emit_1(to_flag ? DECREMENT : INCREMENT,
            for_tp == char_typep ? byte(for_idp) : word(for_idp));
}

/*------------------------------------------------------------*/
/*  case_statement      Process a CASE statement:             */
/*                                                            */
/*                          CASE <expr> OF                    */
/*                              <case-branch> ;               */
/*                              ...                           */
/*                          END                               */
/*------------------------------------------------------------*/

TOKEN_CODE follow_expr_list[]      = {OF, SEMICOLON, 0};

TOKEN_CODE case_label_start_list[] = {IDENTIFIER, NUMBER, PLUS,
                                      MINUS, STRING, 0};

case_statement()

{
    BOOLEAN         another_branch;
    int             case_end_labelx = new_label_index();
    TYPE_STRUCT_PTR expr_tp;

    get_token();
    expr_tp = expression();

    if (   ((expr_tp->form != SCALAR_FORM) &&
            (expr_tp->form != ENUM_FORM) &&
            (expr_tp->form != SUBRANGE_FORM))
        || (expr_tp == real_typep)) error(INCOMPATIBLE_TYPES);

    /*
    -- Error synchronization:  Should be OF
    */
    synchronize(follow_expr_list, case_label_start_list, NULL);
    if_token_get_else_error(OF, MISSING_OF);

    /*
    -- Loop to process CASE branches.
    */
    another_branch = token_in(case_label_start_list);
    while (another_branch) {
        if (token_in(case_label_start_list))
            case_branch(expr_tp, case_end_labelx);

        if (token == SEMICOLON) {
            get_token();
```

```
                another_branch = TRUE;
            }
        else if (token_in(case_label_start_list)) {
            error(MISSING_SEMICOLON);
            another_branch = TRUE;
            }
        else another_branch = FALSE;
        }

    if_token_get_else_error(END, MISSING_END);
    emit_label(STMT_LABEL_PREFIX, case_end_labelx);
}

/*-----------------------------------------------------------*/
/* case_branch              Process a CASE branch:           */
/*                                                           */
/*                          <case-label-list> : <stmt>       */
/*-----------------------------------------------------------*/

TOKEN_CODE follow_case_label_list[] = {COLON, SEMICOLON, 0};

case_branch(expr_tp, case_end_labelx)

    TYPE_STRUCT_PTR  expr_tp;          /* type of CASE expression */
    int              case_end_labelx;  /* CASE end label index */

{
    BOOLEAN          another_label;
    int              next_test_labelx;
    int              branch_stmt_labelx = new_label_index();
    TYPE_STRUCT_PTR  label_tp;
    TYPE_STRUCT_PTR  case_label();

    /*
    -- <case-label-list>
    */
    do {
        next_test_labelx = new_label_index();

        label_tp = case_label();
        if (expr_tp != label_tp) error(INCOMPATIBLE_TYPES);

        emit_1(JUMP_NE, label(STMT_LABEL_PREFIX, next_test_labelx));

        get_token();
        if (token == COMMA) {
            get_token();
            emit_1(JUMP, label(STMT_LABEL_PREFIX, branch_stmt_labelx));

            if (token_in(case_label_start_list)) {
                emit_label(STMT_LABEL_PREFIX, next_test_labelx);
                another_label = TRUE;
            }
            else {
                error(MISSING_CONSTANT);
                another_label = FALSE;
            }
        }
        else another_label = FALSE;
    } while (another_label);

    /*
    -- Error synchronization:  Should be :
    */
    synchronize(follow_case_label_list, statement_start_list, NULL);
    if_token_get_else_error(COLON, MISSING_COLON);

    emit_label(STMT_LABEL_PREFIX, branch_stmt_labelx);
```

```
        statement();

    emit_1(JUMP, label(STMT_LABEL_PREFIX, case_end_labelx));
    emit_label(STMT_LABEL_PREFIX, next_test_labelx);
}

/*-----------------------------------------------------------*/
/* case_label              Process a CASE label and return a */
/*                         pointer to its type structure.    */
/*-----------------------------------------------------------*/

    TYPE_STRUCT_PTR
case_label()

{
    TOKEN_CODE sign    = PLUS;      /* unary + or - sign */
    BOOLEAN    saw_sign = FALSE;    /* TRUE iff unary sign */

    /*
    -- Unary + or - sign.
    */
    if ((token == PLUS) || (token == MINUS)) {
        sign     = token;
        saw_sign = TRUE;
        get_token();
    }

    /*
    -- Numeric constant:  Integer type only.
    */
    if (token == NUMBER) {
        if (literal.type == INTEGER_LIT)
            emit_2(COMPARE, reg(AX),
                   integer_lit(sign == PLUS
                                    ? literal.value.integer
                                    : -literal.value.integer))
        else error(INVALID_CONSTANT);

        return(integer_typep);
    }

    /*
    -- Identifier constant:  Integer, character, or enumeration
    --                       types only.
    */
    else if (token == IDENTIFIER) {
        SYMTAB_NODE_PTR idp;

        search_all_symtab(idp);

        if (idp == NULL) {
            error(UNDEFINED_IDENTIFIER);
            return(&dummy_type);
        }

        else if (idp->defn.key != CONST_DEFN) {
            error(NOT_A_CONSTANT_IDENTIFIER);
            return(&dummy_type);
        }

        else if (idp->typep == integer_typep) {
            emit_2(COMPARE, reg(AX),
                   integer_lit(sign == PLUS
                                    ? idp->defn.info.constant
                                          .value.integer
                                    : -idp->defn.info.constant
                                          .value.integer));
```

```
            return(integer_typep);
        }

    else if (idp->typep == char_typep) {
        if (saw_sign) error(INVALID_CONSTANT);
        emit_2(COMPARE, reg(AL),
                        char_lit(idp->defn.info.constant
                                    .value.character));
        return(char_typep);
    }

    else if (idp->typep->form == ENUM_FORM) {
        if (saw_sign) error(INVALID_CONSTANT);
        emit_2(COMPARE, reg(AX),
                        integer_lit(idp->defn.info.constant
                                    .value.integer));
        return(idp->typep);
    }

    else return(&dummy_type);
}

    /*
    -- String constant:  Character type only.
    */
    else if (token == STRING) {
        if (saw_sign) error(INVALID_CONSTANT);

        if (strlen(literal.value.string) == 1) {
            emit_2(COMPARE, reg(AL), char_lit(literal.value.string[0]));
            return(char_typep);
        }
        else {
            error(INVALID_CONSTANT);
            return(&dummy_type);
        }
```

```
        }
    }

    else {
        error(INVALID_CONSTANT);
        return(&dummy_type);
    }
}

/*----------------------------------------------------------*/
/*  compound_statement       Process a compound statement:  */
/*                                                          */
/*                           BEGIN <stmt-list> END          */
/*----------------------------------------------------------*/

compound_statement()

{
    /*
    -- <stmt-list>
    */
    get_token();
    do {
        statement();
        while (token == SEMICOLON) get_token();
        if (token == END) break;

        /*
        -- Error synchronization:  Should be at the start of the
        --                         next statement.
        */
        synchronize(statement_start_list, NULL, NULL);
    } while (token_in(statement_start_list));

    if_token_get_else_error(END, MISSING_END);
}
```

FIGURE B-6   expr.c

```
/***********************************************************/
/*                                                        */
/*      E X P R E S S I O N   P A R S E R                 */
/*                                                        */
/*      Parsing routines for expressions.                 */
/*                                                        */
/*      FILE:     expr.c                                  */
/*                                                        */
/*      MODULE:   parser                                  */
/*                                                        */
/***********************************************************/

#include <stdio.h>
#include "common.h"
#include "error.h"
#include "scanner.h"
#include "symtab.h"
#include "parser.h"
#include "code.h"

/*----------------------------------------------------------*/
/* Externals                                                */
/*----------------------------------------------------------*/
```

```
extern TOKEN_CODE       token;
extern char             token_string[];
extern char             word_string[];
extern LITERAL          literal;

extern SYMTAB_NODE_PTR  symtab_display[];
extern int              level;

extern TYPE_STRUCT_PTR  integer_typep, real_typep,
                        boolean_typep, char_typep;

extern TYPE_STRUCT      dummy_type;

extern SYMTAB_NODE_PTR  float_literal_list;
extern SYMTAB_NODE_PTR  string_literal_list;

extern int              label_index;
extern char             asm_buffer[];
extern char             *asm_bufferp;
extern FILE             *code_file;

/*----------------------------------------------------------*/
/* Forwards                                                 */
/*----------------------------------------------------------*/
```

```
TYPE_STRUCT_PTR expression(), simple_expression(), term(), factor(),
                constant_identifier(), function_call();

TYPE_STRUCT_PTR float_literal(), string_literal();

/*----------------------------------------------------------*/
/*  integer_operands    TRUE if both operands are integer,   */
/*                       else FALSE.                         */
/*----------------------------------------------------------*/

#define integer_operands(tp1, tp2)  ((tp1 == integer_typep) && \
                                     (tp2 == integer_typep))

/*----------------------------------------------------------*/
/*  real_operands     TRUE if at least one or both operands  */
/*                    operands are real (and the other       */
/*                    integer), else FALSE.                  */
/*----------------------------------------------------------*/

#define real_operands(tp1, tp2) (((tp1 == real_typep) &&       \
                                  ((tp2 == real_typep) ||       \
                                   (tp2 == integer_typep)))      \
                                         ||                      \
                                  ((tp2 == real_typep) &&        \
                                   ((tp1 == real_typep) ||       \
                                    (tp1 == integer_typep))))

/*----------------------------------------------------------*/
/*  boolean_operands   TRUE if both operands are boolean     */
/*                     else FALSE.                           */
/*----------------------------------------------------------*/

#define boolean_operands(tp1, pt2)  ((tp1 == boolean_typep) && \
                                     (tp2 == boolean_typep))

/*----------------------------------------------------------*/
/*  expression          Process an expression consisting of a */
/*                      simple expression optionally followed */
/*                      by a relational operator and a second */
/*                      simple expression.  Return a pointer to */
/*                      the type structure.                   */
/*----------------------------------------------------------*/

TOKEN_CODE rel_op_list[] = {LT, LE, EQUAL, NE, GE, GT, 0};

    TYPE_STRUCT_PTR
expression()

{
    TOKEN_CODE      op;             /* an operator token */
    TYPE_STRUCT_PTR result_tp, tp2;
    int             jump_label_index; /* jump target label index */
    INSTRUCTION     jump_opcode;    /* opcode for cond. jump */

    result_tp = simple_expression();  /* first simple expr */

    /*
    -- If there is a relational operator, remember it and
    -- process the second simple expression.
    */
    if (token_in(rel_op_list)) {
        op = token;                 /* remember operator */

        result_tp = base_type(result_tp);
        emit_push_operand(result_tp);

        get_token();
```

```
        tp2 = base_type(simple_expression());   /* 2nd simple expr */

        check_rel_op_types(result_tp, tp2);

        /*
        -- Both operands are integer, character, boolean, or
        -- the same enumeration type.  Compare DX (operand 1)
        -- to AX (operand 2).
        */
        if (integer_operands(result_tp, tp2) ||
            (result_tp == char_typep) ||
            (result_tp->form == ENUM_FORM)) {
            emit_1(POP, reg(DX));
            emit_2(COMPARE, reg(DX), reg(AX));
        }

        /*
        -- Both operands are real, or one is real and the other
        -- is integer.  Convert the integer operand to real.
        -- Call FLOAT_COMPARE to do the comparison, which returns
        -- -1 (less), 0 (equal), or +1 (greater).
        */
        else if ((result_tp == real_typep) || (tp2 == real_typep)) {
            emit_push_operand(tp2);
            emit_promote_to_real(result_tp, tp2);

            emit_1(CALL, name_lit(FLOAT_COMPARE));
            emit_2(ADD, reg(SP), integer_lit(8));
            emit_2(COMPARE, reg(AX), integer_lit(0));
        }

        /*
        -- Both operands are strings.  Compare the string pointed
        -- to by SI (operand 1) to the string pointed to by DI
        -- (operand 2).
        */
        else if (result_tp->form == ARRAY_FORM) {
            emit_1(POP,  reg(DI));
            emit_1(POP,  reg(SI));
            emit_2(MOVE, reg(AX), reg(DS));
            emit_2(MOVE, reg(ES), reg(AX));
            emit(CLEAR_DIRECTION);
            emit_2(MOVE, reg(CX),
                    integer_lit(result_tp->info.array.elmt_count));
            emit(COMPARE_STRINGS);
        }

        emit_2(MOVE, reg(AX), integer_lit(1));  /* default: load 1 */

        switch (op) {
            case LT:    jump_opcode = JUMP_LT;  break;
            case LE:    jump_opcode = JUMP_LE;  break;
            case EQUAL: jump_opcode = JUMP_EQ;  break;
            case NE:    jump_opcode = JUMP_NE;  break;
            case GE:    jump_opcode = JUMP_GE;  break;
            case GT:    jump_opcode = JUMP_GT;  break;
        }

        jump_label_index = new_label_index();
        emit_1(jump_opcode, label(STMT_LABEL_PREFIX,
            jump_label_index));

        emit_2(SUBTRACT, reg(AX), reg(AX));    /* load 0 if false */
        emit_label(STMT_LABEL_PREFIX, jump_label_index);

        result_tp = boolean_typep;
    }
```

```
        return(result_tp);
}

/*------------------------------------------------------------*/
/*  simple_expression   Process a simple expression consisting */
/*                      of terms separated by +, -, or OR      */
/*                      operators.  There may be a unary + or - */
/*                      before the first term.  Return a       */
/*                      pointer to the type structure.         */
/*------------------------------------------------------------*/

TOKEN_CODE add_op_list[] = {PLUS, MINUS, OR, 0};

    TYPE_STRUCT_PTR
simple_expression()

{
    TOKEN_CODE op;                      /* an operator token */
    BOOLEAN    saw_unary_op = FALSE;    /* TRUE iff unary operator */
    TOKEN_CODE unary_op = PLUS;         /* a unary operator token */
    TYPE_STRUCT_PTR result_tp, tp2;

    /*
    -- If there is a unary + or -, remember it.
    */
    if ((token == PLUS) || (token == MINUS)) {
        unary_op = token;
        saw_unary_op = TRUE;
        get_token();
    }

    result_tp = term();         /* first term */

    /*
    -- If there was a unary operator, check that the term
    -- is integer or real.  Negate the top of stack if it
    -- was a unary - either with the NEG instruction or by
    -- calling FLOAT_NEGATE.
    */
    if (saw_unary_op) {
        if (base_type(result_tp) == integer_typep) {
            if (unary_op == MINUS) emit_1(NEGATE, reg(AX));
        }
        else if (result_tp == real_typep) {
            if (unary_op == MINUS) {
                emit_push_operand(result_tp);
                emit_1(CALL, name_lit(FLOAT_NEGATE));
                emit_2(ADD, reg(SP), integer_lit(4));
            }
        }
        else error(INCOMPATIBLE_TYPES);
    }

    /*
    -- Loop to process subsequent terms separated by operators.
    */
    while (token_in(add_op_list)) {
        op = token;                     /* remember operator */

        result_tp = base_type(result_tp);
        emit_push_operand(result_tp);

        get_token();
        tp2 = base_type(term());        /* subsequent term */

        switch (op) {

            case PLUS:
```

```
            case MINUS: {
                /*
                -- integer <op> integer => integer
                -- AX = AX +|- DX
                */
                if (integer_operands(result_tp, tp2)) {
                    emit_1(POP, reg(DX));
                    if (op == PLUS) emit_2(ADD, reg(AX), reg(DX))
                    else {
                        emit_2(SUBTRACT, reg(DX), reg(AX));
                        emit_2(MOVE, reg(AX), reg(DX));
                    }
                    result_tp = integer_typep;
                }

                /*
                -- Both operands are real, or one is real and the
                -- other is integer.  Convert the integer operand
                -- to real.  The result is real.  Call FLOAT_ADD or
                -- FLOAT_SUBTRACT.
                */
                else if (real_operands(result_tp, tp2)) {
                    emit_push_operand(tp2);
                    emit_promote_to_real(result_tp, tp2);

                    emit_1(CALL, name_lit(op == PLUS
                                         ? FLOAT_ADD
                                         : FLOAT_SUBTRACT));
                    emit_2(ADD, reg(SP), integer_lit(8));

                    result_tp = real_typep;
                }

                else {
                    error(INCOMPATIBLE_TYPES);
                    result_tp = &dummy_type;
                }

                break;
            }

            case OR: {
                /*
                -- boolean OR boolean => boolean
                -- AX = AX OR DX
                */
                if (boolean_operands(result_tp, tp2)) {
                    emit_1(POP, reg(DX));
                    emit_2(OR_BITS, reg(AX), reg(DX));
                }
                else error(INCOMPATIBLE_TYPES);

                result_tp = boolean_typep;
                break;
            }
        }
    }

    return(result_tp);
}

/*------------------------------------------------------------*/
/*  term           Process a term consisting of factors        */
/*                 separated by *, /, DIV, MOD, or AND          */
/*                 operators.  Return a pointer to the          */
/*                 type structure.                              */
/*------------------------------------------------------------*/
```

```
TOKEN_CODE mult_op_list[] = {STAR, SLASH, DIV, MOD, AND, 0};

    TYPE_STRUCT_PTR
term()

{
    TOKEN_CODE op;                      /* an operator token */
    TYPE_STRUCT_PTR result_tp, tp2;

    result_tp = factor();               /* first factor */

    /*
    -- Loop to process subsequent factors
    -- separated by operators.
    */
    while (token_in(mult_op_list)) {
        op = token;                     /* remember operator */

        result_tp = base_type(result_tp);
        emit_push_operand(result_tp);

        get_token();
        tp2 = base_type(factor());      /* subsequent factor */

        switch (op) {

            case STAR: {
                /*
                -- Both operands are integer.
                -- AX = AX*DX
                */
                if (integer_operands(result_tp, tp2)) {
                    emit_1(POP, reg(DX));
                    emit_1(MULTIPLY, reg(DX));

                    result_tp = integer_typep;
                }

                /*
                -- Both operands are real, or one is real and the
                -- other is integer.  Convert the integer operand
                -- to real.  The result is real.
                -- Call FLOAT_MULTIPLY.
                */
                else if (real_operands(result_tp, tp2)) {
                    emit_push_operand(tp2);
                    emit_promote_to_real(result_tp, tp2);

                    emit_1(CALL, name_lit(FLOAT_MULTIPLY));
                    emit_2(ADD, reg(SP), integer_lit(8));

                    result_tp = real_typep;
                }

                else {
                    error(INCOMPATIBLE_TYPES);
                    result_tp = &dummy_type;
                }

                break;
            }

            case SLASH: {
                /*
                -- Both operands are real, or both are integer, or
                -- one is real and the other is integer.  Convert
                -- any integer operand to real. The result is real.
```

```
                -- Call FLOAT_DIVIDE.
                */
                if (real_operands(result_tp, tp2) ||
                    integer_operands(result_tp, tp2)) {
                    emit_push_operand(tp2);
                    emit_promote_to_real(result_tp, tp2);

                    emit_1(CALL, name_lit(FLOAT_DIVIDE));
                    emit_2(ADD, reg(SP), integer_lit(8));
                }
                else error(INCOMPATIBLE_TYPES);

                result_tp = real_typep;
                break;
            }

            case DIV:
            case MOD: {
                /*
                -- integer <op> integer => integer
                -- AX = AX IDIV CX
                */
                if (integer_operands(result_tp, tp2)) {
                    emit_2(MOVE, reg(CX), reg(AX));
                    emit_1(POP, reg(AX));
                    emit_2(SUBTRACT, reg(DX), reg(DX));
                    emit_1(DIVIDE, reg(CX));
                    if (op == MOD) emit_2(MOVE, reg(AX), reg(DX));
                }
                else error(INCOMPATIBLE_TYPES);

                result_tp = integer_typep;
                break;
            }

            case AND: {
                /*
                -- boolean AND boolean => boolean
                -- AX = AX AND DX
                */
                if (boolean_operands(result_tp, tp2)) {
                    emit_1(POP, reg(DX));
                    emit_2(AND_BITS, reg(AX), reg(DX));
                }
                else error(INCOMPATIBLE_TYPES);

                result_tp = boolean_typep;
                break;
            }
        }
    }

    return(result_tp);
}

/*------------------------------------------------------------*/
/*  factor          Process a factor, which is a variable,    */
/*                  a number, NOT followed by a factor, or     */
/*                  a parenthesized subexpression. Return     */
/*                  a pointer to the type structure.          */
/*------------------------------------------------------------*/

    TYPE_STRUCT_PTR
factor()

{
    TYPE_STRUCT_PTR tp;
```

```
switch (token) {

    case IDENTIFIER: {
        SYMTAB_NODE_PTR idp;

        search_and_find_all_symtab(idp);

        switch (idp->defn.key) {

            case FUNC_DEFN:
                get_token();
                tp = routine_call(idp, TRUE);
                break;

            case PROC_DEFN:
                error(INVALID_IDENTIFIER_USAGE);
                get_token();
                actual_parm_list(idp, FALSE);
                tp = &dummy_type;
                break;

            case CONST_DEFN:
                tp = constant_identifier(idp);
                break;

            default:
                tp = variable(idp, EXPR_USE);
                break;
        }

        break;
    }

    case NUMBER: {
        if (literal.type == INTEGER_LIT) {
            /*
            -- AX = value
            */
            emit_2(MOVE, reg(AX),
                    integer_lit(literal.value.integer));
            tp = integer_typep;
        }

        else { /* literal.type == REAL_LIT */
            /*
            -- DX:AX = value
            */
            tp = float_literal(token_string, literal.value.real);
        }

        get_token();
        break;
    }

    case STRING: {
        int length = strlen(literal.value.string);

        if (length == 1) {
            /*
            -- AH = 0
            -- AL = value
            */
            emit_2(MOVE, reg(AX),
                    char_lit(literal.value.string[0]));
            tp = char_typep;
        }
        else {
```

```
            /*
            -- AX = address of string
            */
            tp = string_literal(literal.value.string, length);
        }

        get_token();
        break;
    }

    case NOT:
        /*
        -- AX = NOT AX
        */
        get_token();
        tp = factor();
        emit_2(XOR_BITS, reg(AX), integer_lit(1));
        break;

    case LPAREN:
        get_token();
        tp = expression();

        if_token_get_else_error(RPAREN, MISSING_RPAREN);
        break;

    default:
        error(INVALID_EXPRESSION);
        tp = &dummy_type;
        break;
    }

    return(tp);
}

/*----------------------------------------------------------*/
/* float_literal       Process a floating point literal.    */
/*----------------------------------------------------------*/

TYPE_STRUCT_PTR
float_literal(string, value)

    char    string[];
    float   value;

{
    SYMTAB_NODE_PTR np = search_symtab(string, symtab_display[1]);

    /*
    -- Enter the literal into the symbol table
    -- if it isn't already in there.
    */
    if (np == NULL) {
        np = enter_symtab(string, symtab_display[1]);
        np->defn.key = CONST_DEFN;
        np->defn.info.constant.value.real  = value;
        np->label_index = new_label_index();
        np->next = float_literal_list;
        float_literal_list = np;
    }

    /*
    -- DX:AX = value
    */
    emit_2(MOVE, reg(AX), word_label(FLOAT_LABEL_PREFIX,
                                    np->label_index));
    emit_2(MOVE, reg(DX), high_dword_label(FLOAT_LABEL_PREFIX,
```

```
                               np->label_index));

    return(real_typep);
}

/*------------------------------------------------------*/
/* string_literal      Process a string_literal.        */
/*------------------------------------------------------*/

    TYPE_STRUCT_PTR
string_literal(string, length)

    char string[];
    int  length;

{
    SYMTAB_NODE_PTR np;
    TYPE_STRUCT_PTR tp = make_string_typep(length);
    char            buffer[MAX_SOURCE_LINE_LENGTH];

    sprintf(buffer, "'%s'", string);
    np = search_symtab(buffer, symtab_display[1]);

    /*
    -- Enter the literal into the symbol table
    -- if it isn't already in there.
    */
    if (np == NULL) {
        np = enter_symtab(buffer, symtab_display[1]);
        np->defn.key = CONST_DEFN;
        np->label_index = new_label_index();
        np->next = string_literal_list;
        string_literal_list = np;
    }

    /*
    -- AX = address of string
    */
    emit_2(LOAD_ADDRESS, reg(AX),
        word_label(STRING_LABEL_PREFIX, np->label_index));
    emit_1(PUSH, reg(AX));
    return(tp);
}

/*------------------------------------------------------*/
/* constant_identifier      Process a constant identifier. */
/*------------------------------------------------------*/

    TYPE_STRUCT_PTR
constant_identifier(idp)

    SYMTAB_NODE_PTR idp;                /* id of constant */

{
    TYPE_STRUCT_PTR tp = idp->typep;    /* type of constant */

    get_token();

    if ((tp == integer_typep) || (tp->form == ENUM_FORM)) {
        /*
        -- AX = value
        */
        emit_2(MOVE, reg(AX),
            integer_lit(idp->defn.info.constant.value.integer));
    }
    else if (tp == char_typep) {
        /*
```

```
        -- AX = value
        */
        emit_2(MOVE, reg(AX),
            char_lit(idp->defn.info.constant.value.character));
    }
    else if (tp == real_typep) {
        /*
        -- Create a literal and then call float_literal.
        */
        float value = idp->defn.info.constant.value.real;
        char  string[MAX_SOURCE_LINE_LENGTH];

        sprintf(string, "%e", value);
        float_literal(string, value);
    }
    else  /* string constant */ {
        string_literal(idp->defn.info.constant.value.stringp,
                strlen(idp->defn.info.constant.value.stringp));
    }

    return(tp);
}

/*------------------------------------------------------------*/
/* variable          Process a variable, which can be a       */
/*                   simple identifier, an array identifier    */
/*                   with subscripts, or a record identifier   */
/*                   with fields.                              */
/*------------------------------------------------------------*/

    TYPE_STRUCT_PTR
variable(var_idp, use)

    SYMTAB_NODE_PTR var_idp;    /* variable id */
    USE             use;        /* how variable is used */

{
    TYPE_STRUCT_PTR tp           = var_idp->typep;
    DEFN_KEY        defn_key     = var_idp->defn.key;
    BOOLEAN         varparm_flag = defn_key == VARPARM_DEFN;
    TYPE_STRUCT_PTR array_subscript_list();
    TYPE_STRUCT_PTR record_field();

    /*
    -- Check the variable's definition.
    */
    switch (defn_key) {
        case VAR_DEFN:
        case VALPARM_DEFN:
        case VARPARM_DEFN:
        case FUNC_DEFN:
        case UNDEFINED: break;          /* OK */

        default: {                      /* error */
            tp = &dummy_type;
            error(INVALID_IDENTIFIER_USAGE);
        }
    }

    get_token();

    /*
    -- There must not be a parameter list, but if there is one,
    -- parse it anyway for error recovery.
    */
    if (token == LPAREN) {
        error(UNEXPECTED_TOKEN);
```

```
        actual_parm_list(var_idp, FALSE);
        return(tp);
}


/*
-- Subscripts and/or field designators?
*/
if ((token == LBRACKET) || (token == PERIOD)) {
    /*
    -- Push the address of the array or record onto the
    -- stack, where it is then modified by code generated
    -- in array_subscript_list and record_field.
    */
    emit_push_address(var_idp);

    while ((token == LBRACKET) || (token == PERIOD)) {
        tp = token == LBRACKET ? array_subscript_list(tp)
                               : record_field(tp);
    }

    /*
    -- Leave the modified address on top of the stack if:
    --     it is an assignment target, or
    --     it represents a parameter passed by reference, or
    --     it is the address of an array or record.
    -- Otherwise, load AX with the value that the modified
    -- address points to.
    */
    if ((use != TARGET_USE) && (use != VARPARM_USE) &&
        (tp->form != ARRAY_FORM) && tp->form != RECORD_FORM)) {
        emit_1(POP, reg(BX));
        if (tp == char_typep) {
            emit_2(SUBTRACT, reg(AX), reg(AX));
            emit_2(MOVE, reg(AL), byte_indirect(BX));
        }
        else if (tp == real_typep) {
            emit_2(MOVE, reg(AX), word_indirect(BX));
            emit_2(MOVE, reg(DX), high_dword_indirect(BX));
        }
        else emit_2(MOVE, reg(AX), word_indirect(BX));
    }
}

else if (use == TARGET_USE) {
    /*
    -- Push the address of an assignment target onto the stack,
    -- unless it is a local or global scalar parameter or
    -- variable.
    */
    if (defn_key == FUNC_DEFN)
        emit_push_return_value_address(var_idp);
    else if (varparm_flag || (tp->form == ARRAY_FORM) ||
            (tp->form == RECORD_FORM) ||
            ((var_idp->level > 1) && (var_idp->level < level)))
        emit_push_address(var_idp);
}
else if (use == VARPARM_USE) {
    /*
    -- Push the address of a variable
    -- being passed as a VAR parameter.
    */
    emit_push_address(var_idp);
}
else if ((tp->form == ARRAY_FORM) || (tp->form == RECORD_FORM)) {
    /*
    -- Push the address of an array or record value.
    */
```

```
        emit_push_address(var_idp);
    }
    else {
        /*
        -- AX = scalar value
        */
        emit_load_value(var_idp, base_type(tp));
    }

    return(tp);
}

/*------------------------------------------------------------*/
/*  array_subscript_list      Process a list of subscripts    */
/*                            following an array identifier:   */
/*                                                             */
/*                            [ <expr> , <expr> , ... ]        */
/*------------------------------------------------------------*/

    TYPE_STRUCT_PTR
array_subscript_list(tp)

    TYPE_STRUCT_PTR tp;

{
    TYPE_STRUCT_PTR    index_tp, elmt_tp, ss_tp;
    int                min_index, elmt_size;
    extern TOKEN_CODE  statement_end_list[];

    /*
    -- Loop to process a subscript list.
    */
    do {
        if (tp->form == ARRAY_FORM) {
            index_tp = tp->info.array.index_typep;
            elmt_tp  = tp->info.array.elmt_typep;

            get_token();
            ss_tp = expression();

            /*
            -- The subscript expression must be assignment type
            -- compatible with the corresponding subscript type.
            */
            if (!is_assign_type_compatible(index_tp, ss_tp))
                error(INCOMPATIBLE_TYPES);

            min_index = tp->info.array.min_index;
            elmt_size = tp->info.array.elmt_typep->size;

            /*
            -- Convert the subscript into an offset by subracting
            -- the mininum index from it and then multiplying the
            -- result by the element size.  Add the offset to the
            -- address at the top of the stack.
            */
            if (min_index != 0) emit_2(SUBTRACT, reg(AX),
                                       integer_lit(min_index));
            if (elmt_size > 1) {
                emit_2(MOVE, reg(DX), integer_lit(elmt_size));
                emit_1(MULTIPLY, reg(DX));
            }
            emit_1(POP,  reg(DX));
            emit_2(ADD,  reg(DX), reg(AX));
            emit_1(PUSH, reg(DX));

            tp = elmt_tp;
```

```
        }
        else {
            error(TOO_MANY_SUBSCRIPTS);
            while ((token != RBRACKET) &&
                    (! token_in(statement_end_list)))
                get_token();
        }
    } while (token == COMMA);

    if_token_get_else_error(RBRACKET, MISSING_RBRACKET);
    return(tp);
}
```

```
/*------------------------------------------------------------*/
/*  record_field              Process a field designation     */
/*                            following a record identifier:  */
/*                                                            */
/*                                . <field-variable>          */
/*------------------------------------------------------------*/

    TYPE_STRUCT_PTR
record_field(tp)

    TYPE_STRUCT_PTR tp;

{
    SYMTAB_NODE_PTR field_idp;

    get_token();

    if ((token == IDENTIFIER) && (tp->form == RECORD_FORM)) {
        search_this_symtab(field_idp,
                            tp->info.record.field_symtab);
        get_token();

        /*
        -- Add the field's offset (using the numeric equate)
        -- to the address at the top of the stack.
        */
        if (field_idp != NULL) {
            emit_1(POP,  reg(AX));
            emit_2(ADD,  reg(AX), tagged_name(field_idp));
            emit_1(PUSH, reg(AX));
            return(field_idp->typep);
        }
        else {
            error(INVALID_FIELD);
            return(&dummy_type);
        }
    }
    else {
        get_token();
        error(INVALID_FIELD);
        return(&dummy_type);
    }
}
```

```
            /*******************************/
            /*                             */
            /*       Type compatibility    */
            /*                             */
            /*******************************/
```

```
/*------------------------------------------------------------*/
/*  check_rel_op_types  Check the operand types for a rela-   */
/*                      tional operator.                      */
/*------------------------------------------------------------*/
```

```
check_rel_op_types(tp1, tp2)

    TYPE_STRUCT_PTR tp1, tp2;            /* operand types */

{
    /*
    -- Two identical scalar or enumeration types.
    */
    if (   (tp1 == tp2)
        && ((tp1->form == SCALAR_FORM) || (tp1->form == ENUM_FORM)))
        return;

    /*
    -- One integer and one real.
    */
    if (   ((tp1 == integer_typep) && (tp2 == real_typep))
        || ((tp2 == integer_typep) && (tp1 == real_typep))) return;

    /*
    -- Two strings of the same length.
    */
    if ((tp1->form == ARRAY_FORM) &&
        (tp2->form == ARRAY_FORM) &&
        (tp1->info.array.elmt_typep == char_typep) &&
        (tp2->info.array.elmt_typep == char_typep) &&
        (tp1->info.array.elmt_count ==
                        tp2->info.array.elmt_count)) return;

    error(INCOMPATIBLE_TYPES);
}
```

```
/*------------------------------------------------------------*/
/*  is_assign_type_compatible   Return TRUE iff a value of type */
/*                              tp1 can be assigned to a vari- */
/*                              able of type tp1.              */
/*------------------------------------------------------------*/

    BOOLEAN
is_assign_type_compatible(tp1, tp2)

    TYPE_STRUCT_PTR tp1, tp2;

{
    tp1 = base_type(tp1);
    tp2 = base_type(tp2);

    if (tp1 == tp2) return(TRUE);

    /*
    -- real := integer
    */
    if ((tp1 == real_typep) && (tp2 == integer_typep)) return(TRUE);

    /*
    -- string1 := string2 of the same length
    */
    if ((tp1->form == ARRAY_FORM) &&
        (tp2->form == ARRAY_FORM) &&
        (tp1->info.array.elmt_typep == char_typep) &&
        (tp2->info.array.elmt_typep == char_typep) &&
        (tp1->info.array.elmt_count ==
                    tp2->info.array.elmt_count)) return(TRUE);

    return(FALSE);
}
```

```
/*------------------------------------------------------------*/
/*  base_type           Return the range type of a subrange   */
```

```
/*                    type.                    */
/*------------------------------------------------*/

    TYPE_STRUCT_PTR
base_type(tp)

    TYPE_STRUCT_PTR tp;
```

```
{
    return((tp->form == SUBRANGE_FORM)
              ? tp->info.subrange.range_typep
              : tp);
}
```

FIGURE B-7   scanner.h

```
/****************************************************************/
/*                                                            */
/*        S C A N N E R    (Header)                           */
/*                                                            */
/*    FILE:      scanner.h                                    */
/*                                                            */
/*    MODULE:    scanner                                      */
/*                                                            */
/****************************************************************/

#ifndef scanner_h
#define scanner_h

#include "common.h"

/*------------------------------------------------*/
/* Token codes                                    */
/*------------------------------------------------*/

typedef enum {
    NO_TOKEN, IDENTIFIER, NUMBER, STRING,
    UPARROW, STAR, LPAREN, RPAREN, MINUS, PLUS, EQUAL,
    LBRACKET, RBRACKET, COLON, SEMICOLON, LT, GT, COMMA, PERIOD,
    SLASH, COLONEQUAL, LE, GE, NE, DOTDOT, END_OF_FILE, ERROR,
    AND, ARRAY, BEGIN, CASE, CONST, DIV, DO, DOWNTO, ELSE, END,
    FFILE, FOR, FUNCTION, GOTO, IF, IN, LABEL, MOD, NIL, NOT,
    OF, OR, PACKED, PROCEDURE, PROGRAM, RECORD, REPEAT, SET,
    THEN, TO, TYPE, UNTIL, VAR, WHILE, WITH,
} TOKEN_CODE;

/*------------------------------------------------*/
/* Literal structure                              */
/*------------------------------------------------*/

typedef enum {
    INTEGER_LIT, REAL_LIT, STRING_LIT,
} LITERAL_TYPE;

typedef struct {
    LITERAL_TYPE type;
    union {
        int    integer;
        float  real;
        char   string[MAX_SOURCE_LINE_LENGTH];
    } value;
} LITERAL;

/*------------------------------------------------*/
/* Functions                                      */
/*------------------------------------------------*/

BOOLEAN token_in();

#endif
```

FIGURE B-8   scanner.c

```
/****************************************************************/
/*                                                            */
/*        S C A N N E R                                       */
/*                                                            */
/*        Scanner for Pascal tokens.                          */
/*                                                            */
/*    FILE:      scanner.c                                    */
/*                                                            */
/*    MODULE:    scanner                                      */
/*                                                            */
/****************************************************************/

#include <stdio.h>
#include <math.h>
#include <sys/types.h>
#include <sys/timeb.h>
#include "common.h"
#include "error.h"
```

```
#include "scanner.h"

#define EOF_CHAR        '\x7f'
#define TAB_SIZE        8

#define MAX_INTEGER     32767
#define MAX_DIGIT_COUNT 20
#define MAX_EXPONENT    37

#define MIN_RESERVED_WORD_LENGTH   2
#define MAX_RESERVED_WORD_LENGTH   9

/*------------------------------------------------*/
/* Character codes                                */
/*------------------------------------------------*/

typedef enum {
    LETTER, DIGIT, QUOTE, SPECIAL, EOF_CODE,
```

```
} CHAR_CODE;

/*------------------------------------------------------------*/
/* Reserved word tables                                       */
/*------------------------------------------------------------*/

typedef struct {
    char        *string;
    TOKEN_CODE  token_code;
} RW_STRUCT;

RW_STRUCT rw_2[] = {
    {"do", DO}, {"if", IF}, {"in", IN}, {"of", OF}, {"or", OR},
    {"to", TO}, {NULL, 0 },
};

RW_STRUCT rw_3[] = {
    {"and", AND}, {"div", DIV}, {"end", END}, {"for", FOR},
    {"mod", MOD}, {"nil", NIL}, {"not", NOT}, {"set", SET},
    {"var", VAR}, {NULL , 0  },
};

RW_STRUCT rw_4[] = {
    {"case", CASE}, {"else", ELSE}, {"file", FFILE},
    {"goto", GOTO}, {"then", THEN}, {"type", TYPE},
    {"with", WITH}, {NULL , 0   },
};

RW_STRUCT rw_5[] = {
    {"array", ARRAY}, {"begin", BEGIN}, {"const", CONST},
    {"label", LABEL}, {"until", UNTIL}, {"while", WHILE},
    {NULL , 0   },
};

RW_STRUCT rw_6[] = {
    {"downto", DOWNTO}, {"packed", PACKED}, {"record", RECORD},
    {"repeat", REPEAT}, {NULL , 0   },
};

RW_STRUCT rw_7[] = {
    {"program", PROGRAM}, {NULL, 0},
};

RW_STRUCT rw_8[] = {
    {"function", FUNCTION}, {NULL, 0},
};

RW_STRUCT rw_9[] = {
    {"procedure", PROCEDURE}, {NULL, 0},
};

RW_STRUCT *rw_table[] = {
    NULL, NULL, rw_2, rw_3, rw_4, rw_5, rw_6, rw_7, rw_8, rw_9,
};

/*------------------------------------------------------------*/
/* Token lists                                                */
/*------------------------------------------------------------*/

TOKEN_CODE statement_start_list[]  = {BEGIN, CASE, FOR, IF, REPEAT,
                                      WHILE, IDENTIFIER, 0};

TOKEN_CODE statement_end_list[]    = {SEMICOLON, END, ELSE, UNTIL,
                                      END_OF_FILE, 0};

TOKEN_CODE declaration_start_list[] = {CONST, TYPE, VAR, PROCEDURE,
                                       FUNCTION, 0};
```

```
/*------------------------------------------------------------*/
/* Globals                                                    */
/*------------------------------------------------------------*/

char       ch;           /* current input character */
TOKEN_CODE token;        /* code of current token */
LITERAL    literal;      /* value of literal */
int        buffer_offset; /* char offset into source buffer */
int        level = 0;    /* current nesting level */
int        line_number = 0;  /* current line number */
BOOLEAN    print_flag = TRUE;  /* TRUE to print source lines */
BOOLEAN    block_flag = FALSE; /* TRUE only when parsing a block */

char source_buffer[MAX_SOURCE_LINE_LENGTH]; /* source file buffer */
char token_string[MAX_TOKEN_STRING_LENGTH]; /* token string */
char word_string[MAX_TOKEN_STRING_LENGTH];  /* downshifted */
char *bufferp = source_buffer;    /* source buffer ptr */
char *tokenp  = token_string;     /* token string ptr */

int     digit_count;         /* total no. of digits in number */
BOOLEAN count_error;         /* too many digits in number? */

int page_number = 0;
int line_count  = MAX_LINES_PER_PAGE;   /* no. lines on current pg */

char source_name[MAX_FILE_NAME_LENGTH]; /* name of source file */
char date[DATE_STRING_LENGTH];          /* current date and time */

FILE *source_file;

CHAR_CODE char_table[256];

/*------------------------------------------------------------*/
/* char_code        Return the character code of ch.          */
/*------------------------------------------------------------*/

#define char_code(ch)   char_table[ch]

            /********************************/
            /*                              */
            /*        Initialization        */
            /*                              */
            /********************************/

/*------------------------------------------------------------*/
/* init_scanner        Initialize the scanner globals         */
/*                     and open the source file.              */
/*------------------------------------------------------------*/

init_scanner(name)

    char *name;      /* name of source file */

{
    int ch;

    /*
    -- Initialize character table.
    */
    for (ch = 0;   ch < 256;  ++ch) char_table[ch] = SPECIAL;
    for (ch = '0'; ch <= '9'; ++ch) char_table[ch] = DIGIT;
    for (ch = 'A'; ch <= 'Z'; ++ch) char_table[ch] = LETTER;
    for (ch = 'a'; ch <= 'z'; ++ch) char_table[ch] = LETTER;
    char_table['\''] = QUOTE;
    char_table[EOF_CHAR] = EOF_CODE;

    init_page_header(name);
```

```
    open_source_file(name);
}

/*----------------------------------------------------------*/
/*  quit_scanner        Terminate the scanner.              */
/*----------------------------------------------------------*/

quit_scanner()

{
    close_source_file();
}

                /*********************************/
                /*                               */
                /*      Character routines       */
                /*                               */
                /*********************************/

/*----------------------------------------------------------*/
/*  get_char            Set ch to the next character from the */
/*                      source buffer.                      */
/*----------------------------------------------------------*/

get_char()

{
    BOOLEAN get_source_line();

    /*
    -- If at end of current source line, read another line.
    -- If at end of file, set ch to the EOF character and return.
    */
    if (*bufferp == '\0') {
        if (! get_source_line()) {
            ch = EOF_CHAR;
            return;
        }
        bufferp = source_buffer;
        buffer_offset = 0;
    }

    ch = *bufferp++;    /* next character in the buffer */

    /*
    -- Special character processing:
    --
    --      tab         Increment buffer_offset up to the next
    --                  multiple of TAB_SIZE, and replace ch with
    --                  a blank.
    --
    --      new-line    Replace ch with a blank.
    --
    --      {           Start of comment:  Skip over comment and
    --                  replace it with a blank.
    */
    switch (ch) {

        case '\t':  buffer_offset += TAB_SIZE -
                                    buffer_offset%TAB_SIZE;
                    ch = ' ';
                    break;

        case '\n':  ++buffer_offset;
                    ch = ' ';
                    break;

        case '{':   ++buffer_offset;
```

```
                    skip_comment();
                    ch = ' ';
                    break;

        default:    ++buffer_offset;
    }
}

/*----------------------------------------------------------*/
/*  skip_comment        Skip over a comment.  Set ch to '}'. */
/*----------------------------------------------------------*/

skip_comment()

{
    do {
        get_char();
    } while ((ch != '}') && (ch != EOF_CHAR));
}

/*----------------------------------------------------------*/
/*  skip_blanks         Skip past any blanks at the current */
/*                      location in the source buffer.  Set */
/*                      ch to the next nonblank character.  */
/*----------------------------------------------------------*/

skip_blanks()

{
    while (ch == ' ') get_char();
}

                /*********************************/
                /*                               */
                /*      Token routines           */
                /*                               */
                /*********************************/

        /*  Note that after a token has been extracted, */
        /*  ch is the first character after the token.  */

/*----------------------------------------------------------*/
/*  get_token           Extract the next token from the source */
/*                      buffer.                             */
/*----------------------------------------------------------*/

get_token()

{
    skip_blanks();
    tokenp = token_string;

    switch (char_code(ch)) {
        case LETTER:    get_word();             break;
        case DIGIT:     get_number();           break;
        case QUOTE:     get_string();           break;
        case EOF_CODE:  token = END_OF_FILE;    break;
        default:        get_special();          break;
    }
}

/*----------------------------------------------------------*/
/*  get_word            Extract a word token and downshift its */
/*                      characters.  Check if it's a reserved */
/*                      word.  Set token to IDENTIFIER if it's */
/*                      not.                                */
/*----------------------------------------------------------*/
```

```
get_word()

{
    BOOLEAN is_reserved_word();

    /*
    -- Extract the word.
    */
    while ((char_code(ch) == LETTER) || (char_code(ch) == DIGIT)) {
        *tokenp++ = ch;
        get_char();
    }
    *tokenp = '\0';
    downshift_word();

    if (! is_reserved_word()) token = IDENTIFIER;
}

/*----------------------------------------------------------*/
/*  get_number          Extract a number token and set literal  */
/*                      to its value.  Set token to NUMBER.     */
/*----------------------------------------------------------*/

get_number()

{
    int     whole_count   = 0;     /* no. digits in whole part */
    int     decimal_offset = 0;    /* no. digits to move decimal */
    char    exponent_sign  = '+';
    int     exponent       = 0;    /* value of exponent */
    float   nvalue         = 0.0;  /* value of number */
    float   evalue         = 0.0;  /* value of exponent */
    BOOLEAN saw_dotdot     = FALSE; /* TRUE if encounter .. */

    digit_count = 0;
    count_error = FALSE;
    token       = NO_TOKEN;

    literal.type = INTEGER_LIT;    /* assume it's an integer */

    /*
    -- Extract the whole part of the number by accumulating
    -- the values of its digits into nvalue.  whole_count keeps
    -- track of the number of digits in this part.
    */
    accumulate_value(&nvalue, INVALID_NUMBER);
    if (token == ERROR) return;
    whole_count = digit_count;

    /*
    -- If the current character is a dot, then either we have a
    -- fraction part or we are seeing the first character of a ..
    -- token.  To find out, we must fetch the next character.
    */
    if (ch == '.') {
        get_char();

        if (ch == '.') {
            /*
            -- We have a .. token.  Back up bufferp so that the
            -- token can be extracted next.
            */
            saw_dotdot = TRUE;
            --bufferp;
        }
        else {
            literal.type = REAL_LIT;
```

```
            *tokenp++ = '.';

            /*
            -- We have a fraction part.  Accumulate it into nvalue.
            -- decimal_offset keeps track of how many digits to move
            -- the decimal point back.
            */
            accumulate_value(&nvalue, INVALID_FRACTION);
            if (token == ERROR) return;
            decimal_offset = whole_count - digit_count;
        }
    }

    /*
    -- Extract the exponent part, if any. There cannot be an
    -- exponent part if the .. token has been seen.
    */
    if (!saw_dotdot && ((ch == 'E') || (ch == 'e'))) {
        literal.type = REAL_LIT;
        *tokenp++ = ch;
        get_char();

        /*
        -- Fetch the exponent's sign, if any.
        */
        if ((ch == '+') || (ch == '-')) {
            *tokenp++ = exponent_sign = ch;
            get_char();
        }

        /*
        -- Extract the exponent.  Accumulate it into evalue.
        */
        accumulate_value(&evalue, INVALID_EXPONENT);
        if (token == ERROR) return;
        if (exponent_sign == '-') evalue = -evalue;
    }

    /*
    -- Were there too many digits?
    */
    if (count_error) {
        error(TOO_MANY_DIGITS);
        token = ERROR;
        return;
    }

    /*
    -- Adjust the number's value using
    -- decimal_offset and the exponent.
    */
    exponent = evalue + decimal_offset;
    if ((exponent + whole_count < -MAX_EXPONENT) ||
        (exponent + whole_count >  MAX_EXPONENT)) {
        error(REAL_OUT_OF_RANGE);
        token = ERROR;
        return;
    }
    if (exponent != 0) nvalue *= pow(10, exponent);

    /*
    -- Set the literal's value.
    */
    if (literal.type == INTEGER_LIT) {
        if ((nvalue < -MAX_INTEGER) || (nvalue > MAX_INTEGER)) {
            error(INTEGER_OUT_OF_RANGE);
            token = ERROR;
```

```
                return;
        }
        literal.value.integer = nvalue;
    }
    else literal.value.real = nvalue;

    *tokenp = '\0';
    token   = NUMBER;
}


/*------------------------------------------------------*/
/* get_string          Extract a string token. Set token to  */
/*                     STRING.  Note that the quotes are     */
/*                     stored as part of token_string but not */
/*                     literal.value.string.                 */
/*------------------------------------------------------*/

get_string()

{
    char *sp = literal.value.string;

    *tokenp++ = '\'';
    get_char();

    /*
    --  Extract the string.
    */
    while (ch != EOF_CHAR) {
        /*
        --  Two consecutive single quotes represent
        --  a single quote in the string.
        */
        if (ch == '\'') {
            *tokenp++ = ch;
            get_char();
            if (ch != '\'') break;
        }
        *tokenp++ = ch;
        *sp++     = ch;
        get_char();
    }

    *tokenp      = '\0';
    *sp          = '\0';
    token        = STRING;
    literal.type = STRING_LIT;
}


/*------------------------------------------------------*/
/* get_special         Extract a special token.  Most are  */
/*                     single-character.  Some are double-  */
/*                     character.  Set token appropriately. */
/*------------------------------------------------------*/

get_special()

{
    *tokenp++ = ch;
    switch (ch) {
        case '^':   token = UPARROW;  get_char();  break;
        case '*':   token = STAR;     get_char();  break;
        case '(':   token = LPAREN;   get_char();  break;
        case ')':   token = RPAREN;   get_char();  break;
        case '-':   token = MINUS;    get_char();  break;
        case '+':   token = PLUS;     get_char();  break;
        case '=':   token = EQUAL;    get_char();  break;
        case '[':   token = LBRACKET; get_char();  break;
        case ']':   token = RBRACKET; get_char();  break;
        case ';':   token = SEMICOLON; get_char(); break;
        case ',':   token = COMMA;    get_char();  break;
        case '/':   token = SLASH;    get_char();  break;

        case ':':   get_char();          /* : or := */
                    if (ch == '=') {
                        *tokenp++ = '=';
                        token     = COLONEQUAL;
                        get_char();
                    }
                    else token = COLON;
                    break;

        case '<':   get_char();          /* < or <= or <> */
                    if (ch == '=') {
                        *tokenp++ = '=';
                        token     = LE;
                        get_char();
                    }
                    else if (ch == '>') {
                        *tokenp++ = '>';
                        token     = NE;
                        get_char();
                    }
                    else token = LT;
                    break;

        case '>':   get_char();          /* > or >= */
                    if (ch == '=') {
                        *tokenp++ = '=';
                        token     = GE;
                        get_char();
                    }
                    else token = GT;
                    break;

        case '.':   get_char();          /* . or .. */
                    if (ch == '.') {
                        *tokenp++ = '.';
                        token     = DOTDOT;
                        get_char();
                    }
                    else token = PERIOD;
                    break;

        default:    token = ERROR;
                    get_char();
                    break;

    }
    *tokenp = '\0';
}


/*------------------------------------------------------------*/
/* downshift_word      Copy a word token into word_string    */
/*                     with all letters downshifted.         */
/*------------------------------------------------------------*/

downshift_word()

{
    int offset = 'a' - 'A';   /* offset to downshift a letter */
    char *wp   = word_string;
    char *tp   = token_string;

    /*
```

```
        -- Copy word into word_string.
        */
        do {
            *wp++ = (*tp >= 'A') && (*tp <= 'Z')    /* if a letter,   */
                        ? *tp + offset              /* then downshift */
                        : *tp;                      /* else just copy */
            ++tp;
        } while (*tp != '\0');

        *wp = '\0';
}

/*-------------------------------------------------------------*/
/* accumulate_value    Extract a number part and accumulate    */
/*                     its value.  Flag the error if the first */
/*                     character is not a digit.               */
/*-------------------------------------------------------------*/

accumulate_value(valuep, error_code)

    float     *valuep;
    ERROR_CODE error_code;

{
    float value = *valuep;

    /*
    -- Error if the first character is not a digit.
    */
    if (char_code(ch) != DIGIT) {
        error(error_code);
        token = ERROR;
        return;
    }

    /*
    -- Accumulate the value as long as the total allowable
    -- number of digits has not been exceeded.
    */
    do {
        *tokenp++ = ch;

        if (++digit_count <= MAX_DIGIT_COUNT)
            value = 10*value + (ch - '0');
        else count_error = TRUE;

        get_char();
    } while (char_code(ch) == DIGIT);

    *valuep = value;
}

                /*******************************/
                /*                             */
                /*      Token testers          */
                /*                             */
                /*******************************/

/*-------------------------------------------------------------*/
/* token_in          Return TRUE if the current token is in    */
/*                   the token list, else return FALSE.        */
/*-------------------------------------------------------------*/

    BOOLEAN
token_in(token_list)

    TOKEN_CODE token_list[];
```

```
{
    TOKEN_CODE *tokenp;

    if (token_list == NULL) return(FALSE);

    for (tokenp = &token_list[0]; *tokenp; ++tokenp) {
        if (token == *tokenp) return(TRUE);
    }

    return(FALSE);
}

/*-------------------------------------------------------------*/
/* synchronize         If the current token is not in one of   */
/*                     the token lists, flag it as an error.   */
/*                     Then skip tokens until one that is in    */
/*                     one of the token lists.                 */
/*-------------------------------------------------------------*/

synchronize(token_list1, token_list2, token_list3)

    TOKEN_CODE token_list1[], token_list2[], token_list3[];

{
    BOOLEAN error_flag = (! token_in(token_list1)) &&
                         (! token_in(token_list2)) &&
                         (! token_in(token_list3));

    if (error_flag) {
        error(token == END_OF_FILE ? UNEXPECTED_END_OF_FILE
                                   : UNEXPECTED_TOKEN);

        /*
        -- Skip tokens to resynchronize.
        */
        while ((! token_in(token_list1)) &&
               (! token_in(token_list2)) &&
               (! token_in(token_list3)) &&
               (token != END_OF_FILE))
            get_token();
    }
}

/*-------------------------------------------------------------*/
/* is_reserved_word    Check to see if a word token is a       */
/*                     reserved word.  If so, set token        */
/*                     appropriately and return TRUE.  Else,   */
/*                     return FALSE.                           */
/*-------------------------------------------------------------*/

    BOOLEAN
is_reserved_word()

{
    int      word_length = strlen(word_string);
    RW_STRUCT *rwp;

    /*
    -- Is it the right length?
    */
    if ((word_length >= MIN_RESERVED_WORD_LENGTH) &&
        (word_length <= MAX_RESERVED_WORD_LENGTH)) {
        /*
        -- Yes.  Pick the appropriate reserved word list
        -- and check to see if the word is in there.
        */
```

```
        for (rwp = rw_table[word_length];
            rwp->string != NULL;
            ++rwp) {
            if (strcmp(word_string, rwp->string) == 0) {
                token = rwp->token_code;
                return(TRUE);              /* yes, a reserved word */
            }
        }
    }

    return(FALSE);                         /* no, it's not */
}


            /*******************************/
            /*                             */
            /*      Source file routines   */
            /*                             */
            /*******************************/

/*----------------------------------------------------------*/
/* open_source_file    Open the source file and fetch its   */
/*                     first character.                     */
/*----------------------------------------------------------*/

open_source_file(name)

    char *name;         /* name of source file */

{
    if ((name == NULL) ||
        ((source_file = fopen(name, "r")) == NULL)) {
        error(FAILED_SOURCE_FILE_OPEN);
        exit(-FAILED_SOURCE_FILE_OPEN);
    }

    /*
    -- Fetch the first character.
    */
    bufferp = ""      ;
    get_char();
}

/*----------------------------------------------------------*/
/* close_source_file   Close the source file.               */
/*----------------------------------------------------------*/

close_source_file()

{
    fclose(source_file);
}


/*----------------------------------------------------------*/
/* get_source_line     Read the next line from the source   */
/*                     file. If there is one, print it out  */
/*                     and return TRUE. Else return FALSE   */
/*                     for the end of file.                 */
/*----------------------------------------------------------*/

    BOOLEAN
get_source_line()

{
    char print_buffer[MAX_SOURCE_LINE_LENGTH + 9];
    extern FILE *code_file;

    if ((fgets(source_buffer, MAX_SOURCE_LINE_LENGTH,
```

```
                    source_file)) != NULL) {
        ++line_number;

        if (print_flag) {
            sprintf(print_buffer, "%4d %d: %s",
                    line_number, level, source_buffer);
            print_line(print_buffer);
        }

        fprintf(code_file, "; %4d: %s", line_number, source_buffer);
        return(TRUE);
    }
    else return(FALSE);
}


            /*******************************/
            /*                             */
            /*      Printout routines      */
            /*                             */
            /*******************************/

/*----------------------------------------------------------*/
/* print_line          Print out a line. Start a new page if */
/*                     the current page is full.            */
/*----------------------------------------------------------*/

print_line(line)

    char line[];        /* line to be printed */

{
    char save_ch;
    char *save_chp = NULL;

    if (++line_count > MAX_LINES_PER_PAGE) {
        print_page_header();
        line_count = 1;
    };

    if (strlen(line) > MAX_PRINT_LINE_LENGTH) {
        save_chp = &line[MAX_PRINT_LINE_LENGTH];
        save_ch = *save_chp;
        *save_chp = '\0';
    }

    printf("%s", line);

    if (save_chp) *save_chp = save_ch;
}

/*----------------------------------------------------------*/
/* init_page_header    Initialize the fields of the page    */
/*                     header.                              */
/*----------------------------------------------------------*/

init_page_header(name)

    char *name;         /* name of source file */

{
    time_t timer;

    strncpy(source_name, name, MAX_FILE_NAME_LENGTH - 1);

    /*
    -- Set the current date and time in the date string.
    */
```

```
    time(&timer);
    strcpy(date, asctime(localtime(&timer)));
}


/*----------------------------------------------------------*/
/*  print_page_header   Print the page header at the top of  */
/*                      the next page.                       */
```

```
/*----------------------------------------------------------*/

print_page_header()

{
    putchar(FORM_FEED_CHAR);
    printf("Page %d   %s   %s\n\n", ++page_number, source_name, date);
}
```

FIGURE B-9　　symtab.h

```
/***************************************************************/
/*                                                             */
/*        S Y M B O L   T A B L E   (Header)                   */
/*                                                             */
/*    FILE:       symtab.h                                     */
/*                                                             */
/*    MODULE:     symbol table                                 */
/*                                                             */
/***************************************************************/

#ifndef symtab_h
#define symtab_h

#include "common.h"

/*----------------------------------------------------------*/
/*  Value structure                                          */
/*----------------------------------------------------------*/

typedef union {
    int   integer;
    float real;
    char  character;
    char *stringp;
} VALUE;

/*----------------------------------------------------------*/
/*  Definition structure                                     */
/*----------------------------------------------------------*/

typedef enum {
    UNDEFINED,
    CONST_DEFN, TYPE_DEFN, VAR_DEFN, FIELD_DEFN,
    VALPARM_DEFN, VARPARM_DEFN,
    PROG_DEFN, PROC_DEFN, FUNC_DEFN,
} DEFN_KEY;

typedef enum {
    DECLARED, FORWARD,
    READ, READLN, WRITE, WRITELN,
    ABS, ARCTAN, CHR, COS, EOFF, EOLN, EXP, LN, ODD, ORD,
    PRED, ROUND, SIN, SQR, SQRT, SUCC, TRUNC,
} ROUTINE_KEY;

typedef struct {
    DEFN_KEY key;
    union {
        struct {
            VALUE value;
        } constant;

        struct {
```

```
            ROUTINE_KEY         key;
            int                 parm_count;
            int                 total_parm_size;
            int                 total_local_size;
            struct symtab_node *parms;
            struct symtab_node *locals;
            struct symtab_node *local_symtab;
            char               *code_segment;
        } routine;

        struct {
            int                 offset;
            struct symtab_node *record_idp;
        } data;
    } info;
} DEFN_STRUCT;

/*----------------------------------------------------------*/
/*  Type structure                                           */
/*----------------------------------------------------------*/

typedef enum {
    NO_FORM,
    SCALAR_FORM, ENUM_FORM, SUBRANGE_FORM,
    ARRAY_FORM, RECORD_FORM,
} TYPE_FORM;

typedef struct type_struct {
    TYPE_FORM           form;
    int                 size;
    struct symtab_node *type_idp;
    union {
        struct {
            struct symtab_node *const_idp;
            int                 max;
        } enumeration;

        struct {
            struct type_struct *range_typep;
            int                 min, max;
        } subrange;

        struct {
            struct type_struct *index_typep, *elmt_typep;
            int                 min_index, max_index;
            int                 elmt_count;
        } array;

        struct {
            struct symtab_node *field_symtab;
        } record;
    } info;
```

```
} TYPE_STRUCT, *TYPE_STRUCT_PTR;
```

```
/*--------------------------------------------------*/
/*  Symbol table node                               */
/*--------------------------------------------------*/
```

```
typedef struct symtab_node {
    struct symtab_node *left, *right;  /* ptrs to subtrees */
    struct symtab_node *next;          /* for chaining nodes */
    char               *name;          /* name string */
    char               *info;          /* ptr to generic info */
    DEFN_STRUCT         defn;          /* definition struct */
    TYPE_STRUCT_PTR     typep;         /* ptr to type struct */
    int                 level;         /* nesting level */
    int                 label_index;   /* index for code label */
} SYMTAB_NODE, *SYMTAB_NODE_PTR;
```

```
/*--------------------------------------------------*/
/*  Functions                                       */
/*--------------------------------------------------*/
```

```
SYMTAB_NODE_PTR search_symtab();
SYMTAB_NODE_PTR search_symtab_display();
SYMTAB_NODE_PTR enter_symtab();
SYMTAB_NODE_PTR exit_scope();
TYPE_STRUCT_PTR make_string_typep();
```

```
        /***************************************/
        /*                                     */
        /*    Macros to search symbol tables   */
        /*                                     */
        /***************************************/
```

```
/*--------------------------------------------------*/
/*  search_local_symtab        Search the local symbol */
/*                             table for the current id */
/*                             name.  Set a pointer to the */
/*                             entry if found, else to */
/*                             NULL.                 */
/*--------------------------------------------------*/
```

```
#define search_local_symtab(idp)                         \
    idp = search_symtab(word_string, symtab_display[level])
```

```
/*--------------------------------------------------*/
/*  search_this_symtab         Search the given symbol */
/*                             table for the current id */
/*                             name.  Set a pointer to the */
/*                             entry if found, else to */
/*                             NULL.                 */
/*--------------------------------------------------*/
```

```
#define search_this_symtab(idp, this_symtab)             \
    idp = search_symtab(word_string, this_symtab)
```

```
/*--------------------------------------------------*/
/*  search_all_symtab          Search the symbol table */
/*                             display for the current id */
/*                             name.  Set a pointer to the */
/*                             entry if found, else to */
/*                             NULL.                 */
/*--------------------------------------------------*/
```

```
#define search_all_symtab(idp)                           \
```

```
    idp = search_symtab_display(word_string)
```

```
/*--------------------------------------------------*/
/*  enter_local_symtab         Enter the current id name */
/*                             into the local symbol */
/*                             table, and set a pointer */
/*                             to the entry.        */
/*--------------------------------------------------*/
```

```
#define enter_local_symtab(idp)                          \
    idp = enter_symtab(word_string, &symtab_display[level])
```

```
/*--------------------------------------------------*/
/*  enter_name_local_symtab    Enter the given name into */
/*                             the local symbol table, and */
/*                             set a pointer to the entry. */
/*--------------------------------------------------*/
```

```
#define enter_name_local_symtab(idp, name)               \
    idp = enter_symtab(name, &symtab_display[level])
```

```
/*--------------------------------------------------*/
/*  search_and_find_all_symtab  Search the symbol table */
/*                              display for the current id */
/*                              name. If not found, ID */
/*                              UNDEFINED error, and enter */
/*                              into the local symbol table. */
/*                              Set a pointer to the entry. */
/*--------------------------------------------------*/
```

```
#define search_and_find_all_symtab(idp)                          \
    if ((idp = search_symtab_display(word_string)) == NULL) {    \
        error(UNDEFINED_IDENTIFIER);                             \
        idp = enter_symtab(word_string, &symtab_display[level]); \
        idp->defn.key = UNDEFINED;                               \
        idp->typep = &dummy_type;                                \
    }
```

```
/*--------------------------------------------------*/
/*  search_and_enter_local_symtab  Search the local symbol */
/*                                 table for the current id */
/*                                 name.  Enter the name if */
/*                                 it is not already in there, */
/*                                 else ID REDEFINED error. */
/*                                 Set a pointer to the entry. */
/*--------------------------------------------------*/
```

```
#define search_and_enter_local_symtab(idp)                       \
    if ((idp = search_symtab(word_string,                        \
                       symtab_display[level])) == NULL) {        \
        idp = enter_symtab(word_string, &symtab_display[level]); \
    }                                                            \
    else error(REDEFINED_IDENTIFIER)
```

```
/*--------------------------------------------------*/
/*  search_and_enter_this_symtab  Search the given symbol */
/*                                table for the current id */
/*                                name.  Enter the name if */
/*                                it is not already in there, */
/*                                else ID REDEFINED error. */
/*                                Set a pointer to the entry. */
/*--------------------------------------------------*/
```

```
#define search_and_enter_this_symtab(idp, this_symtab)          \               }                                                         \
    if ((idp = search_symtab(word_string,                       \                   else error(REDEFINED_IDENTIFIER)
                           this_symtab)) == NULL) {             \
       idp = enter_symtab(word_string, &this_symtab);           \       #endif
```

FIGURE B-10   symtab.c

```
/****************************************************************/
/*                                                            */
/*      S Y M B O L   T A B L E                               */
/*                                                            */
/*      Symbol table routines.                                */
/*                                                            */
/*      FILE:       symtab.c                                  */
/*                                                            */
/*      MODULE:     symbol table                              */
/*                                                            */
/****************************************************************/

#include <stdio.h>
#include "common.h"
#include "error.h"
#include "symtab.h"

/*-----------------------------------------------------------*/
/* Externals                                                 */
/*-----------------------------------------------------------*/

extern int level;

/*-----------------------------------------------------------*/
/* Globals                                                   */
/*-----------------------------------------------------------*/

SYMTAB_NODE_PTR symtab_display[MAX_NESTING_LEVEL];

TYPE_STRUCT_PTR integer_typep, real_typep,     /* predefined types */
                boolean_typep, char_typep;

TYPE_STRUCT dummy_type = {       /* for erroneous type definitions */
    NO_FORM,        /* form */
    0,              /* size */
    NULL            /* type_idp */
};

/*-----------------------------------------------------------*/
/* search_symtab      Search for a name in the symbol table. */
/*                    Return a pointer of the entry if found,*/
/*                    or NULL if not.                        */
/*-----------------------------------------------------------*/

    SYMTAB_NODE_PTR
search_symtab(name, np)

    char           *name;       /* name to search for */
    SYMTAB_NODE_PTR np;         /* ptr to symtab root */

{
    int cmp;

    /*
    -- Loop to check each node.  Return if the node matches,
```

```
    -- else continue search down the left or right subtree.
    */
    while (np != NULL) {
        cmp = strcmp(name, np->name);
        if (cmp == 0) return(np);                   /* found */
        np = cmp < 0 ? np->left : np->right;    /* continue search */
    }

    return(NULL);                               /* not found */
}

/*-----------------------------------------------------------*/
/* search_symtab_display   Search all the symbol tables in the */
/*                         symbol table display for a name.    */
/*                         Return a pointer to the entry if    */
/*                         found, or NULL if not.              */
/*-----------------------------------------------------------*/

    SYMTAB_NODE_PTR
search_symtab_display(name)

    char *name;             /* name to search for */

{
    short i;
    SYMTAB_NODE_PTR np;         /* ptr to symtab node */

    for (i = level; i >= 0; --i) {
        np = search_symtab(name, symtab_display[i]);
        if (np != NULL) return(np);
    }

    return(NULL);
}

/*-----------------------------------------------------------*/
/* enter_symtab       Enter a name into the symbol table,    */
/*                    and return a pointer to the new entry. */
/*-----------------------------------------------------------*/

    SYMTAB_NODE_PTR
enter_symtab(name, npp)

    char           *name;       /* name to enter */
    SYMTAB_NODE_PTR *npp;       /* ptr to ptr to symtab root */

{
    int            cmp;         /* result of strcmp */
    SYMTAB_NODE_PTR new_nodep;  /* ptr to new entry */
    SYMTAB_NODE_PTR np;         /* ptr to node to test */

    /*
    -- Create the new node for the name.
    */
    new_nodep = alloc_struct(SYMTAB_NODE);
```

```
    new_nodep->name = alloc_bytes(strlen(name) + 1);
    strcpy(new_nodep->name, name);
    new_nodep->left = new_nodep->right = new_nodep->next = NULL;
    new_nodep->info = NULL;
    new_nodep->defn.key = UNDEFINED;
    new_nodep->typep = NULL;
    new_nodep->level = level;
    new_nodep->label_index = 0;

    /*
    -- Loop to search for the insertion point.
    */
    while ((np = *npp) != NULL) {
        cmp = strcmp(name, np->name);
        npp = cmp < 0 ? &(np->left) : &(np->right);
    }

    *npp = new_nodep;                    /* replace */
    return(new_nodep);
}


/*------------------------------------------------------------*/
/*  init_symtab          Initialize the symbol table with     */
/*                       predefined identifiers and types,    */
/*                       and routines.                        */
/*------------------------------------------------------------*/


init_symtab()

{
    SYMTAB_NODE_PTR integer_idp, real_idp, boolean_idp, char_idp,
                    false_idp, true_idp;

    /*
    -- Initialize the level-0 symbol table.
    */
    symtab_display[0] = NULL;

    enter_name_local_symtab(integer_idp, "integer");
    enter_name_local_symtab(real_idp,    "real");
    enter_name_local_symtab(boolean_idp, "boolean");
    enter_name_local_symtab(char_idp,    "char");
    enter_name_local_symtab(false_idp,   "false");
    enter_name_local_symtab(true_idp,    "true");

    integer_typep = alloc_struct(TYPE_STRUCT);
    real_typep    = alloc_struct(TYPE_STRUCT);
    boolean_typep = alloc_struct(TYPE_STRUCT);
    char_typep    = alloc_struct(TYPE_STRUCT);

    integer_idp->defn.key   = TYPE_DEFN;
    integer_idp->typep      = integer_typep;
    integer_typep->form     = SCALAR_FORM;
    integer_typep->size     = sizeof(int);
    integer_typep->type_idp = integer_idp;

    real_idp->defn.key   = TYPE_DEFN;
    real_idp->typep      = real_typep;
    real_typep->form     = SCALAR_FORM;
    real_typep->size     = sizeof(float);
    real_typep->type_idp = real_idp;

    boolean_idp->defn.key   = TYPE_DEFN;
    boolean_idp->typep      = boolean_typep;
    boolean_typep->form     = ENUM_FORM;
    boolean_typep->size     = sizeof(int);
    boolean_typep->type_idp = boolean_idp;
```

```
    boolean_typep->info.enumeration.max = 1;
    boolean_idp->typep->info.enumeration.const_idp = false_idp;
    false_idp->defn.key = CONST_DEFN;
    false_idp->defn.info.constant.value.integer = 0;
    false_idp->typep = boolean_typep;

    false_idp->next = true_idp;
    true_idp->defn.key = CONST_DEFN;
    true_idp->defn.info.constant.value.integer = 1;
    true_idp->typep = boolean_typep;

    char_idp->defn.key = TYPE_DEFN;
    char_idp->typep    = char_typep;
    char_typep->form   = SCALAR_FORM;
    char_typep->size   = sizeof(char);
    char_typep->type_idp = char_idp;

    enter_standard_routine("read",     READ,     PROC_DEFN);
    enter_standard_routine("readln",   READLN,   PROC_DEFN);
    enter_standard_routine("write",    WRITE,    PROC_DEFN);
    enter_standard_routine("writeln",  WRITELN,  PROC_DEFN);

    enter_standard_routine("abs",      ABS,      FUNC_DEFN);
    enter_standard_routine("arctan",   ARCTAN,   FUNC_DEFN);
    enter_standard_routine("chr",      CHR,      FUNC_DEFN);
    enter_standard_routine("cos",      COS,      FUNC_DEFN);
    enter_standard_routine("eof",      EOFF,     FUNC_DEFN);
    enter_standard_routine("eoln",     EOLN,     FUNC_DEFN);
    enter_standard_routine("exp",      EXP,      FUNC_DEFN);
    enter_standard_routine("ln",       LN,       FUNC_DEFN);
    enter_standard_routine("odd",      ODD,      FUNC_DEFN);
    enter_standard_routine("ord",      ORD,      FUNC_DEFN);
    enter_standard_routine("pred",     PRED,     FUNC_DEFN);
    enter_standard_routine("round",    ROUND,    FUNC_DEFN);
    enter_standard_routine("sin",      SIN,      FUNC_DEFN);
    enter_standard_routine("sqr",      SQR,      FUNC_DEFN);
    enter_standard_routine("sqrt",     SQRT,     FUNC_DEFN);
    enter_standard_routine("succ",     SUCC,     FUNC_DEFN);
    enter_standard_routine("trunc",    TRUNC,    FUNC_DEFN);
}


/*------------------------------------------------------------*/
/*  enter_standard_routine     Enter a standard procedure or  */
/*                             function identifier into the   */
/*                             symbol table.                  */
/*------------------------------------------------------------*/


enter_standard_routine(name, routine_key, defn_key)

    char      *name;          /* name string */
    ROUTINE_KEY routine_key;
    DEFN_KEY    defn_key;

{
    SYMTAB_NODE_PTR rtn_idp = enter_name_local_symtab(rtn_idp, name);

    rtn_idp->defn.key                       = defn_key;
    rtn_idp->defn.info.routine.key          = routine_key;
    rtn_idp->defn.info.routine.parms        = NULL;
    rtn_idp->defn.info.routine.local_symtab = NULL;
    rtn_idp->typep                          = NULL;
}


/*------------------------------------------------------------*/
/*  enter_scope     Enter a new nesting level by creating     */
/*                  a new scope.  Push the given symbol       */
/*                  table onto the display stack.             */
/*------------------------------------------------------------*/
```

```
enter_scope(symtab_root)

    SYMTAB_NODE_PTR symtab_root;

{
    if (++level >= MAX_NESTING_LEVEL) {
        error(NESTING_TOO_DEEP);
        exit(-NESTING_TOO_DEEP);
    }

    symtab_display[level] = symtab_root;
}

/*------------------------------------------------------*/
/* exit_scope        Exit the current nesting level by  */
```

```
/*                              closing the current scope.  Pop the    */
/*                              current symbol table off the display   */
/*                              stack and return a pointer to it.      */
/*------------------------------------------------------------*/

    SYMTAB_NODE_PTR
exit_scope()

{
    SYMTAB_NODE_PTR symtab_root = symtab_display[level--];

    return(symtab_root);
}
```

FIGURE B-11   code.h

```
/*****************************************************************/
/*                                                               */
/*      C O D E   G E N E R A T O R   (Header)                   */
/*                                                               */
/*      FILE:      code.h                                        */
/*                                                               */
/*      MODULE:    code                                          */
/*                                                               */
/*****************************************************************/

#ifndef code_h
#define code_h

#include "common.h"

/*------------------------------------------------------*/
/* Assembly label prefixes                              */
/*------------------------------------------------------*/

#define STMT_LABEL_PREFIX      "$L"
#define FLOAT_LABEL_PREFIX     "$F"
#define STRING_LABEL_PREFIX    "$S"

/*------------------------------------------------------*/
/* Names of library routines                            */
/*------------------------------------------------------*/

#define FLOAT_NEGATE     "_float_negate"
#define FLOAT_ADD        "_float_add"
#define FLOAT_SUBTRACT   "_float_subtract"
#define FLOAT_MULTIPLY   "_float_multiply"
#define FLOAT_DIVIDE     "_float_divide"
#define FLOAT_COMPARE    "_float_compare"
#define FLOAT_CONVERT    "_float_convert"

#define WRITE_INTEGER    "_write_integer"
#define WRITE_REAL       "_write_real"
#define WRITE_BOOLEAN    "_write_boolean"
#define WRITE_CHAR       "_write_char"
#define WRITE_STRING     "_write_string"
#define WRITE_LINE       "_write_line"

#define READ_INTEGER     "_read_integer"
#define READ_REAL        "_read_real"
#define READ_CHAR        "_read_char"
```

```
#define READ_LINE        "_read_line"

#define STD_END_OF_FILE "_std_end_of_file"
#define STD_END_OF_LINE "_std_end_of_line"

#define STD_ABS          "_std_abs"

#define STD_ARCTAN       "_std_arctan"
#define STD_COS          "_std_cos"
#define STD_EXP          "_std_exp"
#define STD_LN           "_std_ln"
#define STD_SIN          "_std_sin"
#define STD_SQRT         "_std_sqrt"

#define STD_ROUND        "_std_round"
#define STD_TRUNC        "_std_trunc"

/*------------------------------------------------------*/
/* Stack frame                                          */
/*------------------------------------------------------*/

#define PROC_LOCALS_STACK_FRAME_OFFSET    0
#define FUNC_LOCALS_STACK_FRAME_OFFSET   -4
#define PARAMETERS_STACK_FRAME_OFFSET    +6

#define STATIC_LINK          "$STATIC_LINK"         /* EQU <bp+4> */
#define RETURN_VALUE         "$RETURN_VALUE"        /* EQU <bp-4> */
#define HIGH_RETURN_VALUE    "$HIGH_RETURN_VALUE"   /* EQU <bp-2> */

/*------------------------------------------------------*/
/* Registers and instruction op codes                   */
/*------------------------------------------------------*/

typedef enum {
    AX, AH, AL, BX, BH, BL, CX, CH, CL, DX, DH, DL,
    CS, DS, ES, SS, SP, BP, SI, DI,
} REGISTER;

typedef enum {
    MOVE, MOVE_BLOCK, LOAD_ADDRESS, EXCHANGE,
    COMPARE, COMPARE_STRINGS, POP, PUSH, AND_BITS, OR_BITS, XOR_BITS,
    NEGATE, INCREMENT, DECREMENT, ADD, SUBTRACT, MULTIPLY, DIVIDE,
    CLEAR_DIRECTION, CALL, RETURN,
    JUMP, JUMP_LT, JUMP_LE, JUMP_EQ, JUMP_NE, JUMP_GE, JUMP_GT,
} INSTRUCTION;
```

```
/**************************************************/
/*                                                */
/*        Macros to emit assembly statements      */
/*                                                */
/**************************************************/


/*-----------------------------------------------*/
/* emit              Emit a no-operand instruction.     */
/*-----------------------------------------------*/


#define emit(opcode)                          \
{                                             \
    operator(opcode);                         \
    fprintf(code_file, "%s\n", asm_buffer);   \
    asm_bufferp = asm_buffer;                 \
}


/*-----------------------------------------------*/
/* emit_1           Emit a one-operand instruction.     */
/*-----------------------------------------------*/


#define emit_1(opcode, operand1)              \
{                                             \
    operator(opcode);                         \
    *asm_bufferp++ = '\t';                    \
    operand1;                                 \
    fprintf(code_file, "%s\n", asm_buffer);   \
    asm_bufferp = asm_buffer;                 \
}


/*-----------------------------------------------*/
/* emit_2           Emit a two-operand instruction.     */
/*-----------------------------------------------*/
```

```
#define emit_2(opcode, operand1, operand2)    \
{                                             \
    operator(opcode);                         \
    *asm_bufferp++ = '\t';                    \
    operand1;                                 \
    *asm_bufferp++ = ',';                     \
    operand2;                                 \
    fprintf(code_file, "%s\n", asm_buffer);   \
    asm_bufferp = asm_buffer;                 \
}


/*-----------------------------------------------------*/
/* emit_label          Emit a statement label.         */
/*-----------------------------------------------------*/


#define emit_label(prefix, index)  fprintf(code_file,   \
                                   "%s_%03d:\n",        \
                                   prefix, index);


/*-----------------------------------------------------*/
/* advance_asm_bufferp   Advance asm_bufferp to the end  */
/*                       of the assembly statement.      */
/*-----------------------------------------------------*/


#define advance_asm_bufferp()   while (*asm_bufferp != '\0') \
                                    ++asm_bufferp;


/*-----------------------------------------------------*/
/* new_label_index           Return a new label index.  */
/*-----------------------------------------------------*/


#define new_label_index()       ++label_index

#endif
```

FIGURE B-12   emitasm.c

```
/*****************************************************************/
/*                                                               */
/*       E M I T   A S S E M B L Y   S T A T E M E N T S          */
/*                                                               */
/*       Routines for generating and emitting                    */
/*       language statements.                                    */
/*                                                               */
/*       FILE:        emitasm.c                                  */
/*                                                               */
/*       MODULE:      code                                       */
/*                                                               */
/*****************************************************************/

#include <stdio.h>
#include "symtab.h"
#include "code.h"

/*-----------------------------------------------*/
/* Globals                                        */
/*-----------------------------------------------*/

int label_index = 0;

char asm_buffer[MAX_PRINT_LINE_LENGTH];   /* assembly stmt buffer */
char *asm_bufferp = asm_buffer;           /* ptr into asm buffer */
```

```
char *register_strings[] = {
    "ax", "ah", "al", "bx", "bh", "bl", "cx", "ch", "cl",
    "dx", "dh", "dl", "cs", "ds", "es", "ss",
    "sp", "bp", "si", "di",
};


char *instruction_strings[] = {
    "mov", "rep\tmovsb", "lea", "xchg", "cmp", "repe\tcmpsb",
    "pop", "push", "and", "or", "xor",
    "neg", "inc", "dec", "add", "sub", "imul", "idiv",
    "cld", "call", "ret",
    "jmp", "jl", "jle", "je", "jne", "jge", "jg",
};


        /**********************************************/
        /*                                            */
        /*      Write parts of assembly statements     */
        /*                                            */
        /**********************************************/


/*-----------------------------------------------------*/
/* label              Write a generic label constructed from */
/*                    the prefix and the label index.   */
/*                                                      */
```

```
/*                  Example:        $L_007              */
/*-----------------------------------------------------*/

label(prefix, index)

    char *prefix;
    int  index;

{
    sprintf(asm_bufferp, "%s_%03d", prefix, index);
    advance_asm_bufferp();
}

/*-----------------------------------------------------*/
/*  word_label        Write a word label constructed from   */
/*                    the prefix and the label index.       */
/*                                                          */
/*                    Example:        WORD PTR $F_007        */
/*-----------------------------------------------------*/

word_label(prefix, index)

    char *prefix;
    int  index;

{
    sprintf(asm_bufferp, "WORD PTR %s_%03d", prefix, index);
    advance_asm_bufferp();
}

/*-----------------------------------------------------*/
/*  high_dword_label  Write a word label constructed from   */
/*                    the prefix and the label index and    */
/*                    offset by 2 to point to the high word  */
/*                    of a double word.                     */
/*                                                          */
/*                    Example:        WORD PTR $F_007+2      */
/*-----------------------------------------------------*/

high_dword_label(prefix, index)

    char *prefix;
    int  index;

{
    sprintf(asm_bufferp, "WORD PTR %s_%03d+2", prefix, index);
    advance_asm_bufferp();
}

/*-----------------------------------------------------*/
/*  reg                Write a register name. Example:  ax  */
/*-----------------------------------------------------*/

reg(r)

    REGISTER r;

{
    sprintf(asm_bufferp, "%s", register_strings[r]);
    advance_asm_bufferp();
}

/*-----------------------------------------------------*/
/*  operator           Write an opcode. Example:  add       */
/*-----------------------------------------------------*/

operator(opcode)
```

```
    INSTRUCTION opcode;

{
    sprintf(asm_bufferp, "\t%s", instruction_strings[opcode]);
    advance_asm_bufferp();
}

/*-----------------------------------------------------*/
/*  byte               Write a byte label constructed from  */
/*                     the id name and its label index.     */
/*                                                          */
/*                     Example:        BYTE_PTR ch_007       */
/*-----------------------------------------------------*/

byte(idp)

    SYMTAB_NODE_PTR idp;

{
    sprintf(asm_bufferp, "BYTE PTR %s_%03d",
                        idp->name, idp->label_index);
    advance_asm_bufferp();
}

/*-----------------------------------------------------*/
/*  byte_indirect      Write an indirect reference to a byte  */
/*                     via a register.                      */
/*                                                          */
/*                     Example:        BYTE PTR [bx]         */
/*-----------------------------------------------------*/

byte_indirect(r)

    REGISTER r;

{
    sprintf(asm_bufferp, "BYTE PTR [%s]", register_strings[r]);
    advance_asm_bufferp();
}

/*-----------------------------------------------------*/
/*  word               Write a word label constructed from  */
/*                     the id name and its label index.     */
/*                                                          */
/*                     Example:        WORD_PTR sum_007      */
/*-----------------------------------------------------*/

word(idp)

    SYMTAB_NODE_PTR idp;

{
    sprintf(asm_bufferp, "WORD PTR %s_%03d",
                        idp->name, idp->label_index);
    advance_asm_bufferp();
}

/*-----------------------------------------------------*/
/*  high_dword         Write a word label constructed from  */
/*                     the id name and its label index and  */
/*                     offset by 2 to point to the high word  */
/*                     of a double word.                    */
/*                                                          */
/*                     Example:        WORD_PTR sum_007+2    */
/*-----------------------------------------------------*/

high_dword(idp)
```

```
    SYMTAB_NODE_PTR idp;

{
    sprintf(asm_bufferp, "WORD PTR %s_%03d+2",
                         idp->name, idp->label_index);
    advance_asm_bufferp();
}

/*-----------------------------------------------------------*/
/*  word_indirect        Write an indirect reference to a word  */
/*                       via a register.                        */
/*                                                              */
/*                       Example:      WORD PTR [bx]            */
/*-----------------------------------------------------------*/

word_indirect(r)

    REGISTER r;

{
    sprintf(asm_bufferp, "WORD PTR [%s]", register_strings[r]);
    advance_asm_bufferp();
}

/*-----------------------------------------------------------*/
/*  high_dword_indirect   Write an indirect reference to the    */
/*                        high word of a double word via a      */
/*                        register.                             */
/*                                                              */
/*                        Example:      WORD PTR [bx+2]         */
/*-----------------------------------------------------------*/

high_dword_indirect(r)

    REGISTER r;

{
    sprintf(asm_bufferp, "WORD PTR [%s+2]", register_strings[r]);
    advance_asm_bufferp();
}

/*-----------------------------------------------------------*/
/*  tagged_name          Write an id name tagged with the id's  */
/*                       label index.                           */
/*                                                              */
/*                       Example:      x_007                    */
/*-----------------------------------------------------------*/

tagged_name(idp)
```

```
    SYMTAB_NODE_PTR idp;

{
    sprintf(asm_bufferp, "%s_%03d", idp->name, idp->label_index);
    advance_asm_bufferp();
}

/*-----------------------------------------------------------*/
/*  name_lit              Write a literal name.                 */
/*                                                              */
/*                        Example:      _float_convert          */
/*-----------------------------------------------------------*/

name_lit(name)

    char *name;

{
    sprintf(asm_bufferp, "%s", name);
    advance_asm_bufferp();
}

/*-----------------------------------------------------------*/
/*  integer_lit           Write an integer as a string.        */
/*-----------------------------------------------------------*/

integer_lit(n)

    int n;

{
    sprintf(asm_bufferp, "%d", n);
    advance_asm_bufferp();
}

/*-----------------------------------------------------------*/
/*  char_lit              Write a character surrounded by single */
/*                        quotes.                               */
/*-----------------------------------------------------------*/

char_lit(ch)

    char ch;

{
    sprintf(asm_bufferp, "'%c'", ch);
    advance_asm_bufferp();
}
```

FIGURE B-13   emitcode.c

```
/*****************************************************************/
/*                                                             */
/*      E M I T   C O D E   S E Q U E N C E S                   */
/*                                                             */
/*      Routines for emitting standard                         */
/*      assembly code sequences.                               */
/*                                                             */
/*      FILE:    emitcode.c                                    */
/*                                                             */
/*      MODULE:  code                                          */
```

```
/*                                                             */
/*****************************************************************/

#include <stdio.h>
#include "symtab.h"
#include "code.h"

/*-----------------------------------------------------------*/
/* Externals                                                   */
/*-----------------------------------------------------------*/
```

```
extern TYPE_STRUCT_PTR   integer_typep, real_typep,
                         boolean_typep, char_typep;

extern int level;

extern char     asm_buffer[];
extern char     *asm_bufferp;
extern FILE     *code_file;

/*-----------------------------------------------------------*/
/* Globals                                                   */
/*-----------------------------------------------------------*/

SYMTAB_NODE_PTR  float_literal_list  = NULL;
SYMTAB_NODE_PTR  string_literal_list = NULL;

                 /****************************************/
                 /*                                      */
                 /*         Emit prologues and epilogues  */
                 /*                                      */
                 /****************************************/

/*-----------------------------------------------------------*/
/* emit_program_prologue       Emit the program prologue.    */
/*-----------------------------------------------------------*/

emit_program_prologue()

{
    fprintf(code_file, "\tDOSSEG\n");
    fprintf(code_file, "\t.MODEL  small\n");
    fprintf(code_file, "\t.STACK 1024\n");
    fprintf(code_file, "\n");
    fprintf(code_file, "\t.CODE\n");
    fprintf(code_file, "\n");
    fprintf(code_file, "\tPUBLIC\t_pascal_main\n");
    fprintf(code_file, "\tINCLUDE\tpasextrn.inc\n");
    fprintf(code_file, "\n");

    /*
    -- Equates for stack frame components.
    */
    fprintf(code_file, "%s\t\tEQU\t<WORD PTR [bp+4]>\n",
                       STATIC_LINK);
    fprintf(code_file, "%s\t\tEQU\t<WORD PTR [bp-4]>\n",
                       RETURN_VALUE);
    fprintf(code_file, "%s\t\tEQU\t<WORD PTR [bp-2]>\n",
                       HIGH_RETURN_VALUE);
    fprintf(code_file, "\n");
}

/*-----------------------------------------------------------*/
/* emit_program_epilogue       Emit the program epilogue,    */
/*                             which includes the data       */
/*                             segment.                      */
/*-----------------------------------------------------------*/

emit_program_epilogue(prog_idp)

    SYMTAB_NODE_PTR prog_idp;    /* id of program */

{
    SYMTAB_NODE_PTR np;
    int             i, length;

    fprintf(code_file, "\n");
    fprintf(code_file, "\t.DATA\n");
```

```
    fprintf(code_file, "\n");

    /*
    -- Emit declarations for the program's global variables.
    */
    for (np = prog_idp->defn.info.routine.locals;
         np != NULL;
         np = np->next) {
        fprintf(code_file, "%s_%03d\t", np->name, np->label_index);
        if (np->typep == char_typep)
            fprintf(code_file, "DB\t0\n");
        else if (np->typep == real_typep)
            fprintf(code_file, "DD\t0.0\n");
        else if (np->typep->form == ARRAY_FORM)
            fprintf(code_file, "DB\t%d DUP(0)\n", np->typep->size);
        else if (np->typep->form == RECORD_FORM)
            fprintf(code_file, "DB\t%d DUP(0)\n", np->typep->size);
        else
            fprintf(code_file, "DW\t0\n");
    }

    /*
    -- Emit declarations for the program's floating point literals.
    */
    for (np = float_literal_list; np != NULL; np = np->next)
        fprintf(code_file, "%s_%03d\tDD\t%e\n", FLOAT_LABEL_PREFIX,
                           np->label_index,
                           np->defn.info.constant.value.real);

    /*
    -- Emit declarations for the program's string literals.
    */
    for (np = string_literal_list; np != NULL; np = np->next) {
        fprintf(code_file, "%s_%03d\tDB\t\"", STRING_LABEL_PREFIX,
                           np->label_index);

        length = strlen(np->name) - 2;
        for (i = 1; i <= length; ++i) fputc(np->name[i], code_file);

        fprintf(code_file, "\"\n");
    }

    fprintf(code_file, "\n");
    fprintf(code_file, "\tEND\n");
}

/*-----------------------------------------------------------*/
/* emit_main_prologue          Emit the prologue for the main */
/*                             routine _pascal_main.          */
/*-----------------------------------------------------------*/

emit_main_prologue()

{
    fprintf(code_file, "\n");
    fprintf(code_file, "_pascal_main\tPROC\n");
    fprintf(code_file, "\n");

    emit_1(PUSH, reg(BP));                /* dynamic link */
    emit_2(MOVE, reg(BP), reg(SP));       /* new stack frame base */
}

/*-----------------------------------------------------------*/
/* emit_main_epilogue          Emit the epilogue for the main */
/*                             routine _pascal_main.          */
/*-----------------------------------------------------------*/

emit_main_epilogue()
```

```
{
    fprintf(code_file, "\n");

    emit_1(POP, reg(BP));           /* restore caller's stack frame */
    emit(RETURN);                   /* return */

    fprintf(code_file, "\n");
    fprintf(code_file, "_pascal_main\tENDP\n");
}

/*----------------------------------------------------------*/
/*  emit_routine_prologue      Emit the prologue for a proce- */
/*                             dure or a function.            */
/*----------------------------------------------------------*/

emit_routine_prologue(rtn_idp)

    SYMTAB_NODE_PTR rtn_idp;

{
    fprintf(code_file, "\n");
    fprintf(code_file, "%s_%03d\tPROC\n",
                       rtn_idp->name, rtn_idp->label_index);
    fprintf(code_file, "\n");

    emit_1(PUSH, reg(BP));             /* dynamic link */
    emit_2(MOVE, reg(BP), reg(SP));    /* new stack frame base */

    /*
    -- Allocate stack space for a function's return value.
    */
    if (rtn_idp->defn.key == FUNC_DEFN) emit_2(SUBTRACT, reg(SP),
                                            integer_lit(4));

    /*
    -- Allocate stack space for the local variables.
    */
    if (rtn_idp->defn.info.routine.total_local_size > 0)
        emit_2(SUBTRACT, reg(SP),
            integer_lit(rtn_idp->defn.info.routine
                                    .total_local_size));
}

/*----------------------------------------------------------*/
/*  emit_routine_epilogue      Emit the epilogue for a proce- */
/*                             dure or a function.            */
/*----------------------------------------------------------*/

emit_routine_epilogue(rtn_idp)

    SYMTAB_NODE_PTR rtn_idp;

{
    /*
    -- Load a function's return value into the ax or dx:ax registers.
    */
    if (rtn_idp->defn.key == FUNC_DEFN) {
        emit_2(MOVE, reg(AX), name_lit(RETURN_VALUE));
        if (rtn_idp->typep == real_typep)
            emit_2(MOVE, reg(DX), name_lit(HIGH_RETURN_VALUE));
    }

    emit_2(MOVE, reg(SP), reg(BP)); /* cut back to caller's stack */
    emit_1(POP, reg(BP));           /* restore caller's stack frame */

    emit_1(RETURN, integer_lit(rtn_idp->defn.info.routine
                                    .total_parm_size + 2));
```

```
                                                   /* return and cut back stack */
    fprintf(code_file, "\n");
    fprintf(code_file, "%s_%03d\tENDP\n",
                       rtn_idp->name, rtn_idp->label_index);
}

            /******************************/
            /*                            */
            /*     Emit equates and data  */
            /*                            */
            /******************************/

/*----------------------------------------------------------*/
/*  emit_declarations   Emit the parameter and local variable */
/*                      declarations for a procedure or a     */
/*                      function.                              */
/*----------------------------------------------------------*/

emit_declarations(rtn_idp)

    SYMTAB_NODE_PTR rtn_idp;

{
    SYMTAB_NODE_PTR parm_idp = rtn_idp->defn.info.routine.parms;
    SYMTAB_NODE_PTR var_idp  = rtn_idp->defn.info.routine.locals;

    fprintf(code_file, "\n");

    /*
    -- Parameters.
    */
    while (parm_idp != NULL) {
        emit_text_equate(parm_idp);
        parm_idp = parm_idp->next;
    }

    /*
    -- Local variables.
    */
    while (var_idp != NULL) {
        emit_text_equate(var_idp);
        var_idp = var_idp->next;
    }
}

/*----------------------------------------------------------*/
/*  emit_numeric_equate     Emit a numeric equate for a field */
/*                          id and its offset.                */
/*                                                            */
/*                          Example:   field_007 EQU 3        */
/*----------------------------------------------------------*/

emit_numeric_equate(idp)

    SYMTAB_NODE_PTR idp;

{
    fprintf(code_file, "%s_%03d\tEQU\t%d\n",
                       idp->name, idp->label_index,
                       idp->defn.info.data.offset);
}

/*----------------------------------------------------------*/
/*  emit_numeric_equate     Emit a numeric equate for a para- */
/*                          meter or a local variable id and  */
/*                          its stack frame offset.           */
```

```
/*                                              */
/*                    Examples:  parm_007   EQU <bp+6>     */
/*                               var_008    EQU <bp-10>    */
/*                               dword_010  EQU <bp-14>    */
/*                               dword_010h EQU <bp-14+2>  */
/*----------------------------------------------------*/

emit_text_equate(idp)

    SYMTAB_NODE_PTR idp;

{
    char *name     = idp->name;
    int  label_index = idp->label_index;
    int  offset    = idp->defn.info.data.offset;

    if (idp->typep == char_typep)
        fprintf(code_file, "%s_%03d\tEQU\t<BYTE PTR [bp%+d]>\n",
                           name, label_index, offset);
    else if (idp->typep == real_typep)
        fprintf(code_file, "%s_%03d\tEQU\t<WORD PTR [bp%+d]>\n",
                           name, label_index, offset);
    else
        fprintf(code_file, "%s_%03d\tEQU\t<WORD PTR [bp%+d]>\n",
                           name, label_index, offset);
}


            /******************************/
            /*                            */
            /*     Emit loads and pushes  */
            /*                            */
            /******************************/


/*----------------------------------------------------*/
/* emit_load_value     Emit code to load a scalar value */
/*                     into AX or DX:AX.                 */
/*----------------------------------------------------*/

emit_load_value(var_idp, var_tp)

    SYMTAB_NODE_PTR var_idp;
    TYPE_STRUCT_PTR var_tp;

{
    int     var_level    = var_idp->level;
    BOOLEAN varparm_flag = var_idp->defn.key == VARPARM_DEFN;

    if (varparm_flag) {
        /*
        -- VAR formal parameter.
        -- AX or DX:AX = value the address points to
        */
        emit_2(MOVE, reg(BX), word(var_idp));
        if (var_tp == char_typep) {
            emit_2(SUBTRACT, reg(AX), reg(AX));
            emit_2(MOVE, reg(AL), byte_indirect(BX));
        }
        else if (var_tp == real_typep) {
            emit_2(MOVE, reg(AX), word_indirect(BX));
            emit_2(MOVE, reg(AX), high_dword_indirect(BX));
        }
        else emit_2(MOVE, reg(AX), word_indirect(BX));
    }
    else if ((var_level == level) || (var_level == 1)) {
        /*
        -- Global or local parameter or variable:
        -- AX or DX:AX = value
```

```
        */
        if (var_tp == char_typep) {
            emit_2(SUBTRACT, reg(AX), reg(AX));
            emit_2(MOVE, reg(AL), byte(var_idp));
        }
        else if (var_tp == real_typep) {
            emit_2(MOVE, reg(AX), word(var_idp));
            emit_2(MOVE, reg(DX), high_dword(var_idp));
        }
        else emit_2(MOVE, reg(AX), word(var_idp));
    }
    else   /* var_level < level */ {
        /*
        -- Nonlocal parameter or variable.
        -- First locate the appropriate stack frame, then:
        -- AX or DX:AX = value
        */
        int lev = var_level;

        emit_2(MOVE, reg(BX), reg(BP));
        do {
            emit_2(MOVE, reg(BP), name_lit(STATIC_LINK));
        } while (++lev < level);

        if (var_tp == char_typep) {
            emit_2(SUBTRACT, reg(AX), reg(AX));
            emit_2(MOVE, reg(AL), byte(var_idp));
        }
        else if (var_tp == real_typep) {
            emit_2(MOVE, reg(AX), word(var_idp));
            emit_2(MOVE, reg(DX), high_dword(var_idp));
        }
        else emit_2(MOVE, reg(AX), word(var_idp));

        emit_2(MOVE, reg(BP), reg(BX));
    }
}


/*----------------------------------------------------*/
/* emit_push_operand   Emit code to push a scalar operand */
/*                     value onto the stack.              */
/*----------------------------------------------------*/

emit_push_operand(tp)

    TYPE_STRUCT_PTR tp;

{
    if ((tp->form == ARRAY_FORM) || (tp->form == RECORD_FORM)) return;

    if (tp == real_typep) emit_1(PUSH, reg(DX));
    emit_1(PUSH, reg(AX));
}

/*----------------------------------------------------*/
/* emit_push_address   Emit code to push an address onto the */
/*                     stack.                                 */
/*----------------------------------------------------*/

emit_push_address(var_idp)

    SYMTAB_NODE_PTR var_idp;

{
    int     var_level    = var_idp->level;
    BOOLEAN varparm_flag = var_idp->defn.key == VARPARM_DEFN;

    if ((var_level == level) || (var_level == 1))
```

```
        emit_2(varparm_flag ? MOVE : LOAD_ADDRESS,
               reg(AX), word(var_idp))

    else   /* var_level < level */ {
        int lev = var_level;

        emit_2(MOVE, reg(BX), reg(BP));
        do {
            emit_2(MOVE, reg(BP), name_lit(STATIC_LINK));
        } while (++lev < level);
        emit_2(varparm_flag ? MOVE : LOAD_ADDRESS,
               reg(AX), word(var_idp));
        emit_2(MOVE, reg(BP), reg(BX));
    }

    emit_1(PUSH, reg(AX));
}

/*-----------------------------------------------------------*/
/*  emit_push_return_value_address      Emit code to push the  */
/*                                      address of the function*/
/*                                      return value in the    */
/*                                      stack frame.           */
/*-----------------------------------------------------------*/

emit_push_return_value_address(var_idp)

    SYMTAB_NODE_PTR var_idp;

{
    int lev = var_idp->level + 1;

    if (lev < level) {
        /*
        -- Find the appropriate stack frame.
        */
        emit_2(MOVE, reg(BX), reg(BP));
        do {
            emit_2(MOVE, reg(BP), name_lit(STATIC_LINK));
        } while (++lev < level);
        emit_2(LOAD_ADDRESS, reg(AX), name_lit(RETURN_VALUE));
        emit_2(MOVE, reg(BP), reg(BX));
    }
    else emit_2(LOAD_ADDRESS, reg(AX), name_lit(RETURN_VALUE));
}
```

```
        emit_1(PUSH, reg(AX));
}

        /***************************************/
        /*                                     */
        /*        Emit miscellaneous code      */
        /*                                     */
        /***************************************/

/*-----------------------------------------------------------*/
/*  emit_promote_to_real         Emit code to convert integer */
/*                               operands to real.            */
/*-----------------------------------------------------------*/

emit_promote_to_real(tp1, tp2)

    TYPE_STRUCT_PTR tp1, tp2;

{
    if (tp2 == integer_typep) {
        emit_1(CALL, name_lit(FLOAT_CONVERT));
        emit_2(ADD,  reg(SP), integer_lit(2));
        emit_1(PUSH, reg(DX));
        emit_1(PUSH, reg(AX));              /* ???_1 real_2 */
    }

    if (tp1 == integer_typep) {
        emit_1(POP,  reg(AX));
        emit_1(POP,  reg(DX));
        emit_1(POP,  reg(BX));
        emit_1(PUSH, reg(DX));
        emit_1(PUSH, reg(AX));
        emit_1(PUSH, reg(BX));              /* real_2 integer_1 */

        emit_1(CALL, name_lit(FLOAT_CONVERT));
        emit_2(ADD,  reg(SP), integer_lit(2));  /* real_2 real_1 */

        emit_1(POP,  reg(BX));
        emit_1(POP,  reg(CX));
        emit_1(PUSH, reg(BX));
        emit_1(PUSH, reg(AX));
        emit_1(PUSH, reg(CX));
        emit_1(PUSH, reg(BX));              /* real_1 real_2 */
    }
}
```

FIGURE B-14   error.h

```
/***************************************************************/
/*                                                           */
/*      E R R O R   R O U T I N E S   (Header)               */
/*                                                           */
/*      FILE:       error.h                                  */
/*                                                           */
/*      MODULE:     error                                    */
/*                                                           */
/***************************************************************/

#ifndef error_h
#define error_h

#define MAX_SYNTAX_ERRORS 25
```

```
/*-----------------------------------------------------------*/
/*  Error codes                                              */
/*-----------------------------------------------------------*/

typedef enum {
    NO_ERROR,
    SYNTAX_ERROR,
    TOO_MANY_SYNTAX_ERRORS,
    FAILED_SOURCE_FILE_OPEN,
    UNEXPECTED_END_OF_FILE,
    INVALID_NUMBER,
    INVALID_FRACTION,
    INVALID_EXPONENT,
    TOO_MANY_DIGITS,
```

```
    REAL_OUT_OF_RANGE,                          NOT_A_CONSTANT_IDENTIFIER,
    INTEGER_OUT_OF_RANGE,                       MISSING_DOTDOT,
    MISSING_RPAREN,                             INCOMPATIBLE_TYPES,
    INVALID_EXPRESSION,                         INVALID_TARGET,
    INVALID_ASSIGNMENT,                         INVALID_IDENTIFIER_USAGE,
    MISSING_IDENTIFIER,                         INCOMPATIBLE_ASSIGNMENT,
    MISSING_COLONEQUAL,                         MIN_GT_MAX,
    UNDEFINED_IDENTIFIER,                       MISSING_LBRACKET,
    STACK_OVERFLOW,                             MISSING_RBRACKET,
    INVALID_STATEMENT,                          INVALID_INDEX_TYPE,
    UNEXPECTED_TOKEN,                           MISSING_BEGIN,
    MISSING_SEMICOLON,                          MISSING_PERIOD,
    MISSING_DO,                                 TOO_MANY_SUBSCRIPTS,
    MISSING_UNTIL,                              INVALID_FIELD,
    MISSING_THEN,                               NESTING_TOO_DEEP,
    INVALID_FOR_CONTROL,                        MISSING_PROGRAM,
    MISSING_OF,                                 ALREADY_FORWARDED,
    INVALID_CONSTANT,                           WRONG_NUMBER_OF_PARMS,
    MISSING_CONSTANT,                           INVALID_VAR_PARM,
    MISSING_COLON,                              NOT_A_RECORD_VARIABLE,
    MISSING_END,                                MISSING_VARIABLE,
    MISSING_TO_OR_DOWNTO,                       CODE_SEGMENT_OVERFLOW,
    REDEFINED_IDENTIFIER,                       UNIMPLEMENTED_FEATURE,
    MISSING_EQUAL,                          } ERROR_CODE;
    INVALID_TYPE,
    NOT_A_TYPE_IDENTIFIER,
    INVALID_SUBRANGE_TYPE,                      #endif
```

FIGURE B-15   error.c

```
/************************************************************/
/*                                                          */
/*       E R R O R   R O U T I N E S                        */
/*                                                          */
/*       Error messages and routines to print them.         */
/*                                                          */
/*       FILE:      error.c                                 */
/*                                                          */
/*       MODULE:    error                                   */
/*                                                          */
/************************************************************/

#include <stdio.h>
#include "common.h"
#include "error.h"


/*----------------------------------------------------------*/
/* Externals                                                */
/*----------------------------------------------------------*/

extern char      *tokenp;
extern BOOLEAN   print_flag;
extern char      source_buffer[];
extern char      *bufferp;


/*----------------------------------------------------------*/
/* Error messages      Keyed to enumeration type ERROR_CODE */
/*                     in file error.h.                     */
/*----------------------------------------------------------*/

char *error_messages[] = {
    "No error",
```

```
    "Syntax error",
    "Too many syntax errors",
    "Failed to open source file",
    "Unexpected end of file",
    "Invalid number",
    "Invalid fraction",
    "Invalid exponent",
    "Too many digits",
    "Real literal out of range",
    "Integer literal out of range",
    "Missing right parenthesis",
    "Invalid expression",
    "Invalid assignment statement",
    "Missing identifier",
    "Missing := ",
    "Undefined identifier",
    "Stack overflow",
    "Invalid statement",
    "Unexpected token",
    "Missing ; ",
    "Missing DO",
    "Missing UNTIL",
    "Missing THEN",
    "Invalid FOR control variable",
    "Missing OF",
    "Invalid constant",
    "Missing constant",
    "Missing : ",
    "Missing END",
    "Missing TO or DOWNTO",
    "Redefined identifier",
    "Missing = ",
```

```
   "Invalid type",
   "Not a type identifier",
   "Invalid subrangetype",
   "Not a constant identifier",
   "Missing .. ",
   "Incompatible types",
   "Invalid assignment target",
   "Invalid identifier usage",
   "Incompatible assignment",
   "Min limit greater than max limit",
   "Missing [ ",
   "Missing ] ",
   "Invalid index type",
   "Missing BEGIN",
   "Missing period",
   "Too many subscripts",
   "Invalid field",
   "Nesting too deep",
   "Missing PROGRAM",
   "Already specified in FORWARD",
   "Wrong number of actual parameters",
   "Invalid VAR parameter",
   "Not a record variable",
   "Missing variable",
   "Code segment overflow",
   "Unimplemented feature",
};

/*----------------------------------------------------------*/
/* Globals                                                  */
/*----------------------------------------------------------*/

int error_count = 0;     /* number of syntax errors */

                 /*****************************/
                 /*                           */
                 /*       Error routines      */
                 /*                           */
                 /*****************************/

/*----------------------------------------------------------*/
/* error            Print an arrow under the error and then */
```

```
/*                   print the error message.              */
/*----------------------------------------------------------*/

error(code)

    ERROR_CODE code;     /* error code */

{
    extern int buffer_offset;
    char message_buffer[MAX_PRINT_LINE_LENGTH];
    char *message = error_messages[code];
    int  offset   = buffer_offset - 2;

    /*
    -- Print the arrow pointing to the token just scanned.
    */
    if (print_flag) offset += 8;
    sprintf(message_buffer, "%*s^\n", offset, " ");
    if (print_flag) print_line(message_buffer);
    else            printf(message_buffer);

    /*
    -- Print the error message.
    */
    sprintf(message_buffer, " *** ERROR: %s.\n", message);
    if (print_flag) print_line(message_buffer);
    else            printf(message_buffer);

    *tokenp = '\0';
    ++error_count;

    if (error_count > MAX_SYNTAX_ERRORS) {
        sprintf(message_buffer,
            "Too many syntax errors.  Aborted.\n");
        if (print_flag) print_line(message_buffer);
        else            printf(message_buffer);

        exit(-TOO_MANY_SYNTAX_ERRORS);
    }
}
```

FIGURE B-16   common.h

```
/****************************************************************/
/*                                                              */
/*      C O M M O N   R O U T I N E S   (Header)                */
/*                                                              */
/*      FILE:     common.h                                      */
/*                                                              */
/*      MODULE:   common                                        */
/*                                                              */
/****************************************************************/

#ifndef common_h
#define common_h
```

```
#define FORM_FEED_CHAR          '\f'

#define MAX_FILE_NAME_LENGTH    32
#define MAX_SOURCE_LINE_LENGTH  256
#define MAX_PRINT_LINE_LENGTH   80
#define MAX_LINES_PER_PAGE      50
#define DATE_STRING_LENGTH      26
#define MAX_TOKEN_STRING_LENGTH MAX_SOURCE_LINE_LENGTH
#define MAX_CODE_BUFFER_SIZE    4096
#define MAX_NESTING_LEVEL       16

typedef enum {
```

```
    FALSE, TRUE,
} BOOLEAN;
```

```
        /****************************************/
        /*                                      */
        /*      Macros for memory allocation    */
        /*                                      */
```

```
        /****************************************/

#define alloc_struct(type)          (type *) malloc(sizeof(type))
#define alloc_array(type, count)    (type *) malloc(count*sizeof(type))
#define alloc_bytes(length)         (char *) malloc(length)

#endif
```

FIGURE B-17   compile2.c

```
/****************************************************************/
/*                                                              */
/*      Program 14-1:  Pascal Compiler II                       */
/*                                                              */
/*      Compile Pascal programs.                                */
/*                                                              */
/*      FILE:       compile2.c                                  */
/*                                                              */
/*      REQUIRES:   Modules parser, symbol table, scanner,      */
/*                      code, error                             */
/*                                                              */
/*      USAGE:      compile2 sourcefile objectfile              */
/*                                                              */
/*          sourcefile      [input] source file containing the  */
/*                              the statements to compile       */
/*                                                              */
/*          objectfile      [output] object file to contain the */
/*                              generated assembly code         */
/*                                                              */
/****************************************************************/

#include <stdio.h>

/*------------------------------------------------------------*/
/* Globals                                                    */
/*------------------------------------------------------------*/

FILE *code_file;   /* ASCII file for the emitted assembly code */
```

```
/*------------------------------------------------------------*/
/* main               Initialize the scanner and call         */
/*                    routine program.                        */
/*------------------------------------------------------------*/

main(argc, argv)

    int  argc;
    char *argv[];

{
    /*
    -- Open the code file.  If no code file name was given,
    -- use the standard output file.
    */
    code_file = (argc == 3) ? fopen(argv[2], "w")
                            : stdout;

    /*
    -- Initialize the scanner.
    */
    init_scanner(argv[1]);

    /*
    -- Process a program.
    */
    get_token();
    program();
}
```

FIGURE B-18   paslib.c

```
/****************************************************************/
/*                                                              */
/*      P A S C A L   R U N T I M E   L I B R A R Y             */
/*                                                              */
/*      Note that all formal parameters are reversed to         */
/*      accomodate the Pascal calling convention of the         */
/*      compiled code.                                          */
/*                                                              */
/*      All floating point parameters are passed in as longs    */
/*      to bypass unwanted type conversions.  Floating point    */
/*      function values are also returned as longs.             */
/*                                                              */
/****************************************************************/

#include <stdio.h>
```

```
#include <math.h>

#define MAX_SOURCE_LINE_LENGTH  256

typedef enum {
    FALSE, TRUE
} BOOLEAN;

union {
    float real;
    long  dword;
} value;

/*------------------------------------------------------------*/
/* Globals                                                    */
/*------------------------------------------------------------*/
```

```
BOOLEAN eof_flag  = FALSE;
BOOLEAN eoln_flag = FALSE;

/*--------------------------------------------------*/
/* main             The main routine, which calls   */
/*                  pascal_main, the "main" of the compiled */
/*                  program.                        */
/*--------------------------------------------------*/

main(argc, argv)

    int  argc;
    char *argv[];

{
    pascal_main();
    exit(0);
}

                /*********************************/
                /*                               */
                /*      Read routines            */
                /*                               */
                /*********************************/

/*--------------------------------------------------*/
/* read_integer      Read an integer value.         */
/*--------------------------------------------------*/

    int
read_integer()

{
    int i;

    scanf("%d", &i);
    return(i);
}

/*--------------------------------------------------*/
/* read_real         Read a real value.             */
/*--------------------------------------------------*/

    long
read_real()

{
    scanf("%g", &value.real);
    return(value.dword);
}

/*--------------------------------------------------*/
/* read_char         Read a character value.        */
/*--------------------------------------------------*/

    char
read_char()

{
    char ch;

    scanf("%c", &ch);
    if (eof_flag || (ch == '\n')) ch = ' ';

    return(ch);
}
```

```
/*--------------------------------------------------*/
/* read_line         Skip the rest of the input record. */
/*--------------------------------------------------*/

read_line()

{
    char ch;

    do {
        ch = getchar();
    } while (!eof_flag && (ch != '\n'));
}

                /*********************************/
                /*                               */
                /*      Write routines           */
                /*                               */
                /*********************************/

/*--------------------------------------------------*/
/* write_integer     Write an integer value.        */
/*--------------------------------------------------*/

write_integer(field_width, i)

    int i;
    int field_width;

{
    printf("%*d", field_width, i);
}

/*--------------------------------------------------*/
/* write_real        Write an real value.           */
/*--------------------------------------------------*/

write_real(precision, field_width, i)

    long i;
    int  field_width;
    int  precision;

{
    value.dword = i;
    printf("%*.*f", field_width, precision, value.real);
}

/*--------------------------------------------------*/
/* write_boolean     Write a boolean value.         */
/*--------------------------------------------------*/

write_boolean(field_width, b)

    int b;
    int field_width;

{
    printf("%*s", field_width, b == 0 ? "FALSE" : "TRUE");
}

/*--------------------------------------------------*/
/* write_char        Write a character value.       */
/*--------------------------------------------------*/

write_char(field_width, ch)
```

```
    int ch;
    int field_width;

{

    printf("%*c", field_width, ch);
}

/*-----------------------------------------------------*/
/* write_string       Write a string value.           */
/*-----------------------------------------------------*/

write_string(length, field_width, value)

    char *value;
    int  field_width;
    int  length;

{

    char buffer[MAX_SOURCE_LINE_LENGTH];

    strncpy(buffer, value, length);
    buffer[length] = '\0';

    printf("%*s", -field_width, buffer);
}

/*-----------------------------------------------------*/
/* write_line         Write a carriage return.        */
/*-----------------------------------------------------*/

write_line()

{
    putchar('\n');
}

            /********************************/
            /*                              */
            /*        Other I/O routines    */
            /*                              */
            /********************************/

/*-----------------------------------------------------*/
/* std_end_of_file    Return 1 if at end of file, else 0.  */
/*-----------------------------------------------------*/

    BOOLEAN
std_end_of_file()

{
    char ch = getchar();

    if (eof_flag || feof(stdin)) eof_flag = TRUE;
    else                         ungetc(ch, stdin);

    return(eof_flag);
}

/*-----------------------------------------------------*/
/* std_end_of_line    Return 1 if at end of line, else 0.  */
/*-----------------------------------------------------*/

    BOOLEAN
std_end_of_line()

{
    char ch = getchar();

    if (eof_flag || feof(stdin))
        eoln_flag = eof_flag = TRUE;
    else {
        eoln_flag = ch == '\n';
```

```
        ungetc(ch, stdin);
    }

    return(eoln_flag);
}

            /************************************************/
            /*                                              */
            /*        Floating point arithmetic routines    */
            /*                                              */
            /************************************************/

/*-----------------------------------------------------*/
/* float_negate       Return the negated value.       */
/*-----------------------------------------------------*/

    long
float_negate(i)

    long i;

{
    value.dword = i;

    value.real = -value.real;
    return(value.dword);
}

/*-----------------------------------------------------*/
/* float_add          Return the sum x + y.           */
/*-----------------------------------------------------*/

    long
float_add(j, i)

    long i, j;

{
    float x, y;

    value.dword = i;  x = value.real;
    value.dword = j;  y = value.real;

    value.real = x + y;
    return(value.dword);
}

/*-----------------------------------------------------*/
/* float_subtract     Return the difference x - y.    */
/*-----------------------------------------------------*/

    long
float_subtract(j, i)

    long i, j;

{
    float x, y;

    value.dword = i;  x = value.real;
    value.dword = j;  y = value.real;

    value.real = x - y;
    return(value.dword);
}

/*-----------------------------------------------------*/
/* float_multiply     Return the product x*y.         */
/*-----------------------------------------------------*/

    long
float_multiply(j, i)
```

```
    long i, j;

{

    float x, y;

    value.dword = i;   x = value.real;
    value.dword = j;   y = value.real;

    value.real = x*y;
    return(value.dword);
}

/*------------------------------------------------------*/
/* float_divide        Return the quotient x/y.         */
/*------------------------------------------------------*/

    long
float_divide(j, i)

    long i, j;

{

    float x, y;

    value.dword = i;   x = value.real;
    value.dword = j;   y = value.real;

    value.real = x/y;
    return(value.dword);
}

/*------------------------------------------------------*/
/* float_convert       Convert an integer value to real and */
/*                     return the converted value.      */
/*------------------------------------------------------*/

    long
float_convert(i)

    int i;

{

    value.real = i;
    return(value.dword);
}

/*------------------------------------------------------*/
/* float_compare       Return -1 if x <  y              */
/*                            0 if x == y               */
/*                           +1 if x >  y               */
/*------------------------------------------------------*/

float_compare(j, i)

    long i, j;

{

    int   comp;
    float x, y;

    value.dword = i;   x = value.real;
    value.dword = j;   y = value.real;

    if (x < y)        comp = -1;
    else if (x == y)  comp =  0;
    else              comp = +1;

    return(comp);
}

        /********************************************/
        /*                                          */
```

```
    /*       Standard floating point functions     */
    /*                                             */
    /***********************************************/

/*------------------------------------------------------*/
/* std_abs             Return abs of parameter.         */
/*------------------------------------------------------*/

    long
std_abs(i)

    long i;

{

    value.dword = i;

    value.real = fabs(value.real);
    return(value.dword);
}

/*------------------------------------------------------*/
/* std_arctan          Return arctan of parameter.      */
/*------------------------------------------------------*/

    long
std_arctan(i)

    long i;

{

    value.dword = i;

    value.real = atan(value.real);
    return(value.dword);
}

/*------------------------------------------------------*/
/* std_cos             Return cos of parameter.         */
/*------------------------------------------------------*/

    long
std_cos(i)

    long i;

{

    value.dword = i;

    value.real = cos(value.real);
    return(value.dword);
}

/*------------------------------------------------------*/
/* std_exp             Return exp of parameter.         */
/*------------------------------------------------------*/

    long
std_exp(i)

    long i;

{

    value.dword = i;

    value.real = exp(value.real);
    return(value.dword);
}

/*------------------------------------------------------*/
/* std_ln              Return ln of parameter.          */
/*------------------------------------------------------*/
```

```
    long
std_ln(i)

    long i;

{

    value.dword = i;

    value.real = log(value.real);
    return(value.dword);
}
```

```
/*----------------------------------------------------------*/
/* std_sin          Return sin of parameter.              */
/*----------------------------------------------------------*/

    long
std_sin(i)

    long i;

{

    value.dword = i;

    value.real = sin(value.real);
    return(value.dword);
}
```

```
/*----------------------------------------------------------*/
/* std_sqrt         Return sqrt of parameter.             */
/*----------------------------------------------------------*/

    long
std_sqrt(i)

    long i;

{
```

```
    value.dword = i;

    value.real = sqrt(value.real);
    return(value.dword);
}
```

```
/*----------------------------------------------------------*/
/* std_round        Return round of parameter.            */
/*----------------------------------------------------------*/

    int
std_round(i)

    long i;

{

    value.dword = i;

    value.dword = (int) (value.real + 0.5);
    return((int) value.dword);
}
```

```
/*----------------------------------------------------------*/
/* std_trunc        Return trunc of parameter.            */
/*----------------------------------------------------------*/

    int
std_trunc(i)

    long i;

{

    value.dword = i;

    value.dword = (int) value.real;
    return((int) value.dword);
}
```

FIGURE B-19   pasextrn.inc

```
EXTRN   _float_negate:PROC          EXTRN   _read_char:PROC
EXTRN   _float_add:PROC             EXTRN   _read_line:PROC
EXTRN   _float_subtract:PROC
EXTRN   _float_multiply:PROC        EXTRN   _std_end_of_file:PROC
EXTRN   _float_divide:PROC          EXTRN   _std_end_of_line:PROC
EXTRN   _float_compare:PROC
EXTRN   _float_convert:PROC         EXTRN   _std_abs:PROC

EXTRN   _write_integer:PROC         EXTRN   _std_arctan:PROC
EXTRN   _write_real:PROC            EXTRN   _std_cos:PROC
EXTRN   _write_boolean:PROC         EXTRN   _std_exp:PROC
EXTRN   _write_char:PROC            EXTRN   _std_ln:PROC
EXTRN   _write_string:PROC          EXTRN   _std_sin:PROC
EXTRN   _write_line:PROC            EXTRN   _std_sqrt:PROC

EXTRN   _read_integer:PROC          EXTRN   _std_round:PROC
EXTRN   _read_real:PROC             EXTRN   _std_trunc:PROC
```

Index